D1881282

A HANDBOOK OF THE SWAHILI LANGUAGE AS SPOKEN AT ZANZIBAR

A HANDBOOK

OF THE

SWAHILI LANGUAGE

AS SPOKEN AT

ZANZIBAR.

EDITED FOR THE UNIVERSITIES' MISSION TO CENTRAL AFRICA

BY

THE LATE EDWARD STEERE, LL.D.,

MISSIONARY BISHOP FOR CENTRAL AFRICA

FOURTH EDITION, REVISED AND ENLARGED BY

A. C. MADAN, M. A.,

SENIOR STUDENT AND FORMERLY TUTOR OF CH. CH. OXFORD.

GYAN

Published by

Gyan Publishing House
5, Ansari Road
Daryaganj, New Delhi-110002
Phone: 011-47034999, 9811692060
E-mail: books@gyanbooks.com

Distribution Network
gyanbooks.com
India, USA, Canada, UK, Australia, France

© Publisher

All rights reserved. No part of this work may be reproduced, stored, adapted, or transmitted in any form or by any means, electronic, mechanical, photocopying, micro-filming, recording or otherwise, or translated in any language, without the prior written permission of the copyright owner and the publisher.

ISBN : 978-81-212-4419-0 (PB)
First Published, 1894

2nd Impression 2020

Printed at: Gyan Press, Delhi.

The book is sold subject to the condition that it shall not, by way of trade or otherwise, be lent, resold, hired out, or otherwise circulated without the prior publisher's written consent.

A Handbook of the Swahili Language
Edited by: Edward Steere

SWAHILI.

COMMON PRAYER. Revised Edition (Zanzibar). Fcap. 8vo. Cloth bds., 1*s*. 6*d*. net.

MISCELLANEOUS STORIES AND TRANSLATIONS. (Visa na Hadithi.) Revised edition. Fcap. 8vo. Cloth, 1*s*. net.

A HANDBOOK OF THE SWAHILI LANGUAGE, as spoken at Zanzibar. Edited by the late BISHOP STEERE. Third Edition, by A. C. MADAN, M.A. Crown 8vo. Cloth boards, 2*s*. 6*d*. net.

SWAHILI GRAMMAR AND VOCABULARY. Drawn up by Mrs. F. BURT. Crown 8vo. Cloth boards, 1*s*. 8*d*. net.

SWAHILI EXERCISES. Compiled for the Universities Mission to Central Africa. By the late BISHOP STEERE, LL.D. Crown 8vo. Cloth boards, 2*s*. net.

STORIES FROM ÆSOP. Cloth, 6*d*. net.

THE LANGUAGE FAMILIES OF AFRICA. By A. WERNER. Crown 8vo. Cloth boards, 3*s*. 6*d*. net.

LONDON:
SOCIETY FOR PROMOTING
CHRISTIAN KNOWLEDGE

First published (third edition) by S.P.C.K. 1884.
Number reprinted since (to February, 1919) 14,000 *copies.*

PREFACE TO THE FIRST EDITION.

THERE is probably no African language so widely known as the Swahili. It is understood along the coasts of Madagascar and Arabia, it is spoken by the Seedees in India, and is the trade language of a very large part of Central or Intertropical Africa. Zanzibar traders penetrate sometimes even to the western side of the continent, and they are in the constant habit of traversing more than half of it with their supplies of Indian and European goods. Throughout this immense district any one really familiar with the Swahili language will generally be able to find some one who can understand him, and serve as an interpreter.

This consideration makes it a point of the greatest importance to our Central African Mission that Swahili should be thoroughly examined and well learnt. For if the members of the Mission can go forth from Zanzibar, or, still better, can leave England already well acquainted with this language, and provided with books and translations adapted to their wants, they will carry with them a key that can unlock the secrets of an immense variety of strange dialects, whose very names are as yet unknown to us. For they will not only be able at once to communicate with new tribes, but in mastering this really simple and far from difficult language they will have learnt how to set about learning and writing all others of the same class, since they agree with Swahili in all the chief respects in which it differs from our European tongues.

The work, then, which is here begun is not to be regarded as though its utility were confined to the islands and the narrow strip of coast of which this language is the vernacular, but much rather as the broad foundation on which our labours in the far interior must for many years be built up. As there is no way by which those inner lands are so ordinarily or can be so easily reached as from Zanzibar and the coast dependent on it, so neither is there any way by which we can make ourselves so readily intelligible, or by which the Gospel can be preached so soon or so well as by means of the language of Zanzibar and its dependencies, to which this work is intended as an introduction —a language which, through its Arabic relations, has a hold on revealed religion, and even on European thought while, through its negro structure, it is exactly fitted to serve as an interpreter of that religion and those thoughts to men who have not yet even heard of their existence.

When Bishop Tozer arrived in Zanzibar at the end of August 1864, the only guides we had to the language were the grammar and vocabulary of Dr. Krapf, and his translation of part of the Book of Common Prayer. During Bishop Tozer's visit to Mombas in November, he made a copy of a revised vocabulary belonging to the Rev. J. Rebmann. However, although one cannot estimate too highly the diligence and linguistic ability displayed by Dr. Krapf and the patient sagacity of Mr. Rebmann, we soon found that, owing partly to the fact of their collections having been made in the dialect of Mombas, and still more to the confused and inexact style of spelling adopted unfortunately by both, their works were of scarcely any use to a mere beginner.

I soon after procured copies of the manuscript vocabularies collected by Mr. Witt and Mr. Schultz, then representing the firm of O'Swald and Co. in Zanzibar, and with such help as I could procure from any quarter, I began in July 1865 to print the first pages of my collections for a "Handbook of Swahili as Spoken in Zanzibar." When I had proceeded as far as page 33, I made the acquaintance of Hamis wa Tani and of his son Mohammed, both of them well acquainted with English and French, and of pure Swahili extraction. To the disinterested kindness of Mohammed, who, while confined to his house by sickness, allowed me to spend every Saturday morning in questioning him about his language, I owe all that is best in my knowledge of African tongues. With his help and revision I completed the list of substantives, and found my way through the intricacies of the adjectives and pronouns. Of how much importance an accurate guide in these matters would be may be seen from the "Table of Concords," first printed in Zanzibar, in a form suggested by Bishop Tozer, and now reprinted as part of this volume.

Mohammed's sickness increasing about the time that

I had begun to print the conjugation of the verb, I was unable to continue my visits, and completed the "Collections" from Dr. Krapf, with the help of the vocabulary collected by the late Baron von der Decken and Dr. Kersten, and of that collected by the Rev. Thomas Wakefield of the United Methodist Free Churches' Mission, both of which I was kindly allowed to copy.

After Mohammed's partial recovery I continued my visits to him, and went through the verbs, making first a list of useful English verbs from a dictionary, and entering all the words contained in the collections of which I had copies. I thus checked and supplemented what others had already done, and obtained a tolerably complete insight into that branch of the vocabulary. Before I could get much beyond this, Mohammed was so far recovered as to be able to sail for Bombay. I have always much pleasure in acknowledging how much I owe to him.

Meanwhile I had begun my collection of short tales in Swahili, the first of which were printed in Zanzibar with an interlinear version, under the title of "Specimens of Swahili," in March 1866, and reprinted in an early number of "Mission Life." I also began to use my Swahili to a practical purpose by making the collections for a handbook of the Shambala language, the first draft of which was completed in May 1866. These collections were made with a view to the mission since commenced in that country by the Rev. C. A. Alington; they were revised by the help of another teacher, and printed in Zanzibar in the year 1867.

Finding the Swahili tales most valuable as well to myself as to those who were studying with me, I proceeded to print a further collection, with the title "*Hadithi za Kiunguja*," in Swahili only. For the tales then printed I was mainly indebted to Hamis wa Kayi, a very intelligent young Swahili, who always comprehended better what a foreigner wanted to know, and explained more clearly what was difficult, than any one else I met with while in Zanzibar.

At the same period I had begun and carried on from time to time the investigation of the Yao or Achowa language, one peculiarly interesting to us, as that of nearly all the released slaves under Bishop Mackenzie's charge, and as having now supplanted the Mang'anja in the country where our Mission was originally settled. From this study I first gained a definite notion of the wonderful effect the letter *n* has in African languages, and so came to understand the origin of several apparent irregularities in Swahili.

I had begun even before Mohammed bin Khamis left Zanzibar to make some essays in translation, the best of which are embodied in a pamphlet printed in Zanzibar, with the title "Translations in Swahili:" it was completed in January 1867.

I was then getting help from many quarters, and on explaining to some of our native friends our wish to make a complete translation of the Bible into their language, one of them, Sheikh 'Abd al 'Aziz, kindly volunteered to translate for me the Arabic Psalter into the best and purest Swahili. I found, before long, that not only did his numerous avocations prevent any rapid progress, but that his language was too learned to suit exactly our purpose in making the version; it did not therefore proceed further than the Sixteenth Psalm. I printed these as at once a memorial of his kindness and a specimen of what one of the most learned men in Zanzibar considers the most classical form of his language.

I cannot but mention at the same time the name of Sheikh Mohammed bin Ali, a man of the greatest research, to whose kindness I was indebted for a copy, made by his own hand, of some very famous Swahili poetry, with an interlinear Arabic version; he also revised for me a paraphrase of it in modern language, for which I was chiefly indebted (as for much other help) to Hassan bin Yusuf, whose interest in our doctrines and teachings has always been most marked. The verses and translation are both printed in the "Swahili Tales."

At the end of 1867 I printed a translation of Bishop Forbes' little primary catechism, chosen as being the shortest and clearest I could find to begin upon. Though very imperfect, I am glad to think that it has been found of use.

When I had completed the Yao collections, I went on to the Nyamwezi language, as being that of the largest and most central tribe with which there is constant and tolerably safe communication.

In November 1867 I lost, by the sadly sudden deaths of the Rev. G. E. Drayton and his wife, most useful helpers, who were beginning to be able to give me substantial assistance. Their places were, however, well supplied by the Rev. W. and Mrs. Lea, who arrived opportunely just before the time of our bereavement. I was then engaged in preparing the translations of St. Matthew's Gospel and of the Psalms, as well as in beginning to put in order the materials for the present work. To Mr. Lea I was indebted, amongst other things, for the first version of the 119th Psalm, and to Mrs. Lea for the arrangement of the Swahili-English Vocabulary. The last thing I printed in Zanzibar was a translation of the Easter and Advent Hymns, and of Adeste Fideles, which I had the pleasure of hearing the girls of the Mission Orphanage sing most sweetly to the old tunes just before I left.

I ought also to mention that, having been often under great obligations to the French Romanist Mission, I had the pleasure of printing for them a Catechism in French and Swahili, which was indirectly valuable to me as showing how the great truths we have in common were rendered by a perfectly independent student of the language. I know not how sufficiently to regret that the excellent compiler, Père Etienne Baur, should have been content to use the jargon (for it is nothing better) commonly employed by Indians and Europeans, and should have adopted an orthography adapted only to a French pronunciation.

Only three weeks before leaving I had the advantage of consulting two large manuscript dictionaries compiled by Dr. Krapf, and brought to Zanzibar by the Rev. R. L. Pennell. I was able to examine about half the Swahili-English volume, with the assistance of Hamis wa Kayi, enough to enrich materially my previous collections, and to show how far even now I fall short of my first predecessor in the work of examining and elucidating the languages of Eastern Africa. There remains for some future time or other hand the examination of the rest of Dr. Krapf's dictionary, as well as the collation of what will no doubt deserve to be the standard Swahili lexicon, on which the Rev. John Rebmann has been for nearly a quarter of a century labouring unweariedly. Even then there will remain many dialectic variations, and many old and poetical words and inflections, so that for many years one who loves such studies might find employment in this one language.

Since my arrival in England, at the end of November 1868, I have been able to superintend the printing of the Gospel of St. Matthew in Swahili, liberally undertaken by the Bible Society, of translations of the Church Catechism and of their Scriptural Reading Lessons out of the Old Testament, kindly undertaken by the Society for Promoting Christian Knowledge. For the Central African Mission I have carried through the press this work and the collection of Swahili Stories with an English version, published by Messrs. Bell and Sons, of which those previously printed at Zanzibar form a small part, and besides these a number of small pamphlets, including translations of the Books of Ruth and Jonah, and some slight specimens of the Gindo, Zaramo, and Ngazidja languages. There remain the Psalms, which the Bible Society has promised to print for us, and the collections in the Yao and Nyamwezi languages, all which I should like to get through the press in the course of this year. I wish there were a chance of the Rev. John Rebmann's Swahili version of St. Luke's Gospel, of which I have seen a large part, being printed at the same time.

This handbook is arranged on the principle of supplying with each portion of it such rules as are required for the practical use of that portion. In the first part, after some introductory observations, Substantives, Adjectives, Pronouns, and Verbs have each a separate section, containing first the rules which govern their inflection and employment, and then an alphabetical list of the Swahili equivalents of our English words belonging to each part of speech. For the mere finding of words one general alphabet would perhaps have been more convenient; but as the object of this work is not merely to tell what the Swahili words are, but also how to employ them correctly, it seems better so to group them as to bring the rules of grammar and the words which they control into as close a connection with one another as possible. The Editor has done what most readers would have had to do—sort out first the word and then the grammatical rules which must be observed in using it. The minor parts of speech are indexed together to avoid a multiplicity of alphabets, except the Interjections, which cannot be said to have exact equivalents in any other language. The part ends with a section on the formation of words, which may be of use where the other alphabets fail to give a satisfactory rendering, and may also be useful as a guide in turning Swahili into English, in the case of the many words which ignorance or some oversight in preparing the second part may have caused to be omitted. The rules and hints prefixed to the second part are intended to enable any one who sees or hears a Swahili word to ascertain the material part of it, so as to be able to use the dictionary which follows. It is evident that there must be great difficulties at first in either using or arranging an alphabetical list of words which may begin with, in some cases, nine or ten different letters, according to the grammatical position they hold in each case However, the difficulty is greater in appearance than in practice.

The Appendices contain some curious or useful matter which could not well find a place in the body of the work. The first contains a specimen of a curious kind of enigmatical way of writing and speaking called Kinyume. The second gives a specimen of the forms used in letter-writing, both in prose and verse. The third is part of a Swahili tale, with all the prefixes separated and the grammatical forms explained, intended as a guide and introduction to the art of reading, and through that of writing the language. The fourth Appendix consists of a small collection of phrases, some of them such as are wanted in ordinary conversation, some of them useful in illustrating the idiom or peculiar constructions used by natives. This collection might have been very much increased had it not been carefully confined to phrases actually met with in conversation with persons reputed to speak correctly.

The name of the language—Swahili—is beyond all doubt a modified form of the Arabic *Sawáhil*, the plural of *Ṡahil*, a coaṣt. The natives themselves jestingly derive it from *Sawa hila*, which a Zanzibar interpreter would explain as "All same cheat."

Little Steeping, May 1870.

ADVERTISEMENT TO SECOND EDITION.

THE First Edition having been at the last sold out with unexpected rapidity, I have not been able to add so much as I should have wished to this. The chief novelty is the omission of what I called the second class of Substantives, which proved to be only the most common instance of the general rule, that Substantives of any and every form denoting animate beings are constructed with Adjectives and Pronouns in the forms proper to the first class. Some words have been added to the Vocabularies and a few mistakes corrected.

During the last four years the work of translation and collection has been going steadily forward, Swahili preaching has been going on, and some Elementary School-books printed in Zanzibar for our vernacular schools. The great work of evangelizing Africa seems to grow in magnitude the more one understands what is required for it; but our hopes still grow with the growth of our knowledge.

EDWARD STEERE.

London, January 1875.

ADVERTISEMENT TO THIRD EDITION.

This Edition may be taken to represent substantially the final form which the Handbook assumed in the hands of its compiler, the late Bishop Steere. No estimate can be attempted here of his services to philology in general, and the student of African languages in particular, still less of their bearing on the spread of Christianity in Central Africa. Whatever the relative purity of the dialects of Mombasa and Zanzibar, and however great the debt Bishop Steere undoubtedly owed to his distinguished predecessor in their study, Dr. Krapf, the broad fact remains that Bishop Steere took the language as he found it spoken in the capital city of the East Coast, reduced its rules to so lucid and popular a form as not only to make it accessible, but easy to all students, and finally made a great advance towards stereotyping its forms and extending its use by embodying it in copious writings and translations.

Some of the last hours of his life were apparently spent in preparing this Handbook for a new edition. Those who were familiar with the many cares and anxieties then pressing on him, will not be surprised that there were signs of haste and pressure in his revision. With Part I., however, he seems to have been satisfied. The corrections of the text were few and unimportant, and though the Lists of Words might have been largely added to, he seems to have preferred leaving them as they were, in view of the strictly practical purpose of the whole book.

With Part II. (the Swahili-English Vocabulary, &c.) the case is rather different. With the aid of various members of the Mission, the Bishop had made somewhat large collections in order to expand and complete it. Probably from the pressure of work before alluded to, he had only prepared a selection of them for this Edition. It has been thought better, however, to incorporate all the words found in his notes and added with his approval. But it must be remembered that the Bishop never regarded Part II. as ranking as a Dictionary, even in embryo, but rather as a tolerably full list of words to serve as a useful companion to Part I. Even with this reservation, there remain many traces of imperfection in arrangement, spelling, and interpretation of words, which would doubtless have been removed if he had been allowed time to pass the whole list under revision finally.

This final revision no one is in a position adequately to supply. Minor corrections and additions have been cautiously and sparingly made. One Appendix (No. V.), likely to subserve the practical aim of the whole, has been added, with the Ven. Archdeacon Hodgson's approval. There still remain among the Bishop's notes some miscellaneous specimens of Swahili verses, proverbs, riddles, &c., which might have formed another.

It is thought best, however, to reserve them, and leave the whole book, as far as possible, as the Bishop left it. Subsequent editors may find something to add. They probably will not find much to alter.

A. C. M.

P.S.—Dr. Krapf's great Dictionary of the Swahili Language, in its printed form, was in the Bishop's hands too short a time to allow of his making any use of it for this Edition of the Handbook.

Zanzibar, Christmas, 1882.

TABLE OF CONTENTS.

PART I.

PART II.

SWAHILI HANDBOOK.

PART I.

The Swahili language is spoken by the mixed race of Arabs and Negroes who inhabit the Eastern Coast of Africa, especially in that part which lies between Lamoo and the neighbouring towns on the north, and Cape Delgado on the south.

It is classified by Dr. Bleek as one of the Zangian genus of the middle branch of the Bantu languages. That is to say, it belongs to one of the subdivisions of that great family of Negro languages, which carries on the work of grammatical inflexion by means of changes at the beginning of the word, similar to that whereby in Kafir, *umuntu*, a man, becomes in the plural *abantu*, people. All these languages divide their nouns into a number of classes, which are distinguished by their first syllable, and bring their adjectives, pronouns, and verbs into relation with substantives by the use of corresponding changes in their first syllables. None of these classes denote sex in any way. Dr. Bleek, in his comparative grammar of South African languages, enumerates eighteen prefixes which are found in one or other of the languages of this family; but it must be remembered that he reckons by the form of the prefix only, so that the singular and plural forms of most words count as two, while the same form will sometimes answer to two or more forms in the other number. Dr. Bleek's arrangement is the most convenient for his purpose, which is the comparison of the formatives used in different languages; but I have not followed it in this work, because I think that for practical purposes such a classification should be used as will enable the learner who sees or hears the noun in the singular at once to put it into the plural. Prefixes may be counted up separately; but in practice we have to do with nouns, not with prefixes, and a noun cannot be put into a different class when it becomes plural or singular without great risk of confusion. Thus in Frédoux' Sechuana grammar, 4 and 6 are the plurals of 3, 10 and 6 are the plurals of 11, and 6 alone is the plural of 5 and 14. Can this be a clear arrangement?

I have very little doubt that Dr. Bleek is right in regarding these classes as substantially the same with the genders in most of the European languages, which are even now only sex-denoting to a very limited extent. There is a distinction in Swahili as to words which denote *living beings*, called by Dr. Krapf, not very happily, a *masculine* gender, though it has no relation to *sex*, but to *life* only.

It is very puzzling to a beginner, accustomed to languages which change at the end, to find the beginnings of words so very uncertain. Thus he hears that *ngema* means *good;* but when he begins to apply his knowledge he finds that natives use for the English word *good*, not only *ngema*, but *mwema*, *wema*, *mema*, *njema*, *jema*, *pema*, *chema*, *vyema*, and *kwema*. Again, *yangu* means *my*, but he will hear also, *wangu*, *zangu*, *changu*, *vyangu*, *langu*, *pangu*, *kwangu*, and *mwangu*. It is necessary therefore to get at the very first a firm hold of the fact that in Swahili it is the end, and not the beginning of a word, which is its substantial and unchanging part. The beginning of the word when taken to pieces denotes its number, time, and agreements.

The "Table of Concords" prefixed to the section on Adjectives, shows at one view the variables of the language; and when that has been mastered, the difficulties for an English student will be over. The various forms will be explained, and the nicer distinctions mentioned in the grammatical parts of the book. In the preliminary observations prefixed to the second part will be found an account of all the changes which may occur at the end of a word, changes which in practice are very soon mastered, relating as they chiefly do to a few points in the conjugation of the verb.

There is a broken kind of Swahili in use among foreigners, Indian as well as European, which serves for very many purposes, though it is of course utterly useless when one has to speak with exactness, or on subjects not immediately connected with the ordinary affairs of life and commerce. Its rules may be briefly laid down as follows:—If you are in doubt about how to make a plural, prefix *ma*, or use *nyingi*, *i.e.* many. In conjugating the verb, always put the subject before and the object after it, for the present tense prefix *na-*, for the past *ma-*, for the future *ta-*. For *no* or *not*, use *hakuna.* It is wonderful how intelligible you can make yourself by these few rules; but it is just as wonderful what absurd broken stuff can be made to do duty for English.

Let any one, however, who really wishes to speak the language get the Table of Concords well into his head, by any means he finds best for the purpose, and he will have no need to resort to broken and incorrect ways of talking.

Swahili, like all languages of the same family, is very rich in Verbs, and poor in Adjectives and Prepositions. There is nothing corresponding to the English Article, the word when standing alone implying the indefinite article, while the definite article can in many cases be expressed by the use and arrangement of the Pronouns, but still must often be left unexpressed. Though the Verb is etymologically the most important part of speech, it is the Substantive which determines the form of all the variable syllables. The Substantive will therefore be first considered, and next the Adjective, which very closely resembles it. The Pronouns will come next, as it is by their help that the Verb is conjugated, then the Verb itself, and after that the minor parts of speech, Adverbs, Prepositions, Conjunctions, and, last of all, the Interjections. A sketch of the grammar of each part of speech, which aims at being sufficient for ordinary and practical purposes, is first given, and after that a list of words belonging to that part of speech, thus forming a combined grammar and English-Swahili dictionary. The second part consists of a Swahili-English vocabulary, and so completes the work.

The Swahili language has been hitherto but little written by those who speak it, and they know and use only the purely Arabic alphabet. There are copies of religious and secular verses, and possibly other works, composed in the old or poetical dialect, which is not now, and I believe never was, thoroughly understood by the mass of the people. The modern dialect is used in letters; but they have always a string of Arabic compliments at the beginning, and Arabic words and phrases freely interspersed throughout.

Any one who tries to read a letter or a poem written in Arabic characters, will at once see why it is impossible to adopt them as the standard Swahili alphabet. It is absolutely necessary to have a good idea of what you are to read before you can read at all. The reason is that Swahili has five vowels, Arabic only three, and of Swahili consonants the Arabic supplies no means of writing *ch*, *g*, *p*, or *v*, nor can consecutive consonants be written without shocking Arabic notions of propriety. Thus the Swahili are driven to write the *ba* for *p* and for *mb* as well as for *b*; the *ghain* for *g*, *ng*, and *ng'*, as well as for *gh*; the *fa* for *v* and *mv*, as well as for *f*; the *ya* for *ny* as well as for *y*; the *shin* for *ch* as well as for *sh*; and to omit altogether the *n* before *d*, *j*, *y*, and *z*. Initial vowels and consecutive vowels are only to be expressed by *hemzas* or *'ains*. In the first piece of written Swahili I ever possessed (the Story of the Ox and the Ass) the words *nq'ombe* and *punda* were written *ghube* and *buda*. It will be easily seen how imperfect and ambiguous a means of writing Swahili the Arabic character must be. An instance occurred while I was in Zanzibar of a letter written from Kilwa with the account of a fight, in which it was said that one of the principal men, *amekufa*, had died, or *amevuka*, had got away, and which it was no one could certainly tell; the last two consonants were *fa* and *qaf*, with three dots over them. If two of the dots belonged to the first letter, the man was dead; if two belonged to the next letter, he was alive: but the dots were so equally placed that no one could tell how to divide them. If the Arabic had possessed a *v*, there could have been no mistake. It would no doubt be possible to express Swahili sounds by using letters with additional dots and affixing arbitrary sounds to the letters of prolongation, as is done in Persian and Hindi, but the result would puzzle a genuine Swahili and could never be quite satisfactory in any respect.

There seems to be no difficulty in writing Swahili in Roman characters, there being no sound which does not so nearly occur in some European language that the proper way of writing it can readily be fixed upon, and illustrated by an example. When this is the case there is no need to look for anything further. I think those who try to settle the alphabets of new languages are too apt to forget how essential simplicity is to a really good alphabet. If the Roman alphabet can be made to distinguish all the sounds used in that language, it does all for it that it does for any. To attempt to distinguish the sounds used in that language, from the sounds used in another, or to mark all the varieties of tone which occur in speaking, is always useless and embarrassing, and not one man in a thousand has sufficient accuracy of ear to do it properly. It is practically easier to learn to attach a new sound to a known letter, than to learn a new sound and a new letter too, especially when the new letter has to be printed and written, and the learner is entangled in a maze of *italics* and letters with a point below and a point above, or a line through them, or some Greek letter which has not the sound one gives it in Greek, or some new invention which will fit well neither into printing nor writing, and looks at its ease neither as a capital nor a small letter. It generally happens that the sounds of a language, though not identical with those of another, correspond with them sufficiently to make the corresponding letters appropriate symbols. Thus an English and a French *t* are not identical; but which nation would or ought to submit always to put a dot somewhere about its *t* to show that it is not the *t* which it never will want to use, and never did, and could not pronounce, if it met with it? Or, to take a stronger instance, ought Germans, Englishmen, and Spaniards always to cross the tails of their *j*'s, or print them in italics, or deform their books with new symbols, merely because they do not pronounce their *j*'s as Frenchmen do theirs?

THE ALPHABET.

The Vowels are to be pronounced as in Italian, the Consonants as in English.

A = *a* in *father.*
B = *b* in *bare.*
Ch = *ch* in *cherry.* Italian *c* before *i* or *e.*
D = *d* in *do.* *D* occurs very frequently in the Mombas dialect where *j* is used in that of Zanzibar.
E = *ai* in *chair.*
F = *f* in *fine.* German *v.*
G = *g* in *gate*, never soft as in *genius.*
H = *h* in *hat.*
I = *ee* in *feet.*
J = *j* in *joy.* Sometimes more like *dy* or *di* in *cordial.* French *di*, German *dj*, Italian *gi.*
K = *k* in *kalendar.*
L = *l* in *long.* *L* and *r* are generally treated as the same letter.
M = *m* in *man.*
N = *n* in *no.*
O = *o* in *boy*, more like *au* than the common English *o.*
P = *p* in *paint.*
R = *r* in *raise.* An English, not a Scotch, Irish, German, or French *r.* See *L.*
S = *s* in *sun.* German *ss.* It is never pronounced like a *z* or the English *s* in *arise.* *S* and *sh* are commonly used for one another indiscriminately.
T = *t* in *ten.* *T* frequently occurs in the dialect of Mombas where *ch* is used in that of Zanzibar.

U = *oo* in *tool.*
V = *v* in *very.* German *w.*
W = *w* in *win.* French *ou.* It is merely a *u* pronounced as a consonant.
Y = *y* in *yonder.* German *j.* It is merely an *i* pronounced as a consonant. *Y* is frequently used in the Lamoo dialect where *j* occurs in that of Zanzibar.
Z = *z* in *zany.* German *s.* *Z* frequently occurs in the dialect of Lamoo where *v* is used in that of Zanzibar.

There are several sounds introduced from the Arabic which do not occur in purely African words.

Gh = the Arabic *ghain;* it is a guttural *g*, resembling the Dutch *g.* It may be obtained by pronouncing a *g* (as nearly as it can be done) with the mouth wide open. Most Europeans imagine, the first time they hear it, that there is an *r* sound after the *g*, but this is a mistake.

Kh = the Arabic *kha;* it is a very rough form of the German *ch*, the Spanish *j*, or the Scotch *ch* in *loch.* It resembles the sound made in trying to raise something in the throat. It may always be replaced in Swahili by a simple *h*, but *never* by a *k.*

Th = the four Arabic letters *tha*, *thal*, *thod*, and *thah*. The first of these is the English *th* in *think*, the second that in *they.* The third and fourth are thicker varieties of the second sound. In Swahili they may all be replaced by a *z.* No attempt is ever made to distinguish the last three letters; but as the first is generally marked in pronunciation, it is in the first part of this handbook marked by printing the *th* in italics wherever it is to be pronounced as in the English word *think.* The sound of the English *th* in *that* occurs in some Swahili as a dialectic variation for *z.* In vulgar Swahili *z* is not merely put for the Arabic *th,* but *th* is also put for the Arabic *z,* as *wathiri* for *waziri,* a vizir.

There are several compound consonantal sounds which require notice.

Ch, a very common sound, representing what is sometimes a *t* and sometimes *ki*—in other dialects. C is not required for any other sound, as it can be always represented by *k* when hard, and by *s* when soft. It would probably be an improvement always to write the *ch* sound by a simple *c.*

Gn, see ng'.

Kw represents the sound of *qu* in *queer.*

M frequently stands for *mu,* in which cases it is pronounced with a half-suppressed *u* sound before it, and is even capable of bearing the accent of the word, as in *mtu,* a person, where the stress of voice is on the *m,* which has a dull nasal semivowel sound, not quite *um.* Where *m* occurs before any consonant except *b* or *w,* it must have this semivowel sound.

M, standing for *mu*, has generally its semivowel sound before *u*. Before *a* or *e* it becomes *mw*, and before *o* it frequently loses the *u* altogether, and is pronounced as a simple *m*.

N has frequently a nasal semivowel sound, a half-suppressed *i* being suggested by it. N has always this semivowel sound where it is immediately followed by *ch*, *f*, *h*, *m*, *n*, or *s*.

Ny has the sound of the Spanish *ñ*, the French and Italian *gn*, the Portuguese *nh*, and the English *ni* in *companion*, only a little thicker and more nasal.

Ng' is a peculiar African sound, much resembling the *-ng* which occurs at the end of many English words. If we could divide *longing* thus, *lo-nging*, without at all altering the pronunciation, it would come very near the African sound, which is never a final, because all Swahili syllables must end in a vowel. Some prefer to write this sound *gn-*, as it resembles the sound given by Germans and others to those letters when they occur as initial letters in Greek. This sound must be distinguished from the common sound of *ng-*, in which the *g* distinctly passes on to the following vowel, as in the English word *engage*; in *ng'-* both sounds are heard, but neither passes on to the vowel.

Sh is the Arabic *shin*, the English *sh*, the French *ch*,

the German *sch.* *Sh* and *s* are commonly treated as identical.

P, T, K, and possibly some other letters, have occasionally an explosive or aspirated sound, such as an Irishman will often give them. This explosive sound makes no change in the letter, but is an addition to it, probably always marking a suppressed *n*. Thus *upepo* is a *wind*, with both *p*'s smooth as in English; but the plural, which should regularly be *npepo*, is *p'epo*, with a strong explosive sound attached to the first letter. This explosive sound may be marked by an apostrophe; it is, however, very seldom necessary to the sense of a word, and is noticeably smoothed down or omitted by the more refined and Arabized Swahili.

There are other niceties of pronunciation which a fine ear may distinguish; but as they are by no means essential, and are seldom noticed by the natives themselves, it is not worth while here to examine them particularly.

As a rule, the vowels are all pronounced distinctly, and do not form diphthongs. When, however, a formative particle ending in *-a* is placed before a word beginning with *e-* or *i-*, the two letters coalesce into a long *e* sound. It is not, however, even in such a case as this, always incorrect to pronounce the two vowels distinctly, though it is not usually done. The instances of and rules for this union of sound will be found where the several prefixes which give occasion to it are dealt with.

When two vowels come together at the end of a word, they are often to the ear one syllable, and have the sound of a diphthong; they are really, however, two syllables of which the former bears the accent. This is at once apparent in the Merima dialect, in which an *l* is put between the vowels. Thus *kufaa*, to be of use, which sounds as if written *kufá*, is in the Merima dialect *kufala*. The shifting of the accent sometimes shows that the vowels are really separate. Thus a common fruit tree is called *mzambarau*, in which word the last two vowels apparently unite into a sound like that in the English word *how;* but when *-ni* is added, making *Mzambaraúni*, at the *zambaráu* tree—the name of one of the quarters of Zanzibar—the *u* is quite separated from the *a*, and the last two syllables are pronounced like the English *-oony*.

It may be assumed in all cases in which two vowels come together that an *l* has been omitted between them, and will appear in some modification of the word or in its derivatives.

The shifting of the accent above referred to takes place in obedience to the universal rule in Swahili, that the main accent of the word is always put upon the last syllable but one, a rule which often changes the sound of a word so materially as to baffle a beginner in his endeavour to seize and retain it. The syllable *-ni* is the chief disturber of accents; and words which end in it may be always suspected of being plural imperatives if they are verbs, or of being in what is known as the locative case if they are nouns. There are only a very few words which end in *-ni* in their simple forms.

The formation or division of syllables is so closely connected with the powers of the letters, that this will be a proper place to mention it. The rule is that all Swahili syllables end in a vowel, and that the vowel must be preceded only by a single consonant, or by one preceded by *n* or *m*, or followed by *w* or *y*.

There are a few half-assimilated Arabic words in which double consonants occur; but there is a strong tendency in all such cases to drop one of the consonants and attach the other to the vowel which follows them.

W can be placed after all the other consonants, simple and compound, except perhaps F and V.

Y can follow F, N, and V.

These two letters are used in the formation of Verbs, *-w-* being the sign of the passive, and *-y-* being used to give a transitive meaning. In several cases *-fy-* stands for *-py-*; *-py-* occurs in one word only, *'mpya*, new.

N can be placed before D, G, J, Y, and Z.

M can be placed before B, and perhaps Ch and V.

M in these instances represents an *n-* used as a substantival and adjectival prefix. Used in this way, *n* before *b* becomes *m*; before *l* or *r* it changes the *l* or *r* into *d*, making *nd-* instead of *nl-* or *nr-*; before *w* it changes into *m*, and the *w* becomes *b*, making *mb-*

instead of *nw-*. It is curious that *w* can be made to follow *n* without any change, but that *n* cannot be put before *w*. Before *k*, *p*, and *t*, the *n* is dropped, and they become *k'*, *p'*, and *t'*; before the other letters *ch*, *f*, *h*, *m*, *n*, and *s*, it is merely dropped.

The resulting syllables are not always easy of pronunciation to a European, as, for instance, *nywa* in *kú-nywa*, to drink, nor is it very easy to pronounce *ngu* or *nda*; but to a native such sounds present no difficulty, whilst he can scarcely pronounce such a word as *black*.

Instances of the division of syllables will be found in the specimen of *Kinyume*, which forms Appendix I. Kinyume is made by taking the last syllable from the end of a word and putting it at the beginning, so that each instance is a specimen of the native idea as to what letters belong to the final syllable. Some Swahili are very ready at understanding and speaking this enigmatical dialect.

At the head of each letter in the second part will be found some observations on its use and pronunciation.

SUBSTANTIVES.

Swahili nouns have two numbers, singular and plural, which are distinguished by their initial letters. Upon the forms of the Substantives depend the forms of all Adjectives, Pronouns, and Verbs governing or governed by them. It is, therefore, necessary to divide them into so many classes as there are different forms either of Substantives or of dependent words, in order to be able to lay down rules for the correct formation of sentences. For this purpose Swahili Substantives may be conveniently divided into eight classes.

I. Those beginning with *M-*, *'M-*, *Mu-*, or *Mw-*, in the singular, and which denote living beings. They make their plural by changing *M-* &c. into *Wa-*.

Mtu, a man ; *watu*, people.

The singular prefix represents in all its forms the syllable *Mu-*, which is itself very rarely heard. Before a consonant it is almost always pronounced as a semi-vowel *m*, with the *u* sound before rather than after it. Before *a* and *e* the *u* becomes a consonant, and the prefix appears as *mw-*. Before *o* and *u* the *u* is very frequently dropped, and the *m* alone is heard. The prefix is treated as a distinct syllable when followed by a consonant, but very rarely so when followed by a vowel.

> *Mchawi*, a wizard; *wachawi*, wizards.
> *Mjusi*, a lizard; *wajusi*, lizards.
> *Mwana*, a son; *waana*, sons.
> *Mwoga*, or *moga*, a coward; *waoga*, cowards.
> *Muumishi*, or *mumishi*, a cupper; *waumishi*, cuppers.

When the plural prefix *wa-* is placed before a word beginning with *a-*, the two *a*'s run together, and are seldom distinguishable by the ear alone. When *wa-* is placed before a word beginning with *e-* or *i-*, the *-a* flows into the other vowel and produces a long *e* sound.

> *Mwenzi*, a companion; *wenzi*, companions.
> *Mwivi*, a thief; *wevi*, thieves.

II. Substantives beginning with *M-*, *'M-*, *Mu-*, or *Mw-*, which do *not* denote living or animate beings. They make their plural by changing *M-* &c. into *Mi-*.

> *Mti*, a tree; *miti*, trees.

The same observations apply to the singular prefix in this class as in Class I.

> *Mfupa*, a bone; *mifupa*, bones.
> *Mwanzo*, a beginning; *mianzo*, beginnings.
> *Mwembe*, a mango tree; *miembe*, mango trees.
> *Mwiba*, a thorn; *miiba*, or *miba*, thorns.
> *Moto*, a fire; *mioto*, fires.

The names of trees belong to this class.

III. Those which do not change to form the plural.

> *Nyumba*, a house; *nyumba*, houses.

The simple description of nouns of this class is that they begin with *n*, followed by some other consonant. It is probable that *Ni-* is the ground form of the prefix of this class, since it always appears as *ny-* before a vowel. The singular powers and antipathies of the letter *n-* very much affect the distinctness of this class of nouns. As *n* must be dropped before *ch*, *f*, *h*, *k*, *p*, *s*, or *t*, nouns beginning with those letters may belong to this class;* and as *n* becomes *m* before *b*, *v*, and *w*, nouns beginning with *mb* or *mv* may belong to it. There is a further complication in Swahili, arising from the fact that foreign words, except only foreign names of persons and offices, whatever their first letters, are correctly placed in this class. The popular instinct, however, refuses this rule, and in the vulgar dialect classes foreign words according to their initial letters, regarding the first syllable as a mere prefix, and treating it accordingly (see also p. 20). In some cases words are handled in this way even in polite Swahili; thus the Arabic *Kitabu*, a book, is very often made plural by treating the *ki-* as a prefix, and saying *Vitabu*, for books.

Kamba, a rope; *kamba*, ropes.
Mbegu, a seed; *mbegu*, seeds.
Nyumba, a house; *nyumba*, houses.
Meza, a table; *meza*, tables.
Bunduki, a gun; *bunduki*, guns.
Ndizi, a banana; *ndizi*, banauas.
Njia, a road; *njia*, roads.

---

* There is nothing to show whether nouns beginning with these letters belong to this class or to the fifth; but it is always safest in cases of doubt to treat them as belonging to this class, unless some special largeness is intended to be intimated concerning them.

IV. Those which begin with *Ki-* before a consonant or *Ch-* before a vowel. They form their plural by changing *Ki-* into *Vi-* and *Ch-* into *Vy-*.

Kitu, a thing; *vitu*, things.
Chombo, a vessel; *vyombo*, vessels.

Substantives are made diminutives by being brought into this class.

Mlima, a mountain; *Kilima*, a hill.
Bweta, a box; *kibweta*, a little box.

If the word stripped of all prefixes is a monosyllable, *ji-* must first be prefixed.

Mti, a tree; *kijiti*, a shrub.
Mwiko, a spoon; *kijiko*, a little spoon.

Words beginning with *Ki-* may be turned into diminutives by inserting *-ji-* after the prefix.

Kitwa, a head; *kijitwa*, a little head.
Kiboko, a hippopotamus; *kijiboko*, a little hippopotamus.

In regard to animals, the use of the diminutive has a depreciating effect.

Mbuzi, a goat; *kibuzi*, a poor little goat.

V. Those which make their plural by prefixing *ma-*.

Kasha, a chest; *makasha*, chests.

Nouns are generally brought into this class by rejecting all prefix in the singular. If, however, the word itself begins with a vowel, *j-* is prefixed; if it be a monosyllable, *ji-* is prefixed. The *j-* or *ji-* is regularly omitted in the plural, but may be retained to avoid ambiguity, where the regular word would have resembled one formed from another root.

Jambo, an affair; *mambo*, affairs.
Jicho, an eye; *macho*, eyes.
Jombo, a large vessel; *majombo*, large vessels.

If the word begin with *i-* or *e-*, the *-a* of the plural prefix coalesces with it and forms a long *-e-*; this distinguishes dissyllables with *j-* prefixed from monosyllables with *ji-* prefixed.

Jino, a tooth; *meno* (not *mano*), teeth.

Foreign names of persons and offices belong to this class.

Waziri, a vizir; *mawaziri*, vizirs.

In the vulgar dialect of Zanzibar all foreign words which have a first syllable that cannot be treated as a prefix, are made to belong to this class, and *ma-* is prefixed to form the plural (see p. 18).

Anything which is to be marked as peculiarly large or important is so described by bringing the word into this class.

Mfuko, a bag; *fuko*, a very large bag.
Mtu, a man; *jitu*, a very large man.
Nyumba, a house; *jumba*, a large house.

If a word is already in this class, it may be described as larger by prefixing *ji-*.

Matanga, sails; *majitanga*, great sails.

Maji, water, *Mafuta*, oil, and other nouns in that form are treated as plurals of this class.

VI. Those which begin with *U-* in the singular. They make their plural by changing *U-* into *Ny-* before a vowel, or *N-* before a consonant.

Uimbo, a song; *nyimbo*, songs.
Udevu, a hair of the beard; *ndevu*, hairs of the beard.

This class is not a large one; but the formation of its plural is full of apparent irregularities produced by the letter *n*.

1. All nouns of this class, which are in the singular dissyllables only, retain the *u-* in the plural, and are treated as beginning with a vowel.

Ufa, a crack; *nyufa*, cracks.
Uso, a face; *nyuso*, faces.

2. Words in which the *U-* is followed by *d, g, j,* or *z*, take *N-* in place of *U-*.

3. Words in which the *U-* is followed by *l* or *r*, take *N-*, but change the *l* or *r* into *d*.

Ulimi, a tongue; *ndimi*, tongues.

4. Words in which the *U-* is followed by *b, v,* or *w*, take *n-*, but change it into *m-*, and their first letter is always *b*.

Ubau, a plank; *mbau*, planks.
Uwingu, a heaven; *mbingu*, the heavens.

5. Words in which the *U-* is followed by *k, p,* or *t*,

drop the *U-*, and give an explosive sound to the first letter.

Upepo, a wind; *p'epo*, winds.

6. Words in which the *U-* is followed by *ch*, *f*, *h*, *n*, or *s*, merely drop the *U-*.

Ufunguo, a key; *funguo*, keys.

Nouns of this class are so few in Swahili that it is scarcely worth while to notice these distinctions; they are, however, important as explaining what would otherwise seem anomalies, and represent influences which have a much larger field in other African languages.

Abstract nouns generally belong to this class.

VII. The one word *Mahali*, place or places, which requires special forms in all adjectives and pronouns.

VIII. The Infinitives of Verbs used as Substantives. All Infinitives may be so used, and answer to the English Verbal Substantives in *-ing*.

Kufa, to die = dying.
Kwiba, to steal = stealing.

All Substantives of both numbers may be put into what may be called the *locative case* by adding *-ni*. This case has three great varieties of meaning, which are marked by differences in all dependent pronouns.

1. In, within, to or from within.
2. At, by, near.
3. To, from, at (of places far off).

Nyumbani mwangu, in my house.
Nyumbani pangu, near my house.
Nyumbani kwangu, to my house.
Mtoni, by the river.
Njiani, on the road.
Vyomboni, in the vessels.
Kitwani, on the head.
Mbinguni, in heaven.
Kuangukani, in falling.

The possessive case is expressed by the use of the Preposition *-a*, which see. The objective or accusative is the same as the subjective or nominative.

In the following list of Substantives the plural form is given in all cases in which, if commonly used, it is not the same as the singular.

LIST OF SUBSTANTIVES

The letters in parentheses denote the several dialects: (A.) Kiamu, that of Lamoo; (M.) Kimvita, that of Mombas; (Mer.) Kimerima, that of the mainland opposite Zanzibar; (N.) Kingozi, the poetical dialect; (Ar.) Arabic.

A what-is-it, a thing the name of which you do not know or cannot recall, dude, *pl.* madude.
Such-a-one, a person whose name is not known or is immaterial, fullani.

A.

Abasement, unenyekeo.
Abhorrence, machukio.
Ability, uwezo.
Abridgment, muhtasari.
Abscess, tumbasi, nasur.
Abundance, wingi, ungi (M.), marithawa.
Abyssinian, Habeshia, *pl.* Mahabeshia.
Acceptance, ukubali.
Accident, tukio, *pl.* matukio.
Accounts, hesabu.
Account book, daftari.
Accusation, matuvumu.
Accusation (before a judge), mshtaka, *pl.* mishtaka.
Ache, maumivu, uchungu.
Action, kitendo, *pl.* vitendo, amali.
Addition (in arithmetic), jumla.
Address (of a letter), anwani.
Adornment, kipambo, *pl.* vipambo, pambo, *pl.* mapambo.
Adultery, zani, uzini, uzinzi.
Advantage (profit), fayida.
Adversity, mateso, shidda.
Advice, shauri, *pl.* mashauri.
Adze, shoka la bapa, sezo.
Affair, jambo.
Affairs, mambo, shughuli, ulimwengu.
Affection, mapenzi, mapendo.
Mutual affection, mapendano
Affliction, teso, *pl.* mateso.
Age, umri.
Old age, uzee.
Extreme old age, ukongwe.
Equal in age, hirimu moja.
Former ages, zamani za kale.
Agent, wakili, *pl.* mawakili.
Agreement, maagano, makatibu, mwafaka, mapatano, sharti.
Aim, shabaha.
Air, hawa, hewa, upepo.
For change of air, kubadili hawa.
Almond, lozi, *pl.* malozi.
Alms, sadaka.

Aloes, subiri, shibiri.
Alocs wood, uudi.
Altar, mathbah, mathabahu.
Alum, shabbu.
Ambergris, ambari.
Amulet, talasimu, *pl.* matalasimu.
Amusement, mazumgumzo, maongezi.
Ancestors, babu, wazee.
Anchor, nanga, baura.
Ancle (*see Anklets*), kiwiko cha mguu, ito la guu (A.).
Angel, malaika.
Anger, hasira, ghathabu.
Angle, pembe.
Angoxa, Ngoje.
Animal, nyama.
The young of a domestic animal, ndama.
A young she-animal that has not yet borne, mtamba, *pl.* mitamba.
Native animals. See under their several names:—
Buku, *a very large kind of rat.*
Toi, *a kind of wild goat.*
Buga (?).
Ndezi (?).
Njiri (?).
Anklets (*see Ancle*), mtali, *pl.* mitali, furungu, *pl.* mafurungu.
Answer, majibu, jawabu.
Antelopes. See Gazelle.
Bara, *Heleobagus arundinaceus.*
Dondoro, *Dyker's antelope.*
Koru, *water buck.*
Kuguni, *haartebeest.*
Mpofu, *pl.* Wapofu, *eland.*
Nyumbo, *wildebeest.*
Parahara.
Kulungu.
Antimony, wanja wa manga.
Ants, chungu, tungu (M.), sisimizi (?).
Siafu, *a large brown kind.*
Maji a moto, *a yellow kind which lives in trees.*
White ants, mchwa.
Ants in their flying stage, kumbi-kumbi.
Anthill, kisugulu, *pl.* visugulu.
Anus, mkunda, fupa.
Anvil, fuawe.
Ape, nyani.
Apostle, mtume, *pl.* mitume.
Appearance, umbo, *pl.* maumbo.
Arab, Mwarabu, *pl.* Waarabu.
Arab from Sheher, Msbihiri, *pl.* Washihiri.
Arab from the Persian Gulf, Mshemali, *pl.* Washemali, Tende halua.
Arabia, Arabuni, Manga.
Arabic, Kiarabu.
Arbitrator, mpatanishi.
Arch, tao, *pl.* matao.
Areca nut, popoo. *See Betel.*
Arithmetic, hesabu.
Addition, jumla.
Subtraction, baki.
Multiplication, tharuba.
Division, mkasama.
Proportion, or division of profits, uirari.
Arm, mkono, *pl.* mikono.
Under the arm, kwapani.
Armpit, kwapa, *pl.* makwapa.
Perspiration of the armpit, kikwapa.
Arrangements, madaraka.
Arrival, kifiko, kikomo.
Arrogance, ghururi.
Arrow, mshale, *pl.* mishale, chembe, *pl.* vyembe (N.).
Arrowroot, uwanga, kanji.
Artery, vein or nerve, mshipa, *pl.* mishipa.

Artifice, kitimbi, *pl.* vitimbi.
Ascriptions of praise, tasbiih.
Ashes, jifu, *pl.* majifu, ivu, pl. maivu (M.).
Ass, punda.
Assafœtida, mvuje.
Assembly, jamaa, jumaa, makutano, makusanyiko.
Place of assembly, makusanyiko.
Asthma, pumu.
Astonishment, mataajabu, msangao.
Astrologer, mnajimu, *pl.* wanajimu.
Astronomy, falaki, fálak.
Attachment, wambiso.
Auction, mnada, *pl.* minada.
Auctioneer, dalali.
Aunt, shangazi, *pl.* mashangazi.
Authority, nguvu, mamlaka, hukumu.
Avarice, choyo, bakhili, tamaa.
Awl, uma, *pl.* nyuma.
Awning, chandalua.
Axe, shoka, *pl.* mashoka.

B.

Baby, mtoto mchanga, kitoto kichanga, malaika.
Back, maungo, mgongo.
Back of the head and neck, kishogo.
Backbone, uti wa maungo.
Badness, ubaya, uovu.
Bag, mfuko, *pl.* mifuko, fuko, *pl.* mafuko, kifuko, *pl.* vifuko.
Mkoba, *pl.* mikoba, *a scrip.*
Kibogoshi, *pl.* vibogoshi, *a small bag made of skin.*
Matting bags.
Kikapu *or* Chikapu, *pl.* vikapu.
Kapu, *pl.* makapu, *very large.*
Kanda, *pl.* makanda, *long and narrow, broadest at the bottom.*
Junia, *used for rice, &c.*, gunia.
Kigunni, *used for dates, sugar, &c.*
Kifumbo, *pl.* vifumbo, *very large, used for cloves.*
Baggage, vyombo.
Bail, lazima.
Bait, chambo, *pl.* vyambo.
Baking place for pottery, &c., jòko.
Balances, mizani.
Baldness, upaa.
A shaved place on the head, kipaa, *pl.* vipaa.
Ball, tufe.
India-rubber ball, mpira, *pl.* mipira.
Any small round thing, donge, *pl.* madonge.
Ballast, farumi.
Bamboo, 'mwanzi, *pl.* miwanzi.
Bananas, ndizi.
Banana tree, mgomba, *pl.* migomba.
Bunchlets of fruit, tana, *pl.* matana.
The fruit stalk, mkungu, *pl.* mikungu.
Band (stripe), utepe, *pl.* tepe.
Band (of soldiers, &c.), kikosi, *pl.* vikosi.
Bandage, utambaa, *pl.* tambaa.
Bangles. *See Anklets.*
Bank (of earth, sand, &c.), fungu, *pl.* mafungu.
Bank of a river, kando.
The opposite bank, ng'ambo.
Baobab. *See Calabash.*
Barber, kinyozi, *pl.* vinyozi.
Bargain, mwafaka, maafikano.
Bargaining, ubazazi.
Bark of a tree, gome (*hard*), ganda (*soft*).

Barley, shairi (Ar.).
Barque (a ship), merikebu ya milingote miwili na nuss.
Barrel, pipa, *pl.* mapipa.
Basin, bakuli, *pl.* mabakuli.
A small basin, kibaba.
A brass basin, tasa, *pl.* matasa. *See Bowl.*
Basket. See Bag.
Chikapu, *pl.* vikapu.
Pakacha, *pl.* mapakacha, *made of cocoa-nut leaves plaited together.*
Dohani, *a very tall narrow basket made of slips of wood supplemented by cocoa-nut leaves.*
Tunga, *a round open basket.*
Ungo, *pl.* maungo, *or* uteo, *pl.* teo (M.), *a round flat basket used for sifting.*
Kiteo, *pl.* viteo, *a very small one.*
Kunguto, *pl.* makunguto, *a basket used as a colander.*
Jamanda, *pl.* majamanda, *a round basket of thick work, with a raised lid.*
Bat, popo.
Batchelor, msijana (?).
Bath, birika, chakogea.
Bath room, choo, *pl.* vyoo. *See Privy.*
Public baths, hamami.
Battle, mapigano.
Battlements, menomeno.
Bay, ghubba.
Beach, pwani, mpwa (M.).
Beads, ushanga, *pl.* shanga.
Kondavi, *pl.* makondavi, *a large kind worn by women.*
(rosary), tasbiih.
Beak, mdomo wa ndege.
A parrot's beak, mbango.

Beam, mti, *pl.* miti, boriti, mhimili, *pl.* mihimili.
Beans, kuunde.
Chooko, *a very small green kind.*
Fiwe, *grow on a climbing plant with a white flower.*
Baazi, *grow on a bush something like a laburnum.*
Beard, ndevu, madevu.
One hair of the beard, udevu.
The imperial, the tuft of hair on the lower lip, kinwa mchuzi, kionda mtuzi (M.).
Beast, nyama.
Beauty, uzuri.
A beauty, kizuri, *pl.* vizuri, haiba.
Bed (for planting sweet potatoes), tuta, *pl.* matuta.
Bedding, matandiko.
Bedstead, kitanda, *pl.* vitanda.
The legs, tendegu, *pl.* matendegu.
The side pieces, mfumbati, *pl.* mifumbati.
The end pieces, kitakizo, *pl.* vitakizo.
The head, mchago.
The space underneath, mvungu kitanda.
Bee, nyuki.
Beehive (a hollow piece of wood), mzinga, *pl.* mizinga.
Beggar, mwombaji, *pl.* waombaji.
Begging, maomvi.
Beginning, mwanzo, *pl.* mianzo.
Start in speaking or doing, feli, *pl.* mafeli.
Behaviour, mwenendo.
Good behaviour, kutenda vema.
Ill behaviour, kutenda vibaya.
Bell, kengele.
Njuga, *a small bell worn as an ornament, a dog bell.*

Bellowing, kivumi, vumi.
Bellows, mifuo, mivukuto.
Belly, matumbo.
Bend, pindo.
The arm stiffened in a bent form, kigosho cha mkono.
Bembatooka bay, Mjanga.
Betel leaf, tambuu. *It is chewed with areca nut, lime, and tobacco folded up in it, and gives its name to the whole.*
Beverage, kinywaji, *pl.* vinywaji.
Bhang, bangi.
Biceps muscle, tafu ya mkono.
Bier, jeneza, jenaiza.
Bifurcation, panda.
Bile, nyongo.
Biliousness, safura (Ar.), marungu (M.).
Bill. *See Beak*
(*account*), hesabu, barua.
Bill of sale, ankra.
(*chopper*), mundu, *pl.* miundu; upamba, *pl.* pamba.
Bird, ndege, nyuni (M.).
Young of birds, kinda, *pl.* makinda.
Birds of the air, ndege za anga.
Bird of ill omen, korofi, mkorofi.
Native birds.
Pugi, *a very small kind of dove.*
Korongo, *crane.*
Mbango, *a bird with a hooked beak.*
Ninga, *a green dove.*
Zawaridi, *a Java sparrow.*
Mbayuwayu, *a swallow.*
Bundi, *an owl.*
Luanga—pungu—tendawala (?).
Birth, uzazi, uvyazi, kizazi, kivyazi.
Biscuit, biskwiti.
A very thin kind, kaki.
Bishop, askafu (Ar.).
A chess bishop, khami.
Bit (*a horse's*), lijamu.
Bitterness, uchungu, ukali.
Blabber of secrets, payo, *pl.* mapayo.
Blacksmith, mfua chuma, *pl.* wafua chuma, mhunzi (Mer.), *pl.* wahunzi.
Blackwood, sesemi.
Bladder, kibofu, *pl.* vibofu.
Blade, kengea.
Blade of grass, uchipuka, *pl.* chipuka.
Blame, matuvumu.
Blanket, bushuti.
Blemish, ila, kipunguo.
Blessing, baraka, mbaraka, *pl.* mibaraka.
Blindness, upofu (*loss of sight*), chongo (*loss of one eye*).
Blinders (*used for camels when grinding in mills*), jamanda (*of basket work*), kidoto (*of cloth*).
Blister, lengelenge, *pl.* malengelenge.
A vesicular eruption of the skin, [uwati.
Block. *See Pulley*.
A block to dry skull caps upon, faroma.
Blood, damu.
Blood-vessel, mshipa, *pl.* mishipa.
Blotch, waa, *pl.* mawaa.
Blowing and bellowing noise (*often made with a drum*), vumi.
Blue vitriol, mrututu.
Board, ubau, *pl.* mbau.
Piece of board, kibau, *pl.* vibau.
Boat, mashua.
Body, mwili, *pl.* miili.
The human trunk, kiwiliwili.
A dead body, mayiti.
The body of soldiers, &c., jamii.

Boil, jipu, *pl.* majipu.
Bomb, kombora.
Bombay, Mombee.
Bone, mfupa, *pl.* mifupa, fupa, *pl.* mafupa (*very large*).
Book, chuo, *pl.* vyuo, kitabu, *pl.* vitabu.
A sacred book, msahafu, *pl.* misahafu.
An account book, daftari.
Booty, mateka, nyara.
Border (*boundary*), mpaka, *pl.* mipaka.
An edging woven on to a piece of cloth, taraza.
Bother, uthia, huja.
Bottle, chupa, *pl.* machupa, tupa (M.), *pl.* matupa.
A long-necked bottle for sprinkling scents, mrashi, *pl.* mirashi.
A little bottle, a phial, kitupa, *pl.* vitupa.
Bottom, chini.
Bough, kitawi, *pl.* vitawi.
Boundary, mpaka, *pl.* mipaka.
Bow, upindi, *pl.* pindi, uta, *pl.* mata, *or* nyuta.
Bowl (*wooden*), fua. *See Basin.*
Bowsprit, mlingote wa maji.
Box, bweta, *pl.* mabweta, ndusi, kisanduku, *pl.* visanduku.
Small, kibweta, *pl.* vibweta.
Large, kasha, *pl.* makasha, sanduku.
Small metal box, kijaluba, *pl.* vijaluba.
Small, long-shaped metal box, often used to keep betel in, kijamanda, *pl.* vijamanda.
Small paper box, kibumba, *pl.* vibumba.
Boy, kijana, *pl.* vijana.
Bracelet, kekee (*flat*).
Kikuku, *pl.* vikuku (*round*).
Kingaja, *pl.* vingaja (*of beads*).
Banagiri(*ornamented with points*).
Timbi.
Braid, kigwe, *pl.* vigwe.
Brains, bongo, mabongo.
Bran, chachu, makapi.
Husks of rice, kumvi.
Branch, tawi, *pl.* matawi, utanzu, *pl.* tanzu.
Brand (*a piece of wood partly burnt*), kinga, *pl.* vinga.
Brass, shaba, nuhás (Ar.).
Brass wire, mazoka (?).
Bravery, ushujaa, u*th*abiti.
Brawler, mgomvi, *pl.* wagomvi.
Bread (*loaf or cake*), mkate.
Breadth, upana.
Break. See Crack, Notch.
Breakfast, chakula cha subui, kifungua kanwa, cha'msha kanwa.
Breaking wind (*upward*), kiungulia, *pl.* viungulia.
(*downward*), jamba, *pl.* majamba, mashuzi.
Breast, kifua, kidari, mtima.
Breasts, maziwa, *sing.* ziwa.
Breath, pumzi, nafusi, roho.
Bribe, rushwa.
Bride, bibi harusi.
Bridegroom, bwana harusi.
Bridle, hatamu (*halter, reins, &c.*), lijamu (*bit*).
Brink, ukingo, mzingo.
Brook, kijito, *pl.* vijito.
Broom, ufagio, *pl.* fagio.
Brother, ndugu, ndugu mume, kaka (Kihadimu).
Foster brother, ndugu kunyonya.
Brother-in-law, shemegi.

Husband's brother, mwamua.
Wife's brother, wifi.
Brow, kikomo cha uso, kipaji.
Bruise, vilio la damu, alama ya pigo.
Brush (*see Broom*), burushi.
Brushwood, koko, makoko.
Bubble, povu, *pl.* mapovu.
Bucket, ndoo.
Buckler, ngao.
Buffalo, nyati.
Bug, kunguni.
Building, jengo, *pl.* majengo.
Building materials, majengo.
Firm and good building, mtomo.
Bull, fahali, *pl.* mafahali, ng'ombe mume or ndume.
Bullet, poopoo, risasi ya bunduki.
Bullock, maksai.
Bunch, tawi, *pl.* matawi, kitawi, *pl.* vitawi, kichala, *pl.* vichala. *The bunch is said to be of the tree and not of the fruit.*
Tawi la mtende, *a bunch of dates.*
Kichala cha mzabibu, *a bunch of grapes. See Bananas.*
Bundle, peto, *pl.* mapeto, mzigo, *pl.* mizigo.
In a cloth, bindo, furushi, kifurushi.
Of straw, mwenge, *pl.* mienge.
Of sticks, titi, *pl.* matiti.
Buoy, chilezo, *pl.* vilezo, mlezo, *pl.* milezo.
Burden, mzigo, *pl.* mizigo.
Burial-place, mazishi, maziko.
Burier (*i.e. a special friend*), mzishi, *pl.* wazishi.
Bush, kijiti, *pl.* vijiti.
Bushes, koko, *pl.* makoko.
Business, shughuli, kazi.
Urgent business, amara.
A complicated business, visa vingi.
His business, amri yake.
I have no business, &c., sina amri, &c.
Butter, siagi.
Clarified butter (*ghee*), samli.
Buttermilk, mtindi.
Butterfly, kipepeo, *pl.* vipepeo.
Buttocks, tako, *pl.* matako.
Button, kifungo, *pl.* vifungo.
Button loop, kitanzi, *pl.* vitanzi.
Button by which the wooden clogs are held on, msuruake, *pl.* misuruake.
Buyer, mnunuzi, *pl.* wanunuzi.

C.

Cabin (*side*), kipenu.
Cable, amara.
Caffre corn, mtama.
Cage, kizimbi, *pl.* vizimbi, tundu, *pl.* matundu.
Cake, mkate, *pl.* mikate.
Cake of mtama meal, mkate wa mofu.
Cake of tobacco, mkate wa tumbako.
Bumunda, *pl.* mabumunda, *a sort of dumpling or soft cake.*
Kitumbua, *pl.* vitumbua, *a cake made like a fritter.*
Ladu, *a round ball made of semsem seed, spice, and sugar.*
Kinyuuya, *pl.* vinyunya, *a little cake made to try the quality of the flour.*
Calabash, buyu, *pl.* mabuyu.
Inner part of the calabash fruit, ubuyu.
Calabash used to draw water, kibuyu, vibuyu.

Calabash tree or baobab, mbuyu, *pl.* mibuyu.
A pumpkin shell used to hold liquids, dundu, *pl.* madundu.
Calamity, masaibu, msiba, *pl.* misiba.
Calico. See Cloth.
Fine, bafta.
Calf, ndama, ndama wa ng'ombe.
Call (calling), mwito, *pl.* miito.
(*a cry*), ukelele, ukemi.
Kikorombwe, *a signal cry.*
Calm, shwali.
Calumba root, kaomwa.
Camel, ngamia.
Camelopard, twiga.
Camphor, karafumayiti, kafuri.
Candle, tawafa, meshmaa.
Candlestick, kinara, *pl.* vinara.
Cannabis Indica, bangi.
Cannon, mzinga, *pl.* mizinga.
Canoe, galawa (*with outriggers*), mtumbwi, *pl.* mitumbwi (*without outriggers*), hori, *pl.* mahori (*with raised head and stern*).
Canter, mghad (*of a horse*).
Thelth (*of an ass*).
Cap, kofia.
A cap block, faroma.
A gun-cap, fataki.
Capacity, kadri.
Cape (headland), rasi.
Captain, nakhotha, naoza, kapitani.
Caravan, msafara, *pl.* misafara.
Caravan porter, mpagazi, *pl.* wapagazi.
Carcase, mzoga, *pl.* mizoga.
Cards (playing), karata.
Cardamoms, iliki.
Care, tunza, *pl.* matunza.
(*caution*), hathari.
Cargo, shehena.
Carpenter, sermala, *pl.* masermala.
Carpet, zulia.
Carriage, gari, *pl.* magari.
A gun carriage, gurudumo la mzinga.
Cartridge, kiass cha bunduki.
Carving, naksh, nakishi.
Case or paper box, kibumba, *pl.* vibumba.
Cashew nut, korosho, *pl.* makorosho
Immature nut, dunge.
Cashew apple, bibo, *pl.* mabibo, kanju (M.), *pl.* makanju.
Cashew nut tree, mbibo, *pl.* mibibo mkanju (M.), *pl.* mikanju.
Cask, pipa, *pl.* mapipa.
Casket, kijamanda, *pl.* vijamanda.
Cassava, muhogo.
A piece of the dried root, kopa, *pl.* makopa.
Castle, gereza, ngome.
A chess castle, fil (Ar. *elephant*).
Castor oil, mafuta ya mbarika, mafuta ya nyonyo (?), mafuta ya mbono (?).
Castor oil plant, mbarika, *pl.* mibarika, mbono (?), *pl.* mibono.
Cat, paka.
Catamite, haniti, hawa, hawara, shoga (A.).
Cattle, ng'ombe, nyama.
Cattle fold, zizi, *pl.* mazizi.
Caudle made on the occasion of a birth, of rice, sugar, and spice, and given to visitors, fuka.
Caulking, khalfati.
Cause, sababu, kisa, asili, maana.
Cautery and the marks of it, pisho, [*pl.* mapisho.
Caution, hathari.
Cave, paango, *pl.* mapaango.
Censer, a small vessel to burn incense in, chetezo, *pl.* vyetezo, mkebe, *pl.* mikebe.

Centipede, taandu.
Certainty, yakini, kite.
Chaff, kapi, *pl.* makapi.
(*of rice*), kumvi.
(*bran and crushed grains*), wishwa.
Chain, mkufu, *pl.* mikufu, mnyo-rero, *pl.* minyororo, silesile,
Door chain, riza.
Chair, kiti, *pl.* viti.
Chalk, chaki.
Chameleon, kinyonga, *pl.* vinyonga, lumbwi (?).
Chance, nasibu.
Chandelier, thurea.
Change or changing, geuzi, *pl.* mageuzi.
Chapter, sura, bab.
Character, sifa.
Characters, herufu.
Charcoal, makaa ya miti.
Charm (*talisman*), talasimu, *pl.* ma-talasimu.
Chatter, upuzi.
Chatterer, mpuzi, *pl.* wapuzi.
Cheat, ayari, mjanja, *pl.* wajanja.
A great cheat, patiala.
Cheek (*the part over the cheek-bone*), kitefute, *pl.* vitefute.
(*The part over the teeth*), chafu, *pl.* machafu, tavu (A.), *pl.* matavu.
Cheese, jibini.
Chess, sataranji.
Chest (*of men*), kifua, *pl.* vifua.
(*of animals or men*), kidari.
(*a large box*), kasha, *pl.* makasha, sanduku.
Chicken, faranga, *pl.* mafaranga, kifaranga, *pl.* vifaranga.
Chief, mfalme, *pl.* wafalme, jumbe, *pl.* majumbe, munyi.
Chieftainship, ujumbe.
Child, mtoto, *pl.* watoto, kitoto, *pl.* vitoto, mwana, *pl.* waana.
A child which cuts its upper teeth first, and is therefore considered unlucky, kigego, *pl.* vigego.
Childhood, utoto.
Chimney, dohaan.
Chin, kidevu, *pl.* videvu, kievu (A.), *pl.* vievu.
Ornament hanging from the veil below the chin, jebu, *pl.* ma-jebu.
Chisel, patasi, chembeu.
Juba, *a mortice chisel.*
Uma, *a small chisel.*
Choice, hiari, hiyari, ikhtiari, na-thari.
Your choice, upendavyo (*as you like*).
Cholera, tauni, wabba, kipindu-pindu.
Church, kanisa, *pl.* makanisa.
Cinders, makaa.
Cinnabar, zangefuri.
Cinnamon, mdalasini.
Cipher (*figure of nought*), sifuru, zifuri.
Circle of a man's affairs, &c., uli-mwengu wake.
Circumcision, tohara, kumbi (Mer.) (?).
Circumference, kivimba, mzingo.
Circumstances, mambo.
A circumstance, jambo.
Cistern, birika.
Citron, balungi, *pl.* mabalungi.
Civet, zabadi.
Civet cat, fungo, ngawa (*a larger animal than the* fungo).
Civilization, ungwana.
Civilized people, wangwana.
Clamp for burning lime, tanuu.
Clap of thunder, radi.
Claret, divai.

Class for study, darasa.

Claw, ukucha, *pl.* kucha.

(*of a crab*), gando, *pl.* magando.

Clay (?), udongo.

Clearness, weupe.

Clerk, karani.

Clergyman, padre *or* padiri, *pl.* mapadiri, khatibu.

Cleverness, hekima.

Climate, tabia.

Clock, saa.

What o'clock is it? Saa ngapi? *According to the native reckoning, noon and midnight are at the sixth hour*, saa a sita; *six o'clock is* saa a *th*enashara.

Clod, pumba, *pl.* mapumba.

Cloth (*woollen*), joho.

(*Cotton*), nguo.

(*American sheeting*), amerikano.

(*Blue calico*), kaniki.

Cloth of gold, zari.

A loin cloth of about two yards, shuka, doti.

A loin cloth with a coloured border, kikoi, *pl.* vikoi.

A turban cloth, kitambi, *pl.* vitambi.

A woman's cloth, kisuto, *pl.* visuto.

A cloth twisted into a kind of rope, used as a girdle, and to make the turbans worn by the Hindis, ukumbuu, *pl.* kumbuu.

Clothes, nguo, miguo, mavazi, mavao.

Cloud, wingu, *pl.* mawingu.

Rain cloud, ghubari, *pl.* maghubari.

Broken scattered clouds, mavundevunde.

Cloves, garofuu, karofuu.

Fruit-stalks, kikonyo, *pl.* vikonyo.

Club, rungu.

Coals, makaa.

Coast, pwani.

Coat, joho (*a long open coat of broadcloth worn by the Arabs*).

Cob of Indian corn, gunzi, *pl.* magunzi.

Cock, jogoo, *pl.* majogoo, jogoi, jimbi.

A young cockerel, not yet able to crow, pora.

A cock's comb, upanga.

A cock's wattles, ndefu.

Cockles, kombe za pwani (?).

Cockroach, mende, makalalao (Malagazy).

Cocoa-nut, nazi.

Cocoa-nut tree, mnazi, *pl.* minazi

Heart of the growing shoot, used as salad, &c., kichilema, shaha.

Cloth-like envelope of young leaves, kilifu.

Leaf, kuti, *pl.* makuti.

Midrib of leaf, uchukuti, *pl.* chukuti.

Leaflets, ukuti, *pl.* kuti.

Leaf plaited for making fences, makuti ya kumba.

Half leaf plaited together, makuti ya pande.

Leaflets made up for thatching, makuti ya viungo.

Part of a leaf plaited into a basket, pakacha, *pl.* mapakacha.

Woody flower sheath, karara.

Bunch of nuts, tawi la mnazi.

Flower and first forming of nuts, upunga, *pl.* punga.

Small nuts, kidaka, *pl.* vidaka.

Half-grown nut, kitale, *pl.* vitale.

Full-grown nut before the nutty part is formed, dafu, *pl.* madafu. *In this stage the shell is perfectly full of the milk or juice* (maji), *and the nuts are often gathered for drinking.*

Half-ripe nut, when the nutty part is formed and the milk begins to wabble in the shell, koroma, *pl.* makoroma.

Ripe nut, nazi.

A nut which has grown full of a white spongy substance without any hollow or milk, joya, *pl.* majoya.

A nut which has dried in the shell so as to rattle in it without being spoilt, mbata.

The fibrous case of the nut, cocoa-nut fibre, makumbi.

Cocoa-nut fibre thoroughly cleaned, usumba.

A stick stuck in the ground to rip off the fibre, kifuo, *pl.* vifuo.

The shell, kifuu, *pl.* vifuu, kifufu (M.).

Instrument for scraping the fresh nut for cooking, mbuzi ya kukunia nazi.

Oily juice squeezed out of the scraped cocoa-nut, tui.

A small bag to squeeze out the tui *in*, kifumbu, *pl.* vifumbu.

The scraped nut after the tui *has been pressed out*, chicha.

Copra, the nut dried and ready to be pressed in the oil mill, nazi kavu.

Cocoa-nut oil, mafuta ya nazi.

Coffee, kahawa, (*plant*) mbuni.

Coffee berries, buni.

Coffee pot, mdila, *pl.* midila.

Coin (*a coin*), sarafu. *See Dollar, Rupee, &c.*

Colander (*in basket work*), kunguto, *pl.* makunguto.

Cold, baridi.

Baridi *and* upepo *are often used to mean wind or cold indifferently.*

Cold in the head, mafua.

I have a cold in the head, siwezi kamasi.

Collar-bone, mtulinga, *pl.* mitulinga.

Colour, rangi.

Colours are generally described by reference to some known substance: rangi ya kahawa, *coffee colour, brown;* rangi ya majani, *leaf colour, green;* rangi ya makuti, *colour of the dry cocoa-nut leaves, grey.*

Comb, kitana, *pl.* vitana, shanuu, *pl.* mashanuu (*a large wooden comb*).

A cock's comb. upanga.

Comfort, faraja.

Comforter, mfariji, *pl.* wafariji.

Coming (*arrival*), kifiko, *pl.* vifiko.

(*Mode of coming*), majilio.

Coming down or out from, mshuko, *pl.* mishuko.

Command, amri.

Commander, jemadari, *pl.* majemadari, mkuu wa asikari.

Second in command, akida.

Commission, agizo, *pl.* maagizo.

Comoro Islands, Masiwa.

Great Comoro, Ngazidja.

Comoro men, Wangazidja.

Johanna, Anzwani.

Mayotte, Maotwe.

Mohilla, Moalli.

Companion, mwenzi, *pl.* wenzi.

Company, jamaa.

Compass (*mariner's*), dira.

Completeness, uzima, ukamilifu, utimilifu,

Compliments, salaamu.
Composition (*of a word*), rakibyueo.
Composition for a murder, money paid to save one's life, dia.
Concealment, mafieho.
Conclusion, mwisho, hatima.
Concubine, suria, *pl.* masuria.
Born of a concubine, suriyama.
Condition (*state*), hali, jawabu.
(*A thing necessarily implied*), kanuni,
Confidence, matumaini.
Confidential servant, msiri, *pl.* wasiri.
Conscience, thamiri, moyo.
Conspiracy, mapatano, mwafaka.
Constipation, kufunga choo.
Constitution, tabia.
Contentment, urathi.
Continent, merima.
Continuance, maisha.
Contract, maagano, sharti.
Conversation, mazumgumzo, maongezi, usemi.
Convert, mwongofu, *pl.* waongofu.
Cook, mpishi, *pl.* wapishi.
Cooked grain, especially rice, wali.
Cooking pot (*metal*), sufuria, *pl.* masufuria, kisufuria, *pl.* visufuria.
(*earthen*), nyungu, chungu, *pl.* vyungu. mkungu, *pl.* mikuugu.
(*a pot to cook meat in with fat, to braze meat in*), kaango, *pl.* makaango, ukaango, kikaango, *pl.* vikaango.
A pot lid, mkungu wa kufunikia.
Three stones to set a pot on over the fire, mafiga, *sing.* figa, mafya, *sing.* jifya.
Cross pieces put in to keep the meat from touching the bottom of the pot and burning, nyalio.

Coolie, hamali, *pl.* mahamali
Copal, sandarusi.
Copper, shaba, sufuria.
Coral (*red*), marijani ya fethaluka (marijani *alone does not always mean the true red coral*).
Fresh coral for building, cut from below high-water mark, matu mbawi.
Cord, ugwe, ukambaa (M.), *pl.* kambaa, kigwe, *pl.* vigwe.
Cork, kizibo, *pl.* vizibo.
Corn, nafaka (*formerly used as money*).
Muhindi, *Indian corn.*
Mtama, *millet* (*the most common grain*).
Mwere, *very small grains growing in an upright head something like the flower of the bulrush.*
Wimbi.
Kimanga.
Corner, pembe.
Corner of a cloth, tamvua, utamvua.
Corpse, mzoga, *pl.* mizoga, mayiti.
Corpulence, unene.
Corruption, uovu, kioza.
Cosmetics.
Dalia, *a yellow composition.*
Yasi, *a yellow powder from India.*
Liwa, *a fragrant wood from Madagascar.*
Kipaji.
Cotton, pamba.
Couch, kitanda, *pl.* vitanda.
Cough, kikohozi.
Council, baraza, diwani.
Councillor, diwani, *pl.* madiwani.
Counsel, shauri.
Countenance, uso, *pl.* nyuso.
Country, inchi, nti (M.). *The names*

of countries are made from the name of the people by means of the prefix U-.

Unyika, *the country of the* Wanyika.

Ugala, *the country of the* Wagala.

Uzungu, *the country of the* Wazungu, *Europe.*

In the country, mashámba.

A country dialect, lugha ya kimashamba.

Courage, ushujaa, u*th*abit, moyo.

Course (of a ship), májira.

Courtesy, jamala, adabu.

Courtyard (enclosure), ua, *pl.* nyua, uanda *or* uanja.

Court within a house, behewa,kati.

Cousin, mjukuu, *pl.* wajukuu.

Covenant, maagano, sharti.

Cover (a lid), kifuniko.

A dish cover made of straw and often profusely ornamented, kawa.

A book cover, jalada.

Covetousness, tamaa, bakhili.

Cow, ng'ombe mke, *pl.* ng'ombe wake.

Coward, mwoga, *pl.* waoga.

Cowardice, uoga.

Cowry, kauri, kete.

Crab, kaa.

Crack, ufa, *pl.* nyufa.

Cramp, kiharusi.

A cramp, gaugo, *pl.* magango.

Crayfish, kamba.

Cream, siagi.

Creed, imani.

Creek, hori.

Crest, shungi (*used also for a way of dressing the hair in two large masses*).

Crew, baharia.

Crime, taksiri.

Crocodile, mamba, mbulu (?).

Crook, kota.

Crookedness, kombo.

A crooked thing, kikombo.

Cross, msalaba, *pl.* misalaba.

Cross roads, njia panda.

Crossing place, kivuko, *pl.* vivuko.

Crow, kunguru.

Crowbar, mtaimbo, *pl.* mitaimbo.

Crowd, kundi, *pl.* makundi, makutano, matangamano, umaati.

Crown, taji.

Crown of the head, upaa, utosi.

Crumbs, vidogo, *sing.* kidogo.

Crutch for oars, kilete, *pl.* vilete.

Cry, kilio, *pl.* vilio, ukelele, *pl.* kelele, ukemi.

(*for help*), yowe.

(*of joy*), hoihoi, kigelegele.

Cucumber, tango, *pl.* matango.

Cubit (from the tip of the middle finger to the point of the elbow), thiraa, mkono, *pl.* mikono.

(*from the point of the elbow to the knuckles when the fist is closed*), thiraa konde.

Cultivation, kilimo.

Cultivator, mkulima, *pl.* wakulima.

Cunning, cherevu, werevu.

Cup, kikombe, *pl.* vikombe.

Cupboard, sanduku.

Cupper, mumishi, *pl.* waumishi.

Cupping horn, chuku.

Curiosity (rarity), kioja, *pl.* vioja, hedaya, tunu.

Curlew, sululu, kipila.

Current, mkondo wa maji.

Curry, mchuzi, mtuzi (M.).

A small seed used in making it, bizari.

An acid thing put into it, kiungo.

Curse, laana, *pl.* malaana.
Curtain, pazia, *pl.* mapazia.
Curve, kizingo.
Cushion, mto, *pl.* mito.
A large cushion, takia, *pl.* matakia.
Custard apple, topetope, mstofele, konokono, matomoko.
Custom, desturi, mathehebu, ada.
Custom-house, fortha.
Customs' duties, ashur.
Cut, a short cut, njia ya kukata.
Cutting (*breaking off*), kato, *pl.* makato.
Cuttle-fish, pweza.
Arms of the cuttle-fish, mnyiriri, *pl.* minyiriri.
Cutwater of a dhow, hanamu.
Cypher. *See Cipher.*
Cymbals, matoazi, *sing.* toazi.

D.

Dagger, jambia (*the curved dagger generally worn*).
Damascus, Sham.
Dance, mchezo, *pl.* michezo.
Names of dances, gungu, msapata, hanzua, kitanga cha pepo, soma.
Dandy, malidadi.
Mtongozi, *pl.* watongozi, *a man who dresses himself up to attract women.*
Danger, hatari, khofu, kicho.
Darkness, kiza, giza (*these are only two ways of pronouncing the same word, but the first is sometimes treated as though the ki- were a prefix and it belonged to the fourth class, while the second is taken as belonging to the fifth; it is probably, however, most correct to refer them both to the fourth*).
Dark saying, fumbo, *pl.* mafumbo, maneno ya fumba.
Darling, kipendi, *pl.* vipendi.
Dates, tende.
Date-tree, mtende, *pl.* mitende.
Daughter, binti, mtoto mke, mwana, kijana.
Daughter-in-law, mkwe, *pl.* wakwe.
Dawn, alfajiri, kucha.
Day (*of twenty-four hours, reckoned from sunset to sunset*), siku.
(*time of daylight*), mchana, mtana (M.).
All day, mchana kutwa.
Day labourer, kibarua, *pl.* vibarua (*so called from the ticket given to workpeople, which they give up again when paid*).
Daylight, mchana, mtana (M.).
Dazzle, kiwi.
Deal (*wood*), sunobari.
Death, kufa (*dying*), mauti, ufu, mafu.
Debt, deni.
Deceit, hila, madanganya, udanganifu, hadaa, uwongo.
Deck, sitaha, dari.
Deep water, kilindi, *pl.* vilindi.
Great depths, lindo, *pl.* malindo.
Defect, upungufu, ila, kombo, kipunguo, *pl.* vipunguo.
Deficiency, kipunguo, upungufu.
Defilement, ujusi.
Deliverance, wokovu.
Demand in marriage, poso, *pl.* maposo.
Dependant, mfuasi, *pl.* wafuasi.
Depth, kwenda, chini, uketo.
Derision, mzaha, thihaka.

Design, kusudi, *pl.* makusudi, nia.
Descent, mshuko, *pl.* mishuko.
Desert, wangwa, jangwa, *pl.* majangwa.
Desolation, ukiwa.
Destruction, kuharibika, kupotea.
Destructiveness, uharibivu, upotevu.
Detachment (*of soldiers, &c.*), kikosi, *pl.* vikosi.
Device, hila, shauri, *pl.* mashauri.
Devil, shetani, *pl.* mashetani.
Devotee, mtaowa, *pl.* wataowa.
Dew, umande.
Dhow (*native craft*), chombo, *pl.* vyombo; *when very large*, jombo, *pl.* majombo.

Kinds of dhows:—

Dau, *pl.* madau, *a small open vessel sharp at the stern, with a square matting sail. They belong to the original inhabitants of* Zanzibar, *and are chiefly employed in bringing firewood to the town.*

Mtepe, *pl.* mitepe, *a large open vessel sharp at the stern, with a large square matting sail; the prow is made to resemble a camel's head, and is ornamented with painting and little streamers. The planks are sewn together. There is always a white pennon at the masthead. These vessels belong chiefly to* Lamoo, *and the country near it.*

Betela, *the common dhow of* Zanzibar: *it has a square stern, with a low poop and a head much like those of European boats.*

Bágala, *pl.* mabágala, *large dhows with very high square sterns and tall poops, and long projecting prows. The Indian dhows are mostly of this class; they have very often a small second mast rising from the poop* (mlingote wa kalmi).

Ghangi, *they resemble the* Bágalas *except in not being so high in the poop or so long in the prow.*

Batili, *a low vessel with a long projecting prow, a sharp stern, and high rudder-head. They have often a flying poop and a second mast. They belong to the piratical Arabs from the Persian Gulf.*

Bedeni, *a dhow with a sharp stern and high rudder-head, and a perpendicular cutwater; there is often a piece of board attached to it, making a kind of head; when this is absent the vessel is an* Awesia. *Bedens may easily be distinguished among other dhows by their masts being upright; in all other dhows the masts incline forward. They belong to the coast of Arabia, especially that on the Indian Ocean.*

Dhow sail, duumi.
Prow, gubeti.
Poop, shetri.
Quarter galleries, makanadili.
Joists of deck, darumeti.
Chunam for bottom, debeni.
Place for stowing things likely to be soon wanted, feuli.

Dialect, maneno, lugha.

Dialects and languages are usually expressed by prefixing ki- *to the name of the place or people.*

Kiunguja (*for* Maneno ya Kiunguja), *the dialect of Zanzibar* (Unguja).
Kimvita, *the dialect of Mombas* (Mvita).
Kiamu, *the dialect of Lamoo* (Amu).

Kigunya, *the dialect of Siwi, &c.*
Kiarabu, *Arabic.*
Kigala, *the Galla language.*
Kimashamba, *a country dialect.*
Kishenzi, *the talk of some uncivilized nation.*
Kiungwana, *a civilized language.*
Kizungu, *the languages spoken by Europeans.*

Diamond, almasi.
Diarrhœa, tumbo la kuenenda.
Diet, maakuli.
Difference, tofauti, sivimoja.
Difficulty, shidda, ugumu, mashaka.
Dinner (mid-day), chakula cha mchana.
Direction (bidding), fundisho, *pl.* mafundisho, agizo, *pl.* maagizo.
Dirt, t'aka.
Disease, marathi, uweli, ugonjwa.
Disfigurement, lemaa.
Disgrace, aibu, ari, fetheha.
Disgust, machukio.
Dish, sahani, kombe, *pl.* makombe, mkungu wa kulia, bungu, kitunga, *pl.* vitunga (*the first is the usual word for European dishes*).
An earthen dish to bake cakes on, waya.
Disorder (confusion), fujo. *See Disease.*
Display, wonyesho.
Disposal, amri.
To put at his disposal, kumwamria.
Dispute, mashindano, tofauti.
Disquiet, fathaa.
Dissipation, asherati, washerati, usherati.
Distortion (by disease), lemaa.
Distress, shidda, thulli, uthia, msiba, mashaka.
District of a town, mta, *pl.* mita.
For the districts of Zanzibar see Part II., p. 330.
Disturbance (riot), fitina.
(*trouble*), kero.
Ditch, handaki, shimo, *pl.* mashimo.
Divine service, ibada ya Muungu.
Division (arithmetical), mkasama.
Divorce, talaka.
Dock for ships, gudi.
Doctrine, elimu, ilm, mathhab.
Document, khati.
Dog, mbwa.
Very large, jibwa, *pl.* majibwa.
Bize, *a wild hunting dog.*
Mbwa wa koko, *the houseless dogs outside Zanzibar.*
Doll, mtoto wa bandia.
Dollar, reale, rea.
Spanish Pillar dollar, reale ya mizinga.
Black dollars, reale ya Sham.
American 20-dollar piece, reale ya thahabu.
French silver 5-franc piece, reale ya kifransa.
For the parts of a dollar see in the section on Adjectives under Numerals—fractions, p. 93.
Dome, zege.
Dominion, mamlaka, hukumu.
Donkey, punda.
Donkey from the mainland, kiongwe, *pl.* viongwe.
Door, mlango, *pl.* milango (*vulgarly*, mwango, *pl.* miango).
Leaf of door, ubau, *pl.* mbau.
Centre piece, mfaa.
Door-keeper, mgoja mlango.
Door chain, riza.
Door frame, top and bottom pieces, kizingiti, *pl.* vizingiti.

Side pieces, mwimo, miimo.
Outer beading, upapi.
Dotage, mapiswa.
Doubt, shaka, *pl.* mashaka, tashwishi, waswas.
Dove, hua. *See Pigeon & Birds.*
Dowry, paid by the husband to the wife's friends, mahari.
Dragon-fly, kering'ende.
Dragon's blood, maziwa (*or* macho), ya watu wawili.
Dream, ndoto.
Dregs, chembe.
Dress, nguo, mavazi, mavao, uvao.

Slaves and very poor men wear generally an nguo *only, that is, a loin cloth of white or blue calico. Women wear a* kisuto, *or long cloth of blue, or printed, or coloured calico wrapped tightly round the body immediately under the arms, and on the head an* ukaya, *a piece of blue calico with two long ends; it has a string passing under the chin, to which a silver ornament,* jebu, *is attached.*

Well-dressed men wear a loin cloth with a coloured border, kikoi, *a long shirt-like garment in white calico,* kanzu, *a shawl,* amazu, *twisted round the waist, a waistcoat,* kisibao, *and a long loose coat,* joho. *On their heads they wear a red or white skull-cap,* kofia, *and twisted round it a turban,* kilemba. *Their feet are slipped into sandals,* viatu.

Women wear trousers, soruali, *a* kanzu *of coloured materials and a* kofia (*cap*) *adorned with gold and spangles, or more commonly a silk handkerchief,* dusamali, *folded and fastened on the head so as to hide the hair. They also wear sometimes a* kisibao (*embroidered waistcoat*), *and nearly always a mask,* barakoa. *When they go out they throw over all a large square of black silk,* lebwani. *On their feet they carry wooden clogs held by a button* (msuruake) *grasped between the toes.*

Dressing of calico, dondo.
Drill, keke. *The iron is called* kekee; *the wood it is fixed in,* msukano; *the handle in which it turns,* jivu; *and the bow,* uta.
Drink, kinwa (*or* kinywa), *pl.* vinwa, kinwaji, *pl.* vinwaji.
Drinker, mnywa, *pl.* waunywa
Dripping (*fat cooked out of meat*), uto wa nyama.
Drop, tone, *pl.* matone, kitone, *pl.* vitone.
Droppings (*dung*), mavi.
Dropsy, istiska.
Drowsiness, leppe, leppe za uzingizi.
Drum, *ngoma.*
Chapuo, *a small drum.*
Kumbwaya, *a drum upon feet.*
Msondo, *a very tall drum, beaten on special occasions.*
The skin of a drum, or anything stretched like it very tightly, kiwambo, *pl.* viwambo.
Drunkard, mlevi, *pl.* walevi
Duck, bata, *pl.* mabata.
Duryan, finessi la kizungu.
Dust, vumbi, *pl.* (*much dust*) mavumbi.
Dust and sand on a road, tifutifu.
Duties. *See Customs.*
Duties of one's position, kiwango, *pl.* viwango.
Dwarf, kibeti, *pl.* vibeti.
Dwelling, makao, makazi, makani, masikani.
Dye, rangi.

Mkasiri, *a tree whose bark is used to dye fishing-nets and lines black.*

Ungamo, *a yellow dye used to dye matting.*

Dysentery, tumbo la kuhara damu.

E.

Eagerness (*excessive haste*), pupa.

Eagle (?) koho, firkomba, tai, pungu, kipanga (*all these words seem to denote some large bird of prey*).

Ear, sikio, *pl.* masikio.

Hole pierced in the lower lobe of the ear, ndewe.

Ear ornaments, a large round ornament in the lower lobe, jassi, *pl.* majassi.

Ornaments in the upper part of the ear, if dangling, kipuli, *pl.* vipuli; *if shaped like a stud*, kipini, *pl.* vipini.

Ear-ring, pete ya masikio.

Ear of corn, suke, *pl.* masuke. *See Bunch, Cob.*

Earnest money, arabuni, stakabathi.

Earth, inchi, udongo.

The earth, inchi, ulimwengu, dunia.

Ease, raha.

After pain, faraja.

East wind, matlaa.

Eaves, mchilizi, *pl.* michilizi.

Eavesdropper, dukizi (*or* duzi), *pl.* madukizi.

Ebony, mpingo.

Echo, mwangwi.

Edge (*of a precipice*), ukingo.

(*Of a piece of cloth*), pindo, *pl.* mapindo.

Edging woven into a piece of cloth, taraza.

Effort, juhudi, bidii.

Effusion (*of blood*), vilio (la damu), *pl.* mavilio.

Egg, yayi, *pl.* mayayi.

White of egg, ute wa yayi.

Yolk of an egg, kiini cha yayi.

Eggshell, ganda la yayi.

Empty eggshell, kaka.

Egypt, Misri, Masri, Mássara.

Elbow, kisigino, *pl.* visigino, kivi, *pl.* vivi.

Elder, mzee, *pl.* wazee, sheki, *pl.* masheki.

Elegance, jamala.

Elephant, tembo, ndovu.

Elephantiasis (*leprosy*), jethamu.

(*Barbadoes leg*), tende.

Embarrassment, matata, uthia, mashaka.

Embroidery, almaria.

(*stitching*), darizi.

(*piping*), kigwe, *pl.* vigwe.

Embroilment, matata.

Emetic, tapisho, *pl.* matapisho, dawa la kutapika.

Employment, kazi, utumwa.

Emulation, bidii.

Encampment (*of a caravan*), kituo, *pl.* vituo.

Enclosure, uanja, ua, *pl.* nyua.

Enclosure made by a fence of cocoa-nut leaves, ua wa makuti.

Enclosure made by a fence of mtama stalks, ua wa mabua.

Enclosure with a stone fence, kitalu, *pl.* vitalu.

End, mwisho, *pl.* miisho (*finishing*), hatima, kikomo, *pl.* vikomo (*leaving off*).

of a journey, kifiko, *pl.* vifiko.

of a piece of cloth, mialamu.

End or corners of a turban cloth, &c., tamvua, kishungi, *pl.* vishungi.
Enemy, adui, *pl.* adui *or* maadui.
Engagement, shughuli, utumwa.
Enigma, kitendawili, *pl.* vitendawili.
Enmity, wadui, adawa, khusuma.
Entrails, matumbo.
Entrance, kuingia, pakuingilia, mlango.
Envy, hasidi, kijicho, kijito (M.).
Epilepsy, kifafa.
Equal (*in age*), hirimu, marika.
Equivalent, badala.
Error, kosa, makosa.
Eructation, kiungulia, *pl.* viungulia.
Escape, wokovu, kuokoka.
(*other course*), buddi.
Esteem, mapendo, maafikano.
Estimate, maafikano.
Eternity, milele.
Eunuch, tawashi, maksai.
Euphorbia, mtupa, *pl.* mitupa.
Europe, Ulaya, Wilaya, Uzungu.
European (*or any one wearing a European dress*), Mzungu, *pl.* Wazungu.
Eve, Hawa.
Evening, jioni.
Event (*startling*), shani.
Evil, uovu.
Exaltation, utukufu, athama.
Example, mfano, *pl.* mifano.
Excrement, mavi.
Expense, gharama.
Extinguisher, mzima (*a person*), *pl.* wazima, kizima (*a thing*), *pl.* vizima.
Eye, jicho, *pl.* macho, jito (M.), *pl.* mato.
Loss of an eye, chongo.
Eyebrow, nyushi, nshi (A.).
Eyelash or Eyelid, kope.
A stye in the eye, chochea.

F.

Fable, ngano.
Face, uso, *pl.* nyuso.
Fæces, mavi.
Faggot, tita, *pl.* matita.
Faith, imani.
Fall, maanguko.
Falsehood, uwongo.
Familiarity, mazoezo.
Family, jamaa, ndugu.
Famine, njaa, ndaa (M.).
Fan, upepeo *pl.* pepeo, pepeo, *pl.* mapepeo, kipepeo, *pl.* vipepeo.
Fare, nauli.
Fast, funga.
Fasting month, Ramathani.
Fat, shahamu, mafuta.
A piece of fat, kipande kilichonona.
Fat cooked out of meat, uto wa nyama.
Fate, ajali.
Father, baba.
In speaking of one's own father it is polite to call him bwana.
Stepfather, baba wa kambo.
Father-in-law, mkwe. *pl.* wakwe.
Fathom, pima, *pl.* mapima.
Fatigue, utufu, ulegevu.
Fatling, kinono, *pl.* vinono.
Fault, hatiya, kosa, *pl.* makosa.
Favour, upendeleo.
A favour, fathili.
Favourite, kipendi, *pl.* vipendi, mpenzi, *pl.* wapenzi.
Fear, khofu, uoga, kitisho, *pl.* vitisho, kicho, *pl.* vicho.
Feast, karamu.
Feast day, siku kuu.

Feather, unyoa, *pl.* nyoa, nyoa (*or* nyoya), *pl.* manyoya.
A wing feather, ubawa, *pl.* mbawa.
Feeder, mlishi, *pl.* walishi.
Fellow-servant, mjoli, *pl.* wajoli.
Fence, ua, *pl.* nyua.
Stone fence, kitalu, *pl.* vitalu.
Fenugreek, watu.
Ferry, kivuko, *pl.* vivuko.
Fetters, pingu.
Fever, homa.
Swelling of the glands of the groin followed by fever, mtoki.
Dengue fever, kidinga popo.
Field, koonde, *pl.* makoonde, mgunda (Yao).
Field labourer, mkulima, *pl.* wakulima.
Fierceness, ukali.
Fig, tini.
Fig-tree, mtini, *pl.* mitini.
Fight, mapigano.
Figure of speech, mfano wa maneno.
Filagree work, temsi.
File, tupa.
Fillet, utepe, *pl.* tepe.
Filth, uchavu, janaba.
Fin, pezi; *pl.* mapezi.
Fine for a murder, dia.
Fineness, uzuri.
Finger, kidole, *pl.* vidole, kidole cha mkono, chanda (M.), *pl.* vyanda.
Fire, moto, *pl.* mioto.
Pieces of wood to get fire by twisting, upekecho.
Firewood, kuni, *one piece*, ukuni.
A half-burnt piece of firewood, kinga, *pl.* vinga.
The act of pushing the wood further into the fire, or an instrument for doing so, kichocheo, kitoteo (M.).
Fireplace, jiko, *pl.* meko, meko, *pl.* mieko, *hence kitchen*, jikoni, mekoni.
Three stones to set a pot over the fire upon, jifya, *pl.* mafya, figa, *pl.* mafiga. Jifya *is the word most used in the town*, figa *that used in the country*.
Firefly, kimurimuri, *pl.* vimurimuri, kimetimeti, *pl.* vimetimeti.
Firmament, anga (?).
Firmness, usimeme, uthabiti, (*in building*) mtomo.
Fish, samaki.
Dagaa, *very small, small fry.*
Njombo, *barred with black and yellow.*
Taa, *a very large flat fish.*
Pono, *a fish said to be nearly always asleep.*
Other kinds, Chafi, Changu, Chewa, Kungu, Mchumbuluru, Mkizo, Mwewe, Mzia, Nguru, Nguva, Panzi, Pungu. *The varieties of fish are exceedingly numerous.*
Chinusi, *a kind of fish or evil spirit never seen, but which is supposed to seize men and hold them under water until they are drowned.*
Fish-trap, dema, lema, ema.
Fish poison from a species of Euphorbia, utupa.
Fisherman, mvuvi, *pl.* wavuvi.
Fist, konde, *pl.* makonde.
Fits, kifafa.
Flag, bandera.
Flat (of a sword, &c.), bapa.
Flatterer, msifu, *pl.* wasifu, msifumno.
Self-flatterer, mwajisifuni.
Flattery, kusifu.

Flavour, luththa, tamu.
Flax, katani, kitani.
Flea, kiroboto, *pl.* viroboto.
Flesh, nyama.
Fleshiness, mnofu.
Flint gun, bunduki ya gumegume.
Flood, gharika.
Floor, chini.
Chunammed floor, sakafu.
Upper floor or roof, dari.
Flower, ua, *pl.* maua.
Flue, vumbi, *pl.* (*much*) mavumbi.
A flue, dohaan.
Flute, filimbi, *pl.* mafilimbi.
Fly, inzi, *pl.* mainzi.
Foam, povu.
Fog, umande, kungu, shemali.
Fold (*of cloth*), upindo.
Cattle-fold, zizi, *pl.* mazizi.
Foliage, majani.
Follower, mfuasi, *pl.* wafuasi, chokora, *pl.* machokora (*a hanger-on*).
Folly, upumbafu.
Fondness, mahaba.
Food, chakula, makuli (Ar.), kande (Mer.).
Food saved from an evening meal to be eaten in the morning, wali wa mwikuu, bariyo (A.).
Bokoboko, *a dish made of wheat and meat.*
Bumbwi, *rice flour pounded up with cocoa-nut.*
Pilao, *an Indian pillaw.*
Birinzi.
Fool, mpumbafu, *pl.* wapumbafu.
Foot, mguu, *pl.* miguu, guu, *pl.* maguu, mjiguu, *pl.* mijiguu (*large*), kijiguu, *pl.* vijiguu (*small*).
Footprint, uayo, *pl.* nyayo.
Footing—to make him pay his footing, kumshika hakali.
Forbidden thing, haramu, marufuku.
Force, nguvu.
Ford, kivuko, *pl.* vivuko.
Forehead, paji la uso.
Brow, kikomo cha uso.
Foreigner, mgeni, *pl.* wageni, mja na maji, *pl.* waja na maji (*from over seas*).
Forelock, panja.
Foreskin, govi mbo.
Forest, mwitu, msitu.
Fork, kiuma, *pl.* viuma.
Forking of a road, tree, &c., panda.
Form (*outward shape*), umbo, *pl.* maumbo.
Fort, gereza, ngome, husuni.
Fortune, bahati, nasibu.
Fortune-teller(*by means of diagrams*), mpiga ramli, *pl.* wapiga ramli.
Foster brother or sister, ndugu kunyonya.
Foundation, msingi *or* msinji, *pl.* misingi.
Fowls, k'uku.
Fox, mbweha.
Fraud, hadaa, madangauya.
Freedom (*from, slavery*) huru, (*permission*) ruksa, ruhusa.
Freight, nauli.
Friday, Jumaa.
Friend, rafiki, *pl.* rafiki *or* marafiki, sahibu, *pl.* as'habu, shoga (*amongst women, and in Zanzibar only. See Catamite*).
Fright, khofu, woga.
(*a start*), kituko.
Fringe, matamvua.
Frog, chula, *pl.* vyula.
Fruit, tunda, *pl.* matunda, zao, *pl.* mazao.

Bungu, *pl.* mabungu, *about the size of a medlar, with a thick russet skin.*

Mazu, *a kind of banana.*

Zambarau, *like a large damson.*

Chokochoko, *a red prickly skin, a large kernel, and white pulp.*

Kunazi, *something like a sloe.*

Kitoria, *pl.* vitoria.—Koma, *pl.* makoma. — Fuu, *pl.* mafuu. —Mtofaa.

Fruit which drops prematurely, pooza, *pl.* mapooza.

Fruit-stalk, (*of cloves*) kikonyo, *pl.* vikonyo, (*of bananas*) mkungu, *pl.* mikungu.

Frying-pan, (*metal*) tawa, *pl.* matawa, (*earthen*) kaango, *pl.* makaango.

Fugitive, mkimbizi, *pl.* wakimbizi.

Fume, azma, fukizo.

Fun, mchezo, mzaha.

Funeral, kuzikani.

Furnace (*for melting metal*), kalibu.

Furniture, pambo la nyumba, vyombo.

G.

Gain, fayida.

Gait, mwendo.

Galago, komba.

Galbanum, ubani.

Gall, safura.

Galla, Mgala, *pl.* Wagala.

Game, (*produce of hunting*) mawindo, (*amusement*) mchezo, machezo.

Bao, *played on a board with thirty-two holes in it.*

Maliyandimu, *a game in which one holds down his head, some other knocks it, and he guesses who struck him.*

Tiabu, *played by throwing up sticks, &c., and watching their fall.*

Dama, *played on a board like chess.*

Tasa, *a game of touch.*

Tinge, *a game consisting in following the movements of a leader.*

Garden, bustani, shamba.

Gate, mlango, *pl.* milango.

Gate of Paradise, kilango cha jaha.

Gazelle, paa.

General, jemadari, *pl.* majemadari.

Generation, kizazi, *pl.* vizazi.

Generosity, ukarimu.

Genius, Jini, *pl.* Majini.

Gentleman, mngwana, *pl.* wangwana.

Gentleness, upole.

Georgian woman, Jorjiya.

Gettings, pato, *pl.* mapato.

Ghee, samli.

Ghost, kivuli, *pl.* vivuli.

Ghoul, zimwi, *pl.* mazimwi.

Giddiness, masua, mbasua, kizunguzungu.

Gift, zawadi (*a keepsake*), tunu (*a choice thing*), bashishi (*largess*), ada (*customary gift*), kilemba (*gift on the completion of a work or to the bride's father*), wapo.

Ginger, tangawizi.

Giraffe, twiga.

Girder, mhimili, *pl.* mihimili.

Girdle, mshipi, *pl.* mishipi, masombo (*of cloth*), maazamu (*a shawl*), kibobwe, *pl.* vibobwe (*a piece of cloth tied round the body during hard work*).

Girl, kijana, *pl.* vijana.

Slave girl, kijakazi, *pl.* vijakazi.

Girth, kivimba.

Gizzard, firigisi.
Gladness, furaha.
Glance, nathiri
Glare. anga.
Glass, kioo.
Looking-glass, kioo, *pl.* vioo.
Drinking-glass, bilauri.
Glitter, kimeta.
Glory, sifa, fakhari, utukufu.
Glue (*or gum*), embwe.
Glutton, mlafi, *pl.* walafi.
Goat, mbuzi.
A strong he-goat, bebera (Ar.).
Go-between, kijumbe, *pl.* vijumbe.
GOD, MUUNGU, *pl.* miungu.
Goitre, tezi.
Gold, thahabu.
Goldsmith, mfua thahabu, *pl.* wafua thahabu.
Good luck, ghanima, jaha.
Goodness, wema.
Goods. mali (*possessions*), vyombo (*utensils*), bithaa (*merchandise*).
Goose, bata la Bukini, *pl.* mabata ya Bukini.
Gonorrhœa, kisunono.
Gourd. *See Pumpkin.*
Gout, jongo.
Governor, wali, liwali, *pl.* maliwali.
Government, serkali, daulati.
An official, mtu wa serkali.
Grain. *See Corn.*
Cleaned grain, mchele.
Cooked grain, wali.
Grains of corn, punje, chembe.
Grandchild, mjukuu, *pl.* wajukuu.
Great-grandchild, kijukuu, *pl.* vijukuu, kitukuu, *pl.* vitukuu, kilembwe, *pl.* vilembwe.
Great-great-grandchild, kiningina, *pl.* viningina.
Grandfather, babu.
Grandmother, bibi.
Great-grandmother, mzaa bibi.
Grammar, sáruf.
Grapes, zabibu.
Gratitude, shukraui.
Grass, nyasi, majani, nyika.
grass cut for fodder, ukoka.
Grasshopper, panzi, *pl.* mapanzi.
Grave, kaburi, *pl.* makaburi.
In the grave, after death, ahera, kuzimu.
Greatness, ukubwa, ukuu, utukufu.
Greediness, choyo, roho, tamaa.
Grey hairs, mvi.
Gridiron, uma wa kuokea nyama, *pl.* nyuma za kuokea nyama.
Grief, sikitiko, kasarani, msiba, huzuni, hamu, simanzi.
(*for a loss*), majonzi.
Grime (*on a pot*), masizi.
Grit (*small stones*), changarawi.
Groom, mchunga, *pl.* wachunga, mtunga (M.), *pl.* watunga.
Ground, chini, inchi.
Ground nuts, mjugu nyasa, (*a hard round kind*) mjugu mawe.
Grudging person, hiana.
Gruel, uji.
Guard, mlinzi, *pl.* walinzi.
Guava, mpera, *pl.* mapera.
Guava-tree, mpera, *pl.* mipera.
Guest, mgeni, *pl.* wageni.
Guide, rubani, kiongozi, *pl.* viongozi, mkuu genzi.
Guitar, kinanda, *pl.* vinanda
Guinea fowl, kanga.
(*a crested kind*), kororo.
Gum (*birdlime, &c.*), ulimbo.
Gum (*of the teeth*), ufizi, *pl.* fizi.
Gum Arabic, haba, sumugh.
Gum Amini or Copal, sandarusi.
Gun, bunduki.

Flint gun, bunduki ya gumegume.
Gun-barrel, kasiba.
Nipple, kifa, *pl.* vifa.
Gun-cap, fataki.
Gun-lock, mtambo, *pl.* mitambo.
(*cannon*), mzinga, *pl.* mizinga.
Gun-carriage, gurudumo la mzinga.
Gunpowder, baruti.
Gut, tumbo, *pl.* matumbo.

H.

H. The guttural Arabic h, ha ngoe.
The softer Arabic h, he mdawari.
Habits, mazoezo, mathehebu.
Hæmorrhoids, bawasir.
Haft, mpini, *pl.* mipini, kipini, *pl.* vipini.
Hair, nyele (*or* nwele), *sing.* unyele.
(*of the beard*), ndevu, *sing.* udevu.
(*of the body, especially of the pubes*), mavuzi, *sing.* vuzi.
(*of the eyebrow*), nyushi, *sing.* unyushi.
(*of the eyelash*), kope, *sing.* ukope.
(*of the hand and arm*), malaika, *sing.* laika.
(*of an animal*), singa.
Straight hair, nyele za singa.
Woolly hair, nyele za kipilipili.
Half, nusu.
A half orange, cocoa-nut, &c., kizio, *pl.* vizio.
Halyards, henza.
Ropes passing through the pulley of the halyards, jarari.
Hammer, nyundo.
Hand (*or arm and hand*), mkono, *pl.* mikono.
Palm of the hand, kitanga cha mkono, *pl.* vitanga vya mikono.
Front of the hand, kofi, *pl.* makofi.
Inside of the fingers, kikofi, *pl.* vikofi.
Handful (*that will lie on the hand*), ukufi, *pl.* kufi.
(*that which will lie on the two hands*), chopa, *pl.* machopa.
(*that can be grasped in the hand*), konzi, *pl.* makonzi.
Handkerchief, leso.
Pocket handkerchief, leso ya kufutia kamasi.
Handle (*like a knife-handle*), mpini, *pl.* mipini, kipini, *pl.* vipini.
(*projecting like that of a saucepan*), kono, mkono, *pl.* mikono.
(*bowed like that of a bucket*), utambo, *pl.* tambo.
Handwriting, khati, mwandiko.
Hanger-on, chokora, *pl.* machokora.
Happiness, furaha, furahani, raba.
Harbour, bandari, bundari.
Hardness, ugumu.
Hare. See Rabbit.
Harm, mathara.
Harness, matandiko.
Harp, kinubi, *pl.* vinubi.
Harpoon, chusa, *pl.* vyusa.
Harvest, mavuno.
Haste, haraka, hima.
Hat, chapeo.
Hatchet, kishoka, *pl.* vishoka, kitoka (M.), *pl.* vitoka, upamba, *pl.* pamba.
Hatred, machukio, buothu.
Hawk, mwewe.
Hawker, dalali.
Head, kitwa (*or* kichwa), *pl.* vitwa.
A little head, kijitwa, *pl.* vijitwa.
Head of a ship, omo.
Head winds, pepo za omo.
Head cloth worn by women, ukaya

(*of blue calico*), dusamali (*of silk*).
Headship, ujumbo.
Healing things, mapoza.
Health, uzima, afia, hali (*state*).
Heap, fungu, *pl.* mafungu, chungu.
of stones, boma, *pl.* maboma.
of wood and sticks, biwi, *pl.* mabiwi, kichaka, *pl.* vichaka.
of earth, kisugulu, *pl.* visugulu.
(*a raised bed*), tuta, *pl.* matuta.
Heart, moyo, *pl.* mioyo, *or* nyoyo, mtima, *pl.* mitima.
Heat, moto, hari (*sweat*), harara (*prickly heat*).
Heaven, mbingu, *sing.* uwingu, samawati (Ar.).
Heaviness (*weight*), uzito.
(*sorrow*), hamu.
Hedge, ua, *pl.* nyua.
Hedge made in the sea for taking fish, uzio, *pl.* nyuzio.
Heel, kifundo (*or* kisigino) cha mguu.
Heifer, mtamba, *pl.* mitamba.
Heir, mrithi, *pl.* warithi.
Help, msaada.
Hem, upindo.
Hemp. *See Cannabis Indica.*
Hempen rope, kamba ulayiti.
Hen, k'uku.
Laying hen, koo, *pl.* makoo.
Hen, full grown, but that has not yet laid, t'embe.
Henna, hina.
Herd, kundi, *pl.* makundi.
Herdsman, mchunga, *pl.* wachunga, mtunga (M.), *pl.* watunga.
Hero, shujaa, *pl.* mashujaa, fahali, *pl.* mafahali.
Heroism, ushujaa.
Hesitation, msangao.
(*in speaking*), kubabaika.
Hickup, kwikwe.
Hidden thing, fumbo, *pl.* mafumbo.
Hide, ngozi.
Hill, kilima, *pl.* vilima.
A rocky hill, jabali, *pl.* majabali.
Hilt, kipini, *pl.* vipini.
Hindrance, kizuizo, kizuio, kizuizi.
It is said that Dr. Krapf, being on one occasion delayed from day to day, in obedience to superior orders, said to those who delayed him:—Kesho na kesho ni madanganya, ao ni makatazanya. "*To-morrow and to-morrow is deceiving or forbidding;*" *to which they replied:*—Si madanganya wala si makatazanya, ni mazuizanya. "*It is not deceiving, and it is not forbidding, it is delaying.*"
Hinge, patta, bawaba.
Hip, nyonga (?), tokono (A.).
Hippopotamus, kiboko, *pl.* viboko, tomondo.
Hire, taja, ijara, ujira.
History, hadithi.
Hoarseness, kupwowa na sauti.
Hoe, jembe (*or* gembe), *pl.* majembe.
Hoeing-up time, mapalilo.
Hold (*of a ship*), ngama.
Hole, tundu, *pl.* matundu.
(*through anything*), kipenyo, *pl.* vipenyo.
(*dibbled for seeds or plants*), korongo, *pl.* makorongo.
Hole to give light and air, mwangaza, *pl.* miangaza.

Hole in the lower lobe of the ear, ndewe.
Holiness, utakatifu, matakatifu.
Hollow (of a tree), mvungu.
Hollowness, uvurungu.
Home, kwangu, kwako, kwake, kwetu, kwenu, kwao, *according to the person whose home it is.*
I have some at home, iko kwangu.
Honey, asali ya nyuki.
Honour, heshima, ukarimu, utukufu.
Hoof, ukwato, *pl.* kwato, kwata.
Hook (fish-hook), doana.
(used to steady work with), kulabu.
Hope, matumaini.
Hordeolum, chokea.
Horn, pembe, *pl.* pembe *or* mapembe.
An antelope's horn used as a trumpet, baragumu. *See Musical Instruments.*
Horse, farasi. fras.
Host (army or multitude), jeshi, *pl.* majeshi.
Host (entertainer), mwenyeji, *pl.* wenyeji.
Hostility, wadui, adawa.
Hour, saa.
House, nyumba.
(large), jumba, *pl.* majumba.
(small), kijumba, *pl.* vijumba.
Household of slaves, kijoli.
Hum, mavumi.
Humility, unenyekeo.
Hump (of an ox), nundu.
(of a humpback), kigongo.
Hunger, njaa, ndaa (M.).
Hundred, mia.
Two hundred, miteen.
Hunter, mwinda, *pl.* wawinda.
Hurry, haraka.
Husband, mume, *pl.* waume.
Husk, ganda, *pl.* maganda.
Husk and bran of rice, kumvi.
Husk of the cocoa-nut, makumbi.
Hut, kibanda, *pl.* vibanda.
Hyæna, fisi, pisi.
Spotted hyæna, kingubwa.
Hydrocele, mshipa, pumbo, kitonga (?)
Hypocrite, mnafiki, *pl.* wanafiki.

I.

Ibo, Wibo.
Idiot, hayawani.
Idleness, uvivu.
Idolater, kafiri. *pl.* makafiri.
Ignorance, ujinga.
Image, sanamu.
Imperial. See Beard.
Imprecation, apizo, *pl.* maapizo.
Imprisonment, kifungo.
Incense, buhuri, ubani, uvumba, uudi. *See Censer.*
Income, pato.
Independence, upweke.
Indian (heathen), Banyani, *pl.* Mabanyani.
Indian (Mahommedan), Muhindi, *pl.* Wahindi.
Indian rubber, mpira.
Indian corn, muhindi. *See Maize.*
Infection, kuambukiza.
Infidel, kafiri, *pl.* makafiri.
Infirmity, uthaifu.
Information, habari.
Ingenuity, uyuzi, umaheli.
Inheritance, urithi.
Inheritor, mrithi, *pl.* warithi.
Ink, wino.
Inkstand, kidau cha wino.
Inlaid work, njumu.

Innovation, mzuzi, *pl.* mizuzi.
Innovator, mzushi, *pl.* wazushi.
Insect, mdudu, *pl.* wadudu.
Paange, *gadfly*.
Manyiga, *hornet*.
Dudu vule, *a boring hornet*.
Bunzi, *pl.* mabunzi, *a stinging fly*.
Vunja jungo, *a mantis*.
Boroshoa, *a long-shaped black insect found in dust-heaps*.
Insolence (*self-sufficiency*), kinaya.
Instruction, mafundisho.
Instruments (*nautical*), vipande vya kupimia.
Insult, tukano, *pl.* matukano.
Intellect, akili (*generally treated as a plural noun of Class III.*).
Intention, nia, kasidi.
Interpretation, tafsiri.
Interpreter, mkalimani, *pl.* wakalimani, posoro.
Intestines, matumbo.
Small intestines, chango.
Interruption, kizuizo, *pl.* vizuizo.
Intoxicating thing, kileo, *pl.* vileo.
Intoxication, kileo, kulewa.
Intruder, kizushi, *pl.* vizushi, fisadi (*one who enters a house without lawful purpose*).
Invalid, mgonjwa, *pl.* wagonjwa.
Iron, chuma.
A piece of iron, chuma, *pl.* vyuma.
Iron bar, mtaimbo, *pl.* mitaimbo.
Island, kisiwa, *pl.* visiwa.
Itch, upele, pele.
Itching, mnyeo.
Ivory, pembe.
a large tusk, buri.

J.

Jackal, mbwa wa mwitu.
Jackfruit, finesi, *pl.* mafinesi.
Jackfruit tree, mfinesi, *pl.* mifinesi.
Jar (*for carrying water*), mtungi, *pl.* mitungi.
Jar (*large*), kasiki.
Jasmine, jasmini.
Jaw, taya.
Jealousy, uwivu.
Jealous anger, gheiri.
To weep for jealousy, kulia ngoa.
Jewel, johari.
Jin, jini, *pl.* majini.
Johanna, Anzwani.
Joint, kiungo, *pl.* viungo.
(*in a cane*), fundo, *pl.* mafundo.
(*piece between two joints in a cane*), pingili.
Joist, boriti.
Joke, ubishi.
Journey, safari, mwendo.
Two days' journey, mwendo wa siku mbili.
Joy, furaha.
Judge, kathi, *pl.* makathi, mwamuzi, *pl.* waamuzi, mwamua, *pl.* waamua.
Judgment, hukumu, maamuzi.
Jug, kopo, *pl.* makopo.
Juice, maji.
Justice, haki.

K.

Keel, mkuku, utako (Mer.).
Kernel, kisa, *pl.* visa.
Kettle, kanderinya.
Key, ufunguo, *pl.* funguo.
Kick, teke, *pl.* mateke.
Kidney, nso, figo (M.).
Kind, namna, ginsi, aina.
Kind, sort or style is expressed by ki. *prefixed to the place, thing,*

or people. Kihindi, *the Indian sort.* Kizungu, *the European sort.*

iatu vya Kihindi, *shoes like those worn by the Indians.*

Viazi vya Kizungu, *sweet potatoes of the European sort*, i.e. *potatoes.*

Mavazi ya kifaume, *robes of the kingly sort, royal robes.*

Kindness, wema.

Every kindness, killa jambo la wema.

A kindness, fathili.

Kindred, ndugu, jamaa.

Utani, *the belonging to a kindred race.*

Mtani, *pl.* watani, *a person of a kindred race.*

King, mfalme, *pl.* wafalme, malki, maliki.

Chess king, shah.

Kingdom, ufalme, ufalume, ufaume, milki, mulki.

Kinsman, ndugu, jamaa. *See Kindred.*

Kiss, busu.

Kitchen, jikoni, mekoni.

Kite (*bird*), mwewe.

(*toy*), tiara.

Knee, gote, *pl.* magote, ondo, *pl.* maondo (A.).

Knife, kisu, *pl.* visu.

(*large*), jisu, *pl.* majisu.

Kotama, *a curved knife used in getting palm wine.*

Shembea, *a kind of curved knife.*

Knight (*chess*), frasi.

Knot, fundo, *pl.* mafundo.

Knowingness, ujuvi, ujuzi, werevu.

Knowledge, maarifa, elimu, hekima.

Koran, korani, furakanu, msahafu.

It is divided into thirty juzuu, *which together make a* khitima nzima.

L.

Labour, kazi.

Labour pains, utungu.

Lac (100,000), lakki.

Ladder, ngazi.

Ladle made out of a cocoa-nut, kata, *pl.* makata (*deep, used to dip up water with*); upawa, *pl.* pawa (*shallow, used for gravy, curry, &c.*).

Lady, bibi, mwana mke wa kiungwana.

Lady of the house, mwana.

Ladylove, mchumba.

Lake, ziwa la maji, *pl.* maziwa.

Lamoo, Amu.

Lamp, taa.

Lampstand, a piece of wood with two flat pieces projecting at right angles on which the lamp is placed, mwango, *pl.* miango.

Lampwick, utambi, *pl.* tambi.

Land, inchi, nti (M.).

Landing-place, diko, *pl.* madiko, liko, *pl.* maliko.

Language, lugha, maneno. *The language of a place or nation is expressed by the use of the prefix* ki-. Maneno ya Kiunguja or Kiunguja, *the language of Zanzibar.* Kinyamwezi, *the language of the* Nyamwezi *tribe. See Dialect.*

Filthy and insulting language, matukano.

Languor, utepetevu.

Lantern, fanusi, kandili, *pl.* makandili.

Lappet, kishungi, *pl.* vishungi.

Largess, takarima, bashishi.
Lathe, keezo.
Laugh, cheko, *pl.* machcko, kicheko, *pl.* vicheko.
Law, sheria, hukumu.
Lead, risasi, rusasi.
(*for sounding*), bildi.
Leader, kiongozi, *pl.* viongozi.
Leaf (*of a tree*), jani, *pl.* majani.
(*of a cocoa-nut tree*), kuti, *pl.* makuti.
Leaf (*of a book*), ukurasa, *pl.* kurasa.
Lean-to, kipenu, *pl.* vipenu.
Learning, elimu.
A man of learning, mwana wa chuoni.
Leather, ngozi, ngovi.
Leave, ruksa, ruhusa.
To take leave, kuaga.
Leaven, chachu, hamira.
Lee side, upande wa chini.
Leech, mruba, *pl.* miruba, mdudu afyonzaye damu.
Lefthandedness, shoto.
Leg (*or foot*), mguu, *pl.* miguu.
(*of a native bedstead*), tendegu, *pl.* matendegu.
Loss of the use of the legs, kitewe, kiwete.
Leg ring. See Anklet.
Legend, hadithi.
Leisure (*private time*), faragha, makini.
Lemon, limao, *pl.* malimao.
Length, urefu.
Leopard, chui, tui (M.).
Leprosy, ukoma, balanga, jethamu, matana.
Letter, waraka, *pl.* nyaraka, barua, khati.
Letter (*of the alphabet*), herufu.
Lever, mvukuto, *pl.* mivukuto.
Liar, mwongo, *pl.* wawongo.
Liberality, ukarimu.
Licentiousness, washerati.
Licorice, sus.
Lid, kifuniko, *pl.* vifuniko, kibia, *pl.* vibia, mkungu wa kufunikia.
Lie, wongo, uwongo.
Life, uzima (*health*), maisha (*continuance*), roho (*soul*).
Light, nuru, weupe, mwanga, *pl.* mianga, anga, *pl.* maanga (*glare*).
Lighthole, mwangaza, *pl.* miangaza.
Lights (*of an animal*), yavuyavu.
Lightning, umeme.
Like (*similar thing*), kifani, *pl* vifani.
Likeness, mfano, *pl.* mifano, kifano *pl.* vifano, sanamu, sura.
Lime, chokaa.
Lime (*fruit*), dimu.
Sweet lime, dimu tamu.
Limit, mpaka, *pl.* mipaka (*boundary*), kinga (*block*), upoo (*what cannot be surpassed*).
Line, mstari, *pl.* mistari (*drawn*), safu (*row*), ugwe (*cord*), shairi (*line of verse*).
Linen, kitani.
Lining of a kanzu *round the throat*, kaba.
Lion, simba.
Lip, mdomo, mlomo, *or* mwomo, *pl.* midomo, milomo, *or* miomo.
Lip-ring, udonya.
Liquid, maji, kiowevu.
Lisp, kitembe.
Litter (*carried by four men*), machera.
Little pieces, vidogo, *sing.* kidogo

Liver, ini, *pl.* maini.
Lizard, mjusi, *pl.* wajusi.
Large water lizard, kenge.
Kinds of lizards, mguruguru, *pl.* waguruguru—gorong'ondwa—kiuma mbuzi—mjumbakaka—mjisikafiri.
Load, mzigo, *pl.* mizigo.
Loaf, mkate, *pl.* mikate.
Loan, maazimo, karatha.
Lock, kitasa, *pl.* vitasa (*box lock*), komeo *or* gomeo (*a native wooden lock*), kufuli, *pl.* makufuli (*padlock*).
Locust, mzige, *pl.* wazige, nzige.
Log, gogo, *pl.* magogo.
(*nautical*), batli.
Loin cloth, nguo, doti, kikoi, *pl.* vikoi (*with a striped border*).
Loins, kiuno, *pl.* viuno.
Longing, uchu, tamaa, hawa.
Look, nathari.
Looking-glass, kioo, *pl.* vioo.
Loop, kitanzi, *pl.* vitanzi.
Loops to haul up a boat by, kishwara.
Loss, hasara.
Lots, kura.
Louse, chawa, tawa.
Love, shauko, mapenzi, habba, mahabu, pendo, mapendo.
Luck, bahati, nasibu.
Messenger of ill luck, korofi.
Lukewarmness, uvuguvugu.
Lumbrici, chango.
Lump, fungo, *pl.* mafungo, fumba, *pl.* mafumba.
Lump (*as in flour*), kidonge, *pl.* vidonge, vumbu, *pl.* mavumbu.
Lump (*of meat*), chinyango.
Lunacy, kichaa, soda.
Lunatic, mwenyi kichaa.
Lungs, pafu, pumu, yavuyavu (*of an animal*).
Lust, hawa.

M.

Mace (*spice*), basbasi.
Machine, samani, mtambo, *pl.* mitambo.
Madagascar, Buki, Bukini.
Madness, wazimo, mahoka (country dialect).
Magadoxa, Mkuchyo.
Magic, uchawi (*black magic*), uganga (*white magic*).
Maggot (funza).
Magnesia (*sulphate of*), chumvi ya haluli.
Maiden, mwana mwali.
Maize (*plant*), muhindi.
half-grown, matindi.
(*corn*), mahindi.
(*corn cob*), gunzi, *pl.* magunzi.
(*young cob*), ngara.
(*parched corn*), mbisi.
Majesty, enzi, ezi.
Malice, uovu.
Man (*person*), mtu, *pl.* watu.
(*male*), mwanamume, *pl.* waanaume.
(*human being*), mwana Adamu, bin Adamu (Ar.).
A very large man, jitu, *pl.* majitu.
A young man whose beard is beginning to appear, mvulana, *pl.* wavulana.
Man of the world, mtu mwerevu.
Mango, embe, embe (M.), *pl.* maembe. Embe za dodo, *large mangoes*.
Mango-tree, mwembe, *pl.* miembe
Mangouste, mohiro, *pl.* wachiro.
Mangrove, mkoko, *pl.* mikoko.

Manner, ginsi.
An elegant manner, madaha.
Manners, desturi, mathehebu.
Good manners, adabu, tasfida.
Mantis, vunja jungo.
Manure, samadi.
Manuscript, mwandiko, *pl.* miandiko.
Mark, alama.
Marks made by dragging anything along, mkokoto, *pl.* mikokoto.
Tribal mark, nemba. *See Spot, Blotch.*
Market, soko, *pl.* masoko.
Marriage, ndoa, mikaha.
(*the ceremony*), harusi.
(*intermarriage*), kuoana.
Marrow, bongo.
Martyr, shahidi, *pl.* mashahidi.
Mask, barakoa.
Mason, mwashi, *pl.* waashi.
Mason's trowel, mwiko, *pl.* miiko.
Mass, the mass of, jamii ya.
Mast, mlingote, *pl.* milingote, mgote, *pl.* migote.
Small mizen-mast, mlingote wa kalmi *or* galmi.
Master (*of a house, or of slaves*), bwana.
Master (*of a school*), mwalimu, *pl.* waalimu.
Master's son, bwana mdogo.
Master workman, fundi.
One's own master, 'mwcza mwenyewe.
Mat (*coarse matting*), jamvi, *pl.* majamvi.
Sleeping mat, mkeka, *pl.* mikeka.
Sleeping mat made like a bag with one side open, fumba.
Oval prayer mat, musala, *pl.* misala.
Round mat on which food is laid out, kitanga, *pl.* vitanga.
Strips of palm leaf for plaiting fine mats, myaa, *pl.* miyaa.
Strips of palm leaf for plaiting coarse mats, mwaa, *pl.* miwaa.
Narrow strips ready to be sewn together to make coarse mats, shupatu, *pl.* mashupatu.
Strips for making fine mats, ukiri, *pl.* kiri.
The thick edge of strips of matting, ng'ong'o.
Busati, *a sort of matting brought from Muscat.*
Matchmaker, kijumbe, *pl.* vijumbe.
Matches, viberiti.
Matter (*pus*), usaha.
A matter, jambo, jawabu.
What is the matter? Kuna nini?
What is the matter with you? Una nini.
Mattress, godoro, *pl.* magodoro.
Mayotte, Maotwe.
Meal (*food*), chakula.
First meal after a fast, futari.
Meal (*flour*), unga.
Meaning, maana.
Meanness, unyonge.
Means, njia.
Measles, churuwa.
Measure, kadri, kiasi, cheo, kipimo.
A measure, kipimo, *pl.* vipimo.
Measuring rod, line, &c., chenezo, *pl.* vyenezo.
See Cubit, Fathom, Span, Weight. The weights are used as measures for such a capacity as would contain that weight of millet [(mtama).
Meat, nyama.
Small pieces cooked on a skewer, mshakiki, *pl.* mishakiki.

Pieces cooked on two parallel sticks, subana.
Meatiness, mnofu.
Meddler, piugamizi.
Mediator (*peace-maker*), mselehisha, *pl.* waselehisha, msuluhisha, *pl.* wasuluhisha, mpatanishi, *pl.* wapatanishi.
Medicine, dawa, *pl.* dawa *or* madawa.
(*medical knowledge*), utabibu, uganga.
Medicine man, mganga, *pl.* waganga.
Meekness, upole.
Melancholy, huzuni, hamu.
Memorandum (*written*), khati.
Memorial, kumbukumbu, ukumbusho.
Memory, ukumbuka, ufahamu.
Menstruation, heth.
Mention, kumbukumbu.
Merchandise, bithaa.
Merchant, mfanyi biashara, *pl.* wafanyi biashara, tajiri, *pl.* matajiri (*a rich man*), ta*th*biri, bazazi (*huckster*).
Mercury, zebakh.
Mercy, rehema, huruma.
Merit, ajara.
Merka, Marika.
Message, maneno, habari.
Messenger, mjumbe, *pl.* wajumbe, mtume, *pl.* watume, tume.
Metal, madini.
Middle, kati.
Middle of a piece of cloth, mji.
Midge, usubi.
Midnight, usiku saa a sita, kati ya usiku, usiku wa manane.
Midwife, mzalisha, *pl.* wazalisha.
Mildew, kawa.
Milk, maziwa.
Curdled milk, maziwa mabivu.
Buttermilk, mtindi.
Mill, dinu, *pl.* vinu.
Steam mill, kinu cha moshi.
Oil mill, kinu cha kushindikia.
Hand mill, mawe ya kusagia (*this last only is used for grinding corn.* Kinu *is properly a wooden mortar, and the common oil mills consist of a lever turned in a mortar by camels*).
Millipede, jongoo.
Millet, mtama.
fully formed but unripe, mtama tete.
Millet stalks, mabua, *sing.* bua.
kinds of millet, kibakuli, kipaje.
Mind, moyo (*heart*), akili (*wits*), nia (*intention*).
Mine, madini.
Mint (*herb*), nana, fidina (?).
Minute, dakika.
Miracle, mwujiza, *pl.* miujiza, ajabu.
Miscarriage, kuharibu mimba.
Mischief, mathara, uharabu.
Miser, bakhili, choyo.
Misery, shidda, thulli.
Misfortune, msiba, *pl.* misiba, taabu.
Missile, kimwondo, *pl.* zimwondo (*used to mean shooting stars, because said to be cast at the Jins by the angels*).
Missionary, mpeekwa, *pl.* wapeekwa.
Mist, kungu, umande, shemali.
Mistake, kosa, makosa.
Mistress (*of slaves*), bibi.
(*of the house*), mwana. *It is reckoned good manners in Zanzibar to speak of one's own mother as* mwana.
Mistress (*kept woman*), kinyumba.
Mistress (*sweetheart*), mchumba.

Mizen-mast, mlingote wa kalmi **or** galmi.
Mockery, usimanga.
Moderation, kadri, kiasi.
Modesty, haya.
Mohilla, Moalli.
Mole, fuko (?).
Mombas, Mvita.
Monday, Juma a tatu.
Money, fetha.
Monfia, Mafya.
Monkey, kima.
Tumbili, *a small light-coloured monkey.*
Ngedere, *a small black monkey.*
Mbega, *pl.* wabega, *a black monkey with long white hair on the shoulders.*
Monsoon (*northerly winds*), musimi.
Month, mwezi, *pl.* miezi.
The months of the Arab year are determined by the sight of the moon, or by the lapse of thirty full days. The months practically begin from the end of the fasting month, and are called Mfunguo wa mosi,—wa pili,—wa tatu,—wa'nne,—wa tano,—wa sita,—wa saba,—wa nane,—wa kenda, Rajabu, Shaabani, Ramathani. *See Time.*
A month of less than thirty days, mwezi mpungufu.
A month of thirty full days, mwezi mwangamu.
Monthly pay, mshaara.
Moon, mwezi.
Moonblindness, kiwi.
Moonlight, bala mwezi.
Morning, subui, assubui, ussubui.
Morning air, umande.
Morocco, Magharibi.
Morsel, kidogo, *pl.* vidogo.
Mortar for pounding and cleaning grain, &c., kinu, *pl.* vinu.
Mortar for throwing shells, kombora.
Builder's mortar, chokaa.
Platters used as mortar boards, chano, *pl.* vyano.
Mosque, méskiti, moskiti, mesjid.
Mosquito, imbu.
Moth, noondo.
Mother, mama. *It is polite in Zanzibar to speak of one's own mother as* mwana.
Step-mother, mama wa kambo.
Mother-in-law, mkwe, *pl.* wakwe.
Mould, kalibu.
(*mouldiness*), ukungu, kawa.
Mound (*of earth*), kisugulu, *pl.* visugulu.
Mound (*of stones*), boma, *pl.* maboma.
Mountain, mlima, *pl.* milima.
Mourning (*grief*), msiba.
To make a formal mourning, kukaa matanga.
To finish a formal mourning, kuondoa matanga.
To live very privately during mourning for a husband, kukalia eda.
The feast with which a mourning concludes, hitimu.
Moustache, muomo, *pl.* miomo.
Mouth, kinwa, *pl.* vinwa, kanwa, *pl.* makanwa.
Mucus (*from the nose*), kamasi.
(*from the vagina*), utoko.
Mud, tope; *much mud*, matope.
Muddiness in water, vumbi.
Mule, nyumbu, búghala. [ruba.
Multiplication (*arithmetical*), thá-

Multitude, makutano, kundi, *pl.* makundi, jeshi, *pl.* majeshi, umaati.
Mummy, mumyani.
Mungoose, mchiro, *pl.* wachiro.
Murderer, muuwaji, *pl.* wauwaji.
Muscle, tafu.
Mushroom, kioga, *pl.* vioga.
Music, ngoma.
Musical Instruments. See Drum.
Baragumu, *a spiral antelope's horn used as a trumpet.*
Kayamba, *a sort of rattle.*
Kinanda, *pl.* vinanda, *a stringed instrument, used of European instruments generally.*
Kinubi, *a harp.*
Matoazi, *sing.* toazi, *cymbals.*
Mbui, *a buffalo's horn played by beating.*
Paanda, *a trumpet.*
Upato, *a plate of copper sounded by beating.*
Vugo, *a large horn sounded by beating.*
Zeze, *a three-stringèd lute.*
Zomari, *a sort of clarionet.*
Musk, mesiki, meski.
Mussel (*shell fish*), kijogoo, *pl.* vijogoo, kome, *pl.* makome.
Mustard, kharadali.
Myriad, kikwi, *pl.* vikwi *or* zikwi.
Myrrh, manemane.

N.

Nail (*finger*), ukucha, *pl.* kucha.
(*iron*), msomari, *pl.* misomari.
Name, jina, *pl.* majina.
What is your name? Jina lako nani?
Namesake, somo, *pl.* masomo.
Nape of the neck, ukosi, kikosi.
Napkin, kitambaa, *pl.* vitambaa.
Table napkin, kitambaa cha meza.
Narcotic, kileo, *pl.* vileo.
Nation, taifa, *pl.* mataifa.
Native, mzalia, *pl.* wazalia, kizao, *pl.* vizao, kivyao, *pl.* vivyao.
Nature, asili, tabia.
Nautical instruments, vipande vya kupimia.
Navel, kitovu, *pl.* vitovu.
Necessaries (*especially as supplied by God's providence*), riziki, ziriki (M.).
(*useful things*), vifaa.
Necessity, farathi, lazima, ukwasefu.
Neck, shingo, *pl.* mashingo. *See Back, Nape.*
Need, uhtaji, kutaka, matakwa.
Needle, sindano.
Neighbour, jirani.
Neighbourhood, upande wa, kiyambo (?).
Nest, tundu, *pl.* matundu.
(*a laying place*), kiota, *pl.* viota.
Net, mshipi, *pl.* mishipi.
used to take gazelles, &c., wavu, *pl.* nyavu, chavu, *pl.* vyavu.
Stake net, hedge made in the sea, uzio, *pl.* nyuzio.
Round casting net, kimia, *pl.* vimia.
Seine made of European cordage, jarifa (*or* jarife), *pl.* majarifa.
Seine made of cocoa-nut fibre, juya, *pl.* majuya.
Fish trap made of basket work, dema.
Nettle, kiwavi, *pl.* viwavi (*used also of sea-nettles*).
News, habari.
Night, usiku.
All night, usiku kucha.

Four whole nights, siku nne usiku kucha.

Four days and nights, siku nne mchana na usiku.

Nightmare, jinamisi.

Nipple, chuchu ya ziwa, titi, bubu (A.).

of a gun, kifa, *pl.* vifa.

Nobody, si mtu.

There is nobody, hapana (*or* hakuna) mtu.

Noise, sauti.

of voices, kelele, *pl.* makelele, uthia.

See Bellow, Roar, Hum, Cry.

Nonsense, upuzi, puo.

Noon, athuuri, jua kitwani.

Noose, tanzi, *pl.* matanzi.

North, kibula, kaskazini.

Northerly winds, kaskazi.

Nose, pua, *pl.* pua *or* mapua.

Nose ornament shaped like a stud, kipini, *pl.* vipini.

Nose ring, azama.

Nostril, tundu ya pua, 'mwanzi wa pua (?).

Notch, a place where a triangular piece is broken out, pengo.

Note, barua, khati.

Number, hesabu, kiwango.

Nurse, yaya (*dry nurse*), 'mlezi, *pl.* walezi (*of a child*), muguzi, *pl.* wauguzi (*of a sick person*).

Nut, kokwa, *pl.* makokwa. *See Ground, Cashew, &c.*

Nutmeg, kungumanga.

O.

Oar, kasia, *pl.* makasia.

Oath, uapo, *pl.* nyapo, kiapo, *pl.* viapo, yamini.

Obedience, mutia.

Objections, makindano, makatazo.

Occupation, shughuli.

Œsophagus, umio.

Offering, sadaka (*gift*), thabihu (*sacrifice*), kafara (*a sacrifice to avert calamity; it is buried or thrown away*).

Officer, akida, mkuu wa asikari.

Officiousness, futhuli, ufuthuli, ujuvi.

Offspring, mzao, *pl.* wazao.

Oil, mafuta.

Castor-oil, mafuta ya mbarika.

Semsem-oil, mafuta ya uta.

Ointment, marhamu.

Old age, uzee, ukongwe (*extreme*).

Old person, mzee, *pl.* wazee, kikongwe, *pl.* vikongwe (*extremely old*).

Omelette, kiwanda, kimanda.

Omen, fali.

Omnipresence, eneo la Muungu (*the spread of God*).

Onion, kitunguu, *pl.* vitunguu.

Open place, kiwanja, *pl.* viwanja, wangwa, wanda.

piece of waste ground in a town, uga.

Opinion, wasia.

Opium, afyuni.

Opportunity, nafasi.

Ophthalmia, weli wa macho.

Orange, chungwa, *pl.* machungwa, chungwa la kizungu, danzi la kizungu.

Bitter or wild oranges, danzi, *pl.* madanzi.

Mandarin oranges, kangaja.

(*a larger sort*), chenza, chenza za kiajjemi.

Order. See Command.

(*regularity, or a regular order*), taratibu.

Ordeal, kiapo, *pl.* viapo.
Origin, asili, chimbuko, mwanzo.
Ornament, pambo, *pl.* mapambo, kipambo, *pl.* vipambo.
Dalia, *a yellow cosmetic.*
Ndonya, *lip-ring worn by the Nyassa women.*
Sarafu, *a small gold plate worn on the forehead.*
Shangwi, *an ornament worn between the shoulders.*
Urembo, *black lines painted upon the face.*
Uzuri, *cosmetic applications.*
Vidani, *collars of gold or silver.*
See Anklets, Bracelets, Ear, Nose.
Orphan, yatima.
Os coccygis, kifundugu.
Ostrich, buni.
Otto of roses, hal wáradi.
Outlet, pakutokea.
Outrigger (of canoes), matengo.
Outskirts of a town, kiunga.
Oven, tanuu, tanuru.
Over-looker, msimamizi, *pl.* wasimamizi, mwangalizi, *pl.* waangalizi.
Owl, bundi.
Owner, mwenyewe.
Ox, ng'ombe *or* gnombe, maksai.
Oyster, cheza, kome (?), *pl.* makome, kombe za pwani.

P.

Pace, mwendo.
Package, packet, or parcel, robota, 'gora. (*of cloth*), peto, *pl.* mapeto.
Small packet, kipeto, *pl.* vipeto.
Pad of grass, &c., used to carry a load on the head upon, generally twisted into a ring, kata.
Pad used as a saddle for donkeys, khorj.
Paddle, kafi, *pl.* makafi.
Padlock, kufuli.
Pail, ndoo.
Pain, maumivu, uchungu, kuuma.
Paint, rangi.
Pair, jozi, jura, jeuzi, jauzi.
Palace, jumba.
Palanquin, machera.
Palate, kaaka, kaa la kinwa.
Palisading, zizi, kizizi.
Palm of the hand, kitanga cha mkono, *pl.* vitanga vya mikono.
A sail-maker's palm, dofra, *pl.* madofra.
Palm-tree. See Cocoa-nut, Date.
Leaf-stem of a palm-tree, upongoe, *pl.* pongoe.
Mkoche, *has an edible fruit.*
Mlala, *hyphæne, branching palm.*
Mvuma, *borassus palm.*
Palm-oil tree, mchikichi, *pl.* michikichi.
its fruit, chikichi, *pl.* machikichi.
the small nuts contained in the fruit, kichikichi, *pl.* vichikichi.
Palm-wine, tembo.
Spirit made from palm-wine, zarambo.
Palm-wine syrup, asali ya tembo.
Palmar abscess, kaka.
Palpitation of the heart, kiherehere cha moyo.
Panniers, shoi, shogi.
Pap, ubabwa.
Papaw, papayi, *pl.* mapapayi.
Papaw-tree, mpapayi, *pl.* mipapayi.
Paper, karatasi.
Parable, methili, methali, mfano, *pl.* mifano.
Paradise, peponi.

Gate of paradise, kilango cha jaha.
Paralysis, kipooza, tiwo (?).
Paralytic, mwenyi kupooza.
Parched maize, nibisi.
Pardon, arathi, musama, masameho, hisa.
Parent, mzaa, *pl.* wazaa, mzazi, *pl.* wazazi, mzee, *pl.* wazee.
Part, fungu, *pl.* mafungu, sehemu, upande, *pl.* pande, kisma.
Partner, msharika, *pl.* washarika.
Partnership, usharika.
Partridge, kwalo (?).
Kering'ende, *the red-legged partridge.*
Party (faction), aria.
Pass, or passport, cheti, *pl.* vyeti.
Passage (by), pito, *pl.* kipito.
(*through*), kipenyo, *pl.* vipenyo.
A very narrow passage, kichochoro, *pl.* vichochoro.
Patch (in cloth), kiraka, *pl.* viraka.
(*in planking*), hasho.
Path, njia, pito, *pl.* mapito.
Patience, saburi, subiri, uvumilivu, utulivu.
Pattern, namna.
(*to work from*) kielezo, *pl.* vielezo.
Pauper, kibapara, *pl.* vibapara (*an insulting epithet*).
Pawn (chess), kitunda, *pl.* vitunda.
Pay, ijara, njia, faritha, mshahara (*monthly*).
Pea, dengu (*they are not grown in Zanzibar, but are brought dry from India*).
A small pea-like bean, chooko, chiroko.
Peace, amani, salamu.
Peace-maker, mpatauishi, mselehisha, msuluhisha.
Peacock, tausi.
Peak, kilele, *pl.* vilele.
Pearl, lulu.
Pebble (very small), mbwe.
(*or small piece of stone*), kokoto, *pl.* makokoto.
Peel, ganda, *pl.* maganda.
Peg, chango, *pl.* vyaugo.
Pelvis, tokoni.
Pen, kalamu.
Reed pen, kalamu ya 'mwanzi.
Penis, mbo.
People, watu.
People of this world, walimwengu.
Other people's, -a watu.
People like us, kina sisi.
Abdallah's people, kina Abdallah.
Pepper, pilipili manga.
Red pepper, pilipili hoho.
Percussion cap, fataki.
Perfection, ukamilifu, utimilivu.
Perfumes, manukato.
Period (or point of time), kipindi, *pl.* vipindi.
Perjury, azúr, zuli.
Permission, ruksa, ruhusa.
Persia, Àjjemi.
Persian Gulf, Bahari il 'ali.
Person, mtu.
A grown person, mtu mzima. *See Old, &c.*
Perspiration, hari, jasho.
Pestilence, tauni, wabba.
Pestle, mchi (*or* mti), *pl.* michi, mtwango, *pl.* mitwango.
Phantom, kivuli, *pl.* vivuli.
Phlegm, belghamu.
Phthisis, ukohozi.
Physic, dawa, *pl.* dawa *or* madawa.
Physician, tabibu, mtabibu, *pl.* watabibu, mganga, *pl.* waganga.

Pice, pesa, *pl.* pesa *or* mapesa.
Pickle, achari.
Picture, taswira, sura, sanamu.
Piece, kipande, *pl.* vipande.
Piece of Madagascar grass cloth, ramba, *pl.* maramba.
Piece let in by way of patch (in planking), hasho. *See Firewood.*
Pig, nguruwe, nguuwe.
Jivi, *a wild hog.*
Pigeon, njiwa, ndiwa (M.).
Tame pigeon, njiwa manga.
Wild pigeon, njiwa wa mwitu.
Pile of sticks, &c., for burning, biwi, *pl.* mabiwi.
Piles (hæmorrhoids), bawasir.
Pilgrimage, haj.
Pill, kidonge, *pl.* vidonge.
Pillar, nguzo.
Pillow, mto, *pl.* mito.
Wooden head rest, msamilo, *pl.* misamilo.
Pilot, rubani.
Pimple, kipele, *pl.* vipele, upele, *pl.* pele (*large*), kiwe, *pl.* viwe (*a small kind*).
Pincers, koleo.
Pine-apple, nanasi, *pl.* mananasi.
Pinna (shell-fish), kaya, *pl.* makaya, panga, *pl.* mapanga.
Pipe (water), nelli.
(*clarionet*), zomari.
(*tobacco*), kiko, *pl.* viko. *The native pipe consists of a bowl* (bora), *a stem* (digali) *leading from the bowl into a small vessel of water, which last is properly the* kiko; *the stem from the* kiko *to the mouth is the* shilamu. *The bubbling of the water when it is being smoked is the* malio ya kiko.
Piping, kigwe, *pl.* vigwe.
Pirate, haramia.
Pistol, bastola.
Pit, shimo, *pl.* mashimo.
Pitch or Tar, lami.
Pity, huruma.
Place, mahali, pahali.
Place may often be expressed by the prefix pa-.
Panyamavu, *a quiet place.*
Pakutokea, *a place to go out at.*
Panginepo, *elsewhere.*
or by the use of penyi.
Penyi mti, *the place where the tree is, or was.*
An open place, kiwanja, *pl.* viwanja.
A clear space in a town, uga.
A place where offerings are made to propitiate spirits supposed to haunt it, mzimu, *pl.* mizimu.
Plague, tauni.
Plain, uwanda.
Plan, shauri, *pl.* mashauri.
Plane, randa.
Plank, ubau, *pl.* mbau.
Planking, mbau.
A plank laid over the body before the earth is filled in, kiunza, *pl.* viunza.
Plant, mbegu, mbeyu.
A young plant, mche, *pl.* miche, chipukizi, *pl.* vipukizi.
Upupu, *cowitch.*
Mbaruti, *a thistle-like plant with a yellow flower.*
Nyinyoro, *a bulbous plant throwing up a head of red flowers.*
Yungiyungi, *the blue water-lily.*
Afu, *the wild jasmine.*
Kirukia, *a parasite on fruit trees.*
Mpungati, *a kind of cactus.*
Plantains, ndizi.

Plantation, shamba, *pl.* mashamba.
Plate, kisabani, *pl.* visabani.
A plate of metal, bamba, *pl.* mabamba.
Platter of wood, chano, *pl.* vyano.
Pleasure, anasa, furaha.
Pleasing things, mapendezi.
Pledge, rahani, amani, kabathi.
Pleiades, kilimia.
Plenty, wingi, ungi (M.), marithawa.
Plumb-line (a stone hung by a strip of banana leaf), timazi.
Plug, nguruzi, zibo, *pl.* mazibo.
Plummet, chubwi.
Pocket, mfuko, *pl.* mifuko.
Pocket-handkerchief, leso.
Poem, mashairi, utenzi (*religious*).
Poet, mtunga mashairi, *pl.* watunga mashairi.
Poetry, mashairi.
One line of poetry, shairi.
Point, ncha.
Poison, sumu, uchungu.
Fish poison, utupa.
Pole, mti, *pl.* miti.
for carrying burdens on, mpiko, *pl.* mipiko.
for propelling a canoe, upondo, *pl.* pondo.
Politeness, adabu.
Pomegranate, kamamanga.
Pomeloe, furungu, *pl.* mafurungu.
Pond, ziwa, *pl.* maziwa.
Pool, ziwa, *pl.* maziwa.
Pool left by the retiring tide, kidimbwi, *pl.* vidimbwi.
Poop, shetri.
Poor free man, maskini ya Muungu.
Porcupine, nungu.
Pores, nweleo, matokeo ya hari.
Porpoise, pomboo.
Porridge, ugali, uji, fuka, hasida.
Porter. *See Doorkeeper*.
(*carrier*), hamali, *pl.* mahamali.
(*in a caravan*), mpagazi, *pl.* wapagazi.
Port Durnford, Burikao.
Position in the world, cheo, kiwango.
Possessions, mali, milki.
Possessor, mwenyewe.
Possessor of, &c., mwenyi, &c., *pl.* wenyi, &c.
Post, mti, *pl.* miti.
Bearing post, mhimili, *pl.* mihimili.
Posterity, wazao.
Pot. *See Cooking-pot, Censer.*
A lobster-pot, dema.
Potash (nitrate of), shura.
Potatoes, viazi vya kizungu.
Sweet potatoes, viazi, *sing.* kiazi.
Raised beds for planting viazi, tuta, *pl.* matuta.
Potsherd (broken piece of pottery or glass), kigai, *pl.* vigai, gai, *pl.* magai (*a large piece*), kigerenyenza, *pl.* vigerenyenza (*a very small piece, a splinter*).
Potter, mfinangi, *pl.* wafinangi, mfinyanzi, wafinyanzi.
A place to bake potter's work, joko.
Poultry, k'uku.
Poverty, umasikini.
Powder, unga.
Gunpowder, baruti.
Power, uwezo, nguvu, mamlaka, enzi.
Practice, mtaala, mazoezo.
Praise, sifa, hamdi.
Prattle, vijineno.
Prayer (worship), ibada.
(*entreaty*), kuomba.

(the prescribed forms), sala. *The regular Mohammedan times of prayer are*, Magaribi, *directly after sunset;* Esha, *an hour or two later;* Alfajiri, *before sunrise;* Athuuri, *at noon;* Alasiri, *about half-way between noon and sunset.*

Preacher, mwenyi kukhutubu, *or* kuayithi.

Precept, mafundisho.

Pregnancy, mimba.

Present (*see Gift*), zawadi.

Customary present, ada, kilemba.

Customary presents at a wedding; to the bride's father, mahari, kilemba; *to the bride's mother*, mkaja, ubeleko; *to the bride's kungu*, kiosha miguu, kifunua mlango; *to the bride herself*, kipa mkono.

Press or Pressure, shinikizo.

Prey, mawindo.

Price, kima, *th*amani.

Prickly heat, vipele vya bahara.

A medicament for it, liwa.

Pride, kiburi.

Priest, kahini, *pl.* makahini (*used in the sense of soothsayer*).

(*Christian*), kasisi, padre *or* padiri, *pl.* mapadiri.

Prison, kifungo, gereza.

Privacy, faragha.

Privy, choo.

Proceeds, pato, *pl.* mapato.

Produce (*fruit, seed, &c.*), zao, *pl.* mazao.

Profit, fayida, ghanima.

Progeny, mzao, *pl.* wazao.

Progress, kiendeleo.

Prohibition, makatazo.

Promise, ahadi, wahadi.

Promissory note, awala.

Pronunciation, mata'mko.

Prop, mhimili, *pl.* mihimili, mategemeo.

A prop to keep a vessel upright when left by the tide, gadi.

Property, mali, milki.

Prophet, nabii, mtume, *pl.* mitume.

Prosecution, mstaki, *pl.* mistaki.

Proselyte, mwongofu, *pl.* waongofu.

Prostitute, kahaba, *pl.* makahaba.

Protection, hami, hamaya.

Under British protection, fi hamayat al Ingrez (Ar.).

Proverb, mfano wa maneno.

Provision, madaraka.

Provisions, vyakula.

Provocation, ekerahi.

Prow, gubeti.

of a small vessel, kikono, *pl* vikono.

(*head*), omo.

Prudence, busara, fikira.

Pulley, kapi, *pl.* makapi, gofia.

Pulpit, mimbara.

Pump, bomba.

Pumpkin, boga, *pl.* maboga.

plant, mboga, *pl.* miboga.

shell used to carry liquids in dundu, *pl.* madundu.

Mumunye, *pl.* mamumunye, *sort of vegetable marrow.*

Tango, *pl.* matango, *eaten raw like cucumber.*

Kitoma, *pl.* vitoma, *a sma round sort.*

Tikiti, *pl.* matikiti, *a round kind of water-melon.*

Punch, keke.

Purchaser, mnunuzi, *pl.* wanunuzi.

Purgative, dawa la kuhara.

Purity, masafi, utakatifu

Purpose, kusudi, *pl.* makusudi, kasidi, nia.
Purse, kifuko cha kutilia fetha.
Push in the cheek, mdukuo.
Putridity, kioza.
Putty, chaki.
Python, chatu.

Q.

Quail, tombo, tomboroko.
Quality, tabia, ginsi, jisi, aina.
Quantity, kiasi. kadiri, cheo (*measurement*).
Quarrel, mateto, tofauti, nazar, ugomvi.
Quarrelsomeness, ugomvi.
Quarter, robo.
Three-quarters of a dollar, kassa robo.
Quarter of a town, mta, *pl.* mita.
Queen, malkia.
(*chess*), kishi.
Question, maulizo, swali.
Quieting thing, kitulizo, *pl.* vitulizo.
Quietness, utulivu, makini, kimya.
Quiver, podo.

R.

Rabbit, sungura, kisungura, *pl.* visungura, kitungule, *pl.* vitungule, kititi.
Race, mashindano.
Rafter, boriti (*for a stone roof*), kombamoyo, *pl.* makombamoyo (*for a thatched roof*), pao, *pl.* mapao (*very thin*).
Rag, kitambaa, *pl.* vitambaa, utambaa, *pl.* tambaa.
Rain, mvua.
Rain cloud, ghubari, *pl.* maghubari.
Rainy season, masika.
Lesser rains, mvua ya mwaka.
Rainbow, upindi wa mvua, kisiki cha mvua (M.).
Rammer for beating roofs, kipande, *pl.* vipande.
Rampart, boma, sera.
Rank, daraja, cheo.
Ransom, kombozi, *pl.* makombozi, ukomboo, ukombozi, fidia, ufidiwa, ukombolewa.
Rarity, t'unu, hedaya.
Rash (*small pimples*), vipele.
Rat, panya.
a very large kind, buku.
Rations, posho.
Rawness (*of meat, &c.*), ubichi.
(*dulness*), ujinga.
Razor, wembe.
Reason, maana, sababu, huja, akili
Reasoning, huja.
Rebellion, maasi.
Recess, kidaka, *pl.* vidaka, kishubaka, *pl.* vishubaka (*a pigeon-hole*).
Wall at the back of a recess, raff.
Recommendation, maagizo.
Rectitude, adili.
Red coral, marijani ya fethaluka.
Red Sea, Bahari ya Sham.
Redeemer, mkombozi, *pl.* wakombozi.
Reed, unyasi, *pl.* nyasi, 'mwanzi, *pl.* miwanzi.
Reference, marejeo.
Refuge, makimbilio.
Regret, majutio.
Regularity, kaida.
Reign, ezi, euzi.
Rein, kigwe, *pl.* vigwe.
Rejoicing, furaha, shangwi.
Relations (*relatives*), akraba, ndugu, jamaa.
A near relative, karibu.

Relaxation (*loosening*), ulegevu.
Religion, dini, dua.
Relish (*something to be eaten with rice or porridge*), kitoweo.
Remainder, msazo, masazo, mabakia, [baki.
Remedy, dawa, mapoza.
Reminder, ukumbusho.
Remission (*of sins*), maghofira, maondoleo.
Remnant, mabakia.
Rent, ijara.
Repentance, toba, majuto.
Representative, wakili.
Reproaches, matayo.
Reprobate, baa, *pl.* mabaa.
Reptile (?).
Kenge, *a monitor* (?), *a very large slender lizard.*
P'ili, *a large snake.*
Chatu, *a python.*
See Snake, Crocodile, &c.
Request, haja, matakwa.
Residue. *See Remainder.*
A little left in a jar, &c., kishinda. *pl.* vishinda.
Resin, ulimbo.
Respiration, kutanafusi, kushusha [pumzi.
Rest, raha, pumziko.
Resting-place, pumzikio, kituo, *pl.* zituo *or* vituo.
Restlessness, fathaa.
Resurrection, ufufuo, ufufulio, kiyama (*the general resurrection*).
Resuscitation, (*actively*) kufufua, kuhuisha, (*neuter*) kufufuka, kuhuika.
Retainer, mfuasi, *pl.* wafuasi.
Retaliation kasasi, kisasi.
Return, maregeo, marejeo kuja zao, &c.
Revenge majilipa.
Reverence, unenyekeo.
Reviling, mashutumu, mashutumio, matayo.
Revival. *See Resuscitation.*
Reward, ijara, ujira, majazo, *thawabu* (*especially from God*).
Reward for finding a lost thing, kiokosi, *pl.* viokosi.
Rheumatism, baridiyabis, uweli wa viungo.
Rhinoceros, kifaru, *pl.* vifaru, pea.
Rib, ubavu, *pl.* mbavu, kiwavu chana (A.).
Rice, growing, or yet in the husk, mpunga.
cleaned from the husk, mchele.
cooked, wali.
watery, and imperfectly cooked mashendea.
cooked so that the grains are dry and separate, pukute ya wali.
scorched in the cooking ukoko, utandu (A.).
left from overnight to be eaten in the morning, wali wa mwikuu.
Kinds of rice, sena, bungala, shindano, garofuu, kapwai, kifungo, madevu, mwanga, sifara, uchukwi.
Riches, mali, utajiri, ukwasi,
Rich man, tajiri, *pl.* matajiri, mwenyi mali, mkwasi, *pl.* wakwasi.
Ridicule, mzaha, thihaka.
Right, haki, wajib, adili.
Righteousness, haki.
Rind, ganda, *pl.* maganda.
Rind of a lemon, &c., after the inside has been squeezed or extracted, kaka.
Ring, pete, *pl.* pete *or* mapete.
Rings on the scabbard of a sword, &c. ukoa, *pl.* koa.

Ring where the blade enters the haft, noleo, *pl.* manoleo.

Ear-ring, pete ya masikio.

Ring-worm, choa.

Ripple, viwimbi.

Risk, in trading, juku.

River, mto, *pl.* mito.

Road, njia.

Roar, ngurumo, vumi.

Robber, mnyang'anyi, *pl.* wanyang'anyi, haramia.

People who wander about at night, robbing and committing violence, mrungura, mpakacha.

Rock, mwamba, *pl.* miamba.

A small rock, kijamba, *pl.* vijamba.

in the sea, kipwa, *pl.* vipwa.

Rolling of a ship, mramma.

Roof, dari, sakafu (*stone roof or floor*), paa, *pl.* mapaa (*thatched roof*). *The thatched roofs consist generally of a front and back slope*, kipaa cha mbele *and* kipaa cha nyuma, *and hips for the ends, which are carried up under and within the main slopes; these hips are called* visusi, *sing.* kisusi.

A lean-to, kipenu, *pl.* vipenu.

The roof over a watching-place in the fields, dungu, *pl.* madungu.

Rook (*chess*), fil.

Room (*space*), nafasi.

(*apartment*), chumba, *pl.* vyumba.

Ukumbi, *hall or porch; it is within a stone house, but outside an earthen one.*

Sébule *or* sebula, *parlour, reception room.*

Orfa, órofa, *or* ghórofa, *an upper room.*

Ghala, *a dark room on the ground-floor, a store-room.*

Root, shina, *pl.* mashina.

Rootlets, mizizi, mizi (M.).

Rope, kamba, ngole (Mer.).

Hempen rope, kamba, ulayiti.

Rosary (*Mohammedan beads*), tasbiih.

Rose, waradi, waridi.

Otto of roses, hal wáradi.

Rose-water, marashi mawaridi.

Rose apple, darabi, *pl.* madarabi.

Roundness, mviringo.

Row (*line*), safu.

Row (*noise*), uthia, kero.

Royalty, kifaume, ufaume.

Rubbish (*from old buildings*), fusi, kifusi.

(*small articles*), takataka.

Rudder, shikio, sakani, msukani, *pl.* misukani, usukani, *pl.* sukani.

Ruddle, used by carpenters to mark out their work, ngeu.

Rudeness, safihi.

Ruin or Ruins, maanguko.

Runaway (*from a master, home, &c.*), mtoro, *pl.* watoro.

(*from a fight, &c.*), mkimbizi, *pl.* wakimbizi.

Rupee, rupia.

Rupia or any similar skin disease, buba.

Rust, kutu.

Rustling, mtakaso.

S.

Sabre, kitara, *pl.* vitara.

Sacrifice, sadaka (*an offering*), fidia (*giving up*), thabihu (*sacrificing*), mathabuha (*the victim*), kafara (*an animal or thing offered but not eaten*).

Saddle, kiti cha frasi, matandiko, seruji (*an Arab saddle*), khorj (*the pad used for a donkey*).
Sadness (*see Grief*), rammu.
Safety, salamu, salama.
Saffron, zafarani.
Sail, tanga, *pl.* matanga.
Dhow-sail, duumi.
Sail-cloth, kitali.
Sailor, baharia.
Saint, walli.
Sake, ajili, huja, maana.
For my sake, unipendavyo (*as you love me*).
Sale (*auction*), mnada.
Salesman, dalali.
Saliva, mate.
Salt, chumvi, munyo (A.).
Saltpetre, shura.
Salute (*fired*), mizinga ya salamu.
(*salutation*), salamu.
Salvation, wokovu, suudi, njema.
Salver, sinia, *pl.* masinia.
Sanction, ithini.
Sand, mchanga, mtanga (M.).
Sandals, viatu, *sing.* kiatu, viatu vya ngozi.
strap of a sandal, gidam.
Sandalwood, liwa (?).
Sandfly, usubi.
Sap, maji.
Saturday, Juma a mosi.
Saucepan, sufuria.
Saviour, mwokozi, *pl.* waokozi.
Savour, luththa, tamu.
Scab, kigaga, *pl.* vigaga.
Scabbard, ala, *pl.* nyala.
The metal rings on a scabbard, ukoa, *pl.* koa.
Scaffold (*for building*), jukwari.
Scales (*of a fish*), magamba, mamba (M.).
Scales (*balances*), mizani.
Scale pans, vitanga vya mizani.
Scar, kovu, *pl.* makovu.
Scarf (*often worn round the waist*), deuli.
Scent, harufu, manuka, nukato, *pl.* manukato, meski, marashi (*a scent for sprinkling*).
Tihu, *a kind of scent.*
See Rose, Ambergris, Aloes wood.
School, chuoni.
Scissors, makasi.
Scoop. See Ladle.
Score (20), korja.
Scorn, tharau, thihaka.
Scorpion, nge.
Scraps left after eating, makombo, *sing.* kombo.
Scrape (*slide*), para.
Scratch, mtai, *pl.* mitai.
Scream, kiowe, *pl.* viowe (*cry for help*), kigelegele, *pl.* vigelegele (*a trilling scream raised as a cry of joy*).
Screw, parafujo.
Scrip, mkoba, *pl.* mikoba.
Scrofulous and gangrenous sores, mti.
Scrotum, pumbo, mapumbu.
Scull, kitwa, *pl.* vitwa, fuvu *or* bupuru la kitwa.
Scum, povu, mapovu.
Sea, bahari.
A sea, mawimbi, wimbi.
A seaman, mwana maji.
One from beyond seas, mja na maji.
Seaweed, mwani.
Seal, muhuri.
Seam, mshono, *pl.* mishono, band (*tacked*), upindo (*a hem*).
Season, wakati.

The principal seasons in Zanzibar are:—Musimi, *the time of the northerly winds* (kazkazi), *that is, December, January, and February. For March, April, and May, the rainy season,* masika; *after that, the cold time,* kipupwe; *then, about the end of August,* demani, *or* mwaka. *The southerly winds* (kusi) *begin to drop in October, and in the intervals between them and the northerly winds come the times of easterly and westerly winds,* malelezi *or* tanga mbili.

Seasoning. See Relish.

Seat, kikao, makazi.

The stone or earth seat near a door, baraza, kibaraza.

Secrecy, siri, faragha.

Secrets, mambo ya siri.

Secretary, mwandishi, *pl.* waandishi, khatibu, karani.

Secretary of State, waziri, *pl.* mawaziri.

Sect, mathhâb, mathehebu.

Sediment, mashapo.

Seed, mbegu, mbeyu.

Seedling, mche, *pl.* miche.

Self, moyo, nafsi, nafusi.

Self-content, kinaya.

Semen, shahawa, manni.

Semsem, ufuta.

Semsem oil, mafuta ya uta.

What is left after the oil has been pressed out, shudu.

Senna, sanamaki.

Sense, akili.

Sentinel, mngoja, *pl.* wangoja.

Servant, mtumishi, *pl.* watumishi, mtumwa, *pl.* watumwa, noker.

One who serves at table, mwandikaji, *pl.* waandikaji.

In a shamba there are generally three chief servants. 1. Msimamizi, *generally a free man.* 2. Nokoa, *the chief slave.* 3. Kadamu, *the second head slave.*

Service, utumwa, hudumu, hidima.

Setting-out, things set out or the place for them, maandiko.

Shaddock, furungu, *pl.* mafurungu.

Shade, uvuli, vuli, mvuli, mvili, kivuli, kitua.

Shadow, kivuli, *pl.* vivuli.

Shame (disgrace), aibu.

(modesty), haya.

(a thing causing confusion), ari, fetheba, hezaya.

having no shame, mjanja, *pl.* wajanja.

Shape, kiasi, kalibu, namna.

Share, fungu, *pl.* mafungu, semehu, kisma.

Sharing, usharika.

Shark, papa.

Sharpness, ukali.

Shaving (of wood), usafi.

Shawl, shali.

worn round the waist, mahazamu.

Sheaf, or bundle of cut rice, mganda, *pl.* miganda.

Sheath, uo, *pl.* mauo, ala, *pl.* nyala.

Sheave (of a pulley), roda, koradani.

Shed, banda, *pl.* mabanda, kibanda, *pl.* vibanda.

Sheep, kondoo.

Sheet, shuka.

of a sail, demani.

of a book, gombo, *pl.* magombo.

of paper, ukurasa, *pl.* kurasa.

Shelf, kibau, *pl.* vibau.

in a recess, rufúf.

Suso, *pl.* masuso, *a kind of hanging shelf.*

Shell (*sea shells*), shelle, *pl.* mashelle.
(*husk*), ganda, *pl.* maganda.
(*empty shell*), fuvu, *pl.* mafuvu, bupuru, *pl.* mabupuru, kaka.

Shepherd, mlishi, *pl.* walishi, mchunga, *pl.* wachunga.

Sherd. *See Potsherd.*

Shield, ngao.

Shin, muundi wa guu (A.).

Ship, merikebu, marikabu, jahasi.
Man-of-war, manowari, merikebu ya mizinga.
Merchant ship, merikebu ya taja,
Steam ship, merikebu ya dohaan, merikebu ya moshi.
Ship belonging to the government, merikebu ya serkali.
Full-rigged ship, merikebu ya milingote mitatu.
Barque, merikebu ya milingote miwili na nuss.
Native craft, chombo, *pl.* vyombo.

Shirt, kanzu.

Shivering, kitapo, kutetema, kutetemeka.

Shoal (*bank*), fungu, *pl.* mafungu.

Shock, shindo.

Shoe, kiatu cha kizungu *or* cha kihindi, *pl.* viatu vya kizungu.

Shoemaker, mshoni viatu, *pl.* washoni viatu.

Shoot, chipukizi, uchipuka, *pl.* chipuka.
A pointed shoot like that containing a spike of flower, kilele, *pl.* vilele.

Shop, duka, *pl.* maduka.
Shops with warerooms, bokhari.

Shot (*small*), marisaa.
Shot-belt, beti.

Shoulder, bega, *pl.* mabega, fuzi, *pl.* mafuzi (A.).
Shoulder-blade, kombe la mkono.

Shout, ukelele, *pl.* kelele, kelele, *pl.* makelele.

Shower, manyunyo.

Showing, wonyesho.

Shrewdness, werevu.

Shroud, saanda.

Shrub, kijiti, *pl.* vijiti.
See Thorn.
Mwango, *pl.* miwango (?).

Sick person, mgonjwa, *pl.* magonjwa, mweli, *pl.* waweli.

Sickness, ugonjwa, uweli, marathi.

Side, upande, *pl.* pande.
Side of the body, mbavu, matambavu.
The other side of a river, &c., ng'ambo.

Siege, mazingiwa.

Sieve, kiyamba.

Siftings of rice after pounding, wishwa.

Sighing, kuugua.

Sign, dalili.

Signal, ishara.
Ukonyezo, *pl.* konyezo, *a sign made by raising the eyebrows.*
Kikorombwe, *a kind of signal cry*

Silence, nyamavu, kimya

Silk, hariri.

Silliness, mapiswa, puo.
Silly talk, upuzi.

Silver, fetha.

Silversmith, mfua fetha, *pl.* wafua fetha.

Simpleton, mjinga, *pl.* wajinga.

Sin, thambi, *pl.* thambi *or* mathambi, makosa, taksiri.

Singleness, upweke.

Sip, funda (?).

Sir! Bwana!
Sister, umbu, *pl.* maumbu, ndugu, ndugu mke.
As a term of endearment, dada.
Foster-sister, ndugu kunyonya.
Sister-in-law, shemegi.
Sitter, mkaa, *pl.* wakaa.
Sitting, kikao, *pl.* vikao, kitako, *pl.* vitako.
Size, ukuu, ukubwa, kiasi, kadiri, cheo.
Skeleton, mzoga (?)
Skilful workman, mstadi, *pl.* wastadi.
Skilled or master-workman, fundi.
Skin, ngozi.
Sky, uwingu.
Slackness, ulegevu.
Slander, masingizio, fitina (*sowing of discord*).
Slaughter-house, matiudo.
Slave, mtumwa, *pl.* watumwa, muhadimu, *pl.* wahadimu, mtwana, *pl.* watwana.
A slave boy, kitwana, *pl.* vitwana.
A slave girl, kijakazi, *pl.* vijakazi.
A slave woman, mjakazi, *pl.* wajakazi.
A concubine slave, suria, *pl.* masuria.
A slave born in the house or country, mzalia, *pl.* wazalia.
A runaway slave, mtoro, *pl.* watoro.
A fellow slave, mjoli, *pl.* wajoli.
A household of slaves, kijoli, *pl.* vijoli.
Piece of land allotted to a slave for his own use, koonde, *pl.* makoonde.
Slavery, utumwa.
Sleep, uzingizi, zingizi.
Sleeping place, malalo.
Things to sleep upon, malazi.
Sleeve, mkono, *pl.* mikono.
Sling, kombeo, *pl.* makombeo.
Slip of a tree, &c., mche, *pl.* miche.
A slip which has put forth leaves, mche uliochanua.
One which has made a new shoot, mche uliochipuka.
Slipperiness, utelezi.
Sloth, uvivu.
Slovenliness, fujofujo.
Smallness, udogo.
Small-pox, ndui.
Smell, harufu, manuka, azma.
Smith (*worker in metal*), mfua, *pl.* wafua. *See Blacksmith, &c.*
Smoke, moshi, *pl.* mioshi.
Snail, koa, *pl.* makoa, konokono.
Snake, nyoka, joka, *pl.* majoka (*large*).
Chatu, *python*.
P'ili, *cobra* (?).
Snare, shabuka.
Sneezing, chafya.
Snoring, kukoroma.
Snuff, tumbako ya kunuka, *or* kunusa.
Snuff-box, tabakelo.
Soap, sabuni.
Soda, magadi.
Solder, lihamu.
Soldier, asikari.
Sole (*of the foot*), uayo, *pl.* nyao.
Solitude, upekee, ukiwa.
Somauli Coast, Banada.
Somebody, mtu.
Some one else's, -a mwenyewe.
Child of somebody, i.e., of respectable parents, mtoto wa watu, mwana wa watu.
Somersault, kitwangomba.

Son, mwana, *pl.* waana, kijana, mtoto mume.
  Wadi Mohammed, *Mohammed's son.*
  Bin Abdallah (Ar.), *Abdallah's son.*
  Hamisi wa Tani, *Hamisi the son of Tani* (*Othman*).
  Son-in-law, mkwe, *pl.* wakwe.
Song, uimbo, *pl.* nyimbo.
Soot, kaa moshi, makaa ya moshi.
Soothing thing, kitulizo, *pl.* vitulizo.
Soothsayer, kahini, *pl.* makahini.
Sore, donda, *pl.* madonda, kidonda, *pl.* vidonda, jeraha.
  Sores in the leg, nyungunyungu, mti.
Sorrow, kasarani, huzuni, sikitiko, matukio.
  Sorrow for a loss, majonzi.
  Sorrow for something done, majutio.
  Excessive sorrow, jitimai.
Sort (*kind*), ginsi, namna, aina.
  The sort is often expressed by the prefix ki-. Kizungu, *the European sort*, kifaume, *the kingly sort.*
Soul, roho.
Sound, sauti.
Soundness, uzima.
Source, asili, chimbuko.
South, kusini, suheli.
Southerly wind, kusi.
Sovereign, mwenyi ezi, mwenyi inchi, mwenyi mji.
  (*coin*), robo Ingrezi.
Sovereignty, ezi, enzi.
Space, nafasi.
  (*of time*), muda.
  (*open space*), uwanda, uga.
Spade, jembe la kizungu.
Span, futuri, shibiri, shibri.
Spangles, puluki.
Spark, chechi, *pl.* machechi.
Sparkle, kimeta.
Speaker, mneni, *pl.* waneni, msemi, *pl.* wasemi, msemaji, *pl.* wasemaji.
Speaking, kusema, kunema.
  A dark obscure way of speaking, kilinge cha maneno.
  An enigmatical way of speaking, in which the last syllable is taken from the end, and made to begin the word, kinyume, kinyuma. (*See Appendix I.*)
Spear, fumo, *pl.* mafumo (*flat-bladed*) mkuke, *pl.* mikuke, (*three-edged*) sagai, *pl.* masagai.
Spectacles, miwani.
Speech (*speaking*), kunena.
  (*oration*), mataguso, milumbe.
Spider, buibui.
Spinal column, uti wa maungo.
Spirits, mvinyo.
  Evil spirit, pepo.
  Kinds of spirits, jini, *pl.* majini, milhoi, mahoka, dungumaro, kitamiri, kizuu, kizuka, koikoi, mwana maua, &c.
Spit, uma, *pl.* nyuma.
Spittle, mate.
Spoil, mateka.
Spleen, wengo.
Splint, gango, *pl.* magango, banzi, *pl.* mabanzi.
Splinter (*of wood*), kibanzi, *pl.* vibanzi.
  (*of glass or earthenware*), kigerenyenza, *pl.* vigerenyenza.
Spoon, mwiko, *pl.* miiko, kijiko, *pl.* vijiko (*a tea-spoon*), mkamshe, *pl.* mikamshe (*a wooden spoon*).

Sport, mchezo, mzaha.
Spot, waa, *pl.* mawaa, kipaku, *pl.* vipaku.
Spout (*from a roof*), kopo la nyumba, marizabu.
Sprain, kuteuka.
Spread, eneo.
Spreading a meal, maandiko.
Spring, mtambo, *pl.* mitambo.
of water, chemchem, jicho la maji.
Sprinkle, manyunyo.
Sprinkler (*for scents*), mrashi, *pl.* mirashi.
Spur of a cock, kipi, kipia, *pl.* vipia.
Spy, mpelelezi, *pl.* wapelelezi, mtumbuizi (A.).
Square, mrabba.
Squint, makengeza.
Stable, banda la frasi, faja la frasi.
Staff, gongo, *pl.* magongo, mkongojo, *pl.* mikongojo.
Stagnation, vilio, *pl.* mavilio.
Stain, waa, *pl.* mawaa.
Stairs, daraja, ngazi.
Up-stairs, juu, darini.
Down-stairs, chini.
Stalks, *of* mtama, bua, *pl.* mabua.
of a kind of millet chewed like sugar-cane, kota, *pl.* makota.
of cloves, &c., kikonyo, *pl.* vikonyo.
Stall keeper, mchuruzi, *pl.* wachuruzi.
Stammering, kigugumizi.
Stamp, muhuri, chapa.
Staple, pete, *pl.* mapete, ṭumbuu.
Star, nyota.
Falling stars, nyota zikishuka.
Shooting stars, kimwondo, *pl.* vimwondo.
Starch, kanji, dondo.
Start (*fright*), kituko.
(*beginning*), feli, *pl.* mafeli.
Startling thing, mzungu, *pl.* mizungu.
A thing to frighten people, kinyago, *pl.* vinyago.
State, hali.
Statue, sanamu.
Stealing, kwiba.
Steam, mvuke.
A steamship, merikebu ya moshi.
Steel, feleji, pua.
Steelyard, mizani.
Steersman, mshiki shikio.
Stem of a tree, shina, *pl.* mashina.
of mtama, bua, *pl.* mabua.
Step (*stepping*), hatua.
(*of stone, &c.*), daraja.
Step-father, baba wa kambo.
Step-mother, mama wa kambo.
Steward, msimamizi, *pl.* wasimamizi.
Stick, fimbo, ufito, *pl.* fito (*thin*), bakora (*a walking-stick with a handle bent at right angles*).
A short heavy stick, kibarango, *pl.* vibarango, mpweke, *pl.* mipweke.
A staff, gongo, *pl.* magongo, mkongojo, *pl.* mikongojo (*an old man's staff*).
Stillness, kimya.
Stirrup, kikuku cha kupandia frasi.
Stocks (*for the feet*), mkatale.
Stomach, tumbo.
Pit of the stomach, chembe cha moyo (A.).
Stone, jiwe, *pl.* mawe *or* majiwe.
A stone house, nyumba ya mawe.
Small stones or pieces of stone, kokoto, *pl.* makokoto.
Very small stones, not larger than an egg, mbwe.
Very small grit, changarawi.
Fresh coral, matumbawi.

Precious stones, kito, *pl.* vito, johari.
Stones of fruit, kokwa, *pl.* makokwa.
Stooping, kiinamizi.
Stop (*end*), kikomo, kinga.
(*stopping*), kizuizo, kizuizi, kizuio.
Stoppage in the nose or wind-pipe, mafua.
(*stagnation*), vilio, *pl.* mavilio.
Stopper, zibo, *pl.* mazibo, kizibo, *pl.* vizibo.
Store (*put by*), akiba.
Store-room, ghala.
Storm, tháruha, tufanu.
Story, hadithi, habari. *See Tale.*
Stoutness, unene.
Strainer, kunguto, *pl.* makunguto (*of basket-work*).
Straits (*distress*), shidda.
(*narrow seas*), kilango cha bahari.
Strands of a cord, meno, ncha.
Stranger, mgeni, *pl.* wageni.
Strap, ukanda.
Stratagem, hila.
Stream, mto, *pl.* mito, kijito, *pl.* vijito.
Strength, nguvu.
String, ugwe, uzi, katani.
String of beads, kigwe, *pl.* vigwe.
String-course, ushi.
Strip. See Mat.
Stripe (*line*), uzi, *pl.* nyuzi, mfuo, *pl.* mifuo, utepe, *pl.* tepe.
Study, mtaala.
Stumble, kwao, *pl.* makwao.
Stumbling-block, kwao, *pl.* makwao.
Stump, shina, *pl.* mashina.
Stupor, kurukwa na akili.
Stye in the eye, chokea.
Style (*of writing*), dibaji, *a good style.*
Subject, rayia.
Substance, asili.
Subtlety, busara, werevu.
Subtraction (*arithmetical*), baki.
Suburbs, kiunga.
Sugar, sukari.
Sugar-cane, mua, *pl.* miwa.
Suit of clothes, kisua.
Sulphate of copper, mrututu.
of magnesia, chumvi ya haluli.
Sulphur, kiberiti.
Sultanship, usultani.
Sum, jumla.
Summary, muhtasari.
Summit, kilele, *pl.* vilele (*used of any sharp-pointed top or peak, of the centre shoot of a cocoa-nut tree as well as of the peak of a mountain*).
Sun, jua, *pl.* majua.
The coming out of the sun after rain, kianga.
Sunday, Juma a pili.
Sundries, takataka.
Sunset, magharibi, maugaribi.
Supercargo, karani.
Superciliousness, kitongotongo.
Superintendent, mwangalizi, *pl.* waangalizi, msimamizi, *pl.* wasimamizi.
Supper, chakula cha jioni.
Suppuration, kutunga.
Surety, mthamini, thámin, thamana, lazima.
Surf, mawimbi.
Swallow (*bird*), barawai, mbiliwili (?), mbayuwayu (A.).
Sweat, hari, jasho, vukuto.
Sweetheart, mchumba.
Sweet lime, dimu tamu.
Sweetness, tamu.
Sweet potatoes, viazi, *sing.* kiazi.

Swindler, thalimu.
Swing, pembea.
Swine, nguruwe, nguuwe.
Switch, ufito, *pl.* fito.
Sword, upanga, *pl.* panga.
  curved sword, kitara, *pl.* vitara.
  straight two-edged sword without any guard, upanga wa feleji.
  with a small cross hilt, upanga wa imani.
Syphilis, sekeneko, kijaraha cha mboni, tego (*a virulent kind supposed to be the result of a charm*).
Syria, Sham.
Syrup, asali.

T.

Table, meza.
  Table-cloth, nguo ya meza.
  Table-napkin, kitambaa cha meza.
Tack of a sail, goshi.
Tacking (*sewing*), bandi.
Tail, mkia, *pl.* mikia.
Tailor, mshoni, *pl.* washoni.
Taking away, maondoleo.
Tale, hadithi, kisa, ngano.
Tale-bearer, mzuzi.
Talipes, kupinda na mguu.
Talk, usemi,
  Silly talk, upuzi.
Talker, msemaji, *pl.* wasemaji.
Tamarind, ukwaju.
  Tamarind tree, mkwaju, *pl.* mikwaju.
Tangle, matata.
Tap, bilula.
Tape, utepe, *pl.* tepe.
Tar, lami.
Tartar on the teeth, ukoga.
Taste, tumu, tamu, luththa, nyonda, maondi, maonji.
Taster, mwonja, *pl.* waonja, mwonda (M.), *pl.* waonda, kionja, *pl.* vionja, kionda (M.), *pl.* vionda.
Tea, chayi, cha.
Teacher, mwalimu, *pl.* waalimu, mkufunzi, *pl.* wakufunzi.
Teaching, mafundisho, elimu.
Teak, msaji.
Teapot, buli, *pl.* mabuli.
Tear, chozi, *pl.* machozi, tozi (M.), *pl.* matozi.
Teazing, thihaka.
Tediousness, uchovu.
Telescope, durabini.
Temper, tabia.
Temperance, tawassuf, kadiri.
Temple, hekalu (*a great thing, the temple at Jerusalem*), baniya (*a building, the temple at Mecca*).
Temptation, majaribu, nyonda.
Ten, kumi, *pl.* makumi.
  a decade, mwongo, *pl.* miongo.
Tent, khema, hema.
Testicles, mapumbu, tamboa.
Testimony, ushahidi.
Thanks, shukuru, ushukura, salamu, ahsanta, marahaba.
Thatch, makuti (*of cocoa-nut leaves*).
  Thin sticks used to tie the makuti *to*, upau, *pl.* pau.
  See Cocoa-nut.
Theft, uizi.
Thicket, kichaka, *pl.* vichaka, koko, *pl.* makoko.
Thickness, unene.
Thief, mwivi, *pl.* wevi, mwibaji, *pl.* webaji.
Thieving, kwiba, uizi, wibaji.
Thigh, upaja, *pl.* paja, paja, *pl.* mapaja.

Thimble, subana.

Sailmaker's palm, dofra, *pl.* madofra.

Thing, kitu, *pl.* vitu (*a thing of the senses*), neno, jambo, mambo (*things of the intellect*).

I have done nothing, sikufanya neno.

I see nothing, sioni kitu.

A kind thing, jambo la wema.

Strange things, mambo mageni.

Third (*a third part*), *th*eluth.

Thirst, kiu.

Thorn, mwiba, *pl.* miiba *or* miba.

Mchongoma, *pl.* michongoma, *a thorny shrub used for hedges.*

Mkwamba, *pl.* mikwamba, *a thorny shrub.*

Thought, wazo, *pl.* mawazo, fikara, thamiri, nia.

Thousand, elfu, *pl.* elfu or alafu.

a thousand or myriad, kikwi, *pl.* zikwi *or* vikwi.

a hundred thousand, lakki.

Thread, uzi, *pl.* nyuzi, katani.

Threat, wogofya, tisho.

Throat, koo, *pl.* makoo.

Thumb, kidole cha gumba.

Thunder, radi (*near*), ngurumo (*distant*).

Thursday, Alhamisi.

Ticket, kibarua, *pl.* vibarua.

Tickling or tingling, mnyeo, kinyenyefu.

Ticks, papasi (*in houses*), kupe (*on cattle*).

Tide, maji kujaa na kupwa.

Spring tides, bamvua.

Neap tides, maji mafu.

Tiller, kana, gana.

Tiller ropes, mijiari, *sing.* mjiari.

Timber, miti, mibau.

Time, wakati, wakti, majira.

(*sufficient*), nafasi.

(*hour*), saa.

(*leisure*), faragha.

(*first, &c.*), mara.

(*fixed term*), mohulla.

Times (*age*), zamani.

Space of time, muda.

Period of time, kipindi.

A short time, kitambo.

Times, in multiplication, fi.

Six times eight, sita fi themanya.

Divisions of Time.

There are two years in use in Zanzibar; that which is most commonly heard of is the Arab year of twelve lunar months. It cannot be more than about 355 days long, and has therefore no correspondence to the seasons. The months are determined by the sight of the new moon, or by the expiration of thirty days since the beginning of the previous month. It happens sometimes that some of the coast towns will begin their months a day before or after what was taken as its first day in Zanzibar. A gun is usually fired from one of the ships when the month begins. Practically the *Ramathan* is treated as the first month, and the rest are reckoned from it; the word by which they are denoted seems to mean *not fasting*, as though the *Ramathan* being the month of *fasting*, the rest were the first, second, third, &c., of *not fasting*, until the months of *Rajab* and *Shauban*, which have both a special religious character

The following are the names of the Arab months, with their Swahili equivalents:

Arab.	Swahili.
Moharram.	Mfunguo a 'nne.
Safr.	Mfunguo a tano.
Rabia al aowal.	Mfunguo a sita.
Rabia al akhr.	Mfunguo a saba.
Jemad al aowal.	Mfunguo a nane.
Jemad al akhr.	Mfunguo a kenda.
Rajab.	Rajabu.
Shaaban.	Shaabani.
Ramathan.	Ramathani.
Shaowal.	Mfunguo a mosi.
Th'il ka'ada.	Mfunguo a pili.
Th'il hajjah.	Mfunguo a tatu.

The two great Mohammedan feasts are held on the first of *Shaowal*, when every one gives presents, and on the tenth of *Th'il hajjah*, when every one is supposed to slaughter some animal and feast the poor.

The other year in use among the Swahili is the Nautical and Agricultural year; it is roughly a solar year, having 365 days. It is reckoned to begin from the *Siku a mwaka* (answering to the Persian *Nairuz*), which now occurs towards the end of August. The last day of the old year is called *Kigunzi*, and the days are reckoned by decades, called *miongo*, sing. *mwongo*. Thus—*Mwongo wa mia* consists of the days between 90 and 100. *Mwongo wangapi?* asks which decade it is. The *Siku a mwaka* is kept as a great day, and formerly had a number of special observances connected with it. In the night or early in the morning every one used to bathe in the sea; the women are particularly careful to do so. They afterwards fill a large pot with grain and pulse, and cook them. About noon they serve out to all friends who come; all the fires are extinguished with water and lighted again by rubbing wood. Formerly no inquiry was made as to any one killed or hurt on this day, and it is still the custom to go armed and to be on the guard against private enemies. It used to be a favourite amusement to throw any Indians that could be caught into the sea, and otherwise ill-use them, until the British Government interfered for their protection. The year is called after the day of the week on which it began; thus, in 1865 it began on Thursday and was *Mwaka Alhamisi;* in 1866 on Friday, and was *Mwaka Juma*, and so on.

The seasons will be found briefly mentioned under that word.

The week has been reconstructed on the Arab week, retaining only the Arab names of two days, *Alhamisi* and *Juma* (Thursday and Friday), which answer to our Saturday and Sunday for Mohammedan religious purposes, and are the days which slaves in the country are generally allowed for their own recreation or profit. *Juma* is so named from the assembly held on that day for public worship; the Arab names of the rest are merely those used by English Quakers, first, second, third, &c.

ENGLISH.	ARABIC.	SWAHILI.
Sunday.	Al ahad.	Juma a pili.
Monday.	Ath theneen.	Juma a tatu.
Tuesday.	Ath theluth.	Juma a 'nne.
Wednesday.	Ar robua'.	Juma a tano.
Thursday.	Al khamis.	Alhamisi.
Friday.	Juma'.	Juma.
Saturday.	As sabt.	Juma a mosi.

The day begins at sunset; *to-night* therefore in the month of a Swahili means what an Englishman would call *last night.* As the days are of a very nearly uniform length there is little practical incorrectness in taking sunset as six o'clock in the evening and reckoning the night first and then the day from it, hour by hour. Thus, seven, eight, and nine are the first, second, and third of the night (*saa a kwanza, a pili, a tatu ya usiku*). Midnight is the sixth hour, *saa a sita.* Five in the morning is the eleventh hour of the night, *saa a edhashara.* Nine o'clock in the morning is the third hour of the day, *saa a tatu.* Twelve at noon is the sixth hour, *saa a sita,* and four and five the tenth and eleventh hours, *saa a kumi, saa a edhashara.* Sunset is determined by observation, and a gun is fired, and the Sultan's flag hauled down to mark it. During the *Ramathan* a gun is fired at half-past two in the morning to warn every one of the approach of morning, that they may get their cooking and eating over before dawn. This gun-fire is called *daakuu.*

There is another way of marking the time by reference chiefly to the hours of prayer (*see Prayer*); the following are the chief points

Magaribi, *sunset.*

Mshuko wa magaribi (*coming out from sunset prayers*), *about half-past six.*

Esha *or* Isha, *from half-past six to eight.*

Mshuko wa esha, *about half-an-hour later.*

Nuss ya usiku, *midnight.*

Karibu na alfajiri, *between three and four in the morning.*

Alfajiri mkuu, *rising of the morning star, about four.*

Alfajiri mdogo, *dawn.*

Assubui, *the morning, i.e., after sunrise.*

Mchana, *the day from* assubui *to* jioni.

Mafungulia ng'ombe (*letting out of cattle*), *about* 8 A.M.

Mafungulia ng'ombe makuu, *is earlier,* mafungulia ng'ombe madogo, *is later than eight o'clock.*

Jua kitwani, *noon.*

Athuuri *or* Azuuri, *noon, and thence till three o'clock.*

Awali athuuri, *between twelve and one.*

Alasiri, *about half-past three, or from three to five.*

Alasiri kasiri, *about five, or thence to half-past.*

Jioni, *evening, from about five or half-past till sunset.*

Tin, bati.

Tip ncha, nta (M.)

Tithes, zaka.

Tobacco, tumbako.

To-day, leo.

Toe, kidole, *pl.* vidole, kidole cha mguu.
Token, dalili, buruhani.
Tomb, kaburi, *pl.* makaburi.
To-morrow, kesho.
the day after, kesho kutwa.
the doy after that, mtondo.
after that, mtondo goo.
Tongs, koleo, *pl.* makoleo.
Tongue, ulimi, *pl.* ndimi.
A piece of cloth, &c., to lie under an opening, lisani.
Tool, samani.
Carpenter's tool for marking lines, mahati.
Tooth, jino, *pl.* meno.
cuspids, chonge.
Dirt on the teeth, ukoga.
He has lost a front tooth, ana pengo.
Tooth stick or brush, msuaki, *pl.* misuaki.
Top, juu.
(*the toy*), pia.
Torpor, utepetefu.
Tortoise, kobe.
Total, jumla.
Towel, kitambaa cha kufutia uso, &c.
Tower, mnara, *pl.* minara.
Town, mji, *pl.* miji.
Trace, dalili.
Track, nyayo.
Trade, biashara.
Trader, mfanyi biashara.
Traitor, khaini.
Trap, mtego, *pl.* mitego.
(*with a spring*), mtambo, *pl.* mitambo.
Traveller, msafiri, *pl.* wasafiri.
Tray, sinia, *pl.* masinia.
Treacle, asali ya mua.
Treasure, hazina, kanzi, khazana.
Treatment, mwamale.
Tree, mti, *pl.* miti.
Mkadi, *Pandanus*.
Mtomondo, *Barringtonia*.
Mtondoo, *Calophyllum inophyllum*.
Trench, handaki.
Trench for laying in foundations, msinji, msingi.
Trial, majaribu.
Tribe, kabila, taifa, *pl.* mataifa.
(taifa *is larger than* kabila).
Of what tribe are you? Mtu gani wee?
Trick, hila, cherevu, madanganya.
Trot, mashindo (*of a horse*), matiti (*of an ass*).
Trouble, taabu, uthia.
Trousers, suruali.
Trowel (*mason's*), mwiko, *pl.* miiko.
Trumpet, paanda.
Trunk, shina, *pl.* mashina, jiti, *pl.* majiti.
(*cut down*), gogo, *pl.* magogo.
(*the human trunk*), kiwiliwili.
Truth, kweli.
A truth teller, msemi kweli.
Trying, maonji, majaribu.
Tub, pipa, *pl.* mapipa.
Tuesday, Juma a nne.
Turban, kilemba, *pl.* vilemba.
A turban cloth, utambi, *pl.* tambi.
ends of turban cloth, utamvua, *pl.* tamvua, kishungi.
Turkey, bata la mzinga, *pl.* mabata ya mzinga.
Turmeric, manjano.
Turn, zamu, *pl.* mazamu.
By turns, kwa zamu.
Turner, mkereza, *pl.* wakereza.
Turnery, zikerezwazo.
Turtle, kasa.
Hawkshead turtle, from which

tortoiseshell is obtained, ug'amba, gnamba.
Turtle-dove, hua.
Twin, pacha.
Twist, pindi, *pl.* mapindi.
Type (*for printing*), chapa, *pl.* machapa.

U.

Udder, kiwele.
Ulcers, donda ndugu.
Umbrella, mwavuli, *pl.* miavuli.
Native umbrella, dapo, *pl.* madapo.
Uncleanness, janaba, uchavu.
Uncle, mjomba, *pl.* wajomba, baba mdogo (*mother's brother*), amu (*father's brother*).
Undergrowth, magugu.
Understanding, akili (*pl.*).
Underwood, makoko.
Unity, umoja.
Universe, ulimwengu.
Uproar, fujo, kelele, makelele, uthia, kero.
Urine, mkojo.
Use, kutumia, kufaa.
(*habit*), mazoezo.
Useful things, vifaa.
Usurer, mlariba, *pl.* walariba.
Usury, iriba.
Utensils, vyombo.
Uterus, mji.
Uvula, kimio.

V.

Vagabond, hana kwao (*homeless*).
Vagina, kuma.
Valley, boonde, *pl*, boonde *or* maboonde.
Value, kima, *th*amani, kadiri, kiasi, upataji, uthani.
What is it worth? Obapataje?
Vapour, mvuke, fukizo.
Vapour bath, mvuke.
Vault, or vaulted place, kuba, kubba.
Vegetables, mboga.
Dodoki, *pl.* madodoki, *a long many-angled seed pod.*
Fijili *or* figili, *a large white radish.*
Jimbi, *pl.* majimbi, *a root very much like a hyacinth root.*
Vegetable marrow, mumunye, *pl.* mamumunye.
Veil, utaji, shela.
Vengeance, kasasi.
Verses, mashairi.
Utenzi, *religious verses.*
Utumbuizo, *verses sung at a dance.*
Vesicular eruption on the skin, uwati.
Vial, kitupa, *pl.* vitupa.
Vice, uovu, ufisadi, ufiski.
(*the tool*), jiliwa, *pl.* majiliwa, iriwa.
Vicegerent, kaimu, *pl.* makaimu, nayibu, kalife.
Victim, mathabuha.
Victuals, vyakula.
Vigil, kesha, *pl.* makesha.
Village, mji, *pl.* miji, kijiji, *pl.* vijiji.
Vine, mzabibu, *pl.* mizabibu.
Vinegar, siki.
Violence, jeuli, nguvu.
Kwa nguvu, *by violence.*
Ana jeuri, *he attacks people wantonly.*
Virgin, bikiri, kizinda.
Viscera, matumbo.
Vizir, waziri, *pl.* mawaziri.
Vizirship, uwaziri.
Voice, sauti.
Vow, nathiri, naziri.

Voyage, safari.
Vulture, tai.

W.

Wages, ujira.
monthly, mshahara.
sailors', halasa.
Wailing, maombolezo.
Waistcoat, kisibau, *pl.* visibau.
sleeved, cha mkono.
sleeveless, kisicho mkono *or* cha vikapa.
Walk, mwendo.
A walk, matembezi.
to go for a walk, kwenda tembea.
Wall, ukuta, *pl.* kuta, kikuta, *pl.* vikuta, kitalu, *pl.* vitalu (*of an enclosure*), kiyambaza (*mud and stud*).
Wall-plate, mbati, mwamba, *pl.* miamba.
Walnut, jozi.
Wandering about, mzunguko, *pl.* mizunguko.
Want, uhtaji, upungufu, kipunguo. (*poverty*), shidda, umasikini.
War, vita, kondo (Mer.).
Wareroom, ghala.
Warehouse and shop, bokhari, bohari.
Warmth moto, uharara.
Lukewarmness, uvuguvugu.
Wart, chunjua.
Washerman, dobi.
Waste, upotevu, uharibivu.
Waster, mpotevu, *pl.* wapotevu, muharibivu, *pl.* waharibivu.
Watch, saa.
(*vigil*), kesha, *pl.* makesha.
(*time or place of watching*), kiugojo. *pl.* vingojo.
(*watching place*), lindo.
Water, maji.
Fresh water, maji matamu, maji ya pepo.
Water-closet, choo, chiro.
Water cooler (*earthen bottle*), guduwia, gudulia, kuzi (*a larger kind with handles and spout*).
Water jar, mtungi, *pl.* mitungi.
Water melon, battikh. *See Pumpkin*.
Water skin, kiriba.
Wave, wimbi, *pl.* mawimbi.
Way, njia.
the shortest way, njia ya kukata.
Weakness, uthaifu.
Wealth, mali mengi, utajiri, ukwasi.
Weapon, selaha, mata (*weapons, i.e., bows and arrows*).
Weather, wakati.
Weather side, upande goshini, upande wa juu.
Weaver, mfuma, *pl.* wafuma.
Wedding, harusi.
Wedge, kabari.
Wednesday, Juma a tano.
Weeds, magugu.
Kinds of weeds, kitawi, mdago, gugu mwitu, mbaruti.
Week, jumaa.
Weight (*see Measure*), uthani.
How much does it weigh? Yapata kassi gani uthani wake?
NATIVE WEIGHTS:
Wakia, *the weight of a silver dollar, about one ounce.*
Rattel, *sixteen* wakia, *about one pound.*
Kibaba, *pl.* vibaba, *one* rattel *and a half.*
Mani, *two* rattel *and three-quarters.*

Table of Concords.

Adjectives and Pronouns are in Swahili made to agree with their Substantives by a change in the first syllable. Swahili Substantives may be conveniently arranged in the eight following Classes.

I. Those which begin with m- *and are the names of living beings.* The plural is made by changing m- into wa- Mtu mmoja, one person: watu wengi, many people. *The names of living beings,* whatever their form, may have their adjectives and pronouns in the forms proper to the first class. Ng'ombe mmoja, one ox: ng'ombe wengi, many oxen. Waziri mmoja, one vizir: mawaziri wengi, many vizirs.

II. Those which begin with m- *and are* not *the names of living beings.* The plural is made by changing m- into mi-. Mti mmoja, one tree: miti mingi, many trees.

III. Those which do not change to form the plural. Nyumba moja, one house: nyumba nyingi, many houses.

IV. Those which begin with ki- or ch-. The plural is made by changing ki- or ch- into vi-. Kitu kimoja, one thing: chombo kimoja, one dhow. Vitu vingi, many things: vyombo vingi, many dhows.

V. Those which make their plural by prefixing ma-. Kasha moja, one chest: makasha mengi, many chests.

VI. Those which begin with u-. If followed by a consonant, the u- is omitted in the plural. If followed by a vowel, the plural is made by changing u- into ny-. Ukucha mmoja, one claw: kucha nyingi, many claws. Uimbo mmoja, one song: nyimbo nyingi, many songs.

VII. The word *mahali*, place. Mahali pamoja, one place: mahali pengi, many places.

VIII. Verbs in the infinitive, used as Substantives. Kufa kwetu, our dying.

The Locative Case made by adding -ni requires special forms, which are the same for all Substantives. When it implies *motion to* or *distance from* the thing named, the Pronouns begin with k-; if it expresses *being within*, they begin with m-; if nearness only, with p-.

Classes.	1		2		3		4		5		6		7	8	9	10
Substantives.	Mtu	Watu	Mti	Miti	Nyumba	Nyumba	Kitu	Vitu	Kasha	Makasha	Uimbo	Nyimbo	Mahali & -ni (*nearness*)	Kufa	-ni (*motion*)	-ni (*in*)
Fine	mzuri	wazuri	mzuri	mizuri	nzuri	nzuri	kizuri	vizuri	zuri	mazuri	mzuri	nzuri	pazuri	kuzuri		
Good	mwema	wema	mwema	mema	njema	njema	chema	vyema	jema	mema	mwema	njema	pema	kwema		
Bad	'mbaya	wabaya	'mbaya	mibaya	mbaya	mbaya	kibaya	vibaya	baya	mabaya	'mbaya	mbaya	pabaya	kubaya		
How many?		wangapi		mingapi		ngapi		vingapi		mangapi		ngapi	pangapi	kwangapi		
All		wote	wote	yote	yote	zote	chote	vyote	lote	yote	wote	zote	pote	kwote	kote	mote
Of		wa	wa	ya	ya	za	cha	vya	la	ya	wa	za	pa	kwa	kwa	mwa
My		wangu	wangu	yangu	yangu	zangu	changu	vyangu	langu	yangu	wangu	zangu	pangu	kwangu	kwangu	mwangu
Thy		wako	wako	yako	yako	zako	chako	vyako	lako	yako	wako	zako	pako	kwako	kwako	mwako
His, her, its		wake	wake	yake	yake	zake	chake	vyake	lake	yake	wake	zake	pake	kwake	kwake	mwake
Our		wetu	wetu	yetu	yetu	zetu	chetu	vyetu	letu	yetu	wetu	zetu	petu	kwetu	kwetu	mwetu
Your		wenu	wenu	yenu	yenu	zenu	chenu	vyenu	lenu	yenu	wenu	zenu	penu	kwenu	kwenu	mwenu
Their		wao	wao	yao	yao	zao	chao	vyao	lao	yao	wao	zao	pao	kwao	kwao	mwao
This & these	huyu	hawa	huu	hii	hii	hizi	hiki	hivi	hili	haya	huu	hizi	hapa		huku	humu
Yonder	yule	wale	ule	ile	ile	zile	kile	vile	lile	yale	ule	zile	pale		kule	mle
That mentioned before	huyo	hao	huo	hiyo	hiyo	hizo	hicho	hivyo	hilo	hayo	huo	hizo	hapo		huko	humo
Which?	yupi	wapi	upi	ipi	ipi	zipi	kipi	vipi	lipi	yapi	upi	zipi	papi			
Where is or are?	yu wapi	wa wapi	u wapi	i wapi	i wapi	zi wapi	ki wapi	vi wapi	li wapi	ya wapi	u wapi	zi wapi	pa wapi			
He is, &c. there (*near*)	yupo	wapo	upo	ipo	ipo	zipo	kipo	vipo	lipo	yapo	upo	zipo	papo			
„ „ (*far*)	yuko	wako	uko	iko	iko	ziko	kiko	viko	liko	yako	uko	ziko	pako		kuko	
„ „ (*within*)	yumo	wamo	umo	imo	imo	zimo	kimo	vimo	limo	yamo	umo	zimo	pamo			mumo
This is he, &c. &c.	ndiyo	ndio	ndio	ndiyo	ndiyo	ndizo	ndicho	ndivyo	ndilo	ndiyo	ndio	ndizo	ndipo	ndiko	ndiko	ndimo
Who or which	aliye, alio	walio	ulio	iliyo	iliyo	zilizo	kilicho	vilivyo	lililo	yaliyo	ulio	zilizo	palipo	kuliko		
	ye	wo	wo	yo	yo	zo	cho	vyo	lo	yo	wo	zo	po	kwo	ko	mo
He, she, it, they	a-	wa-	u- w-	i- y-	i- y-	zi- z-	ki- ch-	vi- vy-	li- l-	ya-	u- w-	zi- z-	pa-	ku-		
Him, it, them	-m- -mw-	-wa	-u		-i-	-zi-	-ki-	-vi-	-li-	-ya-	-u-	-zi	-pa-			

To face page 82.

Pishi, *four* vibaba, *or six* rattel.
Frasila, *thirty-five* rattel, *or twelve* mani.
Farra ya mti, *seventy-two* rattel, *or twelve* pishi.
Well, kisima, *pl.* visima.
Weeping, kilio.
West, maghribi.
West wind, umande.
Wet, rátaba, maji.
Whale, nyamgumi, ngumi.
Wheat, ngano.
Wheel, gurudumu, *pl.* magurudumu.
Wheeled carriage, gari, *pl.* magari.
Whetstone, kinoo, *pl.* vinoo.
Whip, mjeledi, *pl.* mijeledi.
A plaited thong carried by overlookers and schoolmasters, kambaa, kikoto (M.).
Whirlwind, kisusuli, pepo za chamchela.
Whistling, msonyo, miunsi.
White ants, mchwa.
White of egg, ute wa yayi.
Whiteness, weupe.
Whitening, chaki.
Whitlow, mdudu.
Wick of a lamp, utambi, *pl.* tambi.
of a candle, kope, *pl.* makope.
Widow, mjani, mjaani, mke aliofiwa na mumewe.
Width, upana.
Wife, mke, *pl.* wake, mtumke, *pl.* watuwake, mwanamke, *pl.* waanaake.
Wilderness, bara, nyika, unyika.
Wild people, washenzi.
Wild animals, nyama za mwitu, nyama mbwayi, nyama wakali.
Will (mind), moyo, nia, kusudi.
(testament), wasio.
Wind, upepo, *much wind*, pepo.
See Cold, Whirlwind, Storm, East West.
Northerly Winds, which blow from December to March, kaskazi.
Southerly winds, which blow from April to November, kusi.
Head winds, pepo za omo (*also stern winds*).
Wind on the beam, matanga kati.
Winding, kizingo, *pl.* vizingo.
of a stream, maghuba.
Windlass, duara.
Window, dirisha, *pl.* dirisha *or* madirisha.
Wine, mvinyo (*strong wine*), divai (*claret*).
Wing, bawa, *pl.* mabawa.
A wing feather, ubawa, *pl.* mbawa.
Wink, kupepesa.
Wire, masango, uzi wa madini.
Wire-drawer's plate, chamburo.
Wisdom, hékima, busara, akili.
Wit, ujuvi (?).
Witch, mchawi, *pl.* wachawi.
Witchcraft, uchawi.
One who uses witchcraft against another, wanga.
Witness, shahidi, *pl.* mashahidi.
(*testimony*), ushahidi.
Wits, akili.
Wizard, mchawi, *pl.* wachawi.
Woe, msiba. *See Grief.*
Woman, mwanamke, *pl.* waanaake *or* waanawake.
A young woman, kijana, *pl.* vijana.
A young woman who has not yet left her father's house, one whose breasts are not yet flattened, mwanamwali.
A slave woman, mjakazi, *pl.* wajakazi.
See Person, Old, Slave.

Womb, tumbo, matumbo, mji.
Wonder, ajabu.
Wonders, mataajabu.
Wood, mti. *See Firewood, Timber.*
A wood, msitu wa miti.
A piece of wood, kijiti, *pl.* vijiti.
KINDS OF WOOD.
Finessi, *the wood of the jack-fruit tree; it has a yellow colour.*
Mche, *a reddish wood much used in Zanzibar.*
Mkumavi, *a red wood.*
Msaji, *teak.*
Mtobwe, *the wood of which the best* bakora *are made.*
Sesemi, *Indian black wood.*
Simbati, *a kind of wood brought from near Cape Delgado.*
Sunobari, *deal.*
Wooden clogs, viatu vya mti.
The button which is grasped by the toes, msuruaki, *pl.* misuruaki.
Woollen cloth, joho (*broadcloth*).
Thick woollen fabrics, blanketing, bushuti.
Word, neno, *pl.* maneno.
Bad words, matukano.
Work, kazi.
Workman, mtenda kazi.
(*skilled*), fundi.
(*skilful, a good hand*), mstadi, *pl.* wastadi.
Workshop, kiwanda, *pl.* viwanda, kiwanja, *pl.* viwanja.
World, ulimwengu, dunia.
People of this world, walimwengu.
Worldly affairs, malimwengu.
Worm, nangonango, chango, mnio (?).
Worth, kima. *See Value.*
Wound, jeraha, donda, *pl.* madonda, kionda, *pl.* vionda, kidonda, *pl.* vidonda.
Wrath, ghathabu.
Wriggle, pindi, *pl.* mapindi.
Wrist, kiwiko cha mkono, kilimbili.
Writer, mwandishi, *pl.* waandishi, akatabao, *pl.* wakatabao (*writer of a letter*).
Writings, maandiko, maandishi.
Writing-desk, dawati.
Wrong, thulumu, sivyo.

Y.

Yam, kiazi kikuu, *pl.* viazi vikuu.
A kind of yam like a hyacinth root, jimbi, *pl.* majimbi.
Yard (*of a ship*), foramali.
(*an enclosure*), uanda, uanja, ua, [*pl.* nyua.
Yawn, miayo.
Year (*see Time*), mwaka, *pl.* miaka.
Last year, mwaka jana.
The year before last, mwaka juzi.
Yesterday, jana.
The day before yesterday, juzi.
Yolk of an egg, kiini cha yayi.
Young of birds, kinda, *pl.* makinda. *See Chicken, &c.*
Youth, ujana, udogo.
A youth, kijana, *pl.* vijana.

Z.

Zanzibar, Unguja.
The language or dialect of Zanzibar, Kiunguja. *In Zanzibar,* Kiswahili *is understood to mean chiefly the language used on the coast north of Mombas.*
The original inhabitants of Zanzibar, Muhadimu, *pl.* Wahadimu. *Their sultan is the* Munyi [mkuu.
Zeal (*effort*), juhudi.
(*jealousy*), uwivu.
Zebra, punda milia.

ADJECTIVES AND NUMERALS.

ADJECTIVES.

Adjectives always follow the Substantives they agree with.

Mtu mwema, a good man.

Regular Swahili Adjectives are made to agree with the Substantives they qualify by prefixing to them the initial syllables proper to the class of their Substantives, in the singular or plural, as the case may be. The minor rules laid down in regard to the prefixes of Substantives are applicable to Adjectives and their prefixes. The following instances will illustrate the ordinary application of these rules:

CLASS I. *M-tu 'm-baya*, a bad man.
Wa-tu wa-baya, bad men.
M-tu mw-eupe, a white man.
Wa-tu w-eupe, white men.

Substantives of whatever class denoting living beings may have their Adjectives in the forms proper to the first class.

Mbuzi m-kubwa, a large goat.
Mbuzi wa-kubwa, large goats
Mbuzi mw-ekundu, a red goat.
Mbuzi w-ekundu, red goats.

Waziri mwema, a good vizir.
Mawaziri wema, good vizirs.
Kijana mwema, a good youth.
Vijana wema, good youths.

CLASS II. *M-ti m-zuri*, a fine tree.
Mi-ti mi-zuri, fine trees.
M-ti mw-ema, a good tree.
Mi-ti mi-ema, or *m-ema*, good trees.

CLASS III. *Ny-umba n-zuri*, a fine house.
Ny-umba n-zuri, fine houses.
Ny-umba ny-eupe, a white house.
Ny-umba ny-eupe, white houses.

CLASS IV. *Ki-tu ki-refu*, a long thing.
Vi-tu vi-refu, long things.
Ki-tu ch-epesi, a light thing.
Vi-tu vy-epesi, light things.

CLASS V. *Kasha zito*, a heavy chest.
Ma-kasha ma-zito, heavy chests.
Kasha j-ekundu, a red chest.
Ma-kasha m-ekundu, red chests.

CLASS VI. *U-imbo m-zuri*, a beautiful song.
Ny-imbo n-zuri, beautiful songs.
U-bau m-refu, a long plank.
M-bau n-defu, long planks.

CLASS VII. *Mahali pa-pana*, a broad place, *or* broad places.
Mahali p-eusi, a black place, *or* black places.

CLASS VIII. *Ku-fa ku-zuri*, a fine death.
Ku-fa kw-ema, a good death.

It will be seen at once from the above examples how to make the Adjective agree with its Substantive in ordinary cases. The following rules must be remembered in order to avoid mistakes:—

1. Adjectives beginning with a vowel require prefixes which end in a consonant, wherever possible, as in the above instances, *mweupe*, *mwekundu*, *mwema*, *chepesi*, *kwema*.

2. Adjectives beginning with a vowel must have *j-* prefixed when they are made to agree with nouns like *kasha*, as in the instance given above of *kasha jekundu*, a red chest. Monosyllabic adjectives prefix *ji*, as in *kasha jipya*, a new chest.

3. Prefixes ending in *-a*, when they are put before adjectives beginning with *e-*, merge the *a* into the first letter of the adjective, as in the instances, *weupe*, *wekundu*, *mekundu*, *peusi*. This suppression of the *a* is more noticeable in Adjectives than in Substantives, and occurs even in the few Adjectives which begin with *-o-*; *-a* before *i-* coalesces with it and forms *e*.

Weusi = *wa-eusi.*	*Meupe* = *ma-eupe.*
Pema = *pa-ema.*	*Mororo* = *ma-ororo.*
Wengi = *wa-ingi.*	

4. Adjectives beginning with a consonant are subject to the same rules when *n* is to be prefixed as Substantives of the third class and plurals of the sixth. The rules are given at length under Class VI. of Substantives. The following instances will show their application to Adjectives:

Nyumba, *Mbau*, *Nyimbo* { *ndogo*, little; *ngeni*, strange; *nzuri*, fine } *n* prefixed.

ndefu, long—*r* becomes *d*.
mbovu, rotten—*n* becomes *m*.
mbili, two—*nw* becomes *mb*.

kubwa, great; *nene*, thick; *pana*, broad; *tamu*, sweet; *chache*, few; *fupi*, short } *n* suppressed.

Besides the many apparent irregularities in these *n* formations, there are two or three really irregular forms. These are *ngema* or *njema* (not *nyema*), good, and *'mpya* (not *pya*), new.

Adjectives beginning with a vowel are, like the corresponding Substantives, regularly formed by prefixing *ny-*, as in the instance given, *nyeupe*, from *-eupe*, white.

Instances are given in the list of Adjectives where there is likely to be any practical difficulty in knowing what form to use.

-Ote, all, and *-enyi*, or *-inyi*, having or with, are not treated as Adjectives, but as Pronouns. Instances illustrating their changes will be found under each. On the other hand *-ngapi*, how many? is treated as an Adjective.

Irregular Adjectives.

Although Swahili is rich in Adjectives when compared with other African languages of the same family, it is very poor in comparison with English. The place of the English Adjective is supplied—

1. By Arabic words which are used as Adjectives but do not vary.

Rahisi, cheap. *Laini*, smooth.

2. By a verb expressing generally in the present imperfect *to become*, and in the present perfect *to be*, possessed of the quality denoted.

Fimbo imenyoka, the stick is straight.
Fimbo iliyonyoka, a straight stick.
Fimbo imepotoka, the stick is crooked.
Fimbo iliyopotoka, a crooked stick.
Mtungi umejaa, the jar is full.
Mtungi uliojaa, a full jar.

3. By a Substantive connected with the thing qualified by the particle *-a*, of.

Mtu wa choyo, a greedy person.
Mtu wa akili, a man of understanding, a wise man.

If it is wished to predicate the quality of any person or thing, the verb *kuwa na*, to have, must be used.

Ana choyo, he is greedy.
Kina taka, it is dirty.

4. By the use of the word *-enyi* or *-inyi*, which may be translated by *having* or *with.*

Mtu mwenyi afia, a healthy person.
Kitu chenyi mviringo, a round thing.
Kamba zenyi nguvu, strong ropes.
Embe yenyi maji, a juicy mango.

When *-enyi* is followed by a Verb in the Infinitive, it answers to our participle in *-ing.*

Mwenyi kupenda, loving.

5. By the use of Adjectival Substantives which change only to form the plural.

Kipofu, blind, *or* a blind person, pl. *Vipofu*, blind, *or* blind people.

Where in English a special stress is laid upon the Adjective, in Swahili the relative is inserted.

Jiwe kubwa, a large stone.
Jiwe lililo kubwa, a *large* stone, literally, a stone that is large.
Mtu wa haki, a just man.
Mtu aliye wa haki, a *just* man.

The Comparison of Adjectives.

There are not, properly speaking, any degrees of comparison in Swahili.

The COMPARATIVE degree as it exists in English is represented in several ways.

1. By the use of *kuliko*, where there is, the idea being that when the two things are brought together one of them is marked by the possession of the quality mentioned, whence it follows that it must possess it in a more eminent degree than the other.

Saa hii njema kuliko ile, this watch is good (or *the best*) where that is, *i.e.*, this watch is better than that.
Tamu kuliko asali, sweeter than honey.

2. By the use of *zayidi ya*, more than, or of *punde*, a little more.

Unguja mji mkubwa zayidi ya Mvita, Zanzibar is a large town more than Mombas, *i.e.*, Zanzibar is a larger town than Mombas.
Kitu kirefu punde, something a little longer.

3. By the use of *kupita*, to pass or surpass.

Salimu ampita Abdallah, Salim is better than Abdallah.
Ndiyo tamu yapita asali, it *is* sweet, it passes honey, *i.e.*, it is sweeter than honey.

4. Comparison of one time with another may be expressed by the use of the Verbs *kuzidi*, to increase, *kupungua*, to diminish.

Mti umezidi kuzaa, the tree has borne more fruit than it did previously.

The SUPERLATIVE may be denoted by the use of the Adjective in its simple form, in an absolute sense.

Mananasi mema ya wapi? Where are the best pines?
Ndiyo mema, these are the best.
Ni yupi alio mwema? Who is the best of them?

When this form is used of two only, it is more

correctly Englished by the Comparative than by the Superlative. So conversely where the Comparative forms are so used as to apply to many or all, they must be translated by Superlatives.

Saa hii njema kuliko zote, this watch is the best of all.
Ali awapita wote, Ali surpasses them all, or, is the best of all.

Numerals.

There are two sets of numerals in use in Zanzibar; one is properly Swahili, the other Arabic, but in a Swahiliized form.

The numbers from one to ten are as follows:

English.	Swahili.	Arabic.
One	*Mosi*	*Wáhid*
Two	*Pili*	The*neen*
Three	*Tatu*	Th*elatha*
Four	*'Nne*	*'Aroba*
Five	*Tano*	*Hamsi*
Six	*Sita*	*Sita*
Seven	*Saba*	*Saba*
Eight	*Nane*	The*manya*
Nine	*Kenda*	*Tissa* or *Tissia*
Ten	*Kumi*	*'Ashara*

It will be seen that for *six* and *seven* there are only the Arabic names. The other Arabic numbers under ten are not very commonly used, but for numbers above ten the Arabic are more used than the purer Swahili.

English.	Swahili.	Arabic.
Eleven	*Kumi na moja*	*Edashara*
Twelve	*Kumi na mbili*	The*nashara*
Thirteen	*Kumi na tatu*	The*lathatashara*
Fourteen	*Kumi na 'nne*	*Arobatashara*
Fifteen	*Kumi na tano*	*Hamstashara*
Sixteen	*Kumi na sita*	*Sitashara*
Seventeen	*Kumi na saba*	*Sabatashara*

ENGLISH.	SWAHILI.	ARABIC.
Eighteen	*Kumi na nane*	*Themanyatashara*
Nineteen	*Kumi na kenda*	*Tissatashara*
Twenty	*Makumi mawili*	*Asharini* or *Ishrin*
Thirty	*Makumi matatu*	*Thelathini*
Forty	*Makumi manne*	*Arobaini*
Fifty	*Makumi matano*	*Hamsini*
Sixty	*Makumi sita*	*Settini*
Seventy	*Makumi saba*	*Sabwini*
Eighty	*Makumi manane*	*Themanini*
Ninety	*Makumi kenda*	*Tissaini*

The intermediate numbers are expressed in the pure Swahili by adding *na moja, na mbili*, &c. Thus *forty-one* is *makumi manne na moja; forty-five* is *makumi manne na tano*, and so on. In the Arabic, the smaller number precedes the larger. *Twenty-one* is *wáhid u ishrín*, forty-five is *khámsi u arobain.* The mode of counting most usual in Zanzibar is to employ the Arabic names for the larger numbers, but to follow the Swahili order, thus—

Twenty-one . .	*Asharini na moja*
Twenty-two . .	*Asharini na mbili*
Twenty-three . .	*Asharini na tatu*
Twenty-four . .	*Asharini na 'nne*
Twenty-five . .	*Asharini na tano*
Twenty-six . .	*Asharini na sita*
Twenty-seven . .	*Asharini na saba*
Twenty-eight . .	*Asharini na nane*
Twenty-nine . .	*Asharini na kenda*
Thirty-one . .	*Thelathini na moja*
&c. &c.	*&c. &c.*

There is no negro word in use for a hundred; the Arabic *mia* is universally employed, and for several hundreds the numeral follows it, as *mia tatu*, three hundred. If the Arabic numerals are used they precede the word *mia, thelatha mia* = three hundred. The

Arabic dual *miteen* is very commonly used to express two hundred.

There is a Swahili word for a thousand, *kikwi*, but it is very rarely used except in poetry. The common word is the Arabic *elfu*. This is used in the same way as *mia*; thus, *elfu tatu* is three thousand, *elfu tano*, five thousand, &c. The Arabic dual *elfeen*, two thousand, is more common than *elfu mbili*. If the Arabic numerals are employed the small number comes first, the plural form *aláf* is employed, and the final of the small number is heard, thus *theláthat aláf* is three thousand, *khámset aláf*, five thousand, and so on.

Lakki is used for ten thousand, and the word *milyôn* is known, but is rarely employed, and perhaps never with exactitude.

Fungate occurs for *seven*, as denoting the days spent by the bridegroom in his bride's company after marriage.

Mwongo, plur. *miongo*, occurs for a *ten* or a *decade*, in reckoning the nautical year.

Both these words occur in cognate African languages as cardinal numbers.

When used in enumerating actual things, and not in mere arithmetical computation, six of the Swahili numbers are treated as regular Adjectives, the other four remaining unchanged. The following table will show the forms proper to each class of Substantives.

	Mtu	Mti	Nyumba	Kitu
1.	mmoja	mmoja	moja	kimoja
	Watu	Miti	Nyumba	Vitu
2.	wawili	miwili	mbili	viwili
3.	watatu	mitatu	tatu	vitatu

	WATU	MITI	NYUMBA	VITU
4.	wanne	minne	'nne	vinne
5.	watano	mitano	tano	vitano
6.	sita	sita	sita	sita
7.	saba	saba	saba	saba
8.	wanane	minane	nane	vinane
9.	kenda	kenda	kenda	kenda
10	kumi	kumi	kumi	kumi

	KASHA	UIMBO	MAHALI	KUFA
1.	moja	mmoja	pamoja	kumoja

	MAKASHA	NYIMBO	MAHALI	KUFA
2.	mawili	mbili	pawili	kuwili
3.	matatu	tatu	patatu	kutatu
4.	manne	'nne	panne	kunne
5.	matano	tano	patano	kutano
6.	sita	sita	sita	sita
7.	saba	saba	saba	saba
8.	manane	nane	panane	kunane
9.	kenda	kenda	kenda	kenda
10.	kumi	kumi	kumi	kumi

The number always follows the Substantive.

One man, *mtu mmoja.*

If an adjective is employed, the numeral follows the adjective, thus exactly reversing the English order.

Two good men, *watu wema wawili.*

The Ordinal numbers are expressed by the use of the variable particle *-a*. (See Prepositions.)

The third man, *mtu wa tatu.*
The fourth house, *nyumba ya 'nne.*
The fifth chair, *kiti cha tano.*

The Ordinal numbers are:

First, *-a mosi*, or more commonly *-a kwanza.*
Second, *-a pili.*
Third, *-a tatu.*
Fourth, *-a 'nne.*
Fifth, *-a tano.*

Sixth, *-a sita.*
Seventh, *-a saba.*
Eighth, *-a nane.*
Ninth, *-a kenda.*
Tenth, *-a kumi.*
&c. &c.
Last, *-a mwisho.*

Once, twice, &c., are denoted by the use of *marra*, or *mara*, a time.

Once, *mara moja.*
The first time, *mara ya kwanza.*
Twice, *mara mbili.*
The second time, *mara ya pili.*
How many times? *Mara ngapi?*
Often, *mara nyingi.*

FRACTIONS may be expressed by the use of *fungu*, a part, as

Fungu la thelathini, a thirtieth.

The only fractions in common use are the parts of a dollar, which are thus expressed in forms borrowed from the Arabic:

One-sixteenth—*Nuss ya* the*muni.*
One-eighth—The*muni*, or The*mni*, or *Ze'mni.*
Three-sixteenths—The*muni na nuss ya* the*muni.*
One-fifth—*Zerenge.*
One-quarter—*Robo.*
Five-sixteenths—*Robo na nuss ya* the*muni.*
Three-eighths—*Robo na* the*muni.*
Seven-sixteenths—*Robo na* the*muni na nuss ya* the*muni.*
One-half—*Nuss.*
Nine-sixteenths—*Nuss na nuss ya* the*muni.*
Five-eighths—*Nuss na* the*muni.*
Eleven-sixteenths—*Nuss na* the*muni na nuss ya* the*muni.*
Three-quarters—*Kassa robo* [i.e., *a dollar* less by a quarter].
Thirteen-sixteenths—*Kassa robo na nuss ya* the*muni.*
Seven-eighths—*Kassa* the*muni.*
Fifteen-sixteenths—*Kassa nuss ya* the*muni.*

Numbers treated as Substantives make their plurals by prefixing *ma-*:

Makumi mawili, two tens, *i.e.*, twenty.
Mamoja pia, all ones, *i.e.*, all the same.

LIST OF ADJECTIVES.

Those words to which no hyphen is prefixed do not take any variable syllable.

A quality for which one cannot find a word, a sort of a, -nyangálika.

Kitu kinyángálika gani? *What sort of a kind of thing is this?*

A.

Able, having ability for, or power over, mweza.

Abortive (fruit, &c.), -pooza.

Active, -tendaji.

Adjacent.

Mpaka mmoja, *having a common boundary.*

Kutangamana, *to adjoin.*

Alike, sawásawa, -moja.

Alive, hayi.

All, -ote, *or* -ot'e, *varying as a possessive pronoun and not as an adjective.*

CLASS	I.	wote.		
"	II.	*sing.* mote,	*pl.*	yote.
"	III.	" yote,	"	zote.
"	IV.	" chote,	"	vyote.
"	V.	" lote,	"	yote.
"	VI.	" wote,	"	zote.
"	VII.	" pote.		
"	VIII.	" kwote.		

-ote *has special forms after the particles of time and place.*

po pote, *whensoever.*
ko kote, *whithersoever.*
mo mote, *whereinsoever.*

Also after the first and second persons plural.

sisi sote, *we all.*
ninyi nyote, *you all.*

Sote *has the meaning of* together.

tu sote, *we are together.*

Wote *has the meaning of* both.

sisi wote, *both of us.*

2. Pia, *the whole, all of it or them.*

3. Jamii.

Jamii wa asikari, *all the soldiers.*

Almighty, mweza vyote.

Alternate, moja bado wa moja.

Ancient, -a kale, -a zamani, -a kwanza.

Angular.

Kuwa na pembepembe, *to have corners.*

Antique, -a kikale, *of the old style.*

Artful, -a vitimbi.

Awake, macho.

He is awake, yu macho.

B.

Bad, -baya, *making* mbaya *with nouns like* nyumba *or* nyimbo.
-ovu *or* -bovu, *making* mbovu *with nouns like* nyumba *or* nyimbo. -ovu *expresses rather corruptness than mere badness.*
Utterly bad, baa, *pl.* mabaa.
Good for very little, thaifu.
Bare, -tupu, *making* tupu *with nouns like* nyumba *or* nyimbo.
Bareheaded, kitwa kiwazi.
Barren, *of land*, kame.
of animals, tasa.
of persons, si mzazi.
Beautiful, -zuri.
Bent, *of persons*, kibiongo, *pl.* vibiongo.
Best, bora (*pre-eminent*).
Bitter, -chungu (-tungu (M.)), *making* uchungu *with nouns like* nyumba, nyimbo, *or* kasha.
Dawa uchungu, *bitter medicine.*
Tunda uchungu, *bitter fruit.*
Black, -eusi. *Sometimes forms occur as if from* -usi, *such as* wausi *for* weusi, mausi *for* meusi, *and* viusi *for* vyeusi *or* veusi. *It makes* nyeusi *with nouns like* nyumba *or* nyimbo, *and* jeusi *with nouns like* kasha.
Blind, kipofu, *pl.* vipofu.
Blue, samawi (*sky colour*).
Maji a babari (*sea-water colour*).
Blunt, -vivu (*see Idle*).
Kisu bakipati, *the knife is blunt.*
Bold, -jasiri, shujaa, *pl.* mashujaa.
Breeding (*of animals*), koo.
Koo la mbuzi, *a breeding goat.*
Broad, -pana, *making* pana *with nouns like* nyumba *or* nyimbo.

C.

Careless, -zembe.
Castrated, maksai.
Certain, yakini.
A certain man, mtu mmoja.
Cheap, rakhisi, rahisi.
Checkered, marakaraka.
Chief, bora, -kuu. *See Great.*
Choice, -teule, aali.
A choice thing, hedaya, tunu, hikaya.
Civilized, -ngwana, -a kiungwana (*of the civilized sort*).
Clear, safi, fasihi, -eupe (*see White*).
Clear, kweu, mbayani, thahiri (*manifest*), -wazi (*see Open*). -eupe (*see White*).
Clever, hodari, mahiri, -a akili.
Clumsy, -zito (*see Heavy*).
Coloured, -enyi rangi.
Of one uniform colour, -takatifu.
Comic, -chekeshaji, -testeshi.
Common, vivi hivi, zizi hizi, &c., yee kwa yee, &c. (*see Pronouns*).
A common thing, jazi.
Complete, kamili, -kamilifu, -timilivu.
Confident, -tumaini.
Confidential, -siri.
Consecrated, wakf.
Cool, wovisi.
Correct, sahihi, fasihi.
Countrified, -a kimashamba.
Covetous, bakhili, -enyi choyo, -enyi tamaa.
Crafty, -a hila, -erevu.
Crazy, mafuu.
Credible, mutaabir, -tabari.
Crooked, kombokombo, mshithari.
Cross, -kali (*see Fierce*).
Cross roads, njia panda.
Cunning, -erevu, -a hila.

D.

Damp, kimaji.
Daring, -jasiri.
Dark, -a giza (*of darkness*), -eusi (*see Black*).
Dead, -fu.
One whose mother is dead, Mtu aliofiwa na mamaye.
Deaf, kiziwi, *pl.* viziwi.
Dear, ghali.
Deceased, marehemu.
Deformed, kilema, *pl.* vilema.
Destructive, -harabu, -haribivu.
Devout, -taowa.
Different, -ingine (*see Other*), mbalimbali, ihtilafu.
Difficult, -gumu (*see Hard*), -zito (*see Heavy*).
Disfigured by disease, -enyi lemaa.
Disobedient, aasi.
Distinct, mbalimbali.
Double, maradufu.
Dressed-up, -pambi.
Drunken, -levi.
Dry, -kavu, *making* kavu *with nouns like* nyumba *or* nyimbo.
yabis.
Dull, -vivu. *See Idle.*
Dumb, bubu, *pl.* mabubu.

E.

Easy, -epesi. *See Light.*
Elder or *Eldest*, -kubwa. *See Great.*
Eloquent, -semaji, -semi.
Empty, -tupu. *See Bare.*
Equal, sawa, sawasawa,
Eternal, -a milele.
European, Ulayiti, -a Kizungu.
Even (*level*), sawasawa.
(*not odd*), kamili.
Every, killa *or* kulla. *It always precedes its substantive.*
Killa mtu, *every man.*
Killa niendapo, *whenever I go*, or, *every time I go.*
Evident, thahiri, -wazi. *See Open.*
Extravagant, mubatharifu.

F.

Fat, -nono.
Faithful, amini.
Feeble, thaifu.
Female, -ke.
On the female side, kukeni.
Few, haba, -chache, *making* chache *with nouns like* nyumba *or* nyimbo.
Fierce, -kali, *making* kali *with nouns like* nyumba *or* nyimbo.
Filthy, -chavu.
Final, tama.
Fine, -zuri.
Firm, imara (*of things*), thabit (*of persons*).
Fixed (*certain*), maalum.
Flat, sawasawa, panapana.
Foolish, -pumbafu.
Foreign, -geni.
Forgetful, -sahau.
Forgiving, -samehe.
Former, -a kwanza.
Fortunate, heri, -enyi bahati, -a heri.
Free, huru, -ngwana.
Fresh, -bichi. *See Raw.*
Fresh water, maji matamu, maji a pepo.
Full, kujaa, *to become full.*
Full to the brink, fara, farafara.
Full of words, mwingi wa maneno.
Full grown, -pevu.
Future, mkabil.

G.

Generous, karimu, -paji.
Gentle, -anana.
Glorious, -tukufu, -enyi fakhari.
Gluttonous, -lafi.
Good, -ema, *making* njema *or* ngema *with nouns like* nyumba *or* nyimbo, *and* jema *with nouns like* kasha.

The idea of goodness may be expressed by the suffix -to.
Manuka, *smells.*
Manukato, *good smells.*
Kuweka, *to put.*
Kuwekato, *to put properly.*

Greedy, -enyi roho, -enyi tamaa, -enyi choyo.
Great, bora, -kuu *and* -kubwa *or* -kuba, *making* kuu *and* kubwa *with nouns like* nyumba *or* nyimbo. Kuu *is used preferably of moral or figurative greatness.* Kubwa, *of physical size.*

Great, when applied to anything not material, is usually rendered by -ingi.

Green, chanikiwiti, rangi ya majani. (*Fresh, or unripe*), -bichi. *See Raw.*

H.

Handsome, -zuri.
Handy, -a mkono.
A handbook, chuo cha mkono.
Happy, -a heri, furahani.
Hard, -gumu.
Having, *with, being with, or who or which has or have*, -enyi *or* -inyi. *It varies like a possessive pronoun, as in the following examples:—*

Class I. Mtu mwenyi (*or* mwinyi) mali, *a rich man.*
Watu wenyi mali, *rich people.*
Class II. Mti mwenyi (*or* mwinyi) kuzaa, *a tree in bearing.*
Miti yenyi (*or* yinyi) kuzaa, *trees in bearing.*
III. Nyumba yenyi (*or* yinyi) dirisha, *a house with windows.*
Nyumba zenyi (*or* zinyi) dirisha, *houses with windows.*
IV. Kikapu chenyi (*or* kinyi) nguvu, *a strong basket.*
Vikapu vinyi nguvu, *strong baskets.*
V. Neno lenyi kweli, *a true word.*
Mabakuli yenyi mayayi, *basins with eggs in them.*
VI. Upindi wenyi nguvu, *a strong bow.*
Pindi zenyi nguvu, *strong bows.*
VII. Mahali penyi mtende, *the place where the date-tree stands*

Healthy (*of persons*), -enyi afia, -zima (*of places, &c.*), -a afia.
Heavy, -zito.
High, -refu. *See Long.* -kubwa *See Great.*
Hollow, -a uvurungu, -wazi. *See Open.*
A hollow stone, jiwe la uvurungu.
It sounds hollow, panalia wazi.
The hollow or open space in or under anything, mvungu.
Holy, -takatifu.
Hot, -a moto.
I am hot, nina hari.
Hot-tempered, hararii.
Human, -a mwana Adamu, -a binadamu, -a mtu,
Humble, -nyenyekevu.
Humpbacked, -enyi kigongo.

I.

Idle, -vivu.
Ignorant (*like a simpleton*), -jinga.
Ill-omened, -korofi.
Ill-tempered, -kali. *See Fierce.*
Immature, -changa.
Infirm, thaifu.
Ingenious, -juzi.
Inquisitive, -pekuzi, -jasusi, -pelelezi.
Insignificant (*mean*), -nyonge.
(*unimportant*), khafifu.
Insipid, -dufu.

J.

Jealous, -wivu.
Juicy, -enyi maji.
Just, sawa, -a haki, -enyi haki.

K.

Kind, -ema. *See Good.*
(*doing kindnesses*), -fathili.
Knowing, -erevu, -juzi.

L.

Languid, -tepetevu, -chovu.
Large, -kubwa *or* -kuba. *See Great.*
(*well-grown*), -kuza.
Lawful, halali.
Lawful to you, halili yako.
Laying (*of birds*), koo, *pl.* makoo.
Koo la k'uku *a laying hen.*
Lazy. See Idle.
Lee, -a damalini, -a chini.
Left (*hand, &c.*), -a kushoto, -a kuke.
Level, sawa, sawasawa.
Liberal, karimu, -paji.
Light (*not dark*), -eupe. *See White.*
(*not heavy*), -epesi, *making* nyepesi *with nouns like* nyumba *or* nyimbo, *and* jepesi *with nouns like* kasha.
(*unimportant*), khafifu.

Lined (*of clothes*), bitana.
Little, -dogo, katiti (A.). -chache (*few*).
Little water, maji machache. (Maji *and other similar nouns being treated as plurals, and therefore requiring* few *and not* small *as their adjective.*)
Kidogo, *pl.* vidogo, *is used as a substantive for* a little *or* a little piece *of anything.*
Living, hayi, -zima.
Long, -refu, *making* ndefu *with nouns like* nyumba *or* nyimbo.
Long-suffering, -vumilivu.
Lukewarm, -enyi uvuguvugu.

M.

Mad, -enyi wazimu, -enyi mahoka (Country *dialect*).
Male, -ume, *making* mume *or* ndume (*as from* -lume) *with nouns of the second class.*
On the male side, kuumeni.
Manifest, thahiri, waziwazi, mbayani, -wazi. *See Open.*
Manly, -ume. *See Male.*
Bebera (*a strong he-goat*).
Fahali (*a bull*).
Many, -ingi *or* -ngi, *making* nyingi *with nouns like* nyumba or nyimbo, *and* jingi *with nouns like* kasha.
Katháwakatha.
Maternal (*on the mother's side*), -a kukeni.
(*motherly*), -a mama.
Mean, -nyonge.
Merry, -chekeshaji.
Middling, kadiri.
Mischievous, -harabu, -tundu.
Moderate, kadiri.

Much, -ingi (*see Many*), tele.
Murderous, kiuwaji, nduli.

N.

Naked, -tupu, uchi. *See Bare.*
Narrow, -embamba, *making* nyembamba *with nouns like* nyumba *or* nyimbo, *and* jembamba *with nouns like* kasha.
Necessary (*unavoidable*), lazim, farathi.
(*indispensable*), kanuni.
New, -pya, *making* 'mpya *with nouns like* nyumba *or* nyimbo, jipya *with nouns like* kasha, *and* pipya *with nouns of place.*
Noble, bora, -kuu. *See Great.*
Notable, mashuhur, mashur.
Nice, -ema (*see Good*), -tamu. *See Sweet.*
Nipping (*pressing closely and tightly*), -kazo.

O.

Obedient, tayi, -tii.
Obligatory, farathi.
Obstinate, -kaidi, -shindani, -shipavu.
Odd (*not even*), witiru.
Officious, -futhuli, -juvi.
Old (*of things*), -kukuu, *making* kukuu *with nouns like* nyumba *or* nyimbo. Kukuu *implies being worn out. Where mere antiquity is to be expressed see Ancient.*
(*of persons*), -zee.
Extremely old, -kongwe.
How old is he? Umri wake apataje?
One-eyed, -enyi chongo.
Only, -a pekee, peke yake, &c.
Open, -wazi.
Other, -ingine *or* -ngine.
Class I. Mgine *or* mwingine. wangine.
II. Mwingine *or* mgine. mingine.
III. Nyingine (*sing. and pl.*
IV. Kingine *or* chingine. vingine.
V. Jingine. mangine *or* mengine.
VI. Mwingine *or* mgine. nyingine.
VII. Pangine *or* pingine.
(*The*) *other*, -a pili.
Other people's, -a watu.
Another person's, -a mwenyewe.
(*not the same*) *is expressed by adding the relative particle* (*see* p. 117).
pangincpo, *elsewhere, other places.*

P.

Paternal (*on the father's side*), -a kuumeni.
(*fatherly*), -a baba.
Patient, -stahimili, -vumilivu.
Perfect, kamili, -kamilifu, -timilifu.
Perverse, -potoe, -tundu.
Plain (*evident*), thahiri, -wazi.
Pleasant, -tamu (*see Sweet*), -a kupendeza.
Plenty, tele.
Polite, -a adabu.
Poor, masikini, fukara, fakiri.
wretchedly poor, thalili.
utterly destitute, hohe hahe.
Printed, -a chapa.
Profane, -najisi.
Pure, safi, fasihi, -takatifu.

Q.

Quarrelsome, -gomvi.
Quick, -pesi.
Quiet, -tulivu (*still*), -nyamavu (*silent*).

R.

Rare, nadira, -a tunu.
Raw, -bichi, *making* mbichi *with nouns like* nyumba *or* nyimbo. Bichi *is used for raw, unripe, underdone, fresh, or any state which will or might change by keeping or cooking.*
(*inexperienced*), -jinga. *This word is specially applied to newly arrived slaves.*
Ready, tayari.
(*quick*), -pesi, mahiri.
Rebellious, aasi.
Red, -ekundu, *making* nyekundu *with nouns like* nyumba *or* nyimbo, *and* jekundu *with nouns like* kasha.
Regular, -a kaida, taratibu.
Safu za kaida, *regular rows.*
Mtu taratibu, *a person of regular habits.*
Remarkable, mashuhur, mashur.
Rich, -enyi mali, -kwasi, tajiri, *pl.* matajiri.
Right (*hand, &c.*), -a kulia, -a kuume, -a kuvuli.
Ripe, -bivu, *making* mbivu *with nouns like* nyumba *or* nyimbo. Bivu *is used as the contradictory of* bichi. *See Raw.*
Rotten, -ovu *or* -bovu. *See Bad.*
Rough, kuparuza, *to be rough and grating.*
Round, -a mviringo.
Royal, -a kifaume.

S.

Safe, salama.
Same, moja, *pl.* mamoja.
Sanguine, -tumaini.
Satisfied or content, rathi.
Self-satisfied, -kinayi.
Savage, -kali (*see Fierce*), mbwai.
Very savage, nduli.
Second, -a pili.
A second in command, akida.
Secret, -a siri, ndani kwa ndani.
Separate, mbali.
Severe, -zito. *See Heavy.*
Shallow, [maji] baba, [maji] machache.
Sharp, -kali. *See Fierce.*
Short, -fupi, *making* fupi *with nouns like* nyumba *or* nyimbo.
Shrewd, -erevu, -enyi busara.
Sick, -gonjwa, -weli.
Silent, -nyamavu.
A silent man, mtu wa kimya-kimya.
Slim, -embamba. *See Narrow.*
Slender, -embamba. *See Narrow.*
Sleek, -neno. *See Stout.*
Slow, -vivu. *See Idle.*
Smooth, laini.
Soaked (*with rain, &c.*), chepechepe.
Soft, -ororo, *making* nyororo *with nouns like* nyumba *or* nyimbo, *and* jororo *with nouns like* kasha.
-anana, laini.
the soft, teketeke.
Solid, yabisi.
Some, baathi ya, akali ya.
Some— others—, wangine— wangine—.
Sound (*healthy, living, entire*), -zima.
Sour, -kali. *See Fierce.*
Spotted, madoadoa, marakaraka.
Square, mrabba.
Steadfast, thabit.

Steep, -a kusimama.
Still, -anana, -tulivu (*quiet*), -nyamavu (*silent*), -zizima (*very still water, &c.*).
Stout (*plump, thick*), -nene.
Strange (*foreign, surprising*), -geni. (*startling*), mzungu, *pl.* mizungu.
Strong, hodari, -enyi nguvu, -ume.
Sweet, -tamu, *making* tamu *with nouns like* nyumba *or* nyimbo.

T.

Tall, -refu. *See Long.*
A very tall man, -tambo.
Thick, -nene.
Thick syrup, asali nzito. *See Heavy.*
Thievish, kijivi, *pl.* vijivi, mwibaji, *pl.* webaji.
Thin, -embamba (*see Narrow*), -epesi. *See Light.*
Tiresome, -chovu.
True, -a kweli, hakika yako, &c. (*it is true of you, &c.*), yakini (*certainly*).
Trustworthy, amini.
Truthful, -a kweli, -neni kweli.

U.

Uncivilized, -a kishenzi.
Uncultivated, -gugu.
Underdone (*half-cooked*), -bichi. *See Raw.*
Unhealthy, -weli.
Unlawful, haramu.
Unripe, -bichi. *See Raw.*
Usual, -zoea.
We are used to him, tuna mazoea naye.

V.

Vain, ana makuu, *he is vain.*
Valuable, -a thamani.
Vigilant, macho. *See Awake.*

W

Wasteful, -potevu.
Watery, chelema.
Weak, thaifu.
Wealthy. *See Rich.*
Weary, -chovu.
Weather, -agoshini, -a juu.
Well. *See Healthy.*
Well done (*cooked*), -bivu. *See Ripe.*
Wet, majimaji, rátaba.
White, -eupe, *making* nyeupe *with nouns like* nyumba *or* nyimbo, *and* jeupe *with nouns like* kasha.
Very white is expressed by putting a strong accent on the last syllable, and sometimes raising the voice on it into a sort of falsetto.
Whole, -zima. *See Sound.*
pia, pia yote, zote, &c.
Wide, -pana. *See Broad.*
Wild (*of plants*), -gugu.
(*of animals*), -a mwitu.
Willing, -epesi, -pesi.
Worn out, -kukuu (*of things*), -kongwe (*of persons*). *See Old.*

Y.

Yellow, rangi ya manjano.
Young (*immature*), -changa, *making* mchanga *with nouns like* nyumba *or* nyimbo.
Younger, youngest, -dogo.

PRONOUNS.

PERSONAL PRONOUNS.

The full forms of the Personal Pronouns are—

I, *Mimi.*	We, *Sisi* or *Swiswi.*
Thou, *Wewe.*	You, *Nyinyi* or *Nwinyi.*
He or she, *Yeye.*	They, *Wao.*

The second and third persons singular are often contracted into *Wee* and *Yee.* The second person singular is always used where one person only is to be denoted.

There are no special forms for *it* and *they* when referring to inanimate things. If any special emphasis makes it necessary, the Demonstrative Pronouns agreeing with the nouns referred to must be used. Similarly, for *he* or *she* and *they*, the Demonstrative Pronouns proper to the first class may be used, when any special emphasis is to be expressed.

The objective cases, *me*, *thee*, *him*, *her*, *us*, *them*, are expressed by the same forms as those given above for the subjective case, *I*, *thou*, &c.

The possessive case, *of me*, *of thee*, *of him*, &c., is

generally expressed by the Possessive Pronouns (which see, p. 109); there is thus no distinction between *of me* and *mine*, *of thee* and *thine*, &c.

Habari zangu, my news, *or* news of me.

The Possessive Pronouns proper to animate beings may be used of inanimate things also; *-ake*, its, and *-ao*, their, being used for *of it* and *of them*, in reference to all nouns of whatever class they may be.

The possessive case may be regarded as an instance of the Personal Pronouns in a special form subjoined to the variable preposition *-a*, of.

The Preposition *na*, with *or* and, is commonly joined with short forms of the Personal Pronoun to express *and* or *with me*, *and* or *with you*, &c. &c.

Nami, and *or* with me.
Nawe, and *or* with you.
Naye, and *or* with him or her.
Nao, *Nayo*, *Nacho*, *Nalo*, *Napo*, *Nako*, and *or* with it.

Nasi or *Naswi*, and *or* with us.
Nanyi or *Nanwi*, and *or* with you.
Nao, and *or* with them.
Nao, *Nayo*, *Nazo*, *Navyo*, *Napo*, and *or* with them.

The above forms may be used for either the objective or subjective cases after *and*. *Nami* = and I *or* and me, *Nawe* = and thou *or* and thee, &c. &c.

It will be seen that in referring to animate beings the latter half of the full form of the Personal Pronoun is suffixed to the *na-*, and in referring to inanimate things the syllable suffixed is that which denotes the relative (see Relative Pronouns, p. 117), a syllable which occurs also as the final syllable of those Demonstrative Pronouns which refer to a thing mentioned before.

Other Prepositions, that is to say, *kwa* and *katika*, are

constructed with the full form of the Personal Pronoun referring to animate beings, and with the Demonstrative Pronouns, where necessary, referring to inanimate things. This rule distinguishes the preposition *kwa*, for, by, &c., from the form of the variable *-a* required by substantives of the eighth class and sometimes by the case in *-ni*.

Kwa mimi, for me. *Kwangu*, of me *or* my, to my [house].

The prefixes used in conjugating the verb to mark the subject and object may be regarded as shortened forms of the Personal Pronouns. The objective and subjective cases are denoted by slightly different forms.

It will be most convenient to take the prefixes denoting animate beings first, as they alone can be used in the first and second person. The following are the subjective or nominative forms :—

I, *Ni-* or *N-*.	We, *Tu-* or *Tw-*.
Thou, *U-* or *W-*.	You, *Mu-*, *'M-*, or *Mw-*.
He *or* she, *A-* (or *Yu-*).	They, *Wa-*.

The rule for applying these prefixes is that the forms ending with a vowel are used when they are to be immediately followed by a consonant, and those ending in a consonant are used before a vowel. In the third person, both singular and plural, the vowel remains unchanged before *o* or *u*, it coalesces with *e* and *i* into an *e*, and merges into an *a*, so as to be no longer distinguishable. Thus, where the verb or tense prefix begins with *a*, the third person singular is apparently without prefix and the third person plural is marked only by a *w-*. Examples of and further observations on these prefixes will be found under *Verbs*, as playing an important part in their conjugation. The form *yu-* is but seldom used for the third person singular, and very rarely with any but monosyllabic verbs.

The syllables which stand for the *objective* or *accusative* case of the Personal Pronouns denoting animate beings, when they are connected with Verbs, are—

Me,	*-ni-* or *-n-*.	Us,	*-tu-* or *-tw-*.
Thee,	*-ku-* or *-kw-*.	You,	*-wa-*.
Him *or* her,	*-m-* or *-mw-*.	Them,	*-wa-*.

The same rules as above apply to the use of forms ending in a consonant before a vowel, and forms ending in a vowel before a consonant.

As the forms proper to the first class of Nouns denote animate beings, there remain seven classes denoting inanimate things, each of which has its appropriate subjective and objective pronominal forms when conjoined with a verb. The subjective pronominal prefixes are—

CLASS	II.	*sing.*	U-	*or*	W-	*plur.*	I-	*or*	Y-.
„	III.	„	I-	„	Y-	„	Zi-	„	Z-.
„	IV.	„	Ki-	„	Ch-	„	Vi-	„	Vy-.
„	V.	„	Li-	„	L-	„	Ya-.		
„	VI.	„	U-	„	W-	„	Zi-	„	Z-.
„	VII.	„	Pa-	„	P-	„	Pa-	„	P-.
„	VIII.	„	Ku-	„	Kw-	„	Ku-	„	Kw-.

Here also the forms ending in a vowel are used before a consonant, and the forms ending in a consonant are used before a vowel. Examples of their use will be found in the sections on the conjugation of the Verb.

There, used as the subject of a verb, is expressed by *ku-* or *pa-* employed as personal prefixes. *Ku-* is the more indefinite of the two. *One*, *they*, or *people* used to denote what is customary, are expressed by the prefix *hu-*.

The objective forms in reference to inanimate objects are very similar to the subjectives.

CLASS	II.	*sing.*	-u-	*plur.*	-i-.
„	III.	„	-i-	„	-zi-.
„	IV.	„	-ki-	„	-vi-.
„	V.	„	-li-	„	-ya-.
„	VI.	„	-u-	„	-zi-.
„	VII.	„	-pa-	„	-pa-.
„	VIII.	„	-ku-	„	-ku-.

In these forms also *u* becomes *w*, and *i y*, before vowels.

The following examples will illustrate the use of the objective syllables: they are parted off from the rest of the word by hyphens. Instances are given of both vowel and consonantal verbs.

CLASS I. *A-ni-penda*, he loves me.
A-n-ambia, he tells me.
A-ku-penda, he loves you.
A-kw-ambia, he tells you.
Na-m-penda, I love him.
Na-mw-ambia, I tell him
A-tu-penda, he loves us.
A-tw-ambia, he tells us.
A-wa-penda, he loves you.
A-wa-ambia, he tells you.
A-wa-penda, he loves them.
A-wa-ambia, he tells them.

„ II. *A-u-penda*, he likes it (*mti*, a tree).
A-w-ona, he sees it.
A-i-penda, he likes them (*miti*, trees).
A-y-ona, he sees them.

„ III. *A-i-penda*, he likes it (*nyumba*, a house).
A-y-ona, he sees it.
A-zi-penda, he likes them (*nyumba*, houses).
A-zi-ona, he sees them.

CLASS IV. *A-ki-penda*, he likes it (*kitu*, a thing).
A-ki-ona, he sees it.
A-vi-penda, he likes them (*vitu*, things).
A-vi-ona, he sees them.
„ V. *A-li-penda*, he likes it (*kasha*, a chest).
A-li-ona, he sees it.
A-ya-penda, he likes them (*makasha*, chests).
A-ya-ona, he sees them.
„ VI. *A-u-penda*, he likes it (*uimbo*, a song).
A-w-ona, he sees it (*ubau*, a plank).
A-zi-penda, he likes them (*nyimbo*, songs).
A-zi-ona, he sees them (*mbau*, planks).
„ VII. *A-pa-penda*, he likes it *or* them (place *or* places).
A-pa-ona, he sees it *or* them.
„ VIII. *A-ku-penda*, he likes it (*kwiba*, stealing).
A-ku-ona, he sees it.

In all cases the Pronominal Syllable representing the subject is the first prefix, and therefore the first syllable of the word; and the syllable representing the object is the last of the prefixes and immediately precedes the verb.

A-takapo-ku-ona, when he shall see you.
Wa-lipoki-m-penda, when they loved him.
A-ki-kw-ita, if he calls you.

It is quite allowable for the sake of emphasis to use the full forms of the Personal Pronouns as well as the subjective and objective syllables.

Mimi nakupenda wewe, I love you.
Wewe wanipenda mimi, you love me.

When so used, however, a very strong emphasis is put upon the persons loving and loved, and unless such an emphasis is intended the full forms ought not to be used. The above phrases might be better translated by—For myself I love you the best; and, It is you who love *me*.

In poetical Swahili an objective suffix is used as well as the objective prefix. The syllables used as a suffix are the same as those given before with *na* (see p. 103). The suffixes are not used in the dialect of Zanzibar.

U-ni-hifathi-mi, do thou preserve me. (Both the *-ni-* and the *-mi* represent the object of the verb.)
Aka-zi-angusha-zo, and he threw them down. (Both the *-zi-* and the-*zo* represent the object of the verb.)
Na-wa-ambia-ni, I tell you.

The use of the objective prefix implies a reference to some ascertained object: it is therefore properly used wherever in English the object would be expressed by a Pronoun. Where in English the object would not be expressed by a Pronoun, the objective prefix has the effect of a definite article, and its omission that of an indefinite article.

Nataka kununua nyumba (no objective prefix being used), I want to buy a house.
Nataka kuinunua nyumba (the objective prefix *-i-* being used), I want to buy the house.
Naona mtu, I see somebody.
Namwona mtu, I see the man.

Where a Demonstrative Pronoun is used with the object, the objective prefix must always be used.

Nataka kuinunua nyumba hii, I want to buy this house.
Namwona mtu yule, I see that man yonder.

The objective prefix is used where anything about the person or thing is about to be stated.

Na-m-jua aliko [I know of him where he is], I know where he is.
Nali-m-thania amekufa [I thought of him, he had died], I thought he was dead.
Aka-m-kata kitwa [and he cut of him the head], and he cut off his head.

Possessive Pronouns.

The Possessive Pronouns are always placed after the Substantive denoting the thing possessed, and vary according to its Class and Number.

The unvarying parts of the Possessive Pronouns are:

My,	*-angu.*	Our,	*-etu.*
Thy,	*-ako.*	Your,	*-enu.*
His, her, *or* its,	*-ake.*	Their,	*-ao.*

The same forms are used for *its* and *their*, of whatever class the thing possessing may be.

In many dialects of Swahili the form of the third person singular is *-akwe*, and in some that of the second is *-akwo.*

The above forms may be used as enclitics, and frequently are so with some common words, such as *baba*, father, *mama*, mother, *mwana*, child, *mwenzi*, companion, &c. When the final letter of the substantive is *-a*, *-e*, or *-i*, it merges into the first letter of the possessive suffix.

Mwanangu, my child.
Mwenzangu, my companion.
Mwanako, thy child.
Mwenzako, thy compauion.
Mwanake, his *or* her child.
Mwenzake, his *or* her companion.
Mwanetu, our child.
Mwenzetu, our companion.
Mwanenu, your child.
Mwenzenu, your companion.
Mwanao, their child.
Mwenzao, their companion.

The initial letters proper to each class of Substantives are:

Class	I. *sing.*	w-	*plur.*	w-.	Class	V. *sing.*	l-	*plur.*	y-.
„	II. „	w-	„	y-.	„	VI. „	w-	„	z-.
„	III. „	y-	„	z-.	„	VII. „	p-	„	p-.
„	IV. „	ch-	„	vy-.	„	VIII. „	kw-	„	kw-.

Besides these forms proper to the several classes, Substantives in the locative case in *-ni* require special forms of the Possessive Pronouns according to the meaning of the case. These forms are the same for all Substantives, of whatever class or number they may be.

1. When the case denotes *being within*, or *to*, or *from within*, the Possessive Pronouns must begin with *mw-*.

2. Where the case denotes mere nearness, and can be translated *at*, *by*, or *near*, the Possessive Pronouns must begin with *p-*.

3. For all other meanings the Possessive Pronouns must begin with *kw-*.

The following instances will show how all these rules are applied :—

Class I. *Mtu wangu*, my man.
Watu wako, thy men.
Mbuzi wake, his *or* her goat.
Mbuzi wetu, our goats.
Waziri wake, his vizir.
Mawaziri wake, his vizirs.
„ II. *Mti wenu*, your tree.
Miti yao, their trees.
„ III. *Nyumba yangu*, my house.
Nyumbo zako, thy houses.
„ IV. *Kiti chake*, his chair.
Viti vyetu, our chairs.
„ V. *Kasha lenu*, your chest.
Makasha yao, their chests.

CLASS VI. *Uimbo wangu*, my song.
Nyimbo zako, thy songs.
" VII. *Mahali pake*, his, her, *or* its place *or* places.
" VIII. *Kufa kwetu*, our dying.
1. *Nyumbani mwenu*, in your house *or* houses.
2. *Nyumbani pao*, near their house *or* houses.
3. *Nyumbani kwangu*, to my house.

All the Possessive Pronouns will be found in the Table of Concords (p. 82), arranged under the classes to which they are appropriate. The Personal Pronouns may be added to give emphasis.

Kisu changu mimi, my own knife.
Vyangu mimi, they are *mine*.

The Possessive Pronoun is used for the preposition *-a*, of, where it is intended to mark particularly the person whose the thing is.

Kiti cha sultani, the sultan's chair, *or* a sultan's chair.
Kiti chake sultani, the sultan's own chair, *or* this sultan's chair.

There is another and short enclitic form for the Possessive Pronouns of the second and third persons singular, which is much used with some common words, such as *mume*, husband, *mke*, wife, *ndugu*, brother or sister, &c. They consist of *-o* for the second person and *-e* for the third, with the appropriate initial letters for each class as given above (p. 110).

Mumewe, her husband.
Mkewo, or *mkeo*, thy wife.
Mwenziwe, his companion.
Jinalo, thy name.
Shogaye, her friend.

It will be seen from the above tables that there is absolutely nothing to distinguish the singular and plural of Substantives in the form of the third class which denote animate beings, when joined with Possessive Pronouns. It is probably for this reason, and to avoid ambiguity, that they are frequently treated as ordinary Substantives of that class.

Ndugu yangu, my brother.
Nduguye or *Ndugu yake*, his brother.
Nduguzo or *Ndugu zako*, thy brothers.
Mbuzi zetu, our goats.

Possessive Pronouns are sometimes used in English where Personal Pronouns are used in Swahili.

Waka-m-funga mikono nyuma [and they tied him hands behind], and they tied his hands behind him.
Ali-m-kata kitwa [he cut him head], he out off his head.

After verbs of coming and going Possessive Pronouns beginning with *z-* (or in other dialects with *vy-* or *th-*) are used somewhat as—his way, &c., were used in old English.

Amekwenda zake, he has gone away, *or* he has gone off.
Twende zetu, let us be going.
Wamekuja zao, they have come home, *or* they have come away.

Reflective Pronouns.

The Swahili verb is made reflective by prefixing *-ji-*, as if it were a pronoun in the objective form.

Na-ji-penda, I love myself.

Self may be translated by the Arabic word, *nefsi*, *nafsi*, or *nafusi*; or by the word *moyo*, a heart, plur. *mioyo* or *nyoyo*.

Nafsi yangu, or *moyo wangu*, myself.
Nafsi zetu, or *nyoyo zetu*, ourselves.

Itself, themselves, &c., may also be expressed by the word *-enyewe* with the proper prefix.

CLASS I. *Mtu mwenyewe*, the man himself.
Watu wenyewe, the people themselves.
Mbuzi mwenyewe, the goat itself.
Mbuzi wenyewe, the goats themselves.
Waziri mwenyewe, the vizir himself.
Mawaziri wenyewe, the vizirs themselves.
„ II. *Mti mwenyewe*, the tree itself.
Miti yenyewe, the trees themselves.
„ III. *Nyumba yenyewe*, the house itself.
Nyumba zenyewe, the houses themselves.
„ IV. *Kitu chenyewe*, the thing itself.
Vitu vyenyewe, the things themselves.
„ V, *Kasha lenyewe*, the chest itself.
Makasha yenyewe, the chests themselves.
„ VI. *Uimbo mwenyewe*, the song itself.
Nyimbo zenyewe, the songs themselves.
„ VII. *Mahali penyewe*, the place itself.

Mwenyewe may be used for *myself* and *thyself*, as well as for *himself* or *herself*.

Wenyewe may be used for *ourselves* and *yourselves*, as well as for *themselves*.

By myself, by ourselves, &c., are expressed by *peke* with the appropriate Possessive Pronoun.

Peke yangu, by myself, *or* I only.
Peke yetu, by ourselves, *or* we only.

DEMONSTRATIVE PRONOUNS.

There are three Demonstrative Pronouns. 1, denoting objects at no great distance. 2, denoting objects previously mentioned. 3, denoting objects at a distance. They have each forms proper to the several classes of Substantives and to the three meanings of the case in *-ni*.

1. *This* or *that*, *these* or *those*, of objects at no great distance.

CLASS I. *Mtu huyu*, this man.
Watu hawa, these people.
Mbuzi huyu, this goat.
Mbuzi hawa, these goats.
Waziri huyu, this vizir.
Mawaziri hawa, these vizirs.
" II. *Mti huu*, this tree.
Miti hii, these trees.
" III. *Nyumba hizi*, this house.
Nyumba hizi, these houses.
" IV. *Kitu hiki*, this thing.
Vitu hivi, these things.
" V. *Kasha hili*, this chest.
Makasha haya, these chests.
" VI. *Uimbo huu*, this song.
Nyimbo hizi, these songs.
" VII. *Mahali hapa*, this place.
" VIII. *Kufa huku*, this dying.
1. *Nyumbani humo* (*humu* (?)), here, in the house.
2. *Nyumbani hapa*, here, by the house.
3. *Nyumbani huku*, here, to the house.

It will be observed that the second syllable of each of these Demonstratives is the pronominal syllable given at p. 105, and that all begin with *h*-, followed by the vowel of the pronominal syllable.

2. *This* or *that*, *these* or *those*, referring to something mentioned before. Both the other forms can also be used in this sense.

CLASS I. *Mtu huyo*, that man.
Watu hao, those people.
Mbuzi huyo, that goat.
Mbuzi hao, those goats.
" II. *Mti huo*, that tree.
Miti hiyo, those trees.
" III. *Nyumba hiyo*, that house.
Nyumba hizo, those houses.

CLASS IV. *Kitu hicho*, that thing.
Vitu hivyo, those things.
" V. *Kasha hilo*, that chest.
Makasha hayo, those chests.
" VI. *Uimbo huo*, that song.
Nyimbo hizo, those songs.
" VII. *Mahali hapo*, that place *or* those places.
" VIII. *Kufa huko*, that dying.
1. *Nyumbani humo*, in that house.
2. *Nyumbani hapo*, by that house.
3. *Nyumbani huko*, to that house.

3. *That* and *those* or *yonder*, referring to things at a distance.

CLASS I. *Mtu yule*, yonder man.
Watu wale, those people.
Mbuzi yule, that goat.
Mbuzi wale, those goats.
" II. *Mti ule*, that tree.
Miti ile, those trees.
" III. *Nyumba ile*, that house.
Nyumba zile, those houses.
" IV. *Kitu kile* or *chile*, that thing.
Vitu vile, those things.
" V. *Kasha lile*, that chest.
Makasha yale, those chests.
" VI. *Uimbo ule*, that song.
Nyimbo zile, those songs.
" VII. *Mahali pale*, that place *or* those places.
" VIII. *Kufa kule*, that dying.
1. *Nyumbani mle*, in that house.
2. *Nyumbani pale*, by that house.
3. *Nyumbani kule*, to that house.

It will be seen that these last Pronouns are made by adding *-le* to the second syllable of the first set of Demonstratives. Sometimes the whole of the first form is retained, making *huyule, hawale, huule, hiile, hizile, hikile, hivile, hilile, hayale, hapale, hukule.*

An increase of distance is denoted by a stress on the final syllable.

Mtu yule, that man yonder.
Yulee, that one further off.
Yuleee, that one still further.

The more stress is laid on the final syllable, and the more the voice rises into a falsetto, so much the greater is the distance denoted.

When the substantive is mentioned the demonstrative always follows it.

The demonstratives are frequently doubled, and then have the meaning of *just this*, *that very*, &c.

Palepale, just there.
Mti uleule, that very tree.
Maneno yaleyale, just those words.

With the first set of demonstratives the final or true pronominal syllable is doubled and prefixed to the usual form.

Papahapa, just here.
Vivihivi, just these things.
Zizihizi, those very, &c.
Kukuhuku, just to this place.

These forms are also used to denote that there is nothing special about what is mentioned.

Zizihizi, just these and no more.

Huyo is often used when people are chasing a man or an animal.

Huyo! Huyo! = There he is! There he is!

There are other forms which ought probably to be regarded as demonstratives, as they have the force of, This is it, and, This is not it.

Class	I.	*ndimi*, it is I.	*ndisi*, it is we.
		ndiwe, it is thou.	*ndinyi*, it is you.
		ndiye, it is he.	*ndio*, it is they.
,,	II.	*ndio*, this is it.	*ndiyo*, these are they.
,,	III.	*ndiyo*.	*ndizo*.
,,	IV.	*ndicho*.	*ndivyo*.
,,	V.	*ndilo*.	*ndiyo*.
,,	VI.	*ndio*.	*ndizo*.
,,	VII.	*ndipo*.	
,,	VIII.	*ndiko*.	
		ndimo, it is here, *or* it is there.	
		ndipo.	
		ndiko.	

The negative is made by substituting ***si-*** **for** ***ndi.***

Siye, it is not he. *Sicho, &c. &c.*, this is not it.

Both forms may be used interrogatively.

Ndiye? Is it he? *Siye?* Is it not he?

Other demonstratives may be used with these for the sake of greater emphasis or clearness.

Relative Pronouns.

The Relative Pronouns have special forms appropriate to the several classes of Substantives and the three meanings of the *-ni* case.

Class	I.	*Who* and *Whom*, *sing.*	ye *or* yee,	*plur.*	o *or* wo.
,,	II.	*Which*, *sing.*	o *or* wo,	*plur.*	yo.
,,	III.	,, ,,	yo	,,	zo.
,,	IV.	,, ,,	cho	,,	vyo.
,,	V.	,, ,,	lo	,,	yo.
,,	VI.	,, ,,	o *or* wo	,,	zo.
,,	VII.	,, ,,	po	,,	po.
,,	VIII.	,, ,,	ko	,,	ko.
	1.	*Wherein* ,,	mo		
	2.	*Whereat* ,,	po		
	3.	*Whereto* ,,	ko.		

These relatives occur most frequently in their simple forms in connection with *-ote*, all.

yee yote, *wo wote*, whosoever *or* whomsoever.
wo wote, yo yote, zo zote, cho chote, vyo vyote, lo lote, po pote, whatsoever.
mo mote, whereinsoever, inside everything.
po pote, wheresoever *or* whensoever.
ko kote, whithersoever *or* wheresoever.

When connected with the substantive verb, to be, that verb is represented by the syllable *-li-*.

CLASS	I.	*aliye*, [he] who is.	*walio*, [they] who are.
,,	II.	*ulio*, [it] which is.	*iliyo*, [they] which are.
,,	III.	*iliyo*.	*zilizo*.
,,	IV.	*kilicho*.	*vilivyo*.
,,	V.	*lililo*.	*yaliyo*.
,,	VI.	*ulio*.	*zilizo*.
,,	VII.	*palipo*.	*palipo*.
,,	VIII.	*kuliko*.	*kuliko*.
	1.	*mulimo*, wherein there is.	
	2.	*palipo*, where there is.	
	3.	*kuliko*, where there is.	

There is a disposition in Zanzibar to make *-o* the general relative. Thus one very often hears *alio* for *aliye*, *lilio* for *lililo*, and *ilio* for *iliyo*.

When joined with the verb the syllable denoting the relative follows the sign of the tense if there is one.

The relative may be joined with the verb to form the present, or rather, an indefinite tense, without the use of any sign of time whatever. It is made precisely as in the examples given above of the use of the relative with the verb, to be, only substituting the particular verb for the syllable *-li-*.

[he] who loves, *apendaye*.
[they] who love, *wapendao*.

[the tree] which falls, *uangukao.*
[trees] which grow, *imeayo.*
[the house] which falls, *yangukayo.*
[houses] which fall, *ziangukazo.*

Where the relative is the object of the verb the same form may be used, only introducing the objective prefix proper to the substantive referred to, and changing the personal prefix.

[fruit] which I love, *nilipendalo.* *-li-* and *-lo-* being the syllables appropriate to *tunda,* a fruit, and other nouns of the Fifth Class.

When taken to pieces the word is seen to be, *ni-*, I, *-li-*, it, *-penda-*, love, *-lo*, which.

Relatives are rarely used in Swahili with any tenses except the present imperfect (the *-na-* tense), the past perfect (the *-li-* tense), and a peculiar form of the future (the *-taka-* tense). The following instances will show the way in which the relative is expressed with these several tenses both as subject and object.

CLASS	I.	[the man]	who is coming, *ana-ye-kuja.*
		,,	who came, *ali-ye-kuja.*
		,,	who will come, *atuka-ye-kuja.*
		,,	whom he is striking, *ana-ye-mpiga.*
		,,	whom we loved, *tuli-ye-mpenda.*
		[the men]	who will beat us, *wataka-o-tupiga.*
		,,	whom we will beat, *tutaka-o-wapiga.*
		[the ox]	which is eating, *ana-ye-kula.*
		,,	which we shall eat, *tutaka-ye-mla.*
,,	II.	[the tree]	which fell, *uli-o-anguka.*
		,,	which he cut down, *ali-o-ukata.*
		[the trees]	which were visible, *ili-yo-onekana.*
		,,	which we saw, *tuli-yo-iona.*
,,	III	[the house]	which fell down, *ili-yo-anguka.*
		,,	which I bought, *nili-yo-inunua.*

CLASS III.	[the houses]	which fell down,	*zili-zo-anguka.*
	,,	which I bought,	*nili-zo-zinunua.*
,, IV.	[the knife]	which cut me,	*kili-cho-nikata.*
	,,	which I took,	*nili-cho-kitwaa.*
	,,	which I gave you,	*nili-cho-kupa.*
	[the knives]	which fell down,	*vili-vyo-anguka.*
	,,	which I gave you,	*nili-vyo-kupa.*
,, V.	[the chest]	which is unfastened,	*lili-lo-funguka.*
	,,	which I unfastened,	*nili-lo-lifungua.*
	[the chests]	which were carried,	*yali-yo-chukuliwa.*
	,,	which they carried,	*wali-yo-yachukua.*
,, VI.	[the song]	which pleased me,	*uli-o-nipendeza.*
	,,	which I liked,	*nili-o-upenda.*
	[the letters, *nyaraka*]	which I wrote,	*nili-zo-ziandika.*
	,,	which I sent to you,	*nili-zo-kupelekea.*
	,,	which reached me,	*zili-zo-niwasilia.*
,, VII.	[the place]	which I live in,	*nina-po-pakaa.*
	[the places]	which I saw,	*nili-po-paona.*

The particles of place and time, *mo*, *po*, *ko*, are treated as relative particles.

alimo, where he is (within).
alipo, where he is (if near).
aliko, where he is (far off).
anapokwenda, when he is going.
anakokwenda, whither he is going.
alimokwenda, wherein he went.
alipokwenda, when he went.
alikokwenda, whither he went.

There is one ambiguity which cannot be avoided where both subject and object are of the same class. *Aliyempiga* may mean, who beat him, or, whom he beat; *kilichokikata* may mean, which cut it, or, which it cut, supposing *kisu*, a knife, to be one substantive, and *kitu*, a thing, to be the other.

The negative is combined with the relative by the

use of *-si-*. There is but one negative tense, and it embraces all times, past, present, and future.

asiye, [he] who is not, who will not be, who was not.
usioanguka, [the tree] which falls not, which is not falling, which did not fall, or, which will not fall.
nisichokupa, [the knife] which I did not give you, do not give you, or, shall not give you.

Where the relative is used in English with a preposition, the relative particle is sometimes joined with the verb and also with the preposition; but more commonly, the force of the preposition being contained in that of the Swahili verb, no special form is required. See DERIVATIVE VERBS, p. 157.

The man whom I went with, *mtu nali-o-kwenda naye.*
The man I went to, *mtu nali-o-mwendea.*
Where I came from, *nili-po-toka.*
Where I am going to, *nina-ko-kwenda.*

As the Swahili has no proper word for *to have*, but uses for it *kuwa na*, to be with, cases of double relatives are very frequent where *having* is mentioned.

The knife I have, *kisu nilicho nacho.*
The houses you have, *nyumba ulizo nazo.*
The knife I had, *kisu nilichokuwa nacho.*
The houses you had, *nyumba ulizokuwa nazo.*

The relative is used in some cases in which it is not employed in English.

Who went by? *Nani ali-ye-pita* (who is he who passed)?
He likes this fruit, *tunda hili ndilo alipendalo* (this fruit is it which he likes).
The boy is going, *kijana aendao.*
Whosoever may come, *yee yote atakayekuja.*

There is another way of expressing the relative by

means of *ambaye* or *ambaye kwamba*, though not used in Zanzibar. When it is employed the final syllable of *ambaye* changes according to the rules given above, making *ambao*, *ambazo*, *ambacho*, *ambavyo*, &c.

Sometimes an English relative can be expressed by the use of *mwenyi*, &c., having.

The man whose house it is, *mtu mwenyi nyumba*.

INTERROGATIVE AND OTHER PRONOUNS.

There are four Interrogatives which are not variable.

Nani?	Who?	*Nini?*	What?
Lini?	When?	*Gani?*	What sort?

Gani always follows the substantive it is connected with.

Mtu gani? What man? What sort of man?
Kitu gani? What thing? What sort of thing?

What? is sometimes expressed by the syllable *-ni* suffixed to a verb.

Atapatani? What will he get?
Amefanyani? What has he done?
Kunani? What is there? What is the matter?
Kina nini? What has it? What is the matter with it?
Wanani? What have they? What are they at?

What o'clock is it? is rendered by *Saa ngapi?* How many hours?

The interrogative Which? is expressed by *-pi* preceded by the appropriate syllable, which is the same as that used as the subjective personal prefix to verbs. It always follows the noun it refers to,

Class	I.	Which	[man]	*Yupi?*	[men]	*Wapi?*
„	II.	„	[tree]	*Upi?*	[trees]	*Ipi?*
„	III.	„	[house]	*Ipi?*	[houses]	*Zipi?*
„	IV.	„	[thing]	*Kipi?*	[things]	*Vipi?*
„	V.	„	[chests]	*Lipi?*	[chests]	*Yapi?*
„	VI.	„	[song]	*Upi?*	[songs]	*Zipi?*
„	VII.	„	[place]	*Papi?*	[places]	*Papi?*

The Interrogative, if followed by a verb, requires a relative with it.

Mtu yupi apendaye kwenda? Which [or what] man likes to go?
Nyumba ipi ikupendezayo? Which house do you like?

Nani? who? is also generally followed by a relative.

Nani aliopo mlangoni? Who is at the door?

It is, however, allowable to say *nani yupo mlangoni*, which is a literal translation of the English.

The interrogative Where? is *wapi?* or *api?*

Wenda wapi? Where are you going?

When referring to a substantive *wapi* must always be preceded by the syllable which is the proper subjective personal prefix for that substantive. This prefix very probably represents the substantive verb, and may often be translated by *is it?* or *are they?*

Class	I.	*sing.*	Yu wapi?	*plur.*	Wa wapi?
„	II.	„	U wapi?	„	I wapi?
„	III.	„	I wapi?	„	Zi wapi?
„	IV.	„	Ki wapi?	„	Vi wapi?
„	V.	„	Li wapi?	„	Ya wapi?
„	VI.	„	U wapi?	„	Zi wapi?
„	VII.	„	Pa wapi?	„	Pa wapi?

A fuller form to represent *where is it?* or *where are they?* is made by adding *-ko* to the personal prefix.

Yuko wapi? Where is he? *Ziko wapi?* Where are they?

The noun referred to follows this interrogative.

I wapi merikebu? Where is the ship?

How? is expressed by the syllable *-je* suffixed to the verb.

Nitakipataje? How shall I get it?
Chalifanywaje? How was it made?
Ulipendaje, ao kupika, ao bichi? How do you like it, cooked or raw?
Asemaje? [How does he talk?] What does he say?
Urefu wake yapataje? How long is it?
Umri wake apataje? How old is he?
Kwenda chini kwake chapataje [kisima]? How deep is it [a well]?

The use of *kupata*, to get, in these phrases must be noticed. There is no direct way of attaching the *how?* to the adjective; they say therefore, "His age, how gets he it?"

How many? is expressed by *-ngapi*, which is treated as an adjective.

How many people? *Watu wangapi?*
How many goats? *Mbuzi wangapi* or *ngapi?*
How many trees? *Miti mingapi?*
How many houses? *Nyumba ngapi?*
How many chairs? *Viti vingapi?*
How many chests? *Makasha mangapi?*
How many planks? *Mbau ngapi?*
How many places? *Mahali pangapi?*

How? is in some cases expressed by the use of other phrases.

How long ago? *Tangu lini?* [since when?]
How much? *Kadri gani*, or *Kiassi gani?* [what quantity?]
How often? *Marra ngapi?* [how many times?]

The exclamatory What! is rendered by the interrogative pronoun in *-pi*.

Furaha ipi! What joy!

VERBS.

Regular Swahili verbs always end in *-a*, as, *kupenda*, to love, *kupiga*, to beat.

Verbs derived from the Arabic may end in *-e*, *-i*, or *-u*, as, *kusamehe*, to pardon, *kusafiri*, to travel, *kuharibu*, to destroy. Verbs in this form do not change the final vowel, where verbs in *-a* regularly do so.

The simplest form of the verb is used in Swahili, as in English, for the second person singular of the imperative.

Penda!	Love!	*Piga!*	Strike!
Samehe!	Pardon!	*Safiri!*	Travel!
Haribu!	Destroy!		

The second person plural imperative is made by adding *-ni*. All the other tenses and moods are made by prefixing syllables to the simple form, except that verbs in *-a* change *-a* into *-e* in the present subjunctive, and into *-i* in the present negative, and a *-w-* is inserted to mark the passive.

There is a negative as well as an affirmative conjugation, in which the tenses and persons are also distinguished by prefixes.

The various prefixes form in pronunciation one word

with the verb, and when taken to pieces denote its person, number, tense, mood, subject, and object.

Amekwambia = *A-me-kw-ambia* = He-has-you-tell = He has told you.
Waliponipenda = *Wa-li-po-ni-penda* = They-did-when-me-love = When they loved me.
Nitakachokupa = *Ni-taka-cho-ku-pa* = I-shall-which-you-give-to = Which I shall give to you.
Ningalimwona = *Ni-ngali-mw-ona* = I-should-have-him-see = I should have seen him.

The syllables used as prefixes have not the same meaning standing separately as they have when combined with the verb in their proper order; for this reason, therefore, as well as to show the proper pronunciation, they with the verb must all be written as one word.

Lists of the several prefixes will be found at the end of the preliminary observations to the second part of this handbook (p. 237). The personal prefixes will be found described under Pronouns (p. 104), and seen arranged under their appropriate classes of Substantives in the Table of Concords, p. 82.

Indefinite Tenses.

1. Customary actions are expressed by prefixing *hu-* to the verb. In this form there is no distinction of number, person, or time.

Hu-enda, one goes, they go, everybody goes, he used to go.
Hu-penda, one likes, they like, one would like.

2. The relative may be joined with the verb without any sign of time. The personal prefix only is put before the verb, and the relative sign suffixed to it.

Sing. Class I. *Ni-penda-ye*, [I] who love.
U-penda-ye, [thou] who lovest.
A-penda-ye, [he] who loves.
" II. *U-anguka-o*, which falls.
" III. *I-anguka-yo*,
" IV. *Ki-anguka-cho*,
" V. *Li-anguka-lo*,
" VI. *U-anguka-o*,
" VII. *P-anguka-po*, where falls.
" VIII. *Kw-anguka-ko*, whither falls.
Plur. " I. *Tu-penda-o*, [we] who love.
M-penda-o, [you] who love.
Wa-penda-o, [they] who love.
" II. *I-anguka-yo*, or, *Y-anguka-yo*, which fall.
" III. *Zi-anguka-zo*,
" IV. *Vy-anguka-vyo*,
" V. *Y-anguka-yo*,
" VI. *Zi-anguka-zo*,

The relative may represent the object of the verb, but in that case the objective sign (pp. 105–6) ought to be inserted between the personal prefix and the verb.

Class I. *Ni-m-penda-ye*, [he *or* she] whom I love.
Ni-ku-penda-ye, [thou] " " "
Ni-wa-penda-o, [you *or* they] " " "
Sing. " II. *Ni-u-penda-o* [it] which I love.
" III. *Ni-i-penda-yo*,
" IV. *Ni-ki-penda-cho*,
" V. *Ni-li-penda-lo*,
" VI. *Ni-u-penda-o*,
" VII. *Ni-pa-penda-po*,
" VIII. *Ni-ku-penda-ko*,
Plur. " II. *Ni-i-penda-yo*, [those] which I love.
" III. *Ni-zi-penda-zo*,
" IV. *Ni-vi-penda-vyo*,
" V. *Ni-ya-penda-yo*,
" VI. *Ni-zi-penda-zo*,

3. The negative form, expressing Who, or which does

not, is made by the personal prefix, the syllable *-si-* [not] and the relative sign, followed by the verb.

Sing.	Class	I.	*Ni-si-ye-penda*, [I] who love not.
			U-si-ye-penda, [thou] who lovest not.
			A-si-ye-penda, [he or she] who loves not
	"	II.	*U-si-o-anguka*, which falls not.
	"	III.	*I-si-yo-anguka*,
	"	IV.	*Ki-si-cho-anguka*,
	"	V.	*Li-si-lo-anguka*,
	"	VI.	*U-si-o-anguka*,
	"	VII.	*Pa-si-po-anguka*, where falls not.
			Ku-si-ko-anguka, whither falls not,
			Mu-si-mo-anguka, wherein falls not.
Plur.	"	I.	*Tu-si-o-penda*, [we] who love not.
			M-si-o-penda, [you].
			Wa-si-o-penda, [they].
	"	II.	*I-si-yo-anguka*, which fall not.
	"	III.	*Zi-si-zo-anguka*,
	"	IV.	*Vi-si-vyo-anguka*,
	"	V.	*Ya-si-yo-anguka*,
	"	VI.	*Zi-si-zo-anguka*.

Where the relative is the object of the verb, it is expressed as in the affirmative tenses, by the form of the relative particle and the insertion of the objective prefix.

Ni-si-zo-zi-penda, which I do not like.

This negative tense may be applied with equal propriety to past, present, or future time, amounting in effect to a negative of the relation at the time and under the circumstances implied in the context.

The application of the relative to the definite affirmative tenses is explained under Pronouns (p. 119).

The difference between—which I like—and—I who like it—is to be found in the form of the relative particle.

[*Nyumba*] *nili-yo-ipenda*, [the house] which I liked.
nili-ye-ipenda, I who liked it.
[*Kitu*] *nili-cho-kipenda*, [the thing] which I liked.
nili-ye-kipenda, I who liked it.

Definite Tenses.

The important part of each tense is the *tense prefix*. It is preceded by the personal sign of the subject, and may be followed directly by the verb. If any signs of relation are used they are suffixed to the tense prefix, and the objective prefix (if any) must always immediately precede the verb. The tense prefix is the same for all persons and both numbers. The personal prefix is the same for all tenses, except the slight changes dependent upon the question whether the first letter of the tense prefix is a vowel or not.

In order therefore to construct the proper form of verb, it is necessary first to ascertain the proper personal prefix, next the proper tense prefix, then the particles of relation and objective prefix, if they are required, and then to finish with the verb. Thus, to say, A house has fallen down. A house is *nyumba*, a word of the third class; the proper personal prefix for a singular noun of the third class is *-i*, the tense prefix for the present perfect is *-me-*, the verb to fall is *ku - anguka* (the *ku-* being the sign of the infinitive: we have therefore—

Nyumba imeanguka = a house has fallen down.

If we wished to say, Six houses have fallen down; we find that *nyumba* being of the third class keeps the same form in the plural; *sita* is six, and must follow its noun; the subjective prefix proper to plural nouns in the third class is *zi-*; the tense prefix and the verb remain the same.

Nyumba sita zimeanguka, six houses have fallen down.

To take one more complicated example, I saw the knife, which you gave him. The personal prefix for the first person is *ni-* or *n-*, the tense prefix of the past perfect is *-ali-*, to see is *ku-ona*, knife is *kisu*, a substantive of the fourth class. As some particular knife is intended we must use the objective prefix, and that for a singular substantive of the fourth class is *-ki-*. As the tense prefix begins with a vowel we must use the personal prefix which ends in a consonant. We have therefore—

Nalikiona kisu = I saw the knife.

'Which you gave him.' The relative referring to a singular noun of the fourth class is *-cho-*. It must follow the tense prefix, which is *-ali-*, as before, for the past perfect. The sign of the second person singular is *u-* or *w-*; the verb, to give to, is *ku-pa*. The object of the verb is *him*, the objective prefix for nouns of the first class is *-mu-* or *-m-*. Putting these together we have,

Which you gave him, *walichompa*.

And the whole sentence,

I saw the knife which you gave him, *nalikiona kisu walichompa*.

It must not be forgotten that *ku-* and *pa-* may be used for *there* in an impersonal sense.

Kulikuwa or *Palikuwa*, there was *or* there were.
Kukapiga, *&c.*, and there struck, &c.

Indicative Tenses.—Present.

There are in the language of Zanzibar two Presents, one Indefinite and one Imperfect.

1. The Indefinite Present answers to our common English present, I come, I love, &c. It is made by prefixing *-a-* to the verb.

N-	*a-penda*	I love.
W-		Thou lovest.
—		He *or* she loves.
W-, Y-, Ch-, L-, W-, P-, Kw-		It loves.
Tw-		We love.
Mw-		You love.
W-		They love.
Y-, Z-, Vy-, Y-, Z-		They love.

2. The Present Imperfect answers to our tense with *am*, I am coming, I am loving, &c. It is made by prefixing *-na-* to the verb.

Ni-	*na-penda*	I am	loving.
U-		Thou art	
A-, U-, I-, Ki-, Li-, U-		He, she,	
Pa-, Ku-		*or* it is	
Tu-		We are	
'M-		You are	
Wa-, I-, Zi-, Vi-, Ya-; Zi-		They are	

In the first person the *ni-* is often contracted into *'n-*, and sometimes altogether omitted. This tense used after another verb may be translated by an English present participle.

Namwona, or *Nalimwona anakuja*, I see him, *or*, I saw him coming.

In the dialect of Mombas this *-na-* tense is used of past time. In Zanzibar it is the more usual form of the present.

Present Perfect.

The Present Perfect is made by the prefix *-me-*: it denotes an action complete at the time of speaking, and therefore answers to the English tense with *have*.

Ni-	*me-penda*	I have	loved.
U-		Thou hast	
A-		He *or* she has	
U-, I-, Ki- *Li-, Pa-, Ku-*		It has	
Tu-		We have	
'M-		You have	
Wa- *I-, Zi-, Vi-* *Ya-*		They have	

In verbs denoting a state or the possession of a quality the present has the meaning of to enter upon, to acquire, or to become, what the verb denotes. The *-me-* tense must then be translated by to have, or to be, &c. (p. 86).

Inajaa, it is getting full.
Imejaa, it is full.
Inapasuka, it is being torn.
Imepasuka, it is torn.
Inapotea, it is becoming lost.
Imepotea, it is lost.
Anavaa, he is putting on.
Amevaa, he has put on, *therefore*, he wears.

When the *-me-* tense occurs in a narrative, it denotes an action complete at the time referred to, and must generally be translated by *had*.

Nikamwona ameufungua mlango, and I saw that he had unfastened the door.

The *-me-* tense may sometimes be translated as a past

participle, signifying a state arrived at at the time of speaking or at the time referred to.

> *Yu hayi ao amekufa?* Is he alive or dead?
> *Zalikuwa zimepotea,* they were lost.

In this sense it may be used to form compound tenses, somewhat as the past participle is in English.

In some dialects of Swahili the prefix is pronounced *-ma-* rather than *-me-*. See the end of *Appendix II.*

Past Perfect.

The Past Perfect tense is made by the prefix *-li-* or *-ali-*: it denotes an action complete in past time. It must sometimes be translated in English by the tense with *had*, but more commonly it represents the indefinite past, which usually ends in *-ed.*

N-, *W-*, —, *W-*, *Y-*, *Ch-*, *L-*, *P-*, *Kw-*, *Tw-*, *Mw-*, *W-*, *Y-*, *Z-*, *Vy-*, *Y-*	*ali-*	*penda*	I, Thou, He *or* she, It, We, You, They	loved.
Ni-, *U-*, *A-*, *U-*, *I-*, *Ki-*, *Li-*, *Pa-*, *Ku-*, *Tu-*, *M-*, *Wa-*, *I-*, *Zi-*, *Vi-*, *Ya-*	*li-*			

When it is intended to denote the action as a

continuous one, the syllable *-ki-* may be inserted after the tense prefix.

> *N-ali-ki-mpenda*, I loved him [not once but continuously].
> *W-ali-papendana*, when they loved one another.
> *W-ali-po-ki-pendana*, while they loved one another.

Narrative Past.

In telling a story it is usual to begin with one verb in the *-li-* tense, and then to put all that follow in a tense made by the prefix *-ka-*. This tense includes in itself the power of the conjunction *and.* It can never properly stand at the beginning of a narrative, but no other past tense can properly be used for any verb except the first. It may occasionally be used after another verb, where the time being indefinite would in English be represented by a present.

<table>
<tr>
<td>Ni-
U-
A-
U-, I-, Ki-
Li-, Pa-, Ku-
Tu-
M-
Wa-
I-, Zi-, Vi-, Ya-</td>
<td>ka-penda</td>
<td>And I
And thou
And he or she
And it
And we
And you
And they</td>
<td>loved.</td>
</tr>
</table>

Nika- is frequently contracted into *Ha-*.

> *Hamwona* = *Nikamwona* = And I saw him.

The *-ka-* of this tense is often pronounced *-ki-* in rapid or careless talking.

FUTURE.

The Future Tense is made by the prefix *-ta-*.

Ni-	*ta-penda*	I shall	love.
U-		Thou wilt	
A-		He *or* she will	
U-, I-, Ki- / *Li-, Pa-, Ku-*		It will	
Tu-		We shall	
M-		You will	
Wa- / *I-, Zi-, Vi-, Ya-*		They will	

In the first person the prefix *Ni-* is often omitted.

Tapenda = *Nitapenda* = I shall love.

When particles of relation are introduced the prefix *-ta-* is very rarely used; the tense prefix stands almost always as *-taka-*.

Atakayekuja, [he] who will come.

With particles of relation the difference between the present, indefinite, and future times is much more carefully observed in Swahili than in English.

Nilalapo, when I sleep, *i.e.*, in the case of my sleeping.
Ninapolala, when I sleep, *i.e.*, at the time when I am sleeping.
Nitakapolala, when I sleep, *i.e.*, when I shall be sleeping.
Mtu aendaye, the man who goes (at any time).
Mtu anayekwenda, the man who is going (now).
Mtu atakayekwenda, the man who goes (at some future time).

Thus, if it is intended to send a man somewhere and pay him afterwards for his trouble, where it might be said in English—Tell the man who goes that I will pay him when he comes back—the Swahili verbs must all be in the future, *Mwambie yule atakayekwenda kwamba atakaporudi nitamlipia.* Where it is the fact and not the time, person, or thing, that is the important element of the idea, it is better not to use the particles of relation, but to employ the *-ki-* tense, which see.

Conditional Tenses.

There are four tenses which may be called Conditional. The first, made with *-ki-*, expresses a state of things as supposed to be existing. The second, made with *-japo-*, expresses a state of things supposed as possible. The other two refer to contingencies; one of them, made with *-nge-* or *-nga-*, expresses what would now be happening, and the contingency on which it would depend regarded as existing; the other, made with *-ngali-*, expresses what would have happened, and the contingency on which it would have depended regarded as no longer existing.

Actual Conditional *or* Participial Tense.

This tense is made with the prefix *-ki-*, and may be translated by the English present participle, or by as, if, when, since, though, or any other words by which the idea of a state of things can be introduced and connected with the rest of the sentence.

Ni-	*ki-penda*	I	loving.
U-		Thou	
A-		He *or* she	
U-, I-, Ki- *Li-, Pa-, Ku-*		It	
Tu-		We	
M-		You	
Wa- *I- Zi- Vi- Ya*		They	

The prefix *Niki-* may be contracted into *Hi-*.

Hifukuza = *Nikifukuza* = As I was driving.

Viewed as a present participle, the *-ki-* tense can be used to form compound tenses, especially a past imperfect.

Alikuwa akiogolea, he was swimming about.

The following are a few examples of the use of this tense :—

Nitafurahi nikikuona, [seeing you I shall rejoice] I shall be glad to see you.

Akija Abdallah mwambia, [Abdallah coming, tell him] Tell Abdallah when he comes.

Nikiwa nacho, [I having it] If I have it—when I have it—if I should have it—in case of my having it—since I have it.

Alipotea akizunguka kwa siku mbili, [He was lost wandering for two days] He lost his way and wandered about for two days.

Majivuno yakiwa mengi, [Puffings up being many] Much self-exaltation.

Upepo ukiwa moto hutanua, [Air being hot] Air expands when it becomes heated.

Akisema kweli, hasadikiwi, [Telling the truth, he is not believed] If he should tell the truth, he would not be believed.

In this instance the use of the *-ki-* tense and of the negative present are both remarkable. It will be seen, however, upon examination, that there is no real contingency in such a sentence as this. It affirms a fact in a state of things, not a contingency upon a supposed state of things; it is not his telling the truth which prevents his being believed.

A corresponding past tense may be made by the *-li-* tense with the relative particle *-po-*.

Walipopenda, when they loved, being that they then loved.

Possible Conditional.

This tense is made by the prefix *-japo-*, and puts a case; it generally implies that the case is an extreme or unlikely one. It may be translated by *even if*.

Ni- *U-* *A-* *U-, I-, Ki-* *Li-, Pa-, Ku-* *Tu-* *M-* *Wa-* *I-, Zi-, Vi-, Ya-*	*japo-penda*, even if	I thou he *or* she it we you they	love.

The prefix seems to be formed from *kuja*, to come, and *-po*, the particle denoting when or where; so that *ujapo* may be translated, When you come, and so with the other persons; this will give the force of the tense.

Wajapokupiga, when they come to beating you, *i.e.*, even if they beat you.

Japo with the personal signs may be used alone in the sense of—even if.

Ujapo hukioni, even if you do not see it.

Present Contingent.

This tense is formed by the prefix *-nge-* or *-nga-*, and puts a condition and its results as present. It necessarily implies that neither are in existence.

Ni- *U-* *A-* *U-, I-, Ki-* *Li-, Pa-, Ku-* *Tu-* *M-* *Wa-* *I-, Zi-, Vi-, Ya-*	*nge-penda*	I should, *or* if I did Thou wouldest, *or* if thou didst He, she, *or* it would, *or* if he, she, *or* it did We should, *or* if we did You would, *or* if you did They would, *or* if they did	love.

The *-nga-* form is used with monosyllabic verbs—*angawa*—though he be, *or* he would be.

The two branches of the contingency cannot in English be represented by the same tense, as they are in Swahili. The pair would stand in English, (1) If I did—(2) I should, &c. (1) If it were—(2) it would be, &c. Or they might stand, (1) Though I did—(2) yet I should, &c.

The second branch is sometimes represented in English by a past tense; sometimes both are.

> *Kama ungekuwa na akili, mali yako ungedumu nayo,* [If you were with wits, your property you would continue with it] If you were a man of understanding, your property would be (or would have been) yours still.

Past Contingent.

This tense is made with the prefix *-ngali-*. It supposes something at a past time, and concludes that something else would then have happened, also at a past time. It represents the English—If this had happened, that would have happened. It supposes that neither condition nor contingency did ever in fact occur. In English a past tense is often used to express a present contingency, but the Swahili seem to distinguish them more carefully.

Ni- *U-* *A-* *U-, I-, Ki-* *Li-, Pa-, Ku-* *Tu-* *M-* *Wa-* *I-, Zi-, Vi-, Ya-*	*ngali-penda*	Had I, *or* I should have Hadst thou, *or* thou wouldest have Had he, she, or it, *or* he, she, or it would have Had we, *or* we should have Had you, *or* you would have Had they, or they would have	loved.

There is always an accent on the personal prefix and none on the tense prefix, thus *úngalikúja*, *ángalióna*, &c.

Kama ungalikuwapo hapa, ndugu yangu angalipona, If you had been here, my brother would have got well.

THE IMPERATIVE.

It has been mentioned above that the simplest form of the verb may be used for the Imperative as in English. The final letter of verbs in *-a* is frequently changed into *e-*. The plural is made by adding *-ni.*

Penda, or *Pende*, love thou.	*Pendani*, or *Pendeni*, love ye.
Twaa, or *Twae*, take thou.	*Twaani*, or *Twaeni*, take ye.
Sifu, praise thou.	*Sifuni*, praise ye.
Fikiri, consider thou.	*Fikirini*, consider ye.

The form ending in *-e* is the more commonly used in Zanzibar. The other persons are supplied by the use of the Subjunctive.

Ka- may be prefixed to the Imperative to connect it with a preceding verb.

Kajificheni, and hide yourselves.

THE SUBJUNCTIVE.

The Subjunctive is made by prefixing the personal sign, and when the verb ends in *-a* changing that letter into *-e*. It may be translated into a variety of English forms. It may be used as an imperative or jussive, and is the only form that can be so used in the first and third persons.

Nipende, let me love.

When used with an interrogative it may be translated —am I to—is he to, &c.

Nifanyeje? What am I to do?

It is the proper form to express purpose or object—that I may, &c.—and must be used in many cases where in English the infinitive is employed.

> *Mwambie akusayidie,* tell him to help you, *or* speak to him that he may help you.

Where no purpose is implied the infinitive is used as in English.

> I want to sleep, *nataka kulala.*

The force of the conjunction *and* may be expressed by inserting *-ka-* after the personal prefix. *And* is used in English in many cases where the second action is more or less the object with which the first is to be done, as in—try and find, &c. In such cases *-ka-* must not be used, but only the subjunctive in its simple form.

<table>
<tr><td>Ni-
U-
A-, U-, I-
Ki-, Li-, Pa-
Ku-
Tu-
M-
Wa-, I-, Zi-
Vi-, Ya-</td><td>pende, That</td><td>I
thou
he or she
it
we
you
they</td><td>may love.</td></tr>
</table>

Verbs which end in *-i*, *-e*, or *-u*, keep the same final letter in the subjunctive.

The Infinitive.

The Infinitive is made in all cases by prefixing *-ku.*

> *Ku-penda,* to love.
> *Ku-ona,* to see.

The *-u-* becomes *-w-* before *a*, *e*, and *i*, and often disappears before *o*.

Kw-ambia, to tell.
Kw-enda, to go.
Kw-isha, to finish.
K-oga, to bathe.

The Infinitive may always be used to express the action denoted by the verb.

Kwenda, going.
Kufa, dying.
Kupendana, mutual loving.

[There are two idiomatic uses of the Infinitive Mood, which are common, and may be mentioned here, the one a logical, the other a grammatical, contrivance.

Any finite form of a verb may be preceded by the infinitive of the same verb, the effect being rather to particularize and give prominence to the idea conveyed by the verb, than to emphasize the mode of an action.

Thus *kufa utakufa*, as to dying, you will die. Dying, that is what will happen to you. Not, you will certainly die.

Again, when any finite form of the verb, and especially a long form, would be closely followed by another verb in the same form, connected with the former verb by (at most) the simple copula '*na*,' the second verb may be put in the infinitive mood. By this device the cumbrous repetition of a series of personal and other prefixes in a number of successive verbs is neatly avoided.

Thus, "*anayeabudiwa na kutukuzwa*," for *anayetukuzwa*, "who is worshipped and glorified."—A. C. M.]

Participles.

There are properly no Participles in Swahili. The present participle in *-ing* may be represented by the *-ana-* tense of an incomplete action, by the *-ki-* tense of a state of continued action, or by the use of the relative.

The man sitting yonder, *mtu akaaye kule.*

The past participle may be represented by the *-me-* tense of a completed action, or by the relative when used adjectivally.

Nimekiona kisu kilichopotea, I have found the lost knife.

The Negative Conjugation.

All Swahili verbs may be employed with negative prefixes to denote the reverse of their affirmative meaning. It must be observed that the negative forms do not simply deny the affirmative forms but rather reverse them.

Napenda kwenda, I like going.
Nataka kwenda, I want to go.
Sipendi kwenda, I dislike going,
Sitaki kwenda, I want not to go.

In English *I do not want* is not so strong as *I do not like,* but in Swahili *sitaki* is stronger than *sipendi.*

The negative tenses are formed by negative personal prefixes, which, except in the first person singular, are made from the affirmative forms by prefixing *ha-*.

For the negative combined with the relative, see p. 120.

Negative Present.

In this tense verbs ending in *-a* change that letter into *-i*; other final letters remain unchanged.

Si- *Hu-* *Ha-, Hau-, Hai-* *Haki-, Hali-, Hapa-* *Haku-* *Hatu-* *Ham-* *Hawa-, Hai-, Hazi-* *Havi-, Haya-*	*pendi*	I Thou He *or* she It We You They	love not *or* do not love.

This tense is a more general negative than the English *do not* tense. It is used for both past and future wherever the negative depends upon some cause which is not affected by the time referred to.

The *-i* of *si-* in this and other tenses often disappears before a vowel.

Sogopi, I do not fear.

Negative Past.

There is one negative form referring to past time generally; it is made by the negative prefixes followed by *-ku-*.

Si- *Hu-* *Ha-, Hau-, Hai-* *Haki-, Hali-* *Hapa-, Haku-* *Hatu-* *Ham-* *Hawa-, Hai-, Hazi-* *Havi-, Haya-*	*ku-penda*	I Thou He *or* she It We You They	did not love *or* have not loved.

In a few rare instances negative prefixes may be followed by *-me-* or *-li-*.

Simekuwa mwongo? Have I not become a liar?

THE *not yet* TENSE.

There is a negative tense made by the use of the negative prefixes followed by *-ja-*, which is a sort of negative present perfect, denying the action up to the time of speaking.

Prefix	Stem	Subject	Meaning
Si-	*ja-penda*	I	have not yet loved.
Hu-		Thou	
Ha-, *Hau-*, *Hai-*		He *or* she	
Haki-, *Hali-*		It	
Hapa-, *Haku-*		We	
Hatu-		You	
Ham-		They	
Hawa-, *Hai-*, *Hazi-*			
Havi-, *Haya-*			

The word *bado* is often used with this tense where it is intended rather to imply that what has not yet happened will some day come to pass.

Hajaja, he is not yet come, he is not come even now.
Hajaja bado, he is not come, at least not yet.

The *-a-* of *-ja-* coalesces with *i* and *e* into a long *-e-* sound.

Hajesha = *Hajaisha* = He has not yet finished.

NEGATIVE FUTURE.

The negative future is made from the affirmative future by merely using negative instead of affirmative personal prefixes.

Si-	*ta-penda*	I shall not	love.
Hu-		Thou wilt not	
Ha-, *Hau-*, *Hai-*		He, she, *or* it will not	
Haki-, *Hali-*		We shall not	
Hapa-, *Haku-*		You will not	
Hatu-		They will not	
Ham-			
Hawa-, *Hai-*, *Hazi-*			
Havi-, *Haya-*			

CONDITIONAL TENSES.

The case of *not being* or *not doing* is put by a tense formed by the affirmative prefixes followed by *-sipo-*; it may be translated by the present participle with a negative, or by as, if, when, though, since, or any other word by which the case of *not being, having,* or *doing,* may be introduced.

Ni-	*sipo-penda*	I	not loving.
U-		Thou	
A-, U-, I-, Ki-		He *or* she	
Li-, Pa-, Ku-		It	
Tu-		We	
M-		You	
Wa-, I-, Zi-, Vi-		They	
Ya			

This tense may be also used to translate an English affirmative preceded by *except* or *unless.*

Asipojua, unless he knows.
Asipokuwa Abdallah, except Abdallah.

CONTINGENT TENSES.

The negative contingent tenses, present and past, are made from the affirmative forms by merely using negative instead of affirmative personal prefixes.

Si-	*nge-penda*	Did I *or* I should	not love
Hu-		Didst thou *or* Thou wouldest	
Ha-. Hau-, Hai- *Haki-, Hali-* *Hapa-, Haku-*		Did he, she, *or* it, *or* He, she, *or* it would	
Hatu-		Did we *or* We should	
Ham-		Did you *or* you would	
Hawa-, Hai-, Hazi- *Havi-, Haya-*		Did they *or* They would	

Si- *Hu-* *Ha-*, *Hau-*, *Hai-* *Haki-*, *Hali-* *Hapa-*, *Haku-* *Hatu-* *Ham-* *Hawa-*, *Hai-* *Hazi-*, *Havi-* *Haya-*	*ngali-penda*	Had I *or* I should have Hadst thou *or* Thou wouldest have Had he, she, *or* it, *or* He, she, *or* it would have Had we *or* We should have Had you *or* You would have Had they *or* They would have	not loved.

Negative Imperative.

The negative imperative is made by the use of *si* (not), with the affirmative forms.

Si penda, love not. *Si pendeni*, love ye not.
Si sifu, praise not. *Si sifuni*, praise ye not.

The negative subjunctive is more often used in this sense than the imperative form.

Negative Subjunctive.

The negative subjunctive is made from the affirmative form by inserting *-si-* between the affirmative personal prefix and the verb.

Ni- *U-* *A-*, *U-*, *I-* *Ki-*, *Li-*, *Pa-*, *Ku-* *Tu-* *M-* *Wa-*, *I-*, *Zi-* *Vi-*, *Ya-*	*si-pende*, That	I may thou mayest he, she, *or* it may we may you may they may	not love.

The *-i* of *-si-* often disappears before a vowel.

asende, that he may not go.

The negative subjunctive may be Englished in several different ways. It may be used as above of a purpose *not to do*, or it may be used of a purpose to do which fails.

Akamtafuta asimwone, he looked for him, but did not see him *or*, without seeing him.

This form is commonly used for the negative imperative.

Nisende, let me not go. *Usende*, don't go.

A form of subjunctive connected with the *not yet* tense is made by the use of *-sije-* with the affirmative prefixes.

<table>
<tr>
<td>Ni-
U-
A-, U-, I-
Ki-, Li-
Pa-, Ku-,
Tu-
M-
Wa-, I-, Zi-
Vi-, Va-</td>
<td>sije-penda, That</td>
<td>I may
thou mayest
he, she, or it may
we may
you may
they may</td>
<td>not have already loved.</td>
</tr>
</table>

This tense may often be translated by *before*.

Utampata asijelala, you will catch him before he goes to sleep.

-sije with the personal prefixes may be used as a complete word followed by the *-ka-* tense.

Nisije nikafa, that I may not be already dead, *or*, that I may not die before, &c.

Negative Infinitive.

The negative infinitive is made by the use of *kutoa* (to put out), often contracted into *kuto-* and used as a prefix.

Kutoa kupenda, or *Kutopenda*, not to love, *or* not loving, to dislike, *or* disliking.

The Passive Voice.

The Passive is made from the Active by merely inserting *-w-* before the final vowel.

Napenda, I love.	*Napendwa*, I am loved.
Sipendi, I do not love.	*Sipendwi*, I am not loved.
Nimependa, I have loved.	*Nimependwa*, I have been loved.
Kupenda, to love.	*Kupendwa*, to be loved.

Verbs ending in two vowels often use the passive of their applied form. See pp. 151, 161.

The Passive is used in a sort of impersonal way to denote what is intended to be done.

Maji yamekwenda kuletwa, some one has gone to get water.
Pesa zimekwenda kuvunjwa, some one has gone to get pice in exchange for silver.

Auxiliary and Irregular Verbs.

As the Auxiliary verbs are mostly also irregular, it will be best to speak of their irregularities first, and afterwards of their use in making compound tenses.

Monosyllabic verbs and most dissyllabic words beginning with a vowel, retain the *ku-* of the infinitive in those tenses in which the tense prefix ends in a syllable incapable of bearing the accent. These tense prefixes are *-na-*, *-ame-*, *-ali-*, *-ta-*, *-japo-*, *-nge-*, *-ngali-*, and *-sije-*. The other prefixes, *-a-*, *-ka-*, *-ki-*, *-nga-*, *-ku-*, *-ja-*, *-si-*, are capable of bearing the accent, and the *ku-* is not retained when they are used. The personal signs, both subjective and objective, can bear the accent, the relative signs cannot.

Thus, from *kuja*, to come, we have :—

Naja, I come.	*Ninakuja*, I am coming.
Nikaja, and I came.	*Nimekuja*, I have come.
Nikija, I coming.	*Nalikuja*, I came.
Siji, I come not.	*Nitakuja*, I shall come.
Sikuja, I did not come.	*Nijapokuja*, even if I come.
Sijaja, I am not yet come.	*Ningekuja*, I should come.
Nisije, let me not come.	*Ningalikuja*, I should have come.
	Nisijekuja, before I come.
Nije, let me not come.	*Nisipokuja*, when I come not.
Ajaye, he who comes.	*Aliyekuja*, he who came.
Nijaye, I who come.	

It is shown that this irregularity depends upon the power of certain syllables to support the accent by the changes which occur when an objective prefix is inserted.

Amekula, he has eaten.
Ame'mla, he has eaten him.

The verb *kupa*, to give to, is peculiar in always requiring an objective prefix, and therefore never having occasion to be irregular.

With dissyllables beginning with a vowel it is generally indifferent whether the *ku-* is retained or not.

Amekwisha or *Ameisha*, he has finished.
Amekwanza or *Ameanza*, he has begun.

Many verbs occur with or without a *w-*, which seems to be a relic of the *-ku-*.

Kuiva or *Kuwiva*, to ripen.
Kuaza or *Kuwaza*, to consider.

The word *kuja*, to come, stands alone in having an irregular imperative.

Njoo, come. *Njooni*, come ye.

Monosyllabic verbs and some dissyllables make their passives in a more or less irregular way. The following is a list of the monosyllabic verbs with their passives:—

Kucha, to fear.	*Kuchwa*, to be feared.
Kula, to eat.	*Kuliwa*, to be eaten.
Kunywa, to drink.	*Kunywewa*, to be drunk.
Kupa, to give to.	*Kupawa* or *Kupewa*, to receive.

Kucha is used in the dialect of Lamoo for to fear, the word used at Zanzibar being *kuogopa*. *Kucha* means at Zanzibar to rise (of the sun), and *kuchwa* (or, in the dialect of Mombas, *kutwa*) means to set. The other monosyllabic verbs, *kufa*, to die, *kuja*, to come, *kunya*, to fall like rain, *kuwa*, to be, being neuters, do not make a passive.

Two dissyllabic verbs make their passive by merely adding *-wa* to the active form.

Kuua, to kill.	*Kuuawa*, to be killed.
Kufua, to beat.	*Kufuawa*, to be beaten.

Verbs ending in two vowels often insert an *-l-* in making their passive. See under Applied Forms, pp. 158–159.

Kuzaa, to bear.	*Kuzawa* or *Kuzaliwa*, to be born
Kukomboa, to ransom.	*Kukombolewa*, to be ransomed.
Kufungua, to open.	*Kufunguliwa*, to be opened.

The origin of this use lies probably in the difficulty of pronouncing distinctly the regular passive forms.

Verbs ending in *-e* make their passive in *-ewa.*

Kusamehe, to pardon. *Kusamehewa,* to be pardoned.

Verbs ending in *-i* make their passives in *-iwa.*

Kukiri, to confess. *Kukiriwa,* to be confessed.

Verbs in *-u* generally make their passive in *-iwa.*

Kuharibu, to destroy. *Kuharibiwa,* to be destroyed.

Where the *-u* is preceded by a vowel the passive is made in *-uliwa.*

Kusahau, to forget. *Kusahauliwa,* to be forgotten.

The verb *kuwa,* to be, has several peculiarities. The Present tense is very seldom used in its regular form. For the Present tense *ni* (or, in the negative, *si*) may be used for all persons and both numbers, or the personal prefix appropriate to the subject of the verb may stand alone. *Ni* is apparently preferred where *being* is the important part of the idea; the personal prefix is used where the being of that particular thing is intended specially to be noticed. *Yu* (not *A*) is used for he or she is.

Si kweli, ni kusifu tu, it is not true, it is only flattery.
Tu tayari, we are ready.

When joined with a relative the regular form has the meaning of *who may be.*

Awaye yote, whoever it be.

Where no stress is intended to be laid on the *being,* the verb to be, when joined with a relative pronoun. is represented by the syllable *-li-*. See Relatives, p. 118. *Li* is used, though but rarely, with the personal signs to form a tense with the meaning—continuing to be. A narative past is also formed with it in the sense of—I have continued to be.

> *Nili hali ya kuwa juu yake*, I being on his back.
> *Nikali nikipotea*, and I go on wandering.

In many cases where the verb *to be* is used in English merely to connect the parts of the sentence it is in Swahili omitted altogether.

Kwa nini weye kutoa kuonekana hizi siku nyingi? why [have] you [been] invisible, *i.e.*, Why have you kept out of sight so long?
Yupi mkuu wao? who [is] their chief?
Nyama ya kifaro ngumu mno, rhinoceros meat [is] very tough.

The Present Perfect has the meaning of *has become*.

> *Manenoye yamekuwa uwongo*, his words are become false.

The Past Perfect must be used to translate *was* and *were*.

> *Nilipokuwa Sultani*, when I was Sultan.

The English *has* or *have been* must be translated by a present.

> *Nipo hapa siku nyingi*, I have been here many days.

The Imperative is used with an *i* prefixed.

> *Iwe*, be thou. *Iweni*, be ye.*

In the negative present and with relatives *si* is used as *ni* and *-li-* are in the affirmative tense. The regular forms are also used, though but rarely.

* The subjunctive forms *uwe, mwe* are commonly preferred in Zanzibar.—A. C. M.

The verb *to be* is used in English sometimes to denote existence viewed as an ultimate fact, sometimes to denote existence in place and time, sometimes to denote existence as the possessor of certain qualities, or the doer or sufferer of certain acts. In Swahili these three uses are distinguished by the employment of different forms.

The simple form of the verb is used only to denote existence as the possessor of qualities, or the doer or sufferer of acts.

Existence merely in place and time, whether the place and time are in English expressed or no, is denoted in Swahili by the addition to the verb of *-po*, *-mo*, or *-ko*, as the case may be. See Relatives, p. 120.

He is at my house, *Yuko kwangu.*
He is here, *Yupo hapa.*
He is in the house, *Yumo nyumbani.*
When he was here, *Alipokuwapo hapa.*
Where are they? *Ziko wapi?*

Existence viewed as a fact in itself is denoted by the addition of *na* to the verb, being the same form as is used for the verb *to have*. *Na* is joined to the personal prefixes to make the present tense, in all other tenses it is treated as a separate word, and has generally the appropriate relative sign suffixed to it.

Kuna mtu, there is a man.
Kulikuwa na mtu, there was a man.
Zinazo, they are.
Zilikuwa nazo, they were.

In Swahili there is properly no verb *to have*. They employ for it *kuwa na*, to be with.

Nina, I have.
Nalikuwa na, I had.
Nitakuwa na, I shall have.
Niwe na, that I may have.

Where the objective prefix would be used with an ordinary verb, the appropriate relative particle must be suffixed to the *na* as well as to the tense prefix.

Ninazo, I have them.
Aliyekuwa nazo, who had them.
Alizokuwa nazo, which he had.

Auxiliary Verbs.

The Verbs used as Auxiliaries are, *kuwa*, to be, *kutoa*, to take out, *kuja*, to come, *kwisha*, to come to an end.

Can is represented by the appropriate tenses of *kuweza*, to be able. *Must* is expressed by *sharti*, of necessity, or by the negative tenses of *kuwa na buddi*, to have an escape from.

Sina buddi, I must.
Asiwe na buddi, that he may be obliged.

After *kuwa na buddi* either the infinitive or subjunctive may be employed.

Ought may be represented by the tenses of *kupasa*, to concern, or, to come to concern. *Should* is expressed in the same way when it implies obligation, and by the contingent tenses when it expresses a contingency.

Imenipasa kwenda, it concerns me to go, *i.e.*, I ought to go.
Imenipasa nisende, it concerns me that I go not, *i.e.*, I ought not to go.

Kupasa is also used as follows :—

Haikunipasa mimi, it is no business of mine.
Imekupasani? What have you to do with it?
Amenipasa mimi, he is a connection of mine.

May and *might* may be represented by *kuweza* where they imply power, by *halali*, lawful, where they imply lawfulness, and by the subjunctive where they imply a purpose.

The use of *kuja* as an auxiliary has been mentioned under the *-japo-*, *-ja-*, and *-sije-* tenses, pp. 138, 145, 148.

Kutoa is used to convey a negation in cases where the regular negative tenses cannot conveniently be used.

With the infinitive it is frequently contracted into *-to-*, and used as a mere formative.

Kutoa kuja, or *Kutokuja*, not to come.
Kutoa kupenda, or *Kutopenda*, not to love.

The meaning of these negative infinitives may be given as, putting out coming, barring coming, coming not happening. A transitive form may be made by the use of *kutosha*, to make to go out.

Kutosha kumwuliza, to exclude asking him.

In many cases *kutoa* may be translated by, to forbear, or, to neglect.

Ametoa kuja, he has neglected coming, he has not come.
Nikitoa kuja, if I forbear from coming, *or*, so long as I do not come.

The negative tenses do not furnish a true present perfect. The past, *hakuja*, is, he did not come; the present, *haji*, implies rather that he never will, that coming is not to be predicated of him at all. The difference between *nisipokuja* and *nikitoa kuja* is represented in English by that between, if I come not, and, while I come not. In all cases the use of *toa* connects the negation with the tense only; the negative tenses imply that the opposite of the verb might be affirmed.

Kwisha may often be translated by already.

Amekwisha kuja, he has already come.
Nimekwisha kula, I have done eating.

It is used to strengthen the present perfect, conveying the meaning that something is not merely done, but fully done and over.

A somewhat similar effect is produced on the present by using *katika kwisha*.

Ni katika kwisha kula, I am finishing eating, I am just leaving off, I have very nearly done.

Kuwa, to be, is used in Swahili very much as it is in English, the *-ki-* and *-me-* tenses of the principal verb being used as present and past participles.

Nili nikienda, I continuing to be going.
Nikali nikienda, and I am still going.
Nikiwa nikienda, I being going, while going.
Nikiwa nimekwenda, I being gone, having gone.
Nikiwa nimekwisha kwenda, having already gone
Nalikuwa nikienda, I was going.
Nalikuwa nimekwenda, I was gone, I had gone.
Nalikuwa nimekwisha kwenda, I had already gone.
Nitakuwa nikienda, I shall be in the act of going.
Nitakuwa nimekwenda, I shall be gone.
Nitakuwa nimekwisha kwenda, I shall have already gone.
Nitakuwa niliokwenda, I shall be who has gone, I shall have gone, I shall have gone to or been at.

Kuwa na, to have, is not used as an auxiliary.

Derivative Verbs.

There are four derivative forms which may be constructed out of any Swahili verb, where in English we must use either another verb or some compound expression.

1. What may be called the applied form is used in cases where in English a preposition would be employed to connect the verb with its object. By the use of this form verbs which have things for their objects may be made to apply to persons.

This form is made by inserting *i* or *e* before the final *-a* of the simple verb. *I* is used when the vowel of the preceding syllable is *a*, *i*, or *u*. *E* is used when the vowel of the preceding syllable is *e* or *o*.

Kufanya, to make.	*Kufanyia*, to make for.
Kuleta, to bring.	*Kuletea*, to bring for.
Kusikitika, to be sorry.	*Kusikitikia*, to be sorry for, to pity
Kuoka, to bake.	*Kuokea*, to bake for.
Kuanguka, to fall down.	*Kuangukia*, to fall down to.

Where the simple verb ends in two vowels the suppressed *l* appears in the applied form.

Kuzaa, to bear.	*Kuzalia*, to bear to.
Kukwea, to climb.	*Kukwelea*, to climb for.
Kusikia, to hear.	*Kusikilia*, to listen to.
Kukomboa, to redeem.	*Kukombolea*, to redeem for.
Kununua, to buy.	*Kununulia*, to buy for.

The following is a list of the monosyllabic verbs with their applied forms:—

Kucha, to fear.	*Kuchelea*, to fear for.
Kufa, to die.	*Kufia*, to die to.
Kuja, to come.	*Kujia*, to come to.
Kula, to eat.	*Kulia*, to eat with.
Kunya, to fall (like rain).	*Kunyea*, to fall upon.
Kunywa, to drink.	*Kunywea*, to drink with.
Kuwa, to be.	*Kuwia*, to be to.

Kuza, to sell, makes *Kuliza*, to sell to.

Kupa, to give to, having already an applied meaning, has no applied form. There is a difficulty in expressing what would have been the meaning of the simple form. *Kutoa* is used for to give, in the sense of parting with. Such expressions as, which was given you, must be rendered by a change of person—*uliopewa*, which you had given to you, or, which you received. Which he gave me, is very commonly rendered *niliopewa naye*.

Verbs ending in *-i* and *-u* make their applied forms in *-ia*.

Kufasiri, to explain.	*Kufasiria*, to explain to.
Kuharibu, to destroy.	*Kuharibia*, to destroy for.

The great paucity of prepositions in Swahili brings the applied forms of verbs into constant use. The only difficulty in their application lies in the exact discrimination of the meaning of the simple word. Many Swahili verbs imply in their simple form what can only be expressed in English by the use of a preposition. Whenever a really good dictionary shall have been compiled it will supply all the necessary information. The applied form may be rendered by inserting any preposition which will suit the context. Thus, *kushuhudia* is, to bear witness about, for, or against, as the case may be, and *kunenea*, which means to speak about, may have to be translated by, to recommend, or to decry, to scold, or to describe. The simple word *nena* has in itself the force of to mention, so that it is not necessary to use the applied form as a translation of to speak of, where it means no more than to mention.

Sometimes the shape of the word will be a useful

reminder to foreigners of its exact meaning; thus, *kupotea*, which may be roughly translated *to lose*, is in the shape of an applied form, and really is one, its exact meaning being, to become lost to. If, therefore, we want to say, I have lost my knife, the construction must be altered into, my knife has become lost to me (*kisu changu kimenipotea*), the subject and object having to change places.

Where in English a preposition connected with the verb can stand by itself at the end of the sentence, the applied form must be used in Swahili.

A knife to cut with, *kisu cha kukatia.*
Stones to grind wheat with, *mawe ye kusagia ngano.*
A place to come out at, *mahali pa kutokea.*
A bag to put money in, *mfuko wa kutilia fetha.*

In these sentences the use of the possessive particle -*a* for the English *to*, denoting a purpose or employment, must be observed and remembered. This particle turns what follows into a sort of adjective in this, as in all other cases in which it is followed by a word which is capable of denoting a quality. It is somewhat like the English expressions, *a man of sense, a building of great solidity, &c.*

When an applied form is followed by *mbali* it conveys the idea that as a consequence of the action denoted by the simple verb something is put out of the way, or got rid of.

Afile, or *Afie mbali*, that he may die out of our way.
Tumwulie mbali, let us kill him and done with it.
Potelea mbali, perish out of my way = go and be hanged.

The passive of the applied form has a meaning which

it requires some attention to remember and apply rightly, though it is strictly according to the rule that the object of the active becomes the subject of the passive voice.

Kuletea, to bring to.	*Kuletewa*, to have brought to one.
Kufanyia, to make for.	*Kufanyiwa*, to have made for one.

It is often difficult in English to express this passive without using an altogether different word. What suggests itself at first to an English ear, that the passive of *to bring to* would be *to be brought to*, is wrong, and must be carefully avoided. Sometimes a change of prepositions will suffice to render the passive correctly; *kupa* may be translated *to present to*, and then *kupewa* is not *to be presented to*, but *to be presented with.*

Passives made in *-liwa* and *-lewa* are used as the passives of both the simple and the applied form. *Kufunguliwa* may be used as the passive of *kufungua*, meaning, to be unfastened, or as the passive of *kufungulia*, meaning then, to have unfastened for one. It can never mean, to be unfastened for. If it is necessary to express a passive in that form it must be done by changing the construction.

A cry was made at him, *alipigiwa ukelele* [he had made at him a cry].

The door was opened for him, *alifunguliwa mlango* [he had opened for him the door].

2. The Causative form is made by changing the final *-a* into *-sha* or *-za.*

Kupungua, to grow less.	*Kupunguza*, to make to grow less.
Kuzidi, to grow greater.	*Kuzidisha*, to make greater.

When the final *-a* is preceded by a consonant the general rule is to use the applied form as the basis of the causative.

Kupenda, to like.	*Kupendeza*, to please.
Kufanya, to make.	*Kufanyiza*, to cause to make.
Kupanda, to go up.	*Kupandisha*, to make to go up.

Verbs which end in the simple form in *-ta* end in the causative form in *-sa*.

Kutakata, to be clean.	*Kutakasa*, to make clean.

Verbs which end in *-ka* may be turned into causatives by changing *-ka* into *-sha*.

Kuwaka, to be on fire.	*Kuwasha*, to set on fire.
Kulainika, to be soft.	*Kulainisha*, to make soft.
Kutoka, to go out.	*Kutosha*, to make to go out.
Kushuka, to go down.	*Kushusha*, to let down.

The causatives of verbs ending in *-e*, *-i*, or *-u* are constructed on the applied form.

Kukaribu, to come near.	*Kukaribisha*, to make to come near.

3. The Neuter, or quasi passive form is made by changing the final *-a* into *-ka*.

Kufungua, to unfasten.	*Kufunguka*, to be unfastened.
Kuokoa, to save.	*Kuokoka*, to be saved.

Where the final *-a* is preceded by a consonant the neuter is constructed from the applied form.

Kuvunja, to break.	*Kuvunjika*, to be broken.
Kukata, to cut.	*Kukatika*, to be cut.

Causatives in *-sha* may be turned into neuters by changing *-sha* into *-ka*.

Kustusha, to startle. *Kustuka*, to be startled.

Verbs in *-e*, *-i*, and *-u*, construct their neuters on the applied forms.

Kusamehe, to forgive. *Kusameheka*, to be forgiven.
Kufasiri, to explain. *Kufasirika*, to be explained..
Kuharibu, to destroy. *Kuharibika*, to be destroyed.

The *-ka* form is used (like the English passive) to denote what is generally done or doable.

Kulika, to be eaton, or, to be eatable.

4. Reciprocal forms are made by changing *-a* into *-ana*.

Kupenda, to lovo. *Kupendana*, to lovo one another.
Kupiga, to beat. *Kupigana*, to beat one another, to fight.

Verbs in *-e*, *-i*, and *-u* construct their reciprocals upon the applied forms.

Kukaribu, to come near. *Kukaribiana*, to como near to one another.

The reciprocal form of the *-ka* form may be translated by to be to be, &c.

Kupatikana, to be to be got.
Kujulikana, to be to be known, to be knowable
Kuoekana, to be to be seen, to be visible.

The derived forms are conjugated and treated in every way as though they were original words, and other derived forms may be made from them to any extent that may be required.

The applied form of an applied form generally signifies to do a thing to or for a person for a purpose.

Doubling the verb gives an idea of thoroughness.

Kukata, to cut.	*Kukatakata*, to cut up.
Kutafuta, to seek.	*Kutafutatafuta*, to seek all about.
Kuchafuka, to be in a mess.	*Kuchafukachafuka*, to be all in a mess.
Kupasuka, to be torn.	*Kupasukapasuka*, to be torn to shreds.
Kukatika, to be cut.	*Kukatikakatika*, to be all cut about.

LIST OF VERBS.

As it is necessary to put *to* before the English Verb to make the Infinitive, so it is necessary to prefix *ku-* to make the Infinitive in Swahili. Before Monosyllabic Verbs the *ku-* bears the accent, and is retained in several of the tenses. See p. 149.

A.

Abase, thili.
Abhor, chukia.
be Able, weza.
Abolish, batili, tangua, ondosha.
Abound with, jaa.
Absorb, nwa, *pass.* nwewa.
Abstain from, epuka, epushwa (*to be kept from*).
Abuse (*by words*), tukana.
Accept, kubali, takabali, pokea (*receive*).
be acceptable or *accepted*, kubalika.
Accompany, fuatana na, andamana.
(*part of the way*), sindikiza, adi.
Accuse, tuhumu, shtaki.
Accustom, zoeza.
become accustomed, zoea.
Ache, uma.
My head aches, kitwa chauma *or* kinaniuma.
Acknowledge, ungama, kubali, kiri.
Acquiesce, nyamaa, rithia.
Acquit, acha.
be acquitted, toka.
Act, tenda.
Adapt, fanya.
Add to, ongeza, zidisha.
Add up, jumlisha.
Adjoin, tangamana.
Adjourn, akirisha.
stand over, akiri.
be Adjudged, fetiwa.
Adjure, apisha.
Admire, penda.
I admire him, amenipendeza.
Admit, ingiza, acha kuingia.
Adorn, pamba.
Adorn oneself, fanya uzuri.
Adulterate, ghoshi.
commit Adultery, zini, zinga.
Advance, endelea mbele.
Advance money to a trader, kopesha.
be Adverse, gomba, teta.
Advise, pa shauri.
Adze, chonga.
Affect to be, jifanya, jiona.
Afflict, tesa.
be Afraid, ogopa, cha (A.).
Agitate, sukasuka.

Agree (*come to an agreement*), patana, afikana, tuliliana, lekezanya, tuzanya (A.).
(*be mutually satisfied*), rathiana.
(*be alike*), elekea, lingana.
Aim, twaa shabaha.
Alarm, ogofisha, ogofya, tisha.
be alarmed [kú-]wa na khofu, ingiwa na khofu.
Alienate, farakisha.
be alienated, farakana.
Allege a defect in, umbua.
Allot amongst many, awaza.
Allow, acha, pa ruksa, ruhusu.
Alter, (*neut.*) badili, badilika, geuka.
(*act.*) geuza, badili.
Amaze, ajaabisha.
be amazed, toshea.
Amend, fanyiza, tengeneza.
(*of a person reforming*), tulia.
Amuse, zumgumza.
Anchor, tia nanga.
Anger, tia hasira, ghathabisha.
be Angry, [kú-]wa na hasira, ghathabika.
be Angular, [kú-]wa na pembepembe.
Announce, hubiri.
Annoy, sumbua, sumbusha, taabisha, hatiki (A.).
Annul, tangua, batili, ghairi.
be Annulled, tanguka.
Answer, jibu.
Answer when called, itika, itikia.
Anticipate for, onea.
be Anxious, taharuki, taabika.
make Anxious, taharakisha, taabisha.
Apostatize (*become an infidel*), kufuru.
Appear, onekana (*become visible*), tokea (*come out to*).
Apply oneself to, tenda.
Appoint, nasibu, aini, chagua *or* teua (*select*).
Approach, karibia, jongea.
Approach one another, karibiana.
Bring near, jongeza, karibisha.
Approve, kubali, penda, rathi.
Argue, jadiliana, shindana (*dispute together*).
Arise, ondoka.
Arm, pa selaha.
Arm oneself, twaa selaha.
Arrange, panga, andika, pangisha, ratibu, fanya.
be Arrogant, ghurika.
Arrive, fika, wasili.
arrive at one's destination, koma.
make to arrive, fikisha, wasilisha.
reach a person, fikia, wasilia.
Ascend, paa, kwea, panda.
Ascertain, bakiki, uyuzi.
be ascertained, kinika.
be Ashamed, ona haya, tahayari.
make ashamed, tia haya, tahayarisha.
Ask, uliza, uza, saili.
Ask for, taka.
Make inquiries on behalf of anyone, ulizia, uuzia, sailia.
Ask how one does, uliza hali.
Ask in marriage, posa.
Assemble, (*act.*) kusanya, kutanisha.
(*neut.*) kutana, kusanyika, kusanyana.
Assent, kubali, itikiza, afikana, rathiana.
Assert, sema.
He asserts that he saw a ship, kamma aliona jahasi.
He asserts that he walked on the water, kamma alikwenda mtoni kwa mguu.

Astonish, ajabisha, taajabisha.
be astonished, toshea, shangaa, taajabika, toshewa, staajabu.
Astound, shangaza.
Atone for, setiri.
Attach, gandamia, gandamiza, ambisa.
be attached, ambatana (*of things*), ambisana (*of people*).
Attack, shambulia.
Attack people wantonly, [kú-]wa na jeuri.
Attend (*wait upon*), ngojea, fuata.
Attend to, sikia, pulika (A.), sikilia.
not to attend, ghafalika.
refuse to attend, jipurukusha.
be Audible, sikiliana, sikizana.
Avail, faa.
Avoid, epuka.
get out of the way of, epa.
be avoidable, epeka, epukika.
Avow, kubali.
Awake (*neut.*), amka.
waken (*act.*), amsha.

B.

Backbite, chongeleza.
Betray, khini.
Bake, oka.
(*pottery*), tomea, chomea.
Bale out water, vuta maji, teka maji.
Banish, fukuza (*drive away*), ondosha (*make to go away*), hamisha *or* tamisha (M.) *or* gurisha (A.). (*to make to remove*).
Bar (*a door*), pingia.
Bargain, fanya ubazazi.
Bark (*like a dog*), lia.
Barter, badili, awithi.
Batter (*bruise*), chubuachubua.
be battered (*like an old copper pot*), chubukachubuka.
Bathe, oga.
Be, wa. *See Irregular Verbs*, p. 152.
(*to stay*), kaa.
be on one's guard, [kú-]wa na hathari.
be off one's guard, taghafali.
Bear (*fruit, children, &c.*), zaa, vyaa.
(*carry*), chukua, himili.
(*tolerate*), vumilia, stahimili.
bear with another person, chukuliana.
Bear with me, niwie rathi.
bear witness, shuhudu.
about, for or against, shuhudia.
Beat, piga, puta, menya (Kiyao).
Beat up together, funda.
Beat to pieces, ponda.
Beat a roof or floor, pigilia.
be well beaten, putika.
be beaten upon (*as a wreck by the waves*), fuawa.
See Conquer, Thresh.
Beckon to, pungia nguo.
The usual sign to beckon a person to come is to wave a cloth up and down.
Become (*be fitting*), sulihi.
Nimekuwa, *I am become.*
Simekuwa, *am I not become.*
The act of becoming is generally expressed by the present tense of the verb expressing the being in the state or possessing the quality.
Become a fool, pumbazika.
Beg, omba, bembeleza.
(*entreat*), sihi, nasihi.
I beg of you, tafáthal.
Beget, zaa.

Begin, anza.
Begin upon, anziliza.
Begin a work, maliki.
Behave, tenda.
Behave well, tenda vema.
Behave ill. tenda vibaya.
Behave like an invalid, jigonjweza.
Belch, ongulia.
Belch out, kokomoka.
Believe, sadiki.
Believe in, amini.
Bend, (*act.*) pinda, (*neut.*) pindana.
Bend round, (*act.*) peta, (*neut.*) petana, petemana.
Bend down,(*act.*) inamisha, (*neut.*) inama.
Benumb, faganza.
Bequeath, wasia, achia.
Besiege, husuru (Ar.).
Bet, shindania.
Beware, angalia, [kú-]wa na hathari.
Bewilder, tekea.
Bewitch, fanyia uchawi, loga (Mer.).
Bicker, papuriana.
Bid. See Command.
Make a first bid, risimu.
Bind, funga.
Bind books, jelidi.
Bind oneself, fanya sharti.
Bind round (*as when a stick is sprung*), ganga.
Bite, uma.
Blab, payuka.
Blame, laumu, tia hatiyani, nenae (*scold*), patiliza (*visit upon*), karipia (*call out at*).
Blaze, waka.
Bleed, toka damu.
(*copiously*), churuzika damu, tuza damu (M.).
Bless, bariki (*see Copulate*), barikia, jalia.
Blind, povua.
become blind, povuka.
Block, kingamisha, pinga.
Blossom, toa maua (*put forth flowers*), funuka (*to open*).
Blow (*as the wind*), vuma, vuvia.
(*with the mouth*), puzia, puliza.
(*a horn, &c.*), piga zomari, &c.
(*the nose*), futa kamasi.
(*bellows*), vukuta.
Blow away, peperusha.
Blunder, kosa.
Blunt.
The knife is blunt, kisu hakipati, kisu ni kivivu (A.).
Blurt out, kokomoka.
Blush, geuka (*change colour*).
put to the blush, hizika.
Boast, jisifu, jigamba, tamba.
Boil (*bubble up*), che'mka, tutuma.
cook by boiling, tokosa.
be cooked by boiling, tokota.
be well boiled, tokoseka.
boil over, furika.
Bore through, zua, pekecha (*used also of boring with talk*).
with an awl, didimikia.
Border, pakana.
be Born, zawa, vyawa, zaliwa, vyaliwa, pathiwa.
Borrow, azimwa, kirithi.
Bother, sumbua, hatika (A.).
Bow, (*act.*) inamisha, (*neut.*) inama.
Box the ears, piga kofi.
Braise, kaanga.
Bray (*like an ass*), lia
pound in a mortar, ponda.
clean corn by pounding, twanga.
Break, vunja, vunda (M.), (*neut.*) vunjika, katika.

[*Break*] *through*, tobea.
into fragments, setaseta.
by bending, ekua.
to be sprung, ekuka.
off the cobs of Indian corn, goboa, konyoa.
down the branches of a tree, kwanua, *pass.* kwanyuka.
wind, jamba, ongulia.
Breathe, pumua, puzia, tanafusi.
inspire, paaza, pumzi.
expire, shusha pumzi.
hard, koketa roho, tweta (*pant*).
breathe oneself (*rest*), pumzika.
Breed, zaa, lia (M.).
be Brilliant, ng'ara.
Bring, leta.
to or for, letea.
Bring up, lea.
Bring together, pambana.
Bring near, jongeza.
Bring to an agreement, patanisha.
Bring to life again, fufua, huisha.
Bring another! Na ije ngine!
Brighten (*act.*), katua.
be bright, katuka (*polished*), ng'ara (*glistening*).
Bruise, chubua.
be bruised, chubuka.
(*batter*), chubuachubua.
Brush (*clean*), sugua.
Brush off, epua.
Bubble up, che'mka, tutuma.
Bud, chupuza (*spring*), chanua (*put forth leaves*), mea (*grow*).
Build, jenga.
in stone, aka.
to point by putting in small stones, tomea.
(*ships*), unda.
Bully, onea.
be a Burden to, lemea.
Burn, waka (*to be on fire*), teketea (*to be consumed*), washa (*to set on fire*), teketeza (*to consume*), choma *or* chomea (*to apply fire to*), onguza (*to produce a feeling of burning, to scorch*).
Burrow, fukuafukua.
Burst, pasuka, tumbuka.
Burst out, bubujika.
Burst into tears, bubujika machozi.
Bury, zika.
Buy, nunua, zabuni.
Purchase for, nunulia.
Buy back, kemboa.
Buzz, like a bee, vuma.

C.

Cackle, like a hen, tetea.
Call, ita, nena, taja (*name*), amkua (*invite*), lingana (A.).
Call out to, pigia ukelele, pigia ukemi (Mcr.).
Call for help, piga yowe.
Call to prayers, athini.
become Callous, faganza.
Calm, tuliza.
be very calm, zizima.
Can (kuweza, *to be able*).
Siwezi, *I cannot.*
Naweza, *I can.*
Canter (*of a horse*), kwenka kwa mghad; (*of a donkey*) kwenda kwa *thelth*.
Capitulate, selimu, sellim.
Care (*take care*), angalia [kú-]wa na hathari.
take care of, tunza.
consider, waza, tafakari.
be careless, [kú]wa mzembe.
I don't care, haithuru, mamoja pia.

Carry, chukua.
for, chukulia.
on a pole over the shoulder, chukua mpikoni.
on the head or shoulders, pagaa.
a child on the back, beba.
astride on the hip or back, eleka.
in front or on the lap, pakata.
in a bundle or faggot, titika.
off as spoil, teka.
as cargo, pakia.
on freight, takabathi.
Carve wood, &c., kata nakshi.
chora (*adorn with carving*).
be carved, nakishiwa.
Cast, tupa.
upon or at, tupia.
a glance, tupa nathiri.
one's eyes, tupa macho.
(*in a mould*), ita.
off all shame, jipujua.
cast lots, piga *or* fanya kura.
Castrate, hasi.
Catch, daka, nyaka.
in a trap, nasa, tega.
fish, vua samaki.
put something to catch rain-water, kinga mvua.
(*see one who thinks himself unseen*), fathehi, gundua.
be in time to meet with, diriki.
Caulk, kalafati.
Cave in, pomoka.
Cease, koma.
make to cease, komesha.
talking, nyamaza.
(*of pain*), nyamaza.
Cense, fukiza (uudi, &c.).
be Certain about, kinika, tasawari.
Change, (*act.*) geusha, geuza, badili, badilisha, (*neut.*) geuka, badilika.
be changeable, badilibadili, badilika.
change one's mind about, ghairi.
change (a piece of money), vunja.
Charge (direct), agiza, sisitiza (M.).
Chase, winda, winga.
away, fukuza.
Chastise, athibu.
Chatter, puza.
(*of the teeth*), tetemeka.
Cheapen, rakhisisha.
Cheat, danganya, hadaa, ghusubu.
be cheated, danganyika, hadaika.
Cheer, ondolea, huzuni.
Chew, tafuna.
Chirrup (as to a bird), fionya. Both word and thing are used in Zanzibar to express contempt.
Choke (throttle), kaba, sama.
choke oneself with drink or spittle, palia na mate, &c., &c.
irritate the throat, kereketa.
Choose, chagua, teua, khitari, penda, toa (*send*).
as you choose, ikhtiari yako, upendavyo.
Chop, chanja (*cut up*), chinja *or* (M.) tinda (*cut*), tema (*slash*), chonga *or* tonga (*cut to a point*), katakata (*chop up small*).
Circulate (intelligence), tangaza.
Circumcise, tahiri.
Claim, dai.
Clap the hands, piga makofi.
Clasp in the hand, shikana, kamata.
in the arms, kumbatia, kumbatiana.
Claw, papura.
Clean, takasa, fanya safi, safisha.
be clean, takata, safika, takasika.
clean corn by pounding, twanga.
clean a second time, pwaya.

[*Clean*] *be quite clear of husks and dirt*, pwayika.
cotton, cloves, &c., chambua.
cocoa-nuts from the husk, fua.
by scraping, paa.
cleanse by ceremonial ablutions, tohara.
clean out from within a shell, komba.
clean out a man (get all his money), komba.
be cleaned out (lose all one's money), kombeka.
Cleanse. See Clean.
Clear. See Clean.
the sky is clear, uwingu umetakata.
(*make clear or plain*), eleza, yuza, fafanua, fafanulia.
(*be clear*), elea, fafanuka, fafanukia.
ground in a forest, fieka mwitu.
Cleave, (*split*), pasua, chenga.
cleave to, gandama, ambatana.
Click, alika, (*act.*) alisha.
Climb, panda, kwea.
a tree, paraga.
Cling, ambata.
together, guiana, ambatana, fungamana, shikamana.
Clip, kata.
Close the eyes, &c., fumba.
the fist, fumbata.
a door, shindika.
a book, funika.
Clothe, vika.
Coagulate, gandamana.
Coax into, shawishi.
Cock (a gun), panza mtambo.
Coddle, engaenga.
Cohabit with, ingiliza.
Cold. See Cool.
be very cold, zizima.
I have a cold in the head, siwezi kamasi.
Collect, kusanya, jamaa, (*neut.*) kusanyika, kutana.
Comb, chana, chania.
Come, ja, *imp.* njoo, *pl.* njooni.
by, for, to, &c., jia.
to a person on a business, jilia.
(*arrive*), fika, wasili.
out, toka.
in, ingia.
upon (meet with), kuta.
near, karibu, karibia, jongea, fikilia.
Come near! or *Come in!* Karib!
Come no further! Koma usije!
close to, wasili, wasilia.
together. See Assemble.
to life again, fufuka, hui, huika.
to an end, isha, koma, tekeza.
be fully come (of time), wadia.
come to light, fumuka, fumbuka.
come to nothing (of plants, fruit, &c.), fifia, pooza.
come apart, katika.
come out in a rash, tutuka, tutumka, tutusika.
Comfort, fariji, tulizia roho (*calm the soul*), ondolea huzuni (*take away grief*).
Phrases used by way of comforting:—
Shukuru Muungu, *thank God.*
Hemdi Muungu, *praise God.*
Itoe huzuni, *put away sorrow.*
Usiwe na huzuni, *don't grieve.*
be comforted, farajika, shukuru Muungu, pendezewa, tawakali (*trust in God and take courage*).
be Comfortable, tengenea.
I cannot be comfortable in the house, nyumba hainiweki.

Command, a'mru, ambia (*tell*), [amrisha.
Commission, agiza.
Commit. *See Adultery*.
Compare, angalia kwamba ni sawa, pambanisha (*bring together*), pambanua (*distinguish*), linganisha (*match*), fafanisha (*make like*).
Compel, juburu, lazimisha.
Complete, timiza, timiliza, khatimisha, maliza (*finish*).
complete one's education, hitimu.
be complete, timia, timilia, isha (*end*).
Comprehend. *See Understand*.
jua (*know*).
kutana (*take in*).
be comprehended in, ingia.
Conceal, setiri, ficha.
be concealed, stirika.
Concern, pasa.
Conciliate, patanisha.
Condemn, laani (*damn*).
Amefetiwa kuuawa, *he was adjudged to be killed*.
Imempasa kuuawa, *he ought to be killed*.
Condescend, nenyekea.
Condole, hana (*join in a formal mourning*).
Conduct, peleka, leta, chukua.
Confess, kiri, ungama, lalama.
be Confident, tumaini.
have confidence, staamani.
Confide in, amini, tumania.
Confound, changanya (*mix*), batili (*annul*).
be in Confusion, fathaika (*of persons*), chafuka (*of things*).
Confuse, changanisha.,
put into confusion, fathebi.
become confused, fathaika.
Congeal, gandamana.
Congratulate, furahisha, shangilia.
Connect, fungamana (*tie together*), ungana, ungamana.
Conquer, shinda.
Consecrate, fanya wakf.
Consent, kubali, rithia, penda, rathiana.
Consider, fikiri, tafakari, waza.
Console (*see Comfort*), tuliza, tulizia roho.
Conspire, wafikana.
Construct, jenga, jenzi.
Consult, taka shauri (*ask advice*), fanya shauri (*consult together*).
Consume, la, teketeza (*by fire*).
be consumed, isha, lika, teketea (*by fire*).
Contain, chukua (*contain as a bag does rice*).
be contained in, ingia, [ku-]wamo, 'mna (*it is contained in it*).
Contend with, shindana na, husumu.
Content, rithika.
be content, [kú-]wa rathi, kinayi.
Continue, dumu, kaa, shinda (*stay at work*, *&c.*).
make to continue, dumisha.
Contract, punguza (*lessen*), fupiza (*shorten*), fanya ndogo (*make small*), kaza (*press together*).
Contract, fanya sharti (*make a contract*), fanya ubazazi (*make a bargain*).
Contradict, kanya wasa.
Control, at*h*abitisha, zuia.
Converse, zungumza.
Convert, geuza, fanya.
Mwenyiezi Muungu amemwongoa, *God has turned him from his evil way*.
to be converted, ongoka.

Convince, *th*ubutisha, tumainisha.
become convinced, tumaini.
Cook, pika, andaa.
cook with fat, kaanga.
cook without fat, oka.
cook muhogo cut into small pieces, pwaza.
to become cooked enough, iva.
Cool, (*neut.*) poa, poroa, (*act.*) poza (*to cool by pouring backward and forward*), zimua (*cool hot water by pouring in cold*).
Copulate, jami, tomba (*vulgar*).
for the first time, bariki.
Copy, nakili, fanya nakl.
copy from, twaa ya.
Correct, sahihi, sahihisha, rudi.
Correspond (*write to one another*), andikiana.
Corrupt, haribu.
go bad, oza, haribika.
Cost, wakifu, simama.
cost to, wakifia, simamia.
Cough, kohoa.
Count, hesabu, wanga (Mer.), hazibu.
Cover, funika, setiri.
as with a flood, funizika.
cover, with leaves, put into embers, &c.), vumbika.
be covered, stirika.
Covet, tamani.
Crack, tia ufa.
as the earth does in dry weather, atuka.
become cracked, ufa.
Crash, fanya kishindo.
Crawl, tambaa.
be Crazy, zulu.
Crease, kunjia.
be creased, kunjika.
Create, umba.
be created, hulukiwa.

Creep, tambaa.
Crinkle up, finyana.
be Crooked, potoka, komboka.
Cross (*lie across*). pandana.
(*cross a river*), vuka, kwenda ng'ambo ya pili.
(*cross a room*), kwenda upande wa pili.
get cross, vuna.
be cross at having anything to do, kimwa.
Crow, wika.
Crucify, sulibi, sulibisha.
Cruize, vinjari.
Crumble, (*act.*) fikicha, (*neut.*) fujika.
Crush, seta, ponda.
crush and bruise one another, pondekana.
crush up, setaseta.
crush in, (*act.*) bonyesha, (*neut.*) bonyeka.
Cry, lia.
cry about, lilia.
cry out at, pigia, ukelele, karipia.
cry for help, piga yowe.
cry for mercy, lalama.
Cultivate, lima.
Cup, umika.
Curdle, gandamana.
curdled milk, maziwa mabivu.
Cure, ponya, poza, ponyesha.
make better, fanya ashekali.
be cured, poa, pona.
cure fish, &c., ng'onda.
Curse, laani, tukana.
Cut, kata.
cut obliquely, kata hanamu.
cut for, cut out for, katia.
cut up, chanja, chenga.
cut to shreds, pasukapasuka.
be cut off from one another, tindikiana.

D.

Dab, chachaga.
Damage, haribu.
Damn, laani, laanisha.
Dance, cheza.
dance for joy, randa.
Dare, *th*ubutu, weza, jasirisha.
Darken, tia giza.
Darn, tililia.
Dash, chupia.
Daub, paka.
Dawn.
kuna kweupe, *to be grey dawn*.
pambazuka *or* pambauka, *become light*.
Dazzle, choma.
the eyes are dazzled, macho yamefanya kiwi.
Deal in (*trade in*), fanya biashara ya, &c.
Deal cards, gawa karata.
Decay, haribika, oza.
Decease, fariki.
Deceive, danganya, padaa.
deceive by promises, ongofya.
be deceived, hadaika.
Decide, kata maneno.
Deck out, hamba.
Declare, thihirisha, yuza.
Decoy, patia *or* twalia kwa cherevu.
Decrease, pungua, punguza, punguka.
Dedicate, fanya *or* wekea wakf.
Defeat, vunja, kimbiza (*put to flight*).
to be defeated, vunjika, kimbia.
Defend, linda.
guard oneself, kinga.
Deflower, bikiri, vunja ungo.
Defraud, thalimu.
Deign, kubali, nenyekea.
Delay, (*neut.*) kawia, kawa, fawiti. (*act.*) weka, kawisha.
be Delirious, papayuka.
Deliver, okoa, vua, toa.
be delivered, vuka, okoka.
Demand, taka.
demand in marriage, posa.
Demolish, vunja, haribu.
Deny, kana, kanisha.
deny to a person, nyima, hini. (*refuse*), kataa.
deny all credence to, katalia.
Depart, ondoka, toka, enda zangu, zako, &c.
Depart from me! Ondoka mbele yangu!
depart from (*be alienated from*), farakana.
Depend upon, [kú-]wa na.
Kunaye, *depending upon him*.
fungamana na, *be connected with*.
fuata, *be a dependant*.
tungikwa, *hang from*.
Depose, uzulu, uzulia.
Depreciate (*act.*), khashifu, umbua.
Deprive of, twalia.
Deride, cheka, chekea, kufuru, fanyizia mzaha.
Descend, shuka.
Describe, andika, fafanulia (*by likening*), pambanulia (*by distinguishing*.
Desert, acha, hujuru.
Deserve, stahili.
deserve well of, fathili.
Desire, taka, ipa, tamani (*long for*), penda (*like*).
Desolate, vunja, haribu.
Despair, kata tamaa.
Despise, tweza, tharau (*pass.* tharauliwa), hakirisha.
Destroy, haribu, vunja.
be destroyed, haribika, vunjika.

Detain, kawisha, weka.
Deter, kataza, zuia.
Determine, yakinia, ázimu, kaza.
determine a matter, kata maneno.
Devise, fanya shauri.
Die, fa,' fakiri, ondoka katika ulimwengu, toweka (A.), tekeza.
make to die, fisha.
lose by death, fiwa na.
Dig, chimba.
dig out or *away*, chimbua.
fukua, *cut a small hole fit to receive a post.*
Dignify, tukuza.
become dignified, or be raised to dignity, tukuka.
Dilute, tia maji.
Dim, tia giza.
Diminish, (*neut.*) pungua, punguka, tilifika, (*act.*), punguza, tilifisha.
Dip, chovya.
dip and leave in, chovcka.
Direct, agiza (*commission*), ambia (*tell*), amuru (*order*), fundisha (*instruct*), vusha (*put into the right way*).
Disagree, gombana, tetana.
Disappear, toweka.
(*as a scar, &c.*), fifia.
Disarrange, chafua.
Discharge from an obligation, feleti.
Discover, vumbua.
Discriminate, pambanua.
Disembowel, tumbua, tumbuza.
Disgrace, aibisha, hizika.
be disgraced, aibika.
Disgust, chukiza.
be disgusted, chukiwa.
Dish up, pakua.
When you wish a meal to be served you should say, not pakua, *but* lete chakula.
Dislocate, teuka.
Disquiet, fathaisha.
be disquieted, fathaika.
Dismiss, likiza, ondoa.
be dismissed, tolewa.
Disobey, asi.
Disorder (*put things in disorder*), chafua.
put an army in disorder, fathaisha.
be in disorder or dishabille, chafuka.
be all in disorder, chafukachafuka.
Dissipate, tampanyatapanya.
Distinguish, pambanua.
Distort, popotoa.
Distress (*put in low spirits*), kefyakefya.
be in distress, thii.
Distribute, gawanya.
Disturb.
Don't disturb yourself! Starche!
Disunite, farakisha.
be disunited, epukana, farakiana, achana.
Dive, zama.
Divide, tenga, gawa, gawanya, kata, hussu.
Divorce, acha, tokana, tangua ndoa.
Do, fanya, tenda.
I have done nothing, sikufanya neno.
He has done nothing at all, hakufanya lo lote.
be done or doable, tendeka.
do (*be of use*), faa.
It won't do, haifai.
do anything slowly and carefully, kototeza.
do wanton violence, husudu, fanya jeuri.
be done (*finished*), isha.
be done (*cooked*), iva.

Dote, piswa.
Double, rudufya.
Doubt, fanya tashwishi, [kú-]wa na shaka.
There is no doubt, hapana shaka.
Doze, sinzia.
wake up suddenly from a doze, zinduka, zindukana.
Drag, kokota, burura (*haul along*).
drag out of one's hand, chopoa, kopoa.
Drain out, churukiza, churuzika.
Draw, vuta.
Draw water, teka maji.
Draw together, kunyata.
Draw near, karibu, karibia, karibiana.
Draw a line, piga mstari.
Draw out nails, &c., kongoa.
Draw breath, tauafusi.
Draw in the breath, paaza pumzi.
Draw up the earth round growing crops, palilia.
Draw the end of the loin cloth between the legs and tuck it in, piga uwinda.
Dread, ogopa, ogopa mno.
Dream, ota.
Dress, vika.
Dress in, vaa, jitia.
Dress up, pamba, jipotoa.
Dress ship, pamba merikebu.
Dress vegetables for the market, chambua.
Drift, chukuliwa.
Drink, nwa, *or* nywa; *pass.* nwewa.
Drip, tona.
Drive, ongoza (*lead, conduct*), chunga (*as a shepherd*), fukuza (*drive away*), fukuzia (*drive away from*), kimbizia (*make to run away from*).
Drop (down), (*neut.*) anguka, (*act.*) angusha.
into, (*neut.*) tumbukia, (*act.*) tumbukiza.
(*like leaves in autumn*), pukutika.
(*fall in drops*), tona.
drop from, little by little, dondoka.
Drown (*act.*) tosa, (*neut.*) tota, fa maji.
be Drunken, lewa.
Dry, (*neut.*) kauka, nyauka, (*act.*) kausha.
become dry by water leaving it, pwa, pwea, pwewa.
be left high and dry, pweleka.
put out to dry, anika.
dry or cure fish, ng'onda.
Dupe, danganya.
Dust, futa vumbi.
Dwell, kaa, kaa kitako, keti (M.).
Dwindle, kunjana, punguka, angamia (*go down in the world*).
Dye, tia rangi.
kutona hina, *to lay on henna so as to dye the part red.*

E.

Earn, pata.
Ease, fariji, sterehisha.
become easy, farajika.
Ease oneself, kunya.
Eat, la.
in, with, for, &c., lia.
be eaten or eatable, lika.
have eaten enough, shiba.
eat at the expense of each one in turn, la kikoa.
eat where each contributes something to the feast, la kwa kuchanga.
eat all the food away from others, ima.

Ametuima, *he has eaten it all up before we came.*
overeat oneself, vimbiwa.
make a person eat too much, vimbisha.
eat without bounds, papia.
eat over voraciously, la kwa pupa.
Ebb, pwa.
be Eclipsed, patwa.
Educate, funda, fundisha, alimisha, adibu, *or* tia adabu (*teach good manners*), lea (*bring up*).
Elongate. ongeza urefu.
Embalm, tia madawa asioze.
Embark, panda (*go on board*), tahassa (*go on board with the intention of sailing*).
Embrace, pambaja, kumbatia, kumbatiana.
Embroil, tia matata.
Emerge, zuka.
Employ, tuma (*send about*), tumia (*make use of*), tumika (*be employed*).
Empty out, mwaga, mwaya.
Enable, wezesha, jalia.
Encamp, tua (*put down loads*).
Encourage, tia moyo, *th*ubutisha.
End, (*neut.*) isha, koma, (*act.*) maliza, komesha, khatimisha.
Endow with, wekea wakf.
Endure, ishi (*last*), vumilia (*bear with*), stahimili.
Enervate, thoofisha.
Engage, afikana, twaa, fanya sharti.
Engender. zaa, vyaa.
Enjoy, furahi, ona raha, furahiwa na.
Enlarge, ongeza, zidisha.
Enlist (*act.*), tia asikari.
be Enough, tosha, toshelea.
It is enough, bassi.
have had enough food, shiba.

Enquire, uliza (*ask*), huji (*enquire into*), hakiki (*make sure about*), ulizia (*enquire on account of*).
Enrage, ghathabisha.
be enraged, ghathabika.
Enrich, pa utajiri.
Enslave, tia utumwani.
Ensnare, tega.
Entangle, tia matata.
Enter, ingia.
Entice, vuta kwa eherevu, twaa kwa werevu.
Entreat, omba, sihi, nasihi.
Entrust, wekea amana, amini mtu na kitu.
be equal to (*an undertaking, &c.*), weza.
Equalize, sawanisha, sawazisha, fanya sawasawa, linganisha (*by measurement*).
Erect, simikisha.
Err, kosa, kwenda hapa na hapa (*wander*).
Escape, okoka (*be delivered*), pona (*to get well*), vuka (*to get across*), kimbia (*run away*), fiatuka (*to escape as a spring, to get free*).
Establish, tengezeka (?).
Estimate, kadiri, kisi.
Evaporate, nwewa.
Exalt, inua (*lift*), tukuza, athimisha.
be exalted (*great*), tukuka, athimika.
Examine, onja (*taste*), tafiti, fatiishi, sayili (*by questions*).
Exceed, pita.
Excel, pita.
Except, toa, tosha.
Exchange, badili.
Excite, taharrakisha, fitini.
be excited, hangaika.
Excuse, uthuru, samehe (*pardon*).

Exercise, zoea.
exercise authority over, hukumu.
Exert oneself, fanya juhudi, jitahidi.
Exhort, onya, nabihisha.
Exorcise by music, *&c.*, punga.
Expand, tanua, kunjua (*unfold*), zidi (*increase*), funuka *or* kunduka (*become open*).
Expect, ngoja, ngojea, tumaini.
Expel, toa, fukuza.
expel an evil spirit by music, *&c.*, punga pepo.
Expend upon, *be at the expense of*, gharimia.
Explain, eleza, pambanua, fasiri, tafsiri, fumbulia, pambanulia (*explain to*), tambulisha (*make to recognise*).
Explode, pasuka (*burst*), waka (*blaze*).
Explore, fatiishi, jasisi, angalia.
Export, toa.
Express, thahiri, baini.
(*press out*), kamua.
Extend, (*act.*) nyosha, (*neut.*) fika (*reach to*), kunjuka, enea (*be spread over*).
Exterminate, ng'oa pia yote (*root up utterly*).
Extinguish, zima, zimia.
to go out, zimika.
Extort, pokonya.
Extol, sifu.
Extricate from, toa na, namua (Mer.).
Exult, furahi.

F.

Fade, fa, kauka, fifia (*pine away*), pukutika (*wither and drop*), thoofika (*grow weak and thin*).
Fail, punguka.
Faint, zimia roho.
Fall, anguka.
fall like rain, nya.
cause rain to fall, nyesha.
fall into, tumbukia.
let fall into, tumbukiza.
fall flat on the ground, lala inchi.
fall in (*cave in*), pomoka.
fall short, punguka, tindika (A.).
fall sick, ugua,
Falter, shanghaa, sita.
Fan, pepea.
Fancy, kumbuka, fikiri.
fancy oneself, jiona.
Fast, funga.
break a fast, *or eat after a fast*, futuru.
Fasten, funga.
Fatten (*get fat*), nona (*of animals*), nenepa (*of men*).
Fatigue, chosha, taabisha.
be fatigued, choka, taabika.
Favour, pendelea.
Fear, ogopa, cha (A.), [kú-]wa na khofu.
be fearless, peketeka.
Feast, kerimu.
Feed, lisha.
cause to be fed, lishisha.
put morsels into a friend's mouth, rai.
Feel, ona (*perceive*), papasa (*touch*).
Feign, jifanya.
Fell, kata.
Fence, fanya ua.
Fend off a boat, tanua mashua.
Ferment, chacha.
Ferry over, vusha, vukisha, abirisha.
Fetch, leta.
Fight, pigana.
set on to fight, piganisha, piganishana.

Fill, jaza.
fill in [*a hole*], fukia.
become full, jaa. *The passive is used for being filled with some extraneous substance.* Mtungi umejaa maji, *the jar is full of water, but,* maji yamejawa na dudu, *the water is full of insects.*
be half full (by remaining), shinda, maji yashinda ya mtungi, *the jar is half full of water.*
fill up, jaliza.
fill with food, shibisha.
to be full, to have had enough, shiba.
Find, ona, zumbua, vumbua, pata, kuta.
be to be found, zumbukana, patikana.
find out in a trick, fathehi, gundua.
be found out, fetheheka.
find fault with, tia hatiyani.
Finish, (*act.*) maliza, (*neut.*) isha, koma.
finish off, tengeneza, tengeleza.
finish a journey, koma.
finish a scholar, hitimisha.
Fire (set on fire), tia moto, washa moto.
(*apply fire to in any way*), choma.
a gun, &c., piga bunduki, &c.
Fish, vua samaki.
fish a spar, &c., ganga, tia gango.
Fit, faa (*do well*).
Ni kiassi changu kama nalikatiwa mimi, *it fits as though it had been made for me.*
Fix, kaza.
fix the eyes upon, kodolea.
Flame, waka, toa ndimi za moto.
Flap, piga
make a sail flap by going too near the wind, pigiza tanga.
Flash (lighten), piga umeme.
Flatten, tandaza.
Flatter, sifu, sifu mno, jipendekeza (*ingratiate oneself with*).
Flavour, to get the right flavour [kolea.
Flay, chuna, tuna (M.).
lose the skin, chunika, tunika (M.).
Flee, kimbia.
be Flexible, pindana, [kú-]wa laini.
Flicker, sinzia.
Flinch, jikunja, ruka.
Fling, tupa.
Float, elea, ogolea.
Flog, piga.
Flood, gharikisha, furika, tawanyika, funikiza.
be flooded, ghariki.
Flourish, sitawi, fana, fanikiwa.
make to flourish, sitawisha.
Flow, pita (*flow by*), toka (*flow out*), bubujika (*to burst and bubble out*).
Flower, toa maua.
Flurry, zulisha.
Flutter, papatika.
Fly, ruka.
fly off, puruka.
Fold, kunja.
fold together, kunjana.
fold in the arms, kumbatia.
Follow, fuata, andama (M.).
follow a pattern, oleza.
become Foolish, pumbazika.
Forbid, gombeza, kataza.
Force (see Compel), tia nguvu, lazimisha.
He was forced to go, alikwenda kwa nguvu.
Force open, pepetua.

Foretell, agua, tabiri, bashiri.
How has this year been predicted of? Mwaka huu umeaguliwaje?
Forfeit, lazimishwa.
be forfeited by, potea.
Forge iron, &c., fua chuma, &c.
weld on a new point or edge, tambuza.
Forget, sahau.
be forgotten, sahauliwa.
Forgive, samehe, achilia, mwafa.
Forgive me, niwie rathi.
Forsake, acha.
Fortify, tia boma (*put a rampart*).
Foster, lea, lisha.
Free (*from slavery*), weka *or* acha huru.
(*from prison*), acha, fungua.
be set free (*from prison*), tokana.
Freeze, ganda, gandamana.
Freight.
pay freight for, takabathisha.
carry on freight, takabathi.
Frighten, ogofya, tia khofu, ogofisha, khofisha, tisha.
become frightened, ingiwa na khofu.
startle, stusha, kutusha.
Front, kabili, lekea.
put in front of, lekeza.
Frown, kunja uso, kunja vipaji.
He has a frowning face, uso unakunjamana.
Frustrate, batili, vunja.
Fry, kaanga.
Fulfil, timiza, timiliza.
fulfil a promise, fikiliza ahadi.
Furl sails, kunja matanga.
Furnish a house, pamba nyumba.

G.

Gain, pata, pata fayida.
Gallop, piga mbio.
Gape, piga nyayo, funua kinwa.
Garble copal, &c., chagua sandarusi, &c.
Gather (*fruit*), chuma.
into a heap, zoa.
together (*act.*), kusanya, kutanisha, jamaa, jamiisha.
together (*neut.*), kusanyika, kutanika.
up into a small space, finyana.
oneself up for an effort, jitutumua.
little by little, lumbika.
up one's courage, piga moyo konde.
Geld, hasi.
be Genial (*good-humoured and merry*), changa'mka.
Get, pata.
get better, pona.
get a little better, [kú-]wa ashekali.
get drunk, lewa, jilevya.
get dry, kauka.
get fire by working one stick against another, pekecha.
get for, patia.
get foul of one another, pambana.
get goods on credit in order to trade with them, kopa.
get into, ingia.
get into a well, a scrape, &c., (*act.*) tumbukiza, (*neut.*) tumbukia.
get into a passion (*neut.*), ingiwa na ghathabu *or* hasira.
get into a quarrel (*act.*), vumbilia vita.
get [*seeds*] *into the ground*, vumbikia.
get mouldy, fanya ukungu.

get out, toka.
get out of the way, jitonga.
Out of the way! Similla!
get out of one's sight, tokomea.
get palm wine, gema.
get ripe, iva.
get thin and watery, poroa.
get through, (*neut.*) penya, (*act.*) penyesha.
get up, ondoka.
rise to (a person), ondokea.
get up or upon, panda.
get well, pona, poa.
be Giddy, levyalevya.
Gild, chovya.
Give (a thing), toa.
(*to a person*), pa, *pass.* pewa, *to receive.*
give a complaint to, ambukiza.
give a taste, an inkling, or a little specimen, dokeza.
give back, rudisha.
give into the hand, kabithi.
give leave to, pa ruksa *or* ruhusa, rukhusu.
give light to, tia mwangaza.
give mutual gifts, pana.
give presents to, tunza, tunukia.
give rations to, posha.
give room or space, nafisisha.
give to drink to, nywesha.
give to eat to, lisha.
give trouble, taabisha, fanya inda, sumbua.
give way under one, bonyea.
Give way (row)! Vuta!
Glance, nathiri, tupa macho *or* nathari (*cast the eyes or a glance*).
Glare at, ng'ariza.
Gleam, mulika, ng'ara.
Glide, teririka, teleza.
Glisten, zagaa.
Glitter, metameta, mekameka, merimeta, mulika.
Glorify, tukuza, sifu.
Glow, ng'ara.
Gnaw, guguna.
Go, enda, enenda.
you can go, ruksa.
go after or for, endea.
(*follow*), fuata.
go alongside, pambana.
go ashore (of a ship), panda.
be left high and dry, pweleka, pwewa na maji.
go ashore (of a person), shuka.
go away, enda zangu, zako, zake, zetu, zenu, zao, *according to the person.*
toka ondoka.
go away from, acha, toka.
go back, rudi, regea.
go backward, endelea nyuma.
go bad, oza.
go before, tangulia.
go before a judge, enda kwa kathi.
go behind, fuata.
go by, pita.
go crooked, patoa, potoka.
go forward, endelea mbele.
go free, toka.
go into, ingia.
go marketing, enda sokoni.
go off (like a spring), fiatuka.
go on (not to stop), fuliza, fuza, fululiza.
go on (with a work), shinda.
go on board, panda.
go on board in order to sail, tahasa.
go on with by turns, pokezana.
go out, toka.
(*like a candle*), zimika.

He has gone out for the day, amekwenda shinda.
go over, vuka.
go past, pita.
go quickly down a steep place, tele'mka.
go running, enda mbio.
go to expense about or upon, gharimia.
go to meet, laki.
go to meet with shouting and joy, shangilia.
go to law with, teta.
go up (neut.), paa.
(*act.*) kwea, panda.
be Good of its kind, fana.
Gore, piga pembe.
Govern, tawala, miliki.
Grant to, pa, jalia, ruzuku.
Grapple, kamatana, shikana.
Grasp, shika, fumbata.
Grate, paruga, paruza.
Graze, paruga, kwaruza.
graze one another, paruzana.
become Great (of a person), tukuka.
become great to or hard for, kulia.
be Greedy, [kú-]wa na roho *or* choyo, fanya tamaa (*be greedy for*).
Greet, salimu, salimia, amkua, barikia.
Grieve, (*act.*) sikitisha, tia huzuni.
(*neut.*) sikitika, ingiwa na huzuni.
Grin, toa meno.
Grind, saga.
grind coarsely, paaza.
Groan, ugua.
groan at, zomea.
Grope, papasa.
Grow, ota (*of plants*), kua (*to become large*), mea (*of plants, to grow or be growable*).
What is to be grown here? Kilimo cha nini?
grow to its full size, pea.
become full-grown, pevuka, komaa.
grow up quickly, vuvumka.
not to grow (of seeds), fifia.
grow large enough to bear fruit, auka.
grow fat, nenepa (*of persons*), nona (*of animals*).
grow thin and lean, konda.
grow larger, kua, kithiri.
grow less, pungua, tilifika.
make to grow large, kuza.
Growl, nguruma.
Grudge, hini.
grudge at, husudu.
Grumble, nung'unika.
Grunt, guna.
Guarantee payment of a debt, hawili.
a result, tadariki.
Guard, linda, tunza, hami, ngojea.
guard oneself against a blow, kinga.
Guess, bahatisha, kisi, thani.
Guide, onyesha njia (*show the way*), peleka (*take*).
Gulp, gugumiza.
gulp down, ak'ia.

H.

Halt, tua (*put down burdens*), simama (*stand*), sita (*go lame, or to stop*), chechemea (*to put one foot only flat on the ground*).
Hammer, gongomea (*hammer in*), fua *pass.* fuawa (*beat as with a sledge-hammer*).
Hang, angika (*as against a wall*), tungika (*be suspended*), tundika, aliki.
(*strangle*), nyonga, songa.

Happen, tukia.
Which happened to him, kilichompata.
Harass, sumbua, uthi, uthia, chokoza, sumbusha.
be harassed, sumbuka, uthika.
Harm, thuru, hasara.
No harm! Haithuru!
Harpoon, paga.
Hasten, (*act.*) harakisha, himiza.
(*neut.*) fanya hima, haraka.
Hatch, ongua, zaliwa, onguliwa (*be hatched*), angua (*break the shell*).
Hate, chukia, buothu, zira (M.).
Have, [kú-]wa na (see p. 154).
(*possess*), miliki.
on board, pakia.
power over, weza.
in one's debt, wia.
To have things done for one, is expressed by the passive of the applied form (see p. 161).
Hawk about, tembeza.
Heal, poza.
be healed, poa, pona, ongoka.
Heap up, kusanya, fanya fungu.
Hear, sikia, pulika (A.).
hear one another, sikilizana, pulikana.
be to be heard, sikilikana.
Hearken, sikiliza, pulika.
Heat (*get hot*), pata moto. *See Warm.*
Heave the log, tia batli.
be Heavy. See Weigh down.
Help, sayidia, auni.
Hem, kunga.
Hesitate, shangaa, sita, ingiwa na shaka (*get into doubt*).
in speaking, babaika.
Hide, ficha, settiri, sita (A.).
You have hid the cap from me, umenificha kofia.
You have hid my cap, umenifichia kofia.
Hinder, zuia, pinga, fawiti.
Hint, dokeza.
Hire, ajiri, panga (*to rent*).
Hit, piga, pata.
with a spear or arrow, fuma.
Hoard, weka, weka akiba.
be Hoarse, pwelewa sauti.
I am hoarse, sauti imenipwea.
Hoe, lima.
hoe up, palia.
cause to be hoed, palililiza.
Hoist, tweka.
Hold, shika, kamata, fumbata (*grasp*), zuia (*hold in*), zuilia (*hold off from*).
hold in the mouth, vuata.
hold one's clothes or hands between one's knees, fiata.
hold a public audience, or council, barizi.
hold up (*not to rain*), anuka.
hold in contempt. See Scorn.
Hollow out, fukua.
Honour, heshimu, pa heshima, jali.
Hop, rukaruka.
Hope, taraja, tumaini (*feel confident*).
I hope, roho yatumai.
Humble, thili, hakiri.
be humble, nenyekea.
Hunger, [kú-]wa na njaa.
be ravenously hungry, rapa, lapa.
I am very hungry, njaa inaniuma.
Hunt, winda, winga, saka.
Hurry, haraka, himiza.
Hurt, uma, umia, umiza.

Husk (*Indian corn*), menya, ambua (M.).
(*cocoa-nuts*), fua.
(*or shell*), papatua.

I.

be Ill or unwell. Illness is expressed by the use of the negative present of the verb kuweza, *to be able.* Siwezi, *I am ill.* Hawezi, *he is ill, &c.* Nalikuwa siwezi, *I was ill.* Alikuwa hawezi, *he was ill, &c.*
I have been ill for two months, siwezi yapata miezi miwili.
Imitate, oleza, iga, fuata.
Immerse, zamisha, chofya.
Implore, pembeleza.
be Impossible, toa kufanyika.
It is impossible, haiyamkini.
Imprecate against, apiza.
Imprison, tia gerezani, funga.
Improve, tengeleza, silihi, sitawisha.
Incline, (*neut.*) inama, (*act.*) inamisha.
incline to (*like*), penda.
Increase, (*act.*) ongeza, zidisha.
(*neut.*) ongezeka, zidi, kithiri.
be Indebted to, wiwa na.
Indulge in, zoeza, jizoeza.
Infect, ambukiza.
Inform, arifu, hubiri, pa habari.
In letter-writing arifu *is always employed, on other occasions* kupata *or* kuwa na habari *is generally used for to be informed, and* ambia (*tell*) *for to inform.*
Ingratiate oneself, jipendekeza.
Inhabit, kaa, keti.
Inherit, rithi.
Injure, hasira, hasiri, hasirisha
be injured, hasirika.
Innovate, zua.
be Inquisitive, tafiti.
Inspect, kagua.
Instruct, fundisha, funza, elemisha.
Insult, shitumu, tukana, chokoza.
Intend, kusudia (*purpose*), azimu *or* azimia, *or* yakinia (*resolve*), nia, *or* ania, *or* nuia (*have in one's mind*).
Inter, zika.
Intercede for, ombea.
Interpret, fasiri, tafsiri.
Interrupt, zuia, katiza, hanikiza, uthia (*bother*).
Intoxicate, levya.
become intoxicated, lewa.
Intrude, fumania.
Going into another person's house for an unlawful purpose (kufisidi), *or without lawful purpose* (ku-fumaniana), *bars by the law of Zanzibar any claim on the part of the intruder in respect of any assault or injury while there.*
Inundate, gharikisha, furika (*swell*), tawanyika (*spread*).
Invade, shambulia.
Invent, buni, zumbua.
Invite, ita, alika.
invite to come in, karibisha.
Irrigate, tia maji, nywesha.
Irritate, tia hasira, ghathabisha, kasirisha, chokoza.
Itch,—cause to itch, nyea.
I itch, imeninyea.

J.

Jam, kwamisha.
become jammed, kwama, sakama.

Jar the teeth, like grit in food, kwaza meno.

Jerk, kutua.

Jest, fanya ubishi *or* mzaha, thihaki.

Join, (*act.*) unga, (*neut.*) ungana na.

Judge, hukumu, hukumia, amua. *The original meaning of* amua *is to separate, and it is used of separating two persons who have been fighting.*

Jumble together different languages or dialects, goteza.

Jump, ruka.

K.

Keep, weka *or* cheleza (*put away*), tunza (*take care of*), linda (*guard*), hifathi (*preserve*), shika (*hold*), fuga (*keep animals*), weka *or* kawisha (*delay*).

be kept gossiping, puzika.

be kept tame or in a cage, fugika.

It cannot be kept, i.e., *it will either run away or die,* hafugiki.

keep awake, (*neut.*) kesha, (*act.*) kesheza.

keep from, epusha, zuilia.

keep in order (*a person*), rudi.

be kept, or capable of being kept, in order, rudika.

keep on at, shinda.

Keep your distance! Koma usije!

Kick, piga teke.

Kill, ua, *pass.* uawa, waga (*Mer.*), fisha (*to cause to die*).

kill with, &c., ulia.

kill for food, chinja, tinda (M.).

be Kind, tenda mema.

do a kindness to, fathili.

Kindle, washa, tia moto.

Kiss, busu.

lift to the lips and kiss, sogeza.

Knead, kanda.

Kneel, piga magote.

Knit the brows, kunja vipaji.

Knock, gonga, gota, piga.

at a door, or to cry Hodi! if the door be open, bisha.

Know, jua. Kujua *is often used in the sense of to know of, about, how, &c.*

I know where he is, namjua aliko (*I know of him, where he is*).

I know how to speak the language of Zanzibar, najua kusema kiunguja.

I can do blacksmith's work, najua kufua chuma.

(*to recognize*), tambua.

be knowable, julikana.

make to know, julisha, juvisha.

become known, tangaa.

know what to do, tanabahi.

L.

Lace in the rope or matting across a native bedstead, tanda, wamba.

Lacerate, papura.

be lacerated, papurika.

be Lame, tegea, chechemea, tetea, kwenda chopi, tagaa (*walk with the legs far apart*).

Land, (*neut.*) shuka, (*act.*) shusha.

Last, ishi.

Laugh, cheka.

laugh at, chekelea.

Launch, shua, *pass.* shuliwa.

Lay, tia, weka.

lay a wager, pinga, shindania.

lay by, weka akiba.

lay down, laza.

lay eggs, atamia, *or* zaa, *or* nya mayayi.
lay hold of, shika.
lay open, funua, weka wazi.
lay out, andika, tandika, toa.
lay out money, gharimu, gharimia.
lay the beams of a roof, ikiza.
lay the table, andika meza.
lay upon the table, weka mezani.
lay to anyone's charge, tuhumu.
lay upon some one else, kumbisha.
be Lazy, [kú-]wa mvivu.
to be cross at having anything to do, kimwa.
Lead, ongoa, ongoza, peleka, fikisha (*make to arrive*).
lead astray, kosesha.
lead devotions, somesha.
Leak, vuja, fu'mka (*to open at the seams*).
Lean upon, tegemea, egemea.
lean upon a staff, jigongojea.
become lean, konda.
make lean or thin, kondesha.
Leap, ruka.
Learn, jifunza, pata kujua.
learn manners, taadabu.
Leave, acha, ata (M.), toka.
leave by death, fia.
leave to (bequeath), achia.
leave go of, acha.
Leave off! Wacha! Bass! Koma!
leave off fasting, fungua.
leave till fit or ready, limbika.
leave (cause to remain), saza.
be left (remain), saa, salia, baki.
ask leave, taka, ruksa.
give leave, ruhusu, pa ruksa.
give leave about, amria.
take leave of, aga.
take leave of one another, agana.
Leaven, chacha.
Lead, azima, kirithi.
Lengthen, ongeza urefu.
make long, fanya mrefu.
Lessen, (*act.*) punguza, (*neut.*) punguka.
Let (permit), acha, pa ruksa, kubali, kubalisha.
let alone, acha.
let a house. pangisha nyumba.
let down, shusha, tua.
let down a bucket, puliza ndoo.
let free a spring, fiatua, fiatusha.
let go an anchor, puliza.
let loose, fungua.
let on hire, ajirisha.
let water, vuja.
Level, fanya sawasawa, tandaza, tengeneza.
be level with, lingana na.
make level with, linga, linganisha.
level a gun at, lekeza bunduki.
be Liberal to, kerimu.
Liberate, fungua, *pass.* funguliwa.
from slavery, weka, *or* acha huru.
Lick, ramba.
Lie (tell lies), sema uwongo
(to be), kaa, [kú-]wako.
lie across, kingama.
a tree lies across the road, mti umekingama njiani.
lie across one another, pandana.
lie down, jinyosha, jilaza, lala, tandawaa.
lie heavy on, lemea.
lie on the face, wama, fuama (M.)
lie on the side, jiinika.
lie on the back, lala kwa tani.
lie in wait for, otea.
Lift, inua, tweka.
lift up the voice, paliza sauti.

Light, washa, tia moto.
be light, angaza.
show a light, mulika.
Lighten (*lightening*), piga umeme.
Like, penda.
be an object of liking, tamanika.
Liken, fafanisha.
Limit.
reach its limit, pea.
Linger, kawia, kawilia.
Lisp, [kú-]wa na kitembe.
Listen, sikiliza, pulikiza.
listen secretly, dukiza.
Live, kaa (*stay or be*), ishi (*continue*), [kú-]wa hayi (*be alive*), [kú-]wako ulimwenguni (*be in this world*).
Load, chukuza.
a person, twika.
a ship, pakia.
a gun, samiri, shindilia.
be laden with, pakia (*of a ship*), chukua (*carry*).
Lock, funga.
with a native lock, gomea.
Loiter, kawilia.
Loll, tandawaa.
Long for, tamani.
Look, tazama.
look out, or look carefully, angalia.
Look out! Angalia! Jiponye!
look out for, tazamia.
look for, tafuta.
look after, tunza.
look over a property, aua.
look up to see what is going on, tahamaka.
Loose, fungua.
be loose, regea.
Loosen, regeza.
Lose (*money*), pata hasara, potea (*to be lost to*).
I have lost my knife, kisu kimenipotea.
lose by having taken from one, twaliwa.
lose by death, fiwa na.
lose one's senses, rukwa na akili.
Love, penda, ashiiki.
be loved by, kora.
Lower, shusha, tua.
Lull, pembeza, tumbuiza.
Lurk for, otea.
Lust after, tamani.

M.

Magnify, kuza, tukuza.
magnify oneself, jitapa.
Make, fanya, fanyiza.
make to do or be. *See p.* 162.
make a floor or roof, sakifu.
make a pen, chonga kalamu.
make a sign to, ashiria.
make a will, wasia.
make another love one, pendeleza.
make brilliant, ng'aza.
make cheap, rakhisisha.
make clear, thihirisha, eleza, weka wazi.
make confident and hopeful, tumainisha.
make crazy, zulisha.
make dear, ghalisha.
make delirious, papayuza.
make equal, like, &c., sawanisha, sawazisha.
make for, fanyia.
make [*clothes*] *for*, katia [nguo].
make game of, thihaki, fanyizia mzaha.
make haste, fanya hima, enda hima.
make ill, gonjweza.
make into a ring, peta.
make lawful, halilisha.

make light of a matter, jipurukusha.
make like, oleza.
make metal things, fua, fulia.
make over talkative, payuza.
make pastry, andaa, andalia.
make peace between, suluhisha.
make plain, thahiri, eleza, thihirisha, weka wazi.
make pottery, finyanga.
make raw, chubua.
make room for, nafisisha.
make sorry, sikitisha.
make sure, hakiki.
make to agree, patanisha.
make to be at peace, suluhisha.
make to enter, ingiza.
make to go up, pandisha, kweza.
make to grow lean, kondesha.
make to hear or understand, sikiza.
make to weep, liza, lizana.
make unlawful, harimu, haramisha.
make up a fire, chochea moto.
make up one's mind, tanabahi.
make verses, tunga mashairi.
make water, kojoa.
make weak, thoofisha.
make well, ponya, ponyesha.
Don't make a noise! Tulia!
Manage, amili, fanya.
Mark, tia alama.
Marry, oa (*of the husband*), olewa (*of the wife*), oana (*of the couple*), oza (*of the parents*).
ask in marriage, posa.
Master, ghelibu, shinda.
be master of, weza, tamálaki.
Match, lingana
make to match, linga, linganisha.
be a match for, weza.
Mean, taka, nia, kusudia.
Measure, pima, twaa cheo.
measure together, enenza.
Mediate between, selehisha.
Meditate, tafakari, waza.
Meet, onana, kutana, kutanika, kusanyika.
meet with, kuta.
go to meet, laki.
Melt, (*neut.*) yeyuka, ayika, (*act.*) yeyusha.
Mend, fanya, fanyiza.
(*sew up*), shonea.
(*darn*), tililia.
(*bind up*), ganga.
Menstruate, [ku]wa na heth.
Mention, nena, taja.
Mess.
be all in a mess, chafukachafuka.
make a mess of one's work, horongaboronga.
Mercy (*have or show*), rehemu.
Mildew, fanya kawa.
Milk, kama.
Mind, tunza (*take care of*), angalia (*take care*), kumbuka (*bear in mind*).
Never mind, haithuru, usitie shuguli.
I don't mind, mamoja pia.
Mingle, changanya.
be mingled, changanyika.
Miscarry, haribu mimba.
Miss, kosa.
(*to go near to without touching*), ambaa.
(*not to go direct to*), epea.
to be missed (*not found*), kosekana.
Mislead, poteza, kosesha.
Mistake, kosa.
Mix, changanya.
mix up by knocking and beating, buruga, funda.

Mock, iga, thihaki, komaza, kufuru.
be Moderate, [kú-]wa kadiri.
Molest, sumbua, chokoza, basirisha.
Mould (*cast in a mould*), ita, fanya kwa kalibu.
grow mouldy, fanya ukungu.
Moulder, fujika, furijika, haribika.
(*go into lumps like spoilt flour*), fanya madonge.
Mount, panda, kwea.
Mourn (*in a formal manner*), kaa matanga.
join in a formal mourning, hana.
Move, (*neut.*) jongea, (*act.*) jongeza.
Move into the shade, jongea mvulini.
(*as a carpet does when a mouse is under it*), furukuta.
(*shake*), tukusa, tikisa, sukasuka.
(*change place of dwelling*), hama, tama (M.), gura (A.).
cause to remove, hamisha, tamisha, gurisha.
Multiply, (*act.*) zidisha, ongeza, (*neut.*) zidi, ongezeka.
Murder, ua, *pass.* uawa.
Murmur, nung'unika.
Must, lazimu, sharti, hana buddi. *See p.* 155.
Mutilate, kata.

N.

Name, taja, nena, ita, pa jina (*give a name to*).
Need, taka, ihtaji, ihtajia.
Neglect, ghafilika (*not to attend to*), achilia (*leave undone*).
Nibble, tafuna.
Nod, sinzia (*doze*), ashiria kwa twaka (*as a signal*).
Notice, ona, angalia nathiri.
notice a defect, toa kombo.
take no notice, taghafali.
Nourish, lisha.
Nurse (*a child*), lea, lisha.
(*a sick person*), uguza.

O.

Obey, tii, fuata, sikia, tumikia.
Object to, kindana, shindana, rudiana.
Oblige (*compel*), lazimisha, juburu, juzia.
be obligatory upon, lazimu.
hold under an obligation to do, &c., juzu.
(*by kindness*), fathili, tendea zema.
Observe, angalia.
Obstruct, kataza, pinga.
Obtain, pata.
Occupy (*keep engaged*), fawiti.
Offend, chukiza, tia ghairi, tia basira.
be easily offended, [kú-]wa na chuki.
not to be offended, ku-wa rathi.
don't be offended with me, niwie rathi, kunrathi.
I am not at all offended, rathi sana.
Offer to, tolea, jongeleza (*bring near to*).
offer for sale by auction, tembeza.
make a first bid, rissimu.
Omit, acha.
Ooze, tiririka.
ooze out, vujia, tokeza, tokea.
Open (*act.*) funua (*uncover*), fungua (*unfasten*), panua (*make wide*), fumbua (*unclose the eyes, &c.*), sindua (*set open a door*), pepetua (*force open*).
(*neut.*) [kú-]wa wazi (*to lie clear*),

funuka *or* **kunduka** (*to open like a flower*), panuka (*become wide*), funguka (*to get unfastened*).

Oppose, gomba, khalifu, kataza, teta, shindania, ingia kati.

be opposite, lekea, kabili, elekea, elekeana, kabilia.

put opposite, lekeza, kabilisha, elekeza.

Oppress, onea, lemea, thelimu.

Order, amuru, amrisha, ambia, agiza (*commission*).

arrange in order, panga, tunga.

put into good order, fanyiza, tengeneza, ganga.

Ought. *See p.* 155.

ihtajia, taka, pasa.

Overbear, *by loud talking*, *&c.*, pambanya, pambanyiza.

Overburden, lemea.

be Overcast, tanda [wingu].

Overeat oneself, vimbika, vimbiwa.

Overfeed, vimbisha.

Overflow, mimiuika, tawanyika, ghariki, furika.

Oversee, simamia, angalia.

Overturn, pindua.

be overturned, pinduka.

Overtake, pata.

Overwhelm, gharikisha.

Owe, wiwa.

I owe him, aniwia.

to have in one's debt, wia.

Own, miliki (*possess*), kiri (*confess*), ungama (*acknowledge*).

P.

Pack up, funga.

Paddle, vuta kwa kafi *or* kapi.

Pain, uma, umia.

Paint, tia rangi.

Pant, tweta.

Paralyse, poozesha.

be paralysed or paralytic, pooza.

Pare, ambua.

Pardon, samehe, afu, ghofira, ghofiria.

Forgive me, nipe hisa yangu.

Ask mutual pardon and so take a last farewell, takana buriani.

Parry, bekua.

Part out, gawa, gawanya.

Pass, pita, pisha.

make to pass, pitisha.

pass going in opposite directions, pishana.

pass through, penya.

pass over (*a river*), vuka.

(*a fault*), achilia.

pass close to without touching, ambaa,

be passable, endeka.

Pasture, chunga, lisha.

Patch (*thatch*, *&c.*), chomelea.

be Patient, vumilia, subiri.

Paw [*the ground*], parapara.

Pay, lipa.

pay to, lipia.

cause to be paid, lipiza.

pay freight for, takabathisha.

Peck, dona, dondoa.

Peel, ambua, puna.

Peep, chungulia, tungulia (M.).

Pelt, tupia.

Penetrate, penya.

Perceive, ona, sikia, fahamu.

Perfect, kamilisha.

be perfect, kamilika. *See Complete.*

Perforate, zua, zua tundu.

Perform a promise, fikiliza ahadi.

ablutions, tohara.

devotions, sali.
a vow, ondoa nathiri.
Perish, fa, potea, potelea, haribika.
Perjure oneself, apa uwongo, shuhudia zuli *or* azúr.
Permit, ruhusu, pa ruksa, acha.
Perpetuate, dumisha.
Perplex, tia matata, changanyisha.
become perplexed, ingia matata, tanganyika.
Persecute, fukuza, thulumu.
Persevere, dumu, dumia, dawamu.
Perspire, taka hari.
Persuade, shawishi, kinaisha, pa shauri.
Pick (*as with a knife point*), chokora.
(*gather*), chuma.
stalks, &c., from cloves, &c., chambua.
pick out (*select*), chagua, teua.
pick up, okota.
pick up bit by bit, dondoa, lumbika.
pick holes in one another's character, papuriana.
Pickle, fanya achari.
Pierce, zua, penyesha, penya.
Pile up [*plates, &c.*], andikanya.
Pinch, finya.
be pinched up, finyana.
Pine away, fifia.
Pity, hurumia, sikitikia, rehemu.
Place, weka.
an arrow on the string, a knife in the belt, &c., pachika.
There is no place for me in the house, nyumba hainiweki.
Plait, suka, sokota.
Plane, piga randa
Plant, panda.
Plaster, kandika.
prepare a wall for the white plaster by smoothing it and tapping in small stones, tomea.
put on a plaster, bandika.
Play, cheza, laabu.
play the fool, pekoteka.
play upon an instrument, piga zomari, &c.
Please, pendeza, furahisha.
(*like*), penda.
as you please, upendavyo.
Please! Tafathali!
be pleased, pendezewa.
make pleasing, pendekeza.
Pledge, weka rahani.
Pluck, chuma (*gather*), nyakua (*snatch*), nyonyoa (*pick off feathers*).
pluck up a courage, piga moyo [konde.
Plug up, ziba.
Plunder, teka, twaa nyara.
Point, chonga; fanya 'ncha.
point out, onyesha, ainisha.
Poison, pa sumu.
Poke, choma.
Polish, katua.
Ponder, fikiri, waza, tafakari.
Possess, miliki, [kú-]wa na.
(*of an evil spirit*), pagaa.
be possessed by an evil spirit, pagawa na pepo.
be Possible, [kú-]wa yamkini, wezekana, fanyika, tendeka.
Postpone, akirisha.
make Pottery, finyanga
Pound, ponda, funda.
clean corn by pounding, twanga.
Pour, mimina.
pour away, mwaga, mwaya.
have Power over, weza.
Practise, jizoeza, taala.
practise witchcraft, fanya uchawi.

Praise, sifu, hemidi.
praise oneself, jisifu, jigamba.
Prate, puza.
Pray, omba, sali (*perform the fixed devotions*), abudu (*worship*).
pray for, taka (*ask for*), ombea (*intercede for*).
Preach, khutubu, ayithi.
Precede, tangulia.
be Precipitous, chongoka.
Predict, agua, bashiri, tabiri.
Prefer, penda, khitari, stahiba.
be Pregnant, chukua mimba, hamili.
Prepare, weka tayari.
food, andaa, andalia.
Present to, tunikia, pa.
make presents to, pukusa, pa bashishi, tunza.
Preserve, hifathi, afu.
be preserved, hifathika.
Press, kaza, shindilia, sinikiza.
press out, kamua.
press upon, kandamiza.
press heavily upon, lemea.
press with the teeth, vuata.
make an impression (*as with the fingers*), bonyesha.
press and crush food for invalids or children, vinyavinya.
press against one another, like sheep in a flock, songanasongana.
Pretend to be, jifanya.
Prevent, zuia, kataza.
Prick, choma.
Pride oneself, jisifu.
Print, piga chapa.
Prize up, tekua.
Proceed, enenda, fuliza.
Proclaim, tangaza, hubiri, nadi, leleza.
Procure for, patia.
be procurable, patikana.
Profess, ungama.
Profit, pata fayida, fayidi, chuma, tuma (M.).
Prognosticate, bashiri.
by the stars, piga falaki.
Prohibit, kataza, gombeza.
Project, tokeza, tukiza.
Prolong, ongeza urefu, tuiliza, endeleza.
Promise, ahidi, toa ahadi.
give a promise to, pa ahadi.
Pronounce, ta'mka.
Prop up, tegemeza, shikiza.
be propped, tegemea.
prop up a vessel to prevent its falling over when left by the tide, gada.
Propose, nena, toa shauri.
Prosecute, shtaki.
Prosper, fanikiwa, sitawi, kibali, jaliwa.
Prostrate oneself, sujudu.
before, to, &c., sujudia.
Protect, hami, linda, hifathi, kinga (*ward off*).
Prove, *th*ubutisha.
be proved, *th*ubutu.
Provide, weka akiba.
Provoke, kirihi, kirihisha, tia hasira, ghathabisha.
Prune, chenga, feka.
Pry, dadisi, fatiishi.
Puff, puliza.
be puffed up, tuna, fura, jetea, jivuna.
Pull, vuta.
pull out, ng'oa.
be pulled out, ng'oka.
Moyo unaning'oka, *my heart has jumped into my throat, used of a person much startled.*
pull out feathers, nyonyoa.

pull out of one's hand, chopoa.
pull up [*roots*], ng'oa.
Pump, piga bomba.
Punish, athibu, athibisha, tesa (*afflict*), sumbusha (*give annoyance to*), patiliza (*visit upon*).
Purify, takasa, safisha.
by ceremonial ablutions, tohara.
be purified, safika, takasika.
Purpose, kusudia, ania.
Pursue, fuata (*follow*), winda (*chase*), fukuza (*drive away*), tafuta (*seek for*).
Push, sukuma.
push against, kumba.
push aside, piga kikumbo.
push off upon, kumbisha.
Put, tia, weka.
put across [*a river*], vusha.
put a pot on the fire, teleka.
put an end to, komesha, ghairi.
put away, weka.
put down, tua.
put forth leaves, chanua.
put in a line, panga.
put in order, tunga.
put in under anything, vumbika.
put into, tia.
Tia motoni, *put it in the fire.*
Tia moto, *set it on fire.*
put into the right way, vusha.
put off, akirisha.
put off upon another, sukumiza.
put on [*clothes*], vaa.
put on his guard, tahathirisha.
put on a turban by winding the cloth round the head, piga kilemba.
put out, toa.
put out [*fire*], zima, zimia.
put out of joint, shtusha, shtua.
put ready for use, sogezea.
put ropes to a native bedstead tanda wamba.
put to (*shut*), shindika.
put to flight, kimbiza.
put to rights, tengeneza, tengeleza
put to straits, thiiki.
put through, penyesha.
Putrify, oza.
Puzzle, tatanisha.
be puzzled, tatana, tatazana.

Q.

Quake, tetemeka, tetema.
Quarrel, gombana, nenana, naziyana.
with, teta, gomba.
Quarry [*stone*], chimba, vunja.
Quell, tuliza.
Quench, zima.
Quicken, himiza (*make quicker*).
be quick enough (*be in time*) diriki.
Quiet, tuliza.
become quiet, tulia, nyamaza, tulika.
Quit, acha, toka.
Quiver, tetema.

R.

Race, shindania.
Rain, nya.
It rains, mvua inakunya, mvua yanya (M.).
cause it to rain, nyesha.
leave off raining, anuka.
Raise, inua (*lift*), paaza (*make to rise*), tweka, kweza, pandisha, imisha.
raise the eyebrows by way of sign, konyeza.

raise the eyebrows by way of contempt, kuuia.
Range together, pangana.
Ransom, komboa, fidi (*of the price*), fidia (*of the person*).
Rap with the knuckles, piga konzi.
be made Raw, chubuka.
Reach. See Stretch.
(*arrive at*), fika, wasili, pata.
reach a person, fikia, wasilia.
cause to reach, fikisha, wasilisha.
put within his reach, [mw-]eneza.
reach its limit, pea.
Read, soma, fyoma (M.).
teach to read, somesha.
Reap, vuna.
(*break off the heads of Indian corn*), goboa.
Rear [*a child*], lea.
Reason, tefua.
Rebel, asi, khalifu, taghi.
Rebuke, nenea, laumu, lawana.
Rebut, dakuliza.
Receive, pokea, pewa, twaa.
(*accept*), kubali, takabali.
receive for some one else, pokelea.
receive a stranger, karibisha.
Reckon, hesabu, wanga.
Recite, karirisha.
Recline, jinyosha, tandawaa, pumzika.
Recognize, tambua, tambulia, fafanua.
be recognizable, tambulikana.
Recollect, kumbuka, fahamu.
Recommend, nenea, agiza, arifu, peleka.
Reconcile, patanisha, selehisha.
Redeem, komboa, fidia.
Reduce, punguza.
Reef a sail, punguza tanga.
Refer to, regea.
Reflect (*think*), kumbuka, waza, fikiri.
Reform, silihi, silihisha, sahihi, sahihisha.
Refresh, burudisha, sterehisha, taburudu.
Refuse, kataza, kataa, iza.
refuse to, nyima, hini.
refuse to believe, katalia.
Refute, batili.
Regret, juta, sikitika.
Rehearse, karirisha.
Reign, miliki, tawala.
Reject, kataa, kania.
Rejoice, (*neut.*) furahi, furahiwa.
rejoice in, furahia.
make to rejoice, furahisha.
shout and triumph, shangilia.
Relate, hadithia, nena, toa, pa.
Relax, regeza.
be relaxed, regea.
Release, acha, likiza.
from an obligation, feleti.
Relish, ona tamu, ona luththa.
Rely upon, fungamana, jetea.
Remain (*stay*), kaa, kaa kitako, keti (M.).
be left, saa, salia, baki.
remain awake, kesha.
remain quiet, starehe.
to remain as he wishes, kumkalia tamu.
Remedy, poza.
Remember, kumbuka, fahamu.
remember against, patiliza.
Remind, kumbusha, fahamisha.
Remit [*sins*], ghofiri.
remit to, ghofiria, ondolea.
Remove, ondoa, tenga, ondolea.
from an office, uzulu.
Rend, rarua, pasua.
be rent to pieces, pasukapasuka.

Renounce, acha, kana.
Rent, panga (*hire*), pangisha (*let*).
Repair, fanyiza, fanya.
Repay, lipiza.
Repent, tubu.
repent of, tubia.
Reply, jibu (*give an answer*), itika (*answer when called*).
Repay, regeza, lipa.
Reproach, shutumu, kamia, taya.
Request, taka.
Rescue, toa kunako hatari, toa mnamo hatari, okoa.
Resemble, fanana na.
make to resemble, fananisha.
Resent, fanya ghathabu, ingiwa na ghathabu.
Resign, jiuzulu, jitoa katika.
Resist, khalifu.
Resolve, yakinia, ázimu.
Rest (*neut.*) pumzika, tulia, starehe.
(*act.*) pumzisha.
He never rests, hana zituo.
I cannot rest in the house, nyumba hainiweki.
Restore, rudisha, rejeza.
Restrain, zuia.
Resuscitate, fufua, huisha.
Retaliate, twaa kasasi, lipia, sawa, jilipiza.
Retire (*go back*), endelea nyuma.
Return, (*neut.*) rudi, regea.
(*act.*) rudisha, regesha.
Reveal, funua.
Revenge, nahma, lipia maovu, toa kasasi.
revenge oneself, jilipiza (*or* lipia) kasasi.
Reverence, nenyekea.
Reverse, pindua.
Revile, shutumu.
Revive, (*neut.*) fufuka, hui, huika.
Revive, as a plant in water, chupuza.
(*act.*) fufua, huisha.
Revolt (*disgust*), kinaisha.
revolt at, kinai.
Reward, jazi, jazilia, lipia, fathili.
Ride upon, panda.
Ridicule, fanyizia mzaha, thihaki.
Ring a bell, piga kengele.
Rip, pasua.
Ripen, iva.
Rise (*ascend*), paa.
(*get up*), ondoka.
(*stand up*), simama, inuka.
(*rise to, or out of respect for*), ondokea.
(*come to the top of the water*), zuka.
(*of the sun*), [kú-]cha.
Roar, lia, nguruma, fanya kishindo (*make a crash*).
Roast, oka.
Rob, ibia (*steal from*), nyang'anya.
(*take by force*), poka.
Rock, pembeza.
Roll, (*act.*) fingirisha.
(*neut.*) fingirika.
(*of a river, time, &c.*), pita.
Root out, ng'oa.
Rot, oza.
be Rough, paruga, paruza.
be Round, viringa.
(*spherical*), viringana.
Rouse from sleep, amsha.
Row, vuta makasia.
be in rows, pangana.
put in a row, panga.
Rub, sugua.
the skin off, chubua, tuna.
rub to pieces, fikicha.
rub in ointment, &c., paka.
Ruin, angamisha, poteza, vunja korofisha.

be ruined, angamia, tilifu, filisika (*be sold up*).

Rule, tawala.

rule a line, paga mstari.

Ruminate, teuka.

Run, piga mbio, rukhuthu.

run a risk, hatirisha.

run against, fulia.

run away, kimbia

make to run away, kimbiza.

run away from a master, home, &c., toroka.

run ashore, panda, tekeza.

run down, like water, or like a person down a steep place, telem'ka.

run down with blood, churuzika damu.

run hard, kaza mbio.

run over, furika.

run with a shuffling noise like a rat, gugurusha.

run (in sewing), piga bandi.

Rush along, enda kassi.

Rust (neut.), ingia kutu.

Rustle, piga mtakaso.

S.

Salute, salimu, sulimu, amkua, amkia, salimia.

fire a salute, piga mizinga ya salamu.

Salve, bandika.

Sanction, toa ithini.

Satisfy, rithika.

be satisfied or content, [kú-]wa rathi.

satisfy with food, shibisha.

be satisfied, shiba.

be never satisfied, nyeta.

be self-satisfied, kinai.

be enough, tosha.

be of use to, faa.

satisfy lust, timia ngoa.

Save, okoa, ponya, vusha.

be saved, okoka, pona, vuka.

(put away), weka.

Saw, kata kwa msumeno, kereza.

Say, sema.

say to, ambia.

Scald, onguza, unguza.

be scalded, ungua.

Scare, fukuza, tia khofu.

scare birds from corn, &c., linda ndege.

Scatter, tawanya, tapanya (M.), farakisha.

be scattered, tawanyika.

scatter about, tawanyatawanya, tapanyatapanya (M.).

Scent (put scent to), singa.

smell out, nukiza.

Scold, fanyizia ukali, nenea, laumu, karipia.

Scoop up, wangua.

Scorch, unguza, onguza.

be scorched, ungua, ungulia.

Scorn, tharau, tweza, peketeka.

Scour, sugua.

Scrape, kuna.

scrape along, kwaruza.

scrape for, with, &c., kunia.

scrape into a coarse meal, paaza.

scrape off, puna.

scrape off bark, dirt, scales, &c., to clean by scraping, paa.

scrape on the ground, para.

scrape out, komba.

scrape up, kwangua.

Scratch, kuna, kunyua.

(make a scratch), piga mtai.

scratch deeply, papura.

scratch like a hen, pekua.

Scream, piga kiowe, piga yowe.

Scrub, sugua.
Search for, tafuta, tefua.
search all about, tafutatafuta.
Seal, tia muhuri.
Seduce women, tongoza.
See, ona.
be seen, or visible, onekana.
see any one off, safirisha.
Seek, taka.
seek advice, taka shauri.
seek out, huji.
seek for, tafuta, zengea.
seek out for, look out for, tafutia.
Seem.
It seems to me, naiona.
seem sweet to, kora.
Seize, kamata, guia, shika.
seize for debt, filisi.
go quietly and secretly up to anything in order to seize it suddenly, nyemelea.
Select, chagua, teua.
Sell, uza. *The* u- *of this word is very unimportant, it is generally merged in the* -u *of* ku-, *the sign of the infinitive, which is retained in most of the tenses.*
sell to, liza.
be ordinarily sold, uzanya.
Send, peleka, leta.
to a person, pelekea, letea.
cause to reach a person, wasilisha.
send away, ondosha, toa.
send back, rudisha, rejeza.
send upon some business, tuma.
Separate, tenga, weka mbali.
(leave one another), achana, atana (M.), tokana.
(alienate), farakisha.
become alienated, farakana, tangukana.
separate people who are fighting, amua.
(distinguish), pambanua.
be cut off from one another, like friends separated by great distances, tindikiana.
be Serene, [kú-]wa saff, tulika, kunduka.
Moyo wake umekunduka, *his heart is at peace.*
Serve, tumikia, hudumia.
be a servant, tumika.
serve for, faa kwa.
Set, weka.
(plant), panda.
(of the sun), chwa, twa (M.).
The sun is not yet set, jua halijachwa.
set a dog on one, tomesha mbwa.
set a trap, tega.
set aside, tangua, ondoa.
set fire to, tia moto, washa, koka choma.
set in order, panga, tunga.
set on to fight, piganisha, piganishana.
set open [a door], sindua.
set out on a journey, safiri, shika njia.
set the teeth on edge, tia ganzi la meno.
set up (put upwards), panza.
(make to stand), simikisha.
set wide apart, panulia.
Settle, *(neut.)* tuana.
settle an affair, kata maneno.
settle down, tulia.
settle in one's mind, yakinia.
Sew, shona.
sew through a mattress to confine the stuffing, tona godoro.
Shade, tia uvuli.

Shake, (*act.*) tikisa.
(*neut.*) tikitika.
shake off, epua, kupua.
shake out, kung'uta, kumunta (Mer.).
become Shallow, punguka.
Shame, tia haya, tahayarisha.
be put to shame, fetheheka, aibika.
Shampoo, kānda.
Shape, umba.
Share, gawanya.
part out in shares, gawa, hussu.
be partners in, shariki, sharikiana.
Sharpen on a stone, noa.
Shave, nyoa.
shave round the head, leaving hair on the crown only, kata denge.
shave all save one long tuft, kata [kinjunjuri.
Shed, pukutika.
Shell, papatua.
shell beans, &c., pua baazi, &c.
shell nuts, &c., by beating, banja, menya.
Shelter, tia kivuli.
Shift a burden from one to another, pokezanya.
shift over a sail to the other side, kisi tanga.
Shine, ng'ara, zagaa, mekameka.
Shiver (*neut.*), tapatapa, tetema, tetemeka, tapa.
Shoot [*with a gun*], piga [kwa bunduki].
(*as a plant*), chupuka, chupuza.
Shorten, fupiza.
be short and small, kundaa.
fall short, punguka, tindika (A.).
Shout, piga kelele.
Shove out of the way, piga kikumbo.
Show, onyesha, onya.
show a light, mulika.
show one's teeth, toa meno.

become Shrewd and knowing, erevuka.
make Shrewd, erevusha.
Shriek, piga kiyowe.
Shrink (*become smaller*), pungua.
(*from something*), jikunja.
shrink up, jikunyata, fingana.
Shrivel (*neut.*), nyauka, finyana, kunjana.
Shrug the shoulders, inua mabega.
Shudder, tetemeka.
Shun, epuka.
Shuffle along, gugurusha.
shuffle cards, tanganya karata.
Shut (*put to*), shindika.
(*fasten*), funga.
(*close*), fumba.
shut against, fungisha.
be Sick or ill, ugua, [kú-]wa mweli, [kú-]wa hawezi, &c. *See Ill and Vomit.*
He feels sick or sea-sick, moyo wamchafuka, moyo umemwelea (M.), ana ng'onga (A.).
Sift, chunga (*by shaking*), peta *or* pepeta (*by tossing*), pepua (*separate large and small, whole and broken grains*). *Sifting is always done by tossing and shaking in a round flat basket.*
Sigh, ugua, kokota roho (*draw breath with an effort*).
Silence, nyamazisha.
become silent, nyamaza.
continue silent, nyamaa.
be Silly, pişwa.
Sin, fanya thambi, kosa.
Sing, imba, tumbuiza (*lull*).
Sink (*act.*), zamisha, tosa (*drown*), didimisha (*into a solid substance*).
(*neut.*), zama, tota (*drown*), didimia (*sink into a solid substance*).

Sip, nywa funda (*? to take in by gulps*).
Sit, kaa, kaa kitako, keti (M.).
Take a seat, kaa kitako.
sit like a hen, atamia.
Skin, chuna, tuna (M.).
Slander, singizia, fitiui, amba, thumu.
Slap, piga kofi.
Slash, tema.
Slaughter, chinja (*to kill by cutting the throat*), tinda (M.). *It is not lawful to eat any meat that has not been so killed.*
Sleep, lala.
Sleep well! Lala unono!
doze, sinzia.
I am sleepy, ninao uzingizi.
be slept upon, lalika.
Slide, teleza.
Sling, tupa kwa kombeo.
Slip, teleza.
It is slippery, pana utelezi.
slip down a steep place, poromoka, telem'ka.
slip away grain by grain like sand or corn, dondoka.
slip off, or out of one's hand, &c., chopoka, ponyoka.
Slit, pasua.
Slope, inama.
be Sluggish, pumbaa.
Smart, waka.
make to smart, nyonyota.
Smear on, paka.
Smell (*emit a smell*), nuka, nusa.
I smell ambergris, inaninuka ambari (*ambergris makes a smell to me*).
Do you not smell it? Huisikii ikinuka? (*Do you not perceive it making a smell?*)
Smell at, nukiza.
Smile, tabássam, cheka, kunja midomo.
Smoke, toka moshi.
smoke tobacco, vuta tumbako.
smoke (*meat, &c.*), piga mvuke.
Smoothe, lainisha.
Smoulder, vivia.
Smuggle, iba ushuru.
Snap, alika (*neut.*), alisha (*act.*).
Snare, tega.
Snarl, toa meno.
Snatch, nyakua, pokonya.
Sneeze, chafya, shamua, enda *or* piga chafya.
Snore, koroma, piga misono (*make a whistling sound*).
Snort, piga pua.
Snub, kemea.
Soak, woweka.
Sob, ingia na shake la kulia.
Sober, levusha.
become sober, levuka.
Soften, lainisha.
Solve, wathaisha, weka wazi eleza.
Soothe, tuliza, pembeza, tumbuiza.
be Sorry, sikitika, kasirika (*be vexed*), juta (*regret*).
I am sorry for it, sioni vema.
Sound, pima maji.
It sounds hollow, panalia wazi.
Sow seeds, panda, yaa (A.).
sow discord, fitini.
Sparkle, merimeta, mekameka, metuka (A.).
Speak, nena, sema (*say*), tamka (*pronounce*), ambia (*say to*).
speak about, at, for, or against, nenea.
speak against, amba.
speak distinctly, pambazua.

Speak out! Sema sana!
make a speech, tagusa, lumba.
speak Arabic, sema Kiarabu.
speak a jumble of different languages or dialects, goteza.
not to speak, nyamaa.
Spell, endeleza.
Spend, tumia, khárij.
spend upon or about, harijia, gharimia.
spend time, ongea.
Spill, mwaga, mimina.
be spilt, mininika.
Spin, sokota.
Spit, tema mate.
Splash, (*act.*) rushia.
(*neut.*) rukia, tawanya.
Splice [*a rope*], unga.
[*a spar*], ganga.
Split, (*act.*) pasua.
split up, (*neut.*) pasukapasuka.
split down (*branches*), (*act.*) kwanua.
be split down, as when any one has been trying to climb up by them, kwanuka.
Spoil, haribu, vunja.
(*neut.*), haribika, oza.
Sport with, laabu.
Spout out, ruka.
The whale spouts, nyamgumi anatoa moshi.
Sprain, shtusha mshipa, teuka.
be sprained, shtuka mshipa.
Spread, (*neut.*) enea, farishi.
(*act.*) eneza.
be opened and spread over, kunjuka.
spread a cloth or a bed, tandika.
spread out, tanda.
spread [*news*], tangaza.
(*become known*), tangaa.
Sprinkle, nyunyiza.
Sprout, mea, chupuka, tokeza (*show itself*), chanua (*put forth leaves*).
Spy out, peleleza.
Squabble, bishana, gombana.
Squander, fuja, tapanyatapanya.
Squeak, lia.
Squeeze, kamua.
(*grasp*), fumbata.
squeeze together (*act.*), songa.
(*neut.*) songaua.
squeeze oneself into a hedge or against a wall to let others pass, jibanza.
Squint, [kú-]wa na makengeza.
Stab, choma.
Stagger, pepa.
be staggered, toshea, shangaa.
(*astonish*), shangaza.
Stain, tia waa, tia madoadoa (*spot*).
Stalk [*an animal*], nyemelea.
Stammer, [kú-]wa na kigugumizi.
Stamp, piga chapa.
Stand, simama, kaa.
up or still, simama (*of persons*).
make to stand, simamisha, simikisha.
stand aghast, ghumiwa.
stand by, simamia.
stand in the way of, kindana.
stand over, akiri.
stand staring, shangaa.
Stare at, kodolea.
Start (*be startled*), shtuka, gutuka.
(*set out*), ondoka, safiri.
start out of the way, kwepa.
Startle, shtua, stusha, kutusha.
Starve, (*neut.*) fa kwa njaa.
(*act.*) fisha kwa njaa.
Stay, kaa, kaa kitako, keti (M.).
He stayed all day, alishinda kutwa.

(*wait*), ngoja, subiri.
(*loiter*), kawia, kawilia.
(*remain over long*), hajirika.
(*stop*) (*act.*), zuia.
be Steady, tungamana, tulia.
Steal, iba, jepa (A.).
steal from, ibia.
Steep, choveka, owamisha.
be steeped, owama.
Steer, shika shikio.
Steer northwards, shika májira ya jaa.
[*a vessel*], andika.
Step over, kiuka, kia.
Stick, (*neut.*) shika, gandama, ambata.
(*act.*) ambatiza, ganda.
stick together, ambatana, gandamana, guiana (Mer.).
stick fast, kwama, sakama.
stick into [*the embers to be roasted*], vumbika.
stick out, (*neut.*) tokeza.
(*act.*) benua.
Stifle, zuia pumuzi.
Still, tuliza, nyamazisha.
be very still, zizima.
Stimulate, taharrakisha.
Sting, uma.
Stink, nuka, nuka vibaya.
Stir, boruga, vuruga, kologa.
stir up and knock about, tibua.
stir up, turn over, and press together, songa.
stir up (*fire, strife, &c.*), chochelezea.
Stoop, inama.
Stop, (*act.*) zuia (*hold in*), komesha (*make to cease*), kingamisha (*block*).
(*neut.*) simama (*stand*), koma (*leave off*).
stop and stagnate, vilia.
stop short of its purpose or perfection, via.
stop up, ziba.
Store up, weka akiba.
Stow, pakiza.
Straddle (*walk with the legs far apart*), tagaa.
Straighten, nyosha.
be straight, nyoka.
Strangle, nyonga, songa.
Strain (*a liquid*), chuja, tuja (M.).
See Sprain, popotoa.
(*make a violent effort*), kakamuka.
Stray, potea, zunguka.
Strengthen, tia nguvu.
Stretch, nyosha.
stretch up to reach anything, chuchumia.
stretch one's legs, kunjua miguu.
stretch the threads for weaving, tenda nguo.
stretch across an opening (*act.*), tanda, wamba.
Strew, mwagia, nyunyiza.
Strike, piga.
strike on the ground, piga na nchi.
strike the foot against anything, kwaa.
strike with the hoof, piga kwata.
strike out (*in writing*), futa.
strike a sore place, tonesha.
String (*beads, &c.*), tunga.
Strip off, ambua, pua, menya, babua.
(*branches, leaves, &c.*), pagua.
Strive with, shindana na, teta, husumu.
(*make an effort*), fanya bidii *or* juhudi.
strive for breath, tweta.
Stroke, papasa.
Stroll about, zungukazunguka.

be Strong and well-knit, pirikana, kakawana.
Struggle, fanya juhudi.
Study, taali.
meet in a class for study, durusi.
Stumble, jikwaa.
make to stumble, kwaza.
Stun.
be stunned, potea na akili, rukwa na akili.
Stunt, viza.
be stunted, via.
Stutter, [kú-]wa na kigugumizi, babaika.
Subdue, tiisha, shinda.
Submit to, tii, fuata.
Succeed (*follow*), ja mahali pake.
Such a one succeeded him, baada yake alikuja na fullani.
(*prosper*), fanikiwa, kibali.
succeed in doing, pata kufanya.
Suck, nyonya, amwa (M.), fyonda, fyonza.
suck up, nwa.
suck out, sonda.
I have sucked him dry (*got all the information, &c., I can out of him*), nimemzua.
Suckle, nyonyesha, amwisha (M.).
Sue for (*at law*), dai.
Suffer, teswa, taabika, umwa.
what he suffered, mambo yaliompata.
suffer loss, pata hasara.
Suffice, tosha, tosheleza, kifu.
Suggest, násiha.
Suit, faa (*be of use to*), lingana (*match*), wafiki (*be suitable to*).
Sum up, jumlisha.
Superintend, simamia, angalia.
Supply, áwini, ruzuku (*used especially of God*).
supply a trader with goods on credit, kopesha.
Support, tegemeza, himili, chukua.
he supports his parents, awachukua wazee wake.
Suppose, thani (*think*), thania (*think of*), kisi (*guess*).
Suppurate, toa uzaha.
become Surety, thamini.
Surpass, pita.
Surprize, toshea, taajabisha.
be surprized, taajabu, toshewa.
(*come upon suddenly*), fumania, gundua.
Surrender, sellim.
Surround, zunguka, tandama (?), duru.
Survey, aua.
Survive, [kú-]wa hayi baada ya.
Suspect, thania, tuhumu, ingiashaka.
Swagger, tamba, wayawaya.
Swallow, meza.
Sway, punga.
sway about, like a drunken man, lewalewa, umbaumba.
sway backwards and forwards, tangatanga.
sway like a tree loaded with fruit, wayawaya.
sway about in the wind, yumba.
Swear, apa.
swear at, apiza.
make to swear, afya, apisha.
Sweat, toka hari, fanya jasho.
Sweep, fagia, pea (M.).
sweep together, zoa.
sweep away all there is, kumba.
Swell, fura, vimba, tuna, vuna.
rise into little swellings, tutuka, tutumka, tutusika.
Swim (*of a man*), ogolea.
(*float*), elea.

moyo unaelea (M.), *I feel disturbed in my inside.*
(*make to float*), eleza.
Swindle, punja.
Swing. See Sway (*neut.*), ning'inia.
(*act.*), ning'iniza, bembesha.
swing the arms, which is reckoned an elegance in a woman's carriage, punga mikono.
swing round the head in dancing, linga.

T.

Tack (*in sewing*), piga bandi.
(*in sailing*), pindua kwa goshini.
Take, twaa.
(*receive*), pokea, pewa.
(*to a person*), pelekea.
(*to a place*), peleka, chukua, fikiza.
take a portion from the dish in eating, mega, ambua.
take a piece in chess, la.
take a walk, tembea, enda tembea.
take across, vua, vukisha, vusha.
take as spoil, teka.
take away, ondosha, toa.
take away from a person, twalia.
take away from, or off from, epua, okoa.
take away the desire of anything more, kinaisha.
take by force, nyang'anya.
take care, angalia.
take care of, tunza.
take civet from the ngawa, zabidi.
take courage, tawakali, piga moyo konde.
take down, angua.
take leave of, aga, agana na.
take off (*clothes*), vua.
(*the fire*), ipua.
take one's due, jilipiza.
take one's revenge, jilipiza kisasi.
take out, opoa, ondosha, toa.
take out of a trap, namua (Mer.).
take out of the sun or rain, anua.
take out of the pot, pakua.
take suddenly and violently, poka.
take the responsibility, tadariki.
take to pieces, kongoa.
take up, tweka.
take up a little at a time, chota, dokoa.
take upon oneself the obligations of another, hawili.
Talk, nena, sema, jizumgumza.
talk about, to, of, at, for, or against, nenea.
talk against one another, nenana.
talk a person over into doing or telling something, nyenya.
talk and murmur in one's sleep, weweseka.
talk English, &c., sema Kiingrezi, *&c.*
talk nonsense, puza, puzika.
talk scandal about, amba, izara.
talk through the nose, semea puani, [kú-]wa na king'ong'o.
Tangle, tia matata, tatanisha.
be tangled, tatana, tatazana.
Tap, gota, gonga, chapa.
Tarry, kawa, kaa.
Taste, onda, onja, thuku, limbuka (*taste a new crop, &c., for the first time*).
Tax, fanya ushuru (?).
Teach, fundisha, funza, funda, elemisha (*instruct*), juvya, juvisha *or* julisha (*make to know*).
Tear, rarua, babua, papua, papura.
be torn, raruka, babuka, papuka.
tear down [branches, &c.], kwanua.

be torn down and broken, kwanyuka.

Teaze, chokoza, kefyakefya.

Tell, ambia.

tell a tale, hadithi, hadithia, nena *or* toa hadithi.

tell tales about, chongeleza.

Tempt, jaribu (*try*), shawishi (*persuade*).

Tend to, lekea.

Tend (*sheep, &c.*), chunga, tunga (M.), lisha.

Terrify, ogofya, tisha, khofisha.

Testify, shuhudu, shuhudia, sema ushuhuda.

Tether, funga.

Thank, ambia asanti, shukuru (*very seldom used except of God*).

Thank you, assánt, marahaba (*this last is the proper answer to a slave's salutation*).

Thatch, vimba, ezeka.

Think (*consider*), aza, fikiri, tafakari, kumbuka.

(*suppose*), thani, thania.

think oneself, jiona.

think oneself a man, jipevua.

think of, tia maanani, kumbuka (*remember*), nia, ania, *or* nuia (*have in one's mind*).

Thirst, ona kiu (*feel thirst*), [kú-]wa na kiu (*have thirst*).

Threaten, ogofya, ogofisha, khofisha, kamia (?).

Thresh, piga, pura (*beat out corn*), fikicha kwa miguu (*tread out*), fikicha kwa mikono (*rub out*).

Thrill, tetema.

Thrive, sitawi, fanikiwa (*of persons only*).

Throb, puma.

Throttle, kaba.

Throw, tupa.

throw a rider, rusha.

throw a stone, &c., vurumisha.

throw about, tawanya, tapanya (M.), chafua, tefua (M.).

throw at, tupia.

throw away, tupa.

throw down, angusha.

throw overboard, tosa.

throw up, or off, rusha.

throw a burden off the shoulder, &c., bwaga.

Thunder, [kú-]wa na ngurumo (*distant*), piga radi (*near*).

Thwart, halifu.

Tickle in the ribs, tekenya, shtua.

Tie, funga.

tie a knot, piga fundo.

tie up into a bundle or faggot, tita.

Tighten, (*act.*) kaza, tia kassi, (*neut.*) kazana, kazika.

Tingle, ona kinyenyefu.

Tip off the head, shoulder, &c., bwaga.

be Tipsy, lewa, jilevya.

make tipsy, levya.

Tire, chosha, taajazi.

become tired, choka.

be tiresome, refuse to be pleased, deka.

Toast, oka.

be Together.

We are Together, tu sote.

Tolerate, stahimili, vumilia.

Torment, athibu, uthi, athibisha.

Toss, rusha.

Totter, tetemeka (*tremble*), pepesuka (*be shaken*), kongoja (*totter in one's walk*).

Touch, gusa.

touch gently, papasa.

touch up, tengeneza.

Tout for custom, &c., sapa.
Tow, fungasa.
Track, fuata nyayo.
Trade, fanya biashara.
trade in a small way, keep a stall, churuza.
Train up, adibu, lea.
Trample, finyanga, kanyaga.
Transcribe, nakili.
Transform, geuza, badili.
be Transparent, ng'ara.
Transgress, taghi, balifu.
Translate, tafsiri, fasiri, geuza.
Trap, tega.
Travail (of a woman), shikwa na utungu.
Travel, safiri.
Tread, kanyaga, vioga (M.), finyanga (*trample*).
Treat, tendea.
he treats me badly, hunitendea vibaya.
he treats me well, hunitendea zema.
Tremble, tetema, tetemeka, tapatapa.
Trickle, tiririka.
Trim, tengeneza.
trim vegetables, &c., for sale, ehambua.
trim (sail), rausi.
Triumph, shinda, fanya shangwi.
Trot, enda mashindo (*of a horse*), enda matiti (*of an ass*).
Trouble, taabisha, sumbua.
be troubled, taabika, sumbuka, shughulika.
be troubled in mind, fathaika.
Trust in, amini, jetea, tumania.
entrust to, aminisha, weka, amini.
(*have confidence*), tumaini.
trust in God and take courage, tawakali.
Try, jaribu, onja (*taste*).
try hard, jitahidi, fanya bidii.

Tuck into the girdle, &c., futika.
Tumble, anguka, pomoka.
tumbukia (*fall into*).
Turn or turn into, (*act.*) geuza, geua.
(*neut.*) *turn, turn into, turn itself*, geuka.
turn over, or the other way, pindua (*act.*), pinduka (*neut.*).
turn round something else, zunguka (*neut.*), zungusha (*act.*).
He turned round, aligeuka.
The river turns, mto unazunguka.
The ship turned, merikebu ilipinduka.
turn (prevent its going on in the same direction), pinga.
turn aside (neut.), potoa, potoka.
turn bottom upwards, fudikiza.
turn in a lathe, kereza.
turn out well for, fanikia.
Tweak, nyukua.
Twist, (*act.*) nyonga, songa, popotoa.
(*neut.*) potoka.
[*a rope*] sokota, suka, pakasa (Mer.).

U.

Unclose, fumbua.
be Uncomfortable, taabika, sumbuka, toa kuona raha.
Uncover, funua.
Unfasten, fungua.
Understand, sikia, jua, fafanua, tambua (*recognize*).
I understand, yamenielea, yamenitulilia.
make to understand, sikiza.
to be mutually intelligible, make one another understand, sikizana.
Undertake, tnamaini, jilazimisha tadariki.

Undervalue, rakhisisha.
Undo (*unfasten*), fungua.
untie a knot, fundua.
(*ruin*), poteza.
Undress, vua nguo.
Unfold, kunjua.
Unite, unga, ungana.
Unpick or Unrip, fumua.
become unsewn, fumuka.
Unroof, ondoa sakafu (*take off a stone roof*), ezua paa, *or* zumbua paa (A.), (*take off thatch*).
Unsew, fumua.
come unsewn, fumuka.
Unthatch, ezua, zumbua (A.)
Untie, fungua.
a knot, fundua.
Upbraid, nenea, tuhumu, taya.
Upset, pindua.
Urge, sukuma, kaza.
Urinate, kojoa.
Use (*make use of*), tumia.
To have been used for something, kulikuwa na kitu.
be of use, faa.
be of use to one another, faana.
use bad language to, tukana.
use words well and correctly, sarifu.
Use (*accustom*), zoeza.
become used to, zoea.
Utter, ta'mka.

V.

Value, tia kima (*put a price upon*), penda (*like*).
be valuable, faa, faa sana, [kú-]wa na manfaa.
Vanish, toweka, toa kuonekana, potea, tokomea (*get out of one's sight*).
Go and hide yourself! Tokomea!
Venture, hatirisha, thubutu.
Vex, kasirisha.
be vexed, kasirika, chukiwa.
be Visible, onekana.
Visit, enda kuangalia, kutazama, *or* kuzuru, jia (*come to*), endea (*go to*).
be visited, jiwa.
visit upon, patiliza.
Vomit, tapika, kokomoka (*belch out*).
make to vomit, tapisha.
Void, tangua, batili.
be made void, tanguka.
Vow, weka nathiri (*make a vow*), *perform a vow*, ondoa nathiri.

W.

Wail, omboleza.
Wait, or wait for, ngoja, sahuri, subiri.
Wait a bit, ngoja kwanza.
wait upon, ngojea.
Wake, (*neut.*) a'mka.
(*act.*) a'msha.
remain awake, kesha, angaza.
be awake, [kú-]wa macho.
wake up suddenly with a start, zinduka, zindukana.
Wale, alia.
Walk, enda, enda kwa miguu.
(*of a horse or ass*), enda delki.
walk about, tembelea.
take a walk, tembea.
walk up and down, enda masia.
walk lame, chechea, enda chopi.
Wander, zunguka, potea.
in mind, papayuka.
Want (*need*), taka, ihtajia, ihtaji.
(*wish to have*), taka, ipa.
be wanting, ihtajiwa, punguka.
Ward off, kinga (*receive on something*), bekua (*knock off again*).

Warm up, kanga moto, pasha moto.
Warn, onya, ambia, nasi, hatharisha (*put on one's guard*).
Warp, benuka (*as wood does in drying*).
Wash, osha.
wash clothes, fua; *by dabbing gently only*, chachaga.
oneself, nawa.
wash one's hands, nawa mikono.
Waste, (*act.*) tilifu, tilifisha, fuja, thii, haribu, tawanya, tapanya (M.).
(*neut.*) pungua, tilifika.
Watch, (*act.*) vizia, ngojea, angalia.
keep watches, ngojea kwa zamu.
watch over, linda.
(*not to sleep*), kesha, angaza.
Water, tia maji, nywesha maji.
make water, kojoa.
Wave, (*act.*) punga.
(*neut.*) tangatanga.
Waver, shangaa.
Waylay, otea.
Weaken, thoofisha, toa nguvu.
become weak, thoofika.
be Weaned, acha ziwa (*leave the breast*), shishwa.
Wear,—*the past tenses of* kuvaa, *to put on, are used to express wearing.*
He wears, amevaa.
He wore, alivaa.
Wear away, (*neut.*) lika, pungua, punguka.
(*act.*) la, punguza.
Wear out, (*neut.*) chakaa (*by age or use*).
He wore out my patience, alinondelea saburi.
Wear ship, pindua kwa damalini.
Weary, chosha.
become weary, choka.

Weave, fuma.
tenda nguo, *to stretch the threads ready for weaving.*
tarizi, *weave a border on to a piece of cloth. This is the only kind of weaving done in Zanzibar.*
Weed (*hoe up weeds*), boruga, palilia.
Weep, lia.
weep together, lizana.
burst into tears, bubujika machozi.
Weigh, pima.
weigh down, lemea, topeza.
Weld on a piece of steel or iron, tambuza.
Wet, tia maji, chofya majini (*dip in water*).
Whet, noa.
Whisper, nong'ona, nong'onezana, nong'onia.
Whistle, piga mbinda, miunzi, misono, *or* miao. *Most, if not all, of these refer to an involuntary whistling sound; to whistle voluntarily is regarded in Zanzibar as profane.*
Widen, panua (*act.*), panuka (*pass.*).
Will, taka, penda.
If God will, inshallah, Muungu akinijalia (*if God gives me the power*).
Win, pata.
Wind (*neut.*), zongazonga, zungukazunguka.
wind thread, kunja uzi.
Wink, kopesa, pepesa, pesa.
Kukonyesha, *to raise the eyebrows; this is a sign used as winking is in England.*
Wipe, futa, pangusa.
wipe the nose, futa kamasi.
Wish, taka, penda.
Wither, nyauka, fa, fifia

Withhold from, nyima, hini.
Witness, ona (*see*).
bear witness, shuhudu.
witness about, for or against, shuhudia.
Wonder, taajabu, staajabu.
Work, fanya kazi, tenda kazi.
work in metal, fua.
(*ferment*), chacha.
Worry, sumbua, sumbusha.
Worship, abudu, abudia.
be Worth, pata kima (*get a price*).
What is it worth? Chapataje?
Wound, umiza.
be wounded, jeruhi.
wound by striking or piercing unawares, vuaza.
Wrap, kunja.
Wreck, vunja.
be wrecked, vunja, vunjika.
go on shore, panda.
be on shore, pweleka.
Wrestle, pigana kwa mbavu.
Wriggle, nyonganyonga.
Wring, sonjoa, kamua, popotoa.
Wrinkle, nyeuka.
become wrinkled, kunjana.
Writhe (*like a wounded snake*), fingirika.
Write, andika.
Wrong, thulumu.

Y.

Yawn, enda, *or* piga miayo, funua kinwa.

ADVERBS, PREPOSITIONS AND CONJUNCTIONS.

ADVERBS.

Adverbs in Swahili follow the words they qualify.

Sema sana, speak out. *Njema sana*, very good.

Adjectives may be used as Adverbs by prefixing *vi-* or *vy-*.

Kunuka vibaya, to smell badly.

Verbs in the Infinitive and Substantives generally may be made to serve as Adverbs by the use of the Preposition *kwa*.

Kwa uwongo, falsely. *Kwa kujua*, knowingly.

Many English Adverbs may be translated by *sana* (very), which intensifies the action or quality expressed by the word to which it is subjoined.

Vuta sana! Pull hard!
Shika sana! Hold tight!
Enda sana! Go fast!

PREPOSITIONS.

There are in Swahili very few Prepositions. Indeed there are scarcely more than four, *na*, *ya*, *kwa*, and *katika*.

Katika has the same force as the case in *-ni*, it denotes locality in nearly every form in which locality can require to be expressed. *Kwa* denotes instrumentality and object. *Na* is *and* or *with*, and *by* of the agent after a passive Verb; in this last sense *ni* is used at Mombas and in other dialects. *Ya*, or rather *-a* with a variable initial letter, denotes possession; it is treated as a possessive pronoun, and changes its first letter according to the class of the noun which precedes it, that is of the person or thing possessed; it can very nearly always be translated by *of*. Its forms appropriate to each class of substantives are:—

CLASS I. sing. *wa*,	plur. *wa*.		CLASS V. sing. *la*,	plur. *ya*.
„ II. „ *wa*,	„ *ya*.		„ VI. „ *wa*,	„ *za*.
„ III. „ *ya*,	„ *za*.		„ VII. „ *pa*,	„ *pa*.
„ IV. „ *cha*,	„ *vya*.		„ VIII. „ *kwa*,	„ *kwa*.

See p. 209 in original.

Many of our Prepositions are expressed by a Noun or Adverb followed by *-a*. Many others are expressed by Verbs in their simple or applied forms (p. 159). Some can scarcely be expressed at all. The Preposition *from* seems to be almost wholly wanting in Swahili. It is sometimes implied in the Verb, as in *kutoka*, to come or go from, or to come or go out of, but generally it is marked only by *katika* or the case in *-ni*, which denote merely the locality in which the action commenced. *From*, of time, may be translated by *tangu*, or by *toka*, or *tokea*, which do not seem to be used of space or derivation, but to be best translated by *since* or *beginning from*.

Until to, as far as, of time and space, are frequently translated by *hatta*, and (less elegantly) by *mpaka*, followed by a substantive.

CONJUNCTIONS.

Conjunctions are often dispensed with by the use of the tenses with *-ka-*. *And, but*, or any other mere connective in a narrative, is unnecessary where the *-ka-* tense is employed, as in all ordinary cases it must be. The Imperative and Subjunctive may also have *-ka-* prefixed with the force of the Conjunction *and*.

Katupa! And throw it away.

Enenda sokoni kaleta ndizi! Go to the market and fetch some bananas.

Uone, ukasadiki, that you may see and believe.

If and other Conjunctions introducing a state are generally expressed by using the *-ki-* tense of the Verb (see Verbs, p. 136).

In order that is generally expressed only by putting the Verb which expresses the purpose into the subjunctive.

LIST OF ADVERBS, PREPOSITIONS, AND CONJUNCTIONS.

A.

About, (*near*) karibu na, kama.
(*in the neighbourhood of*), upande wa.

Above, (*adv.*) juu.
(*prep.*) juu ya.

Abundantly, tele, sana.

After, (*adv.*) nyuma, baada.
(*prep.*) nyuma ya, baada ya.
Nyuma *is more correctly used of place, and* baada, *of time.*
After this, akiisha (*he finishing*), akaisha (*and he finished*).

Afterwards, nyumaye, baada yake, baadaye, tena, kiisha, halafu, pindi.

Again, mara ya pili, tena.

Against, juu ya. *Against is commonly expressed by the use of the applied form of the verb.*

Ago.
long ago, zamani za kale, zamani, kwanza.
How long ago? Tangu lini?
ten days ago, leo siku kumi, kwa siku kumi, tangu siku kumi.

Alike, sawasawa, ginsi moja, mamoja.

Almost, karibu na.

Alone, peke yake, &c. (*by himself*, *&c.*), tu (*only*). Tu *always follows the word or phrase qualified by it.*

Along, kandokando ya.
along with, pamoja na.

Alongside, mbavuni.

Aloud, kwa sauti kubwa.

Already, mbele (*before*), sasa (*now*).
He is already gone away, amekwisha kwenda zake (p. 155).

Also, na, tena. Na *always precedes what it is connected with.*

Although, kwamba, ikiwa.

Altogether, pia yote, kabisa.

Always, sikuzote, dayima, abadan, kipindi, milele (*for ever*).

Amidst, katikati ya.

Among, katika.
among themselves, wao kwa wao.

Anciently, zamani za kale, kwanza.

And, na.
And he, and I, &c. *See p.* 103.

And *is very often expressed by the use of the* -ka- *tense. See p.* 134 *and p.* 141.

And *followed by a negative must be translated by* wala.

And so, and then, &c., bassi.

Any is expressed by using the word absolutely.

Anywhere, po pote.

I don't see anything, sioni kitu.

Anything whatever, kitu cho chote.

Apart, mbali.

Around, pande zote, mzingo wa.

As (when, or if), -po-, -ki-. *See p.* 136.

(*as if*), kama, kana, kwamba.

(*like*), -vyo, -vyo-, *added to or inserted in the verb.*

As you please, upendavyo.

As it was formerly, yalivyokuwa kwanza.

As *followed by* as *is generally omitted.*

As big as a house, kubwa kama nyumba.

As it stands, shelabela.

Ashore, pwani

go ashore, panda (*of a ship*), shuka (*of a person*).

be ashore (*of a ship*), pwelewa.

Aside, kando.

At, kwa, katika; *case in* -ni, *followed by pronouns in* p-, *when it denotes nearness only, but by pronouns in* kw- *when it is indeterminate.*

At first, awali, kwanza.

At home, kwangu, kwako, kwake, kwetu, kwenu, kwao, nyumbani.

He is not at home, hako. Hayuko *is commonly used by slaves in Zanzibar, but is wholly incorrect.*

At last, mwisho, hatima, hatta.

At length, hatta, hatima.

At night, usiku.

At once, mara, mara moja.

At the top, juu.

At the bottom, chini.

Away.

go away, enda zangu, zako, &c., *according to the person going.*

come away, ja zake, &c.

He is away, hako.

B.

Back, nyuma.

He went back, alirudi nyuma.

upon the back, kwa tani, chali.

Backwards, kingaligali (M.).

Because, kwa sababu.

because of, kwa sababu ya, kwa ajili ya, kwani (*for*).

Before, (*adv.*) mbele, kwanza.

(*prep.*) mbele ya *or* za, kabla ya. Kabla *is used preferably of time*, mbele *of place.*

To go before, tangulia.

Before he goes to sleep, asijelala.

Before I die, kabla sijafa.

Behind, (*adv.*) nyuma.

(*prep.*) nyuma ya.

Below, (*adv.*) chini.

(*prep.*) chini ya.

Beside, kando la, kandokando ya, zayidi ya (*more than*).

Besides, tena, zayidi; na (*also*), *preceding the thing mentioned.*

Better, afathali, heri *or* kheiri.

You had better go, afathali uenende, u heri uenende.

Afathali *is* preferably, heri *means* it would be a good thing.

Between, katikati ya, beina.

Beyond, (*adv.*) kwa kuko.

(*prep.*) zayidiya, juu ya.

beyond (of place), upande wa pili wa.

Both—and—, na—na,

Both of them, wote wawili, zote mbili, &c., &c.

But, lakini, wallakini (*and however*), illakiui (*except however*), illa, bali. *In many cases* but *may be best translated by the use of the* -ka- *tense of the verb.*

By (*after a passive verb*), na, ni (M.).

(*of an instrument*), kwa.

(*near*) katika), *case in* -ni *followed by pronouns in* p-.

C

Certainly, yakini, hakika, hapana shaka.

You certainly, &c., Hakika yako, &c.

Chokefull, tobtob.

Constantly, abadan, dayima.

Crookedly, kombokombo, mishithari.

D.

Daily, killa siku, siku kwa siku.

Directly. See Now.

Distinctly, kiada.

Down, chini.

During, wakati wa.

During his journey, alipokuwa akisafiri, akiwa akisafiri.

E.

Early, mapema.

Easily, upesi.

Either—or—, ao—ao—, ama—ama—.

Elsewhere, panginepo.

Entirely, pia, kabisa, yote, pia yote.

Ere, kabla ya, mbele ya. *See Before.*

Even, hatta.

Even if, -japo. *See p.* 138.

Ever, sikuzote, dayima, kipindi.

for ever, milele.

Everywhere, mahali pote.

Exactly, halisi, khassa, bawaba.

Exceedingly, 'mno *subjoined to the word qualified*, sana.

Except, illa, ela (M.). Except *may often be expressed by the use of the tense with* -sipo. *See p.* 146.

except by, billa.

Excessively, 'mno *subjoined to the word qualified*, chapa, chapara.

F.

Far or far off, mbali.

First, kwauza, mbele.

to go first, kutangulia.

Fluently, kama maji.

For, (*conj.*) kwani.

(*prep.*) kwa. For *is generally expressed by the use of the applied form of the verb.*

(*in the place of*), mahali pa.

for the space of, muda wa.

for the sake of, kwa ajili ya.

for my sake, unipendavyo (*as you love me*).

Formerly, kwanza, zamani.

Forth, 'nje.

to go forth, kutoka.

Forward, mbele.

go forward, endelea mbele.

Forwards (*upon the face*), fulifuli, fudifudi, kwa kufahamia (M.).

Frequently, mara uyingi.

From, katika, *case in* -ni.

from among, miongoni mwa.

from time to time, mara kwa mara.

(*since*), taugu, toka, tokea.

I had it from (of) the Sheikh, nalipokea ya Sheikh.
Further, tena.
Further on, mbele.

G.

Gently, polepole, taratibu, tahafifu.
Gladly, furaha.
Gratis, burre, attia, bilashi.

H.

Hard, kassi.
to work hard, kutenda kazi sana.
to run hard, kaza mbio.
Hastily, hima, kwa haraka.
Here, hapa, huku.
He is here, yupo.
I am here, mimi hapa.
Here and there, hapa na hapa.
Hereafter, baadaye.
Hither, hatta hapa, hapa.
Hither and thither, kuku na huku.
Hitherto, hatta leo, hatta sasa.
How? -je *subjoined to the verb. See p.* 123.
kama ipi? Kwaje?
How is it? Ginsi gani?
How often? Mara ngapi?
How much? Kassi gani? Kadri gani?
How, ginsi *with* -vyo- *joined with the verb; ginsi is often omitted.*
How he was, &c., ginsi alivyokuwa, &c.
However, lakini.

I.

If, kana, kwamba, kama; -ki- *or* -po- *inserted in the verb. See pp.* 136, 146.
Immediately, mara, mara moja.
now immediately, sasa hivi.
In, katika, *case in* -ni *followed by pronouns in* m-.
in the shoulder, ya bega.
in front, pambele, mbele.
[*I*] *in going*, nikienda, nikiwa nikienda.
in good time, at its proper time, tahafifu.
in heaps, chungu chungu.
in order that, illi. *See p.* 141.
in place of, mahali pa.
in the middle, katinakati, kati, katikati.
in the middle of, kati ya, katikati [ya.
in the morning, assubui.
Indeed, kusema kweli.
great indeed, kubwa sana.
Inside, ndani.
inside of, ndani ya, *case in* -ni *followed by pronouns in* m-.
He is inside, yumo ndani.
Into, katika, *case in* -ni *followed by pronouns in* m-.

J.

Just, see p. 116, halisi.
That is just it, ndiyo yalio.

L.

Lastly, kwa mwisho, mwisho.
at last, hatima, mwisho.
Late, kasiri.
Less, duni.
to become less, kupungua.
Less by, kassa.
Like, kama, methili, hesabu ya.
People like us, kina sisi.
Little, kidogo.
a little more, punde.
a little longer, -refu punde.

M.

Merely, tu, bassi. *Both words follow the word or phrase they qualify.*
Moderately, kadiri.
More, zayidi.
more than, zayidi ya.
a little more, punde.
Moreover, tena, na.
Much more, or much less, sembuse, seuze.

N.

Near, (*adv.*), karibu.
Near to, karibu na, karibu ya.
Nearly, karibu na *or* ya, kadri ya.
Necessarily, of necessity, kanuni lazim, ukwasefu.
Neither—nor—, wala—wala—.
Never, kabisa (*with a negative preceding*), kamwi (M.).
Next, -a pili yake, kiisha.
next to, -a pili ya.
No, abaa, habáa, la, siyo, hakuna, hapana, hamna. *These last three words mean*, there is not, *or* there is none.
No, by no means, hasha.
Nor, wala.
Not, si. *See Negative Tenses of Verbs, p. 143.*
Not only—, but also—; si—bassi, —lakini tena; si—tu, illa—.
Not yet, hado, asitasa, haitassa, &c. (M.). *These words are used to denote incompleteness, whatever the subject referred to may be.* Not yet *may generally be expressed by the negative tense with* -ja- (*see p.* 145), *after which tense* bado *is generally added.*
Now, sasa, leo (*to-day*), wakati huu (*at this time*), zamani hizi (*in these times*), zamani zetu (*in our times*), siku hizi (*in these days*).
Now directly, sasa hivi.

O.

Obliquely, hanamu.
Of, -a, *with a first letter varying according to the class of the preceding word, that is of the thing possessed.*

I. Mtu wa Ali, *Ali's man.*
Watu wa Ali, *Ali's people.*
Mbuzi wa Ali, *Ali's goat.*
Mbuzi wa Ali, *Ali's goats.*

II. Mnazi wa Ali, *Ali's cocoanut tree.*
Minazi ya Ali, *Ali's cocoanut trees.*

III. Nyumba ya Ali, *Ali's house.*
Nyumba za Ali, *Ali's houses.*

IV. Kisu cha Ali, *Ali's knife.*
Visu vya Ali, *Ali's knives.*

V Kasha la Ali, *Ali's chest.*
Makasha ya Ali, *Ali's chests.*

VI. Uimbo wa Ali, *Ali's song.*
Nyimbo za Ali, *Ali's songs.*

VII. Mahali pa Ali, *Ali's place.*

VIII. Kufa kwa Ali, *Ali's dying.*

1. Nyumbani mwa Ali, *in Ali's house.*
2. Nyumbani pa Ali, *by Ali's house.*
3. Nyumbani kwa Ali, *to Ali's house.*

Ya *is sometimes pronounced* a.
saa a sita, *twelve o'clock.*
Where it is intended to mark specially the individuality of the possessor the possessive pronoun may be used instead of the preposition -a.

Kiti chake Sultani, *means the chair in which no one but the Sultan sits, or the Sultan's own chair.*

Of *is included in some words which are therefore not followed by* -a.

Kina Abdallah, *Abdallah's people, or people like Abdallah.*

Wadi Mohammed, *Mohammed's son.*

Binti Mohammed, *Mohammed's daughter.*

In some common phrases -a is omitted apparently for shortness only.

Often, mara nyingi.

On, juu ya, *the case in* -ni.

Put it on the table, weka mezani.

Put it on the top of the table, weka juu ya meza.

on both sides, pande mbili.

on every side, kotekote.

on foot, kwa miguu.

on one side, onesidedly, pogo.

on purpose, makusudi.

on the part of, miongoni mwa.

Once, mara moja.

at once, mara moja, mara.

once only, mara moja tu.

Only, peke yake, &c. (*by itself, alone*), tu, bassi, *both following the word or phrase qualified.*

Orderly, taratibu.

Out, nje.

out and out, tama.

Speak out, sema sana.

Outside, nje, kwa nje.

outside of, nje ya.

Outwardly, kwa nje.

Over, juu ya (*of place*), zayidi ya (*of quantity*). Over *in the sense of excess may be expressed by* kupita, *to pass; and in the sense of* finished, *by* kuisha, *to come to an end.*

The battle is over, mapigano yamekwisha.

P.

Patiently, stahimili.

Perhaps, labuda, hwenda, kwenda, kwa nasibu, inshallah.

Perpetually, dayima, ábadan.

Possibly, labuda, yamkini (*it is possible*), kwa yamkini (*by possibility*).

Presently, halafu.

Properly, vema, halisi, bawaba.

-to, *used as an enclitic subjoined to verbs and substantives.*

Amejiwekato, *he has placed himself properly.*

Q.

Quickly, hima, himahima, kwa haraka, upesi, mbio (*running*).

Quietly, taratibu, polepole.

Quite, kabisa, pia hálisi.

R.

Rather, zayidi (*more*), afathali (*preferably*).

much rather, sembuse, seuzo.

S.

Secretly, kwa siri, ndani kwa ndani.

Side by side, kandokando.

Silently, kimyakimya.

Since, tangu, toka, tokea.

Slowly, polepole, taratibu, kiada.

So, *when followed by* as *is generally omitted, when standing alone it may be expressed by* ginsi, *and* -vyo *inserted in the verb.*

He is not so tall as you are, si mrefu kama wewe.

I did not know he was so tall, sikumjua ginsi alivyo mrefu.

So far as, hatta.

Sometimes, mara, mara kwa mara.

Sometimes he laughs, sometimes he cries, mara hucheka, mara hulia.

Soon, sasa hivi (*immediately*), upesi (*quickly*), bado kidogo (*yet a little*), karibu (*near*).

Still, tena, hatta leo.

Strongly, kwa nguvu.

Suddenly, gháfala, mara moja, tháruba moja.

T.

That (how that), kwamba, ya kwamba.

(*in order that*), illi. *See p.* 141.

Then, is often expressed by the use of the -ka- *tense, or by the verbs* kwisha, *to finish, or,* kwenda, *to go.*

Akiisha akatoka, *having finished this, he went out = then he went out.*

Akaenda akamkamata, *and he went and seized him = then he seized him.*

(*after this*), baadaye, baada yake, nyumaye, nyuma yake.

(*then it was*), ndipo.

(*in those days*), zamani zile, siku zile.

(*at that time*). wakati ule.

There, pale, huko, kule. Pale *points to what is nearest,* kule *to what is farthest off.*

Therefore, kwa sababu hii.

Though, kwamba; *the* -ki- *tense, p.* 136, *when the case is put as an existing one; the* -nge- *tense, p.* 138, *where the case is put as not existing.*

Though he is, akiwa.

Though he be, angawa.

(*even if*), -japo, *p.* 138.

Thus (in this way), hivi, hivyo.

just thus, vivi hivi, vivyo hivyo.

(*in the same way*), vivyo.

Till, hatta, mpaka wa.

To (as the sign of the infinitive), ku-; *the* u *becomes* w *before* a, e, *or* i, *and is often omitted before* o *and* u.

Kwisha = ku-isha, *to finish.*

Kwenda = ku-enda, *to go.*

Koga = ku-oga, *to bathe.*

To *before a verb where it expresses the purpose or the object aimed at, is expressed by the use of the subjunctive.*

I stood up to look, nalisimama nione.

Tell him to help you, mwambia akusayidie.

I want him to go, namtaka aende.

I want to go, nataka kwenda. (*In such cases as this the verb in the infinitive is used as a substantive.*)

(*unto*) *is generally contained in the verb,* kupa = *to give to (not to give). If not contained in the meaning of the original verb, it may be expressed by the use of the applied form. In the few cases in which* to *cannot be brought into the meaning of the verb, it must be rendered by* kwa.

(*as far as*), hatta.
(*to the house of*), kwa.
Together, pamoja, wote.
When joined with persons together is expressed by forms of -ote, *all.*
twende sote, *let us go together.*
mwende nyote, *go together.*
wende wote, *let them go together.*
both together, wote, wote wawili.
Topsy-turvy, kitwakitwa, vitwavitwa.
Totally, kabisa, pia.
Truly, kweli, hakika, yakini, inna.
Twice over, kuwili.

U.

Unawares, gbáfala.
Under, chini ya.
Until, hatta.
Up, juu.
Upon, juu ya, *case in* -ni. *See On.*
Upwards, juu.
Utterly, kabisa, pia yote, tikitiki.

V.

Vainly, burre.
Very, sana. Sana *always follows the word qualified by it.*
Vigorously, kwa nguvu, sana.
Violently, kwa nguvu, kassi.

W.

Well, vema, sana, -to. *See Properly.*
What? *See p.* 122.
What do you want? Wataka nini?
What tree is it? Mti gani huu?
What man? Mtu yupi?
What = that which. *See Relatives, p.* 117.
When? Lini?
When (if, as soon as, &c.), the -ki *tense, p.* 136.
(*at the time when*), -po, *treated as a relative particle and joined with the verb, p.* 119.
(*during the time*), wakati wa.
when it rains, wakati wa mvua.
When the harvest comes, wakati wa kuvuna, [wa]vunapo.
(*even if*), -japo, *p.* 138.
Whenever, wakati wote, killa -po.
Whenever I go, killa nendapo.
Where? Wapi, api, *p.* 123.
Where are you going? Wenda wapi?
Where, po, ko, mo, *treated as relative particles and joined with the verb.* Po *implies nearness, and* mo *the being inside.*
I don't know where he is, simjui alipo.
I don't know where I am going, sijui ninapokwenda.
I don't know where I came from, sijui ninakotoka.
Where the tree is (*or was*), penyi mti.
Wherever, po pote, ko kote, mo mote.
Wherever I go, killa nendako.
Wherever I enter, killa uingiamo.
Wherever I am, killa nilipo.
Wherefore, kwa sababu hii *or* hiyo.
Whether—or—, ao—ao—.
Whether it be, licha.
(*if*), kwamba.
While, maadám, maazál.
While, is generally expressed by the use of -ki- *prefixed to the verb, p.* 136.
While it is yet early, kungali na mapema bado.
Why? Mbona? Kwani? Kwa nini? Ya nini? Kwa sababu gani? Ginsi *or* Gissi gani?

With, na, pamoja na.
(*as an instrument*), kwa.
(*containing, having*), -enyi. *See p.* 97.
Within, ndani.
Without, nje.
Without (*prep.*), pasipo (*where there is not*).
Without is generally expressed by the -sipo- *tense* (*p.* 146). *It may be represented by a simple negative.*
He is without shame, hana haya = *he has no shame.*
Without, followed in English by the participial or verbal in -ing, may be rendered by the negative subjunctive of the verb.
Without seeing him, asimwone.
Without there being, pasiwe.
Wonderfully, ajíb, ajabu.

Y.

Yearly, mwaka kwa mwaka.
Yes, aée, eée, na'am, vema, njema, yakini, ndio, kweli.
Ewaa *or* Ee wallah *are often used by slaves or inferiors to express a willing assent.*
Inshallah *is used as a promise to do something.*
Lebeka *or* Labeka, *contracted into* lebék, ebbe *or even* be, *is used by inferiors as an answer when called. Superiors or equals generally use* naam, *the Arabic yes.*
Ndiyo yalio, *that is just it.*
Yonder, kule, kulee, *p.* 115, 116.

Z.

Zigzag, upogoupogo.

INTERJECTIONS.

There are in Swahili, as in all languages, some scarcely articulate Interjections, and many of the natives, especially of the lower class, use a great deal of action, often joined with half-articulate exclamatory sounds, to illustrate and enforce their meaning. The following are the most usual Interjections, and those which can best be written. The words used for Yes and No are given in the preceding list, pp. 216 and 220.

The ordinary salutations are in practice a sort of Interjections, not being very easily explained under any other head.

A slave addressing a superior says *Sikamoo* or *Nasikamoo*, for *nashika miguu*, I embrace your feet. The superior replies *Marahaba*, thank you, or welome, the word being originally an Arabic form of congratulation and well-wishing.

Equals very commonly say when they meet *Jambo* or *Yambo*, to which the reply is *Jambo* or *Jambo sana*. There is a playful or very affectionate way of continuing the dialogue thus—*Jambo. Jambo. Jambo sana. Jambo sana. Sana sana. Sana sana. Kama lulu* (like pearls). *Kama marijani* (like coral), *&c.*, *&c.* The more correct expressions are—*Hu jambo?* Are you well? and the answer, *Si jambo*, I am well. It is difficult to explain these phrases intelligibly. *Hu jambo?* is literally, Are you not a matter or affair? or still more strictly, Are you not a word? The meaning is very nearly that of the English, Is nothing the matter with you? Sometimes *Ha jambo* is used to express, He is well, or *Ha jambo kidogo*, He is not very ill, or He is a little better. One may ask, *U hali gani?* What state are you in? i.e., How are you? to which a proper reply is, *Njema, hemd il Illahi*, Good, praise be to God. The Arabic *Sabalkheir*, Good morning, and *Masalkheir*, Good afternoon, are often heard. The more elegant forms are *Subahk Alláh bilkheir* and *Masak Alláh bilkheir*. It is not usual to inquire about the health of a wife or of the women of a household, unless among very intimate friends, or for some special reason. When necessary, one should say, *Hujambo nyumbani?* or *U hali gani nyumbani?* How are you in the house, i.e., How are your household, or those in your house? It is proper, if you are asked how you are, always to answer, well, for the sake of the omen; and similarly if you are asked *Habari gani?* What news? to answer *Njema*, good, and then afterwards to give a true account of the matter.

In Swahili Interjections a final *h* is often distinctly heard. It requires much practice to enable a European to make this sound properly.

LIST OF INTERJECTIONS.

A.

Ah! An exclamation of mingled grief and surprize. The final *h* must be distinctly sounded.

Ahsánt or *asanti*, thank you. *Ahsánt* is an Arabic word meaning, You have done well. It is sometimes used profusely by way of mere compliment.

Amina. Amen, used at the end of a prayer.

Ati! Look you! I say! It is used generally as a means of calling attention to what has been said, or is about to be said. It is a sort of vocal note of admiration.

B.

Bassi! or *Bass!* That will do! Enough! Stop! No more!

C.

Chub! An exclamation of impatience and contempt; the *ch* is the sound most heard, the vowel being very short and insignificant.

E.

Ee! O! The interjection of invocation.

Ewe! plur. *Enyi!* You there! A rather contemptuous way of demanding attention. It is used for Hi! I say! and any exclamation merely meant to attract notice. It must not be used to a superior and rarely only to an equal. It is customary to call to them *Bwana!* i.e., Master! The answers will be found in the previous list, p. 220, under the word *Yes.*

H.

Haya! An exclamation borrowed from the Arabic; it means, give your attention to this, go on with it. It is used where we say, Come along! Look sharp! Be quick! Go on! If it has been proposed to do anything, *Haya!* means, Let us set about it. *Haya!* is commonly used by a master or overlooker to hasten men about their work.

Hima! Quick! Be quick! Make haste! Often doubled, *Hima hima!*

Hódi! with a great stress on the *o*. It is not right to enter any house or room (not your own) without first crying *Hódi!* and waiting for some one to come, or at least to answer, *Kárib*, Come in!

J.

Je! or *Ye!* Hullo! What now! Well! What is it?

K.

Kárib! i.e., come near! It is used to invite people into a house, to join a party, or to sit down and put themselves at their ease. *Kárib!* may generally be translated, Come and sit with us! and a common answer is, *Nimekaa kitako*, I am set down.

Kéfule! An exclamation of contempt.

Kua heri! Good-bye! Farewell! Sometimes a plural is made, *Kuaherini*, though it seems to be an incorrect form.

Sometimes a special friend adds, *Ya kuonana*, as much as to say, May we soon meet again.

Kumbe! What! What then! An expression of surprize, especially used when things turn out not to be as they were represented to be.

L.

Laiti! Oh that! Would that! An exclamation of regret, a wish that things had been otherwise.

Looo! An exclamation of surprize: the *o* is more dwelt upon in proportion to the amount of surprize.

M.

Marahaba! Thank you! It is well! used by way of acknowledging a gift or a compliment.

Miye! Me! I! I am the one!

Mwenyewe! You did it yourself!

O.

Ole! An exclamation foreboding evil. Woe! *Ole wenu!* Woe unto you! *Ole wangu?* Woe is me!

S.

Saa! You! I say! It is put after a word to give emphasis to it. *Njoo saa!* Come on, do!

Salaam! Peace! Hail! It is used as a salutation by the Indians. The regular Arabic *Salaam aleikum!* Peace be with you! and the answer, *Wa aleik salaam!* And with you peace! is not very commonly heard. *Salaam* is often used in the sense of compliments: *Salaam Bibi!* With the mistress' compliments,—said in presenting anything.

Similla! Out of the way! Originally, as it is said, *Bismillah*, In the name of God. It is now the common cry by which people are warned of something coming. *Simillu punda!* Make way for a donkey! *Similla ubau!* Take care of the plank! Two servants frequently go before a great man to clear the way for him, and call out to any one in the road, *Similla! Similla!*

A plural *Simileni!* is sometimes made as though it were the imperative of a verb. The more correct phrase for Get out of the way! is *Jitenge!*

Starehe! Don't disturb yourself! When a new-comer enters, the rest rise to do him honour, which he tries to prevent by saying, *Starehe! Starehe!* It is properly used to deprecate any trouble or disturbance on the speaker's account.

T.

Tendeni! Go on! Let us go! Probably the imperative of *kutenda*, to do or to be employed about.

Tutu! Don't touch! Used to a child meddling with what he had better leave alone.

V.

Vema! Very well! So be it! That will do!

W.

Weye! You! You are the one! It's you!

FORMATION OF WORDS.

The formation and introduction of new words go on so freely in Swahili, that no guide to the language would be complete without a section on the subject.

Foreign words are adopted in a shape as nearly like their own as the rules in regard to Swahili syllables will allow. At first indeed a word may be used in its crude original shape, but it soon has vowels introduced into, and subjoined to it, so as to bring it into a regular form. Arabic words seldom present great difficulties when once the gutturals have been toned down. Thus *khábar* (news) softens into *habári*, *wakt* (time) becomes first *wákti* and then *wakáti*, *kabr* or *gabr* (a grave) is softened and expanded into *kabúri*. It is seldom that an Arabic word presents so much difficulty as did these three. Portuguese has furnished some words, as *kasha* (caxa), a large box; *meza*, a table; *mvinyo* (vinho), wine. French gives a few, as *bweta* (boite) a box; *divai* (du vin) claret. An instance of English adaptation occurs in *manowari*, which is the current designation of an English man-of-war.

VERBS.

Some rules have been given at the end of the section on Verbs for the formation of several derived forms (p. 157). Verbs in the causative and neuter forms may be made from other parts of speech, especially from foreign Adjectives, by changing their final syllable into *-isha* or *-esha*, *-ika* or *-eka*, as though they had been originally Verbs.

Ghali, dear. *Kughalisha*, to make dear.
Laini, smooth. *Kulainisha*, to make smooth.
Kulainika, to be made smooth.

Beside those formations which are in daily use, it is a great help to the understanding of the language to bear in mind the traces of formations not now ordinarily employed. In regard to Verbs it is a constant rule that those ending in *-ua* reverse the meaning of similar verbs ending in *-a* only.

Kufunga, to fasten. *Kufungua*, to unfasten.
Kufuka, to fill in a hole. *Kufukua*, to clear out a hole.

Several verbs show traces of a rule, which prevails in some other African languages, that the change of *-a* into *-ya* gives the Verb a causative meaning.

Kupona, to get well. *Kuponya*, to cure.
Kuogopa, to fear. *Kuogofya*, to frighten.

There are many questions about the form of Verbs which need much more investigation. What is the rule by which some causatives are made in *-sha* and some in *-za*? Has the *-sha* termination the effect of *to make to be*, and *-za* that of *to make to do*? What is the explanation of the apparently neuter form of some active Verbs, such as *kufunika*, to cover? What is the effect of the terminations *-ma* and *-ta*, as in *kuungama* and *kufumbata?* What dialect did they originate in? What are the rules for the termination *-anya*, which seems to be common in the most northerly Swahili?

It has been shown in the section on verbs how some tenses are formed by the use of an auxiliary, and some by a tense prefix which has no independent meaning. An example of the transition between the two is supplied by the three forms of the negative infinitive: 1. *kutoa kupenda;* 2. *kutoa penda;* 3. *kutopenda.* In the first form both words have a substantial independence; in the second the principal verb, *penda*, is already drawn out of its proper form, and depends for its meaning upon the first verb, *toa*, as upon a prefix; in the third it has swallowed up the final of the first verb and appropriated its prefix *ku-*. The form of the future prefix which is used with relatives points to *taka* as the original form, and the verb *kutaka* is so like our own word *to will* that one can hardly be wrong in supposing that in both cases the change from a verb expressing volition to a mere sign of tense expressing futurity has proceeded in a similar manner. Now, if the tense prefixes were ever independent words, the principal verb must have been in the infinitive; and, if so, the presence of the *ku-* before monosyllabic verbs, wherever the accent requires it, is fully explained; it was dropped wherever it served no purpose, and retained where it was convenient to retain it. The original independence of the tense prefix and of the principal verb would also go to account for the way in which the objective prefix clings to the principal verb; it would then have originally followed the *ku-*, and so been severed by it from all the other prefixes. The only cases in which the natives separate the prefixes from the verbs in writing seem to be where a particle of relation is joined with the *-na-*, *-li-*, and *-taka-* prefixes, and in the past conditional or *-ngali-* tense. It is curious to have in such a word as *atakayekuja* the same letters exactly used to form a tense prefix and to express an independent verb. *Atakaye kuja* means, who desires to come, *atakayekuja*, who will come, in the sense of a simple future.

Adjectives.

Adjectives are made from Verbs in correct Swahili by substituting *-vu* or *-fu* for the final *-a*. Where the final is preceded by a consonant the Adjective is made from the applied form.

Kunyamaa, to remain silent. *-nyamavu*, silent.
Kuharibu, to destroy. *-haribifu*, destructive.

Verbs that end in *-ka* change this into *-vu* in making the Adjective.

Kuchoka, to become tired. *-chovu*, tired.

These forms do not now appear to be freely made or used in the common dialect of Zanzibar. A somewhat similar meaning may be expressed by the use of the variable Preposition *-a* followed by the Infinitive of the Verb.

Substantives.

Substantives may be freely made by prefixing to the simple form of the Verb the initial letters proper to the first, or to the fourth class, according to whether it is a living being or a thing which does what the Verb expresses. It must be observed, that this form is so purely verbal that it takes an object after it just as a Verb would.

Mfanya biashara, a trade maker, *i.e.*, a merchant.
Vifaa, things which are of service, necessaries.
Kifungua mlango, the door opener.

The final letter is sometimes changed into *-i*, and the word ceases to govern an object.

Msemi, a speaker.

Where the final *-a* is preceded by a *-b-* it becomes *-v-*.

Kwiba, to steal. *Mwivi*, a thief.
Kugomba, to quarrel. *Mgomvi*, a quarrelsome person.

Where the above rules would produce a common word with another meaning, the *ku* of the Infinitive is retained.

Kulima, to cultivate. *Mkulima*, a cultivator.
Mlima, a mountain.

There are a few traces of a formation of verbals by changing the last letter into *-e*, as in *-teule*, chosen, from *kuteu*[*l*]*a*, to choose.

The habitual doer of an action may be denoted by adding *-ji* to the simple form of the Verb and prefixing the initial letters proper to the first Class.

Kuomba, to beg. *Mwombaji*, a beggar,
Kuiba, to steal. *Mwibaji*, an habitual thief.

Another way of denoting a person who does what the Verb expresses is formed by changing the final letter into *-si*, *-shi*, or *-zi*, and employing the usual prefixes.

When the Verb ends in *-ka* the *-ka* becomes *shi*; where the Verb ends in *-ta* the *-ta* becomes *-si*.

Kuokoa, to save. *Mwokozi*, a saviour.
Kununua, to buy. *Mnunuzi*, a purchaser.
Kuaka, to build (in stone). *Mwashi*, a mason.
Kufuata, to follow. *Mfuasi*, a follower.

The result of the action denoted by the Verb may be expressed by changing the final *-a* into *-o* and using some appropriate prefix.

Kuzaa, to bear. *Mazao*, fruit, produce.
Kutenda, to do. *Kitendo*, an action.
Kwenda, to go. *Mwendo*, a journey, *or* going.

Of the Substantival prefixes those of the fourth (Ki-) Class are most often used.

The same forms especially in the fifth Class are used to express the place where an action is generally done.

Kuoka, to bake. *Joko*, a baking place.
Kukusanyika, to be assembled. *Makusanyiko*, a gathering place, *or* an assembly.

Words of similar meaning are also made by the terminations *-zi -shi*, *-si*. See above.

Mavao, or *Mavazi*, dress, garments.
Kizao, or *Kizazi*, birth, a generation.
Pendo, or *Penzi*, love.

Where the Verb and Substantive are both borrowed from the Arabic, it is useful to remember that the Substantive has generally *a* where some other vowel occurs in the Verb.

Kuabudu, to worship. *Ibada*, worship.
Kusafiri, to travel. *Safari*, a journey.

Sometimes both the Arabic and the Swahili forms occur.

Kujibu, to answer. *Jawabu* and *majibu*, an answer.

Verbs joined with relatives, or with the particles of place or time, may be treated as Substantives.

Wendako kote, whithersoever thou goest.
Killa nendapo, every time I go.
Zikereziwazo, turnery, turned goods.

Substantives of place may be made from Adjectives by putting them into the form required by *Mahali*, place (Class VII.).

Panyamavu, a quiet place.

The place where something is may be expressed by *penyi*.

Penyi mtende, where the date tree is, or was.

The place for doing anything may be expressed by *pa* followed by the Infinitive of the Verb.

Pakutokea, a place to go out at, an outlet.

Abstract Substantives are ordinarily formed by means of the prefix *U*- or *W*-.

Karimu, generous.	*Ukarimu*, generosity.
-eupe, white.	*Weupe*, whiteness.
Mwizi, a thief.	*Uizi*, thievishness.
Muuaji, a murder	*Uuaji*, murders.
Waziri, a vizier.	*Uwaziri*, viziership.

An instance in which both Arabic and Swahili forms are used occurs in the word for *enmity*.

Adui, an enemy. *Wadui* or *Adawa*, enmity.

Nations, their country and language, are regularly

expressed by the prefixes of the first, sixth, and fourth Classes.

Mgala, a Galla. *Ugala*, Galla land. *Kigala*, the Galla language.

Mzungu, a European. *Uzungu*, the native country of the Europeans. *Kizungu*, the language which Europeans speak.

It is to be observed that the *U-* form would also express *the being* a Galla. European, &c., and that the *Ki-* form denotes the sort or kind of anything, not of language only. It is seldom used absolutely except of the language, but when preceded by *-a* (of) its true meaning becomes evident.

Mavao ya Kizungu, European dress.
Viazi vya Kizungu, potatoes.

The *Ki-* form may be made from other substantives.

Mavao ya kifaume, royal robes (form *mfaume*, a king, and *ufaume*, kingdom or kingship).

The formation of Adverbs and Prepositions has been described in the section on the smaller parts of speech.

Table of Noun Prefixes in various African Languages.

Taken chiefly from Dr. Bleek's "Comparative Grammar."

		Swahili.	Shambala.	[ki] Nyika.	[kt] Kamba.	Nyamwezi.	Yao.	Kafir.	[se] Chuana.	[ochl] Herero.
I.	*Sing.*	M(u)-	M(u)	M(u)-	M(u)-	Mu-	M(u)-	(u)M(u)-	M(u)-	M(u)-
	Plur.	Wa-	Wa-	A-	A-	Wa-	Wa-	(a)Ba-	Ba-	Va-
II.	*Sing.*	M(u)-	M(u)-	M(u)-	Mu-	Mu-	M(u)-	(u)M(u)-	M(u)-	Mu-
	Plur.	Mi-	Mi-	Mi-	Mi-	Mi-	Mi-	(i)Mi-	Me-	Mi-
III.	*Sing.*	N-	N-	N-	N-	N-	N-	(i)N-	N-	N-
	Plur.	N-	N-	N-	N-	N-	N-	(i)Zin-	Lin-	Thon-
IV.	*Sing.*	Ki-	Ki-	Ki-	Ki-	Ki-	Chi-	(i)Si-	Se-	Chi-
	Plur.	Vi-	Vi-	Vi-	I-	Fi-	I-	(i)Zi-	Li-	Vi-
V.	*Sing.*	—	—	—	—	(l)I-	Li-	(i)Li-	(Le)-	E-
	Plur.	Ma-	Ma-	Ma-	Ma-	Ma-	Ma-	(a)Ma-	Ma-	Ma-
VI.	*Sing.*	U-	Lu-	Lu-	U-	Lu-	Lu-	(u)Lu-	Lu-	Lu-
	Plur.	N-	N-	N-	N-	N-	N-	(i)Zin-	Lin-	Thon-
VII.		Pa-	Ha-	Va-	Wa-	H-	Pa-			Po-
VIII.		Ku-	Ku-	Ku-	Ku-	Ku-	Ku-	(u)Ku-	Ku-	Ku-
(IX.)	*Sing.*		Ka-	Ka-	Ka-	Ka-	Ka-			Ka-
	Plur.		(?)Vi-	(?)Vi-	Tu-	Tu-	Tu-			U-

TABLE of the PREPOSITION *-a* (of)

in four Languages.

		SWAHILI.	SHAMBALA.	NYAMWEZI.	YAO.
I.	*Sing.*	Wa	Ywa	Wa	Jwa
	Plur.	Wa	Wa	Wa	Wa
II.	*Sing.*	Wa	Wa	Gwa	Wa
	Plur.	Ya	Ya	Ya	Ja
III.	*Sing.*	Ya	Ya	Ya	Ja
	Plur.	Za	Za	Za	Sya
IV.	*Sing.*	Cha	Kya	Cha	Cha
	Plur.	Vya	Vya	Fya	Ya
V.	*Sing.*	La	Ja	Lya	Lya
	Plur.	Ya	Ya	Ga	Ga
VI.	*Sing.*	Wa	Lwa	Lwa	Lwa
	Plur.	Za	Za	Za	Sya
VII.		Pa	Ha		Pa
VIII.		Kwa	Kwa	Kwa	Kwa
(IX.)	*Sing.*		Ka	Ka	Ka
	Plur.		Vya(?)	Twa	Twa

END OF PART I.

HANDBOOK OF THE SWAHILI LANGUAGE

AS SPOKEN AT ZANZIBAR.

PART II.

SWAHILI-ENGLISH VOCABULARY.

PRELIMINARY OBSERVATIONS.

In using the following Vocabulary it is necessary to remember that Swahili words change very much at the beginning and not often at the end.

In searching for the meaning of a word, which is not to be found exactly as written, it is well to examine first the final syllable, so as to correct, or remove, any termination or enclitic which may be attached to it. These are as follow :—

1. The passive of the verb is made by changing *-a* into *-wa*. Verbs ending in two consecutive vowels frequently use as their passive the passive of the applied form which ends in *-liwa* or *-lewa*.

> *Kupenda*, to love. *Kupendwa*, to be loved.
> *Kufungua*, to unfasten. *Kufunguliwa*, to be unfastened.
> *Kuzaa*, to bear. *Kuzaliwa*, to be born.
> *Kukomboa*, to buy back. *Kukombolewa*, to be bought back.

2. Verbs ending in *-a* change the *-a* into *-e* in the subjunctive and imperative, and into *-i* in the negative present.

> *Pende*, love thou.
> *Apende*, that he may love.
> *Hapendi*, he does not love.

The change of the final vowel distinguishes *hapendi*, he does not love, from *hapenda*, a contracted form of *nikapenda*, and I loved.

3. The plural of the imperative is made by adding *-ni* to the singular.

> *Pendani* or *Pendeni*, love ye.
> *Sifuni*, praise ye.
> *Fikirini*, consider ye.

4. Substantives form the locative case by adding *-ni.*

Nyumbani mwangu, inside my house.
Nyumbani kwangu, to or at my house.
Nyumbani pangu, by or near my house. All from *Nyumba.*

5. *-ni* may stand for *nini?* What?
Watakani? What do you want?

6. *Je?* How? is subjoined to the verb expressing the action inquired about.

Asemaje? How does he speak? *i.e.,* What does he say?

7. *mno,* exceedingly, always follows the word it qualifies, and may be treated as an enclitic.

8. *-to,* which, however, rarely occurs in the dialect of Zanzibar, denotes goodness and fitness.

Kuweka, to place. *Kuwekato,* to place properly.
Manuka, smells. *Manukato,* scents.

9. The relative signs and the particles denoting time and place are subjoined to the verb when there is no tense prefix, otherwise they follow the tense prefix.

Tulala-po, when we sleep.
Tuna-po-lala, while we are sleeping.

The particles denoting time and place are,

-po, when or where.
-ko, whither or whence.
-mo, wherein.

These preceded only by the personal prefix imply the substantive verb *to be.*

Yupo, he is there, not far off.
Zipo, &c., &c., they are there, not far off, &c., &c.
Yuko, he is there, far off.
Ziko, &c., &c., they are there, far off, &c., &c.
Yumo, he is there inside.
Zimo, &c., &c., they are there inside, &c., &c.

The relative signs are, *-cho, -lo, -o, -po, -vyo, -wo, -ye, -yo, -zo.*

These syllables with *na* prefixed have the meaning of *and,* or *with him, her, it,* or *them.*

10. The possessive pronouns may be used in enclitic forms.

Thy, or *your*, may be expressed by subjoining, according to the class of the substantive, *-cho*, *-lo*, *-o*, *-po*, *-vyo*, *-wo*, *-yo*, or *-zo*.

His, *hers*, or *its*, may be expressed by subjoining *-che*, *-e*, *-le*, *-pe*, *-vye*, *-we*, *-ye*, or *-ze*.

Other enclitic forms of the possessive pronouns are,—

-ngu, or *-angu*, my.	*-etu*, our.
-ko, or *-ako*, thy.	*-enu*, your.
-ke, or *-ake*, his, &c.	*-ao*, their.

The final letter of the substantive generally merges into the initial of the pronoun.

Mwanangu, my child.	*Mwanetu*, our child.
Mwanako, thy child.	*Mwanenu*, your child.
Mwanake, his child.	*Mwanao*, their child.

11. New verbs may always be formed when wanted by changing the final vowel into *-ia* or *-ea*, *-lia* or *-lea*, to make the applied form; into *-za* or *-sha*, *-iza* or *-eza*, *-isha* or *-esha*, to make a causative form; into *-ana*, to make a reciprocal form; and into *-ka*, *-ika*, or *-eka*, to make a neuter or quasi-passive form.

12. In old and poetical Swahili the object of the verb is suffixed as well as prefixed, as in *U-ni-hifathi-mi*, Do thou preserve me; where both the *ni* and the *mi* denote the object of the verb.

The syllables thus used are *-cho*, *-lo*, *-ni*, *-nyi*, *-o*, *-po*, *-si*, *-vyo*, *-we*, *-wo*, *-ye*, *-yo*, *-zo*.

Having cleared the word of all adventitious terminations it wil probably be found at once; if not, look for the first syllable, and so on, taking syllable by syllable until the word, its number, person, and tense, will all have been explained. It must, however, be borne in mind that nouns in *u-* or *w-* generally drop the initial letter in the plural and frequently substitute for it *n-* or *ny-*.

Verbs and adjectives are here indexed under the first letter of the simplest form, or of that to which the prefixes are joined.

Kupenda will be found as *Penda ku-*, to love.
Mabaya will be found as *-baya*, bad.

Words which may be used as adjectives or as substantives, but from their nature can hardly be applied to any but animate beings, will be found under *m-* or *mw-*, as they can very rarely in the singular take any other prefix.

Substantives are indexed by the prefix with which they are generally used. It must be remembered, however, that the use of particular prefixes may be nearly always varied to suit any particular shade of meaning, so that if the word is not to be found under one, it may happen that its meaning can be found under some other.

Where no plural is mentioned, it is to be understood that the plural, if used at all, is in the same form as the singular.

The following table of prefixes may be found useful. The use of each will be explained in the Vocabulary.

SUBSTANTIVAL PREFIXES.

Ch-	Ki-	Ma-	Mw-	U-	W-
J-	Ku-	Mi-	N-	Vi-	Wa-
Ji-	M-	Mu-	Ny-	Vy-	

ADJECTIVAL PREFIXES.

Ch-	Ku-	'M-	Mu-	Ny-	Vi-
J-	Kw-	Ma-	Mw-	P-	Vy-
Ki-	M-	Mi-	N-	Pa-	Wa-

PRONOMINAL PREFIXES.

Ch-	Ku-	Li-	Mw-	Vi-	Y-
I-	Kw-	M-	Pa-	W-	Z-
Ki-	L-	Mu-	U-	Wa-	Zi

VERBAL PREFIXES.

1. Personal or subjective prefixes, which take precedence of all others.

A-	*Ki-	*Mw-	Si-	*Vy-	Yu-
*Ch-	*Ku-	N-	*Tu-	*W-	*Z-
Ha-	*L-	Ni-	*Tw-	*Wa-	*Zi-
Hu-	*Li-	*Pa-	*U-	*Y-	
*I-	*M-	*P-	*Vi-	*Ya-	

2. Tense prefixes which precede all except the signs of person.

-a-	-japo-	-ku-	-na-	-si-	-ta-
-ali-	-ka-	-li-	-ngali-	-sije-	-taka-
-ja-	-ki-	-me-	-nge-	-sipo-	

* These may all be preceded by *Ha*, to form negative tenses in the indicative mood, and personal prefixes followed by *-si-* make negative subjunctives.

3. Particles of place, time, and relation, which follow the tense prefix, or, if there is no tense prefix, are subjoined to the verb.

-cho	-mo	-wo
-ko	-o	-ye
-kwo	-po	-yo
-lo	-vyo	-zo

4 Objective prefixes, which always immediately precede the verb.

-i-	-mw-	-u-
-ki-	-n-	-vi-
-ku-	-ni-	-wa-
-li-	-pa-	-ya-
-m-	-tu-	-zi-

A suppressed *l* or *r* always exists between two consecutive vowels. It is often heard in the Merima dialect, and frequently appears where otherwise three or more vowels would follow one another. However, the more classical the Swahili, the less tolerant it is in any case of an *l* between vowels, or even as an initial letter.

keee = *kelele*. *ete* = *lete*.

The following letters are interchanged;

l and *r*, *s* and *sh*, and vulgarly *ki* and *chi*, and *th* and *z*.

Zanzibar ch = t (M.).
" e = a (M.).
" h = kh (Ar.).
" j = d (M.), y (A.) (N.).
" t = ch (Ozi.).
" v = z (A.).
" z = v (Mer.), th (Patta and Ozi.), j (vulgar).

The letters enclosed in parentheses denote the various dialects.

(M.) = Mombas (kimvita). (Mer.) = Southern Coast dialect (kimerima).
(A.) = Lamoo (kiamu). (Ar.) = Arabic.
(N.) = Poetical Swahili (kingozi).

SWAHILI-ENGLISH VOCABULARY.

A

The sound of *a* in Swahili resembles that of *a* in the English word "father." It is, perhaps,—except when doubled—somewhat sharper and lighter.

When the final *a* of any prefix—except the negative prefix *ha*—is brought by composition to precede immediately either *e* or *i*, it coalesces with them and produces the sound of a long *e*.

Aka-enda is pronounced *akenda*.

Akawa-ita is pronounced *akaweta*.

A and *u* have a tendency to coalesce into an *o* sound.

Arabic substantives incorporated into Swahili have often been made by changing *-i-* in the verb into *-a-* in the substantive.

Kubarizi, to hold a public audience. *Baraza*, a public audience.

Kusafiri, to travel. *Safari*, a journey.

A occurs in some dialects where *e* is used in Zanzibar. See *E*.

A = *ya*, of.

-*a* with a varying initial letter, of. -*a* is used in such phrases as the following for *in*: *Unitie wa macho*, put it in my eyes. *Akamchoma ya kitovu*, and he stabbed him in the navel.

A-, the sign of the third person singular prefixed to verbs when governed by substantives which denote animate beings—he, she, or it.

Where the tense prefix begins with *a*, one of the *a*'s disappears.

The following are instances of the way in which this *a* occurs.

A-penda (for *a-a-penda*), he loves.

A-na-penda, he is loving.

A-m-penda, he has loved.

A-li-penda (for *a-ali-penda*), he loved.

A-ka-penda, and he loved.

A-ta-penda, he will love.

A-ki-penda, he being in the condition of loving.

A-nge-penda, he would love.

A-ngali-penda, he would have loved.

A-japo-penda, even if he loves.

A-sipo-penda, he not loving.

A-pende, let him, or that he may love.

A-si-pende, let him not, or that he may not love, or without his loving.

-a-, the sign of the present indefinite; it follows the prefix denoting the person of the subject or nominative, and precedes that denoting the object or accusative.

N-a-m-penda, I love him (I do him love).

Aali, choice, good.

Aasi, disobedient, rebellious.

Abadan, or *abadi*, always, constantly.

Abiri ku-, to pass over, go across (a river, &c.).

Abiria, passengers.

Abirisha ku-, to put across, to ferry over.

Abudia ku-, to give worship to.

Abudisha ku-, to cause to worship.

Abudu ku-, to worship.

Acha ku-, to leave, leave alone, let be, let go, allow, acquit, divorce.

Achana ku-, to leave one another, to, separate.

Achari, pickle, a relish made of lemon-juice and red pepper.

Achia ku-, to leave to *or* for, to bequeath to.

Achilia ku-, to pass over what a person has done, to forgive, to neglect.

Ada, a custom, *especially* a customary gift.

Adabu, good manners, politeness.

Kutia adabu, to make polite, to teach good manners.

Adamu, Adam.

Mwana Adamu, or *Bin Adamu*, a human being, a man.

Adawa, enmity.

Adi ku-, to accompany a person part of his way.

Adibu ku-, to educate, to teach manners.

Adili, right, right conduct.

Adili ku-, to learn to behave rightly.

Adilisha ku-, to teach to behave rightly.

Adui, plur. *Adui* or *maadui*, an enemy.

Aee, Yes.

Afa, plur. *maafa*, an enemy.

Afathali, rather, better of the two, best, preferably.

Afia, health, good health.

Afikana ku-, to come to an agreement, agree.

Afiuni, opium.

Afu, wild jasmine.

Afu ku-, to save, to deliver, to pardon, to preserve. Also, to get well.

Afya. See *Afia*, health.

Afya ku-, to make to swear.

Aga ku-, to take leave of, to agree with.

Agana ku-, to take leave of one another, to make an agreement.

Agga ku-, to be lost, to perish.

Agiza ku-, to commission, direct, give in charge, appoint to.

Agizo, plur. *maagizo*, commission charge.

Agua ku-, to predict.

Agulia ku-, to predict of.

Ahaa! No!

Ahadi (vulgarly *wahadi*), a promise, promises.

Ahadiana ku-, to promise mutually, agree.

Ahili, family, relations.

Ahera, in the grave, under the earth, after death, at the end of the world. [Ar. *akhr*, the other.]

Ahidi ku-, to promise.

Ahsánt, or *Ahsanti*, or *Asanti*, thanks! thank you!

Aibika ku-, to be disgraced, to be put to shame.

Aibisha ku-, to disgrace, to put to shame.

Aibu, a disgrace, a reproach.

Aina, kind.

Aini ku-, to appoint.

Ainisha ku-, to show, point out.

Aitiwalo, pronounced *Etiwalo*, what he is wanted (or called) for, *a-itiwa-lo*.

Ajabisha ku-, to astonish, amaze.

Ajabu, a wonderful thing, wonderfully.

Ajali, fate, death.

Kusalimika ajali, to be altogether come to an end (to be saluted by its fate).

Ajara, merit.

Ajib! or *'Ajab!* Wonderful! Wonderfully.

Ajili, or *ajili*, sake, cause.

Kwa ajili ya, because of, for the sake of.

Ajiri ku-, to hire.

Ajirisha ku-, to cause to hire, to let on hire.

'Ajjemi, Persian.

Aka ku-, to build in stone, to do mason's work.

Akali, some few, some.

Akali ya watu, ya vitu, &c., some few men, things, &c.

-ake, or *-akwe*, his, her, or its, of him, &c.

-ake yeye, his own.

Akenda, for *Akaenda*, and he went.

Akhera = *Ahera*.

Akhtilaf, to quarrel.

Atafanya akhtilaf, she will scold.

Akia ku-, to build for.

Ak'ia ku-, to swallow, gulp down.

Akiba, store, a thing laid by.

Kuweka akiba, to lay up, to put by.

Akida, an officer, a second in command.

Akida wa asikari, an army officer.

Akidi ku-, to suffice.

Akiisha or *Akisha*, then, he having finished this business.

Akika, a funeral feast for a child.

Akili, intelligence, wits, understanding (generally treated as a plural noun).

Akina, you—addressed to young or inferior persons. *Akina bwana* young sirs. *Akina bibi*, my young ladies.

Akiri ku-, to stand over, to remain behind.

Akirisha ku-, to adjourn, put off, make to stand over.

ako, thy, your, of thee.

-ako wewe, your own.

Akraba, relations.

Akraba ya kuumeni, paternal relations.

Akraba ya kukeni, maternal relations.

Al, the Arabic article *the*. It is retained in many words derived from the Arabic, as *Alfajiri* for *Al Fajr*, the dawn. Sometimes its form is varied, as *Liwali* for *Al Wali*, the governor.

In Arabic phrases the definite article prefixed to the second of two nouns is the sign of the possessive case, as *Rayiat a'*

Ingrez, a subject of the English *i.e.*, a British subject.

Ala, plur. *maala* or *nyala*, a sheath, a scabbard.

'*Alaka*, a tusk of ivory.

Alafu, thousands.

Alama, a mark, marks.

Alasiri, one of the Mohammedan hours of prayer, about half-past 3 P.M., afternoon.

Albunseyidi (Ar.), of the sons of princes.

Alf = *Elfu*, a thousand.

Alfajiri, the dawn, the earliest Mohammedan hour of prayer, about 4 A.M. A stress on the second syllable denotes very early dawn.

Alfia.

Kofia alfia, a chief's cap.

Alhamisi, Thursday.

-ali- or *-li-*, the sign of that past tense which denotes an action complete in past time.

-li or *-li-* sometimes stands for the verb *to be*, as in *a-li-ye*, he who is, or merely, who. *A-li*, he is, or, he being. *Nika-li*, and I am.

Alia ku-, to make a mark by striking, to wale.

Alifu, *Alif*, the first Arabic letter, the alphabet.

Alika ku-, to invite, to call, to call invited guests to a wedding, to inform, to split, to click, to give a crack, to snap.

Alikwa ku-, to go through a certain course of medicine, consisting chiefly of various fumigations and a very strict regimen.

Aliki ku-, to hang.

Aliko, where he is, or was.

Alimisha ku-, to instruct.

Aliomo, wherein he is, or was.

Alisa, a dancing place, a house of amusement.

Alisha ku-, to cause to snap.

Kualisha mtambo wa bunduki, to click the lock of a gun.

Allah (Ar.), God, more reverently, *Allah ta'ala*, God the most high.

Allah Allah, without delay or pretence.

Allah billkheir, may God make it good. A common answer to the usual morning and afternoon salutations.

Almaria, embroidery.

Almasi, a diamond.

Ama—ama, either—or.

Ama siyo? Isn't it so?

Amali, an act, a thing done.

Amali, a kind of amulet.

Amama (Ar.), a turban?

Amana, a pledge, a thing entrusted, a deposit, a present sent by another person.

Amani, peace.

Amara, urgent business.

Amara (*ya nanga*), a cable.

Amba ku-, to speak against, to talk scandal, to speak, to say.

Amba. See *Ambaye.*

Ambaa ku-, to go near to without touching, not to reach, to leave unhurt.

Ambari, ambergris.

Ambata ku-, to attach, to stick.

Ambatana ku-, to cleave together, to be mutually attached.

Ambatiza ku-, to make to stick.

Ambaye or *Ambaye kwamba*, who. The final syllable is variable, making *ambazo*, *ambayo*, &c., which.

Ambaza ku-, to cause to pass near without touching.

Ambia ku-, to tell, to say to.
Pass. *Kuambiwa*, to be told, to have said to one.

Ambika ku-, to put (or be put?) firmly together.

Ambilika ku-, to be spoken to.

Ambisana ku-, to be cemented together, to stick together.

Ambisha ku-, to make to hold together.

Ambua ku-, to peel, to husk, to take a morsel in eating.

Ambukiza ku-, to give a complaint to, infect.

Amdelhan, a silky kind of stuff.

Amerikano, American sheeting, best cotton cloth used in trading in the interior.
Njia, &c., *ya Amerikano*, the best way, &c.

Amili ku-, to manage.

Amina, Amen.

Amini ku-, to believe in, trust.
Kuamini mtu na kitu, to trust a man with something, to entrust something to some one.

Amini, or *Aminifu*, trustworthy, faithful.

Aminisha ku-, to entrust to, have perfect confidence in.

Amiri, plur. *maamiri*, an emir, an officer.

Amka ku-, to awake.

Amkia ku-, to salute.

Amkua ku-, to invite, summon (?).

Amrawi, a dipping line, made fast to the foremost yard-arm.

Amri, order, command.
Amri ya Muungu, a matter in God's hands.
Sina amri, &c., I have no business, &c.

Amria ku-, to put a thing at one's disposal, to give leave concerning something.

Amrisha ku-, to cause to be ordered, order.

Amru ku-, to order, command.

Amsha ku-, to waken, cause to awake, rouse.

Amu, Lamoo.
Kiamu, the dialect of Lamoo, of the Lamoo kind.

Amu, father's brother.

Amua ku-, to judge, to separate two people who are fighting.
Passive, *Kuamuliwa*, to be judged.

Amuka ku- = *Amka ku-*.

Amuru ku- = *Amru ku-*.

Amusha ku- = *Amsha ku-*.

Amwa ku-, to suck (M.).

Amwisha ku-, to suckle (M.).

Ana, he has.

Anakotoka, whence he is coming, where he comes from.

-anana, gentle, soft.
Upepo mwanana, a soft breeze.
Maji manana, clear, quiet water.

Anapokwenda, whither he is going.

Anapolala, while he is sleeping.

Anasa, pleasure.

Andaa ku-, to prepare for cooking, to make pastry, &c.

Andalia ku-, to prepare for, to make made dishes for.

Andama ku-, to follow (M.).
Mwezi umeandama, the month is up—the new moon has begun.

Andamana ku-, to accompany (M.).

Andika ku-, to put in order, to lay out, to describe, to write, to steer a vessel.

Andikanya ku-, to put things one upon another, as plates in a pile.

Andikia ku-, to write, to lay out, &c., for or on account of.

Andikiwa ku-, to be written, laid out, &c., for.

Andikiana ku-, to write to one another, to correspond.

Anfu, knowing, ingenious.

Anga, a great light, the firmament.

Ndege za anga, birds of the air.

Anga ku-, to jump or dance about like a wizard.

Angaika ku-, to be in a great bustle.

Angalia ku-, to look attentively, regard, take notice, observe, be careful, beware of.

Angama ku-, to be caught in falling (as by the boughs of a tree).

Angamia ku-, to be ruined, to fall, come to poverty.

utaangamia mwituni, you will be lost in the jungle.

Angamisha ku-, to ruin.

Angaza ku-, to be light, to be bright, to remain awake, to keep watch.

Kutia mwangaza, to give light to.

Angia ku-, to bewitch by dancing and jumping about.

Angika ku-, to hang up, to hang against a wall.

-angu, my, of me.

-angu mimi, my own.

Angua ku-, to take down, to hatch [eggs.

Anguka ku-, to fall down.

Angukia ku-, to fall down to, or before.

Angusha ku-, to make to fall down, throw down.

Ania ku-, to purpose, think of doing.

Anika ku-, to spread out to dry.

Ankra, a bill of sale.

Anua ku-, to take out of the sun or rain.

Anuka ku-, to leave off raining.

Anwani, the address of a letter.

Anza ku-, to begin.

The *ku-* is frequently retained, as *Alikwanza* for *Alianza*.

Anziliza ku-, to make a beginning.

Anzwani, Johanna.

Ao, or.

Ao—ao, either—or.

-ao, their, of them.

Apa ku-, to swear.

Apendalo, what he likes.

Api? where?

The *a* sometimes is so run into the final *a* of the preceding word as to be scarcely separable from it.

Apia ku-, to swear to, or about.

Apisha ku-, to make to swear, to adjure.

Apiza ku-, to swear at, to imprecate against, to wish bad luck to.

Apizo, plur. *maapizo*, an imprecation.

Arabuni, Arabia, in Arabia.

Arabuni, earnest money.

Arathi, pardon.

Arba'a, four.

'Ari, a thing to make one blush a disgraceful thing.

Aria, following, party, faction.

Ariaa, lower! let out the rope!

Arifu, knowing, ingenious.

Arifu ku-, to inform.

Arobaini, forty.

Arobatashara, fourteen.

Asa ku-, to forbid.

Asali, syrup.

Asali ya nyuki, honey.

Asali ya mua, the boiled juice of the sugar-cane, treacle.

Asali ya tembo, fresh palm wine boiled into a syrup.

'Ashara, ten.

Asharini, twenty.

Ashekali, better in health during sickness.

Kuwa ashekali, to improve.

Kufanya ashekali, to make better

Asherati, dissipation, a dissipated person.

Ashiiki ku-, to love, to love exceedingly.

Ashiria ku-, to make a sign to.

Ashúr, customs duties.

Asi ku-, to neglect one's duty to, to rebel, to be disobedient.

Kuasi mkewe, to quarrel with his wife, and not do his duty by her.

Asikari, plur. *asikari*, or *waasikari*, a soldier.

Kutia asikari, to enlist.

Asili, origin, nature, source.

Asisha ku-, to cause to leave, to cause to cease.

Asitasa, not yet.

Assubui, in the morning.

Asusa, that which assuages bitterness or pain, takes away an unpleasant taste. Also *Azuza*.

Ata, *Atana*, *Atia*, *Atilia*, (M.) = *Acha*, *Achana*, &c.

Atamia ku-, to sit on eggs, to hatch eggs.

Atamisha ku-, to put under a sitting [hen.

Atgul, average.

Athabatisha ku-, to control.

Athama, highness.

Mwenyi athama, the Most High.

Athari = *Hathari*.

Athibu ku-, to chastise, to punish.

Athibisha ku-, to punish.

Athima = *Athama*.

Athimika ku-, to be exalted.

Athini ku-, to call to public prayers.

Athuuri, noon, one of the Mohammedan hours of prayer.

Ati! look you! I say!

Atibu, a fragrant herb used in the composition of *kikuba*.

Attia, gratuitously, for nothing.

Atuka ku-, to crack as the earth does in very dry weather.

Aua ku-, to make a survey of, to go over and look at.

Auka ku-, to grow large enough to bear fruit.

Auni ku-, to help.

Avya ku-, to produce, to spend, to give away.

Awa ku-, to go out or away (Mer.).

Awala, a promissory note.

Awali or *Aowali*, first, almost, nearly.

Awaza ku-, to dispose, to allot to each his share.

Awesia, a kind of dhow like a *bedeni* (which see), without any prow or head, with merely a perpendicular cutwater.

Awini ku-, to help, to supply.

Awithi ku-, to barter.

Ayari, a cheat.

Ayari, a pulley, the stay of a dhow's mast.

Ayasi, a sort of grass.

Ayasi ya shaba, brass wire.

Ayika ku-, to dissolve, to melt.

Ayithi ku-, to preach.

Aza ku- = *Waza ku-*, to ponder, think.

Azama, a nose ring.

Azima, a charm used to bring back a runaway slave and to drive away evil spirits.

Azima ku-, to lend.

Azimwa ku-, to borrow.

Azimia ku-, to make an *azima* against.

Azimia ku-, to resolve.

Azimu ku-, to resolve (generally pronounced *ázimu*).

Azizi, a rarity, a curiosity.

Azma, scent, fume.

Azur, perjury.

Azuza. See *Asusa*.

B.

B has the same sound as in English.

N changes into *m* before *b*, as *mbaya* for *n-baya*, bad.

mbwa for *n-bwa*, a dog or dogs.

Nw also becomes *mb*.

mbingu for *n-wingu*, the heavens.

Ba, a shortened form of *bwana*.

Baa, evil

Baa, plur. *mabaa*, a worthless person, an utter reprobate.

Baada, afterwards.

Baada ya, after (used preferably of time).

Baadaye, or *baada yake*, after it, then, afterwards.

Baathi, some.

Baathi ya watu, some persons.

Baazi, a sort of pea growing on a small tree somewhat resembling laburnum.

Bab (Ar.), a gate, chapter.

Bab Ulaya, goods for the European market.

Bab Kachi, goods for the Cutch trade.

Bab il amana, something entrusted, lent to one.

Baba, father.

Baba mdogo, mother's brother.

Baba wa kambo, stepfather.

Baba wa waana, } an owl.
Baba wa watoto, }

Babaika ku-, to hesitate in speaking, to stutter, to talk in one's sleep.

Babata ku-, to pat, to tap, to flatten out.

Babu, grandfather, ancestors

Babua ku-, to strip off.

Babuka ku-, to tear, to become torn.

Badala or *Badali*, a thing given in exchange for something else, an equivalent.

Badani. See *Kansu*.

Badili ku-, to change, exchange, alter, become changed.

Badilika ku-, to be changed, to be changeable.

Bado, not yet, used generally to express that the matter in question is as yet incomplete.

Bado kidogo, soon.

Bafe, a kind of snake.

Bafta, a sort of fine calico.

Bagala or *Bágala*, a buggalo, a large kind of dhow square in the stern, with a high poop and a very long prow. Most of the Indian trading dhows are of this build; they have generally a small mizen-mast.

Bághala, a mule.

Bagua ku-, to separate.

Baguka ku-, to be separate.

Bagukana ku-, to be in hostility, to be on two sides.

Bahari, sea.

Bahari il'ali, the Persian Gulf.

Bahari ya Sham, the Red Sea.

Baharia, a sailor, sailors, the crew.

Bahasha, a square bag or pocket with a three-cornered flap to tie over the opening, frequently used to keep books in.

Bahati or *Bakhti*, luck, good fortune.

Bakhti mtu, that depends on the person.

Bahatisha ku-, to guess.

Baini, &c. See *Bayini*, &c.

Baini ya, between.

Bajia, small cakes of ground beans and pepper.

Bajuni = *Mgunya.*

Bakaku, to dispute, to argue.

Bakhili, a miser, covetous, miserly.

Bakhti. See *Bahati.*

Baki, the remainder, what is left.

Baki (in arithmetic), subtraction.

Baki ku-, to remain, to be over, to be left.

Bakora, a walking stick with the top bent at right angles to the stem. The best are made of a white, straight-grained wood (mtobwe), which will bend nearly double like a piece of lead without breaking or returning.

Baksha, a packet, of clothes, &c.

Bakuli, plur. *mabakuli*, a basin.

Bakwia ku-, to snatch out of the hand.

Balaa, sorrow.

Balamwezi, moonlight, moonshine.

Balanga, leprosy.

Balasi, a large kind of water jar.

Bali, but.

Balighi, a boy who is a virgin, a youth.

Balungi, plur. *mabalungi*, a citron.

Bamba, plur. *mabamba*, a plate, a flat thin piece.

Bambo, an instrument like a cheese-taster thrust into a bag to draw out some of its contents for examination.

Mabambo, large mats for beating out mtama upon.

Bamvua, spring-tides.

Bana ku-, to squeeze, press as in a vice.

Banada, the Somauli coast.

Banajiri or *Banagiri*, a kind of bracelet ornamented with points or blunt spikes, much worn in Zanzibar.

Banda, plur. *mabanda*, a large shed.

Banda la frasi, a stable.

Bandari, a harbour.

Bandera, a flag, red stuff the colour of the Arab flag.

Bandi, a seam.

Kupiga bandi (in sewing), to tack, to run, to baste.

Bandia.

Mtoto wa bandia, a doll.

Bandika ku-, to put on a plaster or any medicament.

Bandua ku-, to strip off, to peel off.

Banduka ku-, to peel off, to come out of its shell, to be peeled.

Bangi, bhang, Indian hemp.

Banika ku-, to roast on a spit over the fire.

Baniya, a temple, a building, especially that at Mecca.

Banja ku-, to crack nuts, &c., to break off the shell or husk by beating.

Banyani, plur. *mabanyani*, used in Zanzibar as a general name for the heathen Indians who come as traders from Cutch.

Banza.

Kujibanza, to squeeze oneself against a wall or into a hedge to allow some one else to pass.

Banzi, plur. *mabanzi*, a small thin piece of wood, a splint.

Bao, the tiller of a small craft (A.).

Bao, a game in card-playing.

Mabao sita = *Mvumo.*

Kutia bao, to mark, in card-playing.

Bao or *Bao la komwe*, a board with thirty-two small holes, each about the size of a teacup, for playing a very favourite game also called *bao*, with *komwe*, or with pebbles. The holes are sometimes merely scooped out in the ground, and any small things used to play with.

Kucheza bao, to play at the above game.

Bapa, the flat of a sword, &c.

Kupiga bapa, to strike with the flat of a sword.

Bara, a species of antelope (Helgobagus arundinaceus).

Bara or *Barra*, wild country, coast. The Arabic name, Zénjibarr, is compounded of this word and *Zenj* or *Zanj*, a negro: hence the Zanguebar and Zanzibar of our maps mean only the negro coast. The Swahili name for Zanzibar is invariably *Unguja*.

Barr Faris, the piece of Persian coast belonging to Oman.

Barr Swáhil, the Swahili coast.

Baraba, proper, just, exactly.

Barabara, a broad open road.

Barafu, ice.

Baragumo, a spiral horn used as a musical instrument; it is blown through a hole at the small end.

Barai, an after brace carried on the lee side to steady the yard of a dhow.

Baraka, a blessing. Also common as a proper name.

Barakoa, a mask reaching down to the mouth, universally worn by the women of Oman and Zanzibar of the upper class.

Barasi, a disease.

Barathuli, an idiot, dupe, simpleton. Also *barazuli*.

Barawai, a swallow.

Baraza, a stone seat or bench table, either outside the house or in the hall, or both, where the master sits in public and receives his friends; hence the durbar, or public audience held by the sultan, and the council then held.

Baridi, cold, wind.

Maji ya baridi, fresh water.

Baridiyabis, rheumatism.

Bariki ku-, to bless.

N.B.—Young people are said in Zanzibar to *bariki*, when they first have connection with the opposite sex. Girls are thought old enough between nine and ten.

Barikia ku-, to give a blessing to, to greet.

Bariyo (A.), what is left from the evening meal to be eaten in the morning.

Barizi ku-, to sit in *baraza*, to hold a public reception.

Barra. See *Bara*.

Barua or *Bárua*, a summons from a judge, a bill, a letter.

Baruti, gunpowder.

Barzuli, a fool.

Basbasi, mace, the inner husk of the nutmeg.

Bashire kheri! may it be lucky!

Bashiri ku-, to prognosticate, to foretell by signs.

Bashishi or *Bakhshishi*, a gift, a largess.

Basiri ku-, to foresee.

Bass or *Bassi*, enough, it will do. When it begins a sentence it means—well, and so, and then. When it follows a word or phrase it means—just this and no more.

Bastola, a pistol.

Bata, plur. *mabata*, a duck.

Bata la bukini, a goose.

Bata la mzinga, a turkey.

Batela, the common dhow of Zanzibar; it has a square stern and an ordinary boat-like head.

Bati, tin, block tin.

Batil. See *Betili.*

Batili ku-, to annul, **to abolish**, to reduce to nothing.

Batli, the log (nautical).

Batobato, plur. *ma-*, various colours and marks on an animal.

Bau, a wizard's fortune-telling board.

Kupiga bau, to divine.

Baura, a European anchor.

Bavuni, alongside, at the side.

Bawa, plur. *mabawa*, the wing of a bird. Also, the scales of a fish.

Bawaba, a hinge.

Bawabu, a house-porter, door-keeper.

Bawasir, hæmorrhoids.

-baya, bad. It makes *mbaya* with nouns like *nyumba*.

Bayini ku-, to recognize, to know.

Bayinika ku-, to be notorious, to be well known.

Bayinisha ku-, to distinguish between, separate distinctly.

Bazazi, a trader, especially a cheating, over-sharp trader, a huckster.

Beba ku-, to carry (a child) on the back in a cloth.

Bebera, a he-goat given to covering, strong, manly.

Bedari, the fixed lower pulley for hoisting a dhow sail and yard, bitts to which and through which the *jirari* are passed and secured.

Bedeni, a kind of dhow with a perpendicular cutwater, or merely a piece of board by way of prow, a sharp stern, and high rudder head. The mast of a *bedeni* is perpendicular; in other dhows it bends forward. They come from the Arab coast.

Bee, a bargain, a trade, transaction.

Beek, for *Lebeka.*

Bega, plur. *mabega*, the shoulder.

Behewa, the inner court in a stone house. All large houses in Zanzibar are built round an inner court.

Beina, between.

Beina yako nini? what do you know about it? Compare *Bayini.*

Bekua ku-, to parry, to knock off a blow.

Belghamu, phlegm.

Bembe, food and confectionery cooked by a woman for her lover, and sent to him during the *Ramathan.*

Bembeleza ku-, to beg.

Bembesha ku-, to swing.

Bembeza ku- } to beg, to caress, to pat.
Bembeleza ku- }

Benua ku-, to put forward, to stick out.

Kubenua kidari, to walk with the chest thrown forward.

Benuka ku-, to warp.

Kubenuka kiko kwa kiko, to warp and twist this way and that.

Besa, vulgar Arabic for *pesa.* *Besteen* = *Pesa mbili.*

Besera, canopy of a bedstead.

Betela = *Batela.*

Beti, a pouch for shot or cartridges.

Beti (Ar.), a house, a line in verses.

Betili or *Batíl*, a dhow with a very long prow, and a sharp stern with a high rudder head. They generally belong to the Shemali, or Persian Gulf Arabs.

Beyana, legible, clear.

Bia.

Kula bia, to subscribe to a meal in common, to go shares in a meal.

Biashara, trade, commerce.

Kufanya biashara, to trade.

Mfanyi biashara, a trader, a merchant.

Bibi, grandmother. It is used as a title answering to *my lady*, and for the *mistress* of slaves.

Bibo, plur. *mabibo*, a cashew apple.

-bichi, fresh, green, unripe, raw, under-done. It makes *mbichi* with nouns like *nyumba*.

Bidii, effort to surpass, emulation.

Bikira, a virgin.

Bikiri ku-, to deflower.

Bilashi, gratis, for nothing.

Bilauri, a drinking glass.

Bildi, the lead (nautical).

Bilisi = *Iblis*, the devil.

Billa, except by.

Bilula, a tap.

Bima, insurance.

Bima ku-, to insure against accidents.

Binadamu, a human being (a son of Adam).

Bindo, the loin-cloth held up to receive or carry things, a bundle in a cloth.

Kukinga bindo, to hold up the loin-cloth to receive things.

Bingwa, shrewd, knowing.

Binti, daughter. Women in Zanzibar are generally mentioned by their father's name only, as, *Binti Mohammed*, Mohammed's daughter.

Birika, plur. *mabirika*, a large vessel for holding water, a cistern.

Birinzi, a dish composed of meat, rice, pepper, &c.

Bisha ku, to knock or cry *Hodi!* at a door to attract the attention of the people within. It is held very wrong to go beyond the entrance hall of a house unless invited in.

Bisha ku-, to work in sailing. Also, to make boards.

Bishana ku-, to squabble, to quarrel.

Bishara, a sign, a good sign.

Bisho, tacking, working to the windward.

Upepo wa bisho, a foul wind.

Bisi, parched Indian corn.

Bitana, lined, double, used of clothes wherever there are two thicknesses.

Bithaa, goods, merchandise.

-bivu or *-wivu*, ripe, well done. It makes *mbivu* with nouns like *nyumba*.

Biwi, plur. *mabiwi*, heaps of garden rubbish, leaves, wood, &c.

Bizari, a small seed used in making curry.

Bize, a wild hunting dog.

Bizima, a buckle.

-bofu or *-ovu*, rotten, bad, malicious.

Boga, plur. *maboga*, a pumpkin.

Boga is used as a general word for edible vegetables.

Bogi = *Pombe*.

Bogoa ku-, to strip off leaves, to tear apart, to chop away wood in making a point?

Bohari or *Bokhari*, a storehouse, a house with a shop and warerooms.

Boko, a buffalo (?).

Bokoboko, a kind of food made of wheat, meat, &c.

Bokwa, jack fruit [Tumbatu].

Boma, plur. *maboma*, a heap of stones, a rampart.

Bomba, a pump.

Bomboromoka, plur. *ma-*. See *Boromoka.*

Bomoa ku-, to make a hole through, to break down.

Bomoka ku-, to have a hole broken through it, to be broken down.

Bongo, plur. *mabongo*, brains, marrow.

Bonth, a bridge, a pier. From the French *pont.*

Bonyea ku-, to give way, to crush in.

Bonyesha ku-, to press so as to sink in, to make an impression with the fingers.

Bonyeza ku-, to examine by feeling and pressing. See *Tomasa.*

Boonde, a valley, a hollow place.

Bora, great, very great, noble, best, most.

Bori, the bowl of a native pipe.

Boriti, a rafter, thick poles cut in the mangrove swamps and laid flat to support the stone roofs.

Borohoa, a dish made of pounded pulse with flavourings.

Boromoka ku-, to fall down a precipice.

Boromoka, plur. *ma-*, precipices, precipitous places. Also *bomboromoka*, plur. *ma-*.

Borongaboronga ku-, to make a mess of one's work.

Boroshoa, a long-shaped black insect found in dunghills.

Boruga ku-, to stir, to cut up weeds.

-bovu or *-ovu*, rotten, bad.

Boza, a narcotic made by mixing bhang with flour and honey.

Bozibozi, idle, dull.

Brámini, an agent (working for two per cent. commission.)

Bua, plur. *mabua*, the stem of millet.

Buba, rupia, applied to various skin diseases.

Bubu, (A.), a teat.

Bubu, plur. *mabubu*, dumb.

Bubujika ku-, to bubble out, burst forth.

Kububujika machozi, to burst into tears.

Bubur (M.), dumb.

Buddi, escape, other course.

Sina buddi, I have no escape, *ie.*, I must.

Bueta, a box. Also *bweta*. (From the French, *boîte.*)

Buga, a hare (?).

Bughuthu ku-, to hate.

Buhuri, incense.

Buibui, a spider.

Buki or *Bukini*, Madagascar.

Buki, a kidney.

Buku, a very large kind of rat.

Buli, plur. *mabuli*, a teapot.

Bumbuazi, perplexity, idiotcy.

Kupigwa na bumbuazi, to become confused and abashed, so as not to be able to go on with one's business.

Bumbwi, rice flour pounded up with scraped cocoa-nut.

Bumia, sternpost.

Bumunda, plur. *mabumunda*, a sort of soft cake or dumpling.

Bundi, a native bird, an owl. Owls are thought very unlucky.

Bunduki, a gun, a musket.

Bungala, a kind of rice.

Bungo, plur. *mabungo*, a kind of fruit something like a medlar.

Bungu, plur. *mabungu*, a dish.

Bungu la kupozea uji, a saucer to cool gruel in.

Buni, raw coffee, coffee-berries.

Buni, an ostrich.

Buni, (Ar.), sons, the sons of.

Buni ku-, to begin, to be the first to do a thing, to invent.

Bunju, a poisonous fish.

Bunzi, plur. *mabunzi*, a stinging fly.

Buothu ku-, to bate.

Bupuru, plur. *mabupuru*, an empty shell.

Bupuru la kitwa, a skull.

Burangeni, of two colours, neither black nor white; also painted of different colours, as a dhow with a white stripe.

Buratangi, a whirring kite.

Burdu.

Marashi ya Burdu, eau-de-Cologne.

Buri, large-sized tusks of ivory.

Buriani, a final farewell, asking a general forgiveness.

Kutakana buriani, to ask mutual pardon and so take a last farewell.

Burikao, Port Durnford.

Burre, for nothing, gratis, in vain, for no good.

Buruda, a book of the prayers used over a dying person.

Burudika ku-, to be refreshed.

Burudisha ku-, to cool, to refresh.

Buruga ku-, to mix up, to knock together.

Buruhani, token, evidence.

Buruji, battlements.

Burura ku-, to drag, to haul along.

Busara, prudence, subtlety, astuteness.

Busati, a kind of matting made at Muscat.

Bushashi, a thin sort of stuff.

Bushu, tow, a gun-wad.

Bushuti, woollen stuff, blanket.

Bustani, a garden.

Busu, a kiss.

Busu ku-, to kiss.

Buu, plur. *mabuu*, maggots in meat (M.).

Buyu, plur. *mabuyu*, a calabash, the fruit of the baobab tree, used to draw water with.

Buzi, plur. *mabuzi*, a very large goat.

Bwaga ku-, to throw down what one has been carrying; to tip off one's head, &c.; to rest by throwing down one's burden.

Kubwaga nazi, to throw down cocoa-nuts.

Bwana, master of slaves, master of the house, lord, sir, used politely in speaking of one's own father.

Bwana mdogo, master's son.

Bwanda = *Gwanda*.

Bwara.

Reale ya bwara, a dollar under full weight, a 5-franc piece.

Bweta. See *Bueta*.

C.

C is required only in writing the sound of the English *ch* or of the Italian *c* before *i* and *e*.

In the dialect of Zanzibar *ch* frequently stands for the *t* of more northern Swahili, as—

Chupa, a bottle (Zanzibar) = *Tupa* (Mombas).

Kucheka, to laugh (Zanz.) = *Kuteka* (Momb.).

Chi, in the vulgar dialect, and amongst the slaves in Zanzibar, stands for *ki* in the more correct language. Several of the tribes in the interior follow the same rule as the Italian in always pronouncing the same root letter *ch* before *i* and *e*, and *k* before *a* and *o*.

Thus slaves commonly say, *Chitu chidogo*, a little thing, for *Kitu kidogo*.

As a rule, in all Swahili where the preformative *ki* has to be prefixed to an adjective or pronoun or tense prefix beginning with a vowel, it becomes *ch*, thus—

Kisu changu, my knife, not *Kisu kiangu*.

Kisu chakata, the knife cuts, not *Kisu kiakata*.

Kitu chema cho chote, every good thing whatsoever, not *Kitu kiema kio kiote*.

Where *ch* represents *ki*, as the initial sound of a substantive, the plural is made by changing *ch* into *vy*.

Chombo, a vessel, *Vyombo*, vessels.

But where *ch* stands for *t*, the plural is made by prefixing *ma*.

Machupa, bottles.

Machungwa, oranges.

The Arabs confound in their pronunciation *ch* with *sh*, though the sounds are in Swahili perfectly distinct.

It would perhaps be an improvement to write all *ch*'s which represent *ki* by a simple *c*, which has been used for this sound in Sechuana, and to write all *ch*'s which represent *t* by *ty*, which has been used for this sound in writing Zulu. But both are here represented by *ch*, because at least in the infancy of our studies it is puzzling to have two signs for one sound, and neither way of writing might be quite satisfactory in all cases.

There is little doubt that the northern *t* becomes *ch* by the addition of a *y* sound, as the same sort of change takes place with *d*, which becomes *dy* or *j*, and sometimes with *n*, making it *ny* or the Spanish ñ. The same sort of change in English vulgarizes *nature* into *nachur*, and *Indian* into *Injun*.

Ch- = *ki-*, which see.

Ch-, a prefix required by substantives beginning with *ki-* or *ch-* representing *ki-*, in all pronouns and adjectives beginning with a vowel, and in tenses of the verb where the tense prefix begins with a vowel.

Cha, of.

Many quasi-substantives may be made by prefixing *cha* to a verb, *kitu* being understood, as *chakula* (a thing), of eating, food.

Cha or *Chayi*, tea.

Cha kú-, to fear [A.] (the *ku-* bears the accent, and is retained in the usual tenses).

Cha kú-, to dawn, to rise [of the sun] the *ku-* bears the accent, and is retained in the usual tenses.

Kumekucha, the dawn (it has dawned).

Kunakucha, the dawning.

Usiku kucha, all night till dawn, all night long. See *Chwa*.

Chaanzu, the beginning of a piece of *ukiri*.

Chacha ku-, to ferment, leaven, work.

Chachaga ku-, to wash clothes by

dabbing them gently on a stone or board, not to beat them so hard as is implied in the more common word *kufua*.

-chache, few, little, not many or much. It makes *chache* with nouns like *myumba*.

Chachia ku-, to come with a press, to come much at once, to burst upon one.

Chachu, bran, leaven, ferment.

Chafi, a kind of fish.

Chafi.

Chafi cha mguu, calf of the leg = *tafu*.

Chafu, plur. *machafu*, the cheek, especially that part which is over the teeth.

Chafua ku-, to put in disorder, disarrange.

Chafuka ku-, to be in disorder, in dishabille.

Moyo umechafuka, (I) feel sick.

Chafukachafuka ku-, to be all in a mess, to be all tumbled about and in confusion.

Chafuo, a poisonous horse-fly.

Chafya ku-, or *kupiga chafya*, or *kwenda chafya*, to sneeze.

Chagaa = *Tagaa*.

Chago, land crabs.

Chago, the place where the head is laid (on a kitanda, etc.).

Chagua, ku-, to pick out, select, garble.

Chai, or *Chayi*, tea.

Chakaa ku-, to become worn out, to become good for nothing through age or use.

Chake, or *chakwe*, his, her, its. See *-ake*.

Chaki, chalk, whitening, putty.

Chako, thy. See *-ako*.

Chakogea = *[Kitu] cha ku-ogea*, a thing to bathe in, a bath.

Chakula, something to eat, food, a meal.

Chakula cha subui, breakfast.

Chakula cha mchana, dinner.

Chakula cha jioni, supper, which is the chief meal of the day.

Plur. *vyakula*, victuals.

Chale, a cut or gash made for ornament.

Chali, backward, on his back.

Chama, a club, guild, band of people.

Waana chama, members of it

Chamba cha jicho, a white film over the eye.

Chambo, plur. *vyambo*, a bait.

Chambua ku-, to dress, clean, pick over, as to pluck off the outer leaves of vegetables when sending them to market, to pick the sticks and dirt out of cotton, to pick cloves off their stalks, &c.

Chambulia ku-, to clean up, to dress up work or things.

Chamburo, a plate for wire drawing.

Chamchela.

Pepo za chamchela, a whirlwind.

Cha'msha kanwa (something to wake the mouth), something eaten first thing in the morning.

Chana = *Tana*.

Chana ku-, to comb.

Chanda, plur. *vyanda* (M.), a finger, a toe.

Chandalua, an awning, a mosquito net.

-changa, young, immature.

Changa ku-, to sift away chaff and husks.

Kula kwa kuchanga, a feast

where each contributes something to the entertainment.

Changa'mka ku-, to be genial, to be hearty and pleasant.

Changamusha ku-, to cheer up.

Changanya ku-, to mix.

Changanyika ku-, to be mixed.

Changanyisha ku-, to perplex.

Changarawi, girt, little white stones like those in coarse sand.

Chango, plur. *vyango*, a peg to hang things upon.

Chango, small intestines, round worms.

Changu, a kind of fish.

Changu, a tribal mark (?).

Changu, my. See *-angu*.

Chani = *Tani*, on the back, backward.

Chania ku-, to comb for, &c.

Chanikiwiti, green.

Chanja ku-, to cut up [firewood, &c.].

Chanjiwa ku-. ndui, to be cut for small-pox, to be vaccinated.

Chano, plur. *vyano*, a large wooden platter, a mortar-board.

Chanua ku-, to put forth leaves.

Chao, their. See *-ao*.

Chapa, plur. *machapa*, a stamp, [type, *-a chapa*, printed.

Kupiga chapa, to print.

Chapa ku-, to beat, to stamp.

Chapachapa, wet through, all dripping.

Chapeo, a hat. From the French *chapeau* (?).

Chappa or *Chappara*, excessively.

Chapuo, a sort of small drum.

Chatu, a python, a crocodile (?).

Chavu, plur. *vyavu*, a net.

-chavu, filthy, unwashed.

Chawa, a louse.

Chayi, tea.

Chaza, an oyster.

Chazo, a sucker fish.

Cheche, a small box (such as a lucifer-box).

Cheche, a brown mangouste. Also = *chechi*.

Cheche, a spark.

Chechea ku-, to walk lame.

Chechele, an absent person, one who goes far beyond where he intended to stop through inattention.

Chechemea ku-, to be lame. Also, to reach up, stretch up to.

Chechi, plur. *machechi*, a spark.

Chegua ku-, to choose.

Cheka ku-, to laugh, to laugh at.

Chekelea ku-, to laugh at, because of.

Cheko, plur. *macheko*, a laugh, a loud laugh.

Chelea ku-, to fear for, about, &c.

Chelema, watery.

Chelewa ku, to be overtaken by something through thoughtlessness, to wake up and find it broad daylight, to be struck foolish, to be dumbfounded. Also, to be too late.

Sikukawia wala sikuchelewa, I did not delay, and I was not late.

Cheleza ku-, to keep, to put on one side, to put off.

Chelezea ku-, to keep or put aside [for.

Chelezo = *Chilezo*.

Chembe, a grain, grains.

Chembe, plur. *vyembe* (N.), an arrow, the head of an arrow or a harpoon.

Chembe cha moyo (A.), the pit of the stomach.

Chembeu, a chisel.

Chemchem, a spring of water.

Che'mka ku-, to boil, to bubble up.

Chenezo, plur. *vyenezo*, a measuring rod, line, &c.

Chenga ku-, to cleave, to cut wood, to prune.

Chenge chenge, small broken bits.

Chenja = *Chenza.*

Chenu, your. See *-enu.*

Chenyi, having, with. See *-enyi.*

Chenza, a large kind of mandarin orauge.

Chenza za kiajjemi, Persian, *i.e.*, good chenzas.

Cheo, plur. *vyeo*, measurement, measure, length, breadth, &c., position in the world, station.

Chepechepe, wet, soaked with rain, wetted.

Chepuka ku- = *Chipuka.*

Cherawi, a well-known mangrove swamp in the island of Zanzibar.

Cheree, a grindstone.

Chercvu, cunning, subtlety.

Cherkhana, machine.

Cherkhana cha kushona, a sewing machine.

Cheruwa, measles.

Chetezo, plur. *vyetezo*, a censer, a pot to fume incense in.

Cheti, plur. *vyeti*, a pass, a passport.

Chetu, our. See *-etu.*

Chewa, a kind of fish.

Cheza ku-, to play, to dance.

Kucheza gwaridi, to be drilled in European fashion.

Kucheza komari, to play for money.

Cheza, a kind of oyster.

Cheza ku-, to play with.

Kuchezea unyago, to deflower a virgin (?).

Chi = *Ki-*.

Chicha, the scraped cocoa-nut after the oil has been squeezed out. It is sometimes used to rub on the hands to clean them of grime, but is generally thrown a way as refuse.

Chichiri, a bribe.

Chikapo = *Kikapu*, a basket.

Chikichi, plur. *machikichi*, the fruit of the palm-oil tree.

Kichikichi, plur. *vichikichi*, the small nuts contained in the fruit of the palm-oil tree.

Chilezo, plur. *vilezo*, a buoy.

Chimba ku-, to dig (M. *timba*).

Chimbia ku-, to dig for (M. *timbia*).

Chimbia ku- = *Kimbia ku-*, to run away.

Chimbua ku-, to dig out or away.

Chimbuko, origin, first beginning. source.

Chini, down, bottom, below.

Yuko chini, he is down stairs.

Chini ya, under, below.

Chinja ku-, to cut, to slaughter animals by cutting the throat, which is the only manner allowed by the Mohammedan law, hence generally to kill for food (M. *kutinda*).

Chinki, a small yellow bird kept in cages.

Chinusi, a kind of water sprite, which is said to seize men when swimming, and hold them under water till they are dead, (?) cramp.

Chinyango, a lump of meat.

Chipuka, &c. = *Chupuka*, &c.

Chipukizi, a shoot, a young plant. See *Tepukuzi.*

Chipukizi ndio mti, children will be men in time.

Chiriki, a small yellow bird often kept in cages.

Chiro, chironi = *Choo, chooni.*

Chiroko = *Chooko*, a kind of pulse.

Chiti = *Cheti*, a note of hand, a note of any kind.

Cho, *-cho*, *-cho-*, which.
Cho chote, whatsoever.
Choa, ringworm.
Chocha ku-, to poke out from, out of a hole.
Chochea ku-, to make up a fire, to turn up a lamp.
Chochelezea ku-, to stir up and increase discord, to add fuel to the fire.
Chofya ku-. See *Chovya*.
Choka ku-, to become tired.
Nimechoka, I am tired.
Chokaa, lime.
Chokea, a stye in the eye, hordeolum.
Chokoa ku-, to clear out, to free from dirt, enlarge a small hole.
Chokochoko, a kind of fruit with a red prickly rind, white pulp, and a large kernel.
Chokora ku-, to pick (with a knife, &c.).
Chokora, plur. *machokora*, a hanger-on, a follower, a dependant.
Chokoza ku-, to teaze, to irritate.
Chole, a place on the island of Zanzibar famous for cocoa-nuts; also, the chief town of Monfia.
Choma ku-, to stab, to stick, to prick, to dazzle. Vulgarly in Zanzibar—to use fire to in any way, to burn, to roast, to parch, to fire, to apply cautery, to bake pottery.
Chombo, plur. *vyombo*, a vessel, a pot, a dhow.
Vyombo is used for household utensils, things used in a house, goods.
Chomea ku-. See *Choma ku-*.
Chomeka ku-, to be stuck into, to be set on fire.
Chomelea ku-, to take out a bad piece of cloth, thatch, &c., and put in a new one.
Chomoza ku-, to be hot.
Chonga ku-, to cut, to adze, to hollow out, to cut to a point.
Kuchonga kalamu, to make a pen.
Chonge, canine teeth, cuspids.
Chongea ku-, to cut for, or with.
Chongea ku-, to do a mischief to, to get (a person) into trouble, to inform against.
Chongeleza ku-, to carry tales, to backbite.
Chongo, loss of an eye.
Kuwa na chongo, to have lost an eye.
Mwenyi chongo, a one-eyed person.
Chongoka ku-, to be precipitous.
Choo, plur. *vyoo*, a privy, the bath-room, which always contains one.
Chooko, a small kind of pea, very much resembling the seeds of the everlasting pea of English gardens.
Chopa, plur. *machopa*, such a quantity as can be carried in the two hands.
Chopi.
Kwenda chopi, to walk lame in such a manner as that the lame side is raised at every step.
Chopoa ku-, to drag out of one's hand.
Chopoka ku-, to slip out of the hand.
Chora ku-, to carve, to adorn with carving, to draw on a wall.
Chorochoro, scratches, marks.
Choropoka ku-, to slip out of one's hand.
Choveka ku-, to put into water, to steep.
Chovya ku-, to dip, to gild.
Chosha ku-, to tire, to make tired.

Chosi = *Kisoze.*
Chota ku-, to make up a little at a time.
Chote, all. See *-ote.*
Chovu, weary, tired.
Choyo, greediness, avarice.
Mwenyi choyo, a miser.
Chozi, plur. *machozi*, a tear, a tear-drop.
Chub! sht! nonsense!
Chubua ku-, to take the skin off, to bruise.
Chubuachubua ku-, to bruise about, to batter.
Chubuka ku-, to be raw, to be bruised.
Chubwi, a plummet.
Chuchu ya ziwa, a teat.
Chuchumia ku-, to stretch up to reach something.
Chui, a leopard, leopards.
Chuja ku-, to strain.
Chujuka ku-, to have the colour washed out.
Chuki, the being easily disgusted or offended.
Ana chuki huyu, he is easily put out.
Chukia ku-, to be disgusted at, to abhor, to hate, not to bear.
Chukiwa ku-, to be offended.
Chukiza ku-, to disgust, to offend.
Chukizisha ku-, to make to offend.
Chuku, a cupping horn.
Chukua ku-, to carry, to carry off, to bear, to support, to sustain.
Kuchukua mimba, to be pregnant.
Chukulia ku-, to carry for a person.
Pass. *kuchukuliwa*, to be carried for, to have carried for one, to be borne, to drift.
Chukuliana ku-, to bear with one another.
Chukuza ku-, to make, to carry, to load.
Chula or *Chura*, plur. *vyula*, a frog.
Chuma, plur. *vyuma*, iron, a piece of iron.
Chuma ku-, to pluck, to gather, to make profit.
Chumba, plur. *vyumba*, a room.
Chumvi, salt.
Chumvi ya haluli, sulphate of magnesia.
Chuna ku, to flay.
Chunga ku-, to pasture, to tend animals.
Chunga ku-, to sift.
Chungu, plur. *vyungu*, an earthen cooking pot.
Chungu, ants.
Chungu, a heap.
Chungu chungu, in heaps.
-chungu, bitter (*uchungu*, the quality of bitterness).
Chungulia ku-, to peep.
Chungwa, plur. *machungwa*, an orange.
Chungwa la kizungu, a sweet orange.
Chunika ku-, to lose the skin, to be flayed.
Chunjua, a wart.
Chunuka ku-, to love exceedingly, to long for.
Chunuzi = *Chinusi.*
Chunyu, an incrustation of salt, as upon a person after bathing in salt water.
Chuo, plur. *vyuo*, a book.
Chuoni, school.
Mwana wa chuoni, a scholar, learned man.
Chupo, plur. *machupa*, a bottle.
Chupia ku-, to dash.
Chupuka ku- or *Chipuka ku-*, to sprout, become sprouted, to shoot, to spring.

Chupuza ku-, or *Chipuza ku-*, to sprout, to throw out sprouts, to shoot, to spring.

Churukiza ku-, to drain out.

Chururika ku- = *Churuzika ku-*.

Churuwa, measles.

Churuza ku-, to keep a stall, to trade in a small way.

Churuzika ku-, to run down with.

Kuchuruzika damu, to bleed freely.

Chussa, plur. *vyussa*, a harpoon.

Chuuza = *Churuza*.

Chwa kú-, to set (of the sun). The *kú-* bears the accent and is retained in the usual tenses.

Mchana kuchwa, or *kutwa*, all day till sunset, all day long.

D.

D has the same sound as in English. It occurs as an inital letter chiefly in words derived from the Arabic.

L or *r* and *t* become *d* after an *n*. *Refu*, long, makes *kamba ndefu*, a long rope, not *nrefu*.

Kanitafutia, and seek out for me, when pronounced quickly becomes *Kandaftia*.

D in the dialect of Mombas becomes *j* or *dy* in that of Zanzibar.

Ndoo! Come (Momb.). *Njoo!* (Zanz.)

See *C* and *J*.

Daba, a small tin box. Also, a fool.

Dacha ku, to drop.

Dada, sister, a term of endearment among women.

Dadisi ku-, to pry into things, to ask impertinent and unnecessary questions.

Dafina, a hidden treasure.

Daftari, an account book.

Dafu, plur. *madafu*, a cocoa-nut fully grown before it begins to ripen, in which state it supplies a very favourite drink. When the shell has begun to harden and the nutty part to thicken, it ceases to be a *Dafu* and becomes a *Koroma*.

Dagaa, a kind of very small fish like whitebait.

Daggla, a short coat.

Dai ku-, to claim, to sue for at law.

Daka ku-, to catch, to get hold of.

Dakika, a minute, minutes.

Daku, the midnight meal during the Ramathan. A gun is fired from one of the ships at Zanzibar about 2 A.M., to give notice that the time for eating is drawing to a close. The name is said to be derived from the saying:—

> "*Leni upesi, kesho kuna ndaa kuu.*"
> "Eat quickly, to-morrow there will be great hunger."

Dakuliza ku-, to coutradict, to deny formally, to rebut.

Dalali, a salesman, a hawker, an auctioneer.

Dalia, a yellow composition much used as a cosmetic: it is said to give softness and a sweet smell to the skin.

Dalili, a sign, a token.

Hatta dalili, anything at all, even a trace.

Dama, a game played on a board like chess.

Damani = *Demani*.

Damu, blood.

Danga ku-, to take up carefully, as they take up a little water left at the bottom of a dipping place to avoid makiug it muddy.

Danganika ku-, to be cheated.

Danganikia ku-, to put to confusion.

Danganisha ku-, to confuse.

Danganya ku-, to cheat, to humbug, to impose upon.

Danzi, plur. *madanzi*, a bitter, scarcely eatable sort of orange. The *Danzi* is reputed to be the original orange of Zanzibar. The name is sometimes applied to all kinds of oranges, and sweet oranges are called *madanzi ya Kizungu*, European (Portuguese) oranges.

Dao. See *Dau*.

Dapo, plur. *madapo*, a native umbrella.

Darabi, plur. *madarabi*, a rose apple.

Daraja, a step, a degree, a rank, a staircase, a bridge, a league.

Darasa, a class for reading, a regular meeting for learning.

Dari, a roof, an upper floor.

Darini, up-stairs, or, on the roof.

Darizi, embroidery, quilting. See also *Kanzu*.

Darumeti, part of a dhow, inner planking.

Dasili, a detergent powder made of the dried and powdered leaves of the *mkunazi*.

Dasturi. See *Desturi*.

Dau, plur. *madau*, a native boat sharp at both ends, with a square mat sail. They are the vessels of the original inhabitants of Zanzibar, and chiefly bring firewood to tbe town from the south end of the island.

Daulati, tho government.

Dawa, plur. *dawa* or *madawa*, a medicine.

Dawa ya kuhara, a purgative.

Dawa ya kutapika, an emetic.

Dawamu ku-, to persevere.

Dawati, a writing desk.

Dayima, always, perpetually.

Dayimara = *Dayima*.

Debe, tin can. See *Daba*.

Deheni, lime and fat for *chunamming* the bottoms of native craft.

Deheni ku-, to *chunam* the bottom of a dhow.

Deka ku-, to refuse to be pleased, to be perverse, to be teazing.

Delki, a donkey's walk.

Kwenda delki, to walk (of a donkey).

Dema, a kind of fish-trap.

Demani, the sheet of a sail.

Demani, the season of gentle southerly winds, beginning about the end of August. It is applied less correctly to the whole season of southerly wiuds from April to the end of October.

Dendaro, a sort of dance.

Denge.

Kukata denge, to shave the hair except on the crown of the head.

Dengu, peas, split peas. They are not grown in Zanzibar, but are brought dry from India.

Deni, debt, a debt, debts.

Deraye (?), armour.

Desturi, a sort of bowsprit, to carry forward the tack of a dhow-sail.

Desturi, custom, customs.

Deuli, a silk scarf worn round the waist.

Devai, claret, light wine.

Dia, composition for a man's life, fine paid by a murderer.

Dibaji, elegance of composition, a good style.

Didimia ku-, to sink.

Didimikia ku-, to bore with an awl, &c.

Didimisha ku-, to sink, to cause to sink.

Digali, part of a native pipe, being the stem which leads from the bowl into a vessel of water through which the smoke is drawn.

Diko, plur. *madiko*, a landing-place.

Dimu, a lime.

Dimu tamu, a sweet lime.

Dini, religion, worship.

Dira, the mariner's compass.

Diriki ku-, to succeed in one's purpose by being quick, to be quick enough to catch a person, to be in time.

Dirisha, plur. *madirisha*, a window.

Diwani, plur. *madiwani*, a councillor, a title of honour among the coast people.

Doana, a hook.

Dobi, a washerman.

Doda ku-, to drop.

Dodo. See *Embe*.

Dodoki, plur. *madodoki*, a long slender fruit eaten as a vegetable.

Dodoa ku-, to take up a little at a time.

Dofra, plur. *madofra*, a sailmaker's palm.

-dogo, little, small, young, younger.

Dohaan, *Dokhaan*, or *Dohani*, a chimney.

Marikebu ya dohaan, a steamship.

Hence *Dohani*, or *Dokhani*, a sort of tall basket in which fruit is brought on men's heads to market. The foundation is made of sticks about two feet long, loosely tied together, which are supplemented with plaited cocoa-nut leaves, until the whole becomes perhaps six feet high and fifteen to twenty inches in diameter. These *dohani* are often decked with flowers and green leaves.

Dokaa ku-, to nibble.

Dokeza ku-, to give a little part of anything, to give a hint.

Dokra, a cent.

Domo.

Kupiga domo, to tell a person in confidence.

Dona ku-, to peck.

Donda, plur. *madonda*, large sores.

Donda ndugu, malignant ulcers.

Dondo, pl. *madondo*, a tiger cowry. Used to smooth down seams with.

Dondo, starch, the dressing of calico.

Dondoa ku-, to pick up small fragments, to pick up rice, &c., to pick up bit by bit.

Dondoka ku-, to drop from little by little.

Mbegu zimenidondoka, the seeds dropped from my hand one by one.

Dondoro, Dyker's antelope.

Donea ku-, to flutter like a bird.

Donge, plur. *madonge*, a small round thing, a ball.

Donoa ku-, to peck, to sting.

Doti, a loin-cloth, a piece of cloth a little less than two yards long.

Doya ku-, to go as a spy.

Dua, worship, theology.

Duara, a windlass, anything round.

Dude, plur. *madude*, a what-is-it? a thing of which you don't know or have forgotten the name.

Dudu, plur. *madudu*, an insect, insects.

Duduvule, a kind of hornet which bores in wood.

-dufu, insipid, tasteless.

Duka, plur. *maduka*, a shop.

Dukiza ku-, to listen secretly.

Dukizi, plur. *madukizi*, an eavesdropper, a tale-bearer.

Dumbuza, a plant having big yellow flowers with dark centres.

Dumia ku-, to persevere.

Dumisha ku-, to make to continue.

Dumu, a jar (?).

Dumu ku-, to continue, to persevere.

Dun, a fine.

Dundu, plur. *madundu*, a large pumpkin shell used to hold liquids.

Dunge, the green skin of the cashew nut, an immature cashew nut.

Dungu, plur. *madungu*, the roof over the little stages for watching corn, &c.

Dumgumaro, a kind of spirit, also the drum, &c., proper for expelling him.

Duni, below, less.

Dunia, the world, this world.

Durabini, a telescope, an eyeglass.

Kupiga durabini, to use a glass, telescope.

Duru ku-, to surround.

Durusi ku-, to meet in a regular class for study.

Dusamali, a striped silk scarf or handkerchief worn upon the head by women.

Duumi, a dhow sail.

Duzi, plur. *maduzi*, one who delights to find out and proclaim secrets and private matters.

E.

E has a sound between those of *a* in gate and of *ai* in chair.

In the dialect of Zanzibar it is often substituted for the *a* of more northern Swahili, especially as representing the Arabic *fet'ha*.

Merikebu, a ship, is in the Mombas dialect *Marikabu*, and in the Arabic *Markab*.

The sound of *e* often arises from the fusion of the final *a* of a prefix with an *e* or *i* which follows it, as—

Akenda for *A-ka-enda*, and he went.

Akaweta for *A-ka-wa-ita*, and he called them.

Some of the cases in which *e* in the Zanzibar dialect stands for *a* in northern Swahili may be explained by the substitution at Zanzibar of *in* for a mere *'n*, as in the word for "land" or country," which is *'nti* at Mombas, with so mere an *'n* that the vowel of the preceding word may be run into it, as in the saying—

"*Mvundánti, mwanánti.*"
"A country can be ruined only by its own children."

Whereas in Zanzibar, besides the usual change of *t* into *ch*, the first syllable has generally a distinct *i* sound, and may be better written *inchi*.

Thus at Mombas the root of the adjective "many" seems to be *ngi*, making the substantive "plenty," or "a large quantity," *ungi*, and with the proper prefix "many people," *wa-ngi*. But in Zanzibar "plenty" is *w-ingi*, and "many people" *wengi*, as if *wa-ingi*.

Ebbe, for *Lebeka*.

Ebu! Ee bo! well then! come then!

Eda.

Ku kalia eda, to remain in extreme privacy and quiet for five months, as is usual by way of mourning for a husband.

Edashara, eleven.

Ee! O!

Ee Waa! or *Ee Wallah!* the common answer of slaves and inferiors when called to do something, a strong assent.

Eema (M.) = *Dema*, a kind of fish-trap.

Egemea ku-, to lean.

Ehee! Yes!

Ekerahi, a provocation, an irritating word or thing.

Ekua ku-, to break by bending.

Ekuka ku-, to be sprung, to be broken.

-ekundu, red. It makes *jekundu* with nouns like *kasha*, and *nyekundu* with nouns like *nyumba*.

Ela (M.), except.

Elafu, thousands.

Elea ku-, to float, to become clear.

Moyo wamwelea, he feels sick (M.)

Yamekuelea? Do you understand? Have they (my words) become clear to you?

Eleka ku-, to carry a child astride on the hip or back.

Elekea ku-, to be right, to agree, to be opposite to.

Elekeana ku-, to be opposite to one another.

Elemisha ku-, to teach, instruct.

Eleza ku-, to make to float, to swim a boat, to make clear, to explain.

Elfeen or *Elfain*, two thousand.

Elfu, a thousand.

Elimisha ku-, to instruct, to make learned.

Elimu, or *élimu-*, learning, doctrine.

-ema, good, kind. It makes *jema* with nouns like *kasha*, and *njema* or *ngema* with nouns like *nyumba*.

-embamba, narrow, thin, slim. It makes *jembamba* with nouns like *kasha*, and *nyembamba* with nouns like *nyumba*.

Embe, a mango. In Mombas the plural is *Maembe*, in Zanzibar it is *Embe*.

Embe dodo, or *Embe za dodo*, a very large kind of mango, so named from a plantation in Pemba, where they first grew.

Embe kinoo, a small kind of mango which is very sweet.

Embwe, glue, gum.

Embwe la ubuyu, a kind of paste made from the fruit of the calabash tree.

Enda kw-, to go. The *kw-* is retained in the usual tenses.

Kwenda is often used merely to carry on the narration without any distinct meaning of going. Sometimes it is employed as an auxiliary, nearly as we say in English, *he is going to do it*. Sometimes it expresses an action merely, as *Kwenda chafya*, to sneeze. *Kwenda* and *Kupiga* used in this way cannot be exactly translated.

Kwenda kwa mguu, to walk.

Kwenda tembea, to go for a walk.

Kwenda mghad, &c., to go cantering, &c.

Kwenda zangu, zako, zake, &c., in other dialects, *vyangu, vyake*, &c., and *thangu, thake*, &c., to go away, to go, to go one's way, to depart.

Imekwenda twaliwar, they have gone to fetch it.

Endea kw-, to go for, to, or after.

Endeka kw-, to be passable, to be capable of being gone upon, to be gone upon.

Endelea kw-, to go either forward or backward.

Kwendelea mbele, to advance.

Kwendelea nyuma, to retire.

Endeleza ku-, to spell, to prolong.

Enea ku-, to spread, to become known.

Enenda ku-, to go, mostly in the sense of to go on, to proceed, to go forward.

Enenza ku-, to measure together, to try which exceeds the other.

Eneo, the spread, the extent covered.

Eneo la Muungu, God's omnipresence.

Eneza ku-, to spread, to cause to spread, to cause to reach.

Muungu amemweneza killa mtu riziki zake, God has put within the reach of every man what is necessary for him.

Enga ku-, to split mahogo for cooking.

Engaenga ku-, to coddle, to tend over carefully.

Engua ku-, to skim.

-enu, your, of you.

-enu ninyi, your own.

Enyi or *Enyie*, You there! You there, I say!

-enyi, having, possessing, with. It makes *mwenyi, wenyi, yenyi, zenyi, lenyi, chenyi, vyenyi*, and *penyi*, which see.

Enza ku-, to ask news of a person.

Enzi, or *Ezi*, sovereignty, dominion, majesty.

Mwenyi ezi, the sovereign, he who is supreme. See *Ezi*.

Epa ku-, to endeavour to avoid (a stone, stroke, &c.)

Epea ku-, not to go direct to, to miss a mark, not to shoot straight (of a gun).

Epeka ku-, to be avoidable, to be what can be got out of the way of.

-epesi, light, not heavy, easy, quick, willing. It makes *jepesi* with nouns like *kasha*, and *nyepesi* with nouns like *nyumba*.

Epua ku-, to brush or shake off, to take away.

Epuka ku-, to be kept from, to avoid, to abstain from.

Epukana ku-, to be disunited.

Epukika ku-, to be evitable.

Haiepukiki, it is inevitable.

Epusha ku-, to make to avoid, to keep from.

Epushwa ku-, to be kept from, to be forbidden something.

-erevu, subtle, shrewd, cunning.

Erevuka ku-, to become shrewd, to get to know the ways of the world, to grow sharp.

Erevusha ku-, to make sharp and knowing.

Eria ku-, to ease off, let down. See *Ariaa*.

Esha, the latest Mohammedan hour of prayer, which may be said to be from half-past 6 to about 8 P.M.

Esse (?), a screw.

-etu, our, of us.

-etu sisi, our own.

Eua ku-, to sprinkle with water after praying by way of charm against a disease.

-eupe, white, clear, clean, light-coloured. It makes *jeupe* with nouns like *kasha*, and *nyeupe* with nouns like *nyumba*.

-eupee, very white.

-eusi, black, dark-coloured. It makes *jeusi* with nouns like *kasha*, and *nyeusi* with nouns like *nyumba*.

Ewaa = *Ee Waa*.

Ewe! You there! Hi! I say, you! plur. *Enyi*.

Eza ku-, to measure.

Ezeka ku-, to thatch, to cover with thatch.

Ezi = *Enzi*, sovereignty.

Mwenyi ezi Muungu, or *Mwenyezímngu*, Almighty God, God the Lord, representing in Swahili the *Allah ta'ala*, God the Most High, of the Arabic.

Ezua ku-, to uncover.

Kuezua paa, to strip a roof.

F.

F has the same sound as in English.

F and *v* are confounded by the Arabs, though in Swahili perfectly distinct, thus:—

Ku-faa means—to be profitable to.

Ku-vaa means—to put on.

There is, however, in some cases a little indistinctness, as in the common termination *ifu* or *ivu*; the right letter is probably in all cases a *v*.

The Arabs in talking Swahili turn *p*'s into *f*'s, and say *funda* for *punda*, a donkey; and conversely, some slaves from inland tribes turn *f*'s into *p*'s. *P*, however, does sometimes become *f* before a *y* sound, as *kuogopa*, to fear, *kuogofya*, to frighten.

There is a curious *fy* sound used in some dialects of Swahili, which is rarely heard in Zanzibar.

Fa kú-, to die, perish, cease, fade away. The *ku-* bears the accent, and is retained in the usual tenses.

Faa ku-, to be of use to, to avail, to be worth something.

Haifai, it is of no use, it won't do.

Faana ku-, to be of use to one another, to help one another.

Fafanisha ku-, to liken.

Fafanua ku-, to recognize, to understand.

Fafanuka ku-, to become clear.

Fafanukia ku-, to be clear to.

Fafanulia ku-, to make clear to.

Faganzi ku-, to become callous.

Mguu wangu umenifaganzi, my foot is asleep.

Fagia ku-, to sweep.

Fahali, plur. *mafahali*, a bull, used of men in the sense of manly, strong.

Fahamia.

Kwa kufahamia (M.), on the face, forward.

Fahamisha ku-, to make to understand, to remind.

Fahamu ku-, to understand, to remember.

Fahari = *Fakhari*, glory.

Kufanya fahari, to live beyond one's means and station.

Faja la frasi, a stable.

Fakefa, generous,a generous person.

Fakhari, glory.

Fakiri, poor, a poor person.

Fala ku-, (Mer.) = *Faa ku-*.

Falaki, or *fálak*, astronomy.

Kupiga falaki, to prognosticate by the stars.

Fali, an omen, omens.

Fana ku-, to be very good of its kind, to become like (?).

Fanana ku-, to become like, to resemble.

Fananisha ku-, to make to resemble.

Fanikia ku-, to turn out well for.

Kufanikiwa, to prosper.

Fanusi, a lantern.

Fanya ku-, to make, to do, to adapt, to mend.

Kujifanya, to make one's self, to pretend to be.

Kufanya kura, to cast lots.

Kufanya shauri, to take counsel.

Fanyia ku-, to do or make for or to.

Nikufanyieje? What am I to do with you?

Fanyika ku-, to be made or done, makable or doable.

Fanyiza ku-, to amend, to mend.

Fanyizika ku-, to be very good, to be well done.

Fara or *Farafara*, brimful, full to the brink.

Faragha, privacy, secrecy, leisure.

Faraja, comfort, ease after pain.

Farajika ku-, to be comforted, to be eased.

Farakana ku-, to be alienated.

Farakiana ku-, to be alienated in regard to one another.

Farakisha ku-, to alienate.

Faranga, pl. *mafaranga*, a chicken, a young fowl.

Farasi or *Frasi*, a horse, in Arabic a mare.

Fariji ku-, to comfort, to console.

Fariki ku-, to become separated, to decease.

Fárine, a kind of rice and milk gruel.

Farishi ku-, to spread.

Faritha, pay.

Faroma, a block to put caps on after washing them, to prevent their shrinking.

Farrathi, necessity, obligation, obligatory.

Farrathi, a place one habitually goes to.

The *th* of this word is the English *th* in that, the *th* of the preceding word is a little thicker.

Farumi, ballast.

Fashifashi, nonsense.

Fashini, the sternpost of a dhow.

Fasihi, correct, clean, pure.

Fasili, spreading.

Huna ásili, wala fásili, you have neither root nor branches, *i.e.*, neither good birth nor great connections.

Fasiri ku-, to explain, to interpret.

Fasiria ku-, to explain to, to interpret to.

Fataki, a percussion cap, a gun cap.

Fathaa, restlessness, disquiet.

Fathaika ku-, to be troubled, disquieted, thrown into confusion.

Fathali = *Afathali*, preferably.

Fathali = *Fathili*.

Fathehi ku-, to put to confusion, to find out a person in a trick, &c.

Fathili, a favour, a kindness, kindnesses.

Fathili ku-, to do a kindness, to deserve well.

Fatiha, a Mohammedan form of prayer.

Fatiishi ku-, to pry, to be over curious.

Fauluku-, to get past, to get through, to weather.

Fawiti ku-, to delay, to occupy, to hinder.

Fayida, profit, gain, advantage, interest.

Fayidi ku-, to get profit.

Fayiti ku-, to delay.

Fayitika ku-, to be delayed.

Fazaa, trouble, confusion, anxiety.

Feka ku- = *Fieka ku-*, to clear forest lands.

Felefele, an inferior kind of millet.

Feleji or *Felegi*, a choice kind of steel.

Upanga wa feleji, a long straight two-edged sword, used by the Arabs.

Feleti ku-, to discharge, to release from an obligation, to release.

Feli, plur. *mafeli*, a beginning of speaking or doing.

Fereji, a channel, a drain.

Ferusaji = *Forsadi*.

Fetha, silver, money.

Fethaluka. *Marijani ya fethaluka*, the true red coral.

Fetheha, a disgraceful thing, a shame.

Fetheheka ku-, to be found out in a disgraceful thing, to be put to shame.

Fetiwa ku-, to be condemned or adjudged to [a punishment].

Fetwa ku-, to give judgment on a question of Mohammedan law.

Feuli, the place in a dhow where they stow things which may be wanted quickly.

Fi, by.

Saba fi saba, seven times seven.

Fia ku-, to leave behind, to die to. Pass. *Kufiwa na*, to lose by death.

Fiata ku-, to hold one's hands or one's clothes between one's legs.

Fiatika ku-, to be kept back, to be delayed.

Fiatua ku-, to allow a spring to escape, to let off.

Fiatuka ku-, to escape (as a spring)

Ficha ku-, to hide.

Kunifieha kofia-, to hide a cap from me.

Kunifichia kofia, to hide my cap.

Fidi ku-, to ransom (of the price paid).

Fidia, a ransom, a sacrifice (giving up).

Fidia ku-, to ransom (of the person paying).

Fidina, mint (?).

Fieka ku-, to clear.

Kufieka mwitu, to clear ground in a forest.

Fifia ku-, to disappear, to cease to be visible (as a scar or a mark; it does not imply motion), to pine away, (of seeds) not to come up.

Figa, plur. *mafiga*, the three stones used to set a pot over the fire upon. See *Jifya*.

Figao, a movable fireplace.

Figili, a kind of large white radish.

Figo, kidney (M.).

Fika ku-, to arrive, to reach, to come.

Fikara, thought.

Fikia ku-, to reach a person.

Fikicha ku-, to crumble, to rub to pieces, to rub hard, to thresh corn. (Used also obscenely).

Fikilia ku-, to come to a person on business of his, to arrive and return without delay.

Fikiliza ku-, to cause to arrive for.
Kufikiliza ahadi, to fulfil a promise.

Fikisha ku-, to make to arrive, to lead, to take.

Fikira, thought, consideration.

Fikiri ku-, to consider, to ponder.

Fil, a chess castle or rook (in Arabic, an elephant).

Fila ku- = *Fia ku-*.
Afile mbali, that he may die out of the way.

Filimbi, a flute.

Filisi ku-, to take away a man's property, to seize for debt.

Filisika ku-, to come to want, to have been sold up, to have run through all one's money.

Fimbo, a stick.

Finessi, plur. *mafinessi*, a jack fruit.
Finessi la kizungu, a duryan.

Fingirika ku-, to roll along, to be rolled, to writhe like a wounded snake.

Fingirisha ku-, to roll, to make to roll.

Finya ku-, to pinch.

Finyana ku-, to be pinched together, to be gathered up small.

Finyanga ku-, to do potter's work, to make pots, to tread and trample.

Fionya ku-, to chirp, to make a chirruping noise with the mouth, to do so by way of showing contempt.

Fira ku-, to commit sodomy.

Firana ku-, to commit sodomy together.

Firigisi, the gizzard.

Firinghi = *Firigisi*.

Firkomba, an eagle (?).

Firuzi, a turquoise.

Fisadi, one who enters other people's houses for a wrongful purpose.

Fisha ku-, to cause to die.

Fisi, a hyæna.

Fisidi ku-, to enter other people's houses for a wrongful purpose, to commit an offence in another man's house.

Fithuli = *Futhuli*, officious, over talkative.

Fitina, slander, sowing of discord, a disturbance.

Fitini ku-, to slander, to sow discord.

Fitiri, alms and presents given at the end of the Ramathan.

Fito (plur. of *ufito*), long slender sticks.

Fiwa ku-, to be died to, to lose by death.
Mwanamke aliofiwa na mumewe, a widow.

Fiwe, a sort of bean growing on a climbing plant with a white flower.

Fofofu.
Kufa fofofu, to die outright.

Fola, a gift expected from those who first touch a new-born baby, paying your footing.

Foramali, a ship's yard.

Formash.
Dawati ya formash, a workbox.

Forsadi, a small kind of edible fruit, mulberries.

Fortha, a custom-house.
Forthani, at the custom-house.

Fras, *Frasi*, or *Farasi*, a horse, a mare.

Frasi, a chess knight.

-fu, dead.

Maji mafu, neap tides.

Fua, a wooden bowl.

Fua ku-, to beat (?), to wash clothes, to clear the husk from cocoanuts, to work in metal, to make things in metal.

Kufua chuma, to be a blacksmith.

Kufua fetha, to be a silversmith.

Kufua thahabu, to be a goldsmith.

Kufua kisu, &c., to forge a knife, &c.

Fuama ku-, to lie on the face (Momb.).

Fuata ku-, to follow, to imitate, to obey.

Fuatana ku-, to accompany, to go with.

Fuatanisha ku-, to make to accompany.

Fuawa ku-, to lie on the side and be beaten by the waves, as when a vessel goes ashore broadside on. Pass. of *fua* (?).

Fuawe, an anvil.

Fucha = *Futa*.

Fudifudi, on the face (of falling or lying).

Fudikiza ku-, to turn bottom upwards, to turn cards backs uppermost.

Fufua ku-, to cause to revive, to resuscitate.

Fufuka ku-, to revive, to come to life again.

Fufuliza ku-, to cause to come to life again for some one.

Fufumonye, in the kitchen (Pemba).

Fuga ku-, to keep animals either tame or in captivity.

Fugika ku-, to be capable of being kept, to be capable of domestication, not to die in captivity.

Fuja ku-, to waste, to squander, to leak. See *Vuja*.

Fujika ku-, to moulder, waste away.

Fujo, disorder, uproar.

Fujofujo, slovenliness, laziness.

Fuka, a kind of thin porridge.

Fuku ku-, to fill in a small hole.

Fuka moshi ku-, to throw out smoke, to fume. See *Vuke*.

Fukara, very poor.

Fukia ku-, to fill up a small hole.

Fukiza ku-, to cense, to put the fuming incense-pot under a person's beard and into his clothes, by way of doing him honour.

Fukizo, vapour, fumes.

Fuko (?), a mole.

Fuko, plur. *mafuko*, a large bag.

Fukua ku-, to dig a small narrow hole, such as those to receive the posts of houses; to dig into a grave so as to get at the body; to dig out, to dig up.

Fukuafukua ku-, to burrow.

Fukuta ku-, to blow with bellows.

Fukuza ku-, to drive away, to chase.

Fukuzana ku-, to chase one another.

Fukuzia ku-, to drive away from.

Fulia ku-, to work in metal for, to make things in metal for.

Fulifuli, on the face, forwards.

Fuliza ku-, to go on, not to stop; also, to blow upon, to kindle.

Fullani, such a one, such and such men or things.

Fululiza ku-, not to stop or delay to go on fast.

Fuma ku-, to weave.

Fuma ku-, to hit with a spear, to shoot with arrows.

Fumania ku-, to come suddenly upon, to surprise, intrude.

Fumaniana ku-, to intrude into people's houses without reasonable cause. Those who do so have no remedy if they are beaten or wounded.

Fumatiti, an owl (?).

Fumba ku-, to close, to shut (used of the eyes, the mouth, the hand, &c.).

Maneno ya fumba, a dark saying.

Makuti ya fumba, cocoa-nut leaves plaited for making enclosures.

Fumba, a lump.

Fumba, a kind of sleeping mat, which is doubled and sewn together at the ends, so as to make a large shallow bag. The sleeper gets inside, and draws the loose edge under him, so as to be completely shut in.

Fumbata ku-, to close the fist, to grasp.

Fumbatika ku-, to be grasped.

Fumbia ku-, to talk darkly.

Fumbo, plur. *mafumbo*, a dark saying, a hidden thing.

Fumbua ku-, to unclose, to open the eyes, &c.

Fumbuka ku-, to come to light.

Fumbulia ku-, to lay open to, to explain.

Fumi, a kind of fish.

Fu'mka ku-, to become unsewn, to open at the seams, to leak (of a boat).

Fumo, plur. *mafumo*, a flat-bladed spear.

Fumo, a chief (Kingozi and Nyassa).

Fumua ku-, to unrip, to unpick.

Kufumua moto, to draw out the pieces of wood from a fire.

Fumuka ku- = *Fu'mka ku-*.

Funda, a large mouthful making the cheeks swell out, a sip (?), a draw at a pipe.

Kupiga funda, to take large mouthfuls one by one.

Funda ku-, to beat up, to mix by beating, to pound.

Funda ku-, to teach.

Fundi, a skilled workman, a master workman, a teacher of any handicraft.

Fundisha ku-, to teach, to instruct.

Kujifundisha, to learn.

Fundisho, plur. *mafundisho*, instruction, direction, teaching.

Fundo, plur. *mafundo*, a knot.

Kupiga fungo, to tie a knot.

Fundua ku-, to untie.

Funga, a civet cat.

Funga ku-, to fasten, to tie, to bind, to imprison, to fast.

Kufunga choo, to become constipated.

Fungamana ku-, to cling together, to connect, to tie together, to rely upon.

Fungana ku-, to bind, to stick together.

Fungasa ku-, to tow.

Fungate, a period of seven days after the completion of the wedding, during which the bride's father sends food to the bridegroom and his friends.

Fungisha ku-, to shut against.

Fungo, a civet cat.

Fungu, plur. *mafungu*, a bank, a shoal, a heap, a part, a week.

Fungua. See *Mfunguo*.

Fungua ku-, to unfasten, to open, to let loose, to leave off fasting.

Funguka ku-, to become unfastened, to be unfastenable.

Funguliwa ku-, to have unfastened for one, to be unfastened.

Funguo (plur. of *Ufunguo*), keys

Funguza ku-, to present with food during the Ramathan.

Funika ku-, to cover (as with a lid), to close a book.

Funikika ku-, to become covered.

Funikiza ku-, to cover (as with a flood).

Funo, a kind of animal.

Funua ku-, to lay open, to uncover, to open a book, to unpick sewing, to show cards.

Kufunua macho, to open one's eyes.

Funuka ku-, to become opened, to open like a flower, &c.

Funza, a maggot.

Funza ku-, to teach.

Kujifunza, to learn.

Fupa, plur. *mafupa*, a large bone, the anus (?).

-fupi, short. It makes *fupi* with nouns like *nyumba*.

Fupiza ku-, to shorten.

Fura ku-, to swell, to be puffed up from the effects of a blow only.

Furaha, gladness, joy, pleasure, gladly.

Furahani, with gladness, happiness.

Furahi ku-, to rejoice, to be glad.

Furahia ku-, to rejoice in.

Furahisha ku-, to make glad.

Furahiwa ku-, to be made glad, to be rejoiced.

Furijika ku-, to moulder away.

Furika ku-, to run over, to boil over, to inundate.

Furukuta ku-, to move, as of something moving under a carpet.

Furumi, ballast.

Furungu, plur. *mafurungu*, a large citron, a shaddock, a kind of anklet.

Furushi, a bundle tied up in a cloth.

Fusfus or *Fussus*, precious stones.

Fusi, rubbish.

Futa ku-, to wipe.

Kufuta kamasi, to blow the nose.

Futa ku-, to draw a sword (=*vuta?*).

Futari, the first food taken after a fast.

Futi, plur. *mafuti*, the knee (A.)

Futhuli, officiousness.

Futika ku-, to tuck into the girdle or loin-cloth.

Futua ku-, to open out a bundle, take out what was tucked in.

Futuka ku-, to get cross or angry.

Futukia ku-, to get cross with.

Futuri, a span.

Futuru ku-, to eat at the end of a fast, to break a fast.

Fuu, plur. *mafuu*, a small black fruit.

Fuvu, plur. *mafuvu*, an empty shell.

Fuvu la kitwa, a skull.

Fuza ku-, to go on, not to stop.

Fuzi, plur. *mafuzi*, a shoulder (A.).

Fwata ku- = *Fuata ku-*.

Fyoa ku-, to answer abusively.

Fyolea ku-, to answer a person with abuse and bad language.

Fyonda ku- or *Fyonja ku-*, to suck out.

Fyonya ku-, to chirrup. See *Fionya*.

Fyonza ku-, to suck.

Fyoma ku-, to read (M.).

Fyuka ku-, to go off, to drop, to escape like a spring.

G.

G is always to be pronounced hard, as in "gate." Much confusion arises from the way in which the Arabic letters *jim* and *kaaf* or *qaf* are pronounced by different Arabs. *Jim* is properly an English *j*, and is so used by the Swahili, and *qaf* is properly a guttural *k*, but most Arabs in Zanzibar pronounce either *jim* or *qaf* as a hard *g*. This must be remembered in writing or looking for many Swahili words.

The Arabic *Ghain* is retained in many Swahili words borrowed from the Arabic, and a similar sound occurs in African languages also. It is here written *gh*. Most Europeans think it has something of an *r* sound, but this is a mistake; it is a hard grating *g*, made wholly in the throat. It resembles the Dutch *g*, and the German *g* approaches it. See *N*.

Gaagaa ku-, to turn over restlessly, to roll like a donkey.

Gabri. See *Kaburi*.

Gadi, a wooden prop to keep a vessel from falling over when left by the tide.

Gadimu ku-, to put *gadi*.

Gaga, plur. *magaga*, rubbish, dirt.

Gai, plur. *magai*, a large piece of potsherd.

Galme. See *Kalme*, the small mizen mast of a dhow.

Galawa, a canoe, a small canoe with outriggers. *Galawas* are hollowed out of the trunk of a tree, and have two long poles tied across, to the end of which pieces of wood pointed at both ends are attached, which serve to prevent the canoe upsetting. These outriggers are called *matengo*. See *Mtumbwi*.

Gamba. See *Jigamba*.

Gana, the tiller, the rudder handle.

Ganda, plur. *maganda*, husk, rind, shell, hard bark.

Ganda la tatu, the three of cards.

Ganda ku-, to stick, to freeze.

Gandama ku-, to cleave, to stick.

Gandamana ku-, to cleave together, to coagulate, to curdle, to freeze.

Gandamia ku-, to stick to, to cleave to.

Gando, plur. *magando*, the claw of a crab.

Ganga ku-, to bind round, as when a stick is sprung to bind it round with string, to splice, to mend, to cure.

Gange, a soft white limestone.

Gango, plur. *magango*, a cramp, a splint, something which holds other things together in their right place.

Gani! What? What sort of? The name of the thing queried about always precedes the word *gani*.

Ganzi.

Imekufa ganzi, it has lost all feeling. See *Faganzi*.

Kutia ganzi la meno, to set the teeth on edge.

Gari, plur. *magari*, a carriage, a wheeled vehicle.

Garofuu, cloves. Also, a kind of rice.

Gauza, *Gauka*, etc. See *Geuza*, *Geuka*, etc.

Gawa ku, to divide, to part out.
Kugawa karata, to deal cards.

Gawanya ku-, to divide, to share.

Gaya ku-, to change one's mind, to vacillate.

Gayami, a post with a cleat at the side of the poop, to fasten the sheet of a dhow sail to.

Gayogayo, a flat fish, (?) a sole.

Gema ku-, to get palm wine. They cut the immature flowering shoot and hang something under to catch what flows from the wound, which is the *tembo*, or palm wine. The cutting is renewed from time to time to keep up the flow.

Gembe, plur. *magembe*, a hoe. See *Jembe*.

-geni, foreign, strange.

Genzi.
Mkuu genzi, one who knows the roads well, a guide.

Gereza, a fort, a prison.

Geua ku-, to turn, to change (Mer.).

Geuka ku-, to become changed, to turn, to change.

Geuza ku- or *Geusha ku-* (?), to cause to change, to turn, to change.

Geuzi, plur. *mageuzi*, a change, changes.

Gháfala, suddenly.

Ghafalika ku-, to be imprudent, not to attend to, to neglect.

Gháfula = *gháfala*.

Ghairi ku-, to annul, change one's mind as to, put an end to.
Kutia ghairi, to offend, to irritate.

Ghala, a wareroom, a store place, especially the rooms on the ground-floor of Zanzibar houses, which have generally no windows, but merely a few small round holes (*miangaza*) near the ceiling.

Ghali, dear.

Ghalime. See *Galme*, *Kalme*

Ghalisha ku-, to make dear.

Ghangi, a kind of dhow resembling a bágala, except that it has not so long a prow.

Ghanima, good luck, profit.

Gharama, expense, payment to a native chief by a caravan.

Gharika, a flood, the flood.

Ghariki ku-, to be flooded, to be covered with water.

Gharikisha ku-, to flood, to overwhelm.

Gharimia ku-, to go to expense about, to be at the expense of.

Ghasi, a measure of about a yard.

Ghasi, rebellion.

Ghasi ku-, to bother, worry.

Ghasia, bother, coming and going, want of privacy.

Ghathabika ku-, to be enraged, to be angry.

Ghathabisha ku, to enrage, to make angry.

Ghathabu, anger.

Ghelibu ku-, to master.

Gheiri, jealousy, jealous anger.

Ghiana, an aggravating person.

Ghofira, plur. *maghofira*, pardon.

Ghofiri ku-, to forgive sins; used of God only.

Ghofiria ku-, to forgive a person.

Ghórofa, an upper room.

Ghoshi ku-, to adulterate.

Ghuba (?), a sheltered place, a screen.

Ghubari, plur. *maghubari*, a rain cloud.

Ghubba, a bay.

Ghumiwa ku-, to be startled, to stand aghast.

Ghurika ku-, to be arrogant.

Ghururi, arrogance.

Ghushi ku- = *Ghoshi ku-*, to adulterate.

Ghusubu ku-, to cheat, to swindle.

Gidam, the strap of a sandal, passing between the toes.

Ginsi, sort, kind.

Ginsi ilivyokuwa njema, &c., it was so good, &c.

Ginsi gani? or *Gissi gani?* Why? How is it?

Giza or *Kiza*, darkness.

Gnamba or *Ng'amba*, a hawk's-head turtle.

Gnombe or *Ng'ombe*, an ox, cattle.

Goa. See *Goo*.

Goboa ku-, to break off the cobs of Indian corn.

Godoro, plur. *magodoro*, a mattress.

Gofia, a pulley.

Gogo, plur. *magogo*, a log of timber, the trunk of a tree when felled.

Gomba ku-, to be adverse to, to oppose, to quarrel with.

Gombana ku-, to squabble, to quarrel.

Gombeza ku-, to forbid.

Gombo, plur. *magombo*, a sheet of a book.

Gome, plur. *magome*, bark of a tree.

Gomea ku-, to fasten with a native lock.

Gomeo, a native lock.

Gonga ku-, to knock.

Gonjweza ku-, to make ill.

Kujigonjweza, to make oneself out an invalid, to behave like a sick man.

Gongo, plur. *magongo*, a large stick.

Gongojea ku-.

Kujigongojea, to prop oneself with a staff, to drag oneself along by the help of a stick.

Gongomea ku-, to hammer in.

Goo. See *Mtondo goo*.

Gora, a piece of cloth, a package of cloth. See *Jura*.

Gorong'ondwa, a kind of lizard.

Goshi, the tack of a sail.

Upande wa goshini, the weather side.

Kupindua kwa goshini, to tack.

Gota ku-, to tap, to knock.

Gote, plur. *magote*, the knee.

Kupiga magote, to kneel.

Goteza ku-, to jumble together different dialects or languages.

Govi mbo, uncircumcised.

Gubeti, prow of a dhow.

Gubiti, barley-sugar (?).

Gudi, a dock for ships.

Gudulia or *Guduwia*, a water-cooler, a porous water-bottle.

Gugu, plur. *magugu*, undergrowth, weeds.

Gugu mwitu, a weed resembling corn.

-gugu, wild, uncultivated.

Gugumiza ku-, to gulp, to swallow with a gulping sound.

Guguna ku-, to gnaw.

Gugurusha ku-, to run with a shuffling noise like a rat, to drag along with a scraping noise.

Guia ku-, to seize (Mer.).

Guiana ku-, to cling together.

Gulegule, a dolphin.

Gumba.

Kidole cha gumba, the thumb.

Gumegume.

Bunduki ya gumegume, a flint gun.

-gumu, hard, difficult.

Guna ku-, to grunt, to make a dissatisfied noise.

Gundua ku-, to see one who thinks himself unseen, to discover unawares, to catch.

Gunga ku-, (1) to warn against doing something, (2) to refuse temptation.

Gungu, a kind of dance.

Gungu la kufunda, danced by a single couple.

Gungu la kukwaa, danced by two couples.

Gunia, a kind of matting bag.

Gunzi, plur. *magunzi*, a cob of Indian corn.

Gura ku-, to change one's place of residence (A.).

Gurisha ku-, to make to remove, to banish (A.).

Guru.

Sukari guru, half-made sugar.

Gurudumo, plur. *magurudumo*, a wheel.

Gurudumo la mzinga, a gun-carriage.

Guruguru, a large kind of burrowing lizard.

Gusa ku-, to touch.

Gutuka ku-, to start, to be startled.

Guu, plur. *maguu*, leg (A.).

Gwa ku-, to fall [Tumbatu].

Gwanda, a very short *kanzu*.

Gwia ku- = *Guia ku-*.

Gwiana ku- = *Guiana ku-*.

H.

H has the same sound as in the English word "hate."

There are in Arabic two distinct *h*'s, one wholly made in the throat, the other somewhat lighter than the English *h*. In Swahili there is only one *h* sound, which is used for both.

The Arabic *kh* is pronounced as a simple *h* in all words which are thoroughly incorporated into Swahili. The *kh* is used by Arabs and in words imperfectly assimilated. Some people regard it as a mark of good education to give the proper Arabic sounds to all words of Arabic origin.

In Arabic a syllable often ends with *h*, which is then strongly pronounced; but in Swahili the *h* is generally transposed so as to precede the vowel.

Kuih'timu, to finish one's education = *Kuhitimu*.

H-, sign of the negative in the second and third persons singular.

H-upendi, thou lovest not.

H-apendi, he lovest not.

Ha-, sign of the third person singular negative when referring to animate beings, and of the negative when prefixed to the affirmative prefixes in the plural, and in the third person singular when not referring to animate beings.

Ha-tupendi, we love not.

Ha-'mpendi, you love not.

Ha-wapendi, they love not.

Ha-ifai, it is of no use.

The final *a* of this *ha-* never coalesces with the following letter.

Ha-, a contraction for *nika*.

Hamwona, and I saw him.

The third person singular present negative is distinguished by the final *i*.

Hamwoni, he does not see him.

Haba, little, few, shallow.

Habibi, my lord.

Habari, news, information, message, story.

Habari zangu zilizonipata, an account of what had happened to me.

Habushia, plur. *mahabushia*, an Abyssinian. Many Galla women are called Abyssinians, and the name is sometimes used for a concubine of whatever race.

Hadaa, deceit, cheating.

Hadaa ku-, to cheat.

Hadaika ku-, to be cheated, to be taken in.

Hadidi, the semicircular ornament to which Arab women attach the plaits of their hair.

Hadimu, a servant, slave. See *Muhadimu*.

Hadithi, a tale, a story, especially one bearing upon Mohammedan tradition.

Hadithia ku-, to relate to.

Hafifu, light, insignificant.

Hafithika ku- = *Hifathika ku-*, to be preserved.

Hahithawahetha (Ar.), these and these.

Haiba, a beauty, not beauty generally, but one good point.

Hai-, sign of third person singular negative agreeing with nouns which do not change to form the plural.

Sign of the third person plural negative agreeing with nouns in *mi-*.

Hai = *Hayi*, alive.

Haina, it is not, there is not.

Haitassa, not yet.

Haithuru, it does not harm, it is of no consequence, never mind, it would be as well.

Haj, the pilgrimage to Mecca.

Haja, a request.

Hana haja, he is good for no purpose, he has no occasion.

Hajiri ku-, to go to live elsewhere.

Hajirika ku-, to remain overlong, delay.

Hakali.

Kumshika hakali, to require a stranger who goes upon workmen's work to pay for his intrusion, to make him pay his footing.

Haki-, sign of the third person singular negative, agreeing with nouns in *ki-* or *ch-*.

Haki, justice, right, righteousness.

Hakika, true, certain, certainly.

Hakika yako, it is true of thee, thou certainly.

Hakiki ku-, to make sure, to ascertain, to prove.

Hakiri ku-, to humble.

Hakirisha ku-, to despise.

Hako, he is not there.

Haku-, sign of the third person negative indefinite.

Haku-, sign of the third person singular of the negative past, referring to animate beings. This form is distinguished from the preceding by the final letter of the verb, which is *-i* in the indefinite and *-a* in the past tense.

Hakuna, there is not, it exists not, no.

Hal wáradi, otto of roses.

Halaf bilkithib, perjury.
Halafu, afterwards, presently.
Halali, lawful.
Halasa, sailors' wages.
Hali, state, condition, health.
U hali gani? How are you?
Wa hali gani? How are they?
Amekuwa hali ya kwanza, he is reduced to his former condition, he is as he used to be.
It is also used as a kind of conjunction, being, if it be, when it is, supposing, so it was.
Hali for *Ahali*, family, connections.
Hali-, sign of the third person singular negative, agreeing with nouns which make their plural in *ma-*.
Halilisha ku-, to make lawful.
Halili yako, at your disposal.
Halisi or *Hálisi*, exactly, without defect or variation.
Halua, a sweetmeat made of ghee, honey, eggs, arrowroot (?), and spice.
Haluli.
Chumvi ya haluli, sulphate of magnesia.
Ha'm-, sign of the second person plural negative.
Hama ku-, to change houses, to move.
Hamali, plur. *mahamali*, a porter, a coolie.
Hamami, a public bath. There are now public baths in Zanzibar.
Hamaya, protection.
Fi hamayat al Ingrez, under British protection.
Hamdi, praise.
Hami, protection.
Hami ku-, to protect.
Hamili ku-, to be pregnant.
Hamira, leaven, made by mixing flour and water and leaving it to turn sour.
Hamisha ku-, to cause to remove, to cause to change one's place of residence, to banish.
Ha'mna, there is not inside, no!
Hamo, he is not inside.
Hamsi, five.
Hamsini, fifty.
Hamstashara, fifteen.
Hamu, grief, heaviness.
Hamwimbi? Don't you sing?
Hana, he has not.
Hana ku-, to mourn with, to join in a formal mourning.
Hana kwao, he has no home, a vagabond.
Hanamu, obliquely.
Hanamu, the cutwater of a dhow.
Handaki, a dry ditch, a trench.
Hangaika ku-, to be excited.
Hangoe, the guttural Arabic *h*, the *hha*. See *Mdawari*.
Hanikiza ku-, to interrupt people, to talk so loud and long as to prevent other people from doing anything.
Hanisi, a man sexually impotent.
Haniti, a catamite, a sodomite.
Hanzua, a kind of dance.
Hao, or *Hawò*, these or those before mentioned, referring to animate beings.
Hapa-, sign of the third person negative, agreeing with *mahali*, place or places.
Hapa, here, this place, in this place.
Hapana, there is not, no!
Hapana refers rather to a particular place, *Hakuna* is general.
Hapo, here, this or that time.

Tangu hapo, once upon a time.
Hapo kale, in old times.
Tokea hapo, ever so long.
Toka hapo! get away! get out of this!

Hara ku-, to be purged.
Harisha ku-, to act as a drastic purgative.

Haraka, haste.

Haraka ku-, to make haste.

Harakisha ku-, to hasten.

Haramia, a pirate, a robber.

Haramu, unlawful, prohibited.

Harara, prickly heat, heat, hot temper.

Harara, quick-tempered.

Hararii, hot-tempered.

Hari, heat, perspiration.
Kutoka hari, to perspire.

Haribika ku-, to be destroyed, to spoil.

Haribu ku-, to destroy, to spoil.
Kuharibu mimba, to miscarry.

Harijia ku-, to spend money, to lay out money, to provide (a feast), &c.

Harimisha ku-, to make or declare unlawful.

Harimu ku- = *Harimisha ku-*.

Harioe, a cry raised on seeing a dhow come in sight (M.).

Hariri, silk.

Harufu, *Harufi*, or *Herufu*, a letter of the alphabet, letters, characters.

Harufu, a scent, a smell of any kind.

Harusi, a wedding; vulgarly, the bride.
Bwana harusi, the bridegroom.
Bibi harusi, the bride.

Hasai = *Maksai*, castrated.

Hasara, loss.
Kupata hasara, to lose.

Hasara ku-, to spoil a thing so that its value is gone.

Hasha, not at all, not by any means, a very strong negative.

Hasha, a patch in planking, a piece let in.

Hasi ku- or *Khasi ku-*, to geld, to castrate.

Hasibu ku-, to count.

Hasida, a kind of porridge.

Hasidi, envy.

Hasira, anger.
Kuwa na hasira, to be angry.
Kutia hasira, to make angry.

Hasira ku-, to injure.

Hasiri ku-, to vex, to do harm to.

Hasirika ku-, to be injured, to be grieved.

Hasirisha ku-, to injure.

Hassa, exactly.

Hata. See *Hatta*.

Hatamu, a bridle.

Hatari, danger, fear.

Hathari, caution, care.
Kuwa na hathari, to beware, to be on one's guard.
Kufanya hathari, to become careful, to become anxious.

Hâtif, an angel.

Hatiki ku-, to bother, to annoy (A.).

Hatima = *Khatima*, end, conclusion, at last.

Hatirisha ku-, to venture, to run the risk.

Hatiya = *Khatiya*, fault.
Kutia hatiyani, to find fault with.
Mwenyi hatiya nami, who has done me wrong.

Hatta, until, so far as, to, at length, when a certain time had arrived. It is used to introduce the time when something fresh happened.

Hatta siku moja, one day.

Hatta assubui, in the morning, but in the morning.

Hatta baada ya mwezi kupita, and when a month had passed.

Hattia, for nothing.

Hattiya = *Hatiya*.

Hatu-, sign of the first person plural negative.

Hatua, a step, steps.

Hau-, sign of the third person singular negative agreeing with nouns in *m-* or *mw-*, not denoting animate beings, or with those in *u-*.

Havi-, sign of the third person plural negative agreeing with plural nouns in *vi-* or *vy-*.

Hawa-, sign of the third person plural negative.

Hawa-, Eve.

Hawa, these, referring to animate beings.

Hawa or *Hewa*, air.

Hawa or *Hawat*, longing, lust, loving.

Usifanye hawa nafsi, don't be partial, don't show favour.

Hawa or *Hawara*, a catamite, a paramour.

Hawala, transfer of a debt, bill of exchange.

Hawezi, he is ill. See *Weza ku-*.

Hawi, he is not.

Hawili ku-, to take upon oneself what was due from another, to guarantee a debt, &c.

Haya-, sign of the third person plural negative agreeing with plural nouns in *ma-*.

Haya, these, referring to a plural substantive in *ma-*.

Haya, shame, modesty.

Hana haya, he is shameless.

Kuona haya, to feel ashamed, to be bashful.

Kutia haya, to abash, to make ashamed.

Haya! Work away! Be quick! Come along!

Hayale, those, those things.

Hayamkini, it is impossible.

Hayawani, a man without his proper senses, an idiot.

Hayi, plur. *wahayi* (?), alive.

Hayo, these or those before mentioned, referring to plural substantives in *ma-*.

Hayuko, vulgarly used in Zanzibar for *hako*, he is not there.

Hazi-, sign of the third person plural negative agreeing with nouns which do not change to form the plural, or with those which begin in the singular with *u-*.

Hazibu ku- = *Hesabu ku-*.

Hazina, a treasure.

Hazitassa, not yet.

Hedaya, a choice thing, a tale.

Hejazi, the *Hejaz* in Arabia.

Hekalu, the temple at Jerusalem, a great or famous thing.

Hékima, wisdom, cleverness.

Hekimiza ku-, to make a man understand, to put him in possession of knowledge.

Hemidi ku-, or *Hamidi ku-*, to praise.

Henza, halyards.

Henzarani, cane-work.

Heri = *Kheiri*, happy, fortunate, it is well.

Ni heri, I had better, it will be well for me.

Kua heri, good-bye.

Mtu wa heri, a fortunate man.

Heria, a cry raised on first seeing a dhow coming. Compare *Hariowe*.

Herimu = *Marika*.

Hero, a wooden platter.

Herufu or *Harufu*, a letter of the alphabet.

Hesabu, accounts, an account.

Hesabu ku-, to count, to reckon.

Heshima, honour.

Heshimu ku-, to honour.

Heth, menstruation, menses.

Kuwa na heth, to menstruate.

Hetima.

Kusoma hetima, to pray for one's [ancestors.

Hewa or *Hawa*, air.

Hezaya, a shame, a thing causing confusion.

Hi-, for *Niki-*. See *-ki-*.

Hiana, a grudging person, one who withholds things. Compare *Ghiana*.

Hiari, choice.

Hiba, property left after death.

Hidima, service.

Hifathi ku-, to preserve, to keep.

Hifathika ku-, to be preserved.

Hifukuza = *Nikifukuza*.

Hii, this, referring to singular nouns which do not change to form the plural; these, referring to plural nouns in *mi-*.

Hiile, that, those.

Hikaya = *Hedaya*, a wonderful thing.

Hiki, this, referring to singular nouns in *ki-* or *ch-*.

Hikile, that, yonder.

Hila, a device, a stratagem, a deceit.

Mtu wa hila, a crafty man.

Hili, this, referring to singular nouns which make their plural in *ma-*.

Hilo, this or that before mentioned, referring to singular nouns which make their plural in *ma-*.

Hima, haste, hastily, quickly.

Himahima! be quick!

Himili ku-, to bear, to support.

Himiza ku-, to hasten.

Hina, henna, a very favourite red dye, used by women to dye the palms of their hands and the soles of their feet, often used to dye white donkeys, &c., a pale red brown.

Hini ku-, to refuse to give, to withhold.

Hirizi, a written charm worn on the side.

Hirimu, an equal in age.

Hirimu moja, of the same age

Hisa, pardon.

Nipe hisa yangu, pardon me.

Hitari ku-, to prefer, choose. See *Ikhtiari*.

Hitima, the feast which concludes a formal mourning.

Hitimu ku-, to finish one's learning, to leave off school, to know one's trade.

Hitimisha ku-, to finish a scholar, to bring to the end of his learning of whatever kind.

Hivi, thus, these, referring to plural nouns in *vi-* or *vy-*.

Hivile, those.

Hivyo, after which manner, these mentioned before, referring to plural nouns in *vi-* or *vy-*.

Hiyari, choice.

Hiyo, this mentioned before, referring to singular nouns which do not change to form the plural; these mentioned before, referring to plural nouns in *mi-* or in *ma-*.

Hizi, these, referring to plural nouns which do not change to form the plural, or which begin in the singular with *u-* or *w-*.

Siku hizi, some days ago, some days hence, now.

Hizi ku-, to treat with contumely, to groan at, to cry out against.

Hizile, those.

Hizika ku-, to be put to the blush.

Hobe! now go on, be off.

Kwenda hobe, to go wherever it may be.

Hobu, grandchild.

Hodari, strong.

Hodi! a cry made by way of inquiry whether any one is within. No one ought to enter a house until he has received an answer.

Hogera ku-, to perform a particular washing customary after circumcision.

Hogo, plur. *mahogo*, a very large root of cassava.

Hohe hahe, a phrase used to denote extreme poverty and destitution.

Hoho.

Pilipili hoho, red pepper.

Mkate wa hoho, a cake made with fresh palm-oil.

Hoja = *Huja*.

Homa, fever.

Hongo, a present demanded by a local chief for liberty to pass through his country.

Hongua, a Comoro dance.

Horari, clever (?).

Hori, or *Khori*, a creek, a small arm of the sea.

Hori, plur. *mahori*, a kind of canoe with a raised head and stern.

Hu-, a quasi-personal prefix denoting a customary action. It applies to all persons and both numbers.

Hunijibu, it is in the habit of answering me.

Huenda, he, &c., commonly goes.

Husema, they say.

Hu- = *h-u-*, the negative prefix of the second person singular. This form is distinguished from the preceding by the termination of the verb.

Huenda, people go.

Huendi, you do not go.

Hua, a dove. They are said to cry, *Mama akafa, Baba akafa, nimesalia mimi, tu, tu, tu, tu, tu*, My mother is dead, my father is dead, I am left alone—lone—lone—lone. Another cry of the same class of birds is explained as, *Kuku mfupa mtupu, mimi nyama tele tele tele*, A fowl is bare bones. I am meat plenty, plenty, plenty.

Hubba, love, affection.

Hubiri, to announce, to give news.

Hudumia ku-, to serve.

Hudumu, service.

Hui ku-, to revive, to come to life again.

Huika ku-, to be brought to life again, to live again.

Huisha ku-, to revive, bring to life again, resuscitate.

Huja or *hoja*, sake, account, concernment, reasoning.

Kina huja nyingi, it is full of bother, it is troublesome.

Hakina huja, it is all clear, it is plain sailing.

Hujambo? Are you well?

Huji ku-, to inquire into, seek out.

Hujuru ku-, to desert.

Huko, there, at a distance.
Huko na huko, hither and thither.
Huku, here, there, near.
Huku na huku, this way and that.
Hukumu, judgment, authority, law.
Hukumu ku-, to act as judge, to have supreme authority over.
Hukumia ku-, to judge, to exercise authority upon.
Hulukiwa ku, to be created, to be a creature.
Humuma, plur. *ma-*, a man who knows no religion.
Hundi, a draft, a bill of exchange.
Huo, this or that before mentioned, referring to singular nouns in *u-* or *w-*, or which make their plural in *mi-*.
Huru, free, not a slave.
Kuweka or *Kuacha huru*, to set free from slavery.
Huru, plur. *mahuru*, a freed man.
Mahuru wa Balyozi, or *Baruzi*, slaves freed by the British consulate.
Huru, diamonds in cards.
Huruma, pity.
Hurumia ku-, to pity, to have pity upon.
Hussu ku-, to divide into shares, to put each one's share separate.
Husudu ku-, to do wanton violence, to grudge at, to envy.
Husumu ku-, to strive, to contend with.
Husuni, a fort.
Husuru ku-, to besiege.
Huthuria ku-, to be present.
Huu, this, referring to nouns in the singular which make their plural in *mi-*, or to singular nouns beginning with *u-* or *w-*.
Huule, that.
Huyo, this or that before mentioned, referring to an animate being.
In chasing a man or animal, any one who sees him cries out, *Huyo! huyo! huyo!* Here he is!
Huyu, this, this person, this one, referring to an animate being.
Huyule, that.
Huzuni, grief, heaviness.
Hwenda, perhaps.

I.

I is pronounced like *ee* in feel.

I before a vowel generally becomes *y*. It is in many cases immaterial whether *i* or *y* be written, but where the accent would otherwise fall upon it, its consonantal character becomes obvious.

An unaccented *i* is often interchanged with a short *u* sound. Thus the word for *lead* may be pronounced either *risasi* or *rusasi*.

N has generally an *i* sound implied in it. It is sometimes expressed following the *n*, as in the prefix *ni*. The final *i* of *ni-* disappears in rapid pronunciation, and in the first person of the future, as *n'* cannot coalesce with *t*, both letters are often omitted. When *n* is followed by a vowel, or by *d*, *g*, *j*, or *z*, the *i* sound is lost. When *n* is followed by other consonants it either disappears altogether or the *i* sound is more or less distinctly prefixed, so as to make the *n* a syllable by itself. The *i* sound is more distinct in the dialect of Zanzibar than in more northern Swahili.

Where *i* follows the final *a* of a

prefix (except the negative prefix *ha*) it coalesces with *a* into the sound of a long *e*.

I, is or was, governed by a singular noun of the class which does not change to form the plural; are or were, governed by a plural noun in *mi-*.

I-, or before a vowel, *y-*, the personal prefix used with verbs whose subject is a singular noun of the class which does not change to form the plural, or a plural in *mi-*, it or they.

-i-, the prefix representing the object of the verb when it is a singular noun of the class which does not change to form the plural, or a plural noun in *mi-*.

-i-, the reflective prefix in *King'ozi* (and in *Nyamwezi*), self.

Iba kw- (the *kw-* is frequently retained in the usual tenses), to steal, to take surreptitiously.

Ibada, worship.

Ibia kw-, to rob, to steal from.

Idadi.

Hayana idadi, there is no counting them.

Idili = *Adili*, right conduct.

Idili ku-, to learn right conduct.

Idilisha ku-, to teach right conduct.

Iftahi, bringer of luck.

Iga ku-, to mock, to imitate (M. *igiza*).

Ih-. See *Hi-*.

Ihtahidi ku-, to strive.

Ih'taji ku-, to be wanting.

Ih'tajia ku-, to want, to be wanting to.

Ih'tilafu, different. Also a fault, difference.

Ih'timu ku-, to finish learning, to complete one's education.

Ijara, pay, hire, rent.

Ijaza, a reward.

Ijaza ku-, to grant permission for worship.

Ikhtiari, choice.

Ikhtiari ku-, to wish.

Ikiza ku-, to lay the beams of a roof.

Kuku ya kuikiza, a fowl cooked with eggs.

Iko, there is, it is there.

Ila, a defect, a blemish.

Ile, that yonder, referring to a singular noun of the class which does not change to form its plural; those yonder, referring to a plural noun in *mi-*.

Ili = *Illi*.

Iliki, cardamoms.

Ilioko, which is, or was there.

Iliopandana, the composition of a word.

Ilizi, a small round thing held to be a great charm against lions.

Illa, except, unless, but.

Illakini, but.

Illi, in order that.

Ilmu, learning.

Ima—ima, either—or.

Ima ku-, to stand up (*King'ozi* and *Yao*).

Njia ya kwima, a straight road.

Ima ku-, to eat up food provided for other people.

Ametuima, he has eaten our share as well as his own.

Imani, faith.

Imara, firm.

Imba kw-, to sing.

Imbu, mosquito, mosquitoes.

Imisha ku-, to set up, to make to stand.

Imma.

Wa imma, to a certainty.

Ina, it has, they have.

Inama ku-, to bow, to stoop, to bend down, to slope.

Inamisha ku-, to make to bend down, to bow.

Inang'ara, it is bright. See *ng'aa.*

Inchi, land, country, earth.

Inda.

Kufanya inda, to give trouble.

Inga ku-, to scare away birds.

-ingi, many, much. It makes *jingi* with nouns like *kasha*, and *nyingi* with nouns like *nyumba.*

Ingia ku-, to enter, to go or come into.

Ingilia ku-, to go or come into, for, or to.

Ingiliza ku-, to cohabit with.

ingine, other, different. It makes *mgine* or *mwingine* with nouns like *mtu* and *mti*; *jingine* with nouns like *kasha*; *ngine* or *nyingine* with nouns like *nyumba*; and *pingine* or *pangine* with nouns of place.

Wangine—wangine, some—others.

Ingiza ku-, to make or allow to enter.

Ini, plur. *maini*, the liver.

Inika ku-, to hang down, to lay upon its side. See *Jiinika.*

Inna, truly.

Inshallah, if God will, perhaps. It is used as a general promise to do as one is asked to do.

Inta = *Nta.*

Inua ku-, to lift, to lift up.

Inuka ku-, to be lifted, to become raised.

Inya, mother (A.).

-inyi = *-enyi*, having, with. It makes *mwinyi, wenyi, yinyi, zinyi, linyi, kinyi, vinyi*, and *penyi.*

Inzi, plur. *mainzi*, a fly.

Ipa ku-, to want, desire to have.

Kuipa roho mbele, to long for everything one sees, to have unrestrained desires.

Ipi

Kupiga ipi, to slap (N.).

Ipi? what?

Kama ipi? how?

Ipua kw-, to take off the fire.

Iriba, usury.

Iriwa, a vice (the tool).

Isha kw, to finish, to come to an end. The *kw-* is retained in the usual tenses, but sometimes the *w* is dropped, as *amekisha* for *amekwisha*, he has done.

Kwisha is commonly used as an auxiliary: thus, *Amekwisha kuja*, he has come already. *Alipokwisha kuja*, when he had come.

Akaisha, or *Akesha*, after that, when he had done this.

Ishara, a sign, signal.

Ishi ku-, to last, to endure, to live.

Isimu or *Ismu*, name, especially the name of God.

Ma ismak (Ar.)? What is your name?

Istara, a curtain.

Istiska, dropsy.

Ita kw-, to call, to call to, to name, to invite. The *kw-* is frequently retained.

Kwitwa, to be called, is sometimes constructed as if it were *kuwitwa.*

Ita ku-, to cast in a mould.

Italassi, satin.

Ithini, sanotion.

Kutoa ithini, to sanction.

Ithneen, two.

Itia ku-, to call for some purpose.

Itika ku-, to answer when called.

Itikia ku-, to reply to, to answer a person when called to.

Itikiza ku-, to assent to.

Ito la guu (A.), the ankle.

Iva ku- or *Wiva ku-*, to become ripe, to become completely cooked, to get done. The *ku-* is frequently retained.

Ivu, plur. *maivu*, ash, ashes (M.).

I wapi? where is it?

Iza ku-, to refuse.

Izara ku-, to tell scandal about, to make things publio about a person improperly.

J.

J. The correct pronunciation of this letter, and especially that of the Mombas dialect, is a very peculiar one. The most prominent sound is that of *y*, but it is preceded by another resembling *d*. The French *di* is perhaps the nearest European representative. The Swahili write it by the Arabic *jim*, which is exactly an English *j*.

In the more northern dialects and in the old poetical Swahili the *j* is represented by a pure *y*.

Moya = *moja*, one.

Mayi = *maji*, water.

A *d* in the dialect of Mombas very commonly becomes a *j* in that of Zanzibar.

Ndia (M.), a road, *Njia* (Zanz.).

Kutinda (M.), to slaughter; *Kuchinja* (Zanz.).

Many words which are properly spelt with a *z* are vulgarly pronounced with a *j* in Zanzibar, as,

Kanju, for *kanzu*.

Chenja, for *chenza*.

This is only carrying to excess the rule that a *z* in the neighbouring mainland languages becomes a *j* in Swahili.

The Arabs and some Swahili confuse *j* with *g*. Thus the late ruler of Zanzibar was often spoken of as *Bwana Magídi*, his proper title being *Seyid Májid*.

J-, a prefix applied to substantives and adjectives in the singular of the class which make their plural in *ma-*, when they begin with a vowel. See *ji-*.

Ja, like.

Ja kú- (the *ku-* carries the accent and is retained in the usual tenses), to come. The imperative is irregular, *Njoo*, come. *Njooni*, come ye.

Ja is used to form several tenses.

1. With *-po-* added, meaning even if; *wa-japo-kupiga*, even if they beat you.
2. With negative prefixes meaning not yet; *ha-ja-ja*, he is not yet come.
3. With negative prefix and subjunctive form. *Asi-je-lala*, before he goes to sleep, or that he may not have already gone to sleep.

Jaa ku-, to become full, to fill, to abound with.

Maji yanajaa, the tide is coming in.

Mtungi umejaa maji, the jar is full of water.

See *Jawa ku-*.

Jaa.
Shika májira ya jaa, steer northwards.
Jaa, a dust heap.
Jabali, plur. *majabali*, a rocky hill. Also see *Kanza.*
Jabari, absolute ruler, a title of God.
Jadiliana ku-, to argue with.
Jaha, good luck, unexpected good fortune.
Kilango cha jaha, the gate of Paradise.
Jahazi, a vessel, a ship.
Jahili ku-, to dare, not to fear.
Jalada, the cover of a bound book.
Jali ku-, to give honour to.
Jalia ku-, to bless, to enable, to grant to.
Muungu akinijalia, God willing.
Jaliwa ku-, to be enabled, to have power, &c., given one.
Jaliza ku-, to fill up, used of vessels which have already something in them.
Jamaa, family, assembly, gathering, society, company.
Jamaa ku-, to collect together, gather.
Jamaat (Hind.), a council of elders.
Jamala, courtesy, good manners, elegance.
Jamanda, plur. *majamanda*, a solid kind of round basket with a lid.
Jamba, breaking of wind downwards.
Jamba ku-, to break wind downwards.
Jambia, plur. *majambia*, a curved dagger always worn by Muscat Arabs.
Jambo, plur. *mambo* (from *kuamba*,) a word (?), a matter, a circumstance, a thing, an affair.
Akanitenda killa jambo la wema, and he showed me all possible kindness.
Jambo for *si jambo*, *hu jambo*, *ha jambo*, &c., I am well, are you well? he is well, &c., &c.
Jambo sana, I am very well, are you very well? &c.
Jami ku-, to copulate, to have connection with.
Jamii, many, a good collection, the mass, the company of, the body of.
Jamiisha ku-, to gather.
Jamvi, plur. *majamvi*, a coarse kind of matting used to cover floors.
Jana, yesterday.
Mwaka jana, last year.
Janna, paradise.
Janaba, filth, uncleanness.
Janga, punishment.
Jangwa, plur. *majangwa*, a large desert.
Jani, plur. *majani*, a leaf. *Majani* is commonly used for any grass or herbage.
Janvia = *Jambia.*
-japo-, sign of a tense signifying even if.
Ujapofika, even if you arrive.
Jarari, the ropes passing through the pulley attached to a dhow's halyards.
Jaribu ku-, to try.
Jarifa, plur. *majarifa*, a seine or drag-net made of European cordage. See *Juya.*
Jasho, sweat.
Kufanya jasho, to sweat.
Jasirisha ku-, to dare.
Jasisi ku-, to explore.
Jasmini or *Jasmin*, jasmine. The flowers are sold in the streets of Zanzibar for their scent.

Jassi, plur. *majassi*, the ornament in the lobe of the ear. It is generally a silver plate about an inch and a half across.

Jathari, take care!

Jawa, a coarse kind of Indian earthenware.

Kikombe cha Jawa, a cup of coarse Indian ware.

Jawa ku-, to be filled with, to be full of: used of something which ought not, or could not be expected to be there.

Maji yamejawa dudu, the water is full of insects; but *mtungi umejaa maji*, the jar is full of water.

Jawabu, an answer, a condition, a matter.

Jawahir (Ar.), jewels.

Jaza ku-, to fill.

Jazi, a common thing, a thing which is abundant.

Jazi ku-, to supply, to maintain.

Jazilia ku-, to reward.

Je! Hullo! Well! What now!

-je? how?

Jebu, an ornament worn by women, hanging under the chin.

Jekundu, red. See *-ekundu*.

Jelidi ku-, to bind books.

Jema, good. See *-ema*.

Jemadari, plur. *majemadari*, a commanding officer, a general.

Jembamba, narrow, thin. See *-embamba*.

Jembe, plur. *majembe*, a hoe.

Jembe la kizungu, a spade.

Jenaiza or *Jeneza*, a bier.

Jenga ku-, to construct, to build.

Jengea ku-, to build for, or on account of.

Jengo, plur. *majengo*, a building.

Majengo, building materials.

Jenzi ku-, to construct.

Jepa ku- (A.), to steal.

Jepesi, light, not heavy. See *-epesi*.

Jeraha, a wound.

Jeribu ku- = *Jaribu ku-*, to try.

Jeruhi ku-, to be wounded.

Jeshi, plur. *majeshi*, a host, a great company.

Jetea ku-, to be puffed up, to be over proud, to rely upon, to trust in.

Jethamu, a leprosy in which the fingers and toes drop off, elephantiasis (?).

Jeuli or *Jeuri*, violence.

Ana jeuli, he attacks people wantonly.

Jeupe, white. See *-eupe*.

Jeusi, black. See *eusi*.

Ji-, a syllable prefixed to substantives which make their plural in *ma-*, if they would otherwise be of one syllable only. This syllable is sometimes inserted after a prefix to give the idea of largeness, or to prevent confusion with someother word. Before a vowel it becomes *j-* only.

-ji-, an infix giving a reflective meaning to the verb.

Kupenda, to love.

Kujipenda, to love oneself.

Kuponya, to save.

Jiponye, save yourself, look out!

Jia ku-, to come for, by, to.

Njia uliyojia, the road you came by.

Jibini, cheese.

Jibiwa ku, to receive an answer, be answered.

Jibu ku-, to answer, to give an answer.

Jibwa, plur. *majibwa*, an exceedingly large dog.

Jicho, plur. *macho*, the eye.

Jicho la maji, a spring of water.

Jifu, plur. *majifu*, ashes.

Jifya, plur. *mafya*, one of three stones to support a pot over the fire. *Mafya* is the usual word in the town, *mafiga* is commonly used in the country.

Jigamba ku-, to boast, to praise oneself.

Jiinika ku-, to lie on the side.

Jiko, plur. *meko*, a fireplace, one of the stones to rest a pot on (?).

Jikoni, in the kitchen, among the ashes.

Jilia ku-, to come to a person on some business.

Jiliwa, plur. *majiliwa*, a vice (the tool).

Jimbi, a cock.

Jimbi, Allocasia edulis. Both leaves and root are eaten: (a sort of Arum).

Jimbo, plur. *majimbo*, a place, a part of the country (Old Swahili).

Jimbo.

Kuosha na jimbo, to wash a new-born child with water and *medicine*.

Jina, plur. *majina*, a name.

Jina lako nani? what is your name?

Jina la kupangwa, a nickname.

Jinamisi, nightmare.

Jingi, much. See *-ingi*.

Jingine, other. See *-ingine*.

Jini, plur. *majini*, jins, spirits, genii.

Jino, plur. *meno*, a tooth, a twist or strand of rope, or tobacco, &c

Kamba ya meno matatu, a cord of three strands.

Jioni, evening.

Jipu, plur. *majipu*, a boil.

Jipotoa ku-, to dress oneself up excessively.

Jipya, new. See *-pya*.

Jirani, a neighbour, neighbours.

Jisi, quality.

Jisu, plur. *majisu*, a very large knife.

Jitenga ku-, to get out of the way.

Jiti, plur. *majiti*, a tree trunk.

Jitimai, excessive sorrow.

Jito, plur. *mato* = *Jicho*, the eye (M.).

Jitu, plur. *matu* or *majitu*, a great large man, a savage.

Jituza ku-, to make oneself mean or low. See *Tuza*.

Jivari, purchase (of a dhow halyards).

Jivi, a wild hog.

Jivu = *Jifu*.

Jiwa ku-, to be visited.

Jiwe, plur. *mawe*, a stone, a piece of stone. Plur. *majiwe*, of very large pieces of stone.

Jiwe la manga, a piece of freestone.

Nyumba ya mawe, a stone house.

Jodari, a kind of fish.

Jogoi = *Jogoo*.

Jogoo, plur. *majogoo*, a cock.

Johari, a jewel.

Joho, woollen cloth, a long loose coat worn by the Arabs.

Joka, plur. *majoka*, a very large snake.

Joko, a place to bake pots in.

Jokum, charge, responsibility.

Jombo, plur. *majombo*, an exceedingly large vessel.

Jongea ku-, to approach, come near to, move.

Jongea mvulini, move into the shade.

Jongeleza ku-, to bring near to, to offer.

Jongeza ku-, to bring near, move towards, move.

Jongo, gout.

Jongoe, a large kind of fish.

Jongoo, a millepede.

Jorjiya, a Georgian, the most valued and whitest of female slaves.

Jororo, soft. See *-ororo*.

Josh, a voyage, a cruize.

= *Goshi*, Luff!

Jotojoto.

Kupata jotojoto, to grow warm.

Joya, plur. *majoya*, a cocoa-nut which is filled with a white spongy substance instead of the usual nut and juice. They are prized for eating.

Jozi, *Jeozi*, or *Jauzi*, a pair, a pack of cards.

Jozi, a walnut.

Jua, plur. *majua*, the sun.

Jua kitwani, noon.

Jua ku-, to know how, to understand, to know about, to know.

Namjua aliko, I know where he is.

Najua kiunguja, I understand the language of Zanzibar.

Najua kufua chuma, I know how to work in iron.

Juba, a mortice chisel.

Juburu ku-, to compel.

Jugo, ground nuts.

Juhudi, an effort, efforts.

Kufanya juhudi, to exert oneself.

Juju, plur. *majuju*, a fool.

Juku, risk, a word used by traders.

Jukwari, a scaffold, scaffolding.

Julia ku-, to know about, see to.

Julisha ku-, to make to know.

Juma, Friday, a week.

Juma a mosi, Saturday.

Juma a pili, Sunday.

Juma a tatu, Monday.

Juma a 'nne, Tuesday.

Juma a tano, Wednesday.

Juma, small brass nails used for ornamentation.

Jumaa, an assembly.

Jumba, plur. *majumba*, a large house.

Jumbe, plur. *majumbe*, a chief, a head-man, a prince, a sultan.

Jumla, the sum, the total, addition (in arithmetic).

Jumlisha ku-, to add up, sum up, put together.

Junia, a kind of matting bag. See *Gunia*.

Jura, a pair; a length of calico, about thirty-five yards.

Jusi.

Haijusi, it is unfitting.

Jut Kásam (Hind.), perjury.

Juta ku-, to be sorry for, to regret.

Juu, up, the top, on the top.

Yuko juu, he is up-stairs.

Juu ya, upon, above, over, on the top of, against.

Juvisha ku-, to make to know, to teach.

Juvya ku-, to make to know.

Juya, plur. *majuya*, a seine or drag-net made of cocoa-nut fibre rope.

Juza, obligation, kindness.

Juza ku-, to make to know.

Juzi, the day before yesterday.

Mwaka juzi, the year before last.

Juzijuzi, a few days ago.

Juzia ku-, to compel, to have power to compel.

Juzu, necessity.

Jambo la juzu, a necessary thing.

Juzu ku-, to oblige, to hold bound, to have under an obligation to do something.

Juzuu, a section of the Koran. There are in all thirty, which are often written out separately. All the *Juzuu* together are *Khitima nzima*.

K.

K is pronounced as in English.

The Arabs have two *k*'s, one, the *kef* or *kaf*, a little lighter than the English *k;* and one, the *kahf* or *qaf*, made wholly in the throat, and confounded by many Arabs with a hard *g*. There is a curious catch in the throat between the preceding vowel and the *qaf*, very hard to explain, but easy enough to imitate. Although the correct pronunciation of these two *k*'s is an elegance, it is not necessary nor very commonly observed in speaking Swahili.

Ki is very commonly pronounced *chi* in Zanzibar, especially by slaves of the Nyassa and Yao tribes.

Kh, the Arabic *kha*, occurs only in words borrowed from the Arabic, and subsides into a simple *h* so soon as the word is thoroughly naturalized.

Khabari or *Habari*, news.

Kheiri or *Heri*, well, good, fortunate.

Ka-, *-ka-*, a syllable prefixed to or inserted in the imperative and subjunctive of verbs, with the force of the conjunction "and."

-ka-, the sign of a past tense, used in carrying on a narration; it includes the force of the conjunction "and."

Akamwambia, and he said to him.

Nika- is often contracted into *ka-*.

Kaa ku-, to sit, to dwell, to stay, to live, to be, to stand, to remain, to continue, to live in, or at.

Kukaa kitako, to sit down, to remain quietly.

Kaa, plur. *makaa*, a piece of charcoal.

Makaa, coals, charcoal, embers.

Kaa la moshi or *Makaa ya moshi*, soot.

Kaa, a crab.

Kaa makoko, small mud crabs with one large claw.

Kaa la kinwa, the palate.

Kaaka or *Kaakaa*, the palate.

Kaanga ku-, to fry, to braze, to cook with fat.

Kaango, plur. *makaango*, an earthen pot to cook meat in.

Kaba ku-, to choke, to throttle.

Kaba la kanzu, a sort of lining round the neck and a short way down the front of a *kanzu*, put in to strengthen it.

Kabari, a wedge.

Kabibu, narrow.

Kabila, a tribe, a subdivision less than *taifa*.

Kabili ku-, to be before, to be opposite.

Kabilisha ku-, to put opposite, to set before.

Kabisa, utterly, altogether, quite.

Kabithi ku-, to give into the hand.

Kabla, before, antecedently.

Kabla ya, before (especially of time).

Kabuli, acceptance.

Kabuli, pillaw.

Kaburi, plur. *makaburi* (pronounced

by many Arabs *Gabri*), a grave, a tomb.

Kadamu, a servant, the lowest of the three chief men usually set over the slaves on a plantation. On the Zambezi the man who stands at the head of the canoe to look out for shoals is called *Kadamo*.

Kadiri or *Kadri*, measure, moderation, capacity, middling, moderate, about, nearly, moderately.

Kadri gani? how much?

Kadiri ya, as, whilst.

Kadiri ku-, to estimate.

Kadri = *Kadiri*.

Kafara, an offering to avert evil, a sacrifice of an animal or thing to be afterwards buried or thrown away, a charm made of bread, sugar-cane, &c., thrown down in a cross-way. Any one who takes it is supposed to carry away the disease, misfortune, &c.

Kafi, plur. *makafi*, a paddle.

Kafiri, plur. *makafiri*, an infidel, an idolater, one who is not a Mohammedan.

Kafuri, camphor.

Kaga ku-, to put up a charm to protect something.

Kago, plur. *mago*, a charm to protect what it is fastened to.

Kagua ku-, to go over and inspect.

Kahaba, plur. *makahaba*, a prostitute.

Kahawa, coffee.

Kahini, plur. *makahini*, a priest, a soothsayer.

Kai ku-, to fall down to, embrace the knees.

Kaida, regularity.

Ya kaida, regular.

-kaidi, obstinate.

Kaimu, plur. *makaimu*, a vicegerent, a representative.

Kaka, a lemon after it has been squeezed, the rind of a lemon, the shell of an egg, &c.

Kaka, a brother (*Kihadimu*, see *Muhadimu*).

Kaka, a disease with swelling of the hand and opening into sores.

Kakakaka, very many.

Kakamia, hard of heart.

Kakamia ku, to be longsuffering, slow to be affected.

Kakamuka ku-, to make an effort, to strain (as at stool, or in travail).

Kakawana ku-, to be strong, capable of great exertion, well-knit and firm in all the muscles.

Kaki, a very thin kind of biscuit or cake.

Kalafati ku-, to caulk.

Kalamika ku-, to prevaricate in giving evidence (?), to cry from pain caused by medicine (?).

Kala'mka ku-, to be sharp, to have one's eyes open.

Kala'mkia ku-, to outdo, to be too sharp for.

Kalamu, a pen. The pens for writing Arabic are made of reed, and the nibs are cut obliquely.

Kalamu ya mwanzi, a reed pen.

Kalamuzi, cunning, crafty.

Kalasia, little brass pots.

Kale, old time, formerly.

-a kale, old, of old time.

Zamani za kale, old times.

Hapo kale, once upon a time.

Kalfati or *Kalafati*, caulking.

-kali, sour, sharp, keen, savage

cross, severe, fierce. It makes *kali* with nouns like *nyumba*.
Jua kali, a hot sun.

Kalia ku-, to remain for.
Ku'mkalia tamu, to remain as he would wish.

Kalibu, a mould, a furnace.

Kama, *Kamma*, *Kana*, or *Kwamba*, as, as if, like, if, supposing.

Kama ku-, to milk, to squeeze.

Kamamanga, a pomegranate.

Kamali, a game played by chucking pice into a hole. If only one goes in they say "*Maliza*," and the player throws a flat stone on the one that is out.

Kamasi, mucus from the nose.
Kufuta kamasi, to blow the nose.
Siwezi kamasi, I have a cold in my head.

Kamata ku-, to lay hold of, take, seize, clasp.

Kamatana ku-, to grapple, to seize one another.

Kamati, balls of wheat-flour leavened with *tembo*.

Kamba, a crayfish.

Kamba, rope.
Kamba ulayiti, European or hempen rope.

Kambaa, plur. of *ukambaa*, cord, string (M.).
Kambaa, a plaited thong or whip kept by schoolmasters and overlookers in Zanzibar.

Kambali, plur. *makambali*, a cat-fish living in fresh water.

Kambarau, a forebrace carried to the weather side to steady the yard of a dhow.

Kambi, plur. *makambi*, a circular encampment, a place where a caravan has hutted itself in.

Kambo.
Baba wa kambo, stepfather.
Mama wa kambo, stepmother.

Kame, quite dried up, utterly barren.

Kami, a bulbous plant with large head of red flowers.

Kamia ku-, to reproach.
Kujikamia, to reproach oneself.

Kamili, perfect, complete.

-kamilifu, perfect, wanting nothing.

Kamilika ku-, to be perfect.

Kamilisha ku-, to make perfect.

Kamua ku-, to press, to press out.

Kamusi, an Arabic lexicon.

Kamwe (M.), not at all, never.

Kamwi = *Kamwe*.

Kana, a tiller.

Kana, if, as. See *Kama*.

Kana ku-, to deny.

Kanda, plur. *makanda*, a long narrow matting bag, broader at the bottom than at the mouth.

Kanda ku-, to knead dough, to knead the limbs, to shampoo.

Kandamiza ku-, to press upon.

Kande, food (Mer.).

Kanderinya, a kettle.

Kandika ku-, to plaster.

Kandili, plur. *makandili*, a lantern.

Kando, side, aside.
Kando ya or *Kandokando ya*, beside, along by the side.

Kanga, a guinea fowl.

Kanga, a dry stem after the cocoanuts have been taken off.

Kanga ku-.
Kukanga moto, to warm.

Kangaja, a small mandarin orange.

Kania ku-, to deny a person.

Kaniki, dark blue calico.

Kanisa, plur. *makanisa*, a church.

Kanisha ku-, to deny, to make to deny.

Kanji, starch, arrowroot.

Kanju, plur. *makanju*, a cashew apple (M.).

Kanju, vulgarly used for *Kanzu*.

Kanuni, a thing implied, a necessary condition, of necessity.

Kanwa, plur. *makanwa*, the mouth.

Kanya ku-, to contradict.

Kanyaga ku-, to tread, to tread upon, trample on.

Kanyassa ku-, to scold.

Kanzi, a treasure.

Kanzu, a long shirt-like garment worn both by men and women in Zanzibar. Men's *kanzus* are white or of a brown yellow colour, with ornamental work in red and white silk round the neck and down the breast; they reach to the heels. Women's *kanzus* are generally shorter, and are made of every variety of stuff, frequently of satin or brocade, but are always bound with red.

Parts of a *Kanzu* (men's):

Tao la kanzu, bottom hem.

Magongo nene, seams.

Badani, front and back pieces. Also *Kimo*.

Taharizi, side pieces.

Sijafu, pieces turned in at the wrists, to receive the *darizi*.

Vikwapa, gores.

Lisani, flap under the opening in front.

Jabali, red line across the back.

Mhalbori, lining at the back of the *darizi* in front.

Kaaba, lining of the neck and shoulders.

Shada, tassel at the neck.

Kitanzi, loop opposite the tassel in front.

Kazi ya shingo, the elaborately worked border round the neck, including—

Tiki, red sewing over of the edge of the neck.

Mrera, lines of red round the neck.

Viboko, small zigzag ornament in the middle of the neck-border.

Vinara, small spots forming the outer edge of the border.

Darizi, lines of silk worked round the wrists and down the front.

Mjuzi (Ar. *shararaji*), ornament at the bottom of the strip of embroidery in front.

Mkia wa mjuzi, line of silk running up the front from the *mjuzi*.

Vipaji, or *viguu*, four little projections on the sides of the *mjazi*.

Kanzu ya ziki, worked with white cotton round the neck instead of red silk.

Kaoleni, one whose words are not to be trusted, a double-tongued man.

Kaomwa, calumba root.

Kapi, plur. *makapi*, a pulley.

Kapi, plur. *makapi*, bran, husks.

Kapiana ku- (*mikono*), to shake hands.

Kapu, plur. *makapu*, a large basket or matting bag.

Kapwai, a kind of rice.

Karafati ku- = *Kalafati*.

Karafu mayiti, camphor.
Karama, a special gift of God, an answer to a holy man's prayer, an honour.
Karamu, a feast.
Karani, a secretary, a clerk, a supercargo.
Karani, tucks.
Karara, the woody flower-sheath of the cocoa-nut tree.
Karata, playing-cards.
Karatha, a loan of money.
Karatasi, paper.
Karib, near, come near, come in.
Karibia ku-, to approach, to draw near to.
Karibiana ku-, to be near to one another.
Karibisha, to make to come near, to invite in.
Karibu, near, a near relative.
Karibu na or *ya*, near to, near.
Karimu, liberal, generous.
Karipia ku-, to cry out at, scold.
Karirisha ku-, to recite.
Kasa, a turtle.
Kasarani, sorrow, grief.
Kasasi, retaliation, revenge, vengeance.
Kasha, plur. *makasha*, a chest, a large box.
Kashifu ku-, to depreciate.
Kashmir, the ace of spades.
Kasia, plur. *makasia*, an oar.
Kuvuta makasia, to row.
Kasiba, a gun barrel.
Kasidi, intention, purpose.
Kasifa, inquisitiveness.
Kasifu ku-, to be inquisitive.
Kasiki, a large earthen jar for ghee.
Kasimele, the juice of grated cocoa-nut before water is put to it.
Tui la kasimele. See *Tui*.
Tui la kupopoloa, the same after mixing with water, and straining again.
Kasiri, towards the end, late.
Kasirika ku-, to become vexed.
Kasirisha ku-, to vex.
Kasiri ku-, to hurt, vex.
Kaskazi, the northerly wind which blows from December till March.
Kaskazini, in a northerly direction.
Kasoro, less by.
Kassa, less by.
Kassa robo, three-quarters of a dollar.
Kassi. See *Kiassi*.
Kasi, hard, with violence.
Kwenda kassi, to rush along.
Kutia kassi, to tighten.
Kasumba, a preparation of opium.
Kataa ku-, to refuse.
Kata, plur. *makata*, a ladle made of a cocoa-nut, only about a third of the shell being removed. A *kata* holds from a quarter to half a pint.
K'ata, a ring of grass or leaves put on the head under a water-pot or other burden.
Kata ku-, to cut, clip, divide.
Kujikata, to cut oneself.
Kukata hananu, to cut obliquely.
Kukata maneno, to settle an affair, to decide.
Kukata nakshi, to ornament with carving, to carve.
Kukata tamaa, to despair.
Njia ya kukata, a short cut, the nearest way.
Kátaba ku-, to write.
Katakata ku-, to chop up.
Katalia ku-, to deny all credence, to refuse to be convinced.

Katani, flax, thread, string, cotton-thread.

Kataza ku-, to prohibit, to deter.

Kathâlika, in like manner.

Kathâwakatha, many, many more.

Watu kathâwakatha, such and such people.

Kathi, plur. *makathi*, a judge, a cadi.

Kati, inside, middle, the court within a house.

Katia ku-, to cut for.

Kukatiwa, to have cut, or cut out for one.

Ni kiasi changu kama nalikatiwa mimi, it fits as though I had been measured for it.

Katika, among, at, from, in, about.

Katika implies nearness at least at the beginning of the action; it has very nearly the same meaning as the case in *-ni*.

Katika safari mle, during that journey.

Katika ku-, to come apart, to be cut, to break, to be decided.

Katikati, in the midst.

Katikati ya, &c., in the midst of, between.

Katili, a murderous, bloodthirsty person, an infidel.

Katinakati, in the middle.

Katiti (A.), little.

Katiza ku-, to put a stop to, to break off, to interrupt.

Kato, plur. *makato*, a cutting, a breaking off.

Katu, a kind of gum chewed with betel.

Katua ku-, to polish, to brighten.

Katuka ku-, to be polished, to be bright.

Kauka ku-, to get dry, to dry.

Sauti imekauka, I am hoarse.

Kauli, a word.

Kauri, a cowry.

Kausha ku-, to make dry, to dry.

-kavu, dry. It makes *kavu* with nouns like *nyumba*.

Kawa, a conical dish-cover of plaited straw, often ornamented with spangles, &c.

Kawa, mildew, spots of mould.

Kufanya kawa, to get mildewed or mouldy.

Kawa ku-, to be delayed, to tarry, to be a long while.

Kawadi (a term of reproach), a bad man.

Kawaida, necessity, custom.

Kawe, a pebble, a small stone (M.).

Kawia ku-, to delay.

Kawilia ku-, to loiter about a business.

Kawisha ku-, to keep, to delay, to cause to stay.

Kaya, plur. *makaya*, a pinna, a kind of shell-fish.

Kayamba, a sieve, a sort of rattle.

Kaza ku-, to fix, to tighten, (of clothes) to fit tightly, to go hard at anything.

Kukaza kwimba, to sing louder.

Kukaza mbio, to run hard.

Kazana ku-, to fix one another, to tighten together, to hold together tightly, to be robust.

Kazi, work, labour, employment, business.

Ndio kazi yake, that is what he always does.

Kazi mbi si mtezo mwema? Is not poor work (as good as) good play (*mbi* for *n-wi*)?

Kazika ku-, to become tight, to become fixed.

-kazo, nipping, pressing tight.

-ke, female, feminine, the weaker.

Kee = *Kelele* (N.).

Keezo, a lathe, a machine for turning.

Kéfule! an exclamation of contempt.

Kefyakefya ku-, to teaze, to put in low spirits.

Keke, a drill. The carpenters in Zanzibar always use drills, which are much better suited to the native woods than gimlets are. The iron is called *kekee*, the wood in which it is fixed *msukano*, the handle in which it turns *Jivu*, and the bow by which it is turned *Uta*.

Kekee, a kind of silver bracelet.

Kelele, plur. *makelele*, noise, uproar, shouting.

Kem (Ar.), How much? How many?

Kemea ku-, to rebuke, to snub, to scold.

Kenda = *Kwenda* and *Kaenda*.

Kenda, nine.

Ya kenda, ninth.

Kendapi? for *kwenda wapi*, going where, *i.e.*, where are you going?

Kenge, a large water-lizard with slender body and long limbs and tail.

Kengea, the blade of a sword, knife, &c.

Kengele, a bell.

Kupiga kengele, to ring a bell.

Kera ku-, to worry, to nag at.

Kerani = *Karani*.

Kereketa ku, to irritate the throat, to choke.

Kereza ku-, to saw, to turn, to cut a tree half through, and lay it down, so as to make a fence.

Kerimu ku-, to feast, to be liberal to.

Kering'ende, a dragon-fly, the red-legged partridge.

Kero, trouble, disturbance, uproar.

Kesha, a watch, a vigil.

Kesha ku-, to watch, to remain awake, not to sleep.

Kesheza ku-, to make, to watch, to keep awake.

Kesho, to-morrow.

Kesho kutwa or *kuchwa*, the day after to-morrow.

Kete, a cowry.

Keti ku-, to sit down, stay, live (M.).

Khabari, news, information.

Khadaa, fraud.

Khafifu, light, unimportant.

Khaini, a traitor.

Khalás, the end, there is no more.

Khálifu ku- or *Halifu ku-*, to resist, oppose, rebel against.

Khalisi ku-, to deliver.

Khami, a chess bishop.

Khamsi, five.

Khamsini, fifty.

Khamstashara, *fifteen*.

Kharadali, mustard.

Khárij ku-, to spend.

Khashifu ku- = *Kashifu ku-*.

Khatari, danger.

Khati, a note, letter, document, memorandum, writing, handwriting.

Khatibu, plur. *makhatibu*, a secretary, a preacher.

Khatima, end, completion.

Khatimisha ku-, to bring to an end, complete.

Khatiya, fault. See *Hatiya*.

Khazana, a treasure.

Khema, a tent.

Kheiri = *Heri*, well, fortunate, happy, good.

Mtu wa kheiri, a happy man.
Kwa kheiri, for good.
Ni kheiri, I had better.

Khini ku-, to betray.

Khitari ku-, to choose.

Khitima nzima, a complete copy of the Koran. See *Juzuu*.

Khofisha ku-, to frighten.

Khofu, fear, danger.
Kuwa na khofu, } to become
Kuingiwa na khofu, } afraid.
Kutia khofu, to frighten.

Khorj, a pad used as a saddle for donkeys.

Khoshi (?), paint, colour.

Khubiri ku-, to inform, give news.

Khusumu, enmity.

Khutubu ku-, to preach.

Khuzurungi or *Huthurungi*, a stuff of a brown yellow colour, of which the best men's kanzus are made.

Ki-, a prefix forming a diminutive. It becomes *ch-* before a vowel, and in the plural it becomes *vi-* and *vy-*, or in other dialects *zi-* or *thi-*.
Ki- as a prefix also means (especially if prefixed to proper names), such a sort; and when used alone, words of such a sort, *i.e.* such a language.
Mavazi ya kifaume, royal robes.
Viazi vya kizungu, European potatoes.
Kiarabu, Arabic.
Kiyao, the Yao language.

Ki- or *ch-*, the adjectival and pronominal prefix proper to words agreeing with substantives of the above forms.

Ki- or *ch-*, the personal prefix of verbs having substantives of the above form as their subject.

-ki-, the objective prefix of verbs having substantives of the above form as their object.

-ki-, the sign of that tense which expresses a state of things, *being that*, which may be translated by the help of the words, if, supposing, when, while, or be treated as a present participle in *-ing*.
Niki- may be contracted into *hi-*.
Alikuwa akiogolea, he was bathing.
Akija, if he comes, or when he comes.
The syllable *-ki-* is inserted in the past perfect tense to denote a continuing action or state.
Walipo-ki-pendana, when or while they loved one another.

Kia, plur. *via*, a piece of wood, a kind of latch, a bar.

Kia ku-, to step over.

Kiada, slowly, distinctly.

Kialio, plur. *vialio*, cross pieces put in a cooking pot to prevent the meat touching the bottom and burning.

Kianga, the coming out of the sun after rain.

Kiapo, plur. *viapo*, an ordeal, an oath.

Kiarabu, Arabic.
Ya kiarabu, Arabian.

Kiasi = *Kiassi*.

Kiass cha bunduki, a cartridge.

Kiassi, measure, moderation.
Kiassi gani? or *Kassi gani?* How much?

Kiatu, plur. *viatu*, a shoe, a sandal.
Viatu vya mti, a sort of tall wooden clog worn in the house,

and especially by women. They are held on by grasping a sort of button (*msuruaki*) between the great and second toe.

Kiazi, plur. *viazi*, a sweet potato.

Kiazi kikuu, plur. *viazi vikuu*, a yam.

Kiazi sena, with white skin.

Kiazi kindoro, with red skin.

Kiba haluli, a knot of *makuti* to light a pipe with.

Kibaba, a measure, about a pint basin full, a pint basin, about a pound and a half.

Kibakuli, a kind of *mtama*.

Kibali ku-, to prosper.

Kibanda, plur. *vibanda*, a hut, a hovel, a shed.

Kibanzi, plur. *vibanzi*, a splinter, a very small piece of wood.

Kibao, plur. *vibao*, a shelf, a small piece of plank. In Tumbatu a chair is called *kibao*.

Kibapara, a pauper, a destitute person (an insulting epithet).

Kibarango, a short heavy stick.

Kibaraza, plur. *vibaraza*, a small stone seat.

Kibarua, plur. *vibarua*, a note, a ticket. *Kibarua* is now used in Zanzibar to denote a person hired by the day, from the custom of giving such persons a ticket, to be delivered up when they are paid.

Kiberiti, sulphur.

Viberiti, matches.

Kibeti, a dwarf.

Kuku kibeti, a bantam.

Kibia, plur. *vibia*, an earthen pot-lid.

Kibiongo, plur. *vibiongo*, a person bent by age or infirmity.

Kibobwe, plur. *vibobwe*, a piece of cloth tied round the loins during hard work.

Kibofu, plur. *vibofu*, a bladder.

Kibogoshi, plur. *vibogoshi*, a small skin bag.

Kiboko, plur. *viboko*, a hippopotamus. See also *Kanzu*.

Kibua, a small fish.

Kibueta, plur. *vibueta*, a box.

Kibula, the *kebla*, the point to which men turn when they pray. Among the Mohammedans the *kibula* is the direction in which Mecca lies, which is in Zanzibar nearly north. Hence *kibula* is sometimes used to mean the north.

Kibula ku-, to point towards, to be opposite to.

Kibumba, plur. *vibumba*, a small paper box or case of anything.

Kiburi, pride.

Kiburipembe, a native bird.

Kichaa, lunacy.

Mwenyi kichaa, a lunatic.

Kichaka, plur. *vichaka*, a thicket, a heap of wood or sticks.

Kichala, plur. *vichala*, a bunch.

Kichala cha mzabibu, a bunch of grapes.

Kicheko, plur. *vicheko*, a laugh, a giggle.

Kichikichi, plur. *vichikichi*, the small nuts contained in the fruit of the palm-oil tree.

Kichilema, plur. *vichilema*, the heart of the growing part of the cocoa-nut tree, which is eaten as a salad, and in various ways.

Kicho, plur. *vicho*, fear, a fear.

Kichocheo, the act of pushing wood further into the fire, an instrument for doing it, exciting words to stir up a quarrel.

Kichochoro, plur. *vichochoro*, a very narrow passage, such as is generally left between the houses in Zanzibar.

Kichwa, plur. *vichwa*, for *Kitwa*, the head.

Kidaka, plur. *vidaka*, a recess in the wall.

Kidaka, plur. *vidaka*, a cocoa-nut when just formed.

Kidaka tonge, the uvula.

Kidanga, a very small fruit, before it gets any taste.

Kidari, the chest: *kidari* is used of both men and animals, *kifua* of men only.

Kidau, plur. *vidau*, a small vessel.

Kidau cha wino, an inkstand.

Kidevu, plur. *videvu*, the chin.

Kidimbwi, plur. *vidimbwi*, a pool left on the beach by the falling tide.

Kidinga popo, the *dengue* fever.

Kidogo, plur. *vidogo*, a little, a very little, a little piece, a morsel, a crumb.

Kidoko.

Kupiga kidoko, to click with the tongue.

Kidole, plur. *vidole*, a finger, a toe.

Kidole cha gumba, the thumb.

Kidonda, plur. *vidonda*, a sore, a small sore, a wound.

Kidonge, plur. *vidonge*, a very small round thing, a lump in flour, a pill.

Kidoto, plur. *vidoto*, a small piece of cloth tied over a camel's eyes while turning an oil press.

Kielezo, plur. *vielezo*, a pattern, something to make something else clear.

Kievu (A,) = *Kidevu*.

Kiendelezo, progress.

Kifa, plur. *vifa*, the nipple of a gun.

Kifa uwongo, the sensitive plant.

Kifafa, epilepsy, fits.

Kifafa, plur. *vifafa*, sparks and crackling of damp firewood.

Kifani, plur. *vifani*, the like, a similar thing.

Kifano, plur. *vifano*, a likeness.

Kifaranga, plur. *vifaranga*, a chick, a very small chicken.

Kifaru, plur. *vifaru*, a rhinoceros, a small rhinoceros.

Kifaume, royalty, a royal sort.

Ya kifaume, royal.

Kifiko, plur. *vifiko*, arrival, point of arrival, end of journey.

Kifu ku-, to suffice.

Kifu ndugu, the os coccygis, the bone which the Mohammedans say never decays.

Kifua, plur. *vifua*, the chest, the bosom.

Kifufu, plur. *vifufu*, the shell of the cocoa-nut (M.).

Kifuko, plur. *vifuko*, a little bag, a pocket, a purse.

Kifuko cha kutilia fetha, a purse.

Kifumbu, plur. *vifumbu*, a small round basket or bag for squeezing scraped cocoa-nut in to get out the *tui*.

Kifumbo, plur. *vifumbo*, a very large kind of matting bag.

Kifundo cha mguu, the ankle.

Kifundo cha mkono, the wrist.

Kifungo, plur. *vifungo*, anything which fastens, a button, prison, imprisonment, a kind of rice.

Kifungua, an unfastener, an opener.

Kifungua kanwa, early food, breakfast.

Kifungua mlango, a present made by the bridegroom to the *kungu* of the bride before she allows him to enter the bride's room, on the occasion of his first visit to her.

Kifuniko, plur. *vifuniko*, a lid, a cover.

Kifuo, plur. *vifuo*, a stick stuck in the ground to rip the husk off cocoa-nuts with.

Kifurushi, something tied up in the corner of a cloth.

Kifusi, rubbish, rubbish from old buildings.

Kifuu, plur. *vifuu*, a cocoa-nut shell.

Kigaga, plur. *vigaga*, a scab.

Kigai, plur. *vigai*, a piece of broken pottery or glass, a potsherd.

Kiganda cha pili, the two of cards.

Kigaogao, the Pemba name for a chameleon, meaning changeable.

Kigego = *Kijego*.

Kigerenyenza, plur. *vigerenyenza*, a very small piece of broken pottery or glass, a splinter.

Kigelegele, plur. *vigelegele*, a shrill trilling scream much used as a sign of joy, especially on the occasion of a birth.

Kigogo, a little block of wood.

Kigogo cha kushonea, a small oblong piece of wood used by shoemakers.

Kigongo, the bump of a humpbacked person.

Mwenyi kigongo, a humpback.

Kigono, plur. *vigono* (Yao), a sleeping place.

Kigosho, a bend.

Kigosho cha mkono, an arm that cannot be straightened.

Kigugumizi, stammering, a stammer.

Kigulu, lame.

Kigunni, plur. *vigunni*, an oblong matting bag of the kind in which dates are brought to Zanzibar.

Kigunzi, the day before the *Siku a mwaka*.

Kigwe, plur. *vigwe*, a plaited cord, reins, a string of beads, a piping on the edge of a dress.

Kiharusi, cramp.

Kiherehere (*cha moyo*), trepidation, palpitation (of the heart).

Kihindi, the Indian sort, an Indian language.

Ya kihindi, Indian.

Kihoro, sorrow at a loss, fright, homesickness.

Kiini, kernel, the heart of wood.

Kiini cha yayi, the yolk of an egg.

Kiinimacho, a conjuror.

Kiisha or *Kisha*, afterwards, next, this being ended.

Kijakazi, plur. *vijakazi*, a slave girl.

Kijamanda, plur. *vijamanda*, a small long-shaped box commonly used to carry betel and areca-nut in.

Kijana, plur. *vijana*, a youth, a young man, a complimentary epithet, a boy or girl, a son or daughter.

Kijaluba, plur. *vijaluba*, a small metal box.

Kijamba, plur. *vijamba*, a small rock.

Kijaraha, plur. *vijaraha*, a small wound.

Kijaraha cha booni, sores on the penis, syphilis.

Kijego, plur. *vijego*, a child which cuts its upper teeth first. They are reckoned unlucky, and among the wilder tribes are often killed. Applied by way of abuse to bad children.

Kijiboko, plur. *vijiboko*, a little hippopotamus.

Kijicho, envy, an envious glance.

Kijiguu, plur. *vijiguu*, a little leg.

Kijiko, plur. *vijiko*, a small spoon, a spoon.

Kijiti, plur. *vijiti*, a little tree, a bush, a shrub, a small pole, a piece of wood.

Kijito, plur. *vijito*, a small stream, a brook.

Kijito (M.) = *Kijicho*.

Kijitwa or *Kijichwa*, plur. *vijitwa*, a little head.

Kijivi, thievish.

Kijogoo, plur. *vijogoo*, a mussel, a kind of shell-fish.

Kijoli, the slaves belonging to one master.

Kijomba, Swahili (M.).

Kijongo = *Kigongo*, a humpback.

Kijukuu, plur. *vijukuu*, a great-grandchild.

Kijumbe, plur. *vijumbe*, a go-between, a match-maker.

Kijumba, plur. *vijumba*, a little house, a hovel.

Kikaango, plur. *vikaango*, a small earthen pot for cooking with oil or fat.

Kikaka, over-haste.

Kikale, old style, the antique.

Ya kikale, of the ancient kind, antique, of old times.

Kikao, plur. *vikao*, a seat, sitting, dwelling-place.

Kikapu, plur. *vikapu*, a basket, a matting bag.

Kikaramba, a very old person (disrespectful).

Kikisa ku-, to understand half of what is said.

Hatti hii yanikikisa, I know some of the words, but not all.

Kiko, plur. *viko*, a tobacco pipe, a pipe. The native pipes consist of a vessel half full of water with two stems, one leading to the bowl and one to the mouthpiece: the water vessel is properly the *kiko*. See *bori*, *digali*, *malio*, and *shilamu*.

Kikoa, plur. *vikoa*.

Kula kikoa, to eat at the expense of each one in turn.

Kikofi, the inside of the fingers.

Kikohozi, a cough.

Kikoi, plur. *vikoi*, a white loin-cloth with coloured stripes near the border.

Kikombe, plur. *vikombe*, a cup.

Kikombo, a little crooked thing.

Kikomo, plur. *vikomo*, end, end of journey, arrival.

Kikomo cha uso, the brow, especially if prominent.

Kikondoo. See *Kondoo*.

Kikongwe, plur. *vikongwe*, an extremely old person, a feeble old woman.

Kikono, plur. *vikono*, the prow of a small native vessel.

Kikonyo, plur. *vikonyo*, flower and fruit stalks, the stalks of cloves.

Kikorombwe, a cry made into the hand by way of signal, a call.

Kikosi or *Ukosi*, the nape of the neck.

Kikoto, plur. *vikoto* (M.), a plaited thong or whip carried by an overlooker and used in schools.

Kikozi, plur. *vikozi*, a detachment, a band, company, division.

Kikuba, plur. *vikuba*, a small packet

of aromatic leaves, &c., worn in the dress by women. It is composed of *rehani*, sprinkled with *dalia*, and tied up with a strip of the *mkadi.*

Kikuku, plur. *vikuku*, a bracelet, an arm ring.

Kikuku cha kupandia frasi, a stirrup.

Kikunazi (?), labia (obscene).

Kikumbo.

Kupiga kikumbo, to push aside, to shove out of the way.

Kikuta, plur. *vikuta*, a small stone wall.

Kikwapa, the perspiration from the armpit. See also *Kanzu.*

Kikwi, plur. *vikwi*, a thousand, ten thousand.

Kilango, a narrow entrance.

Kilango cha bahari, straits.

Kilango cha jaha, the gate of Paradise.

Kile, that, yonder.

Kileji, a round flat wheaten cake.

Kilele, plur. *vilele*, a peak, a summit, a pointed top, a pointed shoot in a tree or plant.

Kilema, plur. *vilema*, a deformed person.

Si vema kucheka kilema, it is wrong to laugh at one who is deformed.

Kilemba, plur. *vilemba*, a turban, a customary present at the completion of a job and on many other occasions.

Kilembwe, a great-grandson.

Kileo, plur. *vileo*, intoxication, an intoxicating thing.

Kilete, plur. *vilete*, metal rowlocks, crutches.

Kilevu = *Kidevu.*

Kilifu, plur. *vilifu*, the cloth-like envelope of the young cocoa-nut leaves.

Kilima, plur. *vilima*, a hill, a rising ground, a mound of earth.

Kilimbili, the wrist.

Kilimia, the Pleiades (?).

Kilimo, cultivation, the crop planted.

Kilimo cha nini? what is the crop to be?

Kilindi, plur. *vilindi*, the deeps, deep water.

Kilinga popo (?), rheumatism.

Kilinge cha maneno, cha uganga, speaking in a dark manner not generally understood.

Kilio, plur. *vilio*, a cry, weeping.

Kiliza ku-, to chink money.

Killa or *Kulla*, every.

Killa nendapo, wherever I go, or, every time I go.

Kiluthu, velvet.

Kima, a monkey.

Kima, price, measure.

Kimaji, damp.

Kimanda, an omelette.

Kimandu, the piece of wood put on behind the sill and lintel of a door to receive the pivots on which it turns.

Kimanga, a small kind of grain.

Kimanga, of the Arab sort. See *Manga.*

Kimango.

Chui kimango, a full-grown leopard.

Kimashamba, belonging to the country, a country dialect.

Ya kimashamba, countrified.

Kimbaumbau, a chameleon.

Kimbia ku-, to run away, to flee.

Kimbiza ku-, to make to run away, to put to flight.

Kimbizia ku-, to make to run away from.

Kimerima. See *Merima.*

Kimeta, a sparkling, a glitter.

Kimetimeti, plur. *vimetimeti*, a fire-fly.

Kimia, plur. *vimia*, a circular casting-net.

Kimio, the uvula, an enlarged uvula.

Kimo, it is or was inside.

Kimoja, one. See *Moja.*

Kimporoto, nonsense.

Kimurimuri, plur. *vimurimuri*, a fire-fly.

Kimvunga, a hurricane.

Kimwa ku-, to be tired, disgusted, to be cross at having anything to do.

Kimwondo, plur. *vimwondo*, a missile, a shooting star, because they are said to be thrown by the angels at the Jins.

Kimya, silence, perfect stillness.

Mtu wa kimyakimya, a still man.

Kina.

Kina sisi, people like us.

Makasha haya ya kina Abdallah, these chests belong to Abdallah's people.

Kina, plur. *vina*, a verse, the final syllable of the lines, which is the same throughout the poem.

Kinai ku-, to be content without, to withhold oneself from desiring, to be self-satisfied, to revolt at, to nauseate.

Kinaisha ku-, to revolt, to make unable to eat any more, to take away the desire of.

Kinamizi or *Kiinamizi*, stooping to one's work.

Kinanda, plur. *vinanda*, a stringed instrument, applied to nearly all European instruments.

Kinara, plur. *vinara*, a little tower, a candlestick. See also *Kanzu.*

Kinaya, self-content, insolence.

Kinayi ku- = *Kinai ku-*.

Kinda, plur. *makinda*, a very young bird, the young of birds.

Kindana ku-, to object to, to stand in the way of.

Kinena, the abdomen.

Kinga, plur. *vinga*, a brand, a half-burnt piece of firewood.

Kinga, a stop, a limit put to a thing.

Kinga ku-, to put something to catch something, to guard oneself, to ward a blow.

Kukinga mvua, to put something to catch the rainwater.

Kingaja, plur. *vingaja*, a bracelet of beads.

Kingalingali, on the back (of falling or lying).

Kingama ku-, to lie across.

Mti umekingama njiani, a tree lies across the road.

Kingamisha ku-, to block, to stop, to spoil.

Kinge, too little.

Chakula kinge, too little food.

Kingojo, a watch, time or place of watching.

Kingozi, the old language of Melinda, the poetical dialect, difficult and ill-understood language.

Kingubwa, the spotted hyæna.

Kinika ku-, to be certain or ascertained about a person.

Kinjunjuri.

Kukata kinjunjuri, to shave all the hair except one long tuft.

Kinono, plur. *vinono*, a fatling.

Kinoo, plur. *vinoo*, a whetstone.

Kinoo.

Embe kinoo, a small yellow kind of mango.

Kinu, plur. *vinu*, a wooden mortar for pounding and for cleaning corn, an oil-mill, a mill.

Kinu cha kushindikia, a mill for pressing oil.

Kinu cha moshi, a steam mill.

Kinubi, plur. *vinubi*, a harp.

Ya Kinubi, Nubian.

Kinwa = *Kinywa*.

Kinwa, plur. *vinwa*, a mouth.

Kinwa mchuzi, the imperial, the place where the imperial grows.

Kinyaa, filth, dung.

Kinyago, plur. *vinyago*, a thing to frighten people, such as a mock ghost, &c., &c.

Kinyegere, a small animal, a skunk.

Kinyemi, pleasant, good.

Kinyenyefu, a tickling, a tingling.

Kinyezi. See *Kinyaa*.

Kinyi, having. See *-inyi*.

Kinyonga, plur. *vinyonga*, a chameleon.

Kinyozi, plur. *vinyozi*, a barber, a shaver.

Kinyuma = *Kinyume*.

Kinyume, afterwards.

Kinyume, going back, shifting, alteration, an enigmatic way of speaking, in which the last syllable is put first. See Appendix I.

Kinyumba, a kept mistress.

Kinyunya, plur. *vinyunya*, a kind of cake, a little cake made to try the quality of the flour.

Kingwa, plur. *vinywa*, a drink, a beverage.

Kinywaji, plur. *vinywaji*, a beverage, a usual beverage.

Kinza ku-, to contradict, deny.

Kioga, plur. *vioga*, a mushroom.

Kiokosi, plur. *viokosi*, a reward for finding a lost thing and returning it to the owner.

Kioja, plur. *vioja*, a curiosity.

Kionda, a taster.

Kionda mtuzi, the imperial, the place where the imperial grows (M.).

Kiongozi, plur. *viongozi*, a leader, a guide, a caravan guide.

Kiongwe, plur. *viongwe*, a donkey from the mainland; they are reputed very hard to manage.

Kioo, plur. *vioo*, glass, a glass, a looking-glass, a piece of glass,—a fish-hook (M.).

Kiopoo, a pole or other instrument to get things out of a well, &c., with.

Kiosha miguu, a present made by the bridegroom to the *kungu* of the bride on the occasion of his first visit.

Kiota, plur. *viota*, a hen's nest, a laying place, a bird's nest.

Kioto = *Kiota*.

Kiowe.

Kupiga kiowe, to scream, cry for help.

Kiowevu, a liquid.

Kioza, putridity.

Kipa mkono, a present made by the bridegroom to the bride when he first sees her face.

Kipaa, plur. *vipaa*, a thatched roof, the long sides of a roof.

Kipaa cha mbele, the front slope of the roof.

Kipaa cha nyuma, the back slope of the roof.

Kipaje, a kind of *mtama*.

Kipaji, a kind of cosmetic. See also *Kanzu*.

Kipaku, plur. *vipaku*, a spot or mark of a different colour.

Kipambo, adornment.

Kipande, plur. *vipande*, a piece, an instrument, a small rammer for beating roofs.

Vipande vya kupimia, nautical instruments.

Kipande kilichonona, a piece of fat.

Kipanga, a large bird of prey, a horse-fly.

Kipangozi, a sluggish incurable sore on a horse or ass.

Kipara, plur. *vipara*, a shaved place on the head.

Kipele, plur. *vipele*, a pimple.

Kipendi, a darling, a favourite.

Kipenu, plur. *vipenu*, a lean-to, the side cabins of a ship.

Kipenyo, a small place where something passes through.

Kipepeo, plur. *vipepeo*, a fan for blowing the fire, a butterfly.

Kipeto, plur. *vipeto*, a packet.

Kipi or *Kipia*, a cock's spur.

Kipigi, a rainbow (?).

Kipila, a curlew.

Kipilipili.

Nyele za kipilipili, woolly hair.

Kipindi, a time, a period of time, an hour.

Kipindi chote, at every period.

Kipindi cha aththuuri, the hour of noon.

Kipinda.

Kufa kipinda, to die a natural death, as cattle, &c.

Kipindupindu, cholera.

Kipingwa, plur. *vipingwa*, a bar.

Kipini, plur. *vipini*, a hilt, a haft, a handle of the same kind as a knife handle, a stud-shaped ornament worn by women in the nose, and sometimes in the ears also.

Kipimo, plur. *vipimo*, a measure.

Kipofu, plur. *vipofu*, a blind person.

Kipolepole, a butterfly.

Kipooza, paralysis.

Kipukuba, dropped early, cast fruit, etc.

Kipukute, *Kipukuse* = *Kipukuba*.

Ndizi kipukute, little bananas.

Kipuli, plur. *vipuli*, a dangling ornament worn by women in the ear; they are often little silver crescents, five or six round the outer circumference of each ear.

Kipunguo, plur. *vipunguo*, defect, deficiency.

Kipupwe, the cold season (June and July).

Kipwa, plur. *vipwa*, rocks in the sea.

Kiraka, plur. *viraka*, a patch.

Kiri ku-, to confess, accept, acknowledge, assert.

Kiriba, plur. *viriba*, a water-skin.

Kirihi ku-, to provoke.

Kirihika ku-, to be provoked, to be offended.

Kirihisha ku-, to make offended, to aggravate.

Kirimba, a cage for wild animals, a meat-safe.

Kirimu ku-, to feast.

Kirithi ku-, to borrow, specially to borrow money.

Kiroboto, plur. *viroboto*, a flea. The Hathramaut soldiers are nicknamed *Viroboto*, and their song as they march is parodied by, *Kiroboto, Kiroboto, tia moto, tia moto.*

Kirukarjia, a kind of mouse found in Zanzibar.

Kirukia, a kind of parasite growing on fruit trees.

Kiruu, blind rage.

Kisa, plur. *visa*, a cause, a reason, a short tale.

Visa vingi, many affairs, a complicated business.

Kisa cha koko, kernel of a stone.

Kisaga, a measure equal to two *Kibabas*.

Kisahani, plur. *visahani*, a plate, a small dish.

Kisanduku, plur. *visanduku*, a small chest, a box.

Kisarani, a greedy fellow, a miser.

Kisasi, revenge, retaliation.

Kishada, a tailless kite.

Kishaka, plur. *vishaka*, a thicket.

Kisheda, a bunch of grapes, a paper fluttering in the air like a kite.

Kishenzi, of the wild people.

Lugha ya kishenzi, a language of the interior.

Kishi, a chess-queen.

Kishigino = *Kisigino*.

Kishinda, a small residue left in a place or inside something, as in a water-jar less than half full.

Vishinda vingapi umetia? How many portions (of grain) have you put (in the mortar, to be cleaned)?

Kishindo, noise, shock.

Kishogo, the back of the head and neck.

Akupaye kishogo si mwenzio, one who turns his back upon you is not your friend.

Kishwara, a loop of rope to haul by in dragging a vessel into or out of the water, a loop in the side of a dhow to pass an oar through for rowing.

Kisi ku-, to guess.

Kukisi tanga, to shift over a sail to the opposite side.

Kisi, Keep her away!

Kisibao, plur. *visibao*, a waistcoat with or without sleeves; they are very commonly worn in Zanzibar.

Kisibao cha mikono, a sleeved waistcoat.

Kisibao cha vikapa or *vikwapa*, a sleeveless waistcoat.

Kisibu (?), a nickname.

Kisigino or *Kishigino*, the elbow.

Kisigino cha mguu, the heel.

Kisiki, plur. *visiki*, a log. Used in slang language for a prostitute.

Kisiki cha mvua, a rainbow (M.).

Kisima, plur. *visima*, a well.

Kisimi (obscene), the clitoris.

Kisitiri, a screen, screen-wall, parapet.

Kisiwa, plur. *visiwa*, an island.

Kisiyangu [Tumbatu] = *Kizingiti*.

Kisiwiso.

Kisiwiso cha choo chauma, constipation.

Kishoka, plur. *vishoka*, a hatchet, a small axe.

Kishubaka, plur. *vishubaka*, a small recess, a pigeon-hole.

Kishungi, plur. *vishungi*, the ends of the turban cloth, lappets.

Kisma, a part.

Kisombo, a paste made of beans, *mahogo*, &c.

Kisongo, plur. *visongo*, a piece of wood to twist cord or rope with.

Kisoze, a very small bird with back blue, and breast yellow.

Kisu, plur. *visu*, a knife.

Kisua, a suit of clothes.

Kisugulu, plur. *visugulu*, a mound of earth, an ant-hill.

Kisungura, plur. *visungura*, a little rabbit or hare (?).

Kisunono, gonorrhœa.

Kisunono cha damu, with passing blood.

Kisunono cha uzaha, with passing matter.

Kisunono cha mkojo, with constant micturition.

Kisusuli, a whirlwind (?) a boy's kite (?).

Kisusi, plur. *visusi*, the hip of a roof. The main roof starts from the long front and back walls, and is called the *paa;* small roofs start from the end walls, and are carried to the ridge under and within the *paa:* these are the *visusi*.

Kisuto = *Kisutu*.

Kisutu, plur. *visutu*, a large piece of printed calico, often forming a woman's whole dress, a coverlid.

Kiswa = *Kisa*.

Kitabu, plur. *vitabu*, a book.

Kitagalifa, a small matting bag for *halua*, &c.

Kitakizo, plur. *vitakizo*, the head and foot-pieces of a bedstead.

Kitako, sitting.

Kukaa kitako, to sit down, to remain in one locality.

Kitale, plur. *vitale*, a cocoa-nut just beginning to grow.

Kitali, sailcloth.

Kitalu, a stone fence, a wall.

Kitambaa, plur. *vitambaa*, a small piece of cloth a rag.

Kitambaa cha kufutia mkono, a towel.

Kitambaa cha meza, a table napkin.

Kitambi cha kilemba, a piece of stuff for making a turban.

Kitambo, a short time.

Kitamiri, a kind of evil spirit.

Kitana, plur. *vitana*, a small comb.

Kitanda, plur. *vitanda*, a bedstead, a couch.

Kitanga, plur. *vitanga*, a round mat used to lay out food upon.

Kitanga cha mkono, the palm of the hand.

Kitanga cha mzani, a scale pan.

Kitanga cha pepo, the name of a dance.

Kitani, flax, linen, string.

Kitanzi, plur. *vitanzi*, a loop, a button-loop.

Kitaowa, the kind proper for a devotee.

Amevaa nguo za kitaowa, he is dressed like a devotee.

Kitapo, plur. *vitapo*, a shivering, a shiver.

Kitara, plur. *vitara*, a curved sword.

Kitara, an open shed in a village, where people sit to talk and transact business.

Kitasa, a box lock, a lock.

Kitatangi, a cheat. Also a very bright-coloured sea-fish with spines, a sea-porcupine.

Kitawi, a kind of weed.

Kitawi, plur. *vitawi*, a branch, a bough, a bunch.

Kite, feeling sure, certainty, faithfully (?), affection.

Kana kite haye, he has no affection.

Kupiga kite, to cry or groan from inward pain.

Kiteflefu, sobbing before or after crying.

Kitefute, the cheek, the part of the face over the cheek-bone.

Kiteku, a tosser.

Kitembe, a lisp.

Kitembwi, a thread of flax or fine grass.

Kitendawili, plur. *vitendawili*, an enigma. The propounder says *Kitendawili;* the rest answer *Tega;* he then propounds his enigma.

Kitendo, plur. *vitendo*, an action.

Kitengenya, a small bird spotted with white, yellow, and red.

Kiteo, plur. *viteo*, a small sifting basket.

Kiteso, a vase.

Kitewe, loss of the use of the legs.

Kithiri ku-, to grow large, increase.

Umekithiri kuzaa, it has borne more than before.

Kiti, plur. *viti*, a chair, a seat.

Kiti cha frasi, a saddle.

Kitimbi, plur. *vitimbi*, an artifice, an artful trick.

Kitinda mimba, the last child a woman will bear;

Kitindi. See *Vitindi*.

Kitisho, plur. *vitisho*, fear, a terrifying thing.

Kititi, plur. *vititi*, a hare, a rabbit, a little thing (M.).

Kititi, to the full, entirely, altogether, all at once.

Kititi cha bahari, the depths of the sea.

Kititia, a child's windmill.

Kitiwanga, chicken-pox. The natives say an epidemic of *kitiwanga*, always precedes one of small-pox. Also *titiwanga*, and perhaps *tete ya kwanga*.

Kito, plur. *vito*, a precious stone.

Kitoka (M.) = *Kishoka*.

Kitoma, plur. *vitoma*, a small round pumpkin.

Kitoma, orchitis.

Kitone, plur. *vitone*, a drop.

Kitonga, hydrocele (?).

Kitongoji, a village.

Kitongotongo.

Kutezama kitongotongo, to glance at contemptuously with half-shut eyes.

Kitoria, a kind of edible fruit.

Kitoteo (M.) = *Kichocheo*.

Kitoto, plur. *vitoto*, a little child.

Kitovu, plur. *vitovu*, the navel.

Kitoweo, plur. *vitoweo*, a relish, a something to be eaten with the rice or other vegetable food, such as meat, fish, curry, &c.

Kitu, plur. *vitu*, a thing, especially a tangible thing.

Si kitu, nothing, worthless.

Kitua, plur. *vitua*, the shade of a tree, &c.

Kituko, startledness, fright.

Kitukuu, plur. *vitukuu*, a great grandchild.

Kitulizo, plur. *vitulizo*, a soothing, quieting thing.

Kitumbua, plur. *vitumbua*, a sort of cake or fritter made in Zanzibar.

Kitunda, plur. *vitunda*, a chess pawn.

Kitundwi, a water-jar [Tumbatu].

Kitunga, plur. *vitunga*, a small round basket.

Kitungu (?) a small round earthen dish.

Kitungule, plur. *vitungule*, a hare or rabbit (?).

Kitunguu, plur. *vitunguu*, an onion.
Kitunguu somu, garlic.
Kitungwa, a small bird like a sparrow.
Kituo, plur. *vituo*, an encampment, a resting-place, a putting down.
Hana kituo, he is always gadding about.
Kitupa, plur. *vitupa*, a little bottle, a vial.
Kitutia.
Bahari ya kitutia, a boiling sea, deep and rough.
Kitwa, plur. *vitwa*, the head.
Kitwangomba, a somersault.
Kitwakitwa, topsy-turvy.
Kitwana, plur. *vitwana*, a slave boy
Kiu, thirst.
Kuwa na kiu, to be thirsty.
Kuona kiu, to feel thirst.
Kiua, plur. *viua*, an eyelet hole.
Kiuka ku-, to step over.
Kiukia = *Kirukia.*
Kiuma, plur. *viuma*, a fork.
Kiuma mbuzi, a small dark-coloured lizard.
Kiumbe, plur. *viumbe*, a creature, created thing.
Kiumbizi, a peculiar way of beating the drum; the people sing the while, *Sheitani ndoo tupigane fimbo.*
Kiunga, plur. *viunga*, a suburb, the outskirts of a town.
Kiungani, near the town, in the suburbs.
Kiungo, plur. *viungo*, a joint,—an acid thing put into the *mchuzi.*
Kiunguja, the language of Zanzibar.
Kiungwana, the free or gentlemanly sort.
Ya kiungwana, civilized, courteous, becoming a free man.
Mwanamke wa kiungwana, a lady.
Kiungulia, plur. *viungulia*, an eructation, a breaking of wind.
Kiuno, plur. *viuno*, the loins.
Kiunza, plur. *viunza*, the plank laid over the body before the grave is filled in. (Coffins are never used.)
Kiuwaji, murderous, deadly.
Kivi, the elbow.
Kivimba, plur. *vivimba*, the girth of a tree, the circumference.
Kivimbi, a small swelling.
Kivuko, plur. *vivuko*, a ford, a ferry, a crossing-place.
Kivuli, plur. *vivuli*, a shadow, a shade, a ghost.
Kivumbazi, a strong-smelling herb said to scare mosquitoes: washing in water in which it has been steeped is said to be a preventive of bad dreams.
Kivumbo, lonely (?).
Kivumi, plur. *vivumi*, a roaring, bellowing sound.
Kivyao = *Kizao.*
Kivyazi, birth.
Kiwambaza, plur. *viwambaza*, a mud and stud wall.
Kiwambo, something strained tightly over a frame, like the skin of a drum, a weaving frame.
Kiwanda, plur. *viwanda*, a workshop, a yard, a plot of land.
Kiwango, plur. *viwango*, a number, position in the world, duties belonging to one's position, a man's place.
Kiwanja = *Kiwanda.*
Kiwao, a great feast [Tumbatu].
Kiwavi, plur. *viwavi*, a nettle, a sea-nettle.
Kiwavu chana (A.), ribs.

Kiwe, plur. *viwe*.
Kiwe cha uso, a small kind of pimple on the face.
Kiwele, an udder.
Kiwembe, a pocket-knife.
Kiweo (M.), thigh, lap.
Kiwete, loss of the use of the legs.
Kiwi, moon-blindness, a dazzle.
Kufanya kiwi, to dazzle.
Kiwi, plur. *viwi*, a small stick, a piece of wood, a bar.
Kiwiko.
Kiwiko cha mkono, the wrist.
Kiwiko cha mguu, the ankle.
Kiwiliwili, the human trunk, the body without the limbs.
Kiyama, the resurrection.
Kiyambaza, a bulkhead, partition. Also = *Kiwambaza*.
Kiyambo, neighbourhood, a village.
Kiza or *Giza*, darkness.
Kutia kiza, to darken, to dim.
Kizao, plur. *vizao*, a native, one born in the place.
Kizazi, plur. *vizazi*, a generation.
Kizee, diminutive of *mzee*, generally used of an old woman.
Kizibo, plur. *vizibo*, a stopper, a cork.
Kizio, plur. *vizio*, half of an orange, cocoa-nut, &c.
Kizimbi, plur. *vizimbi*, a cage.
Kizinda, a virgin.
Kizinga, plur. *vizinga*, a large log half burnt.
Kizingiti, threshold, the top and bottom pieces of a door or window frame, bar of a river.
Kizingo, turnings, curves of a river, &c., (?) a burial ground.
Kizingo, sharp shore sand used for building.
Kiziwi, plur. *viziwi*, deaf.
Kizuio = *Kizuizi*.
Kizuizi, plur. *vizuizi*, a stop, a thing which hinders or stays.
Kizuizo, plur. *vizuizo*, a hindrance.
Kizuka, plur. *vizuka*, a kind of evil spirit, a woman who is staying in perfect secrecy and quiet during the mourning for her husband. See *Eda*.
Kizungu, a European language.
Ya kizungu, European.
Kizunguzungu, giddiness.
Kizuri, beauty, a beauty.
Kizushi, an intruder.
Kizuu, plur. *vizuu*, a kind of evil spirit, which kills people at the order of its master.
Ko, *-ko*, *-ko*, where, whither, whence.
Ko kote, whithersoever.
Koa, plur. *makoa*, a snail.
Koa (plur. of *Ukoa*), the silver rings on the scabbard of a sword, &c., plates of metal.
Kobe, a tortoise.
Koche, plur. *makoche*, the fruit of a kind of palm.
Kodi, rent.
Kodolea ku-, to fix the eyes upon, to stare.
Kofi, plur. *makofi*, the flat of the hand.
Kupiga kofi, to strike with open hand, to box the ears.
Kupiga makofi, to clap the hands.
Kofia, a cap.
Kőfila, a caravan.
Kofua, emaciated.
Koga = *Kuoga*.
Kohani, a small red fish like a mullet.
Koho, a large bird of prey.
Kohoa, *ku-*, to cough.
Kohozi, expectorated matter.

Koikoi, plur. *makoikoi*, a sort of evil spirit.

Koja, a gold ornament for the neck.

Kojoa ku-, to make water.

Koka = *Kuoka*.

Koka ku-, to set on fire.

Koko, plur. *makoko*, kernels, nuts, stones of fruit.

Koko, plur. *makoko*, brushwood, thickets, bushes.

Mbwa koko, a homeless dog that lives in the thickets and eats carrion.

Kokomoka ku-, to vomit, to belch out, blurt out.

Kokota ku-, to drag.

Kukokota roho, to breathe hard.

Kokoteza ku-, to do anything slowly and carefully.

Kokoto, plur. *makokoto*, a small stone, a small piece of stone.

Kokwa, plur. *makokwa*, nuts, stones of fruit.

Kolekole, a kind of fish.

Kolea ku-, to become well flavoured, to get the right quantity of a condiment.

Koleo, plur. *makoleo*, tongs.

Kologa ku-, to stir.

Koma, plur. *makoma*, a kind of fruit.

Koma ku-, to cease, to leave off, to end a journey, to arrive at a destination.

Koma usije! Come no further!

Komaa ku-, to be full grown.

Komaza ku-, to mock, to make game of.

K'omba, a galago.

Komba ku-, to scrape out, to clean out.

Dafu la kukomba, a cocoa-nut in which the nutty part is but just forming, which is then reckoned a delicacy.

Kukomba mtu, to get all his money, to clean him out.

Kombamoyo, plur. *makombamoyo*, one of the rafters of a thatched roof.

Kombe, plur. *makombe*, a large dish.

Kombe la mkono (A.), the shoulder-blade.

Kombe za pwani, oysters (?), cockles (?), sea-shells.

Kombeka ku-, to be cleaned out, to have had all one's money got from one.

Kombeo, a sling.

Kombo, plur. *makombo*, scraps, pieces left after eating.

K'ombo, a defect, crookedness.

Kutoa k'ombo, to notice a defect.

Komboa ku-, to ransom, to buy back.

Komboka ku-, to be crooked.

Kombokombo, crooked.

Kombora, a bomb, a mortar.

Kombozi, a ransom.

Kome, plur. *makome*, a pearl oyster (?), a mussel (?), a shell.

Komea ku-, to fasten with a native lock (*komeo*).

Komeo, a kind of wooden lock.

Komesha ku-, to make to cease, to put a stop to.

Komwe, plur. *makomwe*, the seeds of a large climbing plant abundantly furnished with recurved thorns; they are used to play the game of *bao* with.

Konda ku-, to grow thin and lean.

Kondavi, large beads worn by women, as a belt round the loins.

Konde, a fist.

Kupiga moyo konde, to take heart, to resolve firmly.

Kondesha ku-, to make to grow lean.

K'ondo, war (Merima).

Kondoa, a sheep [Lindi].

Kondoo, sheep.

Yuafa kikondoo, he dies like a sheep, silently (which is high praise).

Konga ku-, to grow old and feeble.

Kongoa ku-, to draw out nails, &c., to take to pieces.

Kongoea, Mombas.

Kongoja ku-, to walk with difficulty, to totter.

Kongolewa ku-, to be taken to pieces.

Kongomero, throat.

Kongoni = *Kunguni*.

Kong'ota, a sort of woodpecker, black and yellow.

Kongwa, a slave-stick.

Kongwe.

Kutoa kongwe, to lead off the solo part of a song, in which others join in the chorus.

-kongwe, over-old, worn out with age.

Kono, a projecting handle, like that of a saucepan.

Konokono, a snail.

Konyesha ku- = *Konyeza ku-*.

Konyeza ku-, to make a sign by raising the eyebrows.

Konzi, what can be grasped in the hand, a fist full.

Kupiga konzi, to rap with the knuckles.

Koo, plur. *makoo*, a breeding animal or bird.

Koo la kuku, a laying hen.

Koo la mbuzi, a breeding goat.

Koo, plur. *makoo*, throat.

Koonde, plur. *makoonde*, cultivated land, fields, the piece of a *shamba* allotted to a slave for his own use.

Konyoa ku-, to break off the cobs of Indian corn.

Kopa, hearts, in cards.

Kopa, plur. *makopa*, a piece of dried *muhogo*, which has been steeped and cooked.

Kopa ku-, to get goods on credit for the purpose of trading with, to cheat, to swindle.

Kope, plur. of *Ukope*, the eyelashes.

Kope, plur. *makope*, the wick of a candle.

Kopesa ku-, to wink.

Kopesha ku-, to supply a trader with goods on credit, to give on trust, to lend.

Kopo, plur. *makopo*, a large metal vessel, a spout.

Kopoa ku-, to drag out of one's hand, = *Chopoa ku-*.

Kora ku-, to seem sweet to, to be loved by.

Koradani, a sheave of a pulley.

Korija, a pucker in sewing. Also, a score.

Korja, a score.

Koroana ku-, to steep in water.

Korofi, a bird of ill omen, a messenger of bad luck.

Korofisha ku-, to ruin a man.

Koroga ku-, to stir, to stir up.

Koroma, plur. *makoroma*, a cocoa-nut in its last stage but one, when the nut is formed but has not yet its full flavour. It has ceased to be a *dafu* and is not yet a *nazi*.

Koroma ku-, to snore.

Korongo, a crane.

Korongo, plur. *makorongo*, a hole dibbled for seed.

Kororo, a crested guinea-fowl.

Korosho, plur. *makorosho*, cashew nuts.

Koru, the waterbuck.

Kosa ku-, to err, mistake, miss, go wrong, do wrong, blunder.

Kosekana ku-, to be missed, not to be there.

Kosesha ku-, to lead astray.

Kosudia ku-, to purpose, to intend, = *Kusudia*.

Kota, plur. *makota*, the stalks of a kind of millet which are chewed like sugar-cane.

Kota, a crook.

Kota ku-.

Kukota moto, to warm oneself.

Kotama, a curved knife used in getting palm wine.

Kote, all. See *-ote*.

Kotekote, on every side.

Koto.

Kupiga koto (M.), to strike with the knuckles.

Kovo, plur. *makovo*, scar.

Ku- or *Kw-*.

1. The indefinite verbal prefix answering to *there* in English.

Ku-likuwa, there was.

Ku-katanda, and there spread.

2. The sign of the infinitive.

Ku-piga, to strike.

Kw-enda, to go.

The infinitive may be used as a substantive answering to the English form in *-ing*.

Kufa, dying, the act of death.

Kwenda, going.

The *ku-* of the infinitive is retained by monosyllabic verbs, and by some others in all tenses in which the tense prefix ends in an unaccented syllable.

3. The prefix proper to adjectives, pronouns, and verbs agreeing with infinitives used as substantives.

Kufa kwetu kwema kutampendeza, our good deaths will please him.

4. The prefix proper to pronouns agreeing with substantives in the locative case (*-ni*), where neither the being or going inside, nor mere nearness, is meant.

Enenda nyumbani kwangu, go to my house.

Ziko kwetu, there are in our possession, at our place.

5. In a few words a prefix signifying locality, commonly so used in other African languages, but generally represented in Swahili by the case in *-ni*.

Kuzimu, among the dead, in the grave.

-ku-.

1. The sign of the negative past always preceded by some negative personal prefix.

Sikujua, I did not know.

Hazikufaa, they were of no use.

2. The objective prefix denoting the second person singular.

Nakupenda, I love thee, or you.

Alikupa, he gave thee, or you.

Sikukujua, I did not know you.

3. The objective prefix referring to infinitives of verbs, or to *huku*, there.

Kua ku-, to grow, to become large.

-kuba or *-kubwa*, great, large.

Kubali ku, to accept, assent to, acknowledge, approve.

Kubalika ku-, to be accepted, to be capable of acceptance.

Kubalisha ku-, to make to accept.

Kubba, a vaulted place.

-kubwa, large, great, elder, chief. It makes *kubwa* with nouns like *nyumba*.

Kucha, or *Kumekucha*, the dawn.
Usiku kucha, all night.
Kuchua ku-.
Kamba imejikuchua, the rope has worn away, chafed, stranded.
Kufuli, a padlock.
Kufuru ku-, to become an infidel, to apostatize.
Kufuru ku-, to mock, to deride.
Kuguni, the hartebeest (boselaphus).
Kuke. See *-ke*.
Mkono wa kuke, the left hand.
Kukeni, on the female side.
Kuko, yonder, to yonder.
Kwa kuko, beyond, on yon side.
K'uku, a hen, a fowl, fowls, poultry.
Kuku na huku, backwards and forwards.
-kukuu, old, worn out. It makes *kukuu* with nouns like *nyumba*.
Kulabu, a hook to steady work with.
Kule, there, far off, yonder.
Kulée, yonder, very far off. As the distance indicated increases the *é* is more dwelt on, the voice raised to a higher and higher falsetto.
Kulekule, there, just there.
Kulia ku-, to become great for, to become hard to.
Kuliko, where there is or was.
Kulikoni? Where there is what = why? (M.).
Kuliko, is used in the ordinary way of expressing the comparative.
Mwema kuliko huyu, good where this man is, and therefore better than he. Because if a quality becomes evident in anything by putting some other thing beside it, the first must possess the quality in a higher degree than the other.

Kulla, often pronounced *killa*, every, each one.
Kululu, nothing at all.
Nikapata kululu = Sikupata neno.
Kululu, tiger cowries, Cypræa tigris.
Kulungu, a sort of antelope.
Kuma, the vagina.
Kumba ku-, to push against, to take and sweep off the whole of anything, *e.g.* to clear water out of a box, to bale a boat.
Kumbatia ku-, to embrace, to clasp.
Kumbatiana ku-, to embrace (of two persons).
Kumbe? What? An expression of surprise used especially when something turns out otherwise than was expected, commonly joined with a negative verb.
Kumbi (Mer.), circumcision.
Anaingia kumbini, he is being circumcised.
Kumbi, plur. *makumbi*, cocoa-nut fibre, the husk of the cocoa-nut and the fibrous mass out of which the leaves grow. Also, at Mgao, gum copal.
Kumbikumbi, ants in their flying stage.
Kumbisha ku-, to push off upon, to lay upon some one else.
Kumbuka ku-, to think of, to remember, to ponder over, to recollect.
Kumbukumbu, a memorial, a mention.
Kumbura, an explosive shell.
Kumbusha ku-, to remind.
Kumbwaya, a kind of drum standing on feet.
Kumekucha, there is dawn, the dawn.
Kumi, plur. *makumi*, ten.
Kumoja, on one side.

Kumpuni, plur. *makumpuni*, a person who has obtained full knowledge of his trade.

Kumunta ku- (Mer.), to shake out or off.

Kumunto, a sieve of basket-work.

Kumutika ku-, to desire (?).

Kumvi, husks and bran of rice.

Kuna, there is,

Kunaye, depending upon him.

Kunani? What is the matter?

Kuna kwambaje? What do you say? [Tumbatu].

Kuna ku-, to scratch.

Kuńakucha, there is dawning, the dawning.

Kunazi, a small edible fruit.

Kunda ku- (M.) = *Kunja ku-*.

Kunda, plur. *makunda*, a green vegetable like spinach.

Kundaa ku-, to be short and small of stature.

Kundamana ku- = *Kunjamana ku-*.

Kunde, beans, haricot beans.

Kundi, plur. *makundi*, a crowd, a herd, many together.

Kundua ku-, to please (?).

-kundufu, giving pleasure.

Nyumba ni kundufu, the house is commodious.

Muungu ni mkundufu, God is the giver of all good things.

Kunduka ku-, to grow larger, to open.

Moyo umekunduka, he is gratified (N.).

Kunga ku-, to hem.

Kunga, cleverness, clever.

Kazi haifai illa kwa kunga, it wants to be done cleverly.

Kungali.

Kungali na mapema bado, while it is yet early.

Kungu, mist, fog.

Kungu manga, a nutmeg.

Kunguni, a bug.

Kunguru, a crow, a bird a little larger than a rook, black, with a white patch on the shoulders and round the neck: it feeds on carrion.

Kung'uta ku-, to shake off, to shake out.

Kung'uto, plur. *makung'uto*, a sort of basket used as a sieve or strainer.

Kuni, firewood. The singular, *ukuni*, means one piece of firewood.

Kunia ku-, to scrape or scratch with, or for.

Kunia ku-, to raise the eyebrows in contempt.

Kuniita, telling me to come.

Kunja ku-, to fold, to wrap up, to furl.

Kukunja uzi, to wind thread.

Kujikunja, to flinch, to shrink.

Kukunja uso or *Kukunja vipaji*, to frown, to knit the brows.

Kunjana ku-, to fold together, to dwindle, to wrinkle.

Kunjamana ku-.

Uso unakunjamana, his face is sad, sour, and frowning.

Kunjia ku-, to fold for, to wrap up for, to crease.

Kunjika ku-, to become folded or doubled up, to be creased.

Kunjua ku-, to unfold.

Kukunjua miguu, to stretch one's legs.

Kunjuka ku-, to become unfolded, to spread over.

Kunjuliwa ku-, to be open and unfolded.

Kunrathi, don't be offended, excuse me, pardon me.

Kunu alamu, be it known.

Kunya ku-, to ease oneself. See *Nya*.

Kunyata ku-, to draw together.

Kujikunyata, to draw oneself together, to shrink.

Kunyua ku- or *Kunyula ku-*, to touch secretly (with a scratching motion) by way of signal or of calling attention privately, to make a scratch on the skin.

Kupaa. See *Makupaa*.

Kupe, a tick, a cattle tick.

Kupua ku-, to shake something off one's dress, out of one's hand, &c.

Kura, the lot.

Kupiga kura, to cast lots.

Kuru, a sphere, a ball.

Kurubia ku-, to come near to.

Nalikurubia, &c., had a good mind to, &c.

Kurumbizi, a small yellow bird, very inquisitive: they say if he sees a man and woman talking together, he cries, "*Mtu anasema na mume*."

Kusa ku, to make to grow.

Kusanya ku-, to collect, gather, assemble.

Kusanyana ku-, to gather together.

Kusanyika ku-, to be gathered, to assemble.

Kushoto, on the left.

Mkono wa kushoto, the left hand.

Kusi, the southerly winds which blow from May till October.

Kusini, in the direction of the *Kusi*, southerly.

Kusudi, plur. *makusudi*, purpose, design.

Kusudia ku-, to purpose, to intend.

Kuta, plur. of *Ukuta*, walls.

Kuta ku-, to meet with, to see, to find, to come upon.

Kutana ku-, to come together, to meet, to assemble.

Kutanika ku-, to become assembled.

Kutanisha ku-, to bring together, to assemble.

Kutu, rust.

Kutuka ku-, to be startled, to be suddenly frightened.

Kutusha ku-, to startle, to alarm suddenly.

-kuu, great, chief, noble. *Kuu* refers more to figurative, *kubwa* to physical greatness. It makes *kuu* with nouns like *nyumba*.

Ana makuu, he is vain.

Kuume. See *-ume*.

Mkono wa kuume, the right hand.

Kuumeni, on the male side.

Kuvuli.

Mkono wa kuvuli, the right hand.

Kuwa, to be, to become (?). See *Wa*.

Kuwadi, also *Kawadi*, a procuress (*Mtu anayewatongosha watu*).

Kuwili, twice over, in two ways.

-kuza, large, full grown.

Kuza ku-, to make bigger.

Kuza, to sell. See *Uza*.

Kuzi, an earthen water bottle larger than a *guduwia*, with a handle or handles and a narrow neck.

Kuzikani, a funeral.

Kuzimu, in the grave, under the earth.

Kw-. See *Ku-*.

Kwa, with, as an instrument, through, to a person, to or at the place where any one lives; for, on account of.

Kwa 'ngi (?), generally.

Kwa, of, after verbs in the infinitive used as nouns, and after the case in *-ni*.

Kwaa ku-, to strike the foot, to stumble.

Kwaje? how?

Kwake, to him, with him, to or at his or her house; his, her, or its, after a verb in the infinitive used as a substantive, or the case in *-ni*.

Kwako, to thee or with thee, to or at thy place, your, thy, of thee or you, after verbs in the infinitive used as a noun, and after the case in *-ni*.

Kwale, a partridge (?).

Kwama ku-, to become jammed, to stick.

Kwamba, saying (?), if, as if, though, that.

Ya kwamba, that.

Kwamisha ku-, to jam, to make to stick in a narrow place.

Kwamua ku-, to unjam, to free, to clear.

Kwangu, to or at my house, to or with me, my, of me, after the infinitives of verbs used as substantives, and after the case in *-ni*.

Kwangua ku-, to scrape up, to scrape one's shoes, &c.

Kwani for, because, wherefore, for why.

Kwanua ku-, to split down, to tear down, to break.

Kwanyuka ku-, to be split down like the boughs and branches of a tree, which some one has been trying to climb by them.

Kwanza, beginning, at first, formerly.

Ya kwanza, first, the first.

Ngoja kwanza, wait a bit.

Kwao, plur. *makwao*, a stumble, a stumbling-block.

Kwao, to or with them, at or to their place; their, of them, after verbs in the infinitive used as nouns, and after the case in *-ni*.

Kwapa, plur. *makwapa*, the armpit.

Kwapani, under the armpit. The people of the African coast wear their swords by a strap over the left shoulder only; the sword hangs under the armpit, and is said to be *kwapani*.

Kwaruza ku-, to scrape along, to slip with a scrape.

Kwata, or *Kwato*, a hoof.

Kupiga kwata, to strike the hoof, to strike with the hoof.

Kwatu, a horseshoe (?).

Kwayo, a stumbling-block.

Kwaza ku-, to make to stumble.

Kukwaza meno, to jar the teeth like grit in food.

Kwea ku-, to ascend, go up, climb.

Kweli, true, the truth.

Ya kweli, true.

Kwelu = *Kweu*.

Kwema, good, well, it is well there.

Kweme, the seed of a gourd, very rich in oil.

Kwenda, to go. See **Enda**, going.

Kwenda, perhaps.

Kwenu, with you, to or at your place, your, of you, after verbs in the infinitive used as nouns or after the case in *-ni*.

Kwenyi, till, since, up to the time of, from the time of.

Kwepa ku-, to start out of the way.

Kweta ku-, to raise.

Kwetu, to or with us, to or at our place, our, of us, after a verb in the infinitive used as a noun, and after the case in *-ni*.

Kweu, clear.

Kweupe, white. See *-eupe*.

Kuna kweupe, grey dawn.

Kweza ku-, to make to go up, to drag up a boat out of the water.

Kweza ku-, to bid up an article at an auction.

Kukwezwa, to have things made dear to one by others bidding them up.

Kwiba. See *Iba ku-*, stealing, to steal.

Kwibana, robbing one another.

Kwikwe, hiccup.

Kwikwe ya kulia, sobs.

Kwisha. See *Isha ku-*, ending, to end.

Kwo, which.

L.

L is pronounced as in English.

L is not distinguished from *r* in African languages of the same family as Swahili. The distinction becomes important in Swahili on account of the Arabic words which have been incorporated into it. Thus—

Mahali, means a place, but *Mahari* a dowry.

Waredi means a rose, but *Waledi* a youth. Slaves, however, frequently confound even these.

When *r* can be used for *l*, it has a light smooth sound, as in English.

There is a latent *l* sound between every two consecutive vowels in Swahili and at the beginning of some verbs, which appears in their derivatives and in other African languages: thus the common passive of *kufungua* is *kufunguliwa*.

So far is this disposition to drop an *l* carried, that even *kuleta*, to bring, is in old Swahili *eta*. It is characteristic of the Merima dialect to retain these *l*'s.

L and *u* are sometimes apparently interchanged.

Mlango, a door, is vulgarly pronounced *Mwango*.

Ufalme, a kingdom, may be written *Ufaume*.

In these cases, however, both forms are probably contractions from *Mulango* and *Ufalume*.

L becomes *d* after *n*, and is sometimes confounded with *d* in inexact pronunciation.

Ndume = *Nlume* or *Nume*, male.

L- or *li-*, the prefix proper to pronouns and verbs governed by words in the singular, of the class which make their plural in *ma-*.

La, no.

La ku-, to eat, to consume, to wear away, to take a piece in chess, &c. The *ku-*, bears the accent and is retained in the usual tenses. The passive of *kula* is *kuliwa*.

Laabu ku-, to play, to sport with.

Laana, plur. *malaana*, a curse.

Laani ku-, to curse, to damn.

Laanisha ku-, to bring a curse upon.

Labeka = *Lebeka*.

Labuda, perhaps.

Ladu, sweet cakes composed of treacle, pepper, and flour or semsem seed, made up into balls.

Laghai, a rascal. Also *Ragai.*

Laika, plur. *malaika*, one of the hairs of the hand or arm.

Laini, smooth, soft.

Lainisha ku-, to make smooth or soft.

Laiti! Would that! Oh that! expressing regret at something past.

Lake or *Lakwe*, his, hers, its. See [*-ake*.

Laki ku-, to go to meet.

Lakini, but, however.

Lakki, a hundred thousand, a lac.

Lako, thy. See *ako*.

Lala ku-, to sleep, to lie down.

Nyumba imelala inchi, the house is fallen flat on the ground.

Lalama ku-, to confess, to cry for mercy; used of extorted confessions.

Lalamika ku-, to be made to cry out, to be quite beaten, to shout, to scream.

Lalika ku-, to be slept upon.

Lalika ku- = *Alika ku-*, to inform, announce to.

Lami, pitch or tar.

Lana ku-, to eat one another.

Landa ku-, to be equal with.

Langu, my. See *-angu*.

Lao, their. See *-ao*.

Laomu ku-, to blame. Also *Laumu*.

Lapa ku-, or *Rapa ku-*, to be ravenously hungry.

Launi, sort, species, form.

Laumu ku-, to blame.

Lawa ku-, to come from (Mer.).

Lawana ku-, to blame, to scold.

Laza ku-, to lay down, to lay at its length.

Kujilaza, to lie down.

Lâzim, of necessity.

Lazima, surety, bail, necessity.

Lazimisha ku-, to compel.

Lazimu ku-, to be obligatory upon.

-le, his, hers, or its.

Lea ku-, to bring up.

Amelewa vema, he is well bred.

Lebeka, the humble manner of replying when called, often shortened into *Ebbe*, or even *Bee*.

Legea ku-, &c., &c. See *Regea ku-*, &c., &c.

Lekea ku-, to be opposite to, to tend to.

Lekeza ku-, to put opposite to.

Kulekeza bunduki, to level a gun at.

Lekezana ku-, to agree, come to an agreement.

Lelam, by auction.

Lelimama, a dance to the music made by beating buffalo horns.

Lema or *Dema*, a kind of fish-trap.

Lemaa, disfigurement.

Mwenyi lemaa, disfigured by disease.

Lembuka ku-, to be weak, limp.

Lemea ku-, to oppress, to lie heavy upon, to overburden.

Lengelenge, plur. *malengelenge*, a blister.

Lenu, your. See *-enu*.

Lenyi. See *-enyi*.

Bakuli lenyi mayayi, a basin with eggs in it.

Leo, to-day.

Leppe, drowsiness, dozes, snatches of sleep.

Leso, a handkerchief.

Leso ya kufutia kamasi, a pocket-handkerchief.

Leta ku-, to cause to arrive at the place where the speaker is, to bring, to send, to fetch.

Letea ku-, to bring or send to or for a person.

Kuletewa, to have brought or sent to one.

Letu, our. See *-etu*.

Levuka ku-, to get sober.

Levya ku-, to intoxicate.

Kujilevya, to make oneself intoxicated, to get drunk.

Levyalevya ku-, to be giddy.

Lewa ku-, to become drunk.

Lewalewa ku-, to swing or sway about like a drunken man.

Li, it is.

Li- or *l-*, the prefix proper to pronouns and verbs governed by a singular noun of the class which makes its plural in *ma-*.

-li-, 1. The objective prefix representing a singular noun of the class which makes its plural in *ma-*, governed by the verb to which it is prefixed.

2. *-li-*, or *-ali-*, the sign of that past tense which denotes an action complete in past time.

3. *-li-* sometimes represents the substantive verb, as in *aliye*, he who is; *nikali*, and I am; *ali*, he is, or he being.

Lia ku-, to breed (M.).

Lia ku-, to eat for, &c.

Chumba cha kulia, a room to eat in.

Mkono wa kulia, right hand, being the only one ever used to eat with.

Lia ku-, to cry, to weep, to cry out; applied to the cries of animals generally. Also, to give a sound.

Kulia ngoa, to weep for jealousy.

Inalia wazi, it sounds hollow.

Libasi, clothes.

Licha, whether it be, though.

Lihamu, solder.

Lihani, a cloth of a particular pattern.

Lijamu, a horse's bit.

Lika ku-, to be eaten, to become worn away, to be eatable.

Likiza ku-, to dismiss, to give leave to go, to release.

Liko, plur. *maliko*, a landing-place.

Lilia ku-, to weep for, to cry about.

Lima ku-, to cultivate, to hoe.

Lima, the feast made by the bridegroom on the first day of the wedding.

Limao, plur. *malimao*, a lemon.

Limatia ku-, to delay, to loiter (A.).

Limbika ku-, to leave till it is fit, to wait for fruit till it is ripe, or for water till it is collected in the dipping hole, to put aside till it is fit.

Limbuka ku-, to taste the first of a new crop.

Limbusha ku-, to bring to be tasted.

Limiza ku-, to make to hoe, &c.

Linalokuja, which is coming.

Linda ku-. to guard, to watch, to keep.

Kulinda ndege, to scare birds from corn, &c.

Lindi, plur. *malindi*, a pit, a deep place.

Lindo, a watching place.

Linga ku-, to swing the head round in dancing.

Linga ku-, to make to match, or to be level.

Lingana ku-, to match, to be level with or like one another.

Lingana ku-, to call, to invite (A.).

Linganisha ku-, to make to match, to compare together.

Lini? When?

Linyi = *Lenyi*.

Lipa ku-, to pay (a debt).

Lipia ku-, to pay (a person).

Lipiza ku-, to cause to be paid.

Kujilipiza, to take one's due, to repay oneself.

Kujilipiza kasasi, to avenge oneself, to take one's revenge.

Lisani, a piece of cloth put in behind an opening, a flap to obviate the effect of gaping at the fastening, a tongue. See *Kanzu*.

Lisha ku-, to feed.

Lishisha ku-, to cause to be fed, to cause people to give one food.

Liwa ku-, to be eaten, to be worn away, to be consumed.

Liwa, a fragrant wood from Madagascar, which is ground up and used as a cosmetic, and as an application to cure prickly heat; Madagascar sandal wood.

Liwali, plur. *maliwali*, for *Al Wali*, a governor

Liza ka-, to sell to.

Liza ku-, to make to weep.

Lizana ku-, to make one another weep, to cry together.

-lo, thy, your.

Lo, *-lo-*, or *-lo*, which, representing a singular noun of the class which makes its plural in *ma*.

Lo lote, whatsoever.

Hakufanya lo lote, he has done nothing at all (*neno* understood).

Loa ku-, to get wet with rain, &c.

Loga ku-, to bewitch, to practise magic (Mer.).

Lo or *Loo!* Hullo! An exclamation of surprise; the number of *o*'s increases in proportion to the amount of surprise.

Lote, all. See *-ote*.

Lo lote, whatsoever.

Lozi, an almond.

Luanga, a kind of bird.

Luba, a leech.

Lugha, language.

Lulu, a pearl.

Lumba ku-, to make a speech.

Lumbika ku-, to gather little by little, to pick up small pieces one by one.

Lumbwi, a chameleon (?).

Luththa, flavour, savour.

Luva, sandal wood (?).

M.

M is pronounced as in English.

M before *b* generally represents an *n*. *Mb* stands sometimes for *nb*, as *nyumba mbaya*, for *nyumba n-baya;* sometimes it represents *nw* or *nv*, as *mbingu* for *n-wingu*.

M is frequently either followed by *w* or *u*, or else has a sort of semi-vowel power, as if preceded by a half-suppressed *u*.

The natives of Zanzibar very rarely say *mu;* they change it into *um* or rather *'m*. Even *Mwenyiezi Muungu*, Almighty God, becomes *'Mnyezimngu*.

It is important to write *'m*, and not *m* only, where it represents *mu* if a *b* or *w* follow, because otherwise the *m* might be supposed to coalesce with them. If any other consonants follow, it is immaterial, for *m* must then always stand for *mu*, and be capable of being pronounced as a separate syllable.

Any verb may be turned into a substantive by prefixing *'m* or *mw* to mean one who does, &c., followed immediately by the object of the verb or the thing done. The last letter is sometimes changed into *i* and if *ji* is added to the substantive it gets the sense of one who habitually does what the verb signifies.

M-, *'m*, *mu-*, or *mw-*, sign of the second person plural prefixed to verbs.

M-, *'m*, *mu*, or *mw-*, the singular prefix of those nouns which make their plural in *wa-*, if they denote animate beings, or in *mi-*, if they do not.

M-, *'m-*, *mu-*, or *mw-*, the prefix proper for adjectives agreeing with a singular substantive denoting an animate being, or with any substantive beginning with *mu-*, *'m-*; *mw-*, or *u-*.

-m-, *-'m-*, or *-mw-*, the objective prefix referring to a singular substantive denoting an animate being.

M-, *mu-*, or *mw-*, the prefix proper to pronouns governed by the case in *-ni*, when it denotes within or inside of.

Ma-, the sign of the plural prefixed to substantives (and to adjectives agreeing with them) which have either no prefix in the singular or begin with *j-* or *ji-*.

All words intended to denote something specially great of its kind make their plural in *ma-*.

Foreign words denoting a person, or an office, make their plural in *ma-*. In the vulgar dialect of Zanzibar nearly all foreign words are made plural by prefixing *ma-*.

Many plural nouns in *ma-* must be translated as though they were singulars, the true singular being used only to denote some one exceptionally large or important instance.

When followed by an *i* or *e*, the *a* of *ma* coalesces with it and forms a long *e* sound.

-ma-. See *-me-*.

Maadám, while, during the time, when.

Maadin = *Madini*.

Maadin ya kinywa, what rises into the mouth without internal cause, water-brash.

Maafikano, bargain, estimate, esteem.

Maagano, contract, agreement, covenant.

Maagizo, commission, direction, recommendation.

Maakuli, diet, food.

Maalúm, fixed, recognizable = *kilichotambulikana*.

Maana, meaning, reason, cause, sake.

Kutia maanani, to remember, think about.

Maandasi, biscuits, cakes, &c., also pastry, preserves.

Maandiko, writing, place for putting out food, the act of spreading a meal, a description, things written.

Maandishi, things which are written, put out, set in order, &c.

Maanguko, ruin, fall, ruins.

Maa'mzi, judgment.

Maarifa, knowledge.

Maarūf, understood, I understand.
Maasi, rebellion.
Maazal, while.
Maazimo, a loan.
Mabaya, bad. See *baya*.
Mabakia, the remnant, what is or was left.
Mabichi, raw. See *-bichi*.
Mabiwi, heaps, piles of sticks and rubbish. See *Biwi-*.
Mabovu, rotten. See *-ovu*.
Machache, few. See *-chache*.
Machela, a litter, a palanquin.
Machezo, a game, games.
Macho (sing. *jicho*), eyes.
Yu macho, he is awake.
Macho ya watu wawili, or *Maziwa ya watu wawili*, dragon's blood.
Macho ya jua, the sun-rising, east.
Machukio, hatred, abomination, disgust.
Machwa ya jua, the sun-setting, west.
Madaha, a graceful manner.
Madanganya, deception, trick.
Madaraka, arrangements, provision.
Madefu, beard.
Madevu, a kind of rice.
Madifu, the fibrous envelope of the cocoa-nut leaves.
Madini, metal, a mine.
Madoadoa, spotted.
Madogovi, a kind of drumming, &c., used in exorcisms.
Maficho, concealment.
Mafu, death, dead things.
Maji mafu, neap tides.
Mafua, a chest complaint causing a cough, a cold in the head, a stoppage in the nose.
Mafundisho, instruction, precept, direction.
Mafundo, cróss-beams in a dhow, to steady the mast, &c.
Mafungulia, unfastening.
Mafungulia ng'ombe, about 8 A.M.
Mafupi, short. See *-fupi*.
Mafusho, steam from a pot of *majani*, used as a vapour-bath in fever, &c.
Mafuta, oil, fat.
Mafuta ya uta, semsem oil.
Mafuta ya mbarika, castor oil.
Mafuu, crazy, cracked.
Mafya, Monfia.
Mafya (sing. *jifya*), the three stones used to put a pot over the fire upon.
Magadi, rough soda.
Magamba, scales of a fish.
Maganda, peel, husks.
Magarasa, 8, 9, and 10 in cards (not used in playing).
Mageuzi, changes.
Maghofira, remission of sins.
Maghrebbi, or *Magaribi*, or *Mangaribi*, sunset, the sunset prayers of the Mohammedans, the west, Morocco.
Maghrib ayuk, N.W.
Maghrib akrab, S.W.
Maghuba, the winding of a stream.
Mago. See *Kago*.
Magongonene. See *Kanzu*.
Magugu, weeds, undergrowth.
Magundalo, an instrument of torture, in which the victim is suspended, and weights being attached to him, he is jerked up and down. Used for extracting evidence.
Mahaba, love, fondness.
Mahala or *Mahali*, place, places.
Mahali pa, in place of, instead of.
Mahali pote, everywhere.

Máhana (Ar.), excessive worry.
Maharazi, a shoemaker's awl.
Mahari, dowry paid by the husband to the wife's relations.
Mahati, a carpenter's tool used for marking lines to a measure.
Mahazamu, a shawl worn round the waist.
Mahindi, Indian corn, maize.
Mahiri, clever, quick.
Mahoka, devil, evil spirits, madness.
Maisha, life, continuance.
  Maisha na milele, now and for ever.
Maiti = *Mayiti*, a dead body, a corpse.
Majahaba, dock for ships.
Majana (?), honeycomb.
Majani, grass. The singular, *jani*, means a leaf.
  Rangi ya majani, green.
  Majani ya pwani, grass wort, samphire (?).
Majaribu or *Majeribu*, trial, temptation.
Majazo, reward.
Majengo, building materials.
Majeribu = *Majaribu*.
Majeruhi, wounded.
Maji, water, liquid, juice, sap.
  Maji maji, wet.
  Kama maji, fluently.
  Maji kujaa na kupwa, the tides.
  Maji ya pepo, *Maji ya baridi*, *Maji matamu*, fresh water.
  Maji mafu, neap-tides.
  Maji a bahari, blue, sea-water colour.
  Maji a moto, hot water, a large yellow kind of ant which makes its nest in trees.
Majibu, an answer.
Majilio, coming, or mode of coming.
Majilipa, revenge.
Majira, time.
Májira, course of a ship.
Majonsi, grief for a loss.
Majori, an elder.
Majuni, a cake made of opium, &c., very intoxicating.
Majutia, regret, sorrow for something done.
Majuto, regret, repentance.
Makaa, coal, coals, embers.
  Makaa ya miti, charcoal.
Makalalao, cockroaches; applied in derision to the Malagazy colony in Zanzibar.
Makali, fierce. See *-kali*.
Makanadili, places in the stern of native craft, the quarter galleries of a dhow.
Makáni, dwelling, dwelling-place.
Makao, dwelling, dwelling-place.
Makasi, scissors.
Makatazo, prohibition, objections.
Makatibu, agreement.
Makavu, dry. See *-kavu*.
Makazi, dwelling.
Makengeza, squinting, a squint.
Maki, thickness.
  Nguo ya maki, stout cloth.
Makimbilio, refuge, place to run to.
Makindano, objections.
Makini, leisure, quietness.
Makiri, a thumb-cleat in the side of a dhow.
Makosa, fault, faults, mistakes, sins.
Makoza (obscene) testicles.
Maksai, a bullock, castrated.
Makubwa or *Makuu*, great. See *-kubwa* and *-kuu*.
Makukuu, old. See *-kukuu*.
Makuli, diet.
Makulya, food [Tumbatu].
Makumbi, cocoa-nut fibre.

Makumbi ya popoo, areca-nut husk.

Makumbi ya usumba, cocoa-fibre cleaned for mattresses, &c.

Makumi, tens.

Makumi mawili, twenty.

Makupaa, the sheaves at the mast-head of a dhow, through which the *henza* leads.

Makusanyiko, place of assembly, assembly.

Makusudi, purpose, design, on purpose, designedly.

Makutano, assemblage.

Makuti, leaves of the cocoa-nut tree.

Makuti ya viungo, leaflets made up for thatching.

Makuti ya kumba, leaves plaited for fences.

Makuti ya pande, half leaves plaited for fences or roofs.

Makwa, the notching and shaping at the end of a pole to receive the wall-plate of a house.

Malaika (plur. of *Laika*), the hair on the hands and arms.

Malaika, an angel, angels. A baby is often called *malaika*.

Malaki or *Malki*, a king.

Malalo, sleeping-place.

Malazi, things to lie upon.

Malazie = *Marathie*.

Malele, orchilla weed.

Malelezi, changes of the monsoon, time of the easterly and westerly winds.

Malenga, a singer.

Mali, goods, property, riches. Properly a singular noun making no change for the plural, but treated sometimes as a plural in *ma-*.

Malidadi, a dandy.

Maliki ku-, to begin a building, a boat, or a house.

Malimo, master, navigator. In the canoes on the Zambezi the steersman is called *malimo*.

Malimwengu, business, affairs, matters of this life.

Malindi, Melinda.

Malio ya kiko, the bubbling sound of the water when a native pipe is being smoked.

Maliza ku-, to complete, to finish.

Malki or *Malaki*, a king.

Malkia, a queen.

Mama, mother.

Mama wa kambo, stepmother.

Mamba, a crocodile.

Mamba, the scales of a fish (M.).

Mambo, circumstances, affairs, things (plur. of *Jambo*).

Mamiye (Mer.), his mother.

Mamlaka, power, authority, dominion.

Mamoja, ones, same.

Mamoja pia, it is all one, I don't care.

Mana = *Mwana*.

Manamize, a name for a hermit crab.

Manane.

Usiku wa manane, the dead of night.

Manda, a loaf.

Mandasi, a pudding. See *Maandasi*.

Manemane, myrrh.

Maneno, language, message, business, matters, things (plur. of *Neno*).

Maneno ya fumba, dark sayings.

Maneno ya Kiunguja, &c., the language of Zanzibar, &c.

Manga, Arabia.

Mangaribi, sunset. See *Maghrebbi*.
Mangi, many. See *-ngi*.
Mangiri or *Mankiri*, a cross-piece at the bows of a dhow for fastening the tack of the sail.
Mango, a round hard black stone used to grind with.
Mang'ung'um, secretly, in fearful expectation.
Mani (obscene), semen.
Mani, a weight, about three rattel.
Manjano, turmeric.
Rangi a manjano, yellow.
Mankiri. See *Mangiri*.
Manoleo (sing. *noleo*), the ring where the blade of a knife issues from the handle.
Manuka, smell, scent.
Manukato, scent, good smells.
Manyang'amba, flour balls in a sweet sauce.
Manyiga, a hornet.
Manyoya, feathers of a bird, hair of a goat.
Manyunyo, a shower, a sprinkle.
Maomboleza, loud wailing.
Maomvi, begging.
Maondi, taste.
Maondoleo, removing, taking away.
Maongezi, conversation, amusement.
Maongo, the back.
Maonji, tasting, trying.
Maoteo, growth from old *mtama* stools.
Maotwe, Mayotte.
Mapalilo, hoeing-up time, hoeing between the crops.
Mapana, broad. See *-pana*.
Mapatano, agreement, conspiracy.
Mapema, early.
Mapendano, mutual affection.
Mapendezi, pleasing things, the being pleased.
Mapendo, affection, esteem.
Mapenzi, liking, affection, pleasure, love, things which are loved.
Mapepeta, a preparation of imma ture rice.
Mapigano, a fight, a battle.
Mapiswa, silliness, dotage.
Mapoza, remedy, healing things.
Mapooza, things which do not serve their purpose, fruit which drops prematurely.
Mapululu, the wilderness.
Mapumbu, testicles, the scrotum.
Mara, a time, sometimes, at once.
Mara moja, once, at once.
Mara mbili, twice.
Mara ya pili, the second time.
Mara nyingi, often.
Mara kwa mara, from time to time.
Mara ngapi? how many times, how often?
Maradufu, double.
Marahaba, thanks, very well, wel-come.
Marakaraka, chequered, spotty.
Marasharasha, a sprinkle, sprink-ling.
Marashi, scents.
Marashi mawaridi or *ya mzomari*, rose-water.
Marathi, disease, sickness.
Marathie, sociable.
Sina kiburi, marathie mimi, I am not above fraternizing.
Marefu, long. See *-refu*.
Maregeo, return, reference.
Marehemu, that has obtained mercy, deceased.
Marejeo, return.
Marfua, a desk, book-rest.
Marhaba = *Marahaba*.
Marhamu, ointment.

Marigeli, a large pot.
Marijani, red coral, imitation coral, gum copal.
Marijani ya fethaluka, the true red coral.
Marika, a person of the same age.
Marika, Merka, a town on the Somauli coast.
Marikabu = *Marikebu* = *Merikebu*, a ship.
Marindi, the little flap of beads worn by a string round the loins by native women.
Marisaa, shot, small shot.
Marithawa, abundance, plenty of space, material, &c.
Marizabu, a spout.
Marra = *Mara*, time, times.
Marufuku, a forbidden thing, prohibited.
Kupiga marufuku, to give public notice against.
Marungu (M.), biliousness.
Masahaba, the companions of Mohammed.
Masafi, purity.
Masaibu, calamity.
Masakasa (Yao), an encampment.
Masakini, or *Maskini*, or *Meskini*, poor, a poor person.
Masalkheiri, good afternoon.
Masameho, pardon.
Masango, wire.
Masanufi, a kerchief used for throwing over the shoulders, &c.
Masazo, what is left, remainder.
Mashairi, verses, poetry.
Shairi, one line of verse.
Mashaka, doubts, difficulty.
Mashamba, the country. Plural of *Shamba*, a plantation.
Mashapo, sediment.
Mashariki, the east, easterly.
Mashendea, rice which is watery and imperfectly cooked.
Mashindano, a race.
Mashindo.
Kwenda kwa mashindo, to trot.
Mashtaka, accusation.
Mashua, a boat, boats, a launch.
Mashúr or *Mashuhur*, remarkable, notable.
Mashutumio, reproaches, revilings.
Mashutumu, reviling.
Mashuzi, breaking wind.
Fathili ya punda ni mashuzi = You cannot make a silk purse out of a sow's ear.
Masia.
Kwenda masia, to walk up and down.
Masika, the rainy season, *i.e.*, March, April, and May.
Masikani, a dwelling.
Masikini = *Masakini*.
Masingizio, slander.
Masiwa, the Comoro Islands and Madagascar.
Masizi, grime, soot, &c., on the bottom of cooking pots.
Maskini = *Masakini*.
Masombo, a girdle of cloth.
Masri = *Misri*, Egypt.
Masrúf, provisions.
Masua, giddiness.
Nina masua, I am giddy.
Masukuo, a whet-stone.
Masuto, reproaches.
Mata, bows and arrows, weapons.
Mataajabu, wonders, astonishment.
Matakatifu, holiness.
Matako, the seat.
Matakwa, request, want, desire.
Matambavu, the side, a man's side.
Mata'mko, pronunciation.
Matamu, sweet. See *-tamu*.

Matamvua, fringe.
Matandiko, bedding, harness, what is spread.
Matana, leprosy.
Matanga, large mats, sails.
Kukaa matanga, to keep a formal mourning, generally for from five to ten days.
Kuondoa matanga, to put an end to the mourning.
Matanga kati, wind abeam.
Matangamano, a crowd.
Matata, a tangle, an embroilment.
Kutia matata, to tangle.
Matayo, reproaches, revilings.
Mate, spittle.
Mategemeo, props, a prop, support, protection.
Mateka, spoil, booty, prisoners.
Matembezi, a walk.
Matengo, the outriggers of a canoe.
Mateso, afflictions, adversity.
Mateto, quarrel.
Mathabahu = *Mathbah*.
Mathabuha, a victim, a sacrifice.
Mathahabi or *Mathháb*, sect, persuasion.
Mathara, mischief, harm.
Mathbah, an altar.
Mathehebu, manners, habits, customs, = *Mathahabi* (?).
Matilo, lift from the after part of a yard to the mast-head of a dhow.
Matindi, half-grown Indian corn.
Matindo, a slaughter-house, a place for killing beasts.
Matiti.
Kwenda kwa matiti, to trot.
Matlaa, the east wind.
Matlaa ayuk, N.E.
Matlaa akrab, S.E.
Matlai = *Matlaa*.
Mato, eyes (M.).
Matoazi, cymbals.
Matokeo, going-out places.
Matokeo ya hari, pores of the skin.
Matomoko, a custard apple.
Matubwitubwi, mumps.
Matukano, filthy and insulting expressions, such as—
Mwana kumanyoko.
Mwana wa haramu.
Kazoakazoa.
Kumanina.
Matukio, accidents, things which happen.
Matumaini, confidence, hope.
Matumbawi, fresh coral, cut from below high-water mark: it is used for roofs and where lightness is an object.
Matumbo, the entrails.
Matupu, bare. See *-tupu*.
Maturuma, stiffeners put on a door, the knees in a dhow, ribs of a boat, &c.
Matusu, bad and abusive language.
Matuvumu, accusation, blame.
Maua (plur. of *Ua*), flowers.
Maulizo, questions, questioning.
Maumivu, pain.
Maungo, the back, the backbone.
Mauthuru, unable.
Mauti, death.
Mavao, dress, dressing.
Mavazi, dress, clothes. Plural of *Vazi*.
Mavi, dung, droppings, excrement.
Mavi ya chuma, dross.
Mavilio. See *Vilio*.
Mavulio, clothes cast off and given to another, clothes worn by one who is not their owner.
Mavunda, one who breaks everything he has to do with.

Mavundevunde, broken, scattered clouds.
Mavumi, hum of voices.
Mavuno, harvest, reaping.
Mavuno ya nyuki, honeycomb.
Mavuzi (plur. of *Vuzi*), the hair of the pubes.
Mawazi, clear. See *wazi*.
Mawe (plur. of *Jiwe*), stones, stone.
Ya mawe, of stone.
Mawe ya kusagia, a hand-mill.
Mawe, a vulgar ejaculation, rubbish!
Mawili, both.
Mawimbi (plur. of *Wimbi*), surf, a sea.
Mawindo, game, produce of hunting.
Mayayi. See *Yayi*.
Mayiti, a dead body.
Mayugwa, a green vegetable cooked like spinach.
Mazao, fruit, produce.
Maziko, burial-place.
Mazinga ombo, sleight of hand (Comoro).
Mazingiwa, a siege.
Mazingombwe, magic, witchcraft.
Mazishi, burial clothes, furniture, &c.
Maziwa, milk, (plur. of *Ziwa*) breasts, lakes.
Maziwa mabivu, curdled milk.
Maziwa ya watu wawili, dragon's blood.
Mazoea, custom.
Mazoezo, habits, customs, practice.
Mazoka, evil spirits.
Mazu, a kind of banana.
Mazumgu'mzo, amusement, conversation.
Mbali, far off, separate.
Mbali mbali, distinct, different.
Potelea mbali! Go and be hanged!
Tumwulie mbali, let us kill him out of the way.
When used with the applied forms of verbs, it means that the person or thing is by that means got rid of, or put out of the way.
Mbango, a bird with a parrot-like beak, a person with projecting teeth.
Mbano, a circumcising instrument.
Mbau (plur. of *Ubau*), planks.
'Mbau, plur. *mibau*, planking, timbers.
'Mbaruti, plur. *mibaruti*, a weed with yellow flowers and thistle-like leaves powdered with white.
Mbasua, giddiness.
Mbata, a cocoa-nut which has dried in the shell so as to rattle, without being spoilt.
Mbati, wall-plate.
Mbavu, ribs, side.
Mbavuni, alongside.
Mbawa, wing feathers. See *Ubawa*.
Mbayani, clear, manifest.
Mbayuwayu, a swallow (A.).
Mbega, a kind of monkey, black, with long white hair on the shoulders.
Mbegu, seed, seeds.
'Mbeja.
'Mbeja wa kani, young man of strength.
Mbele, before, in front, further on.
Mbele ya, before, in front of.
Kuendelea mbele, to go forward.
Mbeleni, in the front. This word is used in Zanzibar with an obscene sense.
Mbeyu = *Mbegu*, seed.
Mbilo, plur. *mibibo*, a cashew-nut tree.

Mbichi, fresh. See *-bichi*.
Mbigili, small thorns, briers.
Mbili, two. See *-wili*.
Mbili mbili, two by two.
Mbiliwili, the wrist (?).
Mbingu, plur. of *Uwingu*, the skies, the heavens, heaven.
Mbio, running, fast.
Kupiga mbio, to run, to gallop.
Mbiomba, mother's sister, aunt.
Mbirambi zako, be comforted. A Swahili greeting to one who has just lost a relative.
Mbisi, parched Indian corn.
Mbiu, a proclamation, public notice.
Mbivu, ripe. See *-bivu* and *-wivu*.
Mbizi.
Kupiga mbizi, to dive.
Mboga, vegetables, greens.
Mboga mnanaa, a kind of mint.
'*Mboga*, plur. *miboga*, a pumpkin plant.
Mboleo, manure.
Mbona? Why? for what reason? Used especially with negatives.
Mboni ya jicho, the apple of the eye.
Mbono, castor-oil plant (?).
Mboo, the penis.
Mboto, a climbing plant yielding a superior kind of oil.
Mbovu, bad, rotten, corrupt. See *-ovu* and *-bovu*.
Mbu = *Imbu*, a mosquito.
Mbui, a buffalo's horn, which is beaten as a musical instrument.
Mbuja, a swell, dandy, gracefully.
Kusema mbuja, to say elegantly.
Mbulu, a crocodile (?).
Mbungu, a hurricane (*Kishenzi*).
Mbuni, an ostrich.
Mbuyu, plur. *mibuyu*, a baobab tree, a calabash tree. They are generally looked upon as haunted.
Mbuzi, a goat, goats.
Mbuzi ya kukunia nazi, an iron to scrape cocoa-nut for cooking with.
Mbwa, a dog, dogs.
Mbwa wa mwitu, a jackal, jackals.
Mbwayi, wild, fierce.
Mbwe, little pebbles, little white stones larger than *changarawi*.
Mbweha, a fox.
Mbweu, eructation, belching.
Mcha, one who fears.
Mcha Muungu, a God-fearing man.
Mchafu, filthy.
Mchago, the pillow end of the bed.
Mchakacho, footsteps (?).
Mchana or *Mtana*, daylight, day-time, day.
Mchanga or *Mtanga*, sand.
Mchawi, plur. *wachawi*, a wizard.
Mchayi, lemon grass.
Mche, plur. *Miche*, a plant, a slip, a seedling.
Mche, a kind of wood much used in Zanzibar.
Mchekeshaji, plur. *wachekeshaji*, a merry body, one who is always laughing.
Mchele, cleaned grain, especially rice.
Mchelema, watery.
Mcheshi, a merry fellow, a laugher.
Mchezo, plur. *michezo*, a game.
Mchezo wake huyu, it is this man's turn to play.
Mchi, plur. *michi*, or *Mti*, plur. *miti*, the pestle used to pound or to clean corn with. Also a screw of paper to put groceries in (?).
Mchicha, plur. *michicha*, a common spinach-like plant used as a vegetable.

Mchikichi, plur. *michikichi*, the palm-oil tree.

Mchilizi, plur. *michilizi*, the eaves.

Mchiro, plur. *wachiro*, a mangouste.

Mchochoro, passage, an opening between.

Mchofu = *Mchovu*.

Mchongoma, plur. *michongoma*, a thorny shrub with white flowers and a small black edible fruit.

Mchorochoro, a rapid writer.

Mchovu, plur. *wachovu*, weary, languid, easily tired, tiring, tiresome.

Mchumba, a sweetheart, one who seeks or is sought by another in marriage.

Mke mchumba, widow (?).

Mchumbuluru, a kind of fish.

Mchunga (or *Mtunga*), plur. *wachunga*, a herdman, a groom, one who has the care of animals.

Mchungoji, a herdsman, shepherd.

Mchuruzi, plur. *Wachuruzi*, one who keeps a stall, a trader in a very small way.

Mchuzi, or *Mtuzi*, curry, gravy, soup.

Mchwa, white ants.

Mda or *Muda*, a space of time, the space, &c.

Mda, plur. *mida* (?), a piece of plank propped up to support a framework, &c. = *'munda*.

Mdago, a kind of weed.

Mdalasini, cinnamon.

Mdarahani, an Indian stuff.

Mdawari.

He mdawari, the softer Arabic *h*, the *he*.

Mdeli = *Mdila*.

Mdila, plur. *midila*, a coffee-pot.

Mdomo, plur. *midomo*, the lip.

Mdomo wa ndege, a bird's beak.

Mdudu, plur. *wadudu*, an insect.

Mdudu, a whitlow.

Mdukuo, a push in the check.

Mdumu, a mug.

Me-, see *Ma-*. Many words are pronounced with *ma-* at Mombas, and with *me-* at Zanzibar.

-me-, the sign of the tense which denotes an action complete at the moment of speaking, answering to the English tense with *have*. Sometimes it is used to denote an action complete at the time referred to, and must then be translated by *had*.

This tense may often be used as a translation of the past participle.

Yu hayi, ao amekufa? Is he alive or dead?

Most Swahili verbs denoting a state have in their present tense the meaning of entering that state or becoming, and in the *-me-* tense the meaning of having entered or being in it.

In some cases the *-me-* tense is best rendered by another verb.

Anavaa, he is putting on, *amevaa*, he wears.

In some dialects the *me* is pronounced *ma*.

Mea ku-, to grow, to be growable.

Medŭn, tortoiseshell.

Mega ku-, to break a piece, or gather up a lump and put it in one's mouth, to feed oneself out of the common dish with one's hand, as is usual in Zanzibar.

Mekameka ku-, to glitter, to shine.

Meko (plur. of *Jiko*), a fireplace.

Mekoni, a kitchen, in the kitchen.

Memetuka ku- (A.), to sparkle.
Mende, a cockroach, cockroaches. Also a slang term for a rupee.
Mengi or *Mangi*, many. See *-ngi.*
Meno (plur. of *Jino*), teeth.
Menomeno, battlements.
Menya ku-, to shell, to husk, to peel.
Menya ku-, to beat (Kiyao).
Merikebu, a ship, ships.
 Merikebu ya serikali, a ship belonging to the government.
 Merikebu ya mizinga or *manowari*, a man-of-war.
 Merikebu ya taja, a merchant ship.
 Merikebu ya milingote mitatu, a full-rigged ship.
 Merikebu ya milingote miwili na nussu, a barque.
 Merikebu ya dohaan or *ya moshi*, a steamship.
Merima, the mainland of Africa, especially the coast south of Zanzibar.
 Wamerima, people who live on the coast south of Zanzibar.
 Kimerima, the dialect of Swahili spoken on the coast south of Zanzibar.
Merimeta ku-, to glitter, to shine.
Meshmaa, a candle, candles.
Mesiki or *Meski*, musk, scent.
Meskiti = *Moskiti*, a mosque.
Metameta, to shine, to glitter.
Methili or *Methali*, like, a parable.
Meza, a table.
Meza ku-, to swallow.
Mezawwereh.
 Waraka mezawwereh, forgery.
Mfaa, centre piece of a door.
Mfalme, plur. *wafalme*, a king.
Mfano, plur. *mifano*, a likeness.
 Mfano wa maneno, a proverb, a parable.
Mfanyi biashara, plur. *wafanyi*, a man who does business, a trader, a merchant.
Mfariji, plur. *wafariji*, a comforter.
Mfathili, plur. *wafathili*, one who does kindnesses.
Mfeleji, a water channel.
Mfilisika, a bankrupt.
Mfinangi, plur. *wafinangi*, a potter.
Mfinessi, plur. *mifinessi*, a jack fruit tree.
Mfu, plur. *wafu*, a dead person.
Mfua, plur. *wafua*, a smith, a worker in metal.
 Mfua chuma, a blacksmith.
 Mfua fetha, &c., a silversmith, &c.
Mfuasi, plur. *wafuasi*, a follower, a retainer, a hanger-on.
Mfuko, plur. *mifuko*, a bag, a pocket.
Mfuma, plur. *wafuma*, a weaver.
Mfumbati, plur. *mifumbati*, the side-pieces of a bedstead.
Mfunguo, a name applied to nine of the Arab months.
 Mfunguo wa mosi, is the Arab *Shaowal.*
 Mfunguo wa pili, is the Arab *Th'il Kaada.*
 Mfunguo wa tatu, is the Arab *Th'il Hajj.*
 Mfunguo wa 'nne, is the Arab *Moharram.*
 Mfunguo wa tano, is the Arab *Safr.*
 Mfunguo wa sita, is the Arab *Rabia al aowal.*
 Mfunguo wa saba, is the Arab *Rabia al akhr.*
 Mfunguo wa nane, is the Arab *Jemad al aowal.*
 Mfunguo wa kenda, is the Arab *Jemad al akhr.*

Mfunguo wa is often so pronounced as to sound like *Fungua*.

The other three months, *Rajab*, *Shaaban*, and *Ramathan*, keep their Arabic names.

Mfuo, plur. *mifuo*, a stripe.

Karatasi ya mifuo, ruled paper.

Mfupa, plur. *mifupa*, a bone.

Mfuto, winning five games out of six at cards.

Mfyozi, an abusive person.

Mgala, plur. *wagala*, a Galla.

Mganda, plur. *miganda*, a sheaf or bundle of rice.

Mganga, plur. *waganga*, a medicine man, a doctor, a dealer in white magic.

Mgao, a place near Cape Delgado.

Mgawo, a deal in card-playing.

Mgeni, plur. *wageni*, a guest, a foreigner.

Mghad, a horse's canter.

Kwenda mghad, to canter.

Mgine = *Mwingine*, another, other.

Mgogoro, an obstacle in a road, a stumbling-block. In slang, a nuisance, crush, worry.

Mgoja or *Mngoja*, plur. *wagoja*, one who waits, a sentinel.

Mgoja mlango, a door-keeper, a porter.

Mgomba, plur. *migomba*, a banana tree.

Mgombwe, bull's-mouth shell, Cassis rubra.

Mgomvi, plur. *wagomvi*, a quarrelsome person, a brawler.

Mgonda, a slave's clout.

Mgongo, plur. *migongo*, the back, the backbone.

Nyumba ya mgongo, a penthouse roof.

Mgonjwa or *Mgonjua*, plur. *wagonjwa*, a sick person, an invalid.

Mgote = *Mlingote*, a mast.

Mgunda, cultivated land.

Mgunya, plur. *Wagunya*, a native of the country between Siwe and the Juba.

Mguruguru, plur. *waguruguru*, a large kind of burrowing lizard.

Mguu, plur. *miguu*, the leg from the knee downward, the foot.

Kwenda kwa miguu, to walk.

Mh-. See *Muh*.

Mhalbori. See *Kanzu*.

Mhimili, plur. *mihilimi*, a girder, a beam, a bearing post, a prop.

Mhulu, a large tree lizard.

Mhunzi, plur. *wahunzi*, a blacksmith.

Mi-, plural prefix of substantives, and of adjectives agreeing with them, which begin in the singular with *m-*, or *'m-*, *mu-*, or *mw-*, and do not denote animate beings.

-mi, an objective suffix denoting the first person singular. This suffix is poetical, not used in Zanzibar.

Mia, a hundred.

Miteen, two hundred.

Mialamu, the ends of a piece of cloth.

Miashiri, pieces lying fore and aft to receive the stepping of the mast.

Miayo, yawning, a yawn.

Miba or *Miiba*, thorns.

Mibau, timbers.

Mifuo, bellows.

Mikaha, marriage.

Mikambe.

Kupiga mikambe, in bathing, to duck down and throw over one leg, striking the water with it.

Mila, a custom.

Milamba.

Kwenda milamba, to go round by a new road to avoid war or some other obstacle, to strike out a new way.

Milele, eternity.

Ya milele, eternal.

Milhoi, jins, which having been merely singed, not killed by the missiles of the angels, lurk in by-places to deceive and harm people.

Miliki = *Milki.*

Miliki ku-, to reign, to possess.

Milki, kingdom, possession, property.

Milumbe, a speech, an over-long speech.

Mimba, pregnancy.

Kuwa na mimba or *Kuchukua mimba*, to be pregnant.

Kuharibu mimba, to miscarry.

Mimbara, the pulpit in a mosque.

Mimi, I, me.

Mimina ku-, to pour, to pour over.

Mimінika ku-, to be poured over, to be spilt, to overflow.

Mingi, many. See *-ingi.*

Mingine, others. See *-ingine.*

Mini (Ar.), right.

Mini wa shemali, right and left.

Minyonoa, a kind of flowering acacia.

Miongoni mwa, in respect of, as to, on the part of, from among.

Miraba, muscles. See *Mraba.*

Mirisaa, shot.

Mishithari, crooked.

Misko, Russia.

Misri, Egypt.

Miteen, two hundred.

Miunsi, a whistling.

Miusi, black. See *-eusi.*

Miwa (plur. of *Mua*), sugar-canes.

Miwali, midribs of a palm-leaf.

Miwani, spectacles.

Miyaa, leaves for making mats.

Miye, me, it is I.

Mizani, balances, steelyard, scales.

Mizi, roots (M.).

Mizizi, roots, rootlets.

Mja na maji, one who has come over the sea, a foreigner. Also, a slave.

Mjakazi, plur. *wajakazi*, a woman slave.

Mjanga, Bembatooka bay in Madagascar.

Mjangao, melancholy, silent sorrow.

Mjanja, plur. *wajanja*, a cheat, a shameless person.

Mjani, a widow.

Mjasiri, plur. *wajasiri*, a bold venturesome man.

Mjassusi, inquisitive.

Mjeledi, a whip.

Mjemba, a plough (?).

Mji, plur. *miji*, a town, a city, a village, the middle part of a piece of cloth.

Mji, the uterus.

Mjiari, plur. *mijiari*, tiller ropes.

Mjiguu, plur. *mijiguu*, large long legs.

Mjinga, plur. *wajinga*, a raw new comer, a simpleton; applied especially to newly arrived slaves, ignorant, inexperienced.

Mjisikafiri, a kind of lizard.

Mjoli, plur. *wajoli*, a fellow-servant.

Mjomba, plur. *wajomba*, uncle.

Mjugu.

Mjugu nyassa, ground-nuts.

Mjugu mawe, a hard kind of ground-nut.

Mjukuu, plur. *wajukuu*, a cousin, a grandchild.

Mjumba, plur. *wajumba*, an uncle.

Mjumbakaka, a kind of lizard.

Mjumbe, plur. *wajumbe*, a messenger.

Mjume, a weapon-smith.

Mjumu, studded with brass.

Mjusi, plur. *wajusi*, a lizard.

Mjusi wa kanzu. See *Kanzu.*

Mjusi kafiri, a rough kind of small lizard.

Mjusi salama, a smooth kind of small lizard.

Mjuvi, plur. *wajuvi*, a chattering, officious person.

Mjuzi, plur. *wajuzi*, a person of information, one who knows.

Mkaa, plur. *wakaa*, one who sits.

Mkaa jikoni, Mr. Sit-in-the-kitchen.

Mkaa, an astringent wood used in medicine.

Mkabala, opposite.

Mkabil, future.

Mkadi, plur. *mikadi*, the pandanus tree; its flowers are valued for their smell.

Mkaidi, obstinate, wilful. See *-kaidi.*

Mkaja, a cloth worn by women, given as a present at the time of a wedding.

Mkali, fierce. See *-kali.*

Mkamilifu, perfect.

Mkamshe, plur. *mikamshe*, a kind of wooden spoon.

Mkandaa, plur. *mikandaa*, a kind of mangrove tree full of a red dye much used for roof beams.

Mkanju, plur. *mikanju*, a cashew tree (M.).

Mkaragazo, a strong tobacco. Also, manfully, again and agaiu (slang).

Mkarakala, a medicinal shrub.

Mkasama (in arithmetic), division.

Mkasasi, a handsome tree, whose wood is useless. Hence the proverb,

Uzuri wa mkasasi,
Ukipata, maji, basi.

Mkasiri, a tree whose bark is used to dye fishing-nets black.

Mkataba, a written agreement.

Mkatale, the stocks.

Mkate, plur. *mikate*, a cake, a loaf.

Mikate ya mofu, cakes of mtama meal.

Mikate ya kusonga, ya kumimina, &c., cakes of batter, &c.

Mkate wa tumbako, a cake of tobacco.

Mkazo, nipping, pressing tight.

Mke, plur. *wake*, a wife, a female.

Mke aliofiwa na mumewe, a widow.

Mkebe, a pot to burn incense in, a drinking pot.

Mkeka, plur. *mikeka*, a fine kind of mat used to sleep upon.

Mkeo = *Mkewo.*

Mkereza, plur. *wakereza*, a turner.

Mkewe, his wife.

Mkewo, your wife.

Mkia, plur. *mikia*, a tail.

Mkimbizi, plur. *wakimbizi*, one who runs away.

Mkindu, plur. *mikindu*, a kind of palm whose leaves are used to make fine mats.

Mkizi, a kind of fish.

Mkoba, plur. *mikoba*, a scrip, a small bag.

Mkoche, plur. *mikoche*, a kind of branching palm with an edible fruit.

Mkojo, urine.

Mkoko, plur. *mikoko*, a mangrove tree.

Mkokoto, plur. *mikokoto*, the mark made by a thing being dragged along.

Mkoma, plur. *mikoma*, a large tree bearing an edible fruit.

Mkombozi, plur. *wakombozi*, a redeemer.

Mkondo.

Mkondo wa maji, a current.

Mkongojo, plur. *mikongojo*, an old man's staff for him to lean upon as he walks.

Mkono, plur. *mikono*, the arm, especially from the elbow to the fingers; the hand, a sleeve, a projecting handle like that of a saucepan, a measure of nearly half a yard, a cubit.

Ya mkono, handy.

Chuo cha mkono, a handbook.

Mkorofi, ill-omened.

Mkubwa, great, the eldest. See *-kubwa*.

Mkuchyo, Magadoxa.

Mkufu, plur. *mikufu*, a chain, especially of a light ornamental kind.

Mkufunzi, plur. *wakufunzi*, a teacher.

Mkuke, plur. *mikuke*, a spear with a sharp point and triangular blade.

Mkuku, the keel of a ship.

Mkule, a gar-fish.

Mkulima, plur. *wakulima*, a cultivator, a field labourer.

Mkulimani, plur. *wakulimani*, an interpreter.

Mkulo, plur. *mikulo*, a pottle-shaped matting bag to strain *tui* through.

Mkumavi, a kind of red wood much used in Zanzibar.

Mkumbi (Mgao.), gum-copal tree.

Mkunga (?), midwife.

Mkungu, plur. *mikungu*, the fruit stalk of the banana.

Mkungu, plur. *mikungu*, a kind of earthen pot.

Mkungu wa kufunikia, a pot lid.

Mkungu wa kulia, a dish.

Mkuu, plur. *wakuu*, a great man, a chief.

Mkuu wa asikari, a commanding officer.

Mkuu wa genzi, a guide.

Mkuza, large, full grown.

Mkwamba, a kind of thorny shrub.

Mkwasi, plur. *wakwasi*, a wealthy person, rich.

Mkwe, plur. *wakwe*, a father or mother-in-law, a son or daughter-in-law.

Mkweme, a climbing plant bearing a gourd with round flat seeds rich in oil.

Mkwezi, a climber, one who goes up.

Mlafi, plur. *walafi*, a glutton.

Mlala, plur. *milala*, hyphæne, a branching palm.

Mlamba, a dark-coloured bird that eats insects, and drives away other birds, even the crows.

Mlango, plur. *milango*, a door, a gate.

Mlanza, a pole for carrying things.

Mlariba, plur. *walariba*, usurer.

Mle, there within.

Mlevi, plur. *walevi*, a drunkard.

Mlezi, plur. *walezi*, a nurse, one who rears children.

Mlezo, plur. *milezo*, a buoy.

Mlima, plur. *milima*, a mountain.

Mlingote, plur. *milingote*, a mast.
Mlingote wa kalmi or *galmi*, the small mizen-mast carried by large dhows.

Mlingote wa maji, the bowsprit.

Mlinzi, plur. *walinzi*, a guard.

Mlishi, plur. *walishi*, a feeder, a shepherd.

Mlisho, the month Shaaban.

Mlizamu, a waterspout on a house.

Mlole, the comb of a cock.

Mlomo, plur. *milomo*, a lip. Also, *Mdomo*.

Mmoja, one, a certain man. See *-moja*.

'Mna, there is, within.

Mnada, plur. *minada*, a sale, an auction.

Mnadi, an auctioneer, huckster.

Mnadi, ku-, to sell by auction.

Mnafiki, plur. *wanafiki*, a hypocrite.

Mnaja, a prophet going to ask a thing of God.

Mnajimu, plur. *wanajimu*, an astrologer.

Mnajisi, plur. *wanajisi*, a profane person, blasphemer.

Mnara, plur. *minara*, a tower, a minaret, a beacon.

Mnazi, plur. *minazi*, a cocoa-nut tree.

Mnena, one who speaks.
Mnena kweli, one who speaks the truth.

Mnene, stout. See *-nene*.

Mneni, plur. *waneni*, a speaker, an eloquent person.

Mngazidja, plur. *Wangazidja*, a native of Great Comoro.

Mngwana, plur. *wangwana*, a gentleman, a free and civilized person.

Mnio (?).

Mno, exceedingly, excessively. *Mno* always follows the word qualified by it.

Mnofu, meatiness, fleshiness.

Mnono, fat. See *-nono*.

Mnunuzi, plur. *wanunuzi*, a buyer, a purchaser, a customer.

Mnyamavu, plur. *wanyamavu*, a silent person, still, quiet.

Mnyang'anyi, plur. *wanyang'anyi*, a robber, one who steals with violence.

Mnyeo, a tickling, itching, a creeping sensation.

Mnyiriri, plur. *minyiriri*, the arms of the cuttle-fish.

Mnyonge, plur. *wanyonge*, an insignificant, mean person.

Mnyororo, plur. *minyororo*, or *mnyoo*, plur. *minyoo*, a chain.

Mnywa, plur. *wanywa*, a drinker, one who drinks.

Mo, *-mo*, or *-mo-*, the particle denoting place inside something else.
Mumo humo, there inside.

Moalli, Mohilla.

Mofa, small round cakes of *mtama* meal.

Mohulla, a fixed time, a term. Also *Muhulla*.

Moja, plur. *mamoja*, one, same.
Mamoja pia, it is all one.

-moja, one.
Moja moja, one by one.
Moja baada wa moja, alternately.
Mtu mmoja, a certain man.
Moja wapo, any one.

Mola, Lord. Used of God.

Moma, a kind of poisonous snake.

Mombee, Bombay.

Moris, Mauritius.
Kutoka Moris, to score twenty-nine or more in a game at cards.

Kwenda Moris, to mark less than twenty-nine in a game at cards.
Mororo, soft. See *-ororo*.
Moshi, plur. *mioshi*, smoke.
Mosi, one (in counting).
Ya mosi, first.
Moskiti, a mosque, the ace of spades.
Mote, all. See *-ote*.
Moto, plur. *mioto*, fire, a fire, heat.
Ya moto, hot.
Kupata moto, to get hot.
Moyo, plur. *mioyo* or *nyoyo*, heart, mind, will, self.
Ya moyo, willingly, heartily.
Mpagazi, plur. *wapagazi*, a caravan porter.
Mpaji, plur. *wapaji*, a giver, a liberal person.
Mpaka, plur. *mipaka*, a boundary, limit.
Mpaka mmoja, adjacent.
Mpaka, until, as far as.
Tutacheka mpaka kulia, we shall laugh till we cry.
Mpambi, plur. *wapambi*, a person dressed up with ornaments.
Mpanzi, a sower.
Mpapayi, plur. *mipapayi*, a papaw tree.
Mparamuzi, plur. *miparamuzi*, a sort of tree said to be unclimbable.
Mpatanishi, plur. *wapatanishi*, a peacemaker, one who brings about an agreement.
Mpato, interlaced work, lattice.
Mpeekwa, plur. *wapeekwa*, a person sent, a missionary, = *Mpelekwa*.
Mpekuzi, plur. *wapekuzi*, one who scratches like a hen, an inquisitive person.
Mpelelezi, plur. *wapelelezi*, a spy.
Mpenzi, plur. *wapenzi*, a person who is loved, a favourite.
Mpera, plur. *mipera*, a guava tree.
'Mpia, new. See *-pya*.
Mpiga ramli, plur. *wapiga*, a fortune-teller, one who prognosticates by diagrams. Formerly they did so by throwing sand, whence the name.
Mpiko, plur. *mipiko*, a pole to carry burdens on.
Kuchukua mpikoni, to carry on a pole over the shoulder.
Mpingo, ebony.
Mpini, plur. *mipini*, a haft, a handle.
Mpira, india-rubber, an india-rubber ball.
Mpishi, plur. *wapishi*, a cook.
Mpofu, plur. *wapofu*, the eland.
Mpotevu, plur. *wapotevu*, a wasteful person.
Mpotoe, plur. *wapotoe*, perverse, wilful, good-for-nothing.
Mpumbafu, plur. *wapumbafu*, a fool.
Mpunga, rice, either growing or while yet in the husk.
Mpungati, plur. *mipungati*, a kind of cactus.
Mpuzi, plur. *wapuzi*, a silly chatterer.
Mpwa, the sea-beach (M.).
Mpweke, plur. *mipweke*, a shor thick stick, a bludgeon.
Mpya, new. See *-pya*.
Mraba, plur. *miraba*, muscles.
Mtu wa miraba minne, a very strong man.
Mrabba, square.
Mradi, preferably (?).
Mramma, the rolling of a ship.
Mrashi, plur. *mirashi*, a long-necked bottle, often of silver, used to sprinkle scent from; a woman's name.

Mremo, plur. *waremo*, a Portuguese. Also *Mrenu*.

Mrenaha, the thorn-apple plant.

Mrenu, plur. *Warenu*, a Portuguese.

Mrithi, plur. *warithi*, an heir, an inheritor.

Mruba, plur. *miruba*, a leech.

Mrungura, people who rob and commit violence at night.

Mrututu, sulphate of copper, blue-stone.

Msaada, help.

Msafara, plur. *misafara*, a caravan.

Msafiri, plur. *wasafiri*, a traveller, one on a journey.

Msahafu, plur. *misahafu*, a koran, a sacred book.

Msahafu wa Sheitani, a butterfly.

Msahau, plur. *wasahau*, one who forgets, a forgetful person.

Msaji, teak.

Msala. See *Musala*.

Msalaba, a cross.

Msaliti, a betrayer of secrets.

Msamehe, plur. *wasamehe*, forgiving.

Msangao, astonishment.

Msapata, a kind of dance.

Msasa, sandpaper, a shrub with leaves like sandpaper.

Msayara, kind, gentle.

Msazo, remainder.

Mselehisha, plur. *waselehisha*, a peacemaker.

Msemaji, plur. *wasemaji*, a talker, an eloquent person.

Msemi, plur. *wasemi*, a talker, a speaker.

Mseto, a sort of food, a mixture of *mtama* and *chooko*.

Msewe, plur. *misewe*, a sort of castanet tied to the leg.

Mshabaha, similar.

Mshahara, plur. *mishahara*, monthly pay, wages.

Mshakiki, small pieces of meat cooked on a skewer.

Mshale or *Mshare*, plur. *mishale*, an arrow.

Msharika, plur. *washarika*, a partner.

Mshayi = *Mchayi*.

Msheheri or *Mshehiri*, plur. *Washeheri*, a native of Sheher in Arabia, many of whom are settled in Zanzibar. The butchers and coarse mat makers are almost all Sheher men.

Mshiki, one who holds.

Mshiki shikio, the steersman.

Mshindani, plur. *washindani*, obstinate, resisting.

Mshindio, woof.

Mshindo (obscene), coitus.

Mshipa, plur. *mishipa*, a blood-vessel, a nerve, any disease affecting these, hydrocele.

Mshipavu, plur. *washipavu*, obstinate.

Mshipi, plur. *mishipi*, a net, a girdle.

Mshoni, plur. *washoni*, a tailor, a sempster.

Mshoni viatu, a shoemaker.

Mshono, plur. *mishono*, a seam.

Mshtaka, plur. *mishtaka*, an accusation, a charge before a judge.

Mshtaki, a prosecutor.

Mshuko, coming down, coming away from performing one's devotions.

Mshuko wa magaribi, about a quarter of an hour after sunset.

Mshuko wa alasiri kasiri, about 5 P.M.

Mshuko wa esha, about an hour after sunset, or from 7 till 8 P.M.

Mshumaa = *Meshmaa*.

Msiba, plur. *misiba*, a calamity, a grief, mourning.

Msifu, a flatterer.

Msifu'mno, plur. *wasifu'mno*, an excessive praiser, a flatterer.

Msijana, a bachelor (?).

Msimamizi, plur. *wasimamizi*, an overlooker, a steward, the head man over a plantation, who is nearly always a free man, often an Arab.

Msinji, plur. *misinji*, foundations, trench for laying foundations.

Msinzi, plur. *misinzi*, a sort of mangrove tree.

Msio, a piece of stone to rub *liwa* on.

Msio, a fated thing, what will destroy or affect a person. See *Mzio*.

Msiri, plur. *wasiri*, a confidential person, one trusted with secrets.

Msitani [Pemba] = *Barazani*.

Msitu, a forest.

Msitu wa miti, a thick wood.

Msomari, plur. *misomari*, a nail, an iron nail. See *Marashi*.

Msondo, a very tall drum, beaten on special occasions.

Msonyo, a whistling.

Mstadi, plur. *wastadi*, a skilful workman, a good hand.

Mstahamili or *Mstahimili*, plur. *wastahimili*, a patient, enduring, long-suffering person.

Mstaki, plur. *wastaki*, a prosecutor.

Mstamu, a shoe; a piece of wood fixed to the keel, with a hole to receive the heel of the mast.

Mstari, plur. *mistari*, a line, a line ruled.

Kupiga mstari, to draw a line.

Mstofele, a custard apple.

Msuaki, plur. *misuaki*, a tooth stick, a little stick of the *zambarau* tree, used as a tooth-brush. It is prepared by chewing the end until it becomes a mere bunch of fibres.

Msufi, plur. *misufi*, a tree bearing a pod of soft cotton, Eriodendron anfractuosum.

Msukani, plur. *misukani*, a rudder.

Msukano. See *Keke*.

Msuluhiwa, a peacemaker.

Msumari = *Msomari*.

Msumeno, plur. *misumeno*, a saw.

Msumkule, the name of Liongo's sword.

Msunobari, fir tree, deal.

Msuruaki, plur. *misuruaki*, the wooden button which is grasped between the toes to hold on the wooden clogs commonly worn by women and in the house.

Msuzo, the handle of a millstone.

Msweni = *Msueni*, cholera.

Mta or *Mtaa*, plur. *mita*, a district, a quarter of a town.

The *mita* of Zanzibar, starting from the western point and going round the outside first, and then into the middle, are: Shangani, Baghani, Gerezani, Forthani, Mita ya pwani, Kiponda, Mbuyuni, Maliudi, Funguni, Jungiani, Kokoni, Mkunazini, Kibokoni, Kidutani, Mzambarauni, Kijukakuni, Vuga, Mnazimoja, Mji mpya, Mtakuja, Jumea, Soko la Mahogo, Kajificheni, Mfuuni, Migomboni, Tiuyani, Sham, Hurumzi, Kutani, Mwavi. All these are on the peninsula, which joins the mainland only at Mnazi moja. Funguni is on the point where the creek enters, which almost surrounds the town. Crossing the creek by the bridge, there are the following *mita*: — Ng'ambo, Mchangani, Gulioni, Kwa Buki, Vikokotoni, Kisimani kwa kema, Mchinjani, Mwembe mjugu, Kikwajuni, Mkadini, and then Mnazi moja again.

Mtaala = *Mtala*.

Mtabari, credible.

Mtai, a scratch, a slight superficial cut.

Kupiga mtai, to scratch.

Mtaimbo, plur. *mitaimbo*, an iron bar, a crowbar.

Mtajiri, plur. *watajiri*, a merchant, a rich man. More correctly *Tajiri*.

Mtakaso, the rustling of new or clean clothes.

Kupiga mtakaso, to rustle.

Mtala = *Mtaala*, practice, study.

Mtali, plur. *mitali*, bangles, anklets.

Mtama, millet, Caffre corn.

Mtama mtindi, half-grown stalks of mtama.

Mtama tete, fully formed but not yet ripe.

Mtamba, plur. *mitamba*, a young she-animal which has not yet borne.

Mtambo, plur. *mitambo*, a spring, a trap with a spring, a machine.

Mtanashati, a swell, dandy.

Mtandi, a loom.

Mtando, the warp in weaving.

Mtani, plur. *watani*, one who belongs to a kindred tribe or race.

Mtaowa, plur. *wataowa*, a devout person.

Mtaramu, shrewd, wise.

Mtatago, a tree or beam thrown across a stream.

Mtego, plur. *mitego*, a trap.

Mtendaji, plur. *watendaji*, an active person.

Mtende, plur. *mitende*, a date palm.

Mtepe, plur. *mitepe*, a kind of dhow or native craft belonging chiefly to Lamoo and the coast near it. *Mitepe* are sharp at the bows and stern, with a head shaped to imitate a camel's head, ornamented with painting and tassels and little streamers. They carry one large square mat sail, and have always a white streamer or pennant at the mast-head: their planking is sewn together, and they are built broad and shallow.

Mtesi, an adversary, a quarrelsome litigious person.

Mtesteshi, comic.

Mteule, plur. *wateule*, chosen, select.

Mthamini, a surety.

Mthulimu, a cheat, a thief.

Mti, plur. *miti*, a tree, pole, wood.

Mti kati, a tall post set in the ground between a prisoner's legs, so that when his feet are fettered together he can only move in a circle round the post.

Mtishamba, a charm of any kind.

Mti, scrofulous and gangrenous sores.

Mtiba, a darling, a term of endearment.

Mtii, plur. *watii*, obedient.

Mtima, heart, chest (old Swahili and Kiyao).

Mtindi, buttermilk.

Mtindo, size, form, shape, pattern.

Mtini, plur. *mitini*, a fig tree.

Mto, plur. *mito*, a river, a stream.

Mto wa kono, a branching river, a delta.

Mto, plur. *mito*, a pillow, a cushion.

Mtobwe, a kind of wood of which the best *bakoras* are made.

Mtofaa, plur. *mitofaa*, an apple-like fruit.

Mtoki, a swelling of the glands at the bend of the thigh followed by fever.

Mtomo, firmness, good building.

Mtomondo, plur. *mitomondo*, the Barringtonia; its fruit is exported to India.

Mtondo, the day after the day after to-morrow.

Mtondo goo, the day after that.

Mtondoo, plur. *mitindoo*, Callophyllum inophyllum; oil is made from its seeds.

Mtongozi, plur. *watongozi*, a man who dresses himself up to allure women.

Mtoro, plur. *watoro*, a runaway.

Mtoto, plur. *watoto*, a child. Used also generally of anything small of its kind, when mentioned in connection with something larger to which it is attached; *e.g.* young shoots, small boats, &c.

Mtoto wa watu, a child of somebody, having relations, a woman of respectable family as distinguished from one of slave parentage, a woman therefore who has somewhere to go if she leaves her husband, or he her.

Mtoto wa meza, a drawer of a table.

Mtovu, without manners, shameless.

Mtu, plur. *watu*, a person, a man, somebody, anybody.

Hakuna mtu, there is nobody.

Mtu gani? of what tribe?

Mtu wa serkali, a man in government employ.

Mtulinga, plur. *mitulinga*, the collar bone.

Mtulivu, plur. *watulivu*, a quiet man.

Mtumaini, plur. *watumaini*, sanguine, confident.

Mtumba, plur. *mitumba*, a bale of cloth made up for a caravan.

Mtumbuizi, plur. *watumbuizi*, a spy, an inquisitive person (A.).

Mtumbwi, plur. *mitumbwi*, a canoe hollowed out from the trunk of a tree, distinguished from a *galawa* by having no outriggers, and being generally of larger size.

Mtume, plur. *mitume*, an apostle, a prophet. Applied especially to Mohammed as a translation of his title, Apostle of God.

Mtumke, plur. *watuwake*, a woman, a wife.

Mtumishi, plur. *watumishi*, a servant.

Mtumwa, plur. *watumwa*, a slave, a servant.

Mtundu, mischievous, perverse, troublesome.

Mtungi, plur. *mitungi*, a water-jar.

Mtupa, plur. *mitupa*, euphorbia.

Mtupu, bare. See *-tupu*.

Mtutu, plur. *mitutu* (Ar.), a mulberry tree.

Mtuzi, curry, gravy (M.). Also *Mchuzi*.

Mtwango, plur. *mitwango*, a pestle for pounding and cleaning corn.

Mu-. See *M-*.

Mua, plur. *miwa*, a sugar-cane.

Mubatharifu, extravagant.

Muda or *Mda*, a space of time, term. *Muda wa*, the space of.

Mudu ku-.

Kujimudu, to gain a little strength after illness.

Muhadimu, plur. *wahadimu*, a servant, one of the original inhabitants of Zanzibar. These *wahadimu* pay two dollars a year for each household to the *Munyi mkuu*, of which *Seyed Majid* now (1870) takes one; they also work for him. They all live in villages in the country, and speak a language of which there are at least two dialects, materially different from the Swahili of the town.

Muharabu, plur. *waharabu*, mischievous, destructive.

Muharibivu, plur. *waharibivu*, a destructive person, one who ruins himself, destroys his own chances.

Muháruma, a kind of silk handkerchief, worn instead of a turban.

Muhindi, plur. *Wahindi*, a native of India, especially an Indian Mussulman, of whom there are two chief sects settled in Zanzibar, the Khojas and Bohras.

Muhindi, plur. *mihindi*, the Indian corn plant. Also *Mahindi*.

Muhogo, cassava, manioc.

Muhtasari, an abridgment, a summary.

Muhulla, time, a fixed period.

Muhuri, a seal.

Mujiza, plur. *miujiza*, a wonderful thing, a miracle. Also *Mwujiza*.

Muli or *Mulia*, clever, knowing.

Mulika ku-, to show a light, to gleam.

Mulki, a kingdom.

Mume, male. See *-ume*.

Mumimi, Azrael, the angel of death.

Mumunye, plur. *mamumunye*, a kind of gourd resembling a vegetable marrow. It often grows of such a shape that its hard rind, when ripe, can be used for bottles, ladles, and spoons.

Mumyani, a mummy. Mummy is still esteemed as a medicament.

Munda, plur. *miunda*, a piece of plank to serve as cap to a post. See also *Mda*.

Mundu, plur. *miundu*, a bill, a small hatchet.

Munyi, a chief, a sheykh. The *Munyi mkuu* is esteemed the true Sultan of the Swahili, at least in the island of Zanzibar and the parts adjacent. He is descended from an ancient Persian family, the heiress of which married, some generations since, an Arab from Yemen. The title is now (1874) in abeyance. His chief residence is at Dunga, near the centre of the island.

Muomo, plur. *miomo*, the moustache, the lip.

Musala, plur. *misala*, an oval mat used to perform the Mohammedan devotions upon.

Musama, pardon.

Musimi, the northerly winds, which blow in December, January, and February. The *musimi* is sometimes reckoned to extend till June.

Musimo = *Musimi*.

Mustarehe, enjoyment.

Mustarifu, with a competency, neither rich nor poor.

Mutaabir, credible.
Mutia, obedience.
Muuaji, plur. *wauaji*, a murderer, a slayer.
Muuguzi, plur. *wauguzi*, a nurse, one who nurses sick people.
Muumishi, plur. *waumishi*, a cupper.
Muundi wa mguu (A.), the shin.
Muungu, God, plur. *miungu*. The Swahili rarely use *Muungu* or *'Mungu* alone. They almost always say *Mwenyiezi 'Mungu.*
Maskini ya Muungu, a poor free person.
Muzimo, a place where offerings are made to some spirit supposed to haunt there. Baobab trees are generally supposed to be haunted by spirits.
Mvi, grey hairs.
Mvili, the shade of a tree.
Mvinje, Cassiorinus.
Mvinyo, strong wine, spirits, wine.
Mviringo, round, roundness.
Mvita, Mombas.
Mvivu, idle. See *-vivu.*
Mvua, rain, rains.
Mvua ya mwaka, the rain which falls about August.
Mvuje, assafœtida.
Mvuke, vapour, steam.
Mvukuto, plur. *mivukuto*, a lever.
Mvulana, plur. *wavulana*, a young man whose beard is just beginning to grow.
Mvule, the lesser rains, about October or November.
Mvulini, in the shade.
Mvuma, plur. *mivuma*, the borassus palm.
Mvumilivu, plur. *wavumilivu*, patient, long-suffering.
Mvumo, a rubber, six games won by one side (in cards).
Mvunda, or *Mvunja*, plur. *wavunda*, a breaker, a destroyer, one who ruins.
Mvungu, the hollow of a tree, a hollow tree.
Mvungu wa kitanda, the space under a bedstead.
Mvuvi, plur. *wavuvi*, a fisherman.
Mw-. See *M-*.
Mwa, of.
Mwaa, plur. *miwaa*, strips of the leaf of a tree called *mkoma* (?), used to make coarse mats and baskets.
Mwafa ku-, to forgive.
Mwafaka, a conspiracy, an agreement, a bargain.
Mwaga ku-, to pour away, to empty out, to spill.
Mwagia ku-, to pour upon, to empty out for.
Mwajisifuni, a self flatterer.
Mwaka, plur. *miaka*, a year. The year commonly used in Zanzibar is the Arab year of twelve lunar months. There is also the Persian year of 365 days, beginning with the *Nairuz*, called in Swahili the *Siku a mwaka*. From this day the year is reckoned in decades, each decade being called a *mwongo*. The year is called from the day of the week on which it commences: *Mwaka juma*, *Mwaka alhamisi*, &c.
Mwaka jana, last year.
Mwaka juzi, the year before last.
Mwaka kwa mwaka, yearly.
Mwake, his, hers, its. See *-ake.*
Mwako, thy. See *-ako.*
Mwali. See *Mwana mwali.*
Mwali, plur. *miwali*, a sort of palm

with very long and strong leaf stalks, which are used for doors, ladders, and other purposes.

Mwalimu, plur. *waalimu*, a teacher.

Mwamale, treatment, mode of treating.

Mwamba, plur. *miamba*, a rock.

Mwamba, plur. *miamba*, the wall plate in a mud and stud house.

Mwamua, plur. *waamua*, a judge.

Mwamua, husband's brother.

Mwamuzi, plur. *waamuzi*, a judge.

Mwana, the mistress of the house, a matron. It is polite in Zanzibar to speak of one's own mother as *mwana*.

Mwana, plur. *waana*, a son, a child.
  Mwanangu, my child.
  Mwanao, your child.
  Mwanawe, his or her child.
  Mwanetu, our child.

Mwana Adamu, a child of Adam, *i.e.*, a human being.

Mwana maji, a seaman.

Mwana maua, a sprite represented as a white woman with an ugly black husband.

Mwana mke, plur. *waana wake* or *waanaake*, a woman.

Mwana mke wa kiungwana, a lady.

Mwana mume, plur. *waana waume* or *waanaume*, a man.
  Mwana mwali, a young woman whose breasts are not yet flattened, one who has not yet left her father's house.

Mwanamizi, a soldier crab.

Mwandikaji, plur. *waandikaji*, a waiter, a table servant.

Mwandiko, plur. *miandiko*, a manuscript, handwriting.

Mwandishi, plur. *waandishi*, a writer, a clerk, a secretary.

Mwanga, plur. *mianga*, light, a light, a kind of rice.

Mwangalizi, plur. *waangalizi*, an overseer, one who overlooks or looks to.

Mwangaza, plur. *miangaza*, a light hole, the small round holes which are often left near the ceilings of rooms in Zanzibar.

Mwango, plur. *miango*, a lamp-stand, a piece of wood about eighteen inches long, from near the bottom of which two small pieces project at right angles, to hold the common clay lamp of the country. The *mwango* is generally hung against a wall.

Mwango = *Mlango*.

'*Mwango*, plur. *miwango*, a kind of shrub.

Mwangu, my. See *-angu*.

Mwangwi, echo.

Mwani, seaweed.

'*Mwanzi*, plur. *miwanzi*, a bamboo.
  Miwanzi ya pua, the nostrils (?).

Mwanzo, plur. *mianzo*, beginning.

Mwao, a worry, bother.

Mwapuza, a simpleton.

Mwashi, plur. *waashi*, a mason.

Mwathini, one who calls to prayer at the mosque, a muezzin. Also *Mueththin*.

Mwavuli, plur. *miavuli*, an umbrella.

Mwawazi, the Disposer, a title of God.

Mwaya ku- = *Mwaga ku-*, to pour away.

'*Mweli*, plur. *waweli*, a sick person.

Mwema, good. See *-ema*.

Mwembamba, thin. See *-embamba*.

Mwembe, plur. *miembe*, a mango tree.

Mwendanguu, a great and irreparable loss.

Mwendo, going, gait, journey.

Mwenendo, going on, behaviour.

Mwenge, plur. *mienge*, a bundle of straw, &c., used to carry a light.

Mwenyeji, plur. *wenyeji*, a host, a person who has a home in the place.

Mwenyewe, plur. *wenyewe*, the owner, self, myself, thyself, himself, &c.

Mbau za mwenyewe, some one else's planks.

Mwenyi, having, possessing. See *-enyi*.

Mwenyi ezi Muungu, Almighty God.

Mwenyi chongo, a one-eyed person.

Mwenyi inchi, the lord of the country.

Mwenyi kichaa, a lunatic.

Mwenyi kuhutubu, a preacher.

Mwenyi kupooza, a paralytic.

Mwenyi mali, a rich man.

Mwenzangu, plur. *wenzangu*, my companion.

Mwenzi, plur. *wenzi*, a companion.

Mwere, a kind of corn or seed like linseed, growing on a close spike like a bulrush flower.

Mwerevu, plur. *werevu*, a shrewd person, a man of the world.

Mwewe, a hawk, a kite, a kind of fish.

Mweya ku-, to steal.

'Mweza, plur. *waweza*, able, having power over.

Mweza mwenyewe, one's own master.

Mwezi, the moon.

Mwezi, plur. *miezi*, a month. The months in Zanzibar begin on the day on which the moon is first seen, unless the old month has already had thirty days; if so, the day which would have been the 31st, is the 1st of the new month.

Mwezi mpungufu, a month of less than thirty days.

Mwezi mwandamu or *mwangamu*, a month of thirty full days.

Mwezi ngapi? what is the day of the month?

Mwezi wa sita, the 6th day of the month.

Mwiba, plur. *miiba*, a thorn.

Mwibaji, plur. *webaji*, an habitual thief, a thievish person.

Mwigo, a sort of large dove with red bill, white neck, and black body. It cries *Kooo!* Then one answers, "*Mwigo!*" *Kooo!*—"*Niagulie!*" *Kooo!* — "*Kwema nendako?*" *Kooo!*—then one may go on. If it answers not, it is a bad omen.

Mwiko, plur. *miiko*, a spoon, a mason's trowel. Also a measure, direction, prohibition, especially of a medical practitioner.

Kushika mwiko, to live by rule, to live abstemiously.

Mwili, plur. *miili*, the body.

Mwimo, plur. *miimo*, side piece of a door frame.

'Mwinda, plur. *wawinda*, a hunter.

Mwinga jini, a common plant whose leaves are said, when rubbed in, to cure the aching of the limbs in fever; a decoction of the roots is said to be useful in dysentery.

Mwingi, much, full.

Mwingi wa maneno, full of words.

Mwinyi = *Mwenyi*, having, with. See *-enyi*.

Mwisho, plur. *miisho*, end, conclusion.

Mwithi (Patta) = *Mwivi.*

Mwito, calling, summons.

Mwitu, forest.

Ya mwitu, wild.

Mbwa wa mwitu, jackals.

Mwivi, plur. *wevi*, a thief.

'*Mwivu*, plur. *wawivu*, a jealous person.

Mwizi (A.) = *Mwivi.*

Mwoga, plur. *waoga*, one who fears, a coward.

Mwokosi, plur. *waokosi*, one who picks up anything.

Mwokozi, plur. *waokozi*, one who saves, a saviour.

Mwombaji, plur. *waombaji*, a beggar.

Mwombezi, plur. *waombezi*, an intercessor.

Mwomo = *Mdomo.*

Mwongo, plur. *miongo*, a decade of ten days, used in reckoning the nautical or Swahili year, from the *siku a mwaka.*

Mwongo mwangapi, in what decade is it?

'*Mwongo*, plur. *wawongo*, a liar, a false person.

Simekuwa 'mwongo? am I not a liar?

Mwongofu, plur. *waongofu*, a convert, a proselyte.

Mwujiza, plur. *miujiza*, a miracle.

Mzaa, plur. *wazaa*, a parent.

Mzaa bibi, a great-grandmother.

Mzabibu. plur. *mizabibu*, a vine.

Mzaha, sport, ridicule, derision.

Kumfanyizia mzaha, to deride him.

Mzalia, plur. *wazalia*, a native, a slave born in the country.

Mzalisha, plur. *wazalisha*, a midwife.

Mzaramu, a pool of water.

Mzazi, plur. *wazazi*, a parent, fruitful.

Si mzazi, barren.

Mzee, plur. *wazee*, an old person, an elder.

Mzembe, plur. *wazembe*, a careless person.

Mzige, a locust.

Mzigo, plur. *mizigo*, a burden, a load.

Mzima, an extinguisher, one who puts out.

Mzima, plur. *wazima*, a living or healthy person.

Mtu mzima, a grown person.

Mzimu. See *Zimwi*, *Muzimo*, *Kuzimu.*

Mzinga, plur. *mizinga*, a hollow cylinder, a hollowed piece of wood used as a beehive, a cannon.

Reale ya mzinga, a pillar dollar.

Mzingi or *Mzinji*, plur. *mizingi*, foundations, trench for laying in the foundation. Also *Msinji.*

Mzingile mwambiji, a puzzle, a labyrinth.

Mzingo, the circumference, brink.

Mzingo wa, around.

Mzio, that which would be deleterious to any one; each person is said to have his special *mzio*—of one it is cuttle-fish, of another, red fish, and so on. Also *Msio.*

Mzishi, plur. *wazishi*, a burier, one who will see to one's funeral, a special friend.

Mzo, sixty *pishi.*

Mzofafa, on tiptoe.

Mzoga, plur. *mizoga*, a dead body, a carcase.

Mzomari. See *Marashi* = *Zomari.*

Mzungu, plur. *mizungu,* a strange and startling thing.

Mzungu, plur. *Wazungu,* a European, one who wears European clothes.

Mzungu wa pili, queen in cards.

Mzungu wa tatu, knave in cards.

Mzungu wa 'nne, king in cards.

Mzunguko, plur. *mizunguko,* a wandering about.

Mzushi, a heretic, an innovator.

Mzuzi, plur. *wazuzi,* a tale-bearer, one who reports maliciously or untruly the word of others.

Mzuzu, plur. *wazuzu,* a simpleton.

Mzwea, used to.

N.

N is pronounced as in English.

An *i* sound is generally connected with an initial *n.* It sometimes precedes more or less distinctly, and may be written *in* or *'n,* making the *n* a distinct syllable. Sometimes the *n* flows into the following letter, so that the *i* sound is altogether lost. Very often it follows it as in the common syllable *ni* or *ny.* It is characteristic of the Zanzibar dialect to make the initial *i* sound distinct. Thus *inchi,* a country, is at Mombas *'nti.*

Ni is often contracted into *'n* or *n,* and where *n* would be dropped *ni* sometimes is so, as in the first person of the future tense, *nitapenda* or *'ntapenda* or *tapenda.*

N cannot be placed before *b, ch, f, k, l, p, r, s, t, v,* or *w.*

Before *b, w,* and perhaps *v,* it becomes *m,* and *w* changes into *b.*

Before *k, p,* and perhaps *t,* it is dropped, and the consonant gets an explosive sound.

Before *l, r,* and perhaps *t,* the *n* remains, but the other consonant becomes a *d.*

Before *ch, j, m, n,* and *s,* it is merely dropped.

N can stand before *d, g, j, y,* and *z.*

N before *k* is in two cases at least contracted into *h.*

Hapenda = *Nikapenda.*

Hipenda = *Nikipenda.*

There is a sound in Swahili which is treated as a simple consonant, which does not occur in European languages as an initial sound. It is very nearly the same with the final *ng* in English, in such words as loving, going, &c. The sounds of *n* and *g* seem both audible, but so blended that neither of them can be carried on to the following vowel. It is here written *ng',* to distinguish it from the common sound *ng,* in which the *g* passes on to the following vowel. There is some little difference in the way in which different persons pronounce it; it has sometimes more of a *gn* sound, and might be so written if it be understood that the two letters are so fused together that neither can be heard as if it stood alone. It has been sometimes written *ñ,* which is either a mistake or very misleading. That the sound really is *ng,* may be proved by the fact that such words as begin with it are treated as words beginning with *n,* and that when other prefixes are applied they are treated as if the root began with *g*. It is not, however, a very common sound in Swahili.

There is another sound compounded of *n* and *i*, which is very fairly represented by the Spanish *ñ*, or by *ni* in such English words as companion, &c. It is pronounced perhaps in Swahili with a slightly broader and more nasal sound. It is here written *ny*, to distinguish it from the common syllable *ni*, in which the *i* has a vowel sound.

The *ny* sound in the dialect of Zanzibar sometimes represents an *n* in more northern Swahili, as in

Kúnwa or *kúnywa*, to drink.

The change from *n* to *ny* has in many verbs the effect of giving a causative meaning, as in *kupona*, to get well, *kuponya*, to make well, to save.

N-, or *ni-*, the sign of the first person singular of verbs, I.

-n-, or *-ni-*, the objective prefix proper to denote the first person, me.

N- (see *ny-*).

1. A prefix frequently occurring in substantives which do not change to form the plural. If followed by *d*, *g*, *j*, or *z*, it is pronounced with them and does not form a distinct syllable. Before other consonants it forms a distinct syllable, and may be written *'n-* or sometimes *in-*.
2. The plural prefix of substantives which begin in the singular with *u-*, followed by a consonant. The *u* is dropped and *n* prefixed before *d*, *g*, *j*, and *z*. Before *b*, and perhaps *v*, the *n* changes into *m*, before *w* the *nw* become *mb*. Before *l* or *r* the *nl* or *nr* become *nd*. Before *k*, *p*, and *t*, the *n* is dropped and the other consonant gets an explosive or aspirated sound, and may be written *k'*, *p'*, and *t'*; before *ch*, *f*, *m*, *n*, and *s*, the *n* is merely dropped. Where, however, dropping the *u-* would leave the word a monosyllable, the *u-* is retained, and *ny* prefixed.

N- (see *ny-*). The prefix proper to adjectives agreeing with substantives of the class which does not change to form its plural of whichever number, or with plural substantives which make their singular in *u-*. Where the simple form of the adjective begins with a vowel, *ny-* is prefixed, except *-ema*, good, which makes *njema* or *ngema*. The changes before a consonant are the same as those given just above for the plural nouns in *u-*.

Nyumba mbaya, not *nbaya*.
" *chache*, not *nchache*.
" *ndogo*.
" *fupi*, not *nfupi*.
" *ngema*.
" *njema*.
" *kubwa*, not *nkubwa*.
" *moja*, not *nmoja*.
" *nane*, not *nnane*.
" *pana*, not *npana*.
" *'mpya*, not *npya* or *pya*.
" *ndefu*, not *nrefu*.
" *tatu*, not *ntatu*.
" *mbili*, not *nwili* or *npili*.
" *nzuri*.

Na, and, also, with; by, of the agent of a passive, and with, of the sharer in the action of a reciprocal verb.

Na when joined with a pronoun commonly forms one word with it.

Nami, and I, or with me.

Nawe, and thou, or with thee.

Nao, *nayo*, *nacho*, *nalo*, and or with them, it, &c., &c., &c.

Na joined with the verb *kuwa*, to be, or with the personal prefix only, constitutes the verb to have. The object is frequently joined with the *na*,—*ana*, or *anazo*, *anacho*, &c., &c., he has.

Alicho nacho, which he has

Alichokuwa nacho, which he had.

Atakachokuwa nacho, which he will have.

Atakuwa nacho, he will have it.

The verb *kuwa na* is used sometimes in the sense of being, as *Palikuwa na mtu*, there was a man.

Hakuna, there is not.

Kuna, there is.

Zinazo, they are.

-na-, the sign of the present tense of a continuing action.

Anakwenda, he is going.

Anasema, he is saying.

This tense has sometimes the effect of a present participle.

Akamwona anakuja, and he saw him coming.

N.B.—At Mombas the *-na-* tense is used as a past tense. At Zanzibar it is the most usual present.

Na or *'Nna* = *Nina*, I have.

Naam or *Na'am*, yes.

Nabihisha ku-, to exhort.

Nabii, a prophet.

Nadi ku, to proclaim, to make a bid for a thing, to sell by auction. See *Mnadi*.

Nádira, rare.

Nafaka, corn, corn used as money.

Mtama, or millet, was formerly used in Zanzibar as small change: it was superseded by the introduction of pice from India about the year 1845.

Nafasi, space, room, time, opportunity.

Nafisisha ku-, to give space, to make space.

Nafsi or *Nafusi*, self, soul, breath.

Nafuu, profitable.

Nahau, spelling, grammar.

Nahma ku, to revenge.

Nahotha ya maji, water-tank.

Nai, a sort of anvil fixed in a forked piece of wood.

Najisi = *Nejjis*, profane.

Nakhotha or *Nahoza*, captain of a vessel, master mariner.

Nakili ku-, to copy, to transcribe.

Nakishi, *Naksh*, or *Nakshi*, carving.

Kukata naksh, to carve, to ornament with carving.

Nakishiwa ku, to be carved or inlaid.

Nakl, a copy.

Nako, and it was there.

Nákudi, cash, ready money.

Nama ku- = *Inama ku-*, to bend down, to bow the head.

Nami, and I, or with me.

Na'mna or *Namuna*, sort, pattern.

Namua ku- (Mer.), to take out of a trap, to extricate.

Nana or *Na'ana*, mint.

Nana, mistress (N.).

Nanazi, plur. *mananazi*, a pine-apple.
Nane, eight.
-*nane*, eight.
Ya nane, eighth.
Nanga, an anchor.
Kutia nanga, to anchor.
Nangonango, a worm (?).
Nani? Who?
Nanigwanzula, a kind of lizard.
Nao, and they or with them, and it or with it.
Naoza = *Nakhotha*, a captain.
Napo, and there, and here.
Nasa ku-, to catch in a trap.
Nasi ku-, to warn.
Nasibu, luck, fortune.
Kwa nasibu, by chance, perhaps.
Nasibu ku, to appoint.
Nasiha ku-, to suggest.
Nasihi ku-, to entreat, to beseech.
Nastahiba, I see it better, prefer.
Nasur, an abscess.
Nata ku-, to be adhesive, to stick.
Nathari, choice.
Nathiri, a look, a glance, a vow.
Kuweka nathiri, to vow.
Kuondoa nathiri, to perform a vow.
Nathiri ku-, to glance.
Natoa, a blemish (?).
Nauli, freight.
Nawa ku-, to wash oneself.
Kunawa mikono, to wash one's hands.
Nazâr, quarrel.
Nazi, a cocoa-nut, a fully ripe nut.
Nazi kavu, copra, cocoa-nuts dried fit for pressing.
Naziri = *Nathiri*.
Naziyana ku-, to quarrel.
'*Ncha*, the point, the end, tip, a strand in cordage.
Nchi. See *Inchi*.
Ndaa (M.), hunger, = *Njaa*.
Ndama, a calf, the young of a domestic animal.
Ndani, within, inside.
Ndani ya, inside of.
Kwa ndani, inner, secret.
Ndani kwa ndani, secretly.
Ndarobo.
Kusema cha ndarobo, to speak a secret language.
Ndefu = *Ndevu*, the beard. Sing. *udevu*, one hair of the beard.
Ndefu, long. See -*refu*.
Ndege, a bird, birds, an omen. To see a woman with a load is lucky, and would be called *ndege njema*. To see a man by himself carrying nothing is unlucky, and is *ndege mbaya*.
Ndere.
Unga wa ndere, a magic poison.
Ndewe, a hole pierced in the lobe of the ear.
Ndezi, a kind of animal.
Ndi-, a prefix used with the short form of the pronoun to express, it is this, this is the one, I am he, you are he, &c.
I, *Ndimi*.
Thou, *Ndiwe*.
He or she, *Ndiye*.
It, *Ndio*, *ndiyo*, *ndicho*, *ndilo*, *ndipo*, *ndiko*, *ndimo*.
We, *Ndisi*.
You, *Ndinyi*.
They, *Ndio*, *ndiyo*, *ndivyo*, *ndizo*.
Ndiyo yalio, that is just it, that is how matters stood.
Ndia (M.) = *Njia*.
Ndimi, tongues. See *Ulimi*.
Ndio, yes.
Ndiwa (M.) or *Njiwa*, a pigeon.
Ndizi, bananas, plantains.

Ndizi Bungala, a thick sweet kind of banana.

Ndizi mjenga, a long kind of banana used in cooking.

Ndizi msusa, a large ridged kind of banana.

Ndoa, marriage.

Ndonya, a lip-ring, worn by the Nyassa.

Ndoo and *Ndooni* (M.) = *Njoo* and *Njooni*, come.

Ndoo, a pail, a bucket.

Ndoto, a dream.

Ndovu, an elephant.

Ndugu, a brother or sister, a cousin, a relation.

Ndugu kunyonya, a foster brother, [&c.

Ndui, small-pox.

Nduli, savage, given to slaying, a man wholly without patience.

Ndume, male, from *-lume* or *-ume*.

Ndusi, a box.

Nebii = *Nabii*, a prophet.

Neema, grace, favour.

Neemesha ku-, to enrich.

Nefsi = *Nafsi* = *Nafusi*, self.

Negesha ku-, to charge with, to attribute falsely to.

Akamnegesha mwivi, and he called him a thief.

Nejjis, or *Nejisi*, or *Najisi*, profane, blasphemous.

Nelli, a pipe, a water-pipe.

Nembo, tribal marks.

Nena ku-, to speak, to name, to mention.

Nenana ku-, to talk against one another, to quarrel.

-nene, thick, stout, fat, whole, complete, plump, sleek.

Nenea ku-, to talk to, of, at, for, or against, to blame, to scold, to recommend.

Nenepa ku-, to grow fat, used especially of persons.

Neno, plur. *maneno*, a word, a thing.

Sikufanya neno, I have done nothing.

Nenyekea ku-, to be humble, to condescend.

-nenyekevu, humble, condescending.

Nepa ku-, to sag, to dip in the middle as a long rope does.

Neupe or *Nyeupe*, white. See *-eupe*.

Neusi or *Nyeusi*, black. See *-eusi*.

-nga- or *-nge-*, the prefix of the present conditional tense.

ni-nge-kuwa, I should be.

Ngadu, land crabs.

-ngawa, though.

Ng'aa ku- = *Ng'ara ku-*, to shine.

-ngali-, the prefix of the past conditional.

ni-ngali-kataa, I should have refused.

Ngama, the hold of a ship.

Ng'amba, a hawkshead turtle, from which tortoiseshell is procured.

Ng'ambo, the other side of a river or creek.

Ngamia or *Ngamiya*, a camel.

Ng'anda, a handful.

Ngano, a tale, a fable.

Ngano, wheat.

Amekula ngano, he has been disgraced; that is, having been as if in paradise, he has now to eat the food of ordinary mortals.

Ngao, a shield or buckler; they are circular and very small.

Ngara, the young cob of Indian corn.

Ng'ara ku-, or *Ng'ala*, or *Ng'aa*, to shine, to glitter, to be transparent, to be clear.

Ngariba, a circumcisor.
N'gariza ku-, to fix the eyes, to glare.
Amening'ariza macho, he glared at me.
Ngawa, a civet cat (?).
The *ngawa* is a larger animal than the *fungo*.
Ng'aza ku-, to make to shine, or to be brilliant.
Ngazi, a ladder.
Ngazidja, Great Comoro.
'Nge, a scorpion.
-nge-, sign of the conditional present, would.
Yangedumu, they would still continue.
Ngedere, a small black monkey.
Ngema, good. See *-ema*.
Ngéu, ruddle used by carpenters to mark out their work.
-ngi or *-ingi*, many, much.
Ngiliza. See *Ingiliza*.
-ngine, other, different.
Wangine—wangine, some—other.
Ng'oa ku-, to pull up, to root up, to pull out.
Ngoa, lust.
Kulia ngoa, to weep for jealousy.
Kutimia ngoa yakwe, to satisfy his desires.
Ng'ofu, the roe of a fish.
Ngoja ku-, to wait, to wait for.
Ngoje, Angoxa.
Ngojea ku-, to wait upon, to watch.
Ng'oka ku-, to be rooted up.
Moyo unaning'oka, I was startled out of my wits.
Ngole, rope.
Ngoma, a drum, a musical performance generally.
Ng'ombe or *Gnombe*, an ox, a cow, a bull, cattle.
Ng'ombe ndume, a bull.
Ngome, a fort.
Ng'onda ku-, to cure or dry fish, &c.
Ng'onga.
Ana ng'onga (A.), he is inclined to vomit.
Ng'ong'e, the strips of leaf or fibre used for sewing matting, and for tying.
Ng'ong'o, the thick edge of a strip of matting.
Ngono, the share of her husband's company which is due to each wife.
Ngovi = *Ngozi*, skin.
Ngozi, skin, hide, leather.
Nguchiro, a mangouste. Also, a sort of bird = *Mchiro*.
Ngumi or *Nyamgumi*, a whale.
Ngumi.
Kupiga ngumi, to strike with the fist.
Ngumu, hard. See *-gumu*.
Nguo, calico, cotton cloth, clothes.
Nguo ya meza, a table-cloth.
Nguo ya maki, stout cloth.
Kutenda nguo, to stretch the threads for weaving.
Nguri, a shoemaker's tool shaped like a skittle.
Nguru, a kind of fish.
Nguruma ku-, to roar, to thunder.
Ngurumo, a roar, distant rolling thunder.
Nguruvu, a kind of jackal with a bushy tail.
Nguruwe or *Nguuwe*, a pig, swine.
Nguruzi, a plug.
Nguue = *Nguruwe*, a pig.
Nguue, red paint.
Nguva, a kind of fish.
Nguvu, strength, power, authority.
Kwa nguvu, by or with strength, by force, strongly, rankly.

Nguzo, a pillar, pillars.

-ngwana, free, civilized.

Ngwe. See *Ugwe.*

Ngwe, an allotment or space for cultivation.

Ngwena, a crocodile, a seal.

Ngwiro, a large kind of ant.

Ni, I am, was, is.

Ni is used to express is or was, for all persons and both numbers.

Ni (M.), by, with the agent of a passive verb.

Ni-, *'N-*, or *N-*, I, the sign of the first person singular. Before the *-ta-* of the future it sometimes disappears.

-ni- or *-n-*, the objective prefix denoting the first person singular.

-ni, added to substantives, forms a sort of locative case, signifying in, at, into, to, from, from out of, near, by.

1. When followed by pronouns, &c., beginning with *'m* or *mw*, this case implies within, inside of, or the coming or going to or from the inside of the thing named.
2. When followed by pronouns, &c., beginning with *p*, it signifies nearness to, or situation at, by, before, near.
3. When followed by pronouns, &c., in *kw*, it denotes going or coming to or from, or at, from, and in, in a vague sense. or of things far off.

-ni, added to verbs in the imperative forms the second person plural. It is sometimes suffixed to common phrases, as *kuaherini*, good-bye, and *twendezetuni*, let us go, and is explained as a short form for *enyi*, or *nyie*, you! you there!

-ni, enclitic form for *nini*, what?

-ni, enclitic for *nyi* as an objective suffix (N.).

Nawaambiani, I tell you.

Nia, mind, intention, what one has in one's mind.

Nia ku, to have in one's mind, to think to do.

Nikaao, which I inhabit.

Nikali, and I am or was.

Nikali nikienda, and I am going.

Nil, blue (for washing).

Nikwata, the little wall lizard.

Nili, I being.

Nili hali ya kuwa juu yake, I being on his back.

Nina, I have.

Nina, mother (N.).

Ninga, a kind of green bird something like a dove, a woman's name.

Ning'inia ku-, to swing.

Ning'iniza ku-, to set swinging.

Nini? What?

Kwa nini, or *Ya nini?* why? what for?

Ninyi, ye, you.

Ninyi nyote, all of you, all together.

Nipe, give me. See *Pa ku-*.

Nira, yoke.

Nisha, starch (?).

Njaa, hunger, famine.

'Nje, outside, forth.

'Nje ya, outside of.

Kwa 'nje, outwardly, on the outside.

Njema, good, very well. See *-ema.*

Njia or *Ndia*, a way, a path, a road means.

Njia panda, cross roads

Njiri, a kind of animal.

Njiwa, a pigeon, pigeons.
Njiwa manga, tame pigeons.
Njiwa ya mwitu, a wild pigeon.

Njombo, a fish barred with black and yellow.

Njoo, come.

Njooni, come ye.

Njozi, an apparition, vision.

Njuga, a dog-bell, a small bell worn as an ornament.

Njugu, ground nuts.
Njugu nyassa, soft ground-nuts.
Njugu mawe, hard ground-nuts.

Njumu, inlaid with silver, inlaying work. See *Mjumu*.

Njuwa = *Njuga*.

Nnaokaa, where I am living, which I am inhabiting.

-'nne, four.
Ya 'nne, fourth.

Noa ku, to whet, to sharpen on a stone.

Noker, a servant.

Nokoa, the second head man at a plantation, generally a slave.

Noleo, plur. *manoleo*, the metal ring round the haft where a knife is set into its handle.

Nona ku-, to get fat, applied especially to animals.

Nong'ona ku-, to whisper, to murmur.

Nong'oneza ku-, to whisper to.

Nong'onezana ku-, to whisper together.

-nona, fat.

Nonoa ku- (?).

Noondo, or *Nondo*, a moth.

Nshi (A.), eyebrow.

Nso, the kidneys.

'Nta, wax, bees'-wax.

Nti = *Inchi*, land, country, earth.

Nuele or *Nwele* = *Nyele*, hair.

Nuia ku-, to have in one's mind, to intend.

Nuka ku-, to give out a smell, to stink.
Tumbako ya kunuka, snuff.

Nukato, plur. *manukato*, a good smell, a scent.

Nukiza ku-, to smell out like a dog.

Nukta, a point, a vowel point.

Nuna ku-, to sulk.

Nundu, a hump, a bullock's hump.

Nungu, a porcupine.

Nungu [Pemba], a cocoa-nut.

Nung'unika ku-, to murmur, to grumble.

Nunua ku-, to buy.

Nunulia ku-, to buy for.
Nunuliwa ku-, to have bought for one.

Nura ku-, to say the words of an oath.

Nuru, light.

Nusa ku-, to smell.
Tumbako ya kunusa, snuff.

Nuss, or *Nusu*, or *Nussu*, half.

Nusuru ku-, to help.

Nwa ku- or *Nywa ku-*, to drink, to absorb.

Nweleo, plur. *manweleo*, pores of the skin.

Nwewa ku-, to be absorbed, to be drunk.

Ny-, a common prefix to substantives which do not change to form the plural, where the root begins with a vowel.
Substantives in *u-* or *w-* followed by a vowel make their plural by substituting *ny-* for the *-u*. Dissyllables in *u-* make their plural by merely prefixing *ny-*.

Ny-, the prefix proper to adjectives,

agreeing with substantives of either number of the class which do not change to form their plural, or with the plural of substantives in *u-*, when the root of the adjective begins with a vowel, except *-ema*, good, which makes *njema* or *ngema*.

Nya kú-, to fall (of rain); the *ku-* bears the accent, and is retained in the usual tenses.

Mvua inakunya, the rain is falling (Zanzibar).

Mvua yanya, rainfalls (M.).

Nyaa, nails of the fingers (N.).

Nyaka ku-, to catch.

Nyakua ku-, to snatch.

Nyala, sheaths. See *Ala*.

Nyalio, cross pieces put in the bottom of a pot to prevent the meat touching the bottom and burning.

Nyama, flesh, meat, an animal, animals, beasts, cattle.

Nyama mbwayi, savage beasts.

Nyamaa ku-, to continue silent, not to speak, to acquiesce.

-nyamavu, silent.

Nyamaza ku-, to become silent, to leave off talking, to cease (of pain).

Nyamgumi, a whale.

Nyanana, gentle. See *-anana*.

-nyangálika, a sort of a.

Kitu kinyangálika, a sort of a thing.

Mnyangálika gani? What sort of a man is it?

Nyang'anya ku-, to rob, to take by force.

Nyangari, large (spider) shells.

Nyani, an ape, apes.

Nyanya, a small red fruit used as a vegetable, &c.

Nyanya ya kizungu, a sort of small tomato.

Nyanyasa ku-, to profane, contemn.

Nyara, booty.

Nyasi, grass, reeds.

Nyati, a buffalo, buffaloes.

Nyatia ku-, to creep up to, to stalk (an animal, &c.).

Nyauka ku-, to dry up, to wither, to shrivel.

Nyawe, his mother (M.).

Nyayo, plur. of *uayo*.

Nyea ku-, to cause to itch, to itch

Imeninyea, I itch

Nyefua ku-, to devour like a beast of prey.

Nyegi.

Kuwa na nyegi, to be in heat.

Nyekundu, red. See *-ekundu*.

Nyele, or *Nuele*, or *Nwele*, the hair, sing. *unyele*, one hair.

Nyele za kipilipili, woolly hair.

Nyele za singa, straight hair.

Nyembamba, thin. See *-embamba*.

Nyemelea ku-, to go quietly and secretly up to a thing in order to seize it.

Nyemi, a great dance.

Nyenya ku-, to talk a person into telling something.

Nyenyekea ku-, to be humble.

Nyenzo, rollers, anything to make things move.

Nyepesi, light. See *-epesi*.

Nyesha ku-, to cause to fall.

Kunyesha mvua, to cause it to rain.

Nyeta ku-, to be teasing, ill-conditioned, never satisfied.

Nyeupe, white. See *-eupe*.

Nyeusi, black. See *-eusi*.

-nyevu, damp.

Nyie or *Enyie*, you there, I say; used in calling people at a distance.

Nyika, wilderness, cut grass (A.).

Nyima ku-, to refuse to, to withhold from, not to give to.

Nyiminyimi, into little bits.

Nyingi, many, much. See *-ingi.*

Nyingine, other, another. See *-ngine.*

Nying'inia ku-, to sway, swing. Also *Ning'inia.*

Nyinyi, you.

Nyinyoro, a bulbous plant which throws up a large head of red flowers.

Nyoa, plur. *manyoa*, a feather, = *Nyoya.*

Nyoa ku-, to shave.

Nyoi (?), a locust.

Nyoka, a snake, a serpent, snakes.

Nyoka ku-, to be straight, to be stretched out.

Nyonda; temptation, trial.

Nyondo; a moth. Also *Noondo.*

Nyonga, the hip.

Nyonga ya sarara (A.), the loins.

Nyonga ku-, to twist, to strangle.

Nyonganyonga ku-, to go from side to side, to wriggle.

-nyonge, mean, insignificant, vile.

Nyongo, bile.

Nyong'onyeya ku-, to be weary, languid, to get slack and powerless.

Nyonya ku-, to suck.

Nyonyesha ku-, to suckle.

Nyonyo.

Mafuta ya nyonyo, castor oil (?).

Nyonyoa ku-, to pluck a bird, to pull out feathers.

Nyonyoka = *Nyonyoa.*

Nyonyota ku-, to make to smart.

Nyororo, soft. See *-ororo.*

Nyosha ku-, to stretch, to straighten, to extend.

Kujinyosha, to lie down, to take a nap.

Nyota, a star, stars, point of the compass.

Nyote, all, agreeing with *ninyi*, you. See *-ote.*

Nyoya, plur. *manyoya*, feather.

Nyoyo, hearts. See *Moyo.*

Nyua, plur. of *ua*, a courtyard, enclosure.

Nyuki, a bee, bees.

Asali ya nyuki, honey.

Nyukua ku-, to tweak, to pinch sharply.

Nyuma, at the back, afterwards

Nyuma ya, behind, after.

Nyumaye, after it, afterwards.

Kurudi nyuma, to go back.

Nyumba, a house, houses.

Nyumbo, the wildebeest, catoblepas gorgon.

Nyumbu, a mule, mules.

Nyundo, a hammer, hammers.

Nyuni, a bird, birds (M.).

Nyungo, plur. of *Ungo.*

Nyungu, a cooking pot.

Nyungunyungu, sores in the leg, said to be caused by the biting of worms bearing the same name.

Nyunyiza ku-, to sprinkle, to sprinkle upon.

Nyunyunika ku-, to murmur (?).

Nyushi, the eyebrow.

Nywa kú- or *Nwa kú-*, to drink, suck up, absorb. The *ku-* bears the accent and is retained in the usual tenses.

Nywea ku-, to get very thin, to waste away.

Nywesha ku-, to give to drink.
Nzi, plur. *manzi*, a fly. Also *Inzi*.
Nzige, a locust.
Nzigunzigu, a butterfly.
Nzima, sound. See *-zima*.
Nzito, heavy. See *-zito*.
Nzuri, fine. See *-zuri*.

O.

O is pronounced a little more like *aw* than is usual in English.

U before *o* sometimes becomes a *w*, but very often disappears, as: *Koga* for *kuoga*, to bathe. This word and some others in *o* are sometimes incorrectly conjugated as if beginning in *ko*.

-o or *-o-*, sign of the relative, referring to substantives in the singular which make their plural in *mi-*, or to singular substantives in *u-*.
-o, the short form of *wao*, they or them.
Oa ku-, to marry, used of the bridegroom. Passive, *kuolewa*.
Oana ku-, to intermarry, to marry one another.
Oawa ku-, to become married (of the man).
Oaza ku-, to marry.
Oga ku-, to bathe, frequently pronounced *koga*.
Ogofisha ku-, to frighten, make afraid, to menace, to threaten.
Ogofya ku-, to frighten.
Ogolea ku-, to swim, to swim about.
Ogopa ku-, to fear, to be afraid.
Oka ku-, to bake, to cook by fire only.
Okoa ku-, to save, to take away.
Okoka ku-, to become saved, to escape.
Okota ku-, to pick up.
Ole, woe.
  Ole wangu, wenu, &c., woe unto me, unto you, &c.
Olewa ku-, to marry or to be married, used of the bride.
Oleza ku-, to make like, to follow a pattern.
Omba ku-, to pray to, to beg of, to beseech.
Ombea ku-, to intercede for, to beg on behalf of, to pray for.
Omboleza ku-, to wail.
Omo, the head of a ship.
  Pepo za omo, head winds (?).
Ona ku-, to see, to perceive, to feel.
  Kuona kiu, to feel thirst.
  Kujiona, to think oneself, to affect to be.
  Naona, I think so.
Onana ku-, to meet.
Onda ku- (M.) = *Onja ku-*, to taste, to try.
Ondo, plur. *maondo* (A.), the knee.
Ondoa ku-, to take away.
Ondoka ku-, to go away, to get up, to arise.
  Ondoka mbele yangu, depart from me.
  Kuondoka katika ulimwengu huu, to depart out of this world.
Ondokea ku-, to rise to, or out of respect to.
Ondokelea ku-, to arise and depart from.
Ondolea ku-, to remove, to take away from.
  Kuondolea huzuni, to cheer.
Ondosha ku-, to make to go away, take away, abolish.
Onea ku-, to see for to anticipate for, to bully, to oppress.

Onekana ku-, to become visible, to appear, to be to be seen.

Ongea ku-, to spend time, to waste time in talking.

Ongeza ku-, to make greater, add to. *Kuongeza urefu*, to lengthen.

Ongezeka ku-, to increase.

Ongoa ku-, to convert, to lead aright.

Ongofya ku-, to deceive by promises.

Ongoka ku-, to be converted, to be led aright, to be healed.

Ongokewa ku-, to prosper.

Ongonga ku-, to feel nausea.

Ongoza ku-, to drive, to lead.

Ongua ku-, to hatch.

Onguliwa ku-, to be hatched.

Onguza ku-, to scorch, to scald.

Onja ku-, to taste, try, examine.

Onya ku-, to warn, to make to see.

Onyesha ku-, to show.

Opoa ku-, to take out, to fish up.

Opolea ku-, to fish up with, for, by, &c.

Orfa, or *Orofa*, or *Ghorofa*, an upper room.

-ororo, soft, smooth. It makes *jororo*, with nouns like *kasha*, and *nyororo* with nouns like *nyumba*.

Osha ku-, to wash.

Osheka ku-, to have been washed.

Osia, learning of old times.

Ota ku-, to dream (*kulota*, Mer.).

Ota ku-, to grow.

-ote or *ot'e*, all, every one, the whole. It varies like the possessive pronouns.

Merikebu zote, all the ships.

Merikebu yote, the whole ship.

Twende sote, let us go together.

Twende wote, let us both go.

Lo lote, cho chote, &c., whatsoever.

Otea ku-, to lie in wait for.

-ovu or *-bovu*, rotten, bad, corrupt, wicked. It makes *mbovu* with nouns like *nyumba*.

Ovyo, trash, any sort of thing.

Owama ku-, to be steeped.

Owamisha ku-, to steep.

Oza ku-, to rot, to spoil, go bad. Also, to marry (of the parents).

P.

P is pronounced as in English.

P, at the beginning of a word, has frequently an aspirated or rather an explosive sound, such as Irishmen sometimes give it. This is very marked in the name of the island of Pemba or P'emba. *P'epo*, the plural of *upepo*, wind, has a very strong explosive sound given to the first *p*, but in *upepo* both *p*'s are smooth, like an ordinary English *p*. It is probable that this explosive sound represents a suppressed *n*.

P followed by a *y* sound sometimes becomes *f*: *kuogopa*, to fear, *kuogofya*, to frighten; *kuapa*, to swear, *kuafya*, to make to swear.

Pa- or *P-*, the prefix proper to adjectives, pronouns, and verbs of both numbers governed by *mahali*, place or places.

The prefix proper to pronouns following the case in *-ni*, when it denotes nearness, at, by, near.

The prefix *pa-* is often applied to a verb in the sense of the English *there*.

Palina or *palikuwa na*, there was. *Hapana*, there is not.

It is not quite so indefinite as *ku-*.

Pa kú-, to present with, to give to. The *ku* bears the accent; *kupa* cannot be used without a person as its object, and the objective prefix bears the accent. *Alikúpa*, he gave you; *ali'mpa*, he gave him. The passive is *kupawa* or *kupewa*, and means, to have given to one, to receive.

Paa, a gazelle, a small kind of antelope.

Paa, plur. *mapaa*, a thatched roof.

Nyumba ya mapaa manne, a roof of four slopes.

Paa ku-, to ascend, to go up.

Paa ku-, to scrape.

Kupaa samaki, to scrape the scales off a fish.

Kupaa sandarusi, to clean gum copal.

Kupaa moto, to take fire and carry it on a potsherd, &c.

Paanda, a trumpet.

Paange, a horsefly, a gadfly.

Paango, plur. *mapaango*, a cave, a den.

Paaza ku-, to make to rise.

Kupaaza pumzi, to draw in the breath.

Paaza ku-, to grind coarsely, not to make fine meal.

Pacha, a twin.

Kuzaliwa pacha, to be born twins.

Pacha ya nje, a child of which its mother was pregnant while suckling a previous child.

Pachika ku-, to *put* an arrow on the string, to *stick* a knife in one's girdle, &c.

Padiri or *Padre*, plur. *mapadiri*, a padré, a priest, a clergyman.

Pafu, lungs.

Paga ku-, to strike hard, to harpoon a whale.

Pagaa ku-, to carry on the shoulders, to possess (of an evil spirit).

Amepagawa na pepo, he is possessed of an evil spirit.

Pagaza ku-, to make to bear, applied to an evil spirit causing a man to fall sick.

Pagua ku-, to take off, strip off (as boughs and leaves).

Pahali, in the place, at the place.

Paja, plur. *mapaja*, the thigh.

Paje, red mtama [Pemba].

Paji la uso, the forehead.

Paka, a cat, cats.

Paka ku-, to rub in, to smear on.

Pakaa ku- = *Paka ku-*.

Pakacha, plur. *mapakacha*, a basket made by plaiting together part of a cocoa-nut leaf.

Pakacha, plur. *mapakacha*, people who prowl about at night to do mischief.

Pakana ku-, to border upon.

Pakanya, rue.

Pakasa ku- (Mer.), to twist rope.

Pakata ku-, to hold a child on the lap or in front.

Pake, his, hers, or its, after *mahali*, or the case in *-ni* signifying nearness. See *-ake*.

Pakia ku-, to load a ship, to be loaded with, to carry as cargo, to have on board.

Pakicha ku-.

Kupakicha miguu, to cross the legs in sitting; reckoned improper in Zanzibar.

Pakilia ku-, to embark for, to put on board for.

Pakiza ku-, to stow on board ship, &c.

Pako, thy, your, after *mahali*, or the case in *-ni* denoting nearness. See *-ako*.

Pakua ku-, to take out of the pot, to dish, to lade out.

Pakuna ku, to scratch.

Pakutokea, a place to go out at, an outlet.

Pale, there, that place, of things not very far off.

Palepale, just there, at that very spot.

Palia ku-, to hoe.

Kupalia moto, to pick up for, and take live embers to a person.

Kupaliwa na mate or *maji*, to choke with spittle or with what one is drinking, so as to send it into one's nose, ears, &c.

Palikuwa na, there was or there were.

Palilia ku-, to hoe up, to draw the earth up round growing crops, to hoe between crops.

Paliliza ku-, to cause to be hoed.

Paliza ku-, to lift up the voice.

Palu, plur. *mapalu*, little cakes of sugar, bhang, and opium.

Pamba, cotton.

Pamba ku-, to adorn, to deck out, furnish.

Kupamba merikebu, to dress a ship.

Ku'mpamba mayiti, to put cotton in ears, mouth, &c. of a dead person before burying him.

Pambaja ku-, to embrace.

Pambana ku-, to meet in a narrow place where two cannot go abreast; applied to ships it means, to go alongside, to get foul of one another.

Pambanisha ku-, to bring together, to compare.

Pambanua ku-, to distinguish, to separate, to discriminate.

Pambanulia ku-, to describe by distinguishing.

Pambanya ku-, or *Pambanyiza ku-*, to overbear by loud talking, &c.

Pambauka or *Pambazuka ku-*, to become light in the morning.

Pambazua ku-, to speak plainly.

Pambele, in front.

Pambo, plur. *mapambo*, adornment, dressing.

Pambo la nyumba, house furniture.

Pamoja, in one place, together.

Pamoja na, together with, with.

Pana, there is or are, was or were.

-pana, broad, wide. It makes *pana* with nouns like *nyumba*.

Pana ku-, to make mutual gifts.

Panapana, flat, level, even.

Panapo, where there is, are, was or were.

Panchayat, five head men (Hind.), governing council.

Panda (M.) = *Panja*.

Panda, a bifurcation, as where a road divides into two, where two streams join, where the bough of a tree forks.

Njia panda, cross roads, or where three ways meet; there is a superstitious custom of emptying rubbish and dirt at such places.

Panda ku-, to mount, to get up, ascend, ride, to go on board, to go ashore (of a ship).

Panda ku-, to set aside.

Panda ku-, to plant, to sow.

Pandana ku-, to lie across one another.

Pande mbili, on both sides. See *Upande*.

Pandisha ku-, to make to go up, to hoist, to raise.

Panga ku-, to rent, to hire a house.

Panga ku-, to put in a line, to set in order.

Panga, plur. of *upanga*.

Pangana ku-, to be in rows.

Pangine, another place, other places. See *-ngine*.

Panginepo, elsewhere.

Pangisha ku-, to let a house to.

Pangisha ku-, to make people sit in rows or in order.

Pangu, my. See *-angu*.

Pangusa ku-, to wipe.

Panja, the forelock.

Mapanja, the receding of the hair on each side of the forelock.

Panua ku-, to widen, to make broad.

Panulia ku-, to widen for, to set wide apart.

Panuka ku-, to become broad, to widen.

Panya, a rat, rats.

Panyamavu, a quiet place, a calm spot. See *-nyamavu*.

Paza ku-, to set up, to raise.

Kupanza mtambo wa bunduki, to cock a gun.

Panzi, a grasshopper, a kind of fish.

Panzi ya nazi, brown rind of the cocoa-nut kernel.

Pao, their. See *ao*.

Pao, clubs (in cards).

P'apa, a shark.

Papa hapa, just here.

Papa ku-, to transude, to allow transudation.

Papasa ku-, to touch gently, to stroke, to feel, to grope.

Papasi, ticks, especially those found in native huts.

Papatika ku-, to flutter like a bird.

Papatua ku-, to shell, to husk.

Papayi, plur. *mapapayi*, papaws, a common kind of fruit.

Papayuka ku-, to be delirious, to wander.

Papayuza ku-, to make delirious.

Papia ku-, to eat all one can get, to eat without bounds.

Papua ku-, to tear.

Papura ku-, to claw, to scratch deeply.

Papuri, thin cakes flavoured with asafœtida.

Papurika ku-, to be lacerated.

Papuriana ku-, to pick holes in one another's reputation.

Para, a scraping, sliding.

Para, plur. *mapara*, cakes of semsem.

Parafujo, a screw.

Paraga ku-, to climb a tree.

Parahara, a large kind of antelope.

Parapara ku-, to paw the ground like a horse.

Paruga ku-, to be rough and grating.

Paruza ku-, to grate, to graze, to be harsh and rough, to strike a match.

Paruzana ku-, to graze (as of two boats, &c.).

Pasa ku-, or *Pasha ku-*, to come to concern, to become a duty.

Imekupasaje? What have you to do with it?

Imenipasa, I ought.

Pasha ku-, to lend money to, to give privately or beforehand.

Kupasha moto, to warm up, to set before the fire.

Pasi, a clothes-iron.

Kupiga pasi, to iron.

Pasipo, without, where there is not.

Pasiwe, without there being.

Pasua ku-, to cleave, to split, to rend.

Pasuka ku-, to become rent, to burst, to crack, to be split.

Pasukapasuka ku-, to be split up, rent to pieces.

Pata, a drawn game at cards where each side marks sixty.

Pata ku-, to get, to reach, to suffer, to find an opportunity, to succeed in doing, to happen to.

Kupata is often used with other verbs where we use may or might :

Apate kuja, that he may come.

Kisu chapata, the knife is sharp.

Kisu hakipati, the knife is blunt.

Kiliehompata, what happened to him.

Chapataje? What is it worth?

Kupata hasara, to lose.

Pata ku, to make a lattice, as by weaving sticks or canework.

Patana ku-, to agree, to come to an agreement.

Patanisha ku-, to bring to an agreement.

Patasi, a chisel.

Pathiwa ku-, to be born.

Pati, a coloured kind of stuff.

Patia ku-, to get for.

Patiala, a great cheat, a thorough rogue.

Patikana ku-, to be procurable, to be got.

Patiliza ku-, to visit upon, to remember against.

Pato, plur. *mapato*, what is got, gettings, income, proceeds.

Patta, a hinge.

Patwa ku-, to be eclipsed.

Properly, to be got, referring to the superstition that a huge snake has seized the moon or sun.

Pau (plur. of *Upau*), the purlins of a roof, the small sticks tied horizontally to fasten the thatch to. Also, rafters (?).

Payo, plur. *mapayo*, one who cannot keep a secret.

Payuka ku-, to blab, to talk without thinking.

Payuza ku-, to make over-talkative.

Tembo limempayuza, the palm wine has made his tongue go.

Pazia, plur. *mapazia*, a curtain.

Pea, a rhinoceros.

Pea ku-, to sweep (M.).

Pea ku-, to grow to full size, to get its growth, to become such that there is nothing more to do, to reach its limit.

Pekecha ku-, to bore a hole, to get fire by twirling a stick, to trouble people by tales and tale-bearing.

Peketeka ku-, to scorn, to have no fear about one.

Pekee, onliness.

Wa pekee, only.

Peke yangu, &c., by myself, I alone.

Peke is never used in Zanzibar without a possessive pronoun following it, and signifies that the person or thing is alone, or that it is the only one.

Pekeyetu, by ourselves, or we alone.

Pekua ku-, to scratch like a hen.

Pele, plur. of *upele*, the itch.

Peleka ku-, to cause to arrive at a place distant from the person speaking, to send, to take, to conduct.

Pelekea ku-, to send, take, or conduct to a person.

Peleleza ku-, to spy out, to look curiously into.

P'embe, horn, corner, ivory.

Pembe ya nyoka, a small white horn, esteemed to be a great medicine.

Kuwa na pembe pembe, to have corners, to be angular, to be all corners.

Pembeni, in the corner.

Pembe za mwaka, the four seasons, points of the world.

Pembea, a swing.

Pembeleza ku-, to beseech.

Pembeza ku-, to rock, to lull.

Penda ku-, to like, to love, to wish, to approve, to choose, to prefer.

Pendekeza ku-, to make pleasing.

Kujipendekeza, to ingratiate oneself with, to flatter.

Pendelea ku-, to favour.

Pendeleo, plur. *mapendeleo*, a favour.

Pendeleza ku-, to make another love one.

Pendeza ku-, to please, to become pleasing.

Pendezewa ku-, to be pleased, to be glad.

Pendo, love.

Pendo la mali, the love of riches.

Pengi, many places. See *-ingi*.

Pengo, a notch, a place where a triangular bit is broken out.

Ana pengo, he has lost a front tooth.

Penu, your. See *-enu*.

Penya ku-, to penetrate.

Penyesha ku-, to pierce, to put through, to cause to penetrate.

Penyi, having (of place), where is or was.

Penyi mtende, where the date tree was.

Pepa ku-, to stagger.

Pepea ku-, to fan.

Pepeo, plur. *mapepeo*, a fan, a screw propeller.

Peperuka ku-, to be blown away.

Peperusha ku-, to blow away.

Pepesa ku-, to wink.

Pepesuka ku-, to totter.

Pepeta ku-, to sift, to toss in a flat basket, so as to separate the chaff and the grain.

Pepetua ku-, to force open.

Pepo, a spirit, a sprite, an evil spirit.

Pepo mbaya, an evil spirit.

Peponi, paradise, in paradise.

Pepo (plur. of *upepo*), much wind.

Pepo za chamchela, a whirlwind.

Maji ya pepo, fresh water.

Pepua ku-, to sift apart the whole from the broken grains.

Pera, plur. *mapera*, a guava.

Pesa, plur. *pesa* or *mapesa*, pice, the Anglo-Indian quarter anna, the only small coin in Zanzibar; sometimes a dollar is worth 140, sometimes only 112.

Pesa ku- (M.) = *Pepesa ku-*.

Peta ku-, to bend round, to make into a ring.

Peta ku- = *Pepeta ku-*.

Petana ku-, to bend round, to be bent in a circle.

Pete, plur. *pete* or *mapete*, a ring.

Pete ya masikio, an earring.

Petemana ku-, to be bent round.

Peto, plur. *mapeto*, a bundle, a thing carried, a large matting bag.

Petu, our. See *-etu*.

-pevu, full grown.

Pevua ku-, to make full grown.

Kujipevua, to think oneself a man.

Pevuka ku-, to become full grown, to reach its full size.

Pewa ku-, to get from some one, to be presented with, to receive.

Pezi, plur. *mapezi*, a fin.

-pi subjoined to the personal sign makes the interrogative which? See *Api*.

Nitawezapi? How can I?

-pia or *-pya*, new.

Pia, all, the whole, entirely.

Pia yote, completely, utterly.

Pia, a top, a humming-top.

Piga ku-, to strike, to beat, to flap.

Kupiga na inchi, to strike on the ground.

Kupiga is used of many actions in which the idea of striking does not always seem to be implied.

Kupiga bomba, to pump.

" *bunduki, bastola*, &c., to fire a gun, a pistol, &c.

" *chapa*, to print.

" *falaki*, to prognosticate by the stars.

" *fundo*, to tie a knot.

" *kelele*, to shout.

" *kengele*, to ring a bell.

" *kilemba*, to wind a cloth round the head so as to make a turban.

" *kiowé*, to scream.

" *kofi*, to box the ears, to slap.

" *kura*, to cast lots.

" *makofi*, to clap the hands.

" *magote*, to kneel.

" *mbinda*, to whistle.

Kupiga mbio, to run, to gallop.

" *mbizi*, to dive.

" *miao, misono*, or *miunzi*, to make a whistling noise.

" *mikambe*, in bathing, to duck under water and fling over one leg.

Kupiga mizinga ya salaamu, to fire a salute.

" *mstari*, to rule a line.

" *mtakaso*, to rustle like new clothes.

" *mvuke*, to smoke meat, &c.

" *nyiayo*, to gape.

" *pasi*, to iron.

" *pembe*, to gore.

" *pigo*, to strike a blow.

" *pua*, to snort.

" *ramli*, to prognosticate by diagrams.

" *randa*, to plane.

" *teke*, to kick.

" *umeme*, to lighten, to flash.

" *uwinda*, to draw the ends of the loin cloth between the legs and tuck them in.

" *yowe*, to cry for help.

" *zomari, kinanda*, &c., to play upon the flageolet, guitar, &c.

Pigana ku-, to fight.

Kupigana kwa mbavu, to wrestle.

Piganisha ku-, to make to fight, to set on.

Piganishana ku-, to set on to fight together.

Pigilia ku-, to beat as the stone roofs are beaten. Small wooden rammers are used, and a great number of people are engaged for about three days, with music and songs; the object of this beating is to prevent the roof cracking as it dries, and to consolidate it while moist.

Pigiza ku-, to make to beat.

Kupigiza tanga, to go so close to the wind that the sail flaps.

Pigo, plur. *mapigo*, a blow.

Pika ku-, to cook.

Pikia ku-, to cook for.

Kupikiwa, to have cooked for one.

Pilao, pillaw, an Indian dish.

P'ili, a large kind of snake.

Pili, two (in counting).

Ya pili, the second.

Ya pili yake, the next.

Yule wa pili, the other.

Mara ya pili, a second time, again.

Philipili hoho, red pepper.

Pilipili manga, common pepper.

Pima, plur. *mapima*, a fathom.

Pima ku-, to measure, to weigh.

Kupima maji, to sound.

Pinda ku-, to bend.

Kupinda na mguu, talipes.

Pindana ku-, to bend together.

Pindi, plur. *mapindi*, a twisting, a wriggle, cramp.

Pindi, if, when (?), although.

Pindo, plur. *mapindo*, the longer edge of a cloth, selvedge.

Pindua ku-, to turn over, to upset.

Kupindua kwa damalini, to wear ship.

Kupindua kwa goshini, to tack.

Pinduka ku-, to be turned over, to be upset.

Pinga ku-, to hinder, to block the way, to lay a wager.

Kupinga chombo kwa shikio, to turn a dhow on one side by means of the rudder.

Pingamizi, a meddler, one who interferes to spoil a bargain, or to give trouble.

Pingia ku-, to fasten a door, &c., by means of a bar.

Pingili.

Pingili ya mua, the piece of a sugar-cane which lies between two knots.

Pingo, plur. *mapingo*, a bar.

Pingu, fetters, consisting generally of two rings and a bar.

Pini, plur. *mapini*, a haft, a hilt.

Pipa, plur. *mapipa*, a barrel, tub, cask, pipe.

Pipya, new. See *-pya*.

Pirikana ku-, to be strong and well knit.

Pisha ku-, to make to pass, especially without intending to do so, let pass, make way for.

Pishana ku-, to pass while going opposite ways.

Pishi, a weight of about 6 lbs. = 4 *ribaba*.

Pisho, cautery, marks of cautery.

Pisi, parched maize.

Pisi = *Fisi*.

Pisiwa ku-, to become silly, to dote.

Pita ku, to pass, surpass, excel.

Pitisha ku-, to make to pass, to pass.

Po, *-po*, or *-po-*, a particle signifying where, or when, while, as, if.

Po pote, everywhere, wherever.

Poa ku-, to become cool, to become well.

Podo, a quiver.

Pofu, plur. *mapofu*, scum, bubble, froth.

Pofua ku-, to spoil the eyes, to make blind.

Pofuka ku-, to have the eyes spoilt, to become blind.

Pogo, on one side.
Kwenda pogo, to go onesidedly, not straight.
Pointa, the wrist-stitching of a coat.
Poka ku-, to take suddenly and violently, to rob.
Kupokwa, to be robbed.
Pokea ku-, to receive, to take from some one else.
Pokelea ku-, to receive for or on account of another.
Pŏkezana ku-, to go on with by turns.
Pokezanya ku-, to shift a burden or work from one to another as each gets tired.
Pokonya ku-, to snatch away, to extort.
Pole, a little, slightly.
Amengua pole, he is not very well.
Polepole, gently, moderately, quietly.
Pombe, native beer.
Pomboo, a porpoise.
Pomoka ku-, to fall in, to cave in. See *Bomoka*.
Pomosha ku-, to cause to fall in.
Pona ku-, to get well, to become safe.
Ponda ku-, to pound, to beat up, to crush.
Pondeka ku-, to be crushed.
Pondekana ku-, to crush and bruise one another, as *mtama* stalks do after much rain and wind.
Pono, a kind of fish said to be nearly always asleep.
Ana usingizi kama pono, he is never awake.
Ponoa ku-, to strip off.
Ponya ku-, to make well, to cure, to save.
Jiponye! Look out!
Ponyesha ku-, to cause to be made well, to cure.
Ponyoka ku-, to slip off, slip out of one's hands.
Ponza ku-, to put in danger.
Poopoo, a bullet, a musket ball.
Pooza, plur. *mapooza*, a thing which never comes to perfection.
Pooza ku-, to become useless, to wither and drop.
Mwenyi kupooza, a paralytic.
Poozesha ku-, to paralyze.
Popo, a bat.
Popoo, the areca nut, commonly chewed with betel-leaf, lime, and tobacco.
Popotoa ku-, to wring, twist, strain, distort.
Popotoka ku-, to be distorted.
Pora, a young cockerel not yet old enough to crow.
Poroa ku-, to cool, to get thin or watery.
Poromoka ku-, to slip down a steep place. Also *Boromoka*.
Posa ku-, to ask in marriage.
Posha ku-, to give rations to.
Posho, rations.
Poso, a demand in marriage.
Posoro, an interpreter, a middleman.
Pote, all, of time or place. See *-ote*.
Potea ku-, to become lost, to get lost, to perish, to become lost to.
Kisu kimenipotea, I have lost my knife.
Potelea ku-, to perish.
Potelea mbali, go and be hanged.
Poteza ku-, to cause to be lost, to cause to perish.
Potoa ku-, to go crooked, to turn aside. See *Jipotoa*.

-potoe, obstinate, good for nothing.

Potoka ku-, to become crooked, to be turned and twisted.

Povu, scum, skimmings, bubble, froth.

Povuka ku- = *Pofuka ku-*, to become blind.

Poza ku-, to cure, to cool by lading up and pouring back again.

Pua, the nose, the apex of an arch.

Mwanzi wa pua, the division between the nostrils, the nostril.

Pua, steol.

Pua ku-, to shell beans, peas, &c.

Pugi, a very small kind of dove.

Pujua ku-.

Kujipujua, to cast off all shame.

Pukusa ku-, to rub the grains off a cob of Indian corn, to make to fall off, to shake fruit from a tree, to throw coins among a crowd, &c.

Pukute.

Pukute ya wali, rice so cooked that the grains are dry and separate.

Pukutika ku-, to shed, to drop like leaves in autumn.

Pulika ku-, to hear, to attend to (A.).

Pulikana ku-, to hear one another.

Puliza ku-, to puff or blow with the mouth. Also, to let go an anchor, to let down a bucket into a well.

Puliki, a spangle, spangles.

Pululu, plur. *mapululu*, wilderness, waste country.

Puluni or *Pululuni*, in the wilderness.

Puma ku-, to throb.

Pumba, plur. *mapumba*, a clod, a lump.

Pumbaa ku-, to be sluggish about.

Pumbazika ku-, to become a fool.

Pumbo or *pumbu*, the scrotum.

Mapumbu, or *koko za pumbu*, or *mayayi ya pumbo*, testicles.

Pumu, an asthma, the lungs.

Pumua ku-, to breathe.

Pumuzi, breath.

Kupaaza pumuzi, to draw in the breath, to inspire.

Kushusha pumuzi, to breathe out, to expire.

Pumzi = *Pumuzi*.

Pumzika ku-, to rest, to breath oneself.

Pumzikio, plur. *mapumzikio*, a resting-place.

Puna ku-, to peel, scrape, scrape off.

Punda, a donkey, donkeys.

Punda milia, a zebra.

Punde, a little more.

Mrefu punde, a little longer.

Punga (sing. *Upunga*), the flower and very first stage of the cocoanut.

Punga ku-, to swing, to sway, to wave. Swaying the arms in walking is thought to give elegance to a womau's carriage.

Kupunga pepo, to expel au evil spirit by music, dancing, &c.

Kukunga upepo, to be fanned by the wind, to beat the air.

Pungia ku-, to wave to, to beckon to.

Kupungia nguo, to wave a cloth up and down by way of beckoning to some one to come.

P'ungu, a kind of fish, a large bird of prey.

Pungua ku-, to diminish, waste, wear away.

Punguani, a defect (M.).

Punguka ku-, to become smaller, to fall short.

Pnnguza ku-, to diminish, to make less, to lessen.

Kupunguza tanga, to reef a sail.

Punja ku-, to swindle, to sell a little for the price of a large quantity.

Punje, grains of corn.

Puo, nonsense.

Pupa, eagerness, excessive rapidity.

Kula kwa pupa, to eat so voraciously that one's companions get little or none.

Puputika ku-, to fall in a shower.

Pura ku-, to beat out corn.

Puruka ku-, to fly off.

Purukusha ku-.

Kujipurukusha, to refuse to attend to, to make light of a matter.

Puta ku-, to beat.

Putika ku-, to be well beaten.

Putugali, a fowl [Pemba].

Puwo, nonsense.

Puza ku-, to talk nonsense, to chatter.

Puzia ku-, to breathe, to blow with the mouth.

Puzika ku-, to talk nonsense, to be detained gossiping.

Pwa ku-, to ebb, to become dry.

Pwaga ku- = *Kupwaya*.

Pwai ku-, to be loose, to waggle about. See *Pwaya*.

Pwani, the shore, on the beach, near the shore.

Pwaya ku-, to give a final cleaning to rice by repounding it.

Pwaya ku-, to be loose (of clothes).

Pwayika ku- to be quite clear of husks, dirt, and dust.

Pwaza ku-, to cook *muhogo* cut up into small pieces.

Pwea ku-, to be dry.

Sauti imenipwea, I am hoarse.

Pwekee, only, alone (A.).

Pweleka ku-, to be dried up, to be left high and dry.

Pwewa ku-, to become or be left dry.

Kupwewa na sauti, to become hoarse.

Pweza, a cuttle-fish.

-pya, new, fresh. It makes *'mpya* with nouns like *nyumba*; *jipya*, with nouns like *kasha*; and *pipya*, with nouns of place.

R.

R is pronounced as in English.

The Arabic *R* is much stronger and more grating than the English, more so perhaps than even the Scotch and Irish *r*. In Arabic words it is correct to give the *r* this strong sound, but in Swahili mouths it is generally smoothed down towards that indeterminate African sound which is frequently written as an *l*. The Swahili, however, often prefer to write and pronounce it as a smooth English *r*. (See L.)

Radi, a crack of thunder, crashing thunder, thunder near at hand.

Radu = *Radi*.

Raff, the wall at the back of a recess.

Rafiki, plur. *rafiki* or *marafiki*, a friend.

Raha, peace, joy, ease, pleasure.

Rahani, a pledge, a mortgage.

Rahisi = *Rakhisi*.

Rahman, a chart, a map.

Rai ku-, to put morsels of food into a person's mouth as a mark of honour or affection.

Rajabu, the seventh month of the Arab year. It is esteemed a sacred month because Mohammed's journey to Jerusalem is said to have taken place on the 27th of it.

Rakhisi, or *Rahisi*, cheap.

Rakhisisha ku-, to make cheap, to undervalue.

Rakibisha ku-, to put together, to set up and put in order.

Rakibyueo, the composition of a word.

Ramathani, the month of fasting.

Ramba, plur. *maramba*, a piece of Madagascar grass cloth.

Ramba ku-, to lick.

Ramba, a chisel-shaped knife used by shoemakers.

Ramli, sand (Ar.).

Kupiga ramli, to divine by diagrams.

Rammu, sadness.

Randa, a plane.

Kupiga randa, to plane.

Randa ku-, to dance for joy.

Rangi, colour, paint.

Rarua ku-, to rend, to tear.

Ras il mali, chief possession.

Rashia ku-, to sprinkle.

Rasi, head, cape.

Rátaba, wet.

Rátel, or *ratli*, a weight of about a pound.

Rathi, satisfied, content, gracious, approving, approval, blessing.

Kuwa rathi, to be satisfied, to be content with.

Niwie rathi, forgive me, excuse me.

Kunrathi, don't be offended.

Rathiana ku-, to consent, assent.

Ratibu ku-, to arrange.

Ratli = *Rátel*.

Rausi ku-, to trim a sail.

Rayia, a subject, subjects.

Rayiat al Ingrez, British subjects.

Re or *Rei*, the ace in cards.

Rea or *Reale*, a dollar.

Reale ya thahabu, an American gold 20-dollar piece.

Reale Fransa or *ya Kifransa*, a French 5-franc piece.

Reale ya Sham or *Fetha ya Sham*, black dollars.

-refu, long. It makes *ndefu* with nouns like *nyumba*.

Regea ku- = *Rejea ku-*.

Regea ku- or *Legea ku-*, to be loose, slack, relaxed, feeble.

Regesha ku- or *Regeza ku-*, to loosen, to relax.

Rehani = *Rahani*.

Kuweka rehani, to pawn.

Rehema, mercy.

Rehemu ku-, to have mercy upon.

Rei = *Re*.

Rejea ku-, to go back, return, refer.

Rejeza ku-, to make to go back, to repay.

Rekabisha ku-, to put on the top of.

Rekebu ku-, to ride.

-remo, Portuguese.

Rihani, a scented herb, sweet basil.

" *ya kipata*, with notched leaves.

" *ya kiajjemi*, with long straight leaves.

Ringa ku- = *Kulinga*, to sway to the tune of a song (only the chief men may do this).

Risasi, lead. Also ***Lisasi***.

Risasi ya bunduki, a bullet.

Risimu ku-, to make a first bid when anything is offered for sale.
Rithi ku-, to inherit (*-th-* as in thing).
Rithia ku- (*-th-* as in this), to be contented with, to acquiesce in.
Rithika ku-, to satisfy, to content.
Riza, a door chain.
Riziki, necessaries, all that a man has need of.
Robo, a quarter, a quarter of a dollar.
Robo Ingreza, an English sovereign.
Robota, a packet or parcel of goods.
Roda, sheave of a pulley.
Rofya.
Kupiga rofya, to fillip.
Roho, soul, spirit, breath, life.
Roho, greediness, the throat.
Rubani, a pilot, a guide.
Rudi ku-, to return, to go back, to correct, to keep in order.
Rudiana ku-, to object to.
Rudika ku-, to be made to return, to be kept in order, to be capable of being kept in order.
Rudisha ku-, to make to return, to give back, to send back.
Rudufya ku-, to double.
Rufuf, the shelf in a recess.
Ruhusa = *Ruksa*, leave.
Ruhusa ku- = *Rukhusu ku-*, to give leave.
Ruka ku-, to fly, to leap.
Rukaruka ku-, to hop.
Rukia ku-, to fly or leap with, &c.
Ruksa, or *Ruhusa*, or *Rukhusa*, leave, permission, liberty.
Kupa ruksa, to give leave, to set at liberty, to dismiss.
Ruksa, you can go.
Rukhusu ku- or *Ruhusu ku-*, to give leave, to permit, to allow, to dismiss.
Rukhuthu ku-, to run.
Rukwa ku-.
Kurukwa na akili, to lose one's senses, to be stunned.
Rungu, a club, a mace.
Rupia, a rupee.
Rupta = *Robota*, a bale.
Rusasi = *Risasi*, lead.
Rusha ku-, to make to fly, to throw up or off, to throw a rider, to splash about.
Rushia ku-, to throw upon, to splash.
Rushwa, a bribe.
Rutuba, dampness.
Rutubika ku-, to be damp.
Rutubisha ku-, to make damp.
Ruwasa, a pattern from which anything is to be made.
Ruzuku ku-, to supply with needful things, especially of God providing for His creatures.

S.

S is pronounced as in *several*, or like the *ss* in German.

Sh is pronounced as in English, or like *sch* in German.

S and *sh* are distinct in Arabic and are generally distinguished in good Swahili. There are, however, many words in which they are used indifferently, and in common talk the *sh* seems to be rather the more common. Many natives seem unconscious of any difference between them.

S is used for the Arabic *tha* by persons who cannot pronounce *th*.

In the Pemba dialect *sh* is often used for *ch*.

Mashungwa = *Machungwa*.

Saa, hour, clock, watch.

Saa ngapi? what o'clock is it? According to Arab reckoning the day begins at sunset. Midnight is *usiku saa ya sita;* four A.M. *saa a kumi;* six A.M. *saa a thenashara;* noon, *saa a sita.*

Saa! You! I say! You now!

Njoo saa! Come along, do!

Saa ku-, to remain over, to be left.

Saala, plur. *masaala*, a question.

Saanda, a shroud, a winding-sheet.

Saba, or *Saba'a*, seven.

Ya saba, seventh.

Sabaa, a stay (in a dhow).

Sababu, cause, reason.

Kwa sababu ya, because of, because.

Sabaini, seventy, = *Sabwini*.

Sabatashara, seventeen.

Sabuni, soap.

Sabuni ku-, to bid, to be in treaty, to buy.

Saburi, patience.

Saburi ku-, to wait.

Sabwini, seventy.

Sadaka, an offering, an alms, an act of charity, anything done for the love of God.

Sadiki ku-, to believe.

Safari, a journey, a voyage, used for "time" or "turn."

Safari hii, this time.

Saff, serene.

Safi, pure, clean.

Safi ku-, to clean.

Safidi ku-, to clear up, to make smooth and neat.

Safihi, rudeness

Safika ku-, to be purified.

Safina (Ar.), a vessel.

Safiri ku- to travel, to set out on a journey, sail, start.

Safirisha ku-, to make to travel, to see any one off.

Safisha ku-, to make pure or clean.

Safu, a row, rows, a line.

Safu za kaida, regular rows.

Safura, biliousness, gall, a complaint in which people take to eating earth.

Saga ku-, to grind.

Kusagwa na gari, to be run over by a cart.

Sagai, a spear, a javelin.

Sagia ku-, to grind with or for.

Mawe ya kusagia, millstones, a mill, a handmill. Two loose stones are often used, the upper one is called *mwana*, and the lower *mama*.

Sahani, a dish.

Sahari, checked stuff for turbans.

Sahau ku- or *Sahao ku-*, to forget, to make a mistake.

Sahauliwa ku-, to be forgotten.

Sahib, sir.

Sahibu, a friend.

Sahili.

Kutia sahili, to sign.

Sahihi, correct, right.

Sahihi ku-, to be correct, to be right.

Sahihisha ku-, to correct.

Saili ku-, to ask, to question.

Sailia ku-, to ask on behalf of.

Saka ku-, to hunt.

Sakafu, a *chunammed* floor, a floor or roof of stone, covered with a mixture of lime and sand, and beaten for about three days with small wooden rammers.

Sakama ku-, to become jammed, to stick fast.

Sakani, a rudder.

Saki ku-, to come close to, to touch, to come home.

Sakifu ku-, to make a *chunammed* floor or roof.

Sala, prayer, the prescribed Mohammedan form of devotion including the proper gestures.

Salaama = *Salama*.

Salaam, or *Salaamu*, or *Salamu*, compliments, safety, peace.

Kupiga mizinga ya salamu, to fire a salute.

Salahisha ku-, or *Selehisha*, or *Suluhisha*, to make to be at peace.

Salala, the meat near the backbone, the undercut of meat.

Salama, safe, safety.

Sali ku-, to use the regular Mohammedan devotions, to say one's prayers.

Salia ku-, to be left, to remain.

Salimu ku-, to salute.

Salimia ku-, to salute, to send compliments to.

Saliti ku-, to betray secrets.

Saluda, a sweetmeat made of saffron, sugar, and starch.

Sama ku-, to choke, to be choked.

Samadi, manure.

Samaki, a fish, fish.

Samani, tools, instruments, machine.

Samawati, the heavens.

Samawi, blue, sky colour.

Sambusa, a little pasty.

Samehe ku-, to forgive, to pass over.

Samiri ku-, to load a gun.

Sa'mli, ghee, clarified butter.

Sana, very, much. It is used to intensify any action.

Sema sana, speak loud.

Vuta sana, pull hard.

Sanamaki, senna.

Sanamu, an image, a likeness, a statue, a picture, an idol.

Sandale, sandal wood.

Sandarusi, gum copal, gum amini.

Sanduku, a chest, a box.

Saniki ku-, to make excuse.

Sapa ku-, to tout for customers.

Sarafu, a small coin.

Sarifa or *Sarf*, exchange, rate of exchange.

Sarifa gani ya niji sasa? What is the current rate of exchange?

Sarifu ku-, to use words well and correctly.

Sáruf, grammar.

Sarufu, a small gold plate with a devout inscription, worn on the forehead as an ornament.

Sasa, now.

Sasa hivi, directly, at once.

Sataranji, chess.

Sauti, voice, sound, noise.

Sawa, equal, right, just.

Kitu kisichokuka sawa naye, something unworthy of him.

Sawanisha ku-, to make alike, equal, even, &c.

Sawasawa, like, alike, even, all the same, level, smooth, equal.

Sawawa, peas (Yao.).

Sawazisha ku-, to make equal or alike.

-sayara, gentle, quiet, long-suffering.

Sayidia ku-, to help.

Sayili ku- = *Saili ku-*.

Saza ku-, to leave over, to make to remain.

Sazia ku-, to leave for.

Sebabu = *Sababu*, cause, reason.

Sebula or *Sebule*, reception room, parlour.

Sefluti, a poultice.

Sehemu, part, share, dividend.

Sekeneko, syphilis.

Selaha, a weapon.

Kupa selaha, to arm.
Selehisha ku- = *Suluhisha*, to make to be at peace, to mediate between.
Selimu ku- or *Sillim ku-*, to capitulate.
Sema ku-, to say, to talk, to speak.
Sema sana, speak out.
Semadari, a bedstead, specially of the Indian pattern.
Sembuse, much less.
Semea ku-, to say about.
Kusemea puani, to talk through the nose.
Semeji = *Shemegi*.
Sena, a kind of rice.
Sengenya ku-, to make secret signs of contempt about some one who is [present.
Senturi, a musical box.
Sera, a rampart.
Serkali or *Serikali*, the court, the government.
Mtu wa serikali, a man in government employ.
Sermala, a carpenter.
Seruji, an Arab saddle.
Sesemi, blackwood.
Seta ku-, to crush.
Setaseta ku-, to crush up, to break into fragments.
Seti, the seven in cards.
Setirika, &c. See *Stirika*, &c.
Settini, sixty.
Settiri, an iron (?).
Settiri ku-, or *Setiri*, or *Sitiri*, to cover, to conceal, to hide, to atone for.
Seuze, much less, much more. Also *Sembuse*.
Seyedia, lordly, belonging to the Seyed.
Seyédina (Ar.), our lord, your majesty.
Sezo, an adze.
Shaabani, the eighth month of the Arab year.
Shaba, copper, brass.
Shabaha, aim.
Kutwaa shabaha, to take aim.
Shabaha, like.
Nyama shabaha mbwa, an animal like a dog.
Shabbu, alum.
Shabuka, a snare.
Shadda, a tassel. See *Kanzu*.
Shah, a chess king.
Shaha, the heart of the cocoa-nut tree.
Shahada, the Mohammedan confession of faith. Also *Ushahada*.
Shahamu, fat.
Shahawa (obscene), semen.
Shahidi, plur. *mashahidi*, a witness, a martyr.
Shaibu (Ar.), an old person.
Shaibu la juzi, exceedingly old.
Shairi, a line of poetry.
plur. *mashairi*, verses, a poem.
Shaka, a bush.
Shaka, plur. *mashaka*, a doubt.
Shake.
Kuingia na shake ya kulia, to sob.
Shali, a shawl.
Sham, Syria, Damascus.
Fetha ya Sham, German dollars.
Shamba, plur. *mashamba*, a plantation, a farm, a piece of land in the country.
Shambulia ku-, to attack.
Shamua ku-, to sneeze. Also *Shumua*.
Shanga, a town near Melinda, long since ruined.
Shanga.
Mwana shanga, a northerly wind, not so strong or persistent as the regular *kaskazi*.

Shangaa ku- or *Sangaa ku-*, to be astonished, to stand and stare, to stop short.

Shangaza ku-, to astound, to astonish.

Shangazi, plur. *mashangazi*, an aunt.

Shangilia ku-, to make rejoicings for, to go to meet with music and shouting, to be glad about.

Shangwi, triumph, shouting and joy, an ornament of gold worn by women between the shoulders.

Shani, a startling, unexpected event.

Shanuu, plur. *mashanuu*, a comb, a large coarse wooden comb.

Sharbu, a moustache.

Shari, evil, the opposite of *Heri*.

Sharia = *Sheria*.

Shariki ku-, to share, to be partners in.

Sharikia ku-, to share with, to be in partnership with.

Sharikiana ku-, to be partners, to share together.

Sharti, or *Sharuti*, or *Shuruti*, or *Shuti*, a contract, of obligation, of necessity, must. Also, the downhaul of a dhow-sail, a truss.

Kufanya sharti, to bind oneself.

Shatoruma, shawl for the waist.

Shauko, love, exceeding fondness, strong desire, will.

Shauri, plur. *mashauri*, advice, counsel, plan.

Kufanya shauri, to consult together.

Kupa shauri, to advise.

Shawi = *Tawi*.

Shawishi ku-, to persuade, to coax over.

Shayiri, barley.

Shehena, cargo.

Sheitani, Satan, the devil, a devil, excessively clever.

Shela, a black veil.

Shelabela, as it stands, in a lot, with all defects.

Shelele ku-, to run a seam.

Shelle, plur. *mashelle*, a shell.

Shema (Ar.), bees-wax.

Shemali (Ar.), the left, the north (because to the left of a person looking east); the Persian Gulf, Arabs (because to the north of Muscat); mist (because it comes on in the Persian Gulf with a northerly wind).

Shembea, a kind of curved knife.

Shemegi, a brother or sister-in-law.

Shena (Ar.), orchilla weed.

Sheria, law.

Sherfz, glue.

Shetani, plur. *mashetani* = *Sheitani*.

Shetri, the poop of a dhow.

Shiba ku-, to have had enough to eat, to be full, to be satisfied.

Shibiri or *Shibri*, a span.

Shibisha ku-, to fill with food, to satisfy with food.

Shidda, difficulty, distress.

Shika ku-, to lay hold of, to hold fast, to keep, to determine.

Kushika njia, to take one's way, to set out.

Shika lako, mind your own business.

Shika ras ile, steer for that point.

Shikamana ku-, to cleave together.

Shikana ku-, to clasp, to grapple, to stick together.

Shikio, a rudder, a thing to lay hold of. See *Sikio*.

Shikiza ku-, to prop up.

Shilamu, the stem leading to the

mouthpiece in a native pipe. See *Kiko.*

Shimo, plur. *mashimo*, a pit, an excavation, a large hole.

Shina, plur. *mashina*, a stump, a trunk, a main root.

Shinda ku-, to overcome, to conquer, to stay, to continue at.

Maji yashinda, it is half full of water.

Amekwenda shinda, he is gone out for the day.

Akashinda kazi, and he went on at his work.

Shindana ku-, to dispute, strive with, race.

Shindania ku-, to bet, to oppose, to object to.

Shindano, plur. *mashindano*, a race. See *Sindano.*

Shindika ku-, or *Sindika*, to shut, to put to, to press in a mill.

Kushindika mafuta ya nazi, to grind cocoa-nuts into oil.

Shindikia ku-, to show any one out, to escort a person on his way. See *Sindikiza.*

Shindilia ku- to press, to load a gun.

Shindo, a shock.

Shingari, a consort, a dhow sailing in company with another.

Shingari ku-, to sail in company (of dhows).

Shingo, plur. *mashingo*, the neck.

Shinikizo or *Sinikizo*, a press.

Shirazi, Shiraz, from Shiraz. Persian work is generally called *shirazi.*

Shishwa ku-, to be weaned.

Shitumu ku-, to insult. See *Shutumu.*

Shoga, a friend; used only by women in speaking of or to one another. In Zanzibar they rarely employ any other word. At Lamoo *shoga* means a catamite.

Shogi, panniers, a large matting bag with the opening across the middle, so as to form two bags when laid across a donkey's back.

Shoi = *Shogi.*

Shoka, plur. *mashoka*, an axe.

Shoka la bapa, an adze.

Shoka la tiss, an axe (Mer.).

Shoka la pwa, an adze (Mer.).

Shola, an ear of corn, a head of grass.

Shona ku-, to sew.

Shonea ku-, to mend for, to sew for, with, &c.

Shonuka ku-, to become unsewn.

Shote.

Kwenda shote, to go with a rush.

Shoto.

Wa kushoto, left.

Ana shoto, he is left-handed.

Shtaki ku-, to prosecute, to charge, to accuse.

Shtua ku-, to startle, to tickle. See *Stusha.*

Shtuka ku-, to be startled, to start.

Shua ku-, to launch. Pass. *kushuliwa.*

Shuba, the elders of a town.

Shubaka, plur. *mashubaka*, a recess in a wall.

Shudu, what is left when the oil has been ground out of *semsem* seed.

Shughuli, business, affairs, occupation, engagement.

Shughulika ku-, to be occupied, to be worried.

Shughulisha ku-, to occupy, to distract attention, to interrupt.

Shuhuda, testimony.

Shuhudia ku-, to bear witness about, for, or against.

Shuhudu ku-, to bear witness.
Shuhuti.
Shuhuti ya kutolea chani, a small piece of wood used by shoemakers in cutting strips of coloured leather.
Shujaa, plur. *mashujaa*, a hero, a brave man.
Shuka, a sheet.
Shuka ku-, to descend, go down, come down, be let down, to land from a ship.
Shuke, the flower of Indian corn.
Shukrani, gratitude.
Shuku ku-, to suspect.
Shukuru, thanks.
Shukuru ku-, to thank. This word is very rarely used in Zanzibar, except in relation to God; and *kushukuru Muungu* means almost always, to take comfort, to leave off mourning, or to become resigned.
Shuliwa ku-, to be launched.
Shumua ku-, to sneeze.
Shumvi, salt [Pemba]. See *Chumvi.*
Shunga ku-, to drive away, to scare.
Shungi, a crest, long hair (?).
Shungi mbili, a way of dressing the hair in two masses.
Shupatu, plur. *mashupatu*, a narrow strip of matting. The broader are sewn together to make floor mats, the narrower are interlaced to make the native couch or bedstead.
Shupaza, spades (in cards).
Shura, saltpetre.
Shuruti = *Sharti*, of necessity.
Shurutiza ku-, to compel, to force.
Alishurutizwa ndani, he was pushed in.
Shusha ku-, to let down, to make to descend, to land goods from a ship.
Kushusha pu'mzi, to breathe out, an expiration.
Shuti or *Shuuti* = *Sharti*, of necessity.
Shutumiwa ku-, to be reviled.
Shutumu ku-, to revile.
Shwali or *Shwari*, a calm.
Si, not.
Si vema, not well.
Si uza, sell not.
Si, is or are not.
Mimi si sultani, I am not a sultan; or, Am I not a sultan?
Si yeye, it is not he or him.
Si-, the opposite of *ndi-*, expressing, This is not it. Is not this it?

Simi,	*Sisisi*,
Siwe,	*Sinyi*,
Siye,	*Sio*, *sivyo*, *siyo*,
Sio, *siyo*, *silo*,	*Sizo*, *simo*.
Sicho, *sipo*, *siko*,	

Si-, sign of the first person negative.
Sikubali, I do not consent.
Sikukubali, I did not consent.
Sitakubali, I shall not consent.
In the present tense the final letter of verbs in *-a* becomes *-i*.
Sioni, I do not see.
-si- inserted between the personal prefix and the verb, is the sign of the negative imperative or subjunctive, the final letter of verbs in *-a* becoming an *-e*.
Nisione, that I may not see, let me not see, or without my seeing.
-si-, sign of the negative in expressing relation.
Asio, he who is or was not, or who will not be. Also *Asiye*.
-sipo-, sign of the tense expressing *not being*.

Asipoona, he not seeing, if he does not see, though he does not see, without his seeing, when he sees not.

Sia ku-, to give a sentence, to pronounce as with authority, to declare.

Siafu, a large reddish brown ant, that travels in great numbers and bites fiercely.

Siagi, cream, butter.

Sibu ku-, to get, to succeed. See *Subu*.

Sifa, praise, character, characteristic.

Sifara, a kind of rice.

Sifu ku-, to praise. Pass. *kusifiwa*.

Kujisifu, to magnify oneself, to boast.

Kusifu'mno, to overpraise, to flatter.

Sifule (a term of reproach), a meddlesome fool.

Sifuru, a cypher, a figure of nought.

Sigizia ku-, to tack (in needlework).

Sihi ku-, to entreat.

Sijafu, the cuff, the hem. See *Kanzu*.

Sijambo, I am well. The invariable answer to *hu jambo?* how are you?

Si jambo punde, I am a little better.

Sikamo or *Sikamoo*, for *Nashika mguu*, the salutation of a slave to a master.

Siki, vinegar.

Sikia ku-, to hear, to obey, to understand.

Sikilia ku-, to listen to, to attend to.

Sikiliana ku-, to be heard, to be audible.

Sikiliza ku-, to listen, to listen to.

Sikilizana ku-, to hear one another.

Sikio or *Shikio*, plur. *masikio*, the ear.

Sikitika ku-, to be sorry.

Sikitikia ku-, to be sorry for, to pity.

Sikitiko, plur. *masikitiko*, sorrow, grief.

Sikitisha ku-, to make sorry.

Sikiza ku-, to make to hear, understand, &c.

Sikizana ku-, to be mutually intelligible, to make one another hear.

Siku, a day of twenty-four hours, from sunset to sunset, days.

Siku kuu, a great day, a feast. The two great feasts are the three days at the end of the Ramathan, when every one makes presents, and three days after the tenth of *Thil hajj* or *Mfunguo wa tatu*, when every one ought to slaughter some animal, and feast the poor.

Siku a mwaka (see *Mwongo*, *Kigunzi*), the *Nairuz*, about the 23rd of August, the beginning of the Swahili and nautical year. The old custom is for every one, but especially the women, to bathe in the sea in the night or morning: then they cook a great mess of grain and pulse, which is eaten about noon by all who like to come. The fires are all extinguished and lighted again by rubbing two pieces of wood together. Formerly no inquiry was made as to any murder or violence committed on this day, and old quarrels used regularly to be fought out upon it.

Siku zote, always.

Silihi ku-, to improve, to reform.

Silihisha ku-, to make to improve, to reform.

Silimu ku-, to become a Mohammedan.

Simama ku-, to stand up, to come to a stand, to stop, to be erect, to stand in, to cost.

Simamia ku-, to stand by, to overlook workmen, to cost to.

Simamisha ku-, to make to stand.

Simanga ku-, to crow over, boast against.

Simanzi, grief, heaviness.

Simba, a lion, lions.

Simba uranga, a well-known mangrove swamp at the mouth of the Lufiji.

Simbati, a kind of wood brought from near Cape Delgado.

Sime, a short straight sword used on the mainland.

Simika ku-, to be erect, to be set up, to stand (often used in an obscene sense).

Simikia ku-.

Kusimikia mlango, to set up and build in a door.

Simikisha ku-, to set up.

Similla, *Simille*, *Simileni*, probably for *Bismillah*, the common cry in Zanzibar, meaning, make way, out of the way.

Similla punda, make way for a donkey.

Similla ubau, make way for a plank.

Simo, I am not in it, am not concerned, have nothing to do with it.

Simo.

Simo hii si njema, this event is not good.

Imeingia simo mpya, something new has turned up.

Simu, the electric telegraph.

Sindano, a needle (or *shindano*).

Sindano, a kind of rice.

Sindi, a long-tailed weasel.

Sindikia ku-, to crush.

Sindikiza ku-, to accompany part of the way.

Sindua ku-, to open, to set open.

Singa, hair of an animal.

Nyele za singa, straight hair, European hair.

Singa ku-, to scent, to put scent.

Singizia ku-, to slander, to spread false reports about.

Sini, China.

Sini, no matter.

Sinia, plur. *masinia*, a circular tray used to carry and set out food upon, generally of copper tinned.

Sinikiza ku-, to press.

Sinzia ku-, to doze, to nod, to flicker.

-sipo-, sign of the tense signifying the case of the thing mentioned not being.

Siri, secrecy.

Mambo ya siri, secret affairs, secrets.

Kwa siri, secretly.

Sisi, we, us. Sometimes pronounced *swiswi*, *suisui*, or *siswi*.

Sisi sote, all of us.

Sisi wote, both of us.

Sisimia ku-, to sigh (?).

Sisimizi, ants (?).

Sisitiza ku- (M.), to charge strictly, to charge to keep secret.

Sita, six.

Ya sita, sixth.

Sita ku-, to halt, to go lame (A.), to hide.

Sitaha, the deck.

Sitashara, sixteen.
Sitawi ku-, to flourish.
Ngoma ipi imesitawi, which dance is going best?
Sitawisha ku-, to make to flourish.
Siti, whistle (of a steamer or engine).
Sitti, my lady, lady.
Sittina, our lady. Applied by the Arabs to St. Mary.
Sivimoja, different.
Sivyo, it is not thus. See *Si-*.
Siwa, an ivory horn only used on great occasions.
Siwezi, I am not well. See *Weza ku-*.
Siyo, that is not it, no. See *Si-*.
Siyu or *Siu*, Siwi, the chief town of the district near Lamoo, the chief seat of old Swahili learning.
Soda, lunacy.
Sodo, a woman's napkin.
Sofe, wool.
Soge, *Sogi*, *Soi*, = *Shogi*.
Sogea ku-, to approach affectionately, to come near to.
Sogeza ku-, to lift to the lips and kiss, to bring near to.
Sogezea ku-, to put ready for, to bring for use.
Soko, plur. *masoko*, a market, a bazaar.
Kwenda sokoni, to go marketing.
Sokota ku-, to twist, to plait, to spin.
Soma ku-, to read, to perform devotions.
Soma, plur. *masoma*, a kind of dance.
Sombela ku-, to work oneself along on one's hands and seat without using the legs.
Somesha ku-, to teach to read, to lead devotions.
Somo, plur. *masomo*, something read, used as a title of friendship, a namesake.
Sonda ku-, to suck out.
Sondo, swelled (?) glands.
Songa ku-, to strangle, to squeeze, to stir together.
Songanasongano ku-, to press against one another like sheep in a flock.
Songea ku-, to push through, to shoulder your way through a crowd.
Sonjoa ku-, to wring.
Sonya ku- = *Kufyonya*.
Soruali, trousers.
Sosoneka ku-, to be hurt or ache, so as to writhe with pain.
Sosonesha ku-, to make to writhe with pain.
Sote, all; agreeing with *sisi*, we or us. See *-ote*.
Tu sote, we are together.
Twende sote, let us go together.
Soza ku-, to beach a boat or vessel.
Ssafi or *Safi*, pure, clean.
Staajabu ku-, to wonder much, to be greatly astonished.
Staamani ku-, to have confidence, to rest trustfully.
Stahabu ku-, to be pleased, to prefer.
Stahamili or *Stahimili*, patiently.
Stahi ku-, to honour, to have respect for.
Stahiba ku- (?), to prefer. See *Stahabu*.
Stahiki ku-, to resemble, to be of one sort with.
Stahili ku-, to deserve, to be worthy of, to be proper, to be right and fitting.
Astahili, serves him right.
Stahimili ku-, to bear, to endure, tolerate.
Stakabathi, earnest, fastening penny.
Stambuli, Constantinople.
Starehe ku-, to sit still, to be at rest, to remain quiet.

Starehe! Don't disturb yourself! don't get up!

Sterehisha ku-, to give rest to, to refresh. Also *Starehisha*.

Stirika ku-, to be covered, to be concealed.

Stusha ku-, to startle, to sprain, to put out of joint.

Subana, small pieces of meat roasted on two parallel sticks.

Subana, a thimble.

Subiri, patience.

Subiri, aloes.

Subiri ku-, to wait.

Subu ku-, to cast in a mould.

Subu ku- or *Sibu ku-*, to happen to.

Subui, morning.

Subulkheiri, good morning.

Suburi, patience.

Subutu ku- = *Thubutu ku-*.

Suduku ku-, to ascertain, to know the truth.

Suff, wool.

Suffi, a devotee, a hermit.

Suffuf, a great variety or number.

Sufi, woollen.

Sufuria, copper.

Sufuria, plur. *sufuria* or *masufuria*, a metal pot.

Sufuria ya chuma, an iron pot.

Sugu, a mark, a callous place. Also, obstinate, insensate.

Sugua ku-, to rub, to scrub, to brush, to scour.

Suheli, south.

Sui, an irrepressible, unconquerable man.

Sujudia ku-, to prostrate oneself to, to adore.

Sujudu ku-, to prostrate oneself, to bow down.

Suka ku-, to plait, to clean.

Sukari, sugar.

Sukari guru, half-made sugar.

Sukasuka ku, to shake, to agitate.

Suke, plur. *masuke* (or *shuke*), an ear of corn, a head of mtama, &c.

Sukua ku-, to slacken, to loose.

Sukuma ku-, to push, to urge.

Sukumi, a steersman, quartermaster.

Sukumiza ku-, to put upon another person, to say it is his business, to throw off from oneself, to push away in anger, to throw (a thing) at a person who wants it. Also, to avert (by sacrifice, &c.).

Sukutua ku-, to rinse out the mouth, to wash one's mouth.

Sulibi ku-, to crucify.

Sulibisha ku-, to crucify.

Sulihi ku-, to become, to be fitting for.

Sulika ku-, to turn about, become giddy

Sulimu ku-, to salute.

Sultani, plur. *masultani*, a sultan, a chief man. *Sultani* at Zanzibar does not mean a king; it is used of the head men of a village.

Sultán Rum, the Sultan of Turkey.

Sulubika ku-, to be strong.

Sulubu, strength, firmness.

Suluhisha ku-, to bring to accord, to make peace between.

Suluhu, concord.

Sululu, a curlew.

Sumba ku-, to sway away, to twist and turn oneself.

Sumbua ku-, to worry, to annoy, to give trouble.

Sumbuana ku-, to worry one another.

Sumbuka ku-, to be put to trouble, to be barassed, to be annoyed.

Sumbulia ku-, to speak sharply to.

Sumbusha ku-, to vex, harass, trouble, worry, annoy.

Sumu, poison.

Sumugh, gum-arabic.

Sungura, a rabbit (?), a hare (?).

Sunni, advisable, recommended, a tradition, what is advisable or recommended, but not compulsory.

Sunobari, deal wood.

Sunza ku-, to search for anything with a lighted brand at night.

Supaa ku-, to be very hard or dry.

Supana = *Supaa*.

Sura, a likeness, a resemblance, a chapter of the Koran.

Suria, plur. *masuria*, a concubine, a female slave.

Suriyama, born of a concubine.

Sururu, an insect that lives in cocoa-nut trees.

Surwali, trousers. See *Soruali*.

Sus, liquorice.

Suso, a kind of hanging shelf, a hammock.

Susupaa = *Supaa*.

Suta ku-, to reproach, to charge a man with slander, to slander, to seek out a man and ask whether he has said such and such things.

Su'udi, or *Suudi njema*, salvation, felicity.

Suza ku-, to stir up. Also, to rinse.

Suzia ku-, to turn with (?).

Swafi = *Safi*.

Swali, a question.

T.

T is pronounced as in English.

There are two *t*'s in Arabic, one much thicker than the English *t*, but only very careful speakers distinguish them in Swahili.

T at the beginning of a word has sometimes an explosive sound, as in *t'aka*, dirt. It is probable that this represents a suppressed *n*.

There is a slight difference in sound between the *t*'s of *tatu*, three, and *tano*, five, the former being the smoother, but natives do not seem conscious of the difference.

T in northern Swahili frequently becomes *ch* in the dialect of Zanzibar.

Kuteka, to laugh (M.) *kucheka* (Zanz.). But *kuteka*, to plunder, or to draw water, does not change.

Kutinda, to slaughter (M.) *kuchinja* (Zanz.).

There is no sound similar to that of the English *th* in the original language of Zanzibar. It occurs in some dialects of Swahili in place of *v* or *z*. There are however in Arabic four *th*'s. 1. *Tha*, pronounced like the English *th* in thing. 2. *Thal*, pronounced like the English *th* in this. 3 and 4. *Thad* and *Tha'* or *Dthau*, which are scarcely distinguished by the Arabs themselves, and have a very thick variety of the *thal* sound. Practically the two English *th*'s are quite sufficient, and the ear soon catches the right method of employing them.

The Indians and many Africans pronounce all these as *z*. Some Swahili confuse the various *th*'s with *z*, and employ the *thal* sound for words properly written with a *z*, as *wathiri* for *waziri*, a vizir.

-ta-, the sign of the future tense.

When the relative or the particles denoting time and place are inserted in the future, the prefix regularly becomes *-taka-*. It is possible however to retain *-ta-* to express a more definite sense.

Atakuja, he will come.

Atakayekuja, who will come.

Atakapokuja, when he shall come.

Atapokuja, when he come, or, if he shall come.

In the first person singular the *ni-*, which is the sign of the person, is often dropped.

Takuja = *Nitakuja*, I shall come.

Ta- at the beginning of Arabic verbs is the mark of the fourth or fifth conjugations or derived forms.

Taa, a lamp, especially the small open earthen lamps made in Zanzibar.

Taa, a large kind of flat fish.

Taa, beneath one's feet.

Taabika ku-, to be troubled.

Taabisha ku-, to trouble, to annoy.

Taabu, trouble.

Taadabu ku-, to learn manners.

Taajabisha ku-, to make to wonder, to astonish.

Taajabu ku-, to wonder, to be astonished. See *Staajabu*.

Taajazi ku-, to tire.

Ta'ali ku-, to study.

Taandu, a centipede.

Taatau ku-, to throw oneself about.

Tabaka, lining.

Tabakelo, a snuff-box.

Tabanja, a pistol (Ar.).

Tabássam ku-, to smile.

Tabia, constitution, temper, temperament, climate.

Tabibia ku-, to doctor.

Tabibu, a physician.

Tabiki ku-, to line, to close to or upon, to cling to as a fast friend.

Tabikiza, to make to cling.

Tabiri ku-, to foretell, to prophesy.

Taburudu ku-, to refresh.

Tadariki ku-, to accept the responsibility of, to guarantee the result of.

Tadi, violence, hurry.

Kwenda kwa tadi, to rush, to go tumultuously.

Tadi ku-, to fight with.

Tafakari ku-, to consider, ponder, think.

Tafáthal or *Tafathali*, please, I beg of you.

Tafiti ku-, to seek out matters secretly, to be over-inquisitive.

Tafsiri ku-, to explain, to interpret.

Tafsiri, interpretation.

Tafsiria ku-, to explain to, to interpret to.

Tafu (M.) = *Chafu*, cheek.

Tafu, gastrocnemic muscles.

Tafu ya mkono, the biceps muscle.

Tafuna ku-, to chew, to nibble.

Tafuta ku-, to look for, seek, search for.

Tafutatafuta ku-, to search all about.

Tafutia ku- or *Taftia*, to seek out for some one, to look for.

Tagaa ku-, to straddle, to walk with one's legs far apart.

Tage, plur. *matage*, bow legs, crookedness.

Taghafali ku-, to be off one's guard, to forget to take notice.

Taghaiari ku-, to be changed.
Taghi ku-, to rebel.
Tagua, branches, main branches.
Tahafifu, gently, in good time, light, thin.
Nguo tahafifu, thin calico.
Tahamaka ku-, to look up to see what is going on.
Taharaki ku-, to be troubled, to be thrown into confusion.
Taharakisha ku-, to put into a state of anxiety, to excite, stimulate.
Taharizi. See *Kanzu.*
Taharuki ku-, to be troubled, to be anxious, to be thrown into confusion. Also, *Taharaki.*
Tahassa ku-, to go on board a ship with a view to sailing.
Tahathari ku-, to beware, to be on one's guard.
Tahatharisha ku-, to warn.
Tahayari ku-, to become ashamed.
Tahayarisha ku-, to shame, to make ashamed.
Tahidi ku-.
Kujitahidi, to exert oneself, to try hard.
Tahiri ku-, to circumcise.
Tahsila, farewell, leave-taking.
Tai, a large bird of prey, a vulture.
Taifa, plur. *mataifa*, a tribe, a nation.
Taja, hire.
Taja ku-, to name.
Taji, a crown.
Tajiri, plur. *matajiri*, a merchant, a rich man, a capitalist, a principal.
-taka-. See *-ta-*.
Taka, dirt.
Takataka, rubbish, sundries, small articles.
Taka ku-, to want, to wish for, to ask for.
Kutaka shauri, to seek advice.
Takabali ku-, to accept; used of God's hearing prayer.
Takabathi ku-, to carry on freight.
Takabathisha ku-, to pay freight for.
Takáddam ku-, to be in advance of, to get before.
Takalika ku-, to be very faint or tired.
Takarimu, gift, largess.
Takasa ku-, to clean, to make clean and clear.
Takasika ku-, to become cleansed.
Takata ku-, to become clean and clear.
Uwingu umetakata, the sky is clear.
-takatifu, holy, cleansed.
Takhari ku-, to stay.
Taki = *Chicha.*
Takia, plur. *matakia*, a large cushion.
Tako, plur. *matako*, the buttock.
Taksiri, a crime.
Takura ku-, to scratch, to dig with claws or fingers.
Talaka, divorce.
Talássim or *Talasimu*, plur. *matalasimu*, a talisman, a charm, a figure divided into squares and marked with magic words and symbols.
Tali ku- or *Ta'ali ku-*, to study.
Talik = *Tarik.*
Taliza ku-, to smooth off, to smooth up, plaster, &c.
Tama, out and out, final.
Tama ku- (M.) = *Hama ku-*, to remove.
Tama ku-, to sit, crouch (Yao.).
Tama.
Kushika tama, to lean the head

on the hand, reckoned unlucky in Zanzibar.

Tamaa, longing, avarice, greediness.

Kukata tamaa, to despair.

Tamálaki ku-, to be master of.

Kujitamálaki mwenyewe, to be one's own master.

Tamani ku-, to long for, to lust after.

Tamanika ku-, to be liked, to be an object of liking.

Tamba ku-, to swagger.

Tàmbaa ku-, to creep, to crawl.

Tambi, vermicelli.

Tambo, a tall man.

Tamboa, testicles.

Tambua ku-, to recognize.

Tambulia ku-, to understand.

Tambulikana ku-, to be recognizable.

Tambulisha ku-, to make to recognize, to explain.

Tambuu, betel leaf chewed with areca nut, lime and tobacco.

Tambuza ku-, to put a new point or edge, to weld on fresh iron or steel.

Tamisha ku- (M.) = *Hamisha ku-*.

Ta'mka ku-, to pronounce.

Tamu, sweetness, flavour, taste.

-tamu, sweet, pleasant. It makes *tamu* with nouns like *nyumba*.

Tamuka ku- = *Ta'mka ku-*.

Tàmvua, ends or corners of turban cloth, &c.

Tana ku-, to divide, to slit, to comb, to part.

Tanatana ku-, to divide up into little bits.

Tana, a bunchlet of bananas, &c. Bananas and plantains grow spirally in a large bunch, not continuously, but in little groups: each group is a *tana*.

Tanabahi ku-, to make up one's mind, to know what to do.

Tanafusi ku-, to draw breath.

Tanda ku-, to spread, to be spread out, to be overcast, to put ropes to a native bedstead.

Kujitanda, to stretch oneself across.

Tandama ku- (?), to surround.

Tandawaa ku-, to recline, to loll at one's ease.

Tandaza ku-, to make flat.

Tandika ku-, to spread, to lay out, to saddle.

Tandu, long slashes made on their faces by Makuas and others.

Tandua ku-, to unsaddle, to take off harness.

Tanga, plur. *matanga* or *majitanga*, a sail. The sails of *mitepe* and *madau* are made of matting.

Tanga mbili, the seasons of changeable winds.

Matanga kati, wind abeam.

Kukaa matanga, to sit at home in sign of mourning, to mourn.

Tangaa ku-, to come to be known.

Tangamana ku-, to adjoin.

Tangamuka ku-, to be cheerful.

Tangamusha ku-, to cheer up.

Tanganya, &c. (M.) = *Changanya*, &c., to mix, to shuffle cards.

Tangatanga ku-, to go backwards and forwards, to wave.

Tangawizi, ginger.

Tangaza ku-, to spread news, to circulate intelligence.

Tange, the trees and rubbish cleared off a new plantation.

Tangisha ku-, to make evident.

Tango, plur. *matango*, a sort of

gourd eaten raw, resembling in taste a cucumber.

Tangu, since, from.

Tangu lini? Since when? How long ago?

Tangua ku-, to annul, to abolish, to separate, untwist, unplait, withdraw a promise, &c.

Kutangua ndoa, to annul a marriage, to divorce.

Tanguka ku-, to be annulled.

Tangukana ku-, to separate.

Tangulia ku-, to precede, to go before, to go first.

Nimetangulia kukuambia, I told you beforehand.

Tangulifu, advanced.

Tani, Othman.

Tani.

Kwa tani, backward, on his back.

Tano or *Tanu*, five.

Ya tano, fifth.

-tano, five.

Tantanbelwa, a great bother, a worry.

Tanua ku, to expand, to spread out, to fend off a boat.

Tanuka ku-, to lie on one's back and spread oneself out, to sprawl.

Tanuru or *Tanuu*, a clamp for burning lime, an oven.

Tanzi, plur. *matanzi*, a noose.

Tanzia, news of a death.

Tao, plur. *matao*, an arch, an arched opening, a bay.

Tapa ku-, to shiver.

Kujitapa, to magnify oneself, to make a great man of oneself.

Tapatapa ku-, to jump about like a fish when taken out of the water, to shiver, to tremble.

Tapanya ku-, to scatter, to throw about.

Tapanyatapanya ku-, to dissipate, to waste.

Tapika ku-, to vomit.

Tapisha ku-, to make to vomit.

Tapisho, plur. *matapisho*, an emetic.

Tapo, plur. *matapo*, a detachment, a division, a part of an army larger than *kikozi*.

Tarabe, side piece of a window, door of planks.

Tarafu, on the part of.

Tarafu yake, on his part.

Taraja ku-, to hope.

Tarathia ku-, to persuade in a friendly way.

Taratibu, carefully, gently, orderly.

Taratibu, orderliness, an order or form.

Taraza, an edging, a narrow silken border usually woven on to turban and loin-cloths in Zanzibar.

Tarazake, business on a small scale.

Tarazaki ku-, to trade in a small way.

Tarik, a date, year, &c., the clew-line or bunt-line of a dhow-sail.

Kitabu cka tarik, a chronicle.

Tarimbo = *Mtaimbo*, an iron bar.

Tarizi ku-, to weave on an edging.

Tartibu = *Taratibu*.

Tasa, a brass basin.

Tasa, a game of touch.

Tasa, a barren animal.

Tasawari ku-, to do with certainty, to be fully able.

Hatasawari, it is certain that he does not do it.

Tasbihi, Mohammedan beads.

Tasfida, good manners.

Tashwishi, doubt.

Tasihili, quickness, quickly.

Taslimu, ready cash.

Tassa = *Tasa*.

Tata. See *Matata.*
Kwenda tatatata, to toddle.
Tataga ku-, to go above or over, to cross a stream on a tree.
Tatana ku-, to be in a tangle, to be puzzled.
Tatanisha ku-, to tangle, to puzzle.
Tatanya ku-, to unravel, disentangle, solve a riddle.
Tatazana ku-, to be tangled.
Tathbiri, a merchant.
Tatia ku-, to wind, to tangle, to complicate.
Tatiza ku-, to wind.
tatu, three.
Ya tatu, third.
Tatua ku-, to tear.
Tatuka ku-, to be torn.
Taumka ku- = *Ta'mka ku-*.
Tauni, plague, cholera.
Tausi, peacock.
Tavu (A.), the cheek.
Tawa, plur. *matawa*, a frying-pan.
Tawa, plur. *tawa*, a louse.
Tawa ku-, to live secluded (Yao.), to tie.
Tawafa, a candle, candles.
Tawakali ku-, to trust in God and take courage.
Tawakáwakatha, many.
Tawala ku-, to govern, to rule.
Tawanya ku-, to scatter.
Tawanyika ku-, to become scattered.
Tawashi, a eunuch.
Tawassuf, temperance.
Tawaza ku-, to make to rule.
Tawaza ku-, to wash the feet, to perform the ablutions.
Tawi, plur. *matawi*, a branch, a bough, a bunch, an ear of millet.
Taya, jaw, jawbone.
Taya ku-, to reproach.
Tayari, ready.
Tayi, obedient.
Tayo, plur. *matayo*, a reproach, reviling.
Tazama ku-, to look.
Tazamia ku-, to look out for.
Tazwi, forgery.
Teende la mguu, Barbadoes leg, elephantiasis (?).
Tefua ku-, to reason, to search, to throw about.
Tega ku-, to set a trap or snare, to snare. See *Kitendawili.*
Tegea ku-, to be lame.
Tegemea ku-, to lean upon, to be propped up.
Tegemeza ku-, to support.
Tego, a virulent kind of syphilis supposed to be the effect of a charm.
Tegu, plur. *mategu*, a tape-worm.
Tegua ku-, to take a pot off the fire, to remove a spell.
Teka ku- (M.) = *Cheka ku-*.
Teka ku-, to plunder, to take as spoil, to draw water.
Kuteka 'mji, to plunder a town.
Kuteka ng'ombe, to carry off an ox.
Kuteka maji, to draw water from a well.
Teke, plur. *mateke*, a kick.
Kupiga teke, to kick.
Tekelea ku-, to prove true, to come to.
Tekeleza ku-, to perform a promise, restore a pledge.
Tekenya ku-, to tickle in the ribs.
Teketea ku-, to be consumed, to be burnt away.
Teketeke, the soft, something soft.
Teketeza ku-, to consume, to cause to be burnt down.
Tekewa ku-, to become bewildered.
Tekeza ku-, to run ashore, to come to an end, to die.

Tekua ku-, to prize up, to toss, to throw up out of a hole

Tele, plenty, abundantly, abundant.

Tele, gold lace or braid.

Telea ku-, to come down, descend, land from.

Teleka ku-, to put a pot on the fire.

Telemua ku-, to pull down, to cause to slip down.

Telemuka ku- or *Telemka ku-*, to go down a steep place, to go quickly down in spite of one's self, to slither down.

Telemuko, the bed of a river.

Teleza ku-, to slip.

Tema ku-, to slash as with a sword.

Tema ku-.

Kutema mate, to spit.

Tembe, a hen full grown but which has not yet laid.

Tembea ku-, to walk about, to take a walk.

Moyo wangu umetembea, my thoughts are wandering.

Tembelea ku-, to walk about.

Tembeza ku-, to offer for sale by auction, to hawk about.

Tembo, palm wine, wine.

Tembo, an elephant.

Te'mka = *Ta'mka*.

Temsi, filigree work.

Tena, afterwards, again, further.

Tenda ku-, to do, to apply oneself to, to act.

Kutenda zema or *vema*, to behave well.

Tenda kani, a pole across a dhow to fasten the sheet to.

Tendawala, a kind of bird.

Tende, a date, dates.

Tenda halwa or *halua*, Arabs from the Persian Gulf, who steal slaves by tempting them into their houses with dates and sweetstuff.

Tendea ku-, to do to, to behave to, to treat.

Tendegu, plur. *matendegu*, the legs of a bedstead.

Tendeka ku-, to be done, to be doable.

Tenga, a sun-fish.

Tenga ku-, to separate, to remove.

Kujitenga, to get out of the way.

Tengea ku-, to be ready and in order.

Duka limetengea, the shop is all ready and open.

Tengeka ku-, to be put on one side.

Tengelea and *Tengeleza* = *Tengeneza* and *Tengenea*.

Tengenea ku-, to be comfortable, to be as it should be.

Tengeneza ku-, to finish off, to put to rights, to touch up.

Tengezeka ku-, to be established, made right.

Tengua ku-, to put aside.

Tepukua ku-, to cut away young shoots.

Tepukuzi, plur. *Matepukuzi*, shoots from the root of a tree.

Terema ku-, to be at ease.

Tesa ku-, to afflict.

Kuteswa, to suffer, to be afflicted.

Teso, plur. *mateso*, afflictions, adversities.

Teta ku-, to oppose, to strive against, to be adverse to, to go to law with, to mention disparagingly.

Tetea ku-, to cackle like a hen.

Tetea ku- (M.) = *Chechea ku-*, to walk lame.

Tete ya kwanga, rubeola.

Tetema ku-, to tremble, to quiver.

Tetemea = *Chechemea*.

Tetemeka ku-, to tremble, to shake, to shiver, to quake (as the earth), to chatter (of the teeth).

Teteri, a small kind of dove.

Teteza ku-, to rattle. Also, to lead a sick person by the hand.

Teua ku-, to choose, select, pick out = *Chagua ku-*.

Teuka ku-, to dislocate, to sprain.

-teule, choice, chosen.

Tezama and *Tezamia* = *Tazama* and *Tazamia*.

Tezi, a fibrous tumour, goître.

Thabihu, an offering, a sacrifice.

Thabit, plur. *mathabit*, firm, brave, steadfast.

Thahabu, gold.

Thahiri, evident, plain.

Thahiri ku-, to make plain, to express.

Thaifu, weak, infirm, bad.

Thalatha, three. Also *Thelatha*, &c.

Thalathatashara, thirteen.

Thalathini, thirty.

Thalimu, a fraudulent person, a swindler.

Thalimu ku-, to wrong, to defraud.

Thalili, very low, very poor.

Thamana (*th* in this), a surety.

Thamani (*th* in thing), a price.

Ya thamani, of price, valuable.

Thambi, sin.

Thámin, surety.

Thamini ku, to become surety.

Thamiri, conscience, thought.

Thani ku-, to think, to suppose.

Thania ku-, to think of a person, to suppose him, to suspect.

Tharau, scorn.

Tharau ku-, to scorn.

Tháruba, (Ar. a stroke), a storm, (in arithmetic) multiplication.

Tháruba moja, at one stroke, suddenly.

Thathu, a kind of jay brought down from Unyanyembe.

Thawabu, a reward; especially rewards from God.

Thelatha, &c. See *Thalatha*, &c.

Thelimu ku-, to oppress.

Thelth, a donkey's canter.

Theluth, a third.

Themanini, eighty.

Themanini, a linen fabric.

Themantashara, eighteen.

Themanya, eight.

Themuni, an eighth.

Thenashara, twelve.

Theneen, two.

Thihaka, ridicule, derision.

Thihaki ku-, to ridicule, to make game of.

Thihirisha ku-, to make clear, to declare.

Thii ku-, to be in distress.

Thiiki ku-, to be put to straits.

Thili ku-, to abase.

Thiraa, a measure of about half a yard, from the point of the elbow to the tips of the fingers.

Thiraa konde, from the point of the elbow to the knuckles of the clenched fist.

Thoofika ku-, to be made weak, to become weak.

Thoofisha ku-, to weaken, to make weak.

Thoumu, garlic.

Thubutisha ku-, to give courage to, to make certain, to convince, to prove.

Thubutu ku-, to dare, to have courage for, to be proved.

Sithubutu, I dare not.

Thuku ku-, to taste.

Thukuru ku-, to invoke.

Thulli, distress, misery.

Thulumu, wrong.

Thulumu ku-, to do wrong, to persecute.

Thuluru, a kind of sandpiper.

Thuluth, a third. Also *Theluth*.

Thumu ku-, to slander.

Thurea, a chandelier.

Thuru ku-, to harm.

Haithuru, no harm, it does not matter.

Tia ku-, to put, to put into.

Kutia nanga, to anchor.

Kutia chuoni, to put to school.

Tiara, a boy's kite.

Tiba, a term of endearment.

Tibika ku-, to be cured.

Tibu ku-, to cure.

Tibu, a kind of scent.

Tibua ku-, to stir up and knock about.

Tifua ku-, to cause to rise like dust or a mist.

Tifuka ku-, to rise in a cloud.

Tii ku-, to obey.

Tiisha ku-, to make to obey, to subdue.

Tika ku-, or *twika*, to put a burden on a man's head for him.

Tiki, just like, exactly as.

Tikia ku-, to reply. See *Itikia*.

Tikisa ku-, to shake.

Tikiti, plur. *matikiti*, a sort of water melon.

Tikitika ku-, to be shaken.

Tikitiki, utterly and entirely, to the last mite. Also, (M.) into little bits.

Tikiza ku-, to have patience with.

Tilia ku-, to put to, for, &c.

Tilifika ku-, to waste, to grow less.

Tilifisha ku-, to diminish, to make to dwindle away.

Tilifu ku-, to ruin, to waste.

Tililia ku-, to darn.

Timazi, a stone hung by a line, used as a plummet by masons.

Timbi, bracelets.

Timbuza ku-, to begin to show itself, like the sun in rising.

Timia ku-, to be complete.

Timilia ku-, to become complete.

-timilifu, complete, perfect.

Timiliza ku-, to make complete.

Timiza ku-, to complete, to make perfect.

Time, a woman's name.

Timvi, an ill-omened child.

Tinda ku- (M.) = *Chinja ku-*, to cut, to cut the throat, to slaughter.

Tindika ku- (A.), to fall short.

Tindikia ku-, to cease to.

Imenitindikia, I am out of it, I have no more.

Tindikiana ku-, to be separated, to be severed, as friends or relations at a distance from one another.

Tinge, a game consisting in imitating all the motions of a leader.

Tini, a fig, figs.

Tini (M.) = *Chini*, down.

Tipitipi, a brown bird, a mocking bird.

Tipua ku-, to scoop out, to dig out, to dip out.

Tiririka ku-, to glide, to trickle.

Tis'a = *Tissia*, nine.

Tisaini, ninety.

Tisatashara, nineteen.

Tisha ku-, to frighten, alarm, make afraid.

Tissia, nine.

Tita ku-, to tie up together.

Tita, plur. *matita*, a faggot, a bundle of firewood.

Titi, the nipple.

Titia ku-, to shake, to sink in.

Also (?) of the sea, when deep and rough, to boil.

Titika ku-, to carry a bundle of sticks, &c.

Titima ku-, to roar and roll like thunder.

Titiwanga, chicken-pox. See ***Kitiwanga***.

Tiwo (?), paralysis.

-to, a suffix, denoting goodness or propriety, rarely used in Zanzibar.

Kuweka, to put;

Kuwekato, to put properly.

Manuka, smells;

Manukato, scents.

Toa ku-, to put out, to take away, give, expel, to deliver, to except, to choose out.

Kutoa meno, to grin, to show the teeth, to snarl.

Toazi, plur. *matoazi*, cymbals.

Toba, repentance.

Toboa ku-, to break through, to break a hole in a wall.

Tobwe, a simpleton, ignoramus.

Tofaa, plur. *matofaa*, a fruit shaped like a codling with rosy-coloured streaks, = *Tomondo*. See *Mtomondo*.

Tofali, plur. *matofali*, a brick.

Tofauti, difference, dispute.

Nimeingia tofauti kwa kuwa wee umeniibia fetha yangu, I have a quarrel with you for stealing my money.

Tofua ku-, to hurt or put out an eye.

Tofuka ku-, to have an eye hurt or put out.

Toga ku-, to pierce the ears.

Togwa, unfermented beer.

Tohara, circumcision.

Tohara ku-, to purify by ablutions, to perform the Mohammedan ablutions.

Toi, a kind of wild goat.

Toja ku-, to slash, cut gashes, as a means of bleeding, &c.

Tojo, a cut made for ornament, &c.

Toka or *Tokea*, from, since.

Toka ku-, to go or come out or away from, to be acquitted, to go free.

Kutoka damu, to bleed.

Kutoka hari, to sweat.

Tokana ku-, to go forth from one another, to divorce, to be set free.

Tokea, from, since. See *Toka*.

Tokea hapo, in old time, from old time.

Tokea ku-, to come out to, or from, to appear.

Tokeza ku-, to ooze out, to project.

Tokomea ku-, to get out of one's sight.

Tokoni, the pelvis.

Tokono (A.), the hips.

Tokora ku-, to pick one's teeth.

Tokosa ku-, to boil, to cook by boiling.

Tokoseka ku-, to be well boiled, to be done.

Tokota ku-, to become boiled, to be cooked by boiling.

Tolea ku-, to put out for, to offer to.

Kutolewa, to have put out for one, or to be put out, to be dismissed.

Toma, orchitis, hydrocele.

Tomasa ku-, to poke with the fingers, to feel, used of examining a living creature, as *Bonyesha*, of inanimate objects.

Tomba ku-, to have sexual connection with.

Tombo, a quail.

Tomea ku- (M.) = *Chomea ku-*.
Tomea ku-, to point by plastering over and putting small stones in to make the work firm.
Tomesha ku-, to set on (a dog, &c.).
Tomo, dross of iron, &c.
Tomise = *Tomo*.
Tomondo, a hippopotamus.
Tomondo, plur. *matomondo* = *Tofua*.
Toha ku-, to drop.
Tona ku-.
Kutona hina, to lay and bind on a plaster of henna until the part is dyed red.
Kutona godoro, to sew through a mattress here and there to confine the stuffing.
Tondoo, a small brown nut containing oil.
Tonesha ku-, to strike against, to touch a sore place, to make a sore run.
Tone, plur. *matone*, a drop.
Toneza ku-, to cause to drop.
Tonga ku- (M.) = *Chonga ku-*, to cut.
Tongea ku- = *Chongea*.
Tongosimba, a small bird black with white neck; it makes a great noise in flying.
Tongoza ku-, to seduce.
Tope, mud, plur. *matope*, much mud.
Topea ku-, to sink in mire, to be stogged.
Topetope, a custard apple.
Topeza ku-, to be too heavy for one.
Topoa ku-, to take out, to break a spell, to clear for cultivation.
Tora, plur. *matora*, a small spear.
Torati, the law of Moses, the Pentateuch.
Toroka ku-, to run away from a master, from home &c.
Torosha ku-, to abduct, to induce to run away.
Tosa ku-, to cause to sink, to drown
Kutosa macho, to spoil the eyes.
Tosa, plur. *matosa*, fruit just beginning to ripen, all but ripe.
Tosha ku-, to suffice, to be enough for, to cause to come out.
Toshea ku-, to be astonished, to be staggered.
Tosheleza ku-, to suffice.
Toshewa ku-, to be astonished.
Tota ku-, to sink.
Totea ku- (M.) = *Chochea ku-*.
Toteza macho ku-, to spoil the eyes.
Totoma ku-, to be lost, to wander.
Totora ku-, to pick one's teeth. Also, *Tokora*.
Tooya = *Chooya*.
Towea ku-, to eat as a relish or *kitoweo*.
Toweka ku-, to vanish. At Lamoo this word is used for *to die*.
Towelea ku-, to eat by mouthfuls.
Towesha ku-, to ruin, to put out of the way.
Toweza ku-, to pour gravy, &c., over the rice.
Tozi, plur. *matozi* (M.), a tear.
Trufu, trump (in cards).
Tu, only, nothing but this, only just. The *-u* of *tu* is very short; it always follows the word or phrase which it qualifies.
Tu, we are or were.
Tu or *Tw-*, the sign of the first person plural, *we*.
-tu- or *-tw-*, the objective prefix denoting the first person plural, *us*.
Tua ku-, to put down, to put down loads, to rest, to halt, to encamp, to set (of the sun).
Jua likitua, at sunset.

Tua ku-, to grind by pushing a stone backwards and forwards.

Tuama ku-, to settle, to clear itself.

Tuana ku-, to settle.

Tubia ku-, to repent of.

Tubu ku-, to repent.

Tufanu, a storm, a tempest.

Tufe, a ball.

Tuhumu ku-, to accuse of, to lay to his charge, to suspect.

Tui (M.) = *Chui*, a leopard.

Tui, the oily juice squeezed out of the scraped cocoa-nut.

Tuiliza ku-, to prolong.

Tuja ku- (M.) = *Chuja ku-*, to strain.

Tuka, posts of a verandah or long eaves.

Tukana ku-, to use bad language to, to abuse, to address with insulting or indecent expressions.

Tukano, plur. *matukano*, bad words, insulting or filthy language.

Tukia ku-, &c. (M.) = *Chukia ku-*, &c.

Tukia ku-, to happen.

Tukio, plur. *matukio*, a thing which happens, an accident.

Tukiza ku-, to project.

Tukua ku-, &c. (M.) = *Chukua*

-tukufu, glorious, great. [*ku-*, &c.

Tukuka ku-, to become exalted, to grow great.

Tukusa ku-, to move, to shake.

Tukuta ku-, to move about restlessly, to shake nervously.

Tukutiza ku- (obscene).

Tukuza ku-, to exalt, to make great.

Tulia ku-, to become quiet, to settle down, to amend from a riotous life.

Tulia, don't make a noise.

Tulia ku-, to grind with. See *Tua*.

Jiwe la kutulia, a stone to grind with.

Tulika ku-, to be serene and tranquil.

Tulilia ku-, to settle down for or in regard to.

Yamekutulilia? have you understood me?

Yamenitulilia, I have.

Tuliliana ku-, to come to an agreement.

Tuliza ku-, to calm, to still.

Tulizia ku-, to calm for.

Kutulizia roho, to calm, to console.

Tuma ku-, to employ, to send about some business.

Tuma ku- (M.) = *Chuma ku-*, to

Tumaa ku-, to hope. [profit.

Tumai ku- = *Tumaa*.

Roho yatumai, I hope.

Tumaini ku-, to be confident, to hope.

Tumainisha ku-, to make confident, to make to hope.

Tumania ku-, to hope in, confide in.

Tumba, a long rice-bag.

Tumbako, tobacco.

Kuvuta tumbako, to smoke.

Tumbako ya kununka or *kunusa*,

Tumbasi, an abscess. [snuff.

Tumbili, a small kind of light-coloured monkey.

Tumbo, plur. *matumbo*, gut, belly, viscera, womb.

Tumbo la kuenenda, diarrhœa.

Tumbo la kuhara damu, dysentery.

Tumbua ku-, to disembowel, cut open, pick a hole in, open (an abscess).

Tumbuiza ku-, to soothe, to sing to, to sing by turns.

Tumbuka ku-, to burst, to be burst, &c. See *Tumbua*.

Tumbukia ku-, to fall into.

Ametumbukia, kisimani, he has got into a scrape.

Tumbukiza ku-, to throw into, to cause to fall into, to get a person into a scrape.
Tumbulia ku-.
Kutumbulia macho, to stare at.
Tumbuu, a staple.
Tumbuza ku-, to disembowel, to penetrate, to get through.
Tume, a messenger.
Tumia ku-, to employ, to spend, to use.
Tumika ku-, to be employed, to serve.
Tumikia ku-, to be employed by, to serve, to obey.
Tumu, taste, tasting.
Tumu, the month Ramathan.
Tuna ku-, &c. (M.) = *Chuna ku*, &c.
Tuna ku-, to swell, to get cross.
Tunda, plur. *matunda*, a fruit.
Tundama ku-, to gather, to settle at the bottom.
Tundika ku-, to hang up, to be suspended.
Tundu, plur. *tundu* or *matundu*, a hole, a cage, a nest.
Tundu ya pua, a nostril.
Tunduaa ku-, to stand stockstill in wonder at, &c.
Tunga, a round open basket.
Tunga ku-, to suppurate.
Tunga ku-, to put together in order, to string beads, to make verses.
Tungama ku-, to clot, to congeal.
Tungamana ku-, to be steady.
Tungia ku-, to thread a needle.
Tungua ku-, to let down, to pull down, to hook down.
Tunguka ku-, to be pulled or let down.
Tungika ku-, to depend upon, to hang from.
Tungu (M.) = *Chungu*, ants.
Tunguja, a common weed, a species of solanum.
Tungulia ku- (M.) = *Chungulia ku-*, to peep.
Tunika ku- (M.), to lose the skin, to be flayed.
T'unu, a rarity, a choice gift, a present.
Tunuka ku-, to love excessively, to long for.
Tunukia ku, to make a present to.
Tunza, plur. *matunza*, care.
Tunza ku-, to take care of, to look after, to make gifts to.
Tupa, a file.
Tupa, plur. *matupa* (M.), a bottle.
Tupa ku-, to throw, to throw away.
Kutupa nathari, or *macho*, to cast a glance, to cast the eyes.
Kutupa mkono, to break off friendship.
Tupia ku-, to throw at, to pelt with.
Tupiza ku-, to pass its proper measure or time.
-tupu, bare, empty. It makes *tupu* with nouns like *nyumba*. See *Utupu*.
Tupua ku-, to root out, to pull up.
Turuhani, tare, allowance for package, &c., in weighing.
Turuma. See *Maturuma*.
Turupuka ku-, to slip out of one's hand.
Tusbiih, ascriptions of praise, a rosary, the beads used by Mohammedans in praying. See *Tasbih*.
Tusha ku-, to lower, to make mean or low.
Tushi, plur. *matushi*, abuse, bad language. See *Matusu*.
Tuswira, a picture.
Tuta, plur. *matuta*, a heap of earth,

a raised bed for planting sweet potatoes.

Tutu! Leave it alone! Don't touch! Used to little children.

Tutuka ku-, or *Tutu'mka* or *Tutusika*, to rise in little swellings, to come out in a rash.

Tutuma ku-, to make a noise of bubbling, to boil up.

Tutumua ku-.

Kujitutumua, to gather oneself up for an effort.

Tuza ku-, or *Tuuza ku-*, to weep (of a wound).

Kutnza damu (M.), to run down with blood, to bleed excessively.

Tuza ku- = *Tunza ku-*.

Kujituza, to make oneself mean or low.

Tuzanya ku-, to come to an agreement (A.).

-tw- = *-tu-*.

Twa ku (M.) = *Chwa ku-*.

Twaa ku-, to take.

Kutwaa nyara, to take as spoil.

Twalia ku-, to take from.

Twaliwa ku-, to be deprived of, to have had taken from one. Used also in the sense of, to be taken.

Twana ku- or *Tuana ku-*, to settle.

Twana ku- = *Twazana*.

Twanga ku-, to clean corn from the husk by pounding it in a wooden mortar.

Twangia ku-, to clean corn for, with, etc.

Twazana ku-, to resemble in face, to be like.

Tweka ku-, to hoist, to raise, to take up.

Twesha ku-, to go by night to see any one.

Tweta ku-, to pant, to strive for breath.

Tweza ku-, to despise, to hold in contempt.

Twiga, a giraffe, a camelopard.

Twika ku-, to put a load on a man's head. Also *Tika*.

U.

U is pronounced like *oo* in food.

U before a vowel takes a consonantal sound, and may be written *w*. This change is not so marked before a *u* as before the other vowels. Sometimes both *u*'s keep their vowel sound. *U* before *o* is frequently dropped:

Moyo = *Muoyo*.

The syllable *mu-* is seldom so pronounced in Zanzibar; it becomes *mw-* or *'m*, or a simple *m*.

L and *u* are sometimes apparently interchanged, as,

Ufalme or *Ufaume*, a kingdom.

Mlango or *Mwango*, a door.

Nouns in *u-* or *w-* generally lose their *u-* in the plural, most of them substituting *n-* or *ny-* for it, but dissyllable nouns keep the *u-* and prefix *ny-*. See *N*.

The insertion of a *-u-* before the final *-a* of a verb reverses its meaning.

Kufunga, to fasten.

Kufungua, to unfasten.

There is a suppressed *l* between the *u* and the *a* (as always in Swahili between two consecutive vowels), which appears in the applied forms.

Kufungulia, to unfasten for.

The passive of the applied forms

of verbs in *-ua* is used also as the passive of the simple form.

Kufunguliwa, to be unfastened, or to have unfastened for one.

Kuua, to kill, is irregular, and makes its passive by adding *-wa*, *kuuawa*, to be killed.

U (Ar.), and.

U, thou art, it is, of nouns in *u-*, and of those which make their plural in *mi-*.

U- or *w-*, the sign of the second person singular.

U- or *w-*, the personal prefix of the third person singular denoting a substantive in *u-*, or one which makes its plural in *mi-*.

-u-, or *-w-*, the objective prefix denoting a substantive in *u-*, or one that makes its plural in *mi-*.

U- as a substantive prefix is used to form abstract nouns, and also to form the names of countries, as,

Unyika, the Nyika country; *Ugala*, the Galla couutry; *Uzungu*, the country of Europeans.

Ua ku-, to kill.

Passive, *kuuawa*, to be killed.

Ua, plur. *maua*, a flower.

Ua, plur. *nyua*, a yard, an enclosure, a fence.

Ua wa mabua, an enclosure fenced with *mtama* stalks.

Ua wa makuti, an enclosure fenced with plaited cocoa-nut leaves.

Uanda, a court, a yard.

Uanda = *Wanda*.

Uanja = *Uanda*.

Uapo, plur. *nyapo*, an oath.

Uawa ku-, to be killed.

Uayo, plur. *nyayo*, the sole of the foot, a footprint.

Ubabwa, pap, a soft food for children.

Ubafu or *Ubavu*, plur. *mbavu*, a rib.

Mbavuni, in or at its side.

Ubani, incense, galbanum.

Ubatili, nullity.

Ubau, plur. *mbau*, a plank.

Ubawa, plur. *mbawa*, a wing feather.

Ubazazi.

Kufanya ubazazi, to make a bargain.

Ubeleko, a cloth worn by women, a customary present to the bride's mother on the occasion of a wedding.

Ubishi, a joke.

Ubuyu, the inside of the calabash fruit.

Uchafu or *Uchavu*, filthiness.

Uchagaa = *Utagaa*.

Uchala, a raised stage to put corn &c. upon.

Uchawi, witchcraft, black magic.

Kufanya uchawi, to practise witchcraft.

Uchi, nakedness.

Uchipuka, plur. *chipuka*, a shoot, a blade of grass.

Uchochoro, a passage, opening between.

Uchovu, tediousness.

Uchu, a longing.

Uchukuti, the leaf stalk of the cocoanut leaf.

Uchukuzi, carriage, cost of carrying.

Uchukwi, a kind of rice.

Uchumi = *Utumi*.

Uchungu, bitterness, pain, poison.

Uchungu, bitter. See *-chungu*.

Dawa uchungu, bitter medicine.

Udaka, babbling, telling secrets.
Udevu, plur. *ndevu*, one hair of the beard.
Udogo, smallness, youth.
Udongo, clay, a kind of earth used to mix with the lime and sand in making mortar.
Ufa ku-, to become cracked.
Ufa, plur. *nyufa*, a crack.
Kutia ufa, to crack.
Ufagio, plur. *fagio*, a brush, a broom, a bundle of the leaves of a palm used to sweep with.
Ufahamu, memory.
Ufajiri = *Alfajiri*.
Ufalme or *Ufaume*, kingdom, royalty.
Ufidiwa, a ransom.
Ufisadi, vice.
Ufiski, vice.
Ufito, plur. *fito*, a thin stick, sticks such as those which are used as laths to tie the *makuti* thatch to.
Ufizi, plur. *fizi*, the gums.
Ufu, death, the state of being dead.
Ufufulio or *Ufufuo*, resurrection, revival.
Ufukara, destitution.
Ufukwe, absolute destitution.
Ufumbi, valley, bottom.
Ufunga, stone bench, = *Kibaraza*.
Ufungu, relatives.
Ufunguo, plur. *funguo*, a key.
Ufuo, sandy beach.
Ufuta, semsem.
Ufuthuli, officiousness.
Uga, an open space in a town where a house has been pulled down, or where a dance could be held.
Ugali, porridge.
Uganga, white magic, medicine.
Ughaibu, the little packet of betel leaf, areca nut, lime, and tobacco made up for chewing.
Ugo, enclosure, close.
Ugomvi, a quarrel, quarrelsomeness.
Ugonjwa, sickness, a sickness.
Ugrani, a general collection of debts.
Ugua ku-, to fall sick, to groan.
Ugumu, hardness, difficulty.
Uguza ku-, to nurse, to take care of a sick person.
Ugwe, string.
Uharabu, mischief.
Uharara, warmth.
Uharibivu, destruction, destructiveness.
Uhtaji, want, thing wanting.
Uhuru, freedom.
Uimbo, plur. *nyimbo*, a song, a ballad.
Uirari (in arithmetic), proportion, division of profits. See *Worari*.
Uizi, theft, thieving.
Ujahili, boldness.
Ujalifu, fulness.
Ujana, youth.
Ujari, tiller-ropes.
Ujenzi, building.
Uji, gruel.
Ujima, help of neighbours, assistance in work.
Ujinga, rawness, dulness, ignorance.
Ujio, coming.
Ujira, hire, reward.
Ujumbe, chiefship, headship.
Ujuvi, knowingness, officiousness, pretended knowledge.
Ujusi, defilement, whatever is removed by ablutions.
Ukaango, plur. *kaango*, an earthen pot for cooking with oil or fat.
Ukafu.
Ukafu wa maji, a bubble on water.
Ukali, fierceness, sharpness.
Kufanya ukali, to scold.
Ukambaa, plur. *kambaa* (M.), cord line.

Ukamilifu, perfectness, perfection.
Ukanda, a strap.
Ukao, stay, stopping.
Ukarimu, generosity, liberality.
Ukawa, delay.
Ukaya, a long piece of blue calico, often ornamented with spangles, worn by slaves and poor women in Zanzibar over their heads: it has two long ends, reaching nearly to the ground.
Ukelele, plur. *kelele*, a cry, a noise.
Akapigiwa ukelele, and a cry was made at him.
Ukemi, a call (Mer.).
Nipigie ukemi, give me a call.
Ukengele, a sort of knife made in Zanzibar.
Ukelo, depth.
Ukingo, the brink, a screen, an enclosure made with cloths.
Ukiri, plur. *kiri*, a strip of fine matting about an inch broad, out of which *mikeka* are made.
Ukiwa, desolation, solitude where people once were.
Uko or *Huko*, there.
Ukoa, plur. *k'oa*, a plate of metal, one of the rings on the scabbard of a sword, &c.
Ukoga, the tartar and dirt on the teeth.
Ukohozi, phthisis.
Ukoka, grass cut for fodder.
Ukoko, the rice on the top of the pot, which is often dry and scorched through the custom of pouring away the water when the rice is done and heaping live embers on the lid of the pot.
Ukoko (A.), a cough.
Ukologefu, decay.
Ukoma, leprosy.
Ukomba, a scraper, a curved knife for hollowing out mortars, &c.
Ukombolewa, a ransom.
Ukombozi or *Ukomboo*, a ransom
Ukonde (*wa tende*), a (date) stone.
Ukongwe, oldness, extreme old age.
Ukonyezo, plur. *konyezo*, a sign made by lifting the eyebrow.
Ukoo, nastiness, uncleanness (?).
Ukoo, ancestry, pedigree, family origin and connections.
Ukope, plur. *kope*, a hair from the eyelash.
Ukosi, the nape of the neck.
Ukubali, acceptance.
Ukubwa, greatness, bigness.
Ukucha, plur. *kucha*, a nail, a claw, a hoof.
Ukufi, plur. *kufi*, a handful, what will lie upon the hand.
Ukumbi, an apartment at the entrance, a hall, a porch. The *ukumbi* is within a stone house and outside a mud house.
Ukumbuka, recollection.
Ukumbusho, memorial, a reminder.
Ukumbuu, plur. *kumbuu*, a girdle made of a narrow cloth, a turban cloth twisted tightly into a sort of rope such as the turbans of the Hindis are made of.
Ukundufu, pleasingness, commodiousness, liberality.
Ukungu, mould, mouldiness.
Kufanya ukungu, to get mouldy
Ukungu, the first light of dawn.
Ukuni, plur. *kuni*, a piece of firewood.
Ukurasa, plur. *kurasa*, a leaf of a book, a sheet of paper.
Ukuta, plur. *kuta*, a stone wall.
Ukuti, plur. *kuti*, a leaflet of the cocoa-nut tree.

Ukuu, greatness, size.
Ukwaju, a tamarind.
Ukwasefu, necessity, having nothing.
Ukwasi, wealth, riches.
Ukwato, plur. *kwato*, a hoof.
Ulalo, a tree or trees cut down so as to fall across a river and make a bridge over it.
Ulaji, gluttony.
Ulambiyambi, a very young *dafu*.
Ulanisi, a foul-mouthed person.
Ulaya or *Wilaya*, home; applied especially to the home of Europeans, Europe.
Ulayiti, European, inferior calico.
Kamba ulayiti, hempen rope.
Ule, that, yonder.
Uledi, a dhow boy, a cabin boy.
Ulegevu, relaxation, the state of being slack.
Ulia ku-, to kill for, with, &c.
Tumulie mbali, let us kill him out of the way.
Ulili, a couch or bedstead (*Kianzwani*).
Ulimbo, birdlime, gum, resin.
Ulimbwende, dandyism.
Ulimi, plur. *ndimi*, the tongue, a tenon, the heel of a mast.
Ulimwengu, the world, the universe, a man's own world or circle of duties and pleasures.
Kuwako ulimwenguni, to be alive.
Ulingo, a raised platform to scare birds from.
Ulio, which is.
Ulitima, the last three cards of the pack.
Uliza ku-, to ask, to inquire of a person.
Kumuliza hali, to ask how he does.
Siwezi kuulizwa uwongo, I cannot tell a lie.
Ulizia ku-, to make inquiries on behalf of.
Ulongo, falsehood. See *Uwongo*.
Uma, plur. *nyuma*, a spit, a large fork, an awl.
Uma wa kuokea nyama, a gridiron.
Uma ku-, to bite, to sting, to hurt, to give pain to, to ache.
Umaheli, ingenuity.
Umalidadi, dandyism.
Umande, dew, morning air, mist, the west wind.
Umasikini, poverty.
Umati, a multitude, people.
Umati Isa, Christians.
Umati Musa, Jews.
Umati Muhammad, Mohammedans.
Umba ku-, to create, to shape.
Umba ku-, to bale out a boat. For *Kumba*.
Umbaumba ku-, to sway about like a drunken man.
Umbo, plur. *maumbo*, form, outward likeness, appearance, character, species.
Najiona umbo la kuwa kiziwi, I feel getting deaf.
Umbu, plur. *maumbu*, a sister.
Umbua ku-, to allege a defect, to depreciate.
Umbwa, or better *Mbwa*, a dog.
-ume (or *-lume*), male, strong. It makes *ndume* with nouns like *nyumba*.
Mkono wa kuume, the right hand.
Umeme, lightning.
Umia ku-, to give pain to.
Umika ku-, to cup.
Umio, the œsophagus.
Umito, heaviness, feeling heavy.
Umiza ku-, to hurt.
Umka ku-, to swell, to rise when leavened.

Umku (?) *ku-*, to call.

Umo or *Humo*, there inside.

Umoja, oneness.

Umri, age.

Umri wake apataje? How old is he?

Umua ku-, to take honey from the hive.

Una, you have, thou hast.

Una nini? What is the matter with you?

Unazozitaka, which you are asking for.

Unda ku-, to build ships or boats.

Undu, the comb of a cock.

Unene, stoutness, thickness.

Unenyekeo, humility, abasement, reverence.

Unga, flour, powder.

Unga wa ndere, a magic poison.

Unga ku-, to unite, to splice, to join.

Ungama, a place near Melinda, swallowed up by the sea.

Ungama ku-, to acknowledge, to confess of one's own accord.

Ungamana ku-, to bring together, connect.

Ungamo, a yellow dye used for dyeing matting.

Ungana ku-, to unite, to join together.

Unge-, the sign of the second person sing. conditional.

Ungedumu, you would continue.

Ungekuwa, you would be.

Ungi, much, plenty.

Ungo, the hymen (?).

Kuvunja ungo, to be deflowered, to begin to menstruate.

Ungo, plur. *maungo*, a round flat basket used in sifting.

Ungua ku-, to be scorched or scalded.

Unguja, Zanzibar.

Ungulia ku-, to scorch or scald.

Unguza ku-, to scorch or scald, to burn.

Ungwana, the state of being a free and civilized man, civilization.

-ungwana, civilized, as opposed to *-shenzi;* free, as opposed to *-tumwa*.

Kiungwana, of a civilized kind.

Unuele, or *Unwele*, or *Unyele*, plur. *nyele*, a hair.

Unyago. See *Kinyago*.

Kuchezea unyago, to teach womanhood.

Unyasi, reed, grass.

Unyayo, plur. *nyayo*, the sole of the foot, a footprint.

Unyele. See *Unuele*.

Unyende.

Kupiga unyende, to cry with a feeble thin voice.

Unyika, the Nyika country.

Unyoa, plur. *nyoa*, a feather.

Unyofu, straightness, uprightness.

Unyogovu, idleness.

Unyonge, vileness, meanness.

Unyungu.

Kupiga unyungu, to strut about, to show oneself off.

Unyushi, plur. *nyushi*, a hair from the eyebrow.

Uo, plur. *mauo*, a sheath.

Uoga or *Woga*, fear.

Uovu, rottenness, badness, corruption, malice, evil.

Uozi, marriage.

Upaa, baldness.

Upaa wa kitwa, crown of the head, baldness.

Upaja, plur. *paja*, the thigh.

Upaji, liberality.

Upamba, plur. *pamba*, a bill, a small hatchet.

Upana, width, breadth

Upande, plur. *pande*, a side, part.
Upande wa Mvita, near or about Mombas.
Upande wa chini, the under side, the lee side.
Upande wa juu, the upper side, the weather side.
Upande wa goshini, the side where the tack of the sail is fastened, the weather side.

Upanga, a cock's comb.

Upanga, plur. *panga*, a sword.
Upanga wa felegi, a long straight two-edged sword carried by the Arabs.
Upanga wa imani, a short sword with a kind of cross hilt.
Kuweka upanga, to set up a sword on its edge.

Upao, plur. *pao*, one of the small sticks used as laths to tie the thatch to.

Upapi, the outer beading of a door frame.

Upataji, value.

Upato, a round plate of copper beaten as a musical instrument.

Upawa, plur. *pawa*, a flat ladle made out of a cocoa-nut shell, used for serving out curry, gravy, &c.
An *upawa* differs from a *kata* in being very much flatter and shallower: more than two-thirds of the shell are cut away to make an *upawa;* scarcely a quarter is cut off in making a *kata*.

Upekecho, the piece of wood used to make fire by rubbing.

Upeketevu, destruction, harm, quarrelling.

Upele, plur. *pele*, a large pimple.
Pele, the itch.

Upembo, curved end, hook, a stick to hook down fruit with.

Upendaji, the habit of liking.

Upendavyo, as you please.

Upendeleo, favour.

Upenzi, love, affection, liking.

Upeo, plur. *peo* (M.), a sweeping brush.

Upeo, the extremest point visible, the extreme limit, something which cannot be surpassed.

Upepeo, plur. *pepeo*, a fan.

Upepo, plur. *pepo*, a wind, cold. See *Pepo*. The plural is used to denote much wind.

Upesi, quickly, lightly.

Upia = *Upya*, newness.

Upindi, plur. *pindi*, a bow.
Upindi wa mvua, the rainbow

Upindo, a fold, a hem.

Upo, a water-dipper for a boat or dhow.

Upofu, blindness.

Upogo, a squint.

Upogoupogo, zigzag.

Upole, gentleness, meekness.

Upondo, plur. *pondo*, a pole used to propel canoes and small vessels.

Upongoe, plur. *pongoe*, the leaf stem of a palm tree.

Upooza, paralysis.

Upote, string, bowstring.

Upotevu, waste, destructiveness, wastefulness.

Upumbofu, folly.

Upunga, plur. *punga*, a flower or embryo nut of the cocoa-nut tree.

Upungufu, defect, defectiveness.

Upupu, cow-itch.

Upuzi, nonsense, chatter, silly talk.

Upweke, singleness, independence.

Upya, newness.

Urathi, contentment.

Urefu, length.

Urembo, ornament, applied especially to the black lines painted on their faces by the women of Zanzibar by way of ornament.

Urithi, inheritance.

Urongo = *Uwongo*.

Urotha, invoice.

Uru, diamonds (in cards).

Usafi. shavings and chips.

Usaha, matter, pus.

Usemi, talk, conversation.

Ushadi, plur. *nyushadi*, verses.

Ushahidi, or *Ushuhuda*, testimony.

Ushambilio, haste, suddenly.

Ushanga, plur. *shanga*, a bead.

Usharika, partnership, sharing.

Ushaufu, deceit.

Usherati, dissipation. Also *Asherati*.

Ushi, a string-course.

Ushujaa, heroism, great courage.

Ushukura, thanks.

Ushungu, a vegetable poison, used to poison arrows.

Ushupafu, perversity, crookedness.

Ushuru, tax, duty, customs.

Usia ku-, to leave directions or orders, by will, &c. See *Wasia*.

Usikizi, hearing, attention, understanding.

Usiku, night. The plur. *siku* is used to denote days of 24 hours. *Four whole nights* must be rendered *siku nne usiku kucha*. Four days and nights, *siku nne mchana na usiku*.

Usimanga, mockery.

Usimeme, firmness.

Usinga, plur. *singa*, a (straight, not woolly) hair. See *Singa*.

Usingizi, plur. *singizi*, sleep. See *Zingizi*.

Usiri, delay.

Usiwa, on the high seas.

Uso, plur. *nyuso*, face, countenance.

Ussubui, for *Assubui*, in the morning, the morning.

Usubi, a sandfly, a midge.

Usufi, silk cotton from the *msufi* tree.

Usukani, plur. *sukani*, a rudder.

Usultani, sultanship.

Usumba, see *Makumbi*.

Uta, plur. *nyuta* or *mata*, a bow, [bow and arrows.

Uta.

Mafuta ya uta, semsem oil.

Utaa, a raised stage to put corn, &c. on.

Utabibu, medical science, being a doctor.

Utagaa, a branch of a tree.

Utaji, a veil.

Utajiri, wealth.

Utakacho, what you wish.

Utakatifu, holiness, purity.

Utako (Mer.), keel of a dhow.

Utambaa, plur. *tambaa*, a bandage, a rag.

Utambi, plur. *tambi*, a lamp-wick, a piece of stuff for a turban.

Utambo (*wa sufuria*, &c.), a swinging handle like that of a pail.

Utamvua, end or corner of a turban, of a cloth, &c.

Utandu (A.) = *Ukoko*.

Utandu? hymen.

Utani, a kindred race, the belonging to a kindred tribe, familiarity.

Utanzu, plur. *tanzu*, a branch.

Utashi, desire.

Utasi, tonguetiedness.

Utawi.

Kupiga utawi, to drink grog together.

Ute.

Ute wa yayi, the white of an egg.

Utelezi, slipperiness.
Utembe, the chewed refuse of betel leaf, &c.
Utenzi, a poem, especially a religious poem.
Uteo, plur. *teo* (M.), a sifting basket.
Utepe, plur. *tepe*, a tape, a band, a fillet, a stripe.
Utepetefu, languor.
Uteti, strife.
Uthabiti, bravery, firmness.
Uthaifu, weakness, infirmity.
Uthani, weight.
Uthi ku-, to harass, trouble.
Uthia, bother, noise, uproar.
Uthia ku-, to harass.
Uthibaji, cheat, deceit, stratagem.
Uthika ku-, to be harassed.
Uthilifu, calamity, great trouble.
Uthuru ku-, to excuse.
Uti.
Uti wa maungo, the backbone.
Utiko, the roof-ridge of a thatched house.
Utiriri, a provoking trick.
Utofu, dull, without amusement.
Utofu, thinness, weakness.
Utoko, mucus from the vagina.
Uto.
Uto wa nyama, fat cooked out of meat, dripping.
Utonwa, thick white sap.
Utondwi, small dhows trading about Zanzibar, coasters.
Utosi, the top of the head.
Utoto, childhood.
Utufu, fatigue.
Utukufu, greatness, exaltation, glory.
Utule, wretchedness, weakness, unfitness.
Utulivu, quietness, patience.
Utumbavu, thickness, swelling, rising.
Utumbuizo, a soothing thing, verses sung during a dance.
Utume, sending people about.
Utumi, use, usage.
Utumo, business, place of business.
Utumwa, slavery, employment, engagement.
Kutia utumwani, to enslave.
Utungu (M.) = *Uchungu.*
Utungu, is used in the dialect of Zanzibar only for the pains of childbirth, *Utungu wa uzazi.*
Utupa, a species of euphorbia used as a fish poison.
Utupu, naked (vulgar).
Mtu utupu, a naked man.
Mtu mtupu, a mere man.
Uuaji, murderousness.
Uudi, aloes wood.
Uuza ku. See *Uza ku-.*
Uvi, a door [Tumbatu].
Uvivu, idleness, sloth.
Uvuguvugu, lukewarmness.
Maji yana uvuguvugu, the water is lukewarm.
Uvuli, shade.
Uvumba, incense, galbanum.
Uvundo, a smell of corruption.
Uvurujika, tendency to crumble, a being spoilt and decayed.
Uvurungu, hollowness.
Jiwe la uvurungu, a hollow stone.
Uvyazi, birth.
Uwanda, a plain.
Uwanga, arrowroot.
Uwanga, a sweet dish made of wheat, flour, sugar, and ghee.
Uwanja, a courtyard, an enclosure.
Uwashi, masonry.
Uwati, a vesicular eruption on the skin.

Uwaziri, the vizirship.
Uweli, sickness, disease.
Uweli wa viungo, rheumatism.
Uwezo, power, ability.
Uwinda.
Kupiga uwinda, to pass the ends of the loin-cloth between the legs and tuck them in, as is done loosely by the Banyans, and tightly by men at work.
Uwingu, plur. *mbingu*, heaven, sky. The plural is the form more commonly used.
Uwivu, jealousy.
Uwongo, falsehood.
Manenoye yamekuwa uwongo, he has become a teller of lies.
Uyajuapo, if you know them.
Uyoga, a mushroom.
Uyuzi, ingenuity.
Uyuzi ku-, to ascertain.
Uza ku-, to ask, to ask questions.
Uza ku- or *Za ku-*, to sell.
The *u* in *kuuza*, or rather *kuza*, to sell, is very short and insignificant: it is possibly only a partial retention of the *ku-*, which bears the accent and is retained entire in the usual tenses. The *u-* in *kuúza*, to ask, is much more important, as is shown clearly in the applied forms.
Kuuliza, to ask of a person; pres. perf. *ameuliza*.
Kuliza, to sell to a person; pres. perf. *ameliza*.
Uzanya ku-, to be ordinarily sold, to be for sale.
Uzazi, birth.
Uzee, old age.
Uzembe, indifference, apathy, slowness.
Uzi, plur. *nyuzi*, thread, string, a stripe.
Uziki, poverty.
Uzima, health, heartiness, completeness, life.
Uzingizi. See *Zingizi* and *Usingizi*.
Uzinguo, disenchantment, as from the power of the evil eye.
Uzini or *Uzinzi*, adultery, fornication.
Uzio, plur. *nyuzio*, a hedge made in the sea to catch fish.
Uzulia ku-, to depose.
Uzulu ku-, to depose, to remove from an office.
Kujiuzulu, to resign, to give up a place or office, to abdicate.
Uzuri, beauty, fineness, ornament.
Kufanya uzuri, to adorn oneself.
Uzushi, raising from the bottom, as in fishing for pearls.
Uzuzu, rawness, greenness (of a simpleton).

V.

V is pronounced as in English.

V, *f*, and *b*, are sometimes a little difficult to distinguish accurately in the dialect of Zanzibar. This is probably owing to the want of a *v* in Arabic.

V and *vy* change in some dialects into *z-*, in others into *th-*.

Mwivi, a thief, becomes *mwizi* at Lamoo, and *mwithi* at Patta.

Vaa ku-, to put on, to dress in.
The past tenses are used in the sense of, to wear.
Amevaa, he wears.
Alivaa, he wore.
Valia ku-.

Mshipi wa kuvalia nguo, a girdle to gird up one's clothes with.

Vao, plur. *mavao*, dress.

Varanga, interrupting and bothering talk.

Vazi, plur. *mavazi*, a dress, a garment.

Vema, well, very well.

Vema or *Vyema*, good. See *-ema*.

Vi- or *Vy-*, the plural prefix of substantives (and of adjectives and pronouns agreeing with them) which make their singular in *ki-* or *ch-*.

Vi- or *Vy-*, sign of the third person plural prefixed to verbs governed by nouns in *vi-* or *vy-*.

Vi- or *Vy-* prefixed to adjectives often gives them an adverbial sense.

-vi-, the objective prefix representing nouns in *vi-* or *vy-*.

Via ku-, to stop short of perfection, to be stunted in its growth, to remain only half cooked for want of fire, &c., &c.

Viaa ku- = *Vyaa ku-*.

Viatu (plural of *Kiatu*), shoes, sandals.

Viatu vya Kizungu, European shoes.

Viatu vya ngozi, leather sandals.

Viatu vya mti, wooden clogs.

Viazi (plur. of *Kiazi*), sweet potatoes.

Viazi vya Kizungu, potatoes.

Viazi vikuu, yams.

Viberiti (plur. of *Kiberiti*), matches, lucifers.

Vidani, collars of gold, &c.

Viembe or *Vyembe*, arrows.

Vifaa, necessaries, useful things.

Vigwe, braid, reins.

Vijineno, little words, prattle.

Vika ku-, to clothe, to dress.

Vile, those yonder.

Vilevile, just those things, like things, in like manner.

Vilia ku-, to stop and stagnate, as the blood does in a bruise.

Vilio, a stagnation, a stoppage.

Mavilio ya damu, bruises, effusion of blood.

Vimba ku-, to swell, to thatch.

Vimbisha ku-, to overfeed a person.

Vimbiwa ku-, to be overstuffed, to overeat oneself.

Vimo, all of one size.

Vinga vya moto, firebrands, sing. *Kinga cha moto*.

Vingi, many. See *-ingi*.

Vingine, others. See *-ngine*.

Vinjari ku-, to cruise about, to go looking out for something, to watch.

Vinyavinya ku-, to press and crush food for children and sick people.

Vinyi. See *Mwenyi*.

Vinyu = *Mvinyo*.

Vioga ku- (M.), to tread.

Viombo = *Vyombo*.

Viote or *Vyote*, all. See *-ote*.

Vipande vya kupimia, nautical instruments, sextants, &c.

Vipele (plur. of *Kipele*), small pimples, a rash.

Vipele vya harara, prickly heat.

Viringa ku-, to become round.

Imeviringa, it is round.

Viringana ku-, to become spherical

Visha ku-, to give clothes to.

Vita, war.

Vitanga vya mizani, scales, scale-pans.

Vitindi vya shaba, brass wire.

Vitwa vitwa, topsy-turvy.

Vivia ku-, to smoulder.
Vivi hivi, common, just there, just so, anyhow.
-vivu, idle, dull, slow.
Kisu ni kivivu, the knife is blunt (A.).
Vivyo, thus, in the way mentioned.
Vivyohivyo, in like manner.
Viwimbi (plur. of *Kiwimbi*), wavelets, a ripple.
Viza ku-, to stunt, to prevent its attaining perfection, to interrupt, to stop or hinder in work.
Vizia ku-, to watch, to spoil one's work for one, to hinder one from working.
Vizuri, fine, finely. See *-zuri*.
Vua ku-, to take off clothes.
Vua ku-, to save, to deliver, to take across.
Vua ku-, to fish, to catch fish.
Vuata ku- or *Vwata ku-*, to press with the teeth, to hold in the mouth.
Vuaza ku-, to wound by striking or running into unawares, to cut.
Vugaza ku-, to put to (a door).
Vugo, a horn played upon by beating.
Vuja ku-, to leak, to let water.
Vujia ku-, to ooze out.
Vuka ku-, to cross, to go over, to pass a river, to be saved.
Vuke, steam, vapour, sweat.
Vukiska ku-, to take across, to ferry over.
Vukiza ku-, to cause to fume, to give off vapour.
Vukuta ku-, to blow bellows.
Vukuto, sweat.
Vule.
Dudu vule, an insect living in wood, a carpenter bee (?).
Vuli, shade.
Mkono wa kuvuli, the right hand.
Vulia ku-, to catch fish for, or with.
Vuma ku-, to blow as the wind, to buzz like a bee.
Vuma ku-, to lose (in card-playing).
Vumbi, plur. *mavumbi*, dust, flue, muddiness in water.
Vumbika ku-, to put in under something, to stick into the embers, to cover with a heap of leaves, &c.
Vumbikia ku-, to put seeds or plants in the ground before rain, to get them into the ground.
Vumbilia ku-.
Kuvumbilia vita, to get into a quarrel.
Vumbu, plur. *mavumbu*, lumps in flour, &c.
Vumbua ku-, to find after a search, to discover.
Vumi, a noise as of blowing or bellowing, often made with a drum.
Vumilia ku-, to endure, to tolerate, to bear.
Vumisha ku-, to win (in card-playing).
Vuna ku-, to reap.
Vuna ku-.
Kujivuna, to swell up, to be puffed up.
Vunda, &c. = *Vunja*, &c.
Vunda ku-, to rot.
-vungu, hollow.
Vunja ku-, to break, to ruin, to spoil, to change a piece of money.
Kuvunja jungo, to have a final feast, as before Ramathan.
Vunja jungo or *chungu*, a mantis (Mantis religiosa), so called from the superstition that a person touching it will break the next

piece of crockery or glass he handles.

Vunjia ku-, to break for, with, &c.

Vunjika ku-, to become broken.

Vuruga ku-, to stir.

Vurujika ku-, to break up into fragments, crumble.

Vurumisha ku-, to throw a stone, &c.

Vusha ku-, to put across, to ferry over, to put into the right way.

Vuta ku-, to draw, to pull.

Kuvuta maji, to bale out water.

Kuvuta makasia, to row.

Kuvuta tumbako, to smoke tobacco.

Vuvia ku-, to blow.

Vuvumka ku-, to grow up quickly.

Vuzi, plur. *mavuzi*, a hair of the pubes. Also, (A.) hair in general.

Vy- = Vi-.

Vya, of.

Vyaa ku-, to bear children, or fruit. Pass. *vyawa* or *vyaliwa*.

Vyake or *Vyakwe*, his, her, its.

Vyako, thy.

Vyakula (plur. of *Chakula*), things to eat, victuals, meals, provisions.

Vyaliwa ku-, to be born.

Vyangu, my, of me. See *-angu*.

Vyao, their, of them. See *-ao*.

Vyetu, our, of us. See *-etu*.

Vyenu, your, of you. See *-enu*.

-vyo or *-vyo-*, as.

Upendavyo, as you please.

Unipendavyo, as you love me, for my sake.

Alivyoagiza, as he directed. See *ginsi*.

Vyo, *-vyo*, *-vyo-*, which. See *-o*.

Vyo vyote, whatsoever.

Vyombo (plur. of *Chombo*), vessels, household utensils, baggage.

W.

W is pronounced as in English.

W is commonly in Swahili a consonantal *u*, and in many words *w* or *u* may be written indifferently. There are other cases, as in the passive termination *-wa*, where the sound can only be expressed by an English *w*.

W- = U-, which see.

W-, the prefix proper to possessive pronouns governed by substantives either singular or plural which denote animate beings.

Wa, of. See *-a*.

Wa nini, why.

Hamisi wa Tani, Tani's Hamisi, *i.e.* Hamisi, the son of Tani.

Wa or *U*, the Arabic *and*.

Wa! an Arabic exclamation.

Wa-, the plural prefix of substantives in *m-*, *'m-*, or *mw-* which denote animate beings.

Wa-, the plural prefix of adjectives and pronouns agreeing with substantives which denote animate beings.

Wa-, the prefix marking the third person plural of verbs governed by nouns denoting animate beings.

Where the tense prefix begins with an *-a-* that of the personal prefix coalesces with it, so that there is no difference between the second person singular and the third plural.

-wa- the objective plural prefix referring to substantives which denote animate beings.

Wa kú-, to be, to become (?): the *ku-* bears the accent and is retained in the usual cases.

The present tense of the substantive verb is generally represented by *ni* or by the personal prefix standing alone.

The present tense with the relative is represented by the syllable *-li-*. *Aliye*, he who is.

The present perfect *amekuwa*, &c. has the sense of, to have become. *Was* is represented by the past perfect tense *alikuwa*, &c.

Kuwa na, to have.

Simekuwa mwongo? should I not be a liar?

Waa ku-, to shine much, like the sun or the moon.

Waa, plur. *mawaa*, a spot, a blotch, a stain.

Wabba, cholera.

Waboondei, the people living in the low country between the sea and the Shambala mountains.

Wadi, son of.

Wadi Mohammed, Mohammed's son.

Wadi ku-, to complete a term.

Watu wa "London" wamewadi, the (H.M.S.) "London's" commission has expired.

Wadia ku-, to be fully come, to be quite time for anything.

Wadinasi for *Walad ennas*, born of people, that is, of decent family.

Wadui, enmity, hostility.

Wafikana ku-, to conspire together.

Wafiki ku-, to suit, to be suitable to.

Waga ku- (Mer.), to kill.

Wagunya, the Swahili living north of Siwi.

Wahadi, plur. *nyahadi* (?), for *Ahadi*, a promise.

Wáhid, one.

Wai ku-, to be in time.

Wainua, verily.

Wájib, rightness, it ought.

Wajihi ku-, to visit, to see face to face.

Wajihiana ku-, to meet face to face, to see one another.

Waka ku-, to blaze, to burn up, to burn.

Wakati, time, season.

Wakati huu, now.

Wake or *Wakwe*, his, her, or its.

Wakf. [See *-ake.*

Kufanya wakf, to dedicate, to set apart for holy uses.

Wakia, the weight of a silver dollar, about an ounce.

Wakifu ku-, to cost.

Wakifia ku-, to cost to.

Wakili, an agent, a representative.

Wako, thy.

Wakti = *Wakati.*

Wakti gani nije? at what time am I to come?

Wala, nor, and not.

Wala—wala—, neither—nor—.

Where *or* would be used in English after a negative *wala* is used in Swahili.

Walai or *Wallaye*, the most common Swahili oath.

Walakini, but, and however.

Walao, not even.

Wale, those yonder.

Wali, cooked grain, especially rice.

Wali wa mwikuu, what is left from some meal overnight to be eaten in the morning.

Wali, a governor.
  Liwali for *Al Wali*, the governor, is more commonly used in Zanzibar.

Walio. See *Nyalio*.

Walio, they who are.

Walimwengu, the people of this world.

Walli, a saint.

Wama ku-, to lie on the face.

Wamba ku-, to lace in the ropes upon the frame of a *kitanda*, to fill up.

Wambiso, attachment.

Wana, they have.
  Hawana, they have not.

Wanda ku-, to get very fat and strong.

Wanda, plur. *nyanda*, a finger, a finger's-breadth.

Wanga ku- (Mer.), to oount, to reckon.

Wanga, one who uses witchcraft against another.

Wanga, arrowroot. Also *Uanga*.

Wanga or *Wangwa*, a cliff.

Wangine, others, other people.
  Wangine — wangine—, some — others—.

Wangu, my. See *-angu*.

Wangua ku-, to scoop up.

Wangwa, a desert, a bare waste place.

Wangwana or *Waungwana*, gentry, free and civilized men.

Wanja.
  Wanja wa manga, antimony.

Wano, plur. *mawano*, the shaft of an arrow or harpoon.

Wao, they.

Wao, their. See *-ao*.

Wapi? which people?

Wapi? or *api?* where? Commonly joined with the personal sign of the noun.
  Yu wapi or *Yuko wapi?* where is [he]?
  Zi wapi or *Ziko wapi?* where are [they]?

Wapilia ku-, to be laden with scent, highly perfumed.

Wapo, a gift.

Waradi, or *Waredi*, or *Waridi*, a rose.

Waraka, plur. *nyaraka*, a letter.

Waria, a clever dhow-builder, a clever man at any business.

Warr, a yard (measure).

Wasa, plur. *nyasa*, small sticks to fill up between larger ones in a wall or roof.

Wasa ku-, to contradict.

Washa ku-, to light, to set fire to.
  Kuwasha moto, to light up a fire.

Washarati, great dissipation, licentiousness.

Washenzi, wild people, uncivilized men.

Wasi, rebellion. Also *Uasi*.

Wasia, sentence, will, declared opinion. Also *Wosia*.

Wasia ku-, to bequeath, to make a will.

Wasili ku-, to arrive, to come close to, to reach.

Wasili, receipt, credit side of account, *i.e.* tho left-hand column.

Wasilia ku-, to reach a person, especially of letters.

Wasilisha ku-, to cause to reach.

Wasio, who are not.

Wasio = *Wasia* and *Wosia*.

Wastani, middling, in the middle

Waswas, doubt.

Wathahisha ku-, to solve.

Wathiki, narrow.

Watia ku-, to sit upon eggs.
Watu, fenugreek.
Watu (plur. of *Mtu*), people.
-*a watu*, other people's.
Wavu, plur. *nyavu*, a net to catch gazelles, &c.
Wawili, two, two persons.
Wote wawili, both.
Waya, an earthen dish to bake cakes on.
Wayawaya ku-, to sway like a bough loaded with fruit, to swagger, to be bent down and burdened.
Wayo, plur. *nyayo*, sole of the foot, footprint. Also *Uayo*.
Waza ku-, to think, consider, reflect.
Wazao, progeny, offspring, posterity.
-*wazi*, open, clear, manifest. It makes *wazi* with nouns like *nyumba*.
Kitwa kiwazi, bareheaded.
Panalia wazi, it sounds hollow.
Waziwazi, manifest.
Wazimu.
Ana wazimu, he is mad.
Waziri, plur. *mawaziri*, a vizier, a secretary of state, a chief officer.
Wazo, plur. *mawazo*, thoughts.
-*we*, his, hers, its, for *wake*.
-*we*, thee, for *wewe*.
Wea ku-, to become the property of.
Weka ku-, to place, to lay, to put away, to keep, to delay.
Nyumba hainiweki, I have no rest in the house, I cannot remain in the house.
Wekea ku-, to put away for.
Kuwekea amana, to entrust to.
Kuwekea wakf, to dedicate.
Weko.
Kutia weko, to weld.
Wekua ku-, to break up, to remove.
Weleko, a cloth worn by women.
Weli, sickness.
Weli wa macho, ophthalmia.
Welii, saintly, a saint.
Wema, goodness.
Wembe, plur. *nyembe* (?), a razor.
Wenga ku-, to cause to break out into sores.
Wengi, many. See -*ingi*.
Wengo, the spleen.
Wenu, your. See -*enu*.
Wenzangu, my companions = *Wa enzi wangu*.
Werevu, cunning, shrewdness.
Weu, a place cleared for planting.
Weupe, whiteness, clearness, light.
Weupe, white. See -*eupe*.
Wevi or *Wezi*, thieves. See *Mwivi*.
Wewe, thou, thee.
Weweseka ku-, to talk and murmur in one's sleep. Also *Weweteka*.
Weye, you! it is you.
Weza ku-, to be able, to be a match for, to have power over, to be equal to.
Siwezi, I cannot, or, I am sick.
Nalikuwa siwezi, I was ill.
Sikuweza, I was not able.
Amehawezi, he has fallen sick.
-*weza*. See *mweza*.
Wezekana ku-, to be possible.
Wezesha ku-, to enable.
-*wi*, bad (old Swahili and Nyamwezi).
Wia ku-, to be to.
Niwie rathi, don't be offended with me.
2. to have in one's debt.
Kuwiwa, to be indebted.
Wibo, Ibo.
Wifi, husband's sister.
Wika ku-, to crow like a cock.
Wilaya = *Ulaya*, home, Europe
-*wili*, two. It makes *mbili* with nouns like *nyumba*.

Wimbi, plur. *mawimbi*, a wave.
Mawimbi, surf.

Wimbi, a very small kind of grain.

Winda ku- or *Winga ku-*, to chase, to hunt.

Wingi = *Ungi*, plenty, a great quantity, much.

Wingu, plur. *mawingu*, a cloud.

Wino, ink.

Wishwa, chaff, the husks of rice, the flour sifted off along with the husks.

Witiru, odd, not even.

Witwa (= *Kwitwa ?*), the being called.

Wiva ku- = *Iva ku-*.

-wivu, jealous.

-wivu = *-bivu*, ripé.

Wiwa ku-, to owe, to be indebted to.

Wiza.
Mayayi mawiza, eggs with chickens formed in them, hard set.

Wo, -wo, -wo-, which, who, whom.
Wo wote, whatsoever, whosoever.

-wo, thy, = *Wako*.

Wogofya, plur. *nyogofya*, a threat.

Wokovu, deliverance, salvation.

Wongo, falsehood. Also *Uwongo*.

Wonyesho, showing, display.

Worari, rateable division, sharing. Ar. *Wora*, to cast pebbles.

Wosia, injunction, sentence, charge, wise saying. Also *Wasia*.

Wote, all, both.
Twende wote, let us both go.
Wote wawili, both.

Wovisi, cool.

Woweka ku-, to soak.

Y.

Y is pronounced as in English.

Y is in Swahili a consonantal *i*, and it is often indifferent whether it be written *i* or *y*. The use of *y* is however important to distinguish such words as *kimia*, a cast-net, and *kimya*, silence.

The insertion of a *y* sound before the final *-a* of a verb has in many cases the effect of giving it a causative meaning. See P.
Kupona, to get well.
Kuponya, to cure.
Kuogopa, to fear.
Kuogofya, to frighten

Y = *I*.

Y-, the prefix proper to possessive pronouns governed by singular substantives of the class which does not change to form the plural, by plural substantives in *mi-*, or by plural substantives in [*ma-*.

Ya, of. See *-a*.
Ya kitovu, in the navel.
Ya kwamba, that.
Ya nini ? Why ?

Ya-, sign of the third person plural prefixed to verbs governed by a plural substantive in *ma-*.

-ya-, objective prefix denoting plural nouns in *ma-*.

Yaa ku-, to sow seeds.

Yábis, or *Yabisi*, dry, solid.

Yai = *Yayi*.

Yaika ku-, to melt.

Yake or *Yakwe*, his, hers, its. See *-ake*.

Yakini, certainly, certainty, it is certain.

Yakinia ku-, to determine, to set one's mind upon.

Yakinisha ku-, to make certain.
Yako, thy, your. See *-ako.*
Yakowapi, where are they?
Yakuti, emerald (?).
Yale, those yonder.
Yaliomo, which are within.
Yambo = *Jambo.*
Yamini, an oath.
Yamkini, possibly, possibility.
Kwa yamkini, possibly.
Yamkini ku- (?), to be possible.
Haiyamkini, it is not possible.
Yamur, deer.
Yange. See *-nge-.*
Yangedumu, they would remain.
Yangu, my, of me. See *-angu.*
Yani = *Ya nini?* for what? why?
Yao, their, of them. See *-ao.*
Yasi, a yellow powder brought from India, and used as a cosmetic.
Yatima, an orphan.
Yavuyavu, lights, lungs.
Yaya, a nurse, an ayah.
Yayi, plur. *mayayi*, an egg.
Yayi ya pumbu, testicles.
Ye! = *Je!* Hullo! Well! What now?
Ye, *-ye*, or *-ye-*, sign of the relative, referring to animate beings, who, which, whom.
Ye yote, whosoever.
Yeekwa yee, common-place people.
-ye, his, hers, or its, = *Yake.*
Yee or *Yeye*, he or she, him or her.
Yei, a child's good-bye, "ta-ta."
Yemkini = *Yamkini.*
Yenu, your, of you. See *-enu.*
Yenyi, having. See *-enyi.*
Yetu, our, of us. See *-etu.*
Yeyuka ku-, to melt, to deliquesce.
Yeyusha ku-, to cause to melt, to melt.
Yinyi = *Yenyi.*
-yo, thy, = *Yako.*
Yo, *-yo*, *-yo-*, sign of the relative, which.
Yo yote, whatsoever.
Yoe = *Yowe.*
Yonga ku-, to sway.
Yote, all. See *-ote.*
Kwa yote, altogether, wholly.
Yowe, a cry for help.
Kupiga yowe, to cry for help.
Yu, he or she is.
Yu-, sign of the third person singular, referring to an animate being. It is used chiefly before monosyllabic verbs and in the Mombas dialect.
Yuqja, he comes.
Yuko, *yumo*, &c., he is there, within, &c.
Yule, yonder person, that person.
Yuma ku-, to sway in the wind.
Yuna, he has.
Yungiyungi, the blue water-lily.
Yuza ku-, to declare, to make clear.

Z.

Z is pronounced as in *zany*, the German *s*. *Z* in some dialects takes the place of *v* or *vy* in that of Zanzibar.

Z is used by people who cannot pronounce *th*, for the Arabic *thal*, *thod*, and *dtha*. See *T.*

Z- or *zi-*, the sign of the third person plural prefixed to verbs which are governed by plural substantives of the class which does not change to form the plural, or of that which makes its singular in *u-*.
Z-, the prefix proper to pronouns

governed by plural nouns of the class which does not change to form the plural, or of that which makes its singular in *u*.

Za, of. See *-a*.

Za ku-. See *Uza ku-*, to sell.

Zaa ku-, to bear, to breed, to beget, to bear fruit.

Zabadi, civet.

Zabibu, plur. *mazabibu* (?), grapes, raisins.

Zabidi ku-, to take civet from the *ngawa*.

Zabuni ku-, to buy.

Zaburi, the psalter, a psalm.

Zafarani or *Zafrani*, saffron, a woman's name.

Zagaa ku-, to shine, to glisten.

Zaidi or *Zayidi*, more.

Zaka, tithes.

Zake or *Zakwe*, his, hers, its. See *-ake*.

Zako, thy, your. See *-ako*.

Zakula (A.) = *Vyakula*, victuals.

Zalia ku-, to bear to.

Zalisha ku-, to beget, cause to bear.

Zaliwa ku-, to be born.

Zama ku-, to sink, to dive.

Zamani, times, long ago.

Zamani za kale, old times, long ago, anciently.

Zamani za Shanga, when Shanga flourished.

Zamani hizi, nowadays.

Zamani zetu, our times.

Zambarau, a kind of fruit, in appearance not unlike a large damson.

Zamisha ku-, to make to sink.

Zamu, a turn, turns.

Kwa zamu, by turns.

Zangefuri, cinnabar.

Zangu, my, of me. See *-angu*.

Zani, adultery.

Zao, plur. *mazao*, fruit, produce.

Zao, their. See *-ao*.

Zarambo, a spirit distilled from palm wine.

Zari, a precious kind of stuff, gold thread, gold brocade.

Zatiti ku-, to set in order, arrange, prepare for.

Zawa ku-, to be born.

Zawadi, a present, a keepsake, a rarity.

Zawaridi, a Java sparrow.

Zayidi, more.

Zazi (?), afterbirth.

-ze, his, her, or its, = *Zake*.

-zee, old, aged.

Zebakh, mercury.

Zege, a dome.

Zelabia, a kind of sweetmeat containing syrup.

Zengea ku-, to seek for.

Zenu, your. See *-enu*.

Zenyi. See *-enyi*.

Zetu, our, of us. See *-etu*.

Zezé, a sort of lute with three strings.

Zi- = *z-*.

-zi-, the objective prefix denoting a plural substantive either of that class which does not change to form the plural or of that which makes its singular in *u-*.

Ziba ku-, to fill up a hole in a wall, &c., to plug up, to stop.

Zibana ku-, to be stopped up, to stop itself up.

Zibo, plur. *mazibo*, a plug, a stopper.

Zibua ku-, to unstop, to bore through.

Zidi ku-, to increase, to do more than before.

Kuzidi kujua, to know more.

Zidisha ku-, to make greater, to add to.
Zifuri, a cipher, a figure of nought.
Zika ku-, to bury, to inter.
Zikerezwazo, turnery, turned goods. See *Kereza.*
Ziki.
Kanzu ya ziki, worked with white cotton round the neck instead of silk. See *Kanzu.*
Zikika ku-, to be impoverished.
Zikwi, plur. *vikwi* (N.), a thousand.
Zile, those yonder.
-zima, sound, whole, healthy, complete.
Zima ku-, to extinguish, to put out.
Kuzima roho, to faint.
Zimia ku-, to put out.
Zimika ku-, to go out, to be extinguished.
Zimiliza ku-, to rub out.
Zimu. See *Wazimu, 'Mzimu, Kusimu, Zimwi.*
Zimua ku-, to cool hot water by adding cold to it.
Zimwi, plur. *mazimwi*, an ogre, a ghoul, an evil being which devours men, &c.
Nazi ina zimwi, i.e. the cocoa-nut has grown without anything inside the shell.
Zina ku-, to commit adultery. See *Zini.*
Zindika ku-, to hold an opening ceremony in, to open for use.
Zindiko, an opening ceremony.
Zinduka ku-, to wake up suddenly from a doze with a nod and a start.
Zindukana ku-, to wake up suddenly.
Zinga ku-, to commit adultery (?).
Zinga ku-, to roll up.
Zingizi, sleep, great sleep. Also *Usingizi.*
Zingizi la ku'mkomesha mzazi, a sleep which is supposed to put an end to all further child-bearing.
Zingulia ku-, to relieve from the evil eye.
Zini ku-, to commit adultery or fornication.
Zira ku-, to hate (M.).
Ziriki (M.) = *Riziki.*
-zito, heavy, difficult, severe, sad, clumsy, thick.
Asali nzito, thick syrup.
Zituo.
Hana zituo, he never rests.
Ziwa, plur. *maziwa*, a lake, a pond, the breasts.
Zizi, plur. *mazizi*, a cow-yard, a cattle-fold, a stable, palisading.
Zizi hizi, just these, common.
Zizima ku-, to become very calm, very still, or very cold.
Zizimia ku-, to sink to the bottom.
Zo, -zo, -zo-, sign of the relative, which.
Zo zote, whatsoever.
-zo, thy, = *Zako.*
Zoa ku-, to gather into little heaps, to sweep together.
Zoea ku-, to become accustomed, to become used to.
Zoeza ku-, to accustom to, to make used to.
Kujizoezá, to practise.
Zomari, a kind of clarionet, a pipe.
Zomea ku-, to groan at.
Zongazonga ku-, to wind.
Zote, all. See *-ote.*
Zua ku-, to pierce, to bore through, to innovate, to invent.
Nimemzua, I have sucked him

dry, I have got all the information I can from him.

Zuia ku-, to hold in, to restrain, to hinder.

Kuzuia pumzi, to stifle.

Zuilia ku-, to hold for, to keep off, to hold in its place.

Zuka ku-, to emerge, to rise.

Zuli, perjury.

Zulia, a carpet.

Zulia ku-, to invent to, to make a false excuse to, to say falsely that one has such and such a message.

Zulisha ku-, to make crazy, to flurry.

Zulu ku-, to be crazy.

Zumarid, an emerald.

Zumbili, consolation.

Zumbua ku-, to find.

Kuzumbua paa (A.), to take off thatch.

Zumbukana ku, to be to be found.

Zumgu'mza ku-, to amuse, converse with.

Kujizumgu'mza, to converse, to amuse oneself.

Zunguka ku-, to go round, to surround, to wind round, to revolve, to wander.

Zungukazunguka ku-, to stroll about.

Zungusha ku-, to make to go round, to turn.

Zuri ku-, to lie, to swear falsely.

-zuri, fine, beautiful, handsome.

Zuru ku-, to visit.

Kwenda kuzuru, to go to visit.

Kuzuru kaburi, to visit a grave.

Zurungi = *Huthurungi*, the brown material of which kanzus are made.

Zuzua ku-, to puzzle a stranger, or a greenhorn.

Zuzuka ku-, to be puzzled or bewildered, not to know what to do.

APPENDICES.

APPENDIX I.

SPECIMEN of Kinyume, as written out by Johari, a native of the Swahili coast a little south of Zanzibar. The Swahili is in the Merima dialect

SWAHILI.	KINYUME.	ENGLISH.
Ng'ombe	*Mbeng'o*	An ox.
Mbuzi	*Zimbu*	A goat.
Punda	*Ndapu*	A donkey.
Ngamiya	*Yangami*	A camel.
Nyumba	*Mbanyu*	A house.
Mkeka	*Kamke*	A sleeping mat.
Kitanda	*Ndakita*	A bedstead.
Mlango	*Ngomla*	A door.
Mijengo	*Ngomije*	Buildings (?).
Udongo	*Ngoudo*	Red earth.
Ngazi	*Zinga*	A ladder.
Daraja	*Jadara*	A staircase.
Maneno	*Nomane*	Words.
Basi	*Siba*	That will do.
Mwanamuke	*Kemwanamu*	A woman.
Uzingizi	*Ziuzingi*	Sleep.
Samaki	*Kisama*	Fish.
Kweli	*Likwe*	Truth.
Nazima	*Manazi*	I lend.
Sikupi	*Pisiku*	I will not give you.
Ntakupa	*Pantaku*	I will give you.
Ntakunyima	*Mantakunyi*	I shall withhold from you.
Macho	*Choma*	Eyes.
Mguru	*Rumgu*	A leg.
Rungu	*Nguru*	A club.
Nakuomba	*Mbanakuo*	I pray you.

SWAHILI.	KINYUME.	ENGLISH.
Njara inaniuma	*Ranja mainaniu*	I ache with hunger.
Vidole	*Levido*	Fingers.
Shingo	*Ngoshi*	The neck.
Si kweli	*Lisikwe*	It is not true.
Fundi	*Ndifu*	A master workman.
Sivyo	*Vyosi*	Not thus.
Karatasi	*Sikarata*	Paper.
Kalamu	*Mukala*	A pen.
Wino	*Nowi*	Ink.
Pakura	*Rapaku*	Dish up.
Twende zetu	*Tutwendeze*	Let us be off.
Senendi	*Ndisene*	I am not going.
Chakula	*Lachaku*	Food.
Utakwenda	*Ndautakwe*	You will go.
Mchanga	*Ngamcha*	Sand.
Samawati (Ar.)	*Tisamawa*	Heaven.
Aruthi (Ar.)	*Thiaru*	Earth.
Mutu	*Tumu*	Man.
Mungwana	*Namungwa*	A free man.
Mtumwa	*Mwamtu*	A slave.
Sitaki	*Kisita*	I dislike it.
Meza	*Zame*	A table.
Bweta	*Tabwe*	A box.
Sanduku	*Kusandu*	A chest.
Kitabu	*Bukita*	A book.
Msahafu	*Fumsaha*	A Koran.

Appendix II.

Specimens of Swahili correspondence in prose and verse, containing:—1. Two Swahili letters, the one on giving, the other on receiving a small present. The forms of address, &c., are those used in all letters, whatever their subject may be 2. Two specimens of verses sent as letters, the first to excuse breaking an appointment, the second sent from Pemba by a Mombas man to his friends at home, who upbraided him for not returning. This form of writing is a very favourite one.

I.

Illa jenáb il mohéb rafiki yangu, bwana wangu, bwana mkubwa, D. S., salamu sana, ama baada ya salamu, nalikuwa siwezi siku nyingi, lakini sasa sijambo kidogo, ama baadahu, nimekuletea kitoweo kidogo tafáthali npokee, nao k'uku saba'a, wa salamu, wa katabahu rafiki yako H. bin A.

To the honourable the beloved, my friend, my master, the great sir, D. S., many compliments, but after compliments, I was unwell for many days, but now I am a little recovered, and after this, I have sent you a little *kitoweo* [*i.e.* something to be eaten with the rice or grain, which forms the bulk of all meals], and I beg your acceptance, they are seven fowls and compliments, and he who wrote this is H. son of **A.**

Illa jenáb, il mohéb, il akram, in nasih, D. S., il Mwingrezi, insha' Allah salaam aleik wa réhmet Allah wa barakátahu; wa baada, nakuarifu hali zangu njema wa *th*ama nawe kathálik ya afia, wa zayidi amana yako ulioniletea imefika kwangu, ahsanta, Mwenyiezi Muungu atakujazi kheiri ukae ukitukumbuka, nasi nyoyo zetu zinakukumbuka sana, tunapenda uje 'nti ya Unguja, wewe na bibi, naye aje tumwangalie, naye aje atazame 'nti ya Unguja, nasi kulla siku tukilala tukia'mka tunakuombea Muungu uje 'nti ya Unguja, tuonane kwa afia na nguvu, nasi twapenda macho yetu yakuone wewe assubui na jioni, na usipokuja wewe, usitusahau kwa nyaraka allah allah. Nisalimie bibi mke wako salamu sana. Nasi tunakutamani, kama tungalikuwa ndege tungaliruka tukija tukaonane nawe mara moja tukiisha tukarudi. Nyumbani kwangu mke wangu salamu sana. M. bin A. akusalimu sana, wa katabahu M. wadi S. 26 mwezi wa mfunguo kenda.

To the honourable, the beloved, the noble, the sincere D. S., the Englishman, please God, peace be with you and the mercy of God and His blessing; and afterwards, I inform you that my health is good, and may you be the same as to health, and further, your pledge which you sent me has reached me, I thank you. Almighty God will satisfy you with good that you may continue to remember us, and as for us, our hearts think much of you; we wish you to come to the land of Zanzibar, you and the mistress, and let her come that we may behold her, and let her come that she may look upon the land of Zanzibar; and we every day when we sleep and when we wake pray for you to God that you come to the land of Zanzibar, that we may meet in health and strength, and we, we wish that our eyes should see you morning and evening, and if you come not yourself, forget us not by letters, we adjure you. Salute for me the mistress your wife with many compliments. And we are longing for you, and if we had been birds we would have come flying to see you once and then return. At home my wife sends many compliments. M. son of A. salutes you much, and he who wrote this is M. the son of S. 26 of the month Jemad al akhr.

II.

Kala es sha'iri.	The Verse says.
Kisala enda kwa hima	Go, message, quickly
Kwa Edward Istira	To Edward Steere,
Umpe yangu salama	Give him health,
Pamwe na kumkhubira,	Together with telling him,
Siwezi yangu jisima	I am ill in my body,
Ningekwenda tesira	I would have gone readily
Kumtazama padira	To see the Padre,
Pamwe na Edward Stira.	Together with Edward Steere.

Pamwe na Edward Stira.	Together with Edward Steere.
Ilimu ya Injili	The doctrine of the Gospel—
Yuaijua habara	He knows how its news
Pia yote kufasili.	To explain,—all of it.
Ni muhebbi akhyara	He is a choice friend,
Kwetu sisi afthali.	Especially in our house;
Edi ni mtu wa kweli.	He is a man of truth.
Rabbi, nipe tesira.	O Lord, give me prosperity.

Hatukiati kisiwa kwa uvambume na upembe
   Tukaifuasa hawa kulewalewa na ombe
Ni mpunga na maziwa na kulla siku ni ngombe
   Twalalia kwa jivumbe, lipangine kwa rihani.

We shall not leave the island for tale-bearing and plotting,
   And follow the fancy to be tossed on the sea.
Here are rice, and milk, and every day an ox;
   We sleep among perfumes, and strings of sweet basil.

Swahili letters are always written with a string of Arabic compliments at the beginning, and Arabic words are freely introduced throughout. In letter-writing *kuarifu* is used for *to inform*, and *kuwasilia* (not *kufikia*) for *to reach*, as in the phrase *your letter has reached me—waraka wako umeniwasilia.* Swahili verses are written in an obsolete dialect full of Arabic words and foreign words generally, called Kingozi. It has not yet been studied by any European. Among its more remarkable peculiarities is the use of a present perfect made by a change in the termination of the Verb, similar to those in use in the Yao and in other languages of the Interior. Thus a poet may write *mbwene* for *nimeona*, and *nikomile* for *nimekoma.* Some specimens of this dialect will be found in the poetry at the end of the "Swahili Tales."

Appendix III.

Part of a Swahili tale with the prefixes marked and explained. It is printed first as in the main it would be written by a native; next the compound forms are marked by hyphens and explained; and last comes an English translation.

Yule kijana akafuta upanga wake, akanena, mimi nitaingia humo I.

The tale, of which this is a part, is called the *Hadithi ya Waridi, na Ureda, na Jindi, na Sinébar*. The portion of it here printed begins with a verb in the *ka* tense, because it is carrying on a narration already commenced. The first words of the story are—*Aliondokea mtu tajiri.* After this first verb in the *li* tense the rest are formed with *ka*, unless they are constructed with a relative or particle of time or place, which cannot be joined with *ka* but only with *li*. II.

Yule, that; demonstrative (p. 115) referring to a singular substantive of the first class, *kijana* being regarded as the name of a person. *Ki-jana*, a young man or woman, here a man. *A-ka-futa*, and he drew; *a-*, sign of third person sing., appropriate to a noun of the first class or to any word denoting a living being; *-ka-*, sign of the narrative past tense; *-futa*, draw. *U-panga*, a sword; a sing. substantive of the sixth class. *W-ake*, his; possessive pronoun, third person sing.; *w-*, prefix proper to a pronoun agreeing with a sing. substantive of the sixth class. *A-ka-nena*, and he said; *a-* and *-ka-*, as before; *-nena*, speak or say out. *Mimi*, I. *Ni-ta-ingia*, I will go in; *ni-*, sign of the first person sing.; *-ta-*, sign of the future tense; *-ingia*, go into, enter. *Humo*, in here; a demonstrative

---

The youth drew his sword, and said, "I will go into this pit, whether III.

I. shimoni, nikafe ao nikapone. Akaingia, akamwona mtoto amefungwa, naye mwanamume. Akamwambia, nifungue nikupe khabari ya humo shimoni. Akamfungua, akaona vichwa vingi vya watu. Aka-

---

II. proper to the *-ni* case, when it denotes being, &c., within. *Shimo-ni*, into the pit; *shimo-*, a singular noun of the fifth class; *-ni*, sign of the locative case. *Ni-ka-fe*, and let me die; *ni-*, sign of first person sing.; *-ka-* and (p. 141); *-fe*, subjunctive form of *fa*, die. *Ao*, or. *Ni-ka-pone*, and let me live; *ni-* and *-ka-*, as before; *-pone*, subjunctive form of *pona*, be saved. *A-ka-ingia*, and he went in; third sing., narrative past of *ingia*, go in. *A-ka-mw-ona*, and saw him; *a-ka-*, and he did; *-mw-*, objective prefix proper to a substantive of the first class (*mtoto*); *-ona*, see. *M-toto*, child; sing. substantive of the first class. *A-me-fungwa*, bound; *a-*, sign of third person sing., governed by a substantive of the first class (*mtoto*); *-me-*, sign of the present perfect, which is here used as a sort of past participle: *-fungwa*, passive of *funga*, bind. *Na-ye*, and he (p. 103). *Mw-ana-m-ume*, a male; *mw-*, sing. prefix of a noun of the first class; *m-* (for *mu-*), prefix agreeing with a substantive of the first class; *-ume*, male; the whole word, *mwanamume*, is used for a man, or any human being of the male sex. *A-ka-mw-ambia*, and he said to him; *a-ka-*, third sing. narrative past; *-mw-*, subjective prefix denoting a person (*kijana*); *-ambia*, say to. *Ni-fungue*, unbind me; *ni-*, objective prefix, first person; *-fungue*, imperative sing. of *fungua*, unbind. *Ni-ku-pe*, that I may give you; *ni-*, subjective prefix first person; *-ku-*, objective prefix, second person; *-pe*, subjunctive of *pa*, give to. *Khabari*, news; sing. substantive of the third class. *Y-a*, of; *y-*, sign of agreement with a sing. substantive of the third class (*khabari*). *Humo*, here in; a demonstrative agreeing with the *-ni* case when denoting *within*. *Shimo-ni*, in the pit; *-ni*, sign of the locative case. *A-ka-m-fungua*, and he loosed him; *a-*, *ka-*, third sing. narrative past; *-m-*, objective prefix referring to a substantive of the first class (*mtoto*); *-fungua*, unbind. *A-ka-ona*, and he saw, third sing., narrative past. *Vi-chwa*, heads or skulls; *vi-*, sign of a plural substantive of the fourth class; *vichwa* is in more elegant Swahili *vitwa*. *V-ingi*, many; *v-* or *vi-*, adjectival plural prefix, marking agreement with a plural substantive of the fourth class (*vichwa*); *-ingi* or *-ngi*, many. *Vy-a*, of; *vy-*, marking the agreement with a plural noun of

---

III. I die or live." And he went in and saw a boy, and he was bound. And [the boy] said, "Unbind me, that I may tell you about what there is in this pit." And he unbound him, and saw many human skulls. And he

mwuliza, habari gani hii? Akamwambia, mna nyoka humo, kazi yake kula watu, na mimi angalinila, lakini amenifanya mtoto wake, miaka mingi nimetoka kwetu. Akamwuliza, sasa yuko wapi nyoka? I.

---

the fourth class (*vichwa*). *Wa-tu*, people; *wa-*, plural prefix first class. II. *A-ka-mw-uliza*, and he asked him; *a-*, *ka-*, third sing. narrative past; *-mw-*, objective prefix referring to a person (*mtoto*); *-uliza*, ask or ask of. *Habari* or *khabari*, news, sing. substantive third class. *Gani*, what sort? *Hii*, this; demonstrative denoting a sing. substantive of the third class (*habari*). *A-ka-mw-ambia*, and he said to him; this word is of constant occurrence, it means that one person told or said to another; there is no mark of sex or means of distinguishing which person of several mentioned before was the speaker, these points must be gathered from the context. *M-na*, there is inside; *m-na* is part of the verb *kuwa na*, to be with or to have, used as it often is to denote mere being (p. 153); it answers to the English *there is; there* may be represented by *ku-*, *pa-*, or *m-;* the last is used where the place suggested is within something, it refers here to *shimoni*, in the pit. *Ny-oka*, a snake, a sing. substantive in the form of the third class, denoting an animate being. *Humo*, there within, referring to *shimoni*. *Kazi*, work or employment, sing. substantive, third class. *Y-ake*, his; *y-*, prefix agreeing with a sing. substantive of the third class; *-ake*, possessive pronoun, third person sing. *Ku-la*, to eat; *ku-*, sign of the infinitive; *-la*, eat. *Wa-tu*, people; *wa-*, plural prefix first class. *Na*, and. *Mimi*, I or me. *A-ngali-ni-la*, he would have eaten me; *a-*, third sing., agreeing with the name of an animal (*nyoka*); *-ngali-*, sign of the past conditional tense; *-ni-*, objective prefix referring to the first person; *-la*, eat; the tense prefix *-ngali-* cannot bear any accent, the word is therefore pronounced *ángalinila*. *Lakini*, but. *A-me-ni-fanya*, he has made me; *a-*, referring to *nyoka; -me-*, sign of present perfect; *-ni-*, objective prefix, first person; *-fanya*, make. *M-toto*, child; *m-*, sing. prefix, first class. *W-ake*, his; *w-*, prefix agreeing with sing. substantive of the first class (*mtoto*). *Mi-aka*, years; plural substantive of the second class (sing. *mwaka*); *mi-*, plural prefix. *M-ingi*, many; *m-* or *mi-*, prefix, denoting agreement with a plural substantive of the second class (*miaka*). *Ni-me-toka*, I have left; *ni-*, first person subjective; *-me-*, present perfect; *-toka*, go out of. *Kw-etu*, home;

---

asked, "What is this?" And he said, "There is a snake in it, that eats men, and would have eaten me, but that it took me for its own son. It is many years since I left home." And he asked, "Where is the snake III.

I. Akamwambia, twende, nikakuonye mahala amelala. Akamwambia, twende. Walipofika, yule kijana akamkata kichwa kimoja, akatoa cha pili, akamkata, hatta vikatimu saba. Wakarudi, wakaenda zao.

II. *kw-*, prefix agreeing with a substantive (perhaps *nyumba*) in the case in *-ni*; *-etu* (our). *A-ka-mw-uliza*, and he asked him; *a-*, third sing. (*kijana*); *-ka-*, narrative past; *-mw-*, third sing. objective (*mtoto*); *-uliza*, ask. *Sasa*, now. *Yu-ko*, he is; *yu-*, sign of third person sing., referring to a substantive of the second class (*nyoka*); *-ko*, denoting existence in space (p. 154). *Wapi*, where? *Ny-oka*, snake; sing. substantive. *A-ka-mw-ambia*, and he said to him. (*See above.*) *Tw-ende*, let us go; *tw-*, sign of the first person plural; *-ende*, subjunctive of *enda*, go. *Ni-ka-ku-onye*, and let me show you; *ni-*, sign of first person sing.; *-ka-*, and (p. 211); *-ku-*, objective second person sing.; *-onye*, subjunctive of *onya*, show. *Mahala*, the place, the place where. *A-me-lala*, he is asleep; *a-*, third sing. animate (*nyoka*); *-me-*, present perfect; *-lala*, lie down to sleep, to go to sleep. *A-ka-mw-ambia*. (*See above.*) *Tw-ende*, let us go; *tw-*, first person plur.; *-ende*, subjunctive of *enda*, go. *Wa-li-po-fika*, when they arrived; *wa-*, sign of third person plural agreeing with substantives denoting persons (*kijana* and *mtoto*); *-li-* or *-ali-*, sign of the past perfect, or of past time generally when joined with a particle of relation; *-po-*, sign of time when; *-fika*, arrive. *Yule*, that; demonstrative denoting a person (*kijana*). *Ki-jana*, youth; sing. substantive fourth class, but denoting a person, and therefore joined as here with pronouns and verbs in forms proper to the first class. *A-ka-m-kata*, he cut him; *a-*, third sing. of a person (*kijana*); *-ka-*, narrative past; *-m-*, objective prefix, referring to the name of an animal (*nyoka*) (see p. 112); *-kata*, cut or cut off. *Ki-chwa*, head, sing. substantive fourth class. *Ki-moja*, one; *ki-*, prefix denoting agreement with a sing. substantive of the fourth class (*kichwa* or *kitwa*); *-moja*, one. *A-ka-toa*, and he put forth; *a-*, third sing., referring to a substantive denoting an animal (*nyoka*); *-ka-*, narrative past; *-toa*, put forth. *Cha pili*, a second (p. 92); *ch-*, referring to a sing. substantive of the fourth class (*kichwa*). *A-ka-m-kata*, and he cut him. (*See above.*) *Hatta*, until. *Vi-ka-timu*, they were complete; *vi-*, third plural refer-

---

III. now?" He said, "Let us go and let me show you where it is sleeping." He said, "Let us go." When they got there the youth cut off one of its heads; it put forth a second, and he cut it off, until he had cut off seven. And they returned, and went on their way.

Akamwambia sasa twende zetu kwetu, lakini tukifika kwetu I
wenende wewe kwanza kwa baba yangu, ukamwambie kana mtoto wako nikikuletea utanipa nini? Akikwambia, nitakupa mali yangu

---

ring to nouns of the fourth class, here to *vichwa*, heads, plural of *kichwa*; II
-ka-, narrative past; *-timu*, be complete. *Saba*, seven. *Wa-ka-rudi*, and they returned; *wa-*, third plural referring to persons (*kijana* and *mtoto*); *-ka-*, narrative past; *-rudi*, return. *Wa-ka-enda z-ao*, and they went away; *wa-*, third plural (*kijana* and *mtoto*); *-ka-*, narrative past; *-enda*, go; *z-ao*, their (ways); *z-*, a prefix denoting agreement with a plural noun of the third or sixth, or in the dialect of Lamoo of the fourth class; *-ao*, their. Possibly *zao* agrees with *njia*, ways. (*See* p. 112.)

A-ka-mw-ambia, and he said to him. *Sasa*, now. *Tw-ende z-etu*. let us go away; *tw-*, sign of first person plural; *-ende*, subjunctive of *enda*, go; *z-*, sign of agreement with a plural noun of the third or the sixth class; *-etu*, our. (*See above.*) *Kw-etu*, home; *kw-*, sign of agreement with the case in *-ni-*; *-etu*, our. *Lakini*, but. *Tu-ki-fika*, when we arrive; *tu-*, sign of the first person plural; *-ki-*, sign of the participial tense (p. 136); *-fika*, arrive. *Kw-etu*, home. *W-enende*, go; *w-*, sign of the second person singular; *-enende*, subjunctive of *enenda*, go, or go on. *Wewe*, thou. *Kwanza*, first; originally the infinitive of the verb *anza*, begin; *kwanza*, to begin, beginning, and therefore first. *Kwa*, to a person, or to his house. *Baba*, father. *Y-angu*, my; *y-*, sign of an agreement with a singular noun of the third class, used here colloquially with one denoting a person (*baba*); *-angu*, my (p. 109). *U-ka-mw-ambie*, and say to him; *u-*, sign of the second person singular; *-ka-*, and; *-mw-*, objective sign referring to a noun denoting a person (*baba*); *-ambie*, subjunctive of *ambia*, tell. *Kana*, if. *M-toto*, child. *W-ako*, thy; *w-*, sign of agreement with a singular substantive of the first class (*mtoto*). *Ni-ki-ku-letea*, if I bring to you; *ni-*, sign of the first person singular; *-ki-*, sign of the participial tense (p. 136); *-ku-*, objective prefix referring to the second person singular; *-letea*, bring to. *U-ta-ni-pa*, you will give me; *u-*, sign of second person sing.; *-ta-*, sign of the future tense; *-ni-*, objective prefix referring to the first person singular; *-pa*, give to. *Nini*, what? *A-ki-kw-ambia*, if he tells you; *a-*, sign of the third person singular referring to a

---

And [the boy] said, "Now let us go to my home; but when we are III
getting near to it do you go first to my father and say to him, 'If I bring your son to you, what will you give me?' If he says to you, 'I will give

I. nussu kwa nussu, usikubali, mwambie nataka kofia yako uliyo ukivaa ujanani mwako. Atakupa kofia ya thahabu, usikubali, ela akupe

---

II. person (*baba*); *-ki-*, sign of the participial tense; *-kw-*, objective prefix referring to the second person singular; *-ambia*, say to. *Ni-ta-ku-pa*, I will give you; *ni-*, sign of the first person sing.; *-ta-*, sign of the future tense; *-ku-*, objective prefix referring to the second person singular; *-pa*, give to. *Mali*, possessions; treated sometimes as a noun of the third class, sometimes as a plural noun of the fifth class. *Y-angu*, my; *y-*, sign of an agreement with a singular noun of the third or with a plural noun of the fifth class. *Nussu*, half. *Kwa*, by. *Nussu*, half. *U-si-kubali*, do not accept; *u-*, sign of second person singular; *-si-*, sign of negative subjunctive (p. 147); *-kubali*, subjunctive of *kubali*, accept. *Mw-ambie*, tell him; *mw-*, objective prefix referring to a person (*baba*); *-ambie*, imperative of *ambia*, tell; *mw-* is known to be the objective third person, and not the subjective second plural, by the form of the word *ambia*; being an applied form it must have the object expressed. *N-a-taka*, I want; *n-*, sign of the first person singular; *-a-*, sign of the present tense; *-taka*, want. *Kofia*, cap; sing. substantive of the third class. *Y-ako*, thy; *y-*, sign of agreement with a sing. substantive of the third class. *U-li-yo*, which you, or which you are, or were; *u-*, sign of the second person sing.: *-li-*, used for the substantive verb; *-yo*, relative sign referring to a singular substantive of the third class (*kofia*). *U-ki-vaa*, putting on; *u-*, sign of the second person singular; *-ki-*, sign of the participial tense; *-vaa*, put on. *U-jana-ni*, in youth; *u-*, sign of a sing. substantive of the sixth class; *-ni-*, sign of the locative case. *Mw-ako*, thy; *mw-*, sign of agreement with a substantive in the locative case with the meaning of *in*. *A-ta-ku-pa*, he will give you; *a-*, sign of third person sing. of a person; *-ta-*, sign of the future; *-ku-*, objective prefix referring to the second person sing.; *-pa*, give to. *Kofia*, cap; sing. substantive of the third class. *Y-a*, of; *y-*, sign of agreement with a sing. substantive of the third class. *Thahabu*, gold; substantive of the third class. *U-si-kubali*, do not accept; *u-*, sign of the second person sing.; *-si-*, sign of the negative subjunctive; *-kubali*, subjunctive of *kubali*, accept. *Ela*, except. *A-ku-pe*, let him give you; *a-*, sign of the third person sing., referring to a person;

III. you half of all I have,' do not accept that, but say, 'I want the cap which you used to wear in your youth.' He will give you a cap of gold; do not accept it, unless he give you a cap quite worn out, take that. And

kofia mbovu kabisa, hiyo pokea. Na mama yangu mwambie nataka taa uliyo ukiwasha ujanani mwako. Atakupa taa nyingi za thahabu, usikubali, ela akupe taa mbovumbovu ya chuma, hiyo pokea. I

-ku-, objective prefix, referring to the second person sing.; *-pe*, subjunctive of *pa*, give to. *Kofia*, sing. substantive third class. *M-bovu*, rotten; *m-*, being *n-* converted into *m-* by standing before *-b* (p. 85), sign of an agreement with a sing. substantive of the third class (*kofia*). *Kabisa*, utterly. *Hiyo*, this one; demonstrative denoting a thing mentioned before, and agreeing with a sing. substantive of the third class (*kofia*). *Pokea*, receive: imperative sing. of *pokea*, receive. *Na*, and. *Mama*, mother: sing. substantive in the form of the third class denoting a person. *Y-angu*, my; *y-*, sign of an agreement with a sing. substantive of the third class, here used colloquially. *Mw-ambie*, tell her; *mw-*, objective prefix referring to a person; *-ambie*, imperative sing. of *ambia*, tell. *N-a-taka*, I want; *n-*, sign of first person sing.; *-a-*, sign of present tense; *-taka*, want. *Taa*, sing. substantive third class. *U-li-yo*, which you, which you were or are; *-u*, sign of the second person sing.: *-li-*, used for the substantive verb (p. 151); *-yo*, relative particle referring to a sing. substantive of the third class (*tao*). *U-ki-washa*, lighting; *u-*, sign of second person sing.; *-ki-*, sign of the participial tense; *-washa*, light. *U-janá-ni*, in youth; *u-*, sign of a sing. substantive of the sixth class; *-ni*, sign of the locative case. *Mw-ako*, thy; *mw-*, sign of agreement with a substantive in the locative case with the meaning *in*. *A-ta- kú-pa*, she will give you; *a-*, sign of third person sing., referring to a person; *-ta-*, sign of the future tense; *-ku-*, objective prefix referring to the second person sing.; *-pa*, give to. *Taa*, lamps; plural substantive of the third class (shown to be plural by the context). *Ny-ingi*, many; *ny-*, sign of agreement with a plural substantive of the third class (*taa*). *Z-a*, of; *z-*, sign of agreement with a plural noun of the third class. *Thahabu*, gold. *U-si-kubali*, do not accept; second person sing. negative subjunctive of *kubali*. *Ela*, except. *A-ku-pe*, let her give you; *a-*, sign of third person sing., referring to *mama*; *-ku-*, objective prefix referring to second person sing.; *-pe*, subjunctive of *pa*, give to. *Taa*, sing. substantive third class. *M-bovu-m-bovu*, all spoilt; *m-* (for *n-* before *-b*), sign of agreement with a sing. substantive of the third class (*taa*); II.

---

say to my mother, 'I want the lamp you used to burn in your youth.' She will give you many lamps of gold; do not accept them, unless she give you an old worn iron lamp, take that." III.

I. **Wakaenda zao hatta walipofika karibu ya mji, yule kijana akamwambia, mimi 'takaa hapa, na wewe enende mjini kwetu, ukafanye shuruti na baba yangu kamma hiyo niliokwambia. Akaenenda. Alipofika akaona mjini watu hawaneni, wana msiba mkuu, akauliza,**

II. the adjective is doubled to show thoroughness. *Y-a*, of; *y-*, sign of agreement with a sing. substantive of the third class. *Ch-uma*, iron; a sing. substantive of the fourth class; it is used in the singular of iron as a metal, and in both sing. and plur. with the meaning of a piece or pieces of iron. *Hiyo*, this one; demonstrative referring to something mentioned before, and agreeing with a sing. substantive of the third class (*taa*). *Pokea*, receive; imperative sing. of *pokea*.

Wa-ka-enda z-ao, and they went their way. (*See above*). *Hatta*, until. *Wa-li-po-fika*, when they arrived. (*See above*). *Karibu ya*, near to. *M-ji*, town; *m-*, sign of a sing. substantive of the second class. *Yule*, that. (*See above*). *Ki-jana*, youth. (*See above*). *A-ka-mw-ambia*, said to him. (*See above*). *Mimi*, I. *'Ta-kaa*, will stay; *ta-*, sign of the future, the prefix of the first person sing. being elided before it; the sign of no other person can be so elided. *Hapa*, here. *Na*, and. *Wewe*, thou. *Enende*, imperative sing. of *enenda*, go, go on. *M-ji-ni*, to the town; *m-*, sign of a sing. substantive second class; *-ni*, sign of the locative case. *Kw-etu*, our; *kw-*, sign of an agreement with a substantive in the locative case. *U-ka-fanye*, and make; *u-*, sign of second person sing.; *-ka-*, and; *-fanye*, subjunctive of *fanya*, make. *Shuruti*, a covenant; sing. substantive third class. *Na*, with. *Baba*, father. *Y-angu*, my. (*See above*, and p. 112). *Kamma*, as. *Hiyo*, that; demonstrative referring to something mentioned before, and agreeing with a sing. substantive of the third class (*shuruti*). *Ni-li-o-kw-ambia*, which I told you; *ni-*, sign of the first person sing.; *-li-*, sign of the past tense which must be used with a relative; *-o-* (for *yo*), relative particle referring to *shuruti* (p. 117); *-kw-*, objective prefix referring to the second person sing. *A-ka-enenda*, and he went on. *A-li-po-fika*, when he arrived. *A-ka-ona*, he saw. *M-ji-ni*, in the town; *m-*, sign of a sing. substantive of the second class; *-ni*, sign of the locative case. *Wa-tu*, people; *wa-*, sign of a plural noun of the first class. *Hawa-neni*, they speak not; *hawa-*, sign of the third person plural negative

---

III. And they went on till they arrived near the town, when the boy said, "I will stay here, and you go on into the town, to our house, and make the agreement with my father as I told you." And he went on and arrived in the city, where he saw the people not talking [but] in great

msiba huu wa nini? Wakamwambia, mtoto wa Sultani amepote siku I.
nyingi. Akauliza, nyumba ya Sultani ni ipi, nipelekeni. Wakampe-
leka watu. Alipofika akamwuliza baba yake, una nini? Akamwa-
mbia, mtoto wangu amepotea. Akamwambia, nikikuletea utanipa

---

agreeing with a plural noun of the first class (*watu*); *-neni*, negative II.
present form of *nena*, speak. *Wa-na*, they have; third person plur. present of *kuwa na*, to have, governed by *watu*. *M-siba*, grief; *m-*, sign of a sing. noun of the second class. *M-kuu*, great; *m-*, sign of agreement with a sing. substantive of the second class (*msiba*). *A-ka-uliza*, and he asked. *M-siba*, grief. *Huu*, this; demonstrative agreeing with a sing. substantive of the second class (*msiba*). *W-a*, of; *w-*, sign of agremeent with a sing. substantive of the second class (*msiba*). *Nini*, what? *Wa-ka-mw-ambia*, and they said to him. *M-toto*, the child. *W-a*, of; *w-*, sign of agreement with a sing. substantive of the first class (*mtoto*). *Sultani*, the sultan; a sing. substantive of the fifth class, but when viewed as denoting a person constructed with adjectives and pronouns as of the first. *A-me-potea*, is lost; third sing. present perfect of *kupotea*, to become lost; he has become lost, *i.e.*, he is lost. *Siku*, days; plural substantive of the third class. *Ny-ingi*, many; *ny-*, sign of agreement with a plural substantive of the third class (*siku*). *A-ka-uliza*, and he asked. *Ny-umba*, house; *ny-*, sign of substantive of the third class. *Y-a*, of; *y-*, sign of agreement with a sing. substantive of the third class (*nyumba*). *Sultani*, sultan. *Ni*, is (p. 152). *I-pi*, which? *i-*, sign of reference to a sing. substantive of the third class (*nyumba*). *Ni-pelekeni*, take me; *ni-*, objective prefix referring to the first person sing.; *pelekeni*, plural imperative of *peleka*, take. *Wa-ka-m-peleka*, and they took him. *Wa-tu*, people. *A-li-po-fika*, when he arrived. *A-ka-mw-uliza*, he asked him; observe here and elsewhere the use of the *ka* tense to carry on the narration, even where there would be no connective employed in English. *Baba*, father. *Y-ake*, his. (*See above*). *U-na nini*, what is the matter with you? *u-na*, second person sing. of the present tense of *kú-wa na*, to have; *nini?* what? *A-ka-mw-ambia*, and he said to him. *M-toto*, child. *W-angu*, my. *A-me-*

---

mourning, and he asked, "What is this mourning for?" They told him, III.
"The Sultan's son has been a long time lost." He asked, "Which is the Sultan's house? Take me there." And the people took him there. When he reached it he asked the boy's father, "What troubles you?" He said, "My son is lost." And he said to him, "If I bring him to you what will

I. nini? Akamwambia, nitakupa mali yangu nussu kwa nussu. Akamwambia, marahaba. Akaenda akamtwaa, akaja naye. Alipomwona babaye na mamaye, ikawa furaha kubwa mjini. Wakapenda sana yule kijana kama mtoto wao.

Hatta alipotaka kwenda zake, yule kijana akamwambia, enende kamwage baba na mama, mwambie akupe kofia na mama akupe taa.

II. *potea*, is lost. (*See* p. 132.) *A-ka-mw-ambia*, and he said to him. *Ni-ki-ku-letea*, if I bring to you. (*See above*). *U-ta-ni-pa*, you will give me. (*See above*). *Nini*, what? *A-ka-mw-ambia*, and he said to him. *Ni-ta-ku-pa*, I will give you. *Mali*, goods. (*See above*). *Y-angu*, my. (*See above.*) *Nussu*, half. *Kwa*, by. *Nussu*, half. *A-ka-mw-ambia*, and he said to him. *Marahaba*, very good. *A-ka-enda*, and he went. *A-ka-m-twaa*, and took him. *A-ka-ja*, and came. *Na-ye*, with him. *A-li-po-mw-ona*, when he saw him. *Baba-ye*, his father; *-ye*, enclitic form of the possessive pronoun proper to the third person; *y-*, sign of agreement with a sing. substantive of the third class, used here with one denoting a person (p. 111). *Na*, and. *Mama-ye*, his mother; *-ye*. (*See above*). *I-ka-wa*, it was; *i-*, sign of agreement with a sing. substantive of the third class (*furaha*). *Furaha*, joy; sing. substantive third class. *Kubwa*, great; agreeing with *furaha*; as *n-*, which would be the regular sign of agreement with a sing. substantive of the third class, cannot stand before *k*, it is omitted altogether (p. 85). *M-ji-ni*, in the town; *m-*, sign of sing. substantive second class; *-ni*, sign of the locative case. *Wa-ka-penda*, and they (the father and mother) loved. *Sana*, much. *Yule*, that. *Ki-jana*, youth. *Kama*, like. *M-toto*, child. *W-ao*, their.

Hatta, at last. *A-li-po-taka*, when he wanted. *Kw-enda z-ake*, to go away. (*See above* and p. 112). *Yule*, that. *Ki-jana*, youth. *A-ka-mw-ambia*, he said to him. *Enende*, go; sing. imperative of *enenda*, go. *Ka-mw-age*, and take leave of him; *ka-*, and; *-mw-*, objective prefix referring to a person; if *mw* had been the subjective second plur. the *ka* would have followed it; *m-ka-age* = and do ye take leave; *-age*,

---

III. you give me?" He said, "I will give you half of all I have." He said, "I am content." And he went and took the boy and brought him. When his father and mother saw him, there was great joy throughout the town. And they loved that youth as though he bad been their own son.

When at last he wished to go away, the boy said to him, "Go and take leave of my father and mother; tell him tc give you the cap and

Akaenda, akawaambia, wakampa kofia nyingi, akakataa akamwambia, I.
nataka hiyo mbovu, wakampa, na mamaye akampa taa. Akawauliza, kofia hii maana yake nini? Wakamwambia, mtu akivaa, haonekani na mtu. Akavaa asionekane akafurahi sana. Akauliza, taa hii maana yake nini? Wakamwambia, ukiwasha hatta hapa watatoka

---

imperative sing. of *aga*, take leave of. *Baba*, father. *Na*, and. II.
Mama, mother. *Mw-ambie*, tell him; *mw-*, objective prefix referring to a person; *-ambie*, imperative sing. of *ambia*, tell. *A-ku-pe*, that he may give you. *Kofia*, cap. *Na*, and. *Mama*, mother. *A-ku-pe*, that she may give you. *Taa*, lamp. *A-ka-enda*, and he went. *A-ka-wa-ambia*, and he told them (the father and mother). *Wa-ka-m-pa*, and they gave him. *Kofia*, caps. *Ny-ingi*, many. *A-ka-kataa*, and he refused. *A-ka-mw-ambia*, and he said to him. *N-a-taka*, I want. *Hiyo*, this one. (*See above.*) *M-bovu*, rotten. (*See above*). *Wa-ka-m-pa*, and they gave him. *Na*, and. *Mama-ye*, his mother. (*See above*, under *babaye*). *A-ka-m-pa*, she gave him. *Taa*, lamp. *A-ka-wa-uliza*, and he asked them. *Kofia*, cap. *Hii*, this; demonstrative referring to a sing. substantive of the third class (*kofia*). *Maana*, meaning, purpose; sing. substantive third class. *Y-ake*, its; *y-*, sign of agreement with a sing. substantive of the third class (*maana*). *Nini*, what? *Wa-ka-mw-ambia*, and they said to him. *M-tu*, person, any one (p. 16); *m-*, sign of sing. substantive of first class. *A-ki-vaa*, if he puts on. *Ha-onekani*, he is not to be seen; *ha-*, negative prefix of the third person sing. referring to a person; *onekani*, negative present form of *onekana*. *Na*, by. *M-tu*, any one (p. 16). *A-ka-vaa*, and he put on. *A-si-onekane*, that he might not be seen: *a-*, prefix of third person sing. referring to a person (*kijana*); *-si-*, sign of negative subjunctive; *-onekane*, subjunctive form of *onekana*. *A-ka-furahi*, and he rejoiced. *Sana*, much. *A-ka-uliza*, and he asked. *Taa*, lamp. *Hii*, this. *Maana*, purpose. *Y-ake*, its. *Nini*, what? *Wa-ka-mw-ambia*, and they told him. *U-ki-washa*, if you light. *Hatta*, as far as. *Hapa*, here. *Wa-ta-toka*, they will come out; *wa-*, sign of third person

---

my mother to give you the lamp." He went and told them, and they III
gave him many caps, but he refused and said, "I want that worn-out one;" and they gave it to him, and the boy's mother gave him the lamp. Then he asked, "What is the object of this cap?" And they told him, "When a man puts it on, no one can see him." He put it on so as to become invisible, and was very glad. "And he asked, What is the object of this lamp?" And they told him, "If you light it as far as this,

I. **watu wawili wakutilie thahabu nyumbani mwako usiku kucha, na ukiwasha hatta hapa watatoka watu wawili wakupige kwa vigo-ngo usiku kucha. Akanena, marahaba. Akafurahi sana, akaenda zake.**

II. plur. referring to a plural substantive of the first class (*watu*). *Wa-tu*, people. *Wa-wili*, two; *wa-*, sign of agreement with a plur. substantive of the first class (*watu*). *Wa-ku-tilie*, that they may put for you; *wa-*, sign of third person plur. referring to a plur. substantive of the first class (*watu*); *-ku-*, objective prefix referring to the second person sing.; *-tilie*, subjunctive form of *tilia*, put for. *Thahabu*, gold. *Ny-umbá-ni*, in house; *ny-*, sign of substantive of the third class; *-ni*, sign of locative case. *Mw-ako*, thy; *mw-*, sign of agreement with a noun in the locative case denoting *within*. *Usiku*, night. *Ku-cha*, dawning or sun-rising; used after *usiku*, it means all night until the morning comes. *Na*, and. *U-ki-washa*, if you light. *Hatta*, as far as. *Hapa*, here. *Wa-ta-toka*, they will come out. *Wa-tu*, people. *Wa-wili*, two. *Wa-ku-pige*, that they may beat you; *-pige*, subjunctive form of *piga*. *Kwa*, with. *Vi-gongo*, cudgels: *vi-*, sign of a plural substantive of the fourth class; *ki-gongo* is a diminutive (p. 19) of *gongo*, a staff. *Usiku*, night. *Ku-cha*, till morning. *A-ka-nena*, and he said. *Marahaba*, thank you. *A-ka-furahi*, and he rejoiced. *Sana*, much. *A-ka-enda z-ake*, and he went away.

III. two men will come out and bring you gold into your house all night long; but if you light it as far as this, two men will come out and beat you with cudgels all night long." And he thanked them, and rejoiced very much, and went his way.

Appendix IV.

USEFUL AND IDIOMATIC PHRASES.

The first fifty-four were collected towards a book of conversations, which was begun with the help of our lamented friend, Mrs. G. E. Drayton; the rest, which are arranged in alphabotical order, were noted from time to time, either as likely to be useful in conversation, or as illustrating some special rule or idiom.

1. How many fowls have you there?
   Unao k'uku ngapi?
2. What do you want for them?
   Kiasi gani unakuza (At how much do you sell)?
3. Have you any eggs?
   Unayo mayayi?
4. I will not give more than a pice apiece for the eggs.
   Nitakupa pesa moja tu kununua yayi, sitatoa zayidi (I will give you one pice only to buy an egg, I will not give more).
5. I don't understand you, say it again.
   Sema mara ya pili, sikusikia.
6. Let me hear it again.
   Sema mara ya pili, nipate kusikia (Say it a second time, that I may get to understand).
7. Fetch me a basin for the eggs.
   Letee bakuli nitie mayayi.
8. Bring the basin with the eggs in it.
   Letee bakuli lenyi mayayi.
9. I don't want any to-day, come to-morrow.
   Leo sitaki, njoo kesho.
10. Are lemons cheap now?
    Malimao rahisi sasa?

11. I won't buy them; they are too dear.
Sitaki kununua, ni ghali.
12. What do you want?
Wataka nini?
13. I don't know what you want.
Sijui ulitakalo.
14. Where do you come from?
Watoka wapi?
15. Don't wait; I will send an answer immediately.
Enenda zako, usingoje, majibu yatakuja sasa hivi (Go your way; do not wait for an answer, it will come immediately).
16. Is your master at home?
Bwana yupo?
17. Master is not at home; he is gone out.
Bwana hako (or *hayuko*) *nyumbani; ametoka.*
18. Where are you going?
Unakwenda wapi?
19. I have lost my way.
Nimepotea, njia sijui (I am lost; the way I don't know).
20. Will you guide me to the English mission?
Nataka unionyeshe mosketini Ingreza?
21. Can you understand English?
Wewe unajua maneno ya Kiingreza?
22. I cannot speak Swahili [of Zanzibar].
Sijui kusema Kiunguja.
23. Did the water boil?
Maji yameche'mka?
24. Does the water boil?
Maji yanache'mka?
25. These plates are not clean.
Sahani hizi zina taka.
26. Wipe them carefully.
Futa vema kwa kitambaa.
27. Sweep this room well.
Fagia vema katika chumba hiki.
28. Dust the furniture.
Pangusa vumbi katika vyombo.
29. You have cracked that cup.
Umekitia ufa kikombe kile.
30. Throw it away.
Katupa.
31. Fetch me the vinegar, the pepper, and the salt.
Niletee siki, na pilipili, na chumvi.

32. Don't make so much noise.
Usifanye uthia.
33. Put a fresh wick in my lamp.
Tia katika taa yangu utambi.
34. Fold up the table-cloth smoothly.
Kunja vema kitambaa cha meza, usikivunje (Fold well the cloth of the table; spoil it not).
35. When you have swept the room put on clean clothes.
Kamma umekwisha kufagia, vaa nguo safi.
36. Take this to Miss T.
Chukua, upeleke kwa bibi T.
37. You have put all these books upside down; turn them.
Umepindua vyuo hivi vyote, uviweke upande mgine.
38. Leave that alone!
Acha!
39. Come here, I want to speak to you.
Njoo hapa, 'nna maneno nitakwambia (I have words I will say to you).
40. Get ready to go for a walk.
Fanya tayari upate kwenda kutembea.
41. Are you ready?
Umekuwa tayari?
42. Which way shall you like to go?
Njia gani utakao kupita?
43. How far is it to your shamba?
Kadri gani mbali ya shamba lako hatta kufika (How much farness of your shamba till getting there)?
44. Not very far; perhaps an hour's walk.
Si mbali sana, labuda ikipata saa moja.
45. Shall you walk, or ride your donkey, or sail?
Utakwenda kwa miguu, ao utapanda punda, ao utakwenda kwa mashua?
46. We will go round the town and home by the bridge.
Tutazunguka katika mji, halafu turudie darajani (Then let us return by the bridge).
47. Bring me some hot water after breakfast.
Niletee maji ya moto, nikiisha kula.
48. Half a bucket full.
Nuss ya ndoo.
49. Turn the mattress over every morning.
Geuza killa siku godoro, chini juu.
50. Turn it top to bottom.
Upande huu uweke upande wa pili.

51. I am very glad to see you.
Umependa moyo wangu kukutazama.
52. What ship is that?
Marikebu gani hii?
53. Has she cast anchor yet?
Imetia nanga?
54. No, she will come nearer the shore.
Bado, inakuja karibu ya pwani.
55. A good man does not desert his friends when they fall into difficulties.
Mtu mwema hawaachi rafiki zake wakipatika na shidda.
56. Are you idle?
Ati mvivu?
57. At what time shall I come?
Wakti gani nije;
58. Did he stay long?
Alikaa sana?
59. No, he went away directly.
Háa, alikwenda zake mara.
60. Does he drink wine?
Hunywa divai?
61. He does not.
Hanywi.
62. Does this boat leak?
Mashua hii yavuja?
63. Do not draw water from the well, the owner forbids it.
Usiteke maji kisimani, mwenyewe agombeza.
64. Don't jerk this rope; if you do it will break.
Kamba hii usiikutue, ukikutua itakatika
65. Eat as much as you like.
Kula kadri utakavyo.
66. Find me a large hen.
Kanitaftia koo la k'uku.
67. Follow this road.
Fuata [or *andama*] *njia hii.*
68. I want you to follow me.
Nataka unifuate [or *uniandame*].
69. Give it only to me and not to them.
Nipe mimi tu, usiwape wale.
70. Go and see if the people have collected.
Kaangalia watu wamekutana.
71. Go and stop that talking.
Enenda kakomesha maneno haya.

72. Stop this outcry.
Makelele haya yakome (Let these cries cease).
73. Go away, whoever you are.
Enda zako, kadri utakaokuwa.
74. Guard yourself, I am going to hit you.
Kinga, takupiga.
75. Has he a large box?
Ana kasha?
76. He has.
Analo kasha.
77. Have you a pipe at home?
Kiko kwako kiko?
78. He built a bridge across the river.
Alijenga bonth katikati ya mto.
79. He built a mosque by the river, and endowed it with a shamba near ours.
Alijenga moskiti ng'ambo, akawekea wakf shamba karibu shamba letu.
80. He described Mombas as it was in early times, as it is now, and as it will be a hundred years hence.
Aliandika Mvita ilivyokuwa kwanza, ilivyo sasa, na itakavyokuwa kwa miaka mia.
81. He does not believe me though I saw it.
Hanisadiki ningawa nimeiona.
82. He had the toothache.
Alikuwa na jino likimwuma.
83. He has been abroad many years.
Alikuwa safarini miaka mingi.
84. He has presence of mind.
Moyo wake uwapo.
85. His mind is absent. *Hapo ati.*
86. He is a troublesome fellow to deal with.
Ana taabu kuingiana naye.
87. He is absorbed in his own thoughts; even if you speak to him he takes no notice.
Yu katika fikara zakwe; ujaponena naye hawepo.
88. He is here.
Yupo hapa.
89. He is not here.
Hapo hapa.
90. He is yonder.
Yuko kule.

91. He is not there.
Hako kule.

92. He is not yet dressed.
Hajavaa.

93. He left us about ten days ago.
Alitwacha kadri ya (or *kama*) *siku kumi.*

94. He ought to be beaten.
Aihtaji kupigwa.

95. He pretends to be satisfied, but do not trust him.
Ajifanya kuwa rathi, usimwamini.

96. He rose up from his chair.
Aliondoka kitini kwake.

97. He runs as fast as he can.
Anakwenda mbio kama awezavyo.

98. He says he will walk on the water!
Ati atakwenda mtoni kwa miguu!

99. He that hateth suretyship is sure.
Mtu asiyekubali kuthamini ni katika amani.

100. He that is not against us is with us.
Mtu asiyekuwa juu yetu, bassi yee pamoja nasi.

101. He that is not with us is against us.
Asiyekuwa pamoja nasi, bassi huyu juu yetu.

102. He tried to make himself agreeable, and he succeeded.
Alijipendekeza ndipo akapendeza.

103. He was changed from a man into a horse.
Alibadiliwa mtu kuwa frasi.

104. He was more energetic than his father.
Huyu alikuwa akiweza zayidi ya baba yake.

105. His non-appearance is unaccountable.
Kutowekana kwake haitambulikani.

106. His self-conceit is no good to him.
Majivuno yake hayamfai neno.

107. How are your household (*i.e.* your wife, daughters, &c.)?
U hali gani nyumbani kwako.

108. How far is it across the island?
Kupataje mbali wake hapa hatta pwani ya pili?

109. A fast walker would take from sunrise to the middle of the afternoon.
Akiondoka mtu assubui hatta alasiri, alio hodari kwenda, kufika.

110. How long has he been ill?
Tangu lini hawezi?

111. How long ago was his illness?
Tangu lini alikuwa hawezi?

112. How pleasant!
Imependeza.

113. How glad you must have been to hear that you were to go home.
Furaha ipi mwaliposikia mwende zenu kwenu.

114. I am amusing myself with a book.
Najizumgumza na chuo.

115. I am here. *Nipo hapa.*

116. I am never without pimples.
Vipele havinitoka kabisa.

117. I am sleepy.
Ninao usingizi.

118. I cannot hold in this horse.
Siwezi kuzuia frasi huyu.

119. I cannot see so far as you can.
Sioni mbali, kama waonavyo wewe.

120. I don't like his way of tying it.
Sipendi ginsi afungavyo.

121. I don't see what you show me.
Sioni ulionyalo.

122. I don't see it, though he does.
Siioni angawa aona.

123. Take care, though you don't see it.
Kaangalia, ujapo hukioni.

124. I feel myself at home.
Hujiona niko kwetu.

125. Make yourself at home.
Usifanye haya, hapa kama kwako (Feel no modesty, here is like your home).

126. I gave him good advice, though he would not take it.
Nimemwonya illakini hakuonyeka.

127. I had almost left off expecting you.
Nalikaribia kukata tamaa ya kukuona.

128. I had lost my way, and I came out close to your shamba.
Nalipotea njia nikatokea shambani kwako.

129. I have asked him again and again, but he will not tell me.
Nimemwuliza mara kwa mara lakini hanambii.

130. I have gained a hundred dollars.
Nalipata fayida reale mia.

131. I have made you my mark, if you step over it, look out (a common defiance).
Nimekupigia mfuo wangu kiuka wangalie.

132. I know where he is.
Namjua mahali alipo.

133. I pray God not to visit it upon me.
Naomba Mwenyiezi Muungu asinipatilize.

134. I saw the flash of the gun, but did not hear the report.
Nimeona mwanga, lakini sikusikia mzinga kulia.

135. I shall go by sea as far as I can.
Nitakwenda kwa bahari, hatta itakaponifikisha.

136. I shall go for a walk to stretch my legs.
Nitakwenda tembea kukunjua miguu.

137. I thought myself a king.
Nalikuwa nikiwaza nimekuwa Sultani.

138. I will shut the door that he may not go out.
Nitafunga mlango asipate kupita.

139. If he strikes you, hit him again.
Akikupiga, nawe mpiga tena.

140. If you had been here he would not have been beaten.
Kama ungalikuwapo hapa, hangalipigwa.

141. It depends upon his coming.
Kuna atakapokuja.

142. It is bad weather.
Kumekaa vibaya.
Hakwendeki.
Hatokeki.

143. It is being hawked about by a salesman.
Kinatembezwa kwa dalali.

144. It is not there, though you say it is.
Hakipo, ungawa wasema kipo.

145. It is time for us to go.
Imekuwa wakati wa sisi kwenda zetu.

146. It is quite time for us to go.
Imewadia wakati wetu wa kwenda zetu.

147. It was a secret, but it oozed out.
Yalikuwa habari ya siri, ikatokeza.

148. Let him go.
Mwacheni enende.

149. Moslems are forbidden wine.
Waslimu wameepushwa divai

150. Much self-exaltation ruins a man's position in the world.
Majivuno yakiwa mengi ya'mvunjia mtu cheo.

151. Nothing I do pleases him.
Killa nafanyalo halimpendezi (everything which I do pleases him not).

152. Whatever I do he finds fault with me.
Killa nafanyalo hunitia khatiyani.

153. Put the water on the fire.
Kateleka maji.
154. Sit down.
Kaa kitako.
155. Don't get up.
Starehe.
156. The baobabs are now coming into leaf.
Siku hizi mibuyu inachanua majani.
157. The fields are flourishing.
Koonde imesitawi.
158. The music is first-rate.
Ngoma inafana.
159. The news has spread.
Khabari zimeenea.
160. Spread the news.
Zieneza khabari.
161. The people who went to Bardera are come back.
Watu waliokwenda Baradera, wamekuja zao.
162. The room wants darkening.
Chumba chataka kutiwa giza.
163. The top of this mountain is inaccessible.
Juu ya mlima huu haupandiki.
164. They [the trees] are almost all dead.
Kama kwamba iliokufa yote.
165. They are badly stowed.
Mapakizo yao mabaya.
166. They cut the boat adrift.
Wakakata kamba ya mashua ikachukuliwa na maji.
167. They like giving and receiving presents.
Hupendelea kupana vitu.
168. They shut themselves up in the fort.
Wakajizuia gerezani.
169. They told me what he had done.
Walinambia alivyofanya.
170. They were fighting, and I passed by and separated them.
Walikuwa wakipigana, hapita mimi nikawaamua.
171. This chest must be taken care of.
Kasha hili la kutunzwa.
172. This has been worn.
Nguo hii imevaliwa.
173. This tree is not so tall as that.
Mti huu si mrefu kama ule.

174. Upon your oath!
Utaapa!

175. Wash me these clothes.
Nioshee nguo hizi.

176. The clothes have been washed.
Nguo zimeosheka.

177. I have washed myself.
Nimenawika.

178. Wash me! *Noshe!*

179. We attacked them and they fell into confusion.
Twaliwashambulia, wakafazaika.

180. We like his company.
Kikao chake chema (his sitting is good).

181. What do you earn by the month?
Upataje killa mwezi?

182. What is become of him?
Amekuwaje?

183. What is this news about Ali?
Habari gani tuzisikiazo za Ali?

184. What are you talking about?
Maneno gani mnenayo?
Muktatha gani?
Mnenani?

185. What will you ferry me over for?
Utánivusha kwa kiasi gani?

186. When I have seen Mohammed, I will give you an answer
Nikiisha mwona Mohamadi, nitakupa jawabu.

187. Where is the knife I saw you with yesterday?
Kiko wapi kisu nalichokuona nacho jana?

188 Where is the pain?
Mahali gani panapouma?

189. Where is your pain?
Wauma wapi?

190. Who is in there?
Mna nani?

191. You cannot teach him anyhow.
Kadri u'mfunzavyo hajui.

192. We do not know whether he will not learn, or whether he cannot.
Hatujui ya kwamba hataki kujifunza ao hana akili za kujifunza.

193. You have made this thread too tight.
Uzi huu umeutia kassi mno.

194. You ought to love him very much.
Wastahili kumpenda sana.

195. *Kuamba na kusengenya.* To talk of a person behind his back, and secretly to make contemptuous signs about him when present. This phrase is often used as a test of a stranger's knowledge of Swahili; what it describes is counted as a special sin.

196. To ask a man his name.
Oh! Rafiki yangu nambie jina lako (Oh! my friend, tell me your name). *Wajua, bwana wee, tumeonana mimi nawe, jina lako nimelisahau, tafáthal nambie jina lako* (You know, sir, you and I have met [before], but I have forgotten your name, please to tell me your name).
When you have heard it, say—*Inshallah, sitalisahau tena* (Please God, I shall not forget it again).

197. A polite question and answer at leave-taking.
Unayo haja tena? (Have you any further desire?)
Haja yangu ya kuishi wewe sana na furaha (My desire is that you may live long and happily).

Appendix V.

ON MONEY, WEIGHTS, AND MEASURES IN ZANZIBAR.

The following account is based on scattered notices in the late Bishop Steere's collections, and on some tables furnished to the Rev. P. L. Jones-Bateman by a well-informed servant of the Mission in Zanzibar.

1. *Money.*

The only copper coin in common use in Zanzibar is the Anglo-Indian quarter-anna, or pice, in Swahili *pesa*, plur. *pesa* or *mapesa*; but the *robo pesa*, or quarter-pice (of which, however, three are equal to one pice), is also current.

The silver coins current are the Anglo-Indian rupee and, less commonly, the Austrian dollar. The eight-anna (half-rupee), four-anna (quarter-rupee), and two-anna pieces are also met with.

The relative values of these coins and their equivalent in English money fluctuate considerably. For practical purposes, it is sufficient to remember that an English sovereign may be generally exchanged for 12 rupees, English bank-notes, cheques, drafts, &c., being subject to a small discount; that an Austrian dollar is reckoned as equal to 2 rupees and 8 pice, and that a rupee is worth usually from 60 to 64 pice. It follows that, though accounts are usually kept in dollars and cents, and 5 dollars reckoned as equal to one pound English, it is more exact to consider—

		s.	*d.*
1 dollar	=	3	7
1 rupee	=	1	8
1 pice	=		$\frac{1}{3}$

In larger sums, the scale of legal tender is to reckon—

47 dollars	=	100 rupees
94 „	=	200 „
141 „	=	300

and so on.

On the mainland, dollars and pice are taken freely on the coast and main lines of traffic, and rupees are met with; but elsewhere, silver dollars only, and such objects of barter as calico, brass-wire, beads, &c.

2. *Measures of Length.*

There is no exact standard or relationship of measures of length. Those in common use are merely taken from parts of the human body, viz.:—

Wanda. plur. *nyanda*, a finger's breadth.

Shibiri, a span, the distance between the tips of the outstretched thumb and little finger.

Mórita, a slightly shorter span, from the tip of the thumb to that of the fore-finger.

Thiraa or *Mkono*, a cubit, the distance from the finger-tips to the elbow joint. Of this again, there are two varieties:—

Thiraa kamili, or full cubit, as just described, and—

Thiraa konde, or fist cubit, from the elbow-joint to the knuckles.

Wari, or yard, is one half of the—

Pima, a man's height, or the distance he can stretch with his arms, a fathom. A *doti* is a measure of similar length.

The *uayo*, or length of the foot, Arab *khatua*, is also used occasionally, and the English foot, *futi*, regularly by Indian carpenters and in other trades. Approximately, the relations of these measures may be tabulated thus:—

1 *wanda*		= 1 inch.
8 or 10 *nyanda*	= 1 *shibiri kamili*	= 1 quarter-yard.
2 *shibiri*	= 1 *thiraa* or *mkono*	= 1 cubit or half-yard.
2 *thiraa*	= 1 *wari*	= 1 yard
2 *wari*	= 1 *pima*	= 1 fathom.

Distance is loosely estimated by the average length of an hour's walking. Dunga, which lies almost exactly halfway across the island of Zanzibar, at a distance of perhaps twelve miles, is described as a walk of four hours, *saa 'nne;* and Kokotoni, at the north end of the island, distant perhaps twenty miles from Zanzibar, as a walk of at least six hours, *saa sita.* On the mainland, a day's march is a common but vague measure of perhaps twenty miles.

3. *Measures of Weight.*

For gold, silver, silk, scent, and other costly articles, the unit is the *wakia*, or weight of an Austrian silver dollar, almost exactly an ounce. For the names of fractional parts of any unit, see "Handbook," p. 93;

but the weight of a pice is often used as a convenient though inexact measure of small quantities.

For heavy articles, the usual unit is a *rátel*, or *rattli*, equal to 16 *wakia*, and corresponding to one pound.

16 *wakia* = 1 *rátel*.
3 *rátel* = 1 *mani*.
6 *rátel* = 1 *pishi*.
6 *pishi* = 1 *frasila*, about 35 lbs. avoirdupois.
10 *frasila* = 1 *mzo*.

Hence, 64 *frasila* or 6⅔ *mizo* may be regarded as = 1 ton.

4. *Measures of Capacity*.

No fixed liquid measure is used by the poorer classes. Shopkeepers sell their oil, treacle, &c., by tin-ladlefuls (*kikombe*), or by the bottle (*chupa*), or by the tin, *i.e.* the tins in which American oil is imported to Zanzibar (*tanaki*, *tini*, also *debe*).

Corn (*nafaka*) or dry measure is, of course, of great importance in a country where grain is the staple of food and chief article of commerce. The smallest unit is the—

Kibaba, a measure of perhaps a pint.

Kibaba cha tele, if the measure is heaped up—the usual proceeding.

Kibaba cha mfuto, if cut off flat.

2 *vibaba* (*vya tele*) = 1 *kisaga*.

2 *visaga* = 1 *pishi*, about half a gallon.

The *pishi* connects the measures of capacity and weight, and for some of the common dry commodities, such as *chiroko* and *kundi*, the *pishi* may be regarded as equivalent either in capacity to 4 *vibaba*, or in weight to 6 *rattli*.

Grain is sold wholesale by the *kanda*, or sack of grass-matting, or (if from India) by the *gunia*, a wide sack. The *gunia* often weighs about 168 lbs. The *kanda* varies, both with the kind of grain and the place from which it is imported. For instance, while at Kwale, Mgao, and Mvita, towns on the Swahili coast, the *kanda* of rice at times contains 10, 11, or 12 *pishi*, and the *kanda* of Indian corn 10 *pishi*, at Pangani, Tanga, and Mtang'ata the *kanda* of rice will contain 15, 16, or 17 *pishi*, and the *kanda* of Indian corn 13 or 13½ *pishi*.

Various other terms are in use for different commodities, *e.g.* poles are sold by the *korja*, or score; stone for building by the *boma*, a heap which may weigh 4 cwt. to 5 cwt.; lime by the *tanuu* (clamp) or *kikapo*; calico by the *jura*, 35 yards; and various other things by the "*mzigo*" or load.